The
Oxford Book
Of English Prose

Impression of 1930
First edition, 1925

The Oxford Book Of English Prose

Chosen & Edited by

Sir Arthur Quiller-Couch

Oxford
At the Clarendon Press

PRINTED IN GREAT BRITAIN

TO

TWO HOUSES

OF LEARNING AND HOSPITALITY

TRINITY COLLEGE, OXFORD

AND

JESUS COLLEGE, CAMBRIDGE

οἴκοθεν οἴκαδε

AND TO

FRIENDSHIP

PREFACE

IT will hardly allure a 'hesitating purchaser' of this book that I open it with a query if it be possible to make a Prose Anthology at all. This doubt I confess has more than once assailed me in the years spent on the attempt. But to be brave is the only way to succeed, and I have hope that this volume will at least establish the possibility.

Yet I must premise that any anthology of English Prose is—for several reasons and of its very nature—difficult.

To begin with, if a man seek to the sources, it demands long and laborious reading, the bulk of our prose being already well-nigh immeasurable. I have read pretty widely among the originals for this book, and during five years for its special purpose. The result leaves me convinced that no honest scholar can pretend an acquaintance with the whole of English prose, or even with the whole that may yield good selections. All one can do is to spread a wide and patient net and report that he brings the best of his haul.

Of this labour upon mere bulk, however, he should despise to complain. It is his business, once undertaken; and it is not the inherent difficulty of his undertaking, which the reader will perhaps most readily understand if he turn to No. 581 of this volume and consider what Mr. Clutton-Brock says of the essential qualities by virtue of which Prose differs from Verse. He hazards that while the cardinal virtue of Verse is Love, the cardinal virtue of Prose is Justice. I should put it a little differently, using other terms. Bearing in mind such lines as Milton's famous invocation:

> Hail holy Light! offspring of Heav'n first-born,

or Macbeth's:

> Tomorrow, and tomorrow, and tomorrow,

or Marvell's *Ode upon Cromwell's return from Ireland*, or Gray's *Elegy*, or many a sonnet of Wordsworth's, I should prefer 'a high compelling emotion' to Mr. Clutton-Brock's 'Love', however widely interpreted, as the virtue of Poetry; and Persuasion rather than Justice as the first virtue of Prose, whether in narrative or in argument. Defoe's art in telling of Crusoe's visits to the wreck is all bent on persuading you that it really happened and *just so*; as Burke, in pleading for conciliation with the American colonists, is bent on marshalling argument upon argument why conciliation is expedient besides being just. In argument, to be sure, the appeal lies always towards an assumed seat of absolute justice to which even in the Law Courts every plea is addressed; Persuasion is, after all, as Matthew Arnold says, the only true intellectual process, or as Socrates, in prison under sentence of death for having failed in it, so nobly proclaimed, the only right way of reforming a commonwealth.

But persuasion, whether in narrative or in argument, is a long process, insinuating, piling up proof ; and Prose its medium is therefore naturally long. So we find ourselves confronted with the material, almost brutal, question, Can any anthology of short passages rightly illustrate an art of which the property is to be long? From this the Devil's Advocate easily goes on to say, 'Prose, being what you allow it to be, on that admission abhors the purple patch. You have admitted many purple patches. Please you, justify yourself.' To this I might answer that the purple patches in this book are actually few in comparison with the mass of its contents : I have very sedulously included all sorts of our prose, choosing often a passage quite pedestrian. Yet the answer would not be quite honest : for some things are here which all men have applauded, and (frankly) because they have been so applauded as well as because my own judgement applauds. Ralegh on Death, for example, some pages of Sir Thomas Browne, Lincoln's Gettysburg Oration. As I wrote in my preface to the *Oxford Book of English Verse*, I have tried to choose the best, and the best is the best though a hundred judges have declared it so.

But I have a bolder word to say for the purple patch. One might, in servility to a catchword of criticism, plead that from a sermon of Donne's, a tract of Milton's, an oration by Chatham or Burke, one must of necessity take the *culmen*, only referring the reader to the winding ways up the heights from which like eagles the impassioned phrases launch themselves. I think that, upon examination, literature—which, after all, is memorable speech—will be found in practice very much more on the side of the purple patch than the generality supposes nowadays. For certain Thucydides sewed on these patches deliberately : so (I think) did Plato, albeit more delicately as a philosopher electing to be a man of the world : so certainly did Cicero : so as certainly in the line of our own prose and in their turn did Malory, Donne, Milton, Browne, Berkeley, De Quincey, Hazlitt —to pursue no farther. Nay, if we go right back, it is arguable that Prose was 'born in the purple': that nine-tenths of the speech-making in the *Iliad* itself, for example, is not poetry at all but rhetoric strung into hexameters; a metre which the tragedians discarded for iambics, 'the most conversational form of verse'. Aristotle himself never troubled to define prose, the medium in which he wrote as it happened to him. In the *Poetics* he just indicates that there is such a thing; that hitherto it has lacked a name; and so (without supplying it) he passes on. He nowhere separates prose from poetry, though we may infer a separation. But in the *Rhetoric* (Book iii) the philosopher, while (man of science as he was) suggesting that bald words, such as he habitually used, are the medium for some definite and ascertained knowledge, does admit the existence of a medium persuading men's opinion; and, while belittling it somewhat, allows its right to cultivate σεμνότης or—shall we call it?—the grand style. The man, after all, could not escape the witchery, the noble charm of Plato, his beloved master. Now we may reasonably argue, I think, that men's opinions about things—their speculations, memories, aspirations, glimpses of the unseen and infinite—are actually of more importance, of more meaning to mankind than any amount of ascertained fact, that all ascertained fact *exit in mysterium*; that when one generation of it has been swallowed, or more frequently ejected, by the next, still man's eternal speculation abides and must abide; and that this is why, while books of exact science may be antiquated by new ones, we can never spare from our shelves a Shakespeare or a Dryden or even a Gibbon. But my immediate point is that even the most austerely practical of philosophers, with his eye intent on prose, admits the value of emotion and the purple patch.

For a last difficulty of the Prose anthologist (or the last to be mentioned here): he can by no contrivance make his book attract the eye as a Verse anthology—with its glancing differences of metre, its stanzas, its long and short lines of type—so easily and naturally does. His type must sit blockishly on the page, broken only by paragraphs or by quotations. There is no help for him here.

In face of all this, on what can he rely even for hope? Simply, I believe, on the courage of a conviction that of his acquaintance with English prose and by driving at practice in the English way, he (or somebody on the strength of an idea) can make a serviceable and portable volume which shall remind not only many stay-at-home quiet-living folk but many an Englishman on his travels and (still better) many a one in exile on far and solitary outposts of duty, of the nobility of this Island, its lineage and its language. I claim here, and with all emphasis, that my book is not one of *Specimens* : that a critic will mistake its purpose who starts judging it by the amount of space, the number of extracts, assigned to so-and-so ; as that he may likely be mistaken in deeming me ignorant of an author not included or, in his opinion, insufficiently represented as against one of acknowledged importance. Mine is not an effort at 'class-listing'—a method always repulsive to me in dealing with literature.

The anthologist, as I understand his trade, must have a 'notion' of his own, a 'pattern in the carpet', though he cannot easily define his pattern. If pressed, I should confess to one or two things.

To begin with, I have tried to make this book as representatively English as I might ; with less thought of robust and resounding 'patriotism' than of that subdued and hallowed emotion which, for example, should possess any man's thoughts standing before the tomb of the Black Prince in Canterbury Cathedral: a sense of wonderful history written silently in books and buildings, all persuading that we are heirs of more spiritual wealth than, may be, we have surmised or hitherto begun to divine.

With this in my mind—keeping English prose as a grand succession while yet trying to release it from any order of 'specimens', I have (and the critics are welcome to the admission) not cared a whit for the number of extracts by which this or that author is over or under 'represented'. All comment directed upon this will simply ignore the book's purpose. There is a great deal of Berners' Froissart. Why? For two reasons: the first that it holds the core of true English gentility: the second that, in the matter of technique, our prose learnt its grace of our dear enemy, France.

For a like reason I have been bold to include an amount of 'out-of-door' matter that may here and there be considered to fall beneath the dignity of high prose and would anyhow overweight a book of 'specimens'. For it is curious to observe, in contrast with our poets who sing of green country all the time, what a disproportionate mass of our prose is urban, and how rarely it contrives, at its best, to get off the pavement. As a countryman I may easily be blamed for a stubborn zeal in redressing this balance.

Yet, this opportunity given, I do not repent of my attempt to redress it. Let me illustrate. When Wolfe crossed the St. Lawrence at night to scale the heights of Abraham, it is recorded that he murmured a stanza or two from Gray's *Elegy*—that his vision on that dark passage went back to a green and English country churchyard; so if the reader will turn to an extract I have taken from Charles Reade (No. 429) he will feel this imperishable land of ours revived, and with tears, in the hearts of its roughest outcasts. Those men had no 'patriotism', no sense of any duty to England: a fair sprinkling of them, perhaps, had been convicts and 'left their country for their country's good'. But what they felt is just what I could wish this book to recall to the breast of any gallant Englishman on outpost duty in fort or tent.

> Nescio qua natale solum dulcedine cunctos
> Ducit et immemores non sinit esse sui.

I propose that, with the aid of the Clarendon Press, this book shall be put upon sale on November 25, 1925, twenty-five years to a day since *The Oxford Book of English Verse* saw the light and started to creep into public recognition, at first (as I remember) very slowly. While no more superstitious than ordinary men, I take a pleasure in observing birthdays and other private anniversaries as well as those of the Church: and it is my fancy to choose this as an omen of continuance in some public favour. A quarter of a century is a large slice in the life of any man who pretends (as in this book must be pretended) some claim to preserve a capacity for discerning good literature from that which is less good : and I feel that the interval may, as happens to men, have somewhat chilled and hardened the judgement. I have, for example, removed out of this anthology many sounding passages for the sole reason that on second thoughts they did not ring true—that is to me, at my time of life, when the instinct to admire is subdued by a scruple against leaving this world with any profession of knowing more than one does. And on a similar principle, in covenant with the years, I have felt it right to concede that my sympathy with prose nowadays being written, though often warm enough, misses a right capacity to discriminate. Therefore I end this book with writers who had already solidified their work by 1914, and trust that the reader will accept this break-off as reasonable and allow me *donatum iam rude* to hang up just there the old harness. Yet, relinquishing it, I look forward in entire faith to the opening fields. The Newspaper Press admits to-day a portentous amount of that Jargon, or flaccid writing to which flaccid thought instinctively resorts. But literature, I repeat, is memorable speech, recording memorable thoughts and deeds, and in such deeds at any rate the younger generation has not failed. Our fathers have, in the process of centuries, provided this realm, its colonies and wide dependencies, with a speech malleable and pliant as Attic, dignified as Latin, masculine, yet free of Teutonic guttural, capable of being precise as French, dulcet as Italian, sonorous as Spanish, and of captaining all these excellencies to its service. Turning over these pages before they go to the printer I recognize (not, I hope, too fondly) that the whole purpose moves to music. So, taking leave of a trade which in these years has at least not lacked the compliment of imitation, I look back somewhat wistfully on the fields traversed, to be searched over by other eyes to which I would fain bequeath, if I could so entreat the gods, a freshness of eyesight more delicate than mine.

My debts to those who have granted me the use of copyright passages are acknowledged elsewhere. I conclude here with a word of special gratitude to one or two helpful friends: to Mr. Charles Whibley, to Professor G. Gordon of Oxford, and to many of the Oxford University Press, at Oxford itself and at Amen House, who on an old tradition would probably resent my particularizing them by name. But, in old regard, I must name two friends: the first, the late Mr. Charles Cannan, sometime Secretary of the Clarendon Press, who suggested this enterprise and nursed its beginnings: the second, the late Mr. A. R. Waller, Secretary of the Cambridge University Press, who fostered it with the purest good-will and of his own wide reading freely bestowed all that was in his power to give. I like to think that, when my time comes in turn, I shall survive in the Oxford Books of English Verse and English Prose along with these two good men.

A. Q-C.

ACKNOWLEDGEMENTS

I must tender my thanks to those many who have helped me with permission to include copyright passages :

Matthew Arnold (Messrs. Macmillan & Co.) ; Sir James Barrie ; Lord Beaconsfield (Messrs. Longmans, Green & Co.) ; Mr. Max Beerbohm (Messrs. Heinemann) ; Mr. Hilaire Belloc (Messrs. Methuen & Co.) ; Mr. Arnold Bennett (Messrs. Chatto & Windus) ; A. C. Benson (Mr. E. F. Benson) ; The Right Hon. Augustine Birrell ; F. H. Bradley (Professor A. C. Bradley) ; Mr. Robert Bridges ; Rupert Brooke (The Literary Executor and Messrs. Sidgwick and Jackson, Ltd.) ; Professor John Burnet ; Samuel Butler (Jonathan Cape, Ltd.) ; Mr. G. K. Chesterton (Messrs. Methuen & Co., and Mr. Cecil Palmer) ; R. W. Church (Messrs. Macmillan & Co.) ; A. Clutton-Brock (Mrs. Clutton-Brock) ; Mary E. Coleridge (Sir Henry Newbolt) ; Joseph Conrad (Messrs. Fisher Unwin and Messrs. J. M. Dent & Sons) ; Lord Courtney of Penwith (Lady Courtney and Messrs. Leonard Parsons, Ltd. ; from 'Cornish Granite') ; Mr. G. Lowes Dickinson (Messrs. J. M. Dent & Sons) ; Austin Dobson (The Executors) ; John Donne (Cambridge University Press) ; Mr. Charles M. Doughty ; George Eliot (Messrs. Wm. Blackwood & Sons) ; 'Michael Fairless' (Messrs. Duckworth & Co.) ; Edward FitzGerald (Messrs. Macmillan & Co.) ; J. A. Froude (Messrs. Longmans, Green & Co.) ; John Galsworthy (Messrs. Heinemann) ; George Gissing (Messrs. Constable & Co.); Sir Edmund Gosse; Mr. R. B. Cunninghame Graham (Messrs. Heinemann); Mr. Kenneth Grahame; J. R. Green (Mrs. Green and Messrs. Macmillan & Co.); H. F. Hall (Messrs. Macmillan & Co., Ltd.); W. E. Hall (The Executors); Mr. Thomas Hardy (Messrs. Macmillan & Co.); Lafcadio Hearn (Messrs. Kegan Paul & Co.); W. E. Henley (The Executrix of Mrs. Henley and Messrs. Macmillan & Co.); Maurice Hewlett (The Executor and Mr. Humphrey Milford); W. H. Hudson (The Royal Society for the Protection of Birds and Messrs. J. M. Dent & Sons); T. H. Huxley (Messrs. Macmillan & Co., Ltd.); Henry James (Messrs. Heinemann and Messrs. Macmillan & Co.); William James (Messrs. Longmans, Green & Co.); Dr. J. H. Jeans; Richard Jefferies (Messrs. Longmans, Green & Co.); W. S. Jevons (Messrs. Macmillan & Co., Ltd.); Lionel Johnson (Messrs. Elkin Mathews, Ltd.); Benjamin Jowett (Jowett Trustees); Mr. Rudyard Kipling (Messrs. Macmillan & Co.); Andrew Lang (Messrs. Longmans, Green & Co.); W. E. H. Lecky (Messrs. Longmans, Green & Co.); Mr. E. V. Lucas (Messrs. Methuen & Co.); The Hon. R. H. Lyttelton (Messrs. Longmans, Green & Co.); Mr. Compton Mackenzie (Mr. Martin Secker); Sir Henry Maine (Messrs. John Murray); F. W. Maitland (Cambridge University Press); Mr. John Masefield (Mr. Grant Richards); George Meredith (Messrs. Constable & Co.); Mr. C. E. Montague (Messrs. Chatto & Windus); Mr. George Moore (Messrs. Heinemann); Lord Morley (Messrs. Macmillan & Co.); William Morris (Mr. Sydney Cockerell); Sir Henry Newbolt; Cardinal Newman (Messrs. Longmans, Green & Co.); Francis Parkman (Messrs. Macmillan & Co.); Walter Pater (Messrs.

Macmillan & Co.); Coventry Patmore (Messrs. G. Bell & Sons, Ltd.); Mark Pattison (The Clarendon Press); F. York Powell (The Clarendon Press); Lady Ritchie (Mr. John Murray); The Earl of Rosebery; John Ruskin (Messrs. Allen & Unwin); W. Clark Russell (Sir Herbert Russell); 'Mark Rutherford' (Mrs. Hale White); Mr. George Saintsbury; Professor George Santayana (Messrs. Constable & Co.); Olive Schreiner (Mr. Cronwright Schreiner and Messrs. Fisher Unwin, Ltd.); Captain R. F. Scott (Mrs. Hilton Young and Mr. John Murray); Mr. G. Bernard Shaw (Messrs. Constable); J. H. Shorthouse (Messrs. Macmillan & Co.); Sir Harry Smith (Mr. John Murray); Miss Somerville; R. L. Stevenson (Mr. Lloyd Osbourne); Mr. Lytton Strachey (Messrs. Chatto & Windus); Lord Sumner of Ibstone (The Incorporated Society of Law Reporters); A. C. Swinburne (Messrs. Constable); J. M. Synge (Messrs. Maunsel & Co.); Francis Thompson (Mr. Wilfrid Meynell and Messrs. Burns, Oates, & Washbourne, Ltd.); T. Traherne (Messrs. P. J. & A. E. Dobell); H. D. Traill (Messrs. Chapman & Hall, Ltd.); Mr. G. M. Trevelyan (Messrs. Longmans, Green & Co.); Mr. A. B. Walkley; Mr. H. G. Wells; Mr. Charles Whibley (Messrs. Macmillan & Co.); J. A. McNeill Whistler (Messrs. Heinemann); Oscar Wilde (Messrs. Methuen & Co.).

I must beg the forgiveness of any one whose rights have been overlooked in the above list.

A. Q-C.

JOHN TREVISA

1326–1402

1 *This Realm, this England*

As *Fraunce* passeth *Bretayne*, so *Bretayne* passeth *Irlond* in faire weder and nobilté, but nought in helthe. For this ilond is best and bringeth forth trees and fruyt and retheren and other bestes, and wyn groweth there in som place. The lond hath plenté of foules and of bestes of dyvers manere kynde; the lond is plenteous and the see also. The lond is noble, copious, and riche of nobil welles and of nobil ryveres with plenté of fische; there is grete plenté of small fische, of samon, and of elys. So that cherles in som place fedith sowes with fische. . .

There beeth schepe that bereth good wolle; there beeth meny hertes and wylde bestes and fewe wolves; therfore the schepe beeth the more sikerliche without kepynge i-lefte in the folde. In this ilond also beeth many cities and townes, faire and noble and riche; many grete ryveres and stremes with grete plenté of fische; many faire wodes and grete with wel many bestes, tame and wylde. The erthe of that lond is copious of metal ore and of salt welles; of quarers of marbel; of dyuers manere stones, of reed, of whyte; of nesche, of hard; of chalk and of whyte lyme. There is also white cley and reed forto make of crokkes and stenes and other vessel, and brent tyle to hele with

4 *retheren) catle* 10 *cherles) peasants* 14 *sikerliche) securely* 20 *quarers) quarries* 21, 23 *reed) red* 22 *nesche) soft* 24 *stenes) pots* *brent) burnt* *hele) roof*

hous and cherches, as hit were in the other *Samia*, that hatte *Samos* also. *Flaundres* loveth the wolle of this lond, and *Normandie* the skynnes and the velles; *Gasquyn* the iren and the leed; *Irlond* the ore and the salt; *Europa* loveth and desireth the white metal of this lond.

From the translation of Higden's *Polychronicon*

2 *The Mettle of Your Pasture*

BUT the Englische men that woneth in *Engelond*, that beeth i-medled in the ilond, that beeth fer i-spronge from the welles that they spronge of first, wel lightliche withoute entisynge of eny other men by here owne assent tornen to contrary dedes. . . .

These men been speedful bothe on hors and on foote, able and redy to alle manere dedes of armes, and beeth i-woned to have the victorie and the maistrie in everich fight wher no treson is walkynge; and beeth curious, and kunneth wel inow telle dedes and wondres that thei haveth i-seie. Also they gooth in dyvers londes; unnethe beeth eny men richere in her owne londe othere more gracious in fer and in strange londe. They konneth betre wynne and gete newe than kepe her owne heritage; therfore it is that they beeth i-spred so wyde and weneth that everich londe is hir owne heritage. The men beeth able to al manere sleithe and witte, but tofore the dede blondrynge and hasty, and more wys after the dede, and leveth ofte lightliche what they haveth bygonne. . .

2 *hatte*) *was called* 3 *velles*) *fells* 5 *white metal*) *tin* 7 *woneth*) *dwell* 8 *i-medled*) (*of race*) *blended* *fer*) *far* 11 *here*) *their* 14 *i-woned*) *accustomed* 16 *kunneth*) *can* *inow*) *enough* 17 *i-seie*) *seen* 18 *unnethe*) *hardly* 19 *othere*) *or* *gracious* (*favour* 22 *weneth*) *think* 24 *sleithe*) *contrivance* *tofore*) *before*

These men despiseth hir owne, and preiseth other menis, and unnethe beeth apaide with hir owne estate; what byfalleth and semeth other men, they wolleth gladlyche take to hemself; therfore hit is that a yeman arraieth hym as a squyer, a squyer as a knyght, a knyght as a duke, a duke as a kyng.

From the translation of Higden's *Polychronicon*

3 *The Thirteenth-Century Maiden*

MEN byhove to take hede of maydens: for they ben hote & tendre of complexion; smale, pliaunt and fayre of disposicion of body; shamfaste, ferdefull and mery touchynge the affeccion of the mynde. Touchinge outwarde disposicion they be well nurtured, demure and softe of speche and well ware what they say: and delycate in theyr apparell. . . Their hondes and the uttermeste party of their membres ben full subtyll and plyaunt, theyr voyce small, theyr speche easy and shorte, lyght in goynge & shorte steppes, and lyght wit and heed; they ben sone angry, and they ben mercyable and envyous, bytter, gylefull, able to lerne. . . And for a woman is more meker than a man, she wepeth soner, and is more envyousse, and more laughinge, & lovinge, and the malice of the soule is more in a woman than in a man. And she is of feble kinde, and she makith more lesynges, and is more shamefaste, & more slowe in werkynge and in mevynge than is a man, as sayth *Aristotle*.

From the translation of Bartholomew de Glanville's *De Proprietatibus Rerum*

2 *apaide) satisfied.* 3 *semeth) beseems* 8 *complexion) temperament* 10 *ferdefull) fearful* *affeccion) disposition* 17 *heed) head* 19 *for) because* 23 *lesynges) lies* 25 *mevynge) moving*

JOHN WYCLIFFE

1324 ?–1384

4 *The Prodigal Son*

LUK seith that Crist tolde how, A man hadde two sones; and the yonger of hem seide unto his fadir, Fadir, gyve me a porcioun of the substance that fallith me. And the fadir departide him his goodis. And soone aftir this yonge sone gederide al that fel to him, and wente forth in pilgrimage into a fer contré; and ther he wastide his goodis, lyvynge in lecherie. And after that he hadde endid alle his goodis, ther fel a gret hungre in that lond, and he bigan to be nedy. And he wente oute, and clevede to oon of the citizeins of that contré, and this citisein sente him into his toun, to kepe swyn. And this sone coveitide to fille his beli with these holes that the hogges eten, and no man gaf him. And he, turninge agen, seide, How many hynen in my fadirs hous ben ful of loves, and Y perishe here for hungre. Y shal rise, and go to my fadir, and seie to him, Fadir, Y have synned in heven, and bifore thee; now Y am not worthi to be clepid thi sone, make me as oon of thin hynen. And he roos, and cam to his fadir. And yit whanne he was fer, his fadir sawe him, and was moved bi mercy, and rennyng agens his sone, fel on his nekke, and kiste him. And the sone seide to him, Fadir, Y have synned in hevene, and bifore thee; now Y am not worthi to be clepid thi sone. And the fadir seide to his servauntis anoon, Bringe ye forth the firste stole, and clothe ye him, and gyve ye a ryng in his hond, and shoon upon his feet. And bringe ye a fat calf, and

4 *departide) divided* 5 *gederide) gathered* 12 *toun) farm* 13 *holes) husks* 15 *hynen) servants* *loves) loaves* 19 *clepid) called* 21 *fer) afar off* 22 *agens) to meet* 26 *stole) robe*

sle him, and ete we and fede us ; for this sone of myn was deed, and is quykened agen, and he was perishid, and is foundun. And thei bigunne to feede hem. And his eldere sone was in the feeld ; and whanne he cam, and was nygh the hous, he herde a symphonie and other noise of mynystralcye. And this eldere sone clepide oon of the servauntis, and axide what weren thes thingis. And he seide to him, Thy brothir is comen, and thi fadir hath slayn a fat calf, for he hath resceyved him saaf. But this eldere sone hadde dedeyn, and wolde not come in ; therfore his fadir wente out, and bigan to preie him. And he answeride, and seide to his fadir, Lo, so many yeeris Y serve to thee, Y passide nevere thi mandement ; and thou gavest me nevere a kide, for to fede me with my frendis. But after that he, this thi sone, that murtheride his goodis with hooris, is come, thou hast killid to him a fat calf. And the fadir seide to him, Sone, thou art ever more with me, and alle my goodis ben thine. But it was nede to ete and to make mery, for he, this thi brothir, was deed and lyvede agen ; he was perishid, and is founden.

Sermons : The Saturday Gospel in the Secunde Weke in Lente

GEOFFREY CHAUCER

1340 ?–1400

5 *Little Lewis and the Astrolabe*

LITEL Lowis my sone, I have perceived wel by certeyne evidences thyn abilité to lerne sciences touchinge noumbres and proporciouns ; and as wel considere I thy bisy preyere in special to lerne the

2 *perishid) lost* 10 *dedeyn) indignation* 14 *passide) overstepped* 17 *hooris) harlots*

Tretis of the Astrolabie. Than, for as mechel as a philosofre seith, 'he wrappeth him in his frend that condescendeth to the rightful preyers of his frend,' therfor have I geven thee a suffisaunt Astrolabie as for oure orizonte, compowned after the latitude of *Oxenford*; upon which, by mediacion of this litel tretis, I purpose to teche thee a certein nombre of conclusions apertening to the same instrument. I seye a certein of conclusiouns, for three causes. The furste cause is this: truste wel that alle the conclusiouns that han ben founde, or elles possibly mighten be founde in so noble an instrument as an Astrolabie, ben unknowe perfitly to any mortal man in this regioun, as I suppose. Another cause is this: that sothly, in any tretis of the Astrolabie that I have seyn, there ben some conclusions that wole nat in alle thinges performen hir bihestes; and some of hem ben to harde to thy tendre age of ten yeer to conseyve. This tretis, divided in fyve parties, wole I shewe thee under ful lighte rewles and naked wordes in English; for Latin ne canstow yit but smal, my lyte sone. But natheles, suffyse to thee thise trewe conclusiouns in English, as wel as suffyseth to thise noble clerkes Grekes thise same conclusiouns in Greek, and to Arabiens in Arabik, and to Jewes in Ebrew, and to the Latin folk in Latin; whiche Latin folk han hem furst out of othre diverse langages, and writen in hir owne tonge, that is to sein, in Latin. And God wot, that in alle thise langages, and in many mo, han thise conclusiouns ben suffisantly lerned and taught, and yit by diverse rewles, right as diverse pathes leden diverse folk the righte wey to *Rome*.

A Treatise on the Astrolabe

1 *mechel*) *much* 9 *a certein of*) *a certain* (*limited*) *number of*
23 *noble clerkes Grekes*) *learned Greeks* 26 *han*) *have*

6 *O stelliferi conditor orbis*

O THOU Maker of the whele that bereth the sterres, which that art y-fastned to thy perdurable chayer, and tornest the hevene with a ravisshing sweigh, and constreinest the sterres to suffren thy lawe; so that the mone somtyme shyning with hir ful hornes, meting with alle the bemes of the sonne hir brother, hydeth the sterres that ben lesse; and somtyme, whan the mone, pale with hir derke hornes, approcheth the sonne, leseth hir lightes; and that the eve-sterre *Hesperus*, whiche that in the firste tyme of the night bringeth forth hir colde arysinges, cometh eft ayein hir used cours, and is pale by the morwe at the rysing of the sonne, and is thanne cleped *Lucifer*. Thou restreinest the day by shorter dwelling, in the tyme of colde winter that maketh the leves to falle. Thou dividest the swifte tydes of the night, whan the hote somer is comen. Thy might atempreth the variaunts sesons of the yere; so that *Zephirus* the deboneir wind bringeth ayein, in the first somer sesoun, the leves that the wind that highte *Boreas* hath reft awey in autumpne, that is to seyn, in the laste ende of somer; and the sedes that the sterre that highte *Arcturus* saw, ben waxen heye cornes whan the sterre *Sirius* eschaufeth hem. Ther nis nothing unbounde from his olde lawe, ne forleteth the werke of his propre estat.

O thou governour, governinge alle thinges by certein ende, why refusestow only to governe the werkes of men by dewe manere? Why suffrest thou that

4 *sweigh*) *movement* 11 *cometh eft ayein*) *returns to* 12 *morwe*) *morning* 14 *dwelling*) *tarrying* 24 *eschaufeth*) *warms* 25 *forleteth*) *leaves*

slydinge *Fortune* torneth so grete entre-chaunginges of thinges, so that anoyous peyne, that sholde dewely punisshe felouns, punissheth innocents? And folk of wikkede maneres sitten in heye chayres, and anoyinge folk treden, and that unrightfully, on the nekkes of holy men? And vertu, cler-shyninge naturelly, is hid in derke derkenesses, and the rightful man bereth the blame and the peyne of the feloun. Ne forsweringe ne the fraude, covered and kembd with a fals colour, ne anoyeth nat to shrewes; the whiche shrewes, whan hem list to usen hir strengthe, they rejoysen hem to putten under hem the sovereyne kinges whiche that poeple with-outen noumbre dreden.

O thou, what so ever thou be that knittest alle bondes of thinges, loke on thise wrecchede erthes; we men that ben nat a foule party but a fayr party of so grete a werk, we ben tormented in this see of fortune. Thou Governour, withdraw and restreyne the ravisshinge flodes, and fastne and ferme thise erthes stable with thilke bonde with whiche thou governest the hevene that is so large.

Boethius *de Consolatione Philosophie*

7 *Sins of the Tongue*

LAT us thanne speken of chydinge and reproche, whiche been ful grete woundes in mannes herte; for they unsowen the semes of frendshipe in mannes herte. For certes, unnethes may a man pleynly been accorded with him that hath him openly revyled and repreved in disclaundre. This is a ful grisly sinne, as Crist seith in the gospel. . . And certes, chydinge

9 *kembd) trimmed (combed)* 10 *shrewes) scoundrels* 25 *unnethes) hardly* 27 *repreved) reproved* *disclaundre) disgrace*

may nat come but out of a vileyns herte. For after the habundance of the herte speketh the mouth ful ofte. . . . Lo, what seith seint Augustin : 'ther is nothing so lyk the develes child as he that ofte chydeth.' Seint Paul seith eek : 'I, servant of god, bihove nat to chyde.' And how that chydinge be a vileyns thing bitwixe alle manere folk, yet it is certes most uncovenable bitwixe a man and his wyf ; for there is nevere reste. And therfore seith Salomon, 'an hous that is uncovered and droppinge, and a chydinge wyf, been lyke.' A man that is in a droppinge hous in many places, though he eschewe the droppinge in o place, it droppeth on him in another place. So fareth it by a chydinge wyf. But she chyde him in o place, she wol chyde him in another. . .

Now comth the sinne of hem that sowen and maken discord amonges folk, which is a sinne that Crist hateth outrely ; and no wonder is. For he deyde for to make concord. And more shame do they to Crist, than dide they that him crucifyede ; for god loveth bettre that frendshipe be amonges folk, than he dide his owene body, the which that he yaf for unitee. Therfore been they lykned to the devel, that evere been aboute to maken discord. . .

Now comth janglinge, that may nat been withoute sinne. And, as seith Salomon, 'it is a sinne of apert folye.' And therfore a philosophre seyde, whan men axed him how that men sholde plese the peple, and he answerde, 'do many gode werkes, and spek fewe jangles.'

After this comth the sinne of japeres, that been the develes apes ; for they maken folk to laughe at hir

6 *how that) whereas* 7 *uncovenable) unsuitable* 13, 15 *o) one*
14 *But) unless* 18 *outrely) utterly* 26 *apert) open*

japerie, as folk doon at the gaudes of an ape. Swiche japeres deffendeth seint Paul. Loke how that vertuouse wordes and holy conforten hem that travaillen in the service of Crist; right so conforten the vileyns wordes and knakkes of japeris hem that travaillen in the service of the devel. Thise been the sinnes that comen of the tonge.

The Persones Tale

SIR JOHN MANDEVILLE

d. 1372

8 *Of Paradise*

OF paradys ne can I not speken propurly for I was not there; it is fer beyonde and that forthinketh me. And also I was not worthi. But as I have herd seye of wyse men beyonde, I schall telle you with gode will. Paradys terrestre, as wise men seyn, is the highest place of erthe that is in all the world and it is so high that it toucheth nygh to the cercle of the mone, there as the mone maketh hire torn. For sche is so high that the flode of Noe ne myght not come to hire, that wolde have covered all the erthe of the world all abowte and aboven and benethen, saf Paradys only allone. And this Paradys is enclosed all aboute with a wall and men wyte not wherof it is. For the walles ben covered all over with mosse, as it semeth. And it semeth not that the wall is ston of nature ne of non other thing that the wall is. And that wall streccheth fro the south to the north And it hath not but one entree that is closed with fyre brennynge, so that noman that is mortall ne dar not

1 *gaudes*) *tricks* 2 *deffendeth*) *forbids* 5 *knakkes*) *tricks*
9 *that forthinketh me*) *I am sorry for that* 15 *torn*) *turn*

entren. And in the most high place of PARADYS, evene in the myddel place, is a welle that casteth out the .iiij. flodes that rennen be dyverse londes. Of the whiche the firste is clept PHISON or GANGES, that is all one, and it renneth thorghout YNDE or EMLAK. In the whiche Ryvere ben manye preciouse stones, and mochel of LIGNUM ALOES, and moche gravell of gold. And that other Ryvere is clept NILUS or GYSON, that goth be ETHIOPE and after be EGYPT. And that other is clept TIGRIS, that renneth be ASSIRYE and be ARMENYE the grete. And that other is clept EUFRATE that renneth also be MEDEE and be ARMONYE and be PERSYE. And men there beyonde seyn that alle the swete watres of the world aboven and benethen taken hire begynnynge of that welle of PARADYS, and out of that welle all watres comen and gon. . . And yee schull understonde that noman that is mortell ne may not approchen to that PARADYS. For be londe noman may go for wylde bestes that ben in the desertes and for the high mountaynes and grete huge roches, that noman may passe by, for the derke places that ben there and that manye. And be the ryveres may noman go, for the water renneth so rudely and so scharply, because that it cometh doun so outrageously from the high places aboven, that it renneth in so grete wawes that no schipp may not rowe ne seyle agenes it. And the water roreth so and maketh so huge noyse and so gret tempest that noman may here other in the schipp, though he cryede with all the craft that he cowde in the hieste voys that he myghte. Many grete lordes han assayed with gret wille many tymes for to passen be tho ryveres toward PARADYS with full grete companyes, but thei myghte

32 *tho*) those

not speden in hire viage. And manye dyeden for weryness of rowynge agenst tho stronge wawes. And many of hem becamen blynde and many deve for the noyse of the water. And summe weren perisscht and loste withinne the wawes. So that no mortell man may approche to that place withouten specyall grace of God, so that of that place I can sey you nomore.

The Voiage and Travaile of Sir John Maundeville

9 *Of the Centre of the Earth*

ALSO yee have herd me seye that JERUSALEM is in the myddes of the world; and that may men preven and schewen, there be a spere that is right into the erthe upon the hour of mydday whan it is EQUENOXIUM, that scheweth no schadwe on no syde. And that it scholde ben in the myddes of the world, *David* wytnesseth it in the psauter where he seyth: DEUS OPERATUS EST SALUTEM IN MEDIO TERRE. Thanne thei that parten fro tho parties of the west for to go toward JERUSALEM, als many jorneyes as thei gon upward for to go thider, in als many journeyes may thei gon fro JERUSALEM unto other confynyes of the superficialtee of the erthe beyonde. And whan men gon beyonde tho journeys toward YNDE and to the foreyn yles, all is envyronynge the roundnesse of the erthe and of the see under oure contrees on this half. And therfore hath it befallen many tymes of o thing that I have herd cownted whan I was yong, how a worthi man departed somtyme from oure contrees for to go serche the world. And so he passed YNDE and the yles beyonde YNDE where ben mo than .v. M[1]. yles. And so

1 *viage*) *journey* 3 *deve*) *deaf* 28 *.v.Ml.*) 5000

longe he wente be see and lond, and so enviround the world be many seisons, that he fond an yle where he herde speke his owne langage, callynge on oxen in the plowgh suche wordes as men speken to bestes in his owne contree. Whereof he hadde gret mervayle, for he knew not how it myghte be.

The Voiage and Travaile of Sir John Maundeville

10 *The Lady of the Land*

AND somme men seyn that in the Ile of LANGO is yit the doughter of *Ypocras* in forme and lykness of a gret dragoun, that is an hundred fadme of lengthe as men seyn, for I have not seen hire. And thei of the Iles callen hire lady of the lond. And sche lyeth in an olde castell in a cave, and scheweth twyes or thryes in the yeer, and sche doth non harm to no man but yif men don hire harm. And sche was thus chaunged and transformed from a fair damysele into lykness of a dragoun be a Goddess that was clept *Deane*. And men seyn that sche schal so endure in that forme of a dragoun unto tyme that a knyght come that is so hardy that dar come to hire and kisse hire on the mouth, and than schall sche turne agen to hire owne kynde and ben a womman agen, but after that sche schall not lyven longe. . . And it is not longe sithen that a yonge man, that wiste not of the dragoun, wente out of a schipp, and wente thorgh the Ile til that he come to the castell, and cam into the cave and wente so longe til that he fond a chambre, and there he saugh a damysele that kembed hire hede and lokede in a myrour. And sche hadde meche tresoure abouten

9 *fadme) fathom* 27 *kembed) combed*

hire and he trowede that sche hadde ben a comoun womman that dwelled there to resceyve men to folye. And he abode till the damysele saugh the schadewe of him in the myrour. And sche turned hire toward him and asked hym what he wolde. And he seyde he wolde ben hire lemman or paramour, and sche asked him yif that he were a knyght, and he seyde nay. And than sche seyde that he myghte not ben hire lemman. But sche bad him gon agen unto his felowes and let make him knyght, and come agen upon the morwe, and sche scholde come out of the cave before him, and thanne come and kysse hire on the mowth. 'And have no drede, for I schall do the no maner harm, all be it that thou see me in lykeness of a dragoun.' For though thou se me hidouse and horrible to loken onne, I do the to wytene that it is made be enchauntement. For withouten doute I am non other than thou seest now, a womman, and therfore drede the nought. And yif thou kisse me thou schalt have all this tresoure, and be my lord and lord also of all that Ile. And he departed fro hire, and wente to his felowes to schippe, and leet make him knyght, and cam agen upon the morwe for to kysse this damysele. And whan he saugh hire comen out of the cave in forme of a dragoun so hidouse and so horrible, he hadde so gret drede that he fleygh agen to the schipp, and sche folewed him. And whan sche saw that he turned not agen, sche began to crye as a thing that hadde meche sorwe. And thanne sche turned agen into hire cave. And anon the knyght dyede, and sithen hiderwardes myghte no knyght se hire but that he dyede anon. But whan a knyght cometh that is so hardy to kisse hire, he schall not dye, but he schall turne the damysele into hire

16 *I do the to wytene*) *I tell thee* 30 *sithen hiderwardes*) *till now*

right forme and kyndely schapp, and he schal be lord of all the contreyes and Iles aboveseyd.

The Voiage and Travaile of Sir John Maundeville

11 *Noes Schipp*

FRA that cytee of ARTYROUN go men to an hill that is clept SABISSOCOLLE; and there besyde is another hill that men clepen ARARATH, but the Jewes clepen it TANEEZ, where Noes schipp rested and yit is upon that montayne. And men may seen it aferr in cleer weder. And that montayne is wel a vij. myle high. And sum men seyn that thei han seen and touched the schipp, and put here fyngres in the parties where the feend went out whan that Noe seyde *Benedicite*. But thei that seyn suche woordes seyn here wille. For a man may not gon up the montayne for gret plentee of snow that is allweys on that montayne, nouther somer ne wynter, so that noman may gon up there, ne neuere man dide, sithe the tyme of Noe, saf a monk that be the grace of God broughte one of the plankes doun, that yit is in the mynstre at the foot of the montayne.

The Voiage and Travaile of Sir John Maundeville

THE LADY JULIAN OF NORWICH

1373

12 *The Courtesy of our Lord*

FLE we to our Lord and we shall be comforted; touch we him and we shall be made clene; cleeve to him and we shall be sekir and safe fro al maner of peril. For our curtes Lord will that we ben as homley

1 *kyndely schapp*) *natural shape* 11 *the feend*) *the Devil* 22 *sekir*) *secure* 23 *curtes*) *courteous*

with him as herte may thinke or soule may desiren. But beware that we taken not so reklesly this homleyhede that we levyn curtesy. For our Lord himselfe is sovereyn homleyhede; and as homley as he is, as curtes he is, for he is very curtes. And the blissid creatures that shall ben in hevyn with him without end, he will have them like to himselfe in all things. And to be like our Lord perfectly it is our very salvation and our full bliss. And if we wott not how we shall don all this, desire we of our Lord and he shal lerne us. For it is his owne likeing and his worship: blissid mot he be.

XVI Revelations of Divine Love

ANONYMOUS

c. 1400

13 *The Magpie and the Eel*

I WOLL tell you an ensaumple of a woman that ete the good morsell in the absence of her husbonde. Ther was a woman that had a pie in a cage, that spake and wolde tell talys that she saw do. And so it happed that her husbonde made kepe a gret ele in a litell ponde in his gardin, to that entent to yeue it sum of his frendes that wolde come to see hym; but the wyff, whanne her husbond was oute, saide to her maide, 'late us ete the gret ele, and y will saie to my husbond that the otour hathe eten hym;' and so it was done. And whan the good man was come, the pye began to tell hym how her maistresse had eten the ele. And he yode to the ponde, and fonde not the ele. And he asked his wiff wher the ele was

2 *homleyhede) (homeliness) intimacy* 3 *levyn) leave* 22 *otour) otter* 25 *yode) went*

become. And she wende to have excused her, but he saide her, 'excuse you not, for y wote well ye have eten yt, for the pye hathe told me.' And so ther was gret noyse betwene the man and hys wiff for etinge of the ele. But whanne the good man was gone, the maistresse and the maide come to the pie, and plucked of all the fedres on the pyes hede, saieng, 'thou hast discovered us of the ele;' and thus was the pore pye plucked. But ever after, whanne the pie sawe a balled or a pilled man, or a woman with an high forhede, the pie saide to hem, 'ye spake of the ele.' And therfor here is an ensaumple that no woman shulde ete no lycorous morcelles in the absens and withoute weting of her husbond, but yef it so were that it be with folk of worshipp, to make hem chere; for this woman was afterward mocked for the pye and the ele.

The Knight de la Tour Landry

JOHN CAPGRAVE

1393–1464

14 *Times of Tribulation*

IN the XXI. yere, whan Kyng Philip of Frauns was fled thus cowardly fro the sege of Caleys, thei of the same town offered the town to Kyng Edward withoute any poyntment. And he lay in the town a month, considering the strong disposicion thereof. Thanne, at instauns of the Pope, was taken trews betwix the two Kyngis for a yere. Aboute the fest of Seynt Michael, the Kyng took the se into Ynglond and there had he grete tempest, and mervelous wyndes;

1 *wende*) *thought* 10 *pilled*) *shaven* 13 *lycorous*) *dainty* *weting*) *knowledge* 14 *but yef*) *unless* 17 *XXI. yere*) *A.D. 1347* 20 *poyntment*) *conditions*

and thanne he mad swech a compleynt onto oure Lady, and seide, O blessed Mayde, what menyth al this? Evyr, whan I go to Frauns, I have fayre wedir, and whanne I turne to Ynglond intollerable tempestes.

In the XXII. yere were grete reynes, whech dured fro the Nativité of Seynt Jon Baptist onto Cristmasse.

And aftir that reyne there folowid a grete pestilens, specialy in the Est side of the world amongst the Sarasines. So many deied, that there left scarsly among hem the tenth man, or the tenth woman. Thei, seyng this veniauns amongst hem, purposed veryly to be Cristen. But whan thei wist that the pestilens was among the Cristen men, than her good purpos sesed.

In the XXIII. yere was the Grete Pestilens of puple. First it began in the north cuntre; than in the south; and so forth thorw oute the reme. Aftir this pestilens folowed a moreyn of bestis, whech had nevir be seyn. For, as it was supposed, there left not in Inglond the ten part of the puple. Than cesed lordes rentis, prestis tithes. Because there were so fewe tylmen, the erde lay untillid. So mech misery was in the lond, that the prosperité whech was before was nevir recured.

The Chronicle of England

SIR JOHN FORTESCUE

1394?–1476?

15 *The Cheap Defence of England*

SOME men haue said that it were good for the kyng, that the commons of Englande were made pore, as be the commons of Fraunce. For than thai wolde not rebelle, as now thai done oftentymes;

9 *left) remained* 11 *veniauns) vengeance* 14 *puple) people* 22 *recured) recovered*

wich the commons of Fraunce do not, nor mey doo; for thai haue no wepen, nor armour, nor good to bie it with all. To theis maner of men mey be said with the phylosopher, *ad pauca respicientes de facili enunciant.* This is to say, thai that see but few thynges, woll sone say thair advyses. For soth theis folke consideren litill the good of the reaume of Englond, wherof the myght stondith most vppon archers, wich be no ryche men. And yf thai were made more pouere than thai be, thai shulde not haue wherwith to bie hem bowes, arroes, jakkes, or any other armour of defence, wherby thai myght be able to resiste owre enymes, when thai liste to come vppon vs; wich thai mey do in euery side, considerynge that we be a Ilelonde; and, as it is said before, we mey not sone haue soucour of any other reaume. Wherfore we shull be a pray to all owre enymyes, but yf we be myghty of owreself, wich myght stondith most vppon owre pouere archers; and therfore thai nedun not only haue suche ablements as now is spoken of, but also thai nedun to be much excersised in shotynge, wich mey not be done withowt ryght grete expenses, as euery man experte therin knowith ryght well. Wherfore the makyng pouere of the commons, wich is the makyng pouere of owre archers, shalbe the distruccion of the grettest myght of owre reaume.

The Governance of England

11 *jakkes) jackets of quilted leather* 20 *nedun) need*

WILLIAM CAXTON

1422?–1491

16 *Discretion*

THER was a child of Rome that was named Papirus that on a tyme went with his fader whiche was a senatour into the chambre where as they helde their counceyll. And that tyme they spak of suche maters as was comanded and agreed shold be kept secrete upon payn of their heedes, and so departed. And whan he was comen home from the senatoire and fro the counceyll with his fader, his moder demanded of hym what was the counceyll and whereof they spack and had taryed so longe there. And the childe answerd to her and sayd he durst not telle ner saye hit for so moche as hit was defended upon payn of deth. Than was the moder more desirous to knowe than she was to fore, and began to flatere hym one tyme, and afterward to menace hym that he shold saye and telle to her what hit was. And whan the childe sawe that he might have no reste of his moder in no wise, he made her first promise that she shold kepe hit secrete and to telle hit to none of the world. And that doon he fayned a lesing or a lye and sayd to her that the senatours had in counceyll a grete question and difference which was this : whether hit were better and more for the comyn wele of Rome that a man shold have two wyvys or a wyf to have two husbondes. And whan she had understonde this, he defended her that she shold telle hit to none other body. And after this she wente to her gossyb and told to her this

12 *defended*) *forbidden*

counceyll secretly, and she told to an other, and thus every wyf tolde hit to other in secrete. And thus hit happend anone after that alle the wyves of Rome cam to the senatorye where the senatours were assemblid, and cryed with an hye voys that they had lever, and also hit were better for the comyn wele that a wyf shold have two husbondes than a man two wyves.

Game and Playe of the Chesse

17 *His Labours*

THUS ende I this book, whyche I haue translated after myn Auctor as nyghe as god hath gyuen me connyng, to whom be gyuen the laude and preysyng. And for as moche as in the wrytyng of the same my penne is worn, myn hande wery and not stedfast, myn eyen dimmed with ouermoche lokyng on the whit paper, and my corage not so prone and redy to laboure as hit hath ben, and that age crepeth on me dayly and febleth all the bodye, and also because I haue promysid to dyuerce gentilmen and to my frendes to adresse to hem as hastely as I myght this sayd book, therfore I haue practysed and lerned at my grete charge and dispense to ordeyne this said book in prynte after the maner and forme as ye may here see, and is not wreton with penne and ynke as other bokes ben, to thende that euery man may haue them attones: for all the bookes of this storye named the Recule of the Historyes of Troyes thus enpryntid as ye here see were begonne in oon day, and also fynysshid in oon day, whiche book I haue presented to my sayd redoubtid lady as

24 *attones*) *at once*

afore is sayd. And she hath well acceptid hit, and largely rewarded me: wherfore I beseche almyghty God to rewarde her euerlastyng blisse after this lyf. Prayng her said grace and all them that shall rede this book not to desdaigne the symple and rude werke, nether to replye agaynst the sayyng of the maters towchyd in this book, thauwh hyt acorde not vnto the translacion of other whiche haue wreton hit: for dyuerce men haue made dyuerce bookes, whiche in all poyntes acorde not . . .; but alle acorde in conclusion the generall destruccion of that noble cyté of Troye. And the deth of so many noble prynces, as kynges, dukes, Erles, barons, knyghtes, and comyn peple, and the ruyne irreperable of that Cyté that neuer syn was reedefyed, whiche may be ensample to all men duryng the world how dredefull and Ieopardous it is to begynne a warre, and what harmes, losses and deth foloweth. Therfore thapostle saith all that is wreton is wreton to our doctryne, whyche doctryne for the comyn wele I beseche God maye be taken in suche place and tyme as shall be moste nedefull in encrecyng of peas, loue, and charyté, whyche graunte vs he that suffryd for the same to be crucyfied on the rood tree. And saye we alle Amen for charyté.

Epilogue to Book III of the *Recuyell of Troy*

18 *His Homage to Chaucer*

THUS endeth this boke whiche is named the boke of Consolacion of philosophie, whiche that Boecius made for his comforte and consolacion, he beyng in exile for the comyn and publick wele, hauyng grete heuynes & thoughtes and in maner of despayr, Rehercing in the sayde boke howe Philosophie appiered to him, shewyng the mutabilité of this transitorie lyfe, and also enformyng howe fortune and happe shold bee vnderstonden, with the predestynacion and prescience of God as moche as maye and ys possible to bee knowen naturelly, as afore ys sayd in this sayd boke . . . And for as moche as the stile of it is harde & difficile to be vnderstonde of simple persones Therfore the worshipful fader & first foundeur & enbelissher of ornate eloquence in our Englissh (I mene, Maister Geffrey Chaucer) hath translated this sayd werke oute of Latyn in to oure vsual and moder tonge, folowyng the Latyn as neygh as is possible to be vnderstande. Wherein in myne oppynyon he hath deseruid a perpetuell lawde and thanke of al this noble Royame of Englond, and in especiall of them that shall rede & vnderstande it. For in the sayd boke they may see what this transitorie & mutable worlde is, and wherto euery man liuyng in hit ought to entende. Thenne for as moche as this sayd boke so translated is rare & not spred ne knowen as it is digne and worthy, for the erudicion and lernyng of suche as ben Ignoraunt & not knowyng of it, atte requeste of a singuler frende & gossib of myne, I William Caxton haue done my debuoir & payne t'enprynte it in fourme as is here afore made, in hopyng that it shal prouffite moche peple to the wele & helth of theire soules, & for to lerne to haue and kepe the better pacience in aduersitees. And furthermore I desire & require you that of your charite ye wold praye for the soule of the sayd worshipful man Geffrey Chaucer, first translatour of this sayde boke into Englissh & enbelissher in making the sayd langage ornate & fayr: whiche shal endure perpetuelly, and therfore he ought eternelly to be remembrid.

Preface to Boethius *de Consolacione Philosophie*

19 *Of Le Morte Arthur*

THENNE al these thynges forsayd aledged I coude not wel denye, but that there was suche a noble kyng named Arthur, and reputed one of the ix Worthy, & fyrst & chyef of the cristen men. And many noble volumes be made of hym & of his noble knyghtes in frensshe, which I have seen & redde beyonde the see, which been not had in our maternal tongue. But in walsshe ben many, & also in frensshe, & somme in englysshe, but no wher nygh alle. Wherfore suche as have late ben drawen oute bryefly in to englysshe, I have after the symple connynge that God hath sente to me, under the favour and correctyon of al noble lordes and gentylmen, enprysed to enprynte a book of the noble hystoryes of the sayd kynge Arthur, and of certeyn of his knyghtes, after a copye unto me delyverd, whyche copye Syr Thomas Malorye dyd take oute of certeyn bookes of frensshe and reduced it in to Englysshe. And I accordyng to my copye have doon sette it in enprynte, to the entente that

12 *of the ix Worthy) of the nine 'Christian Worthies'* 22 *enprysed) undertaken*

noble men may see and lerne the noble actes of chyvalrye, the Ientyl and vertuous dedes that somme knyghtes used in tho dayes, by whyche they came to honour, and how they that were vycious were punysshed and ofte put to shame and rebuke, humbly bysechyng al noble lordes and ladyes wyth al other estates of what estate or degree they been of, that shal see and rede in this sayd book and werke, that they take the good and honest actes in their remembraunce, and to folowe the same. Wherin they shalle fynde many Ioyous and playsaunt hystoryes, and noble & renomed actes of humanyté, gentylnesse and chyualryes. For herein may be seen noble chyualrye, Curtosye, Humanyté, frendlynesse, hardynesse, loue, frendshyp, Cowardyse, Murdre, hate, vertue, and synne. Doo after the good and leue the euyl, and it shal brynge you to good fame and renommee.

Preface to Malory's *Le Morte Arthur*

SIR THOMAS MALORY

fl. 1470

20 *The Month of May*

AND thus it past on from Candylmas untyl after Ester that the moneth of May was come, whan every lusty herte begynneth to blosomme and to brynge forth fruyte. For lyke as herbes and trees bryngen forth fruyte and florysshen in May, in lyke wyse every lusty herte that is in ony maner a lover spryngeth and floryssheth in lusty dedes. For it gyveth unto al lovers courage, that lusty moneth of May, in some thyng to constrayne hym to some

11 *renomed*) *renowned*

maner of thyng more in that moneth than in ony other moneth, for dyverse causes. For thenne alle herbes and trees renewen a man and woman. And lyke wyse lovers callen ageyne to their mynde old gentilnes and old servyse, and many kynde dedes were forgeten by neclygence. For lyke as wynter rasure doth alway arase and deface grene somer, soo fareth it by unstable love in man and woman. For in many persons there is no stabylyté. For we may see al day, for a lytel blast of wynters rasure anone we shalle deface and lay aparte true love, for lytel or noughte, that cost moch thynge. This is no wysedome nor stabylyté, but it is feblenes of nature and grete disworshyp who somever used this. Therfore lyke as May moneth floreth and floryssheth in many gardyns, soo in lyke wyse lete every man of worship florysshe his herte in this world, fyrst unto God, and next unto the ioye of them that he promysed his feythe unto. For there was never worshypful man or worshipfull woman but they loved one better than another. And worshyp in armes may never be foyled, but fyrst reserve the honour to God, and secondly the quarel must come of thy lady, and suche love I calle vertuous love. But now adayes men can not love seven nyghte but they must have alle their desyres. That love may not endure by reason. For where they ben soone accorded, and hasty hete, soone it keleth. Ryghte soo fareth love now adayes: sone hote, soone cold. This is noo stabylyté. But the old love was not so. Men and wymmen coude love togyders seven yeres, and no lycours lustes were bitwene them, and thenne was love trouthe and feythfulnes. And loo in lyke wyse was used love in kynge Arthurs dayes. Wherfor I lyken love now

21 *foyled*) *defiled* 27 *keleth*) *cooleth* 30 *togyders*) *together*

adayes unto somer and wynter. For lyke as the one is hote & the other cold, so fareth love now adayes. Therfore alle ye that be lovers calle unto your remembraunce the moneth of May, lyke as dyd quene Guenever. For whome I make here a lytel mencyon, that whyle she lyved she was a true lover, and therfor she had a good ende.

Le Morte Arthur

21 *The Maid of Astolat*

NOW speke we of the fayre mayden of Astolat, that made suche sorowe daye and nyght that she never slepte, ete, nor drank, and ever she made her complaynt unto sir Launcelot. So when she had thus endured a ten dayes, that she febled so that she must nedes passe out of thys world, thenne she shryved her clene, and receyved her creatoure. And ever she complayned stylle upon sire Launcelot. Thenne her ghoostly fader bad her leve suche thoughtes. Thenne she sayd, Why shold I leve suche thoughtes? am I not an erthely woman? and alle the whyle the brethe is in my body I may complayne me, for my byleve is I doo none offence though I love an erthely man, and I take God to my record I loved none but sir Launcelot du Lake, nor never shall. And a clene mayden I am for hym and for alle other. And sythen hit is the sufferaunce of God that I shalle dye for the love of soo noble a knyghte, I byseche the hyghe fader of heven to have mercy upon my sowle, and upon myn innumerable paynes that I suffred may be allygeaunce of parte of my synnes. For swete lord

28 *allygeaunce*) *alleviation*

Ihesu, sayd the fayre mayden, I take the to record, on the I was never grete offenser ageynst thy lawes, but that I loved this noble knyght sire Launcelot out of mesure, and of my self, good lord, I myght not withstande the fervent love wherfor I have my dethe. And thenne she called her fader sire Bernard and her broder sir Tyrre, and hertely she praid her fader that her broder myght wryte a letter lyke as she did endyte hit: and so her fader graunted her. And whan the letter was wryten word by word lyke as she devysed, thenne she prayd her fader that she myght be watched untyl she were dede: And whyle my body is hote lete this letter be putt in my ryght hand, and my hande bounde fast with the letter untyl that I be cold, and lete me be putte in a fayre bedde with alle the rychest clothes that I have aboute me, and so lete my bedde and alle my rychest clothes be laide with me in a charyot unto the next place where Temse is, and there lete me be putte within a barget, & but one man with me, suche as ye trust to stere me thyder, and that my barget be coverd with blak samyte over and over. Thus, fader, I byseche yow, lete hit be done. Soo her fader graunted hit her feythfully alle thynge shold be done lyke as she had devysed. Thenne her fader and her broder made grete dole, for when this was done, anone she dyed. And soo whan she was dede, the corps and the bedde alle was ledde the next way vnto Temse, and there a man and the corps & alle were put in to Temse. And soo the man styred the barget unto Westmynster, and there he rowed a grete whyle to & fro or ony aspyed hit.

Soo by fortune kynge Arthur and the quene Guenever were spekynge togyders at a wyndowe, and

31 *or) ere* 33 *togyders) together*

soo as they loked in to Temse they aspyed this blak barget, and hadde merveylle what it mente. Thenne the kynge called sire Kay, & shewed hit hym. Sir, said sir Kay, wete you wel there is some newe tydynges. Goo thyder, sayd the kynge to sir Kay, & take with yow sire Brandyles and Agravayne, and brynge me redy word what is there. Thenne these four knyghtes departed and came to the barget and wente in, and there they fond the fayrest corps lyenge in a ryche bedde, and a poure man sittyng in the bargets ende, and no word wold he speke. Soo these foure knyghtes retorned unto the kyng ageyne, and told hym what they fond. That fayr corps wylle I see, sayd the kynge. And soo thenne the kyng took the quene by the hand & went thydder. Thenne the kynge made the barget to be holden fast; & thenne the kyng & the quene entred, with certayn knyghtes wyth them. And there he sawe the fayrest woman lye in a ryche bedde coverd unto her myddel with many ryche clothes, and alle was of clothe of gold, and she lay as though she had smyled. Thenne the quene aspyed a letter in her ryght hand, and told it to the kynge. Thenne the kynge took it, and sayd, Now am I sure this letter wille telle what she was, and why she is come hydder. Soo thenne the kynge and the quene wente oute of the barget, and soo commaunded a certayne wayte upon the barget. And soo whan the kynge was come within his chamber he called many knyghtes aboute hym, & saide that he wold wete openly what was wryten within that letter. Thenne the kynge brake it, & made a clerke to rede hit. & this was the entente of the letter: Moost noble knyghte, sir Launcelot, now hath dethe made us two at debate for your love. I was your lover, that men called the fayre mayden of Astolat: therfor unto alle ladyes I make my mone. Yet praye for my soule, & bery me atte leest, & offre ye my masse peny; this is my last request. And a clene mayden I dyed, I take God to wytnes. Pray for my soule, sir Launcelot, as thou art pierles. This was alle the substance in the letter. And whan it was redde the kyng, the quene and alle the knyghtes wepte for pyté of the doleful complayntes. Thenne was sire Launcelot sente for. And whan he was come kynge Arthur made the letter to be redde to hym. And whanne sire Launcelot herd hit word by word, he sayd, My lord Arthur, wete ye wel I am ryghte hevy of the dethe of this fair damoysel. God knoweth I was never causer of her dethe by my wyllynge, & that wille I reporte me to her own broder: here he is, sir Lavayne. I wille not saye nay, sayd syre Launcelot, but that she was bothe fayre and good, and moche I was beholden unto her, but she loved me out of mesure. Ye myght have shewed her, sayd the quene, somme bounté and gentilnes that myghte have preserved her lyf. Madame, sayd sir Launcelot, she wold none other wayes be ansuerd but that she wold be my wyf, outher els my peramour, and of these two I wold not graunte her. But I proferd her, for her good love that she shewed me, a thousand pound yerly to her and to her heyres, and to wedde ony manere knyghte that she coude fynde best to love in her herte. For, madame, said sir Launcelot, I love not to be constrayned to love. For love muste aryse of the herte, and not by no constraynte. That is trouth, sayd the kynge and many knyghtes: love is free in hym selfe, and never wille be bounden, for where he is bounden he looseth hym self. Thenne

23 *outher) or*

sayd the kynge unto sire Launcelot, Hit wyl be your worshyp that ye over see that she be entered worshypfully. Sire, sayd sire Launcelot, that shalle be done as I can best devyse. And soo many knyghtes yede thyder to behold that fayr mayden. And soo upon the morne she was entered rychely, and sir Launcelot offryd her masse peny, and all the knyghtes of the table round that were there at that tyme offryd with syr Launcelot. And thenne the poure man wente ageyne with the barget.

Le Morte Arthur

22 *The Last Meeting of Launcelot and Guenever*

SO it was no bote to stryve, but he departed and rode westerly, & there he sought a vij or viij dayes, & atte last he cam to a nonnerye, & than was quene Guenever ware of sir Launcelot as he walked in the cloystre. And whan she sawe hym there she swouned thryse, that al the ladyes & Ientyl wymmen had werke ynough to holde the quene up. So whan she myght speke she callyd ladyes & Ientyl wymmen to hir & sayd, Ye mervayl, fayr ladyes, why I make this fare. Truly, she said, it is for the syght of yonder knyght that yender standeth. Wherfore, I praye you al, calle hym to me. Whan syr Launcelot was brought to hyr, than she sayd to al the ladyes, Thorowe this man & me hath al this warre be wrought, & the deth of the moost noblest knyghtes of the world. For thorugh our love that we have loved togyder is my moost noble lord slayn. Therfor, syr Launcelot, wyt

11 *bote*) *good* 20 *fare*) *stir*

thou wel I am sette in suche a plyte to gete my soule hele. & yet I truste thorugh Goddes grace that after my deth to have a syght of the blessyd face of Cryst, and at domes day to sytte on his ryght syde, for as synful as ever I was are sayntes in heven. Therfore, syr Launcelot, I requyre the & beseche the hertelye, for al the love that ever was betwyxte us, that thou never see me more in the vysage, & I comande the on goddes behalfe that thou forsake my companye, & to thy kyngdom thou torne ageyn & kepe wel thy royame from warre & wrake. For as wel as I have loved the, myn hert wyl not serve me to see the, for thorugh the & me is the flour of kynges & knyghtes destroyed. Therfor, sir Launcelot, goo to thy royame, & there take the a wyf, & lyve with hir with Ioye & blysse. & I praye the hertelye praye for me to our Lord, that I may amende my myslyvyng. Now, swete madam, sayd syr Launcelot, wold ye that I shold torne ageyn unto my cuntreye & there to wedde a lady? Nay, Madam, wyt you wel that shal I never do, for I shal never be soo fals to you of that I have promysed, but the same deystenye that ye have taken you to I wyl take me unto, for to plese Iesu, & ever for you I cast me specially to praye. Yf thou wylt do so, sayd the quene, holde thy promyse. But I may never byleve but that thou wylt torne to the world ageyn. Wel, madam, sayd he, ye say as pleseth you, yet wyst you me never fals of my promesse, & God defende but I shold forsake the world as ye have do. For in the quest of the Sank Greal I had forsaken the vanytees of the world had not your lord ben. And yf I had done so at that tyme wyth my herte, wylle and thought, I had passed al the knyghtes that were in the Sanke

10 *torne*) *turn*

Greal, excepte syr Galahad my sone. And therfore, lady, sythen ye have taken you to perfeccion, I must nedys take me to perfection of ryght. For I take recorde of God, in you I have had myn erthly Ioye. And yf I had founden you now so dysposed I had caste me to have had you in to myn owne royame. But sythen I fynde you thus desposed I ensure you faythfully I wyl ever take me to penaunce, & praye whyle my lyf lasteth, yf that I may fynde ony heremyte other graye or whyte that wyl receyve me. Wherfore, madame, I praye you kysse me, & never nomore. Nay, sayd the quene, that shal I never do, but absteyne you from suche werkes ; & they departed.

Le Morte Arthur

23 *Sir Ector's Dirge over Launcelot*

AND soo the bysshop & they al togydere wente wyth the body of syr Launcelot dayly, tyl they came to Ioyous garde. And ever they had an C torches bernnyng aboute hym ; & so within xv dayes they came to Ioyous garde. And there they layed his corps in the body of the quere, & sange & redde many saulters & prayers over hym and aboute hym, & ever his vysage was layed open & naked that al folkes myght beholde hym. For suche was the custom in tho dayes, that al men of worshyp shold so lye wyth open vysage tyl that they were buryed. And ryght thus as they were at theyr servyce there came syr Ector de Maris, that had vij yere sought al Englond, Scotland & Walys, sekyng his brother syr Launcelot. And whan syr Ector herde suche noyse & lyghte in the

9 *other*) *either* 13 *departed*) *separated*

quyre of Ioyous garde he alyght, & put his hors from hym, & came in to the quyre, & there he sawe men synge & wepe. And al they knewe syr Ector, but he knewe not them. Than wente syr Bors unto syr Ector, & tolde hym how there laye his brother syr Launcelot dede. And than Syr Ector threwe hys shelde, swerde & helme from hym; and whan he behelde syr Launcelottes vysage he fyl doun in a swoun, & whan he waked it were harde ony tonge to telle the doleful complayntes that he made for his brother. A, Launcelot, he sayd, thou were hede of al crysten knyghtes; & now I dare say, sayd syr Ector, thou sir Launcelot, there thou lyest, that thou were never matched of erthely knyghtes hande; & thou were the curtest knyght that ever bare shelde; & thou were the truest frende to thy lover that ever bestrade hors; & thou were the trewest lover of a synful man that ever loved woman; & thou were the kyndest man that ever strake wyth swerde; & thou were the godelyest persone that ever cam emonge prees of knyghtes; & thou was the mekest man & the Ientyllest that ever ete in halle emonge ladyes; & thou were the sternest knyght to thy mortal foo that ever put spere in the breste. Than there was wepyng & dolour out of mesure. Thus they kepte syr Launcelots corps on lofte xv dayes, & than they buryed it with grete devocyon.

Le Morte Arthur

15 *curtest) most courteous* 21 *prees) crowd* 26 *on lofte) above ground*

24 *Suffolk dies by Pirates*

5 May 1450

To my ryght worchipfull John Paston, at Norwich

RYGHT worchipfull sir, I recomaunde me to yow, and am right sory of that I shalle sey, and have soo wesshe this litel bille with sorwfulle terys, that onethes ye shalle reede it.

As on Monday nexte after May day there come tydyngs to London, that on Thorsday before the Duke of Suffolk come unto the costes of Kent full nere Dover with his ij. shepes and a litel spynner; the qweche spynner he sente with certeyn letters to certeyn of his trustid men unto Caleys-warde, to knowe howe he shuld be resceyvyd; and with hym mette a shippe callyd Nicolas of the Towre, with other shippis waytyng on hym, and by hem that were in the spyner, the maister of the Nicolas hadde knowlich of the dukes comyng. And whanne he espyed the dukes shepis, he sent forthe his bote to wete what they were, and the duke hym selfe spakke to hem, and seyd, he was be the Kyngs comaundement sent to Caleys-ward, &c.

And they seyd he most speke with here master. And soo he, with ij. or iij. of his men, wente forth with hem yn here bote to the Nicolas; and whanne he come, the master badde hym, 'Welcom, Traitor,' as men sey; and forther the maister desyryd to wete yf the shepmen woldde holde with the duke, and they sent word they wold not yn noo wyse; and soo he was on the Nicolas tyl Saturday next folwyng.

Soom sey he wrotte moche thenke to be delyverd

3 *onethes) with difficulty* 8 *spynner) pinnace* 9 *qweche) which* 27 *thenke) thing*

to the Kynge, but thet is not verily knowe. He hadde hes confessor with hym, &c.

And some sey he was arreyned yn the sheppe on here maner upon the appechementes and fonde gylty, &c.

Also he asked the name of the sheppe, and whanne he knew it, he remembred Stacy that seid, if he myght eschape the daunger of the Towr, he should be saffe; and thanne his herte faylyd hym, for he thowghte he was desseyvyd, and yn the syght of all his men he was drawyn ought of the grete shippe yn to the bote; and there was an exe, and a stoke, and oon of the lewdeste of the shippe badde hym ley down his hedde, and he should be fair ferd wyth, and dye on a swerd; and toke a rusty swerd, and smotte of his hedde withyn halfe a doseyn strokes, and toke awey his gown of russet, and his dobelette of velvet mayled, and leyde his body on the sonds of Dover; and some sey his hedde was sette oon a pole by it, and hes men sette on the londe be grette circumstaunce and preye. And the shreve of Kent doth weche the body, and sent his under shreve to the juges to wete what to doo, and also to the Kenge whatte shalbe doo.

Forther I wotte nott, but this fer is that yf the proces be erroneous, lete his concell reverse it, &c.

Also for alle your other maters they slepe, and the freer also, &c.

Sir Thomas Keriel is take prisoner, and alle the legge harneyse, and abowte iij. m[l]. Englishe men slayn.

Mathew Gooth with xv[c] fledde, and savyd hym

10 *desseyvyd) deceived* 12 *stoke) block* 14 *fair ferd wyth) fairly dealt with* 20 *be grette circumstaunce) in great numbers* 24 *fer) far* 27 *freer) friar* 29 *iij. ml.)* 3000 31 *xvc)* 1500

selfe and hem ; and Peris Brusy was chefe capteyn, and hadde x. ml. Frenshe men and more, &c.

I prey yow lete my mastras your moder knowe these tydyngis, and God have yow all yn his kepyn.

I prey yow this bille may recomaunde me to my mastrases your moder and wyfe, &c.

James Gresham hath wretyn to John of Dam, and recomaundith hym, &c.

Wretyn yn gret hast at London, the v. day of May, &c.

W. L.

The Paston Letters

JOHN FISHER

1459–1535

25 *The Death of the Lady Margaret*

BUT specyally whan they sawe the dethe so hast vpon her and that she must nedes departe from them, and they sholde forgo so gentyll a maystris, so tender a lady, then wept they meruayllously, wepte her ladyes and kynneswomen to whom she was full kynde, wepte her poore gentylwomen whom she had loued so tenderly before, wept her chamberers to whome she was full deare, wepte her chapelaynes and preestes, wepte her other true & faythfull seruauntes. And who wolde not haue wept that there had ben presente. All Englonde for her dethe had cause of wepynge. The poore creatures that were wonte to receyue her almes, to whome she was alwaye pyteous and mercyfull. The studyentes of bothe the vnyuer-

2 *x. ml.*) 10,000

sytees to whome she was as a moder. All the lerned men of Englonde to whome she was a veray patronesse. All the vertuous and deuoute persones to whom she was as a louynge syster, all the good relygyous men and women whom she so often was wont to vysyte and comforte. All good preestes and clerkes to whome she was a true defenderesse. All the noble men and women to whome she was a myrroure and exampler of honoure. All the comyn people of this realme for whom she was in theyr causes a comyn mediatryce, and toke ryght grete dyspleasure for them, and generally the hole realme hathe cause to complayne & to morne her dethe. . .

Now therfore wolde I aske you this one questyon. Were it, suppose ye, al this considerd, a meetly thyng for vs to desyre to haue this noble princes here amongest vs agayn to forgo the ioyous lyfe aboue, to wante the presence of the gloryous Trynyté whom she so longe hathe sought & honoured, to leue that moost noble kyngdome, to be absent frome the moost blessyd company of sayntes & sayntesses, & hether to come agayn to be wrapped & endaungered with the myseries of this wretched worlde, with the paynfull dyseases of her aege, with the other encomberaunces that dayly happethe in this myserable lyfe? Were this a reasonable request of oure partye, were this a kynde desyre, were this a gentyl wysshe, that where she hathe ben so kinde & louyng a maystresse vnto us, all we sholde more regarde our owne prouffytes then her more synguler wele & comfort? The moder that hathe so grete affeccyon vnto her sone that she wyll not suffre hym to departe from her to his promocyon & furtheraunce but alway kepe hym at home, more regardynge her owne pleasure than hys wele, were not she an vnkinde & vngentyl moder? Yes verayly, let vs therfore thynke our moost louyng maystres is gone hens for her promocyon, for her grete furtheraunce, for her moost wele & prouffyte. And herin comforte vs, herin reioyse ourselfe & thanke almyghty God whiche of his infynyte mercy so gracyously hathe dysposed for her.

The Month's Mind of the noble princess Margaret, Countess of Richmond and Derby

THOMAS BETSON

26 *To his Kinswoman Katherine Ryche*

June 1476

Jesus. An°. xvj°.

MY nowne hartely belovid Cossen Kateryn, I recomande me unto you withe all the inwardnesse of myn hart. And now lately ye shall understond that I resseyvid a token from you, the which was and is to me right hartely welcom, and with glad will I resseyvid it; and over that I had a letter from Holake, youre gentyll Sqwyer, by the which I understond right well that ye be in good helth of body, and mery at hart. And I pray God hartely to his plesour to contenew the same: for it is to me veray grete comforth that ye so be, so helpe me Jesu. And yf ye wold be a good etter of your mete allwaye, that ye myght waxe and grow fast to be a woman, ye shuld make me the gladdest man of the world, be my trouth: for whanne I remembre your favour and your sadde lofynge delynge to me-wardes, for

7 *nowne*) *own* 10 *resseyvid*) *received* 22 *sadde*) *serious lofynge*) *loving*

south ye make me evene veray glade and joyus in my hart: and on the tother syde agayn whanne I remembre your yonge youthe, and seeth well that ye be none etter of youre mete, the which shuld helpe you greately in waxynge, for south than ye make me veray hevy agayn. And therfore I praye you, myn nown swete Cossen, evene as you lofe me to be mery and to eate your mete lyke a woman. And yf ye so will do for my love, looke what ye will desyre of me, whatsomever it be, and be my trouth I promesse you by the helpe of our Lord to performe it to my power. I can [no] more say now, but at my comyng home I will tell you mych more betwene you and me and God before. And where as ye, full womanly and lyke a lofer, remembre me with manyfolde recomendacion in dyversse maners, remyttynge the same to my discresscion to depart them ther as I love best, for south, myn nown swete Cossen, ye shall understond that with good hart and good will I resseyve and take to my self the one half of them, and them will I kepe by me; and the tother half with hartely love and favour I send hem to you, myn nown swete Cossen, agayn, for to kepe by you: and over that I send you the blissynge that our Lady gave hir dere sonne, and ever well to fare. I pray you grete well my horsse, and praye hym to gyfe yow iij of his yeres to helpe you with all: and I will at my comynge home gyf hym iiij of my yeres and iiij horsse lofes till amendes. Tell hym that I prayed hym so. And Cossen Kateryn I thannke you for hym, and my wif shall thanke you for hym hereafter; for ye do grete cost apon hym as it is told me. Myn

17 *depart*) *divide* 29 *horsse lofes*) *horseshoes* 32 *do grete cost*) *spend much money*

nown swete Cossen, it was told me but late that ye were at Cales to seeke me, but ye cowde not se me nor fynde me: for south ye myght have comen to my counter, and ther ye shuld bothe fynde me and see me, and not have fawtid off me: but ye sought me in a wronge Cales, and that ye shuld well know yf ye were here and saw this Cales, as wold God ye were and som of them with you that were with you at your gentill Cales. I praye you, gentill Cossen, comaunde me to the Cloke, and pray hym to amend his unthryfte maners: for he strykes ever in undew tyme, and he will be ever afore, and that is a shrewde condiscion. Tell hym with owte he amend his condiscion that he will cause strangers to advoide and come no more there. I trust to you that he shall amend agaynest myn commynge, the which shalbe shortely with all hanndes and all feete with Godes grace. My veray feithefull Cossen, I trust to you that thowe all I have not remembred my right worshipfull maystres your modyr afore in this letter that ye will of your gentilnesse recomaunde me to her maystresshipe as many tymes as it shall ples you: and ye may say, yf it plese you, that in Wytson Weke next I intend to the marte-ward. And I trust you will praye for me: for I shall praye for you, and, so it may be, none so well. And Almyghty Jesu make you a good woman, and send you many good yeres and longe to lyve in helth and vertu to his plesour. At greate Cales on this syde on the see, the fyrst day of June, whanne every man was gone to his Dener, and the Cloke smote noynne, and all oure howsold cryed after me and badde me come down; come down to

4 *counter*) *office* 5 *fawtid off*) *missed* 10 *Cloke*) *clock*
24 *marte-ward*) *to the market*

dener at ones! and what answer I gave hem ye know it of old.

Be your feithefull Cossen and lofer
Thomas Betson.

I sent you this rynge for a token.

To my feithefull and hartely belovid Cossen Kateryn Ryche at Stonor this letter be delyvered in hast.

Stonor Letters and Papers

ADAM OF EYNSHAME. *Englished*

c. 1480

27 *The Monk awakes from his Vision*

How the monke came owte ageyne throw the same gate of paradyse. Ca. 181

THERFORE when y had seyn al these syghtys above seyde and many othyr innumerable, my lorde Sent *Nycholas* that hylde my by the hande seyde schortly thys to me. Loo sonne, he seyde, now a party aftyr thy peticion and grete desir thow haste seyne, and beholde the state of the worlde that ys to cumme as hyt myghte be to possible. . .

Of the swete pele and melodye of bellys that he herde in paradyse and also how he came to hym self ageyne

And whyle the holy confessour Sent *Nycholas* thys wyse spake yet with me, sodenly y herde ther a solenne pele and a rynggyng of a mervelus swetenes, and as al the bellys yn the worlde, or whatsumever ys of sownyng, had be rongen togedyr at onys. Trewly yn thys pele and rynging brake owte also a mervelus swetenes, and a variant medelyng of melody sownyd

26 *medelyng*) *mingling*

wyth alle. . . Sothly anone as that gret and mervelus sownnyng and noyse was cessyd, sodenly y saw myselfe departyd fro the swete feleschippe of my duke and leder Sent *Nicholas*. Than was y returnyd to myselfe ageyne, and anone y herd the voycis of my brethyrne that stode abowte our bedde; also my bodely strenthe cam ageyn to me a lytyl and a litil, and myn yes opinde to the use of seying as ye sawe ryghte wele. . . Ful delectable hyt was to hym, as he seyde, fro that tyme forthe, as ofte as he herde any solenne pele of ryngyng of bellys, bycause hyt wolde then cum to hys mynde ageyne, the ful swete pele and melody the whyche he herde when he was amonge the blessyd sowlys yn paradyse. Sothely aftyr that he was cum to hymselfe, and hys brethirne had tolde hym that now ys the holy tyme of Estyr, than fyrst he belevyd, when he herde hem rynge solenly to complen. For then he knew certenly that the pele and melodye that he herde yn paradyse wyth so grete ioy and gladnes betokynde the same solennyté of Estir yn the whyche owre blessyd lorde and sauyur *Jesus Criste* rose uppe visibly and bodely fro dethe onto lyfe, to whome wyth the Fadyr and the Holy Gooste be now and evermore everlastyng joy and blysse Amen.

The 1482 edition of William de Machlines

JOHN BOURCHIER, LORD BERNERS

1467–1532

28 *The Death of the Bruce*

IT fortuned that kyng *Robert* of *Scotland* was right sore aged, and feble; for he was greatly charged with the great sickenes, so that ther was no way with hym but deth. And whan he felte that his ende drew nere, he sent for suche baronis & lordis of his realme as he trusted best; & shewed them, how there was no remedy with hym but he must nedes leue this transitory lyfe: Commaundyng them on the faith and trouth that they owed hym, truly to kepe the realme, and ayde the yong prince *Dauid* his sonne, and that whan he were of age, they shulde obey hym and crowne hym kyng, and to mary hym in suche a place as was conuenient for his estate. Than he called to hym the gentle knyght sir *William Duglas*, & sayde before all the lordes: Sir *William* my dere frend, ye knowe well that I haue had moche ado in my dayes to vphold and susteyne the ryght of this realme, and whan I had most ado, I made a solemne vow, the whiche as yet I haue nat accomplysshed, whereof I am right sory. The which was, if I myght acheue and make an ende of al my warres, so that I myght ones haue brought this realme in rest and peace, than I promysed in my mynd to haue gone, and warred on Christes enemies, aduersaries to our holy christen faith. To this purpose myn hart hath euer entended, but our Lorde wolde nat consent therto, for I haue had so moche ado in my dayes, & nowe in my last entreprise I haue taken suche a malady that I can nat escape. And syth it is so that my body can nat go nor acheue that my hart desireth, I wyll sende the hart in stede of the body to accomplysshe myn avowe, and bycause I knowe nat in all my realme no knyght more valyaunt than ye be, nor of body so well furnysshed to accomplysshe myn avowe in stede of my selfe: Therfore I require you myn owne dere & speciall frende that ye wyll take on you this voiage for the loue of me, and to acquite my soule agaynst my Lorde God. For I trust so moche in your noblenes and trouth, that and ye wyll take on you,

I doubte nat but that ye shall achyue it, and than shall I dye in more ease and quiete, so that it be done in suche maner as I shall declare vnto you. I will that as soone as I am trepassed out of this worlde that ye take my harte owte of my body, and embawme it, and take of my treasoure as ye shall thynke sufficient for that entreprise, both for your selfe and suche company as ye wyll take with you, and present my hart to the holy Sepulchre where as our Lorde laye, seyng my body can nat come there. And take with you suche company and purueyaunce as shalbe aparteynyng to your estate. And where soeuer ye come let it be knowen howe ye cary with you the harte of kyng *Robert* of *Scotland*, at his instaunce and desire, to be presented to the holy Sepulchre. Than all the lordes that herde these wordes, wept for pitie. And whan this knyght, syr *William Duglas* myght speke for wepyng, he sayd: A, gentle & noble kyng, a .C. tymes I thanke your grace of the great honour that ye do to me, sith of so noble and great treasure ye gyve me in charge. And syr I shall do with a glad harte all that ye haue commaunded me, to the best of my true power, howe be it I am nat worthy nor sufficient to achyve suche a noble entreprise. Than the kyng sayd, A, gentle knyght, I thanke you so that ye wyl promyse to do it. Sir, sayd the knyght, I shall do it vndoubtedly, by the faythe that I owe to God, and to the ordre of knyghthode. Than I thanke you, sayd the kyng: for nowe shall I dye in more ease of my mynde, sith that I knowe that the most worthy and sufficient knyght of my realme shall achyue for me, the whiche I coulde neuer atteyne unto. And thus soone after thys noble *Robert de Bruse* kyng of *Scotland*, trepassed out of this

4 *trepassed) gone forth*

vncertain world, and hys hart taken out of his body, and embaumed, and honorably he was entred in the abbey of Donfremlyn, in the yere of our Lord God, M.CCC.xxvii, the .vii. day of the moneth of Nouembre.

Froissart's *Chronicles*

29 *The Battle of Creçy*

THE valyant kyng of *Behaygne* called Charles of *Luzenbourge*, sonne to the noble emperour Henry of *Luzenbourge*, for all that he was nyghe blynde, whan he vnderstode the order of the batayle, he sayde to them about hym, Where is the lorde *Charles* my son? his men sayde Sir we can nat tell, we thynke he be fightynge. Then he sayde Sirs ye are my men, my companyons and frendes in this iourney. I requyre you bring me so farre forwarde, that I may stryke one stroke with my swerde. They sayde they wolde do his commaundement: and to the intent that they sholde nat lese hym in the prease, they tyed all their raynes of their bridelles eche to other. . . Than the seconde batayle of th'englysshmen came to socour the princes batayle, the whiche was tyme, for they had as than moche ado, and they with the prince sent a messanger to the kynge, who was on a lytell wyndmyll hyll. Than the knyght sayd to the kyng, Sir, th'erle of *Warwyke*, and th'erle of *Canfort*, sir *Reynolde Cobham*, and other suche as be about the prince your sonne ar feersly fought withall and are sore handled: wherfore they desyre you that you and your batayle wold come and ayde them, for if the frenchmen encrease as they dout they wyll, your sonne and they shall haue moche ado. Than the kynge sayde Is my sonne dede or hurt, or on the yerthe felled ? No sir, quoth the knyght, but he is hardely matched, wherfore he hathe nede of your ayde. Well, sayde the kyng, retourne to hym and to them that sent you hyther, and say to them that they sende no more to me for any aduenture that falleth, as long as my sonne is alyue: and also say to them that they suffre hym this day to wynne his spurres, for if God be pleased I woll this iourney be his, and the honoure therof, and to them that be aboute him. Than the knyght retourned agayn to them and shewed the kynges wordes, the which gretly encouraged them, and repoyned in that they had sende to the kynge as they dyd. . .

Whan the nyght was come, and that th'Englysshmen herd no more noyse of the frenchemen, than they reputed themselfe to haue the vyctorie and the frenchmen to be dysconfited, slayne and fledde away. Than they made great fyers and lyghted vp torchesse and candelles, bycause it was very darke. Than the kyng auayled downe fro the lytell hyll where as he stode, and of all that day tyll than his helme came neuer off on his heed. Than he went with all his batayle to his sonne the prince, and enbrased hym in his armes and kyst hym, and sayde Fayre sonne, God gyue you good perseuerance, ye ar my good son, thus ye haue aquyted you nobly: ye ar worthy to kepe a realme.

Froissart's *Chronicles*

30 *The Burghers of Calais*

AFTER that the frenche kyng was thus departed fro *Sangate*, they within *Calays* sawe well howe their socoure fayled them, for the whiche they were in great sorrow. Than they desyred so moche their captayn sir *John* of *Vyen*, that he went to the walles

8 *iourney*) *day* 11 *repoyned*) *repented*

of the towne, and made a sygne to speke with some person of the hoost. Whan the kyng herde therof, he sende thyder sir *Gaultier* of *Manny*, and sir *Basset*. Than sir *John* of *Vyen* sayd to them : Sirs, you be right valyant knyghtes in dedes of armes, and you knowe well howe the kynge my maister hath sende me and other to this towne, and commaunded vs to kepe it to his behofe, in suche wyse that we take no blame nor to hym no dammage ; and we haue done all that lyeth in oure power. Nowe our socours hath fayled vs, and we be so sore strayned that we haue nat to lyue withall, but that we muste all dye, or els enrage for famyn, without the noble and gentyl kyng of yours woll take mercy on vs ; the which to do we requyre you to desyre hym, to haue pytye on vs, and let vs go and depart as we be, and lette hym take the towne and castell and all the goodes that be therin, the whiche is great habundaunce. Than sir *Gaultyer* of *Manny* sayde, Sir, we knowe somwhat of the entencyon of the kynge our maister, for he hath shewed it vnto vs. Surely knowe for trouth it is nat his mynde that ye nor they within the towne shulde depart so, for it is his wyll that ye all shulde put your selfes into his pure wyll to ransome all suche as pleaseth hym and to putte to dethe suche as he lyste, for they of *Calays* hath done hym suche contraryes and despyghtes, and hath caused hym to dyspende soo moche good, and loste many of his menne, that he is sore greued agaynst them. Than the captayne sayde, Sir, this is to harde a mater to vs, we ar here within a small sorte of knyghtes and squyers, who hath trewely serued the kynge our maister, as well as ye serve yours in like case. And we haue endured moche payne and vnease, but we shall yet

30 *sorte*) *company*

endure as moche payne as euer knyghts did rather thanne to consent that the worst ladde in the towne shulde haue any more yuell than the grettest of vs all. Therefore sir we pray you that of your humylité yet that you will go and speke to the kynge of *Englande*, and desyre hym to haue pytie of vs, for we trust in hym so moche gentylnesse, that by the grace of God his purpose shall chaunge. Sir *Gaultier* of *Manny* and sir *Basset* retourned to the kynge, and declared to hym all that hadde ben sayde: the kynge sayde he wolde none other wyse, but that they shulde yelde theym vp symply to his pleasure. Than sir *Gaultyer* sayde, Sir, sauyng your dyspleasure in this, ye may be in the wronge, for ye shall gyue by this an yuell ensample: if ye sende any of vs your servaunts into any fortresse, we will nat be very gladde to go, if ye putte any of theym in the towne to dethe after they be yelded, for in lykewise they will deale with vs, if the case fell lyke: the whiche wordes dyuerse other lordes that were there present sustayned and maynteyned. Than the kynge sayde, Sirs, I will nat be alone agaynst you all, therefore sir *Gaultyer* of *Manny* ye shall goo and say to the capytayne, that all the grace that they shall fynde nowe in me is, that they lette sixe of the chiefe burgesses of the towne come out bare heded, bare foted, and bare legged, and in their shertes, with haulters about their neckes, with the kayes of the towne and castel in their handes, and lette theym sixe yelde themselfe purely to my wyll, and the resydewe I will take to mercy. Than sir *Gaultyer* retourned and founde sir *John* of *Vyen* styll on the wall abydinge for an answere: than sir *Gaultier* shewed hym all the grace that he coulde gette of the kynge. Well, quoth sir *Johan*, Sir, I requyre you tary here a certayne space tyll I go into the towne and shewe this to the commons of the towne who sent me hyder. Than sir *John* went vnto the market place and sowned the common bell: than incontynent men and women assembled there: than the captayne made reporte of all that he had done, and sayde, Sirs, it wyll be none otherwyse, therfore nowe take aduyse and make a shorte aunswere. Thanne all the people beganne to wepe and to make such sorowe that there was nat so hard a hert if they had sene them but that wolde haue had great pytie on theym: the captayne hymselfe wepte pyteously. At last the moost riche burgesse of all the towne called *Ewstace* of saynt *Peters* rose vp and sayde openly. Sirs, great and small, great myschiefe it shulde be to suffre to dye suche people as be in this towne, other by famyn or otherwyse, whan there is a meane to saue theym. I thynke he or they shulde haue great merytte of our lorde God that myght kepe theym fro suche myschiefe: and for my parte I haue so good truste in our lorde God that if I dye in the quarel to saue the residewe that God wolde pardone me. Wherefore to saue them I wyll be the first to putte my lyfe in ieopardy. Whan he had thus sayde euery man worshypped hym, and dyuers kneled downe at his fete with sore wepyng and sore sighes. Than another honest burgesse rose and sayde I wyll kepe company with my gossyppe *Eustace*, he was called *John Dayre*. Than rose up *Jaques* of *Wyssant*, who was riche in goodes and herytage: he sayd also that he wolde holde company with his two cosyns in likwyse: so dyd *Peter* of *Wyssant* his brother, and thanne rose two other: they sayde they wolde do the same. Thanne they went and aparelled them as the kynge desyred. . . . Whan sir *Gaultier* presented these burgesses to the kyng they kneled downe and helde vp their handes and sayd, Gentyll kyng, beholde here we sixe who were burgesses of *Calays* and great marchantes, we haue brought to you the kayes of the towne and of the castell, and we submyt ourselues clerely into your wyll and pleasure, to saue the resydue of the people of *Calays*, who haue suffred great payne. Sir, we beseche your grace to haue mercy and pytie on us through your hygh nobles: than all the erles & barownes, and other that were there wept for pytie. The kyng loked felly on theym, for greatly he hated the people of *Calys*, for the gret damages and dyspleasures they had done to hym on the see before. Than he commaunded their heedes to be stryken off. Than euery man requyred the kyng for mercy, but he wolde here no man in that behalfe. Than sir *Gaultier* of *Manny* said A, noble kyng, for Goddes sake refrayn your courage, ye haue the name of souerayn nobles, therfore nowe do nat a thyng that shulde blemysshe your renome, nor to gyue cause to some to speke of you villany, euery man will say it is a great cruelty to put to deth suche honest persons, who by their owne wylles putte themselue into your grace to saue their company. Than the kyng wryed away fro hym, and commaunded to sende for the hangman, and sayd they of *Calys* hath caused many of my men to be slayne, wherfore these shall dye in like wyse. Than the quene beynge great with chylde, kneled downe & sore wepyng sayd: A, gentyll sir, syth I passed the see in great perill I haue desyred nothyng of you, therfore nowe I humbly requyre you in the honour of the son of the virgyn *Mary* and for the loue of me, that ye will take mercy of these sixe burgesses. The kyng behelde the quene & stode styll in a study a space, and than sayd, A, dame, I wold ye

10 *felly*) *fiercely* 17 *nobles*) *noblesse* 22 *wryed*) *turned*

had ben as nowe in some other place, ye make suche request to me that I can nat deny you; wherfore I gyue them to you to do your pleasure with theym. Than the quene caused them to be brought into her chambre, and made the halters to be taken fro their neckes and caused them to be newe clothed, and gaue them their dyner at their leser. And than she gaue ech of them sixe nobles, and made them to be brought out of thoost in sauegard & set at their lyberté.

Froissart's *Chronicles*

31 *John Ball's Preaching*

THER was an vsage in *England*, & yet is in diuerse countreys, that the noble men hath great fraunches ouer the comons, and kepeth them in seruage: that is to say, their tenauntes ought by custome to laboure the lordes landes, to gather and bring home theyr cornes, & some to threshe and to fanne and by seruage to make theyr hey, and to heaw their wood and bring it home: all these thyngs they ought to do by seruage. And ther be mo of these people in *Englande*, than in any other realme: thus the noble men and prelates arre serued by them, and specially in the countie of *Brendpest*, *Sussetter*, and *Bedford*. These vnhappy people of these sayd countreys began to styre, bycause they sayde they were kept in great seruage. And in the begynning of the worlde, they sayd they were no bonde men. Wherfore they maynteyned that none ought to be bounde withoute he dyd treason to his lorde: as *Lucifer* dyde to God. But they sayd they coude haue no such batayle, for they were nother angelles nor spirittes, but men fourmed to the similytude of their lordes: sayng, why shuld they than

7 *leser*) *ease* 9 *thoost*) *the host* 15 *fanne*) *winnow*

be kept so undre lyke bests, the which they sayd they wold no lengar suffre, for they wolde be all one: and if they labored or dyd any thyng for theyr lordes, they wold haue wages therfore as well as other. And of this imaginacion was a folisshe preest in the countie of *Kent*, called *Johan Ball*, for the which folysshe wordes he had ben thre tymes in the bysshop of *Canterburies* prison. For this preest vsed often tymes on the sondayes after masse, whanne the people were goynge out of the mynster, to go in to the cloyster & preche, and made the people to assemble about hym, and wolde say thus: A, ye goode people, the maters gothe nat well to passe in *Englande*, nor shall nat do tyll euery thyng be common, and that there be no villayns nor gentylmen, but that we may be all vnyed toguyder, & that the lordes be no greatter maisters than we be. What haue we deserued, or why shulde we be kept thus in seruage? We be all come fro one father and one mother, *Adam* and *Eue*. Whereby can they say or shewe that they be gretter lordes than we be, sauynge by that they cause vs to wyn and labour, for that they dispende? they are clothed in Ueluet and chamlet furred with grise, and we be vestured with pore clothe: they haue their wynes, spyces, and good breed, and we haue the drawynges out of chaffe, & drinke water. They dwell in fayre houses, and we haue the payne and traveyle, rayne, and wynde in the feldes. And by that, that cometh of our labours, they kepe and maynteyne their estates. We be called their bondmen, and without we do redilye them seruyce, we be beaten. And we haue no souerayne to whom we may complayne, nor that wyll here vs, nor do vs right. Lette vs go to the kyng, he is yonge: & shewe hym what seruage we be in: and shewe him howe we wyll haue it otherwyse, or els we wyll prouyde vs of some remedy. And if we go togyder, all maner of people that be nowe in any bondage wyll folowe vs, to thentent to be made fre. And whan the kyng seyth vs, we shall haue some remedy, outher by fayrnesse or otherwyse. Thus *John Ball* sayd on sundayes, whan the people issued out of the churches in the vyllages. Wherfore many of the meane people loued him, & such as entended to no goodnesse sayde, howe he sayd trouth: and so they wolde murmure one with anothere in the felds and in the wayes, as they went togyder: Affirming how *Johan Ball* sayd trouthe.

Froissart's *Chronicles*

SIR THOMAS MORE

1478–1535

32 *How far is Honest Mirth lawful*

VINCENT. . . And first, good uncle, ere we procede farther, I wil be bold to move you one thing more of that we talked when I was here before. For when I revolved in my minde againe the thinges that were concluded here by you, methought ye would in no wyse that in any tribulacion men shoulde seke for comforte eyther in worldly thing or fleshly, which mynde uncle of yours, semeth somewhat hard, for a mery tale with a frende refresheth a man much, & without any harme lyghteth hys mynde, and amendeth his courage and hys stomake, so that it semeth but well done to take suche recreacion. And Salomon sayeth I trowe that men should in heavines geve the sory man wine to make hym forgeat his sorowe. And saynct Thomas saieth that propre pleasaunte talking which is called ἐυτραπελια is a good vertue seruing to refreshe the minde, & make it quicke and lusty to labor and study againe, where continuall fatigacion would make it dull and deadly.

Anthony. Cosen, I forgat not that point, but I longed not muche to touche it . . . Of trueth Cosin, as you knowe very well, myselfe am of nature even halfe a gigglot and more. I woulde I coulde as easely mende my faulte as I wel knowe it, but scant can I restraine it as olde a foole as I am : howbeit so parcial wil I not be to my fault as to praise it. . . Cassianus that very verteous man rehearseth in a certayne collacion of his, that a certaine holy father in making of a sermon, spake of heaven and heavenly thynges, so celestially, that much of his audience with the swete sounde therof, began to forget all the world and fall aslepe : whiche when the father beheld, he dissembled their sleping, and sodeinly sayd unto them : I shal tell you a mery tale. At which worde they lyfte up their heades and harkened unto that. And after the slepe therwith broken, heard hym tel on of heaven agayne. In what wyse that good father rebuked than their untowarde myndes so dull unto the thyng that all our lyfe we labor for, & so quicke and lusty towarde other tryfles, I neither beare in mynde, nor shal here nede to rehearse. But thus much of that matter suffiseth for our purpose, that wheras you demaunde me whither in tribulacion men may not sometyme refreshe themselfe with worldlye myrth & recreacion, I can no more say, but he that cannot long endure to holde up his head and heare talking of heaven except he be now & than betwene (as though heaven were heavines) refreshed with a mery folishe tale, there is none other remedy but you must let him have it : better would I wishe it, but I cannot helpe it. *A Dialogue of Comfort against Tribulation*

33 *His Last Letter to his Daughter Margaret*

OURE Lorde blesse you, good doughter, and youre good housbande, and youre lyttle boye, and all yours, and all my chyldren, and all my Goddechyldren and all oure frendes. Recommende me whan ye maye, to my good doughter Cicily, whom I beseche oure Lorde to coumforte. And I sende her my blessyng, and to all her children, and praye her to praye for me. I sende her an handkercher: and God coumfort my good sonne her husbande. My good doughter Daunce hathe the picture in parchemente, that you delyuered me from my ladye Coniers, her name is on the backeside. Shewe her that I hartelye praye her, that you may sende it in my name to her agayne, for a token from me to praye for me. I lyke speciall wel Dorothe Coly, I pray you be good unto her. I woulde wytte whether thys be she that you wrote me of. If not yet I praye you bee good to the tother, as you maye in her affliccion, and to my good doughter Joone Aleyn too. Geve her I praye you some kynde aunswere, for she sued hither to me this day to pray you be good to her. I comber you good Margaret much, but I would be sory, if it should be any lenger than tomorow. For it is saint Thomas euen, and the utas of saint Peter: & therfore tomorow long I to go to God: it were a day verye mete and conuenient for me. I never liked your maner toward me better, than when you kissed me laste: for I love when doughterly loue and deere charitye hath no laysure to loke to worldlye curtesy. Fare well my dere chylde, and pray for me, and I shall for you and all

24 *utas*) *octave*

youre frendes, that we may merelye mete in heauen. I thanke you for youre gret cost. I sende now to my good doughter Clement her algorisme stone, and I send her and my godsonne and all hers, Gods blessing and myne. I praye you at time conuenient recommende me to my good sonne John More. I liked wel his naturall fashion. Our Lord blesse hym & his good wyfe my louyng doughter, to whom I praye him be good as he hathe greate cause: and that yf the lande of myne come to his hande, he breake not my wyll concernynge hys sister Daunce. And oure Lord blisse Thomas and Austen and all that they shal haue.

The Workes of Sir Thomas More

MILES COVERDALE

1488–1568

34 *The Boke of Wysdome*

FOR the ungodly talke and ymagin thus amonge themselves (but not right:) The tyme of oure life is but short and tedious, and when a man is once gone, he hath nomore joye ner pleasure, nether knowe we eny man that turneth agayne from death: for we are borne of naught, and we shal be herafter as though we had never bene. For oure breth is as a smoke in oure nostrels, and the wordes as a sparck to move oure herte. As for oure body, it shalbe very asshes that are quenched, and oure soule shal vanish as the soft ayre. Oure life shall passe awaye as the trace of a cloude, and come to naught as the myst that is dryven awaye with the beames of the Sonne, and put downe with the heate therof. Oure name also shalbe forgotten by litle and litle, and no man shal have oure workes in remembraunce.

3 *algorisme stone*) *counter*

For oure tyme is a very shadow that passeth awaye, and after oure ende there is no returnynge, for it is fast sealed, so that no man commeth agayne. Come on therfore, let us enjoye the pleasures that there are, and let us soone use the creature like as in youth. We wil fyll oure selves with good wyne and oyntment, there shal no floure of the tyme go by us. We wil crowne oure selves with roses afore they be wythered. There shal be no fayre medowe, but oure lust shal go thorow it. Let every one of you be partaker of oure volupteousnes. Let us leave some token of oure pleasure in every place, for that is oure porcion, els gett we nothinge. . . .

Soch thinges do the ungodly ymagin, and go astraye, for their owne wickednes hath blynded them. As for the misteries of God, they understonde them not: they nether hope for the rewarde of righteousnesse, ner regarde the worshipe that holy soules shall have. For God created man to be undestroied, yee after the ymage of his awne licknesse made he him. Neverthelesse thorow envye of the devell came death in to the worlde, and they that holde of his syde, do as he doth.

But the soules of the righteous are in the hande of God, and the payne of death shal not touch them. In the sight of the unwyse they appeare to dye, and their ende is taken for very destruccion. The waye of the righteous is judged to be utter destruccion, but they are in rest. And though they suffre payne before men, yet is their hope full of immortalite.

The Boke of Wysdome, ii. 1–9, 21–4, iii. 1–4

1549

35 Collects from the First Prayer Book of Edward VI

i. *Fourth Sunday after Easter*

ALMIGHTIE God, whiche doest make the myndes of all faythfull men to be of one wil: graunt unto thy people, that they maye loue the thyng, whiche thou commaundest, and desyre, that whiche thou doest promes, that emong the sondery and manifold chaunges of the worlde, oure heartes maye surely there bee fixed, whereas true ioyes are to be founde: through Christe our Lorde.

ii. *Trinity Sunday*

ALMIGHTYE and euerlastyng God, whiche haste geuen unto us thy seruauntes grace by the confession of a true fayth to acknowlege the glorye of the eternall trinitie, and in the power of the diuyne maiestie to wurshippe the unitie: we beseche thee, that through the stedfastnes of thys fayth, we may euermore be defended from all aduersitie, whiche liueste and reignest, one God, worlde without end.

iii. *All Saints' Day*

ALMIGHTIE God, whiche haste knitte together thy electe in one Communion and felowship, in the misticall body of thy sonne Christe our Lord; graunt us grace so to folow thy holy Saynctes in all virtues, and godly liuyng, that we maye come to those unspeakeable ioyes, whiche thou hast prepared for all them that unfaynedly loue thee: through Jesus Christe.

iv. *Collect from the Communion Office*

ALMIGHTIE God, the fountayn of all wisdome, which knowest our necessities beefore we aske, and our ignoraunce in asking: we beseche thee to haue compassion upon our infirmities, and those thynges, whiche for our unwoorthines we dare not, and for our blindnes we cannot aske, vouchsaue to geue us for the woorthines of thy sonne Jesu Christ our Lorde. Amen.

Psalms in the Version of the Great Bible

v. *Psalm xlv*

MY heart is enditing of a good matter: I speake of the thinges, which I haue made vnto the king. My tonge is the pen of a ready writer. Thou art fairer than the children of men, full of grace are thy lippes, bicause God hath blessed thee for euer. Girde thee with thy sweard vpon thy thigh (O thou most mightie) according to thy worship and renowne. Good lucke have thou with thy honour, ride on bicause of the worde of truth, of mekenes and righteousness, & thy right hande shall teach thee terrible thinges. Thy arowes are very sharpe, and the people shalbe subdued vnto thee, euen in the middest among the kinges enemies. Thy seate (O God) endureth for euer: the scepter of thy kingdom is a right scepter. Thou hast loued righteousnes, and hated iniquitie: wherfore God (euen thy God) hath anointed thee with the oyle of gladnesse aboue thy fellowes. Al thy garments smel of Mirre, Aloes and Cassia, out of the yuory palaces, wherby they haue made thee glad. Kynges daughters wer among thy honorable women: vpon thy right hand did stand the Quene in a vesture of golde (wrought about with diuers coloures.) Hearken (O daughter) and consider : encline thyne eare : forget also thyne own people, and thy fathers house. So shall the kyng haue pleasure in thy beauty, for he is thy Lord God, and worship thou hym. And the daughter of Tyre shalbe ther with a gift lyke as the rich also among the people shall make their supplication before thee. The kynges daughter is all glorious within, her clothing is of wrought golde. She shalbe brought vnto the kyng in rayment of nedle work : the virgins that be her felowes, shal beare her companye, and shalbe brought vnto thee. With ioy and gladnesse shall they be brought, and shal enter into the kynges palace. In stede of thy fathers thou shalt haue children, whom thou mayest make Princes in al landes. I wil remember thy name from one generation to another : therfore shall the people geue thankes vnto thee world without ende.

vi. *Psalm cxxvi*

WHEN the Lorde turned again the captiuitie of Sion, then were we lyke vnto them that dreame. Then was our mouth fylled with laughter : and our tong with ioy. Then said they among the Heathen : the Lord hath done great thinges for them. Yea, the Lord hath done great thynges for vs already, wherof we reioyce. Turne our captiuitie, O Lorde, as the riuers in the South. They that sow in teares, shall reape in ioye. He that now goeth in his way weping and beareth forth good sede, shal come again with ioy, & bring his sheaues with him.

vii. *Psalm xxiii*

THE Lorde is my shepehearde : therfore can I lacke nothing. He shall fede me in a grene pasture, and lead me forth beside the waters of comfort. He shall conuerte my soule, and bryng me foorth in the pathes of righteousnesse for his name sake. Yea, though I walke through the valley of the shadow of death, I will feare no euil : for thou art with me, thy rod and thy staffe comfort me. Thou shalt prepare a table before me, against them that trouble me : thou haste anointed my hed with oyle, and my cup shalbe full. But thy louing kindnesse and mercy shal folow me al the dayes of my lyfe : and I will dwell in the house of the Lorde for euer.

viii. *Psalm xc*

LORDE, thou hast bene oure refuge from one generation to another. Before the mountayns were brought foorth, or euer the earth & the worlde were made, thou art God from euerlasting, and world without ende. Thou turnest manne to destruction. Agayne thou sayeste, come agayne ye chyldren of men. For a thousand yeres in thy sight ar but as yesterday, seing that is paste as a watche in the night. Assoone as thou scatterest them they ar euen as a slepe, and fade away sodeinly lyke the grasse. In the morning it is greene & groweth vp, but in the euening it is cut downe, dried vp and withered. For we consume away in thy displeasure : and are afrayde at thy wrathfull indignation. Thou hast set our misdedes before thee, and our secrete sinnes in the lyght of thy countenaunce. For when thou art angry, al our dayes are gone : we bryng our yeares to an end, as it were a tale that is tolde.

The Navy Prayer

[*added to the Book of Common Prayer 1662, and probably composed by Bishop Sanderson*]

O ETERNAL Lord God, who alone spreadest out the heavens, and rulest the raging of the sea; who hast compassed the waters with bounds until day and night come to an end; Be pleased to receive into thy Almighty and most gratious protection the persons of us thy servants, and the Fleet in which we serve. Preserve us from the dangers of the sea, and from the violence of the enemy, that we may be a safe-guard unto our most gratious soveraign lord King Charles and his Kingdoms, and a security for such as pass on the seas upon their lawfull occasions; that the inhabitants of our Island may in peace and quietness serve thee our God, and that we may return in safety to enjoy the blessings of the land, with the fruits of our labours; and with a thankfull remembrance of thy mercies to praise and glorifie thy holy Name, through Jesus Christ our Lord.

THOMAS CRANMER

1489–1556

36 *Uses of Holy Scripture*

DOEST thou not mark, & consider how the smith, mason, or carpenter, or any other handy craftesman, what nede soeuer he be in, what other shift so euer he make, he wil not sel, nor lay to pledge the toles of his occupation, for then how should he worke his feate or get his liuing therby? Of like minde & affection ought we to be towardes holy Scripture, for as mallets, hammers, sawes, chesils, axes, & hatchets

23 *worke his feate*) *do his job*

be the toles of their occupation : So be the bokes of the Prophetes, & Apostles & al holy writers inspired by the holy ghost the instrumentes of our saluation. Wherfore let vs not sticke to bye & prouide vs the Bible, that is to say, the bokes of holy Scripture. And let vs thinke that to be a better Iuel in our house then either gold or siluer. For like as theues bene lothe to assault an house, where they know to be good armoure & artillary, so wheresoeuer these holy & ghostly bokes bene occupied, there nether the deuil, nor none of his angels dare come nere. And they that occupy them bene in much sauegarde, & haue a great consolation, and bene the readier vnto all goodnesse, the slower to al euil : and if they haue done any thing amisse anone euen by the sight of the bokes, their consciences ben admonished, & they waxen sory and ashamed of the facte. *Preface to the Great Bible*

HUGH LATIMER

1491–1555

37 *Decay of the Yeomanry*

MY father was a Yoman, and had no landes of hys own, only he had a farme of iii. or iiii. pound by yere at the uttermooste, and here upon he tilled so much as kept halfe a dosen men. He had walke for a hundred shepe, and my mother milked xxx. kyne. He was able and did finde the kyng a harnesse, with himselfe, and his horse, whyle he came to the place that he shoulde receive the kynges wages. I can remembre, that I buckled hys harnesse, when he wente unto Blacke heathe felde. He kept me to schole, or els I hadde not bene able to have preached before

21 *walke*) *pasture*

the kinges majesty now. He maryed my systers wyth v. pounde, or xx. nobles a piece, so that he brought them up in godlinesse, and fear of God. He kepte hospitality for his pore neighboures. And some almesse he gave to the pore, and al thys dyd he of the said farm. Where he that now hath it, payeth xvi. pound by yere or more, and is not able to do any thing for his prince, for him selfe, nor for his children, or geve a cup of drink to the pore. Thus al the enhansyng and rearing goth to your private commodity and welth. So that where ye had a single to much, you have that: and sins the same, ye have enhansed the rent, and so have encresed another to muche. So nowe ye have double to muche, which is to to muche. But let the precher preach til his tong be worn to the stomps, nothing is amended. We have good statutes made for the common wealth as touching commeners, enclosers, many metings and sessions, but in the end of the matter, there commeth nothing forthe. Well, well, thys is one thing I wil say unto you, from whence it commeth I know, even from the devil. I know his intent in it. For if ye bring it to passe, that the yomanry be not able to put their sonnes to schole (as in dede universities do wondrously decay al redy) and that they be not able to marrye theyr daughters to the avoidynge of whoredome I say ye plucke salvation from the people, and utterly destroye the realme. For by yomans sonnes, the faith of Christe is, and hath bene maintayned chieflye. Is this realme taughte by rich mens sonnes? No, no, read the chronicles, ye shall finde somtime noble mennes sonnes, whych have bene unpreaching bishops and prelates, but ye shal fynde none of them learned men. But verily, they that shoulde looke to the redresse of these thinges, be the greatest againste them. In thys realme are a great many of folkes, and amongest many, I knowe but one of tender zeale, at the mocyon of his pore tenauntes, hath let down his landes to the old rentes for their relief. For Gods love, let not him be a Phenix, let him not be alone, let him not be an Hermite closed in a wal, some good man folow him, and do as he geveth example.

First Sermon preached before King Edward VI

38 Cause and Effect

AND here by the way I wyll tel you a mery toy. Maister Moore was once sent in commission into Kent, to help to try out (if it might be) what was the cause of *Goodwin* sandes, and the shelfe that stopped up *Sandwich* haven. Thyther commeth maister More, and calleth the country afore him, such as wer thought to be men of experience and men that could of lykelyhod best certify hym of that matter concerning the stopping of *Sandwich* haven. Among others came in before hym an olde man with a white head, and one that was thought to be lytle lesse then an hundereth yeares olde. When maister Moore saw thys aged man, he thought it expedient to heare hym say hys mynd in thys matter (for being so olde a man it was lykely that he knewe most of any man in that presence and company.) So Maister Moore called this old aged man unto hym, and sayd: Father (sayd he) tel me if ye can what is the cause of thys great arising of the sandes and shelves here about thys haven, the which stop it up that no shippes can arive here? Ye are the eldest man that I can espye in al thys company, so that it any man can tell any cause of it, ye of lykelyhode can say most in it, or at leastwyse more then any other man here assembled. Yea forsooth good Maister (quod this old man) for I am wel nighe an hundreth yeares old, and no man here in this company any thing nere unto mine age.

Well then (quod Maister Moore) howe saye you in thys matter? what thincke ye to be the cause of these shelves and flattes that stoppe up *Sandwiche* haven? Forsoth syr (quoth he) I am an olde man, I thyncke that *Tenterton* steeple is the cause of *Goodwyn* sandes. For I am an old man syr (quod he) and I may remember the building of *Tenterton* steeple, and I may remember when there was no steeple at al there. And before that *Tenterton* steeple was in building, there was no maner of speaking of any flats or sands that stopped the haven, and therfore I thinke that *Tenterton* steple is the cause of the destroyng and decaying of *Sandwych* haven. And even so to my purpose is preaching of Gods word the cause of rebellyon, as *Tenterton* steple was cause that *Sandwich* haven is decayed.

Last Sermon preached before King Edward VI

WILLIAM TYNDALE

1496 ?–1536

39 *A Vision of Judgement*

WHEN the Sonne of Man shall come in hys maiestie, and all hys holy angelles with him, then shall he sytt uppon the seate of his maiestie, and before hym shalbe gaddred all nacions. And he shall sever them won from another, as a shepherde putteth asunder the shepe from the gootes. And he shall sett the shepe on his right honde, and the gotes on his lyfte honde. Then shall the Kynge saye to them on his right honde: Come ye blessed children of my father, inheret ye the kyngdome prepared for you from the beginninge of the worlde. For I was anhongred, and ye gave me meate. I thursted, and ye gave me drinke. I was herbroulesse, and ye lodged me. I was naked and ye clothed me: I was sicke and ye visited me. I was in preson and ye cam unto me.

Then shall the juste answere hym sayinge: Master, when sawe we the anhongred, and feed the? or a thurst, and gave the drynke? when sawe we the herbroulesse, and lodged the? or naked and clothed the? or when sawe we the sicke, or in preson and cam unto the? And the Kynge shall answere, and saye unto them: Verely I saye unto you: in as moche as ye have done it unto won of the leest of these my brethren: ye have done it to me.

Then shall the Kynge saye unto them that shalbe on the lyffte hande: Departe from me, ye coursed, into everlastinge fire, which is prepared for the devyll and hys angels. For I was an hungred, and ye gave me no meate. I thursted, and ye gave me no drynke. I was herbroulesse, and ye lodged me nott. I was naked, and ye clothed me nott. I was sycke and in preson, and ye visited me not.

Then shall they also answere hym sayinge: Master when sawe we the anhungred, or a thurst, or herbroulesse, or naked, or sicke, or in preson, and have not ministred unto the? Then shall he answere them, and saye: Verily I say unto you, in as moche as ye dyd

9 *herbroulesse*) *homeless*

it nott to won of the leest of these, ye dyd it nott to me. And these shall go into everlastinge payne : And the rightous into lyfe eternall.

St. Matthew xxvi. 31–46

WILLIAM ROPER

1496–1578

40 *Sir Thomas More parts from his Daughter Margaret*

WHEN Sir *Thomas More* came from *Westminster* to the *Tower*-ward again, his daughter, my wife, desirous to see her father, whom she thought she should never see in this world after, and also to have his final blessing, gave attendance about the *Tower Wharf*, where she knew he should pass by before he could enter into the *Tower*. There tarrying for his coming home, as soon as she saw him, after his blessing upon her knees reverently received, she hastening towards him, and without consideration or care of herself pressing in among the midst of the throng and company of the guard that with halberds and bills went round about him, hastily ran to him, and there openly in the sight of them all embraced him, took him about the neck, and kissed him. Who well liking her most natural and dear daughterly affection towards him, gave her his fatherly blessing, and many godly words of comfort besides. From whom after she was departed, she, not satisfied with her former sight of him, and like one that had forgotten herself, being all ravished with the entire love of her dear father, having respect neither to herself nor to the press of the people and multitude that were about him, suddenly turned back again, ran to him as before, took him about the neck, and divers times together most lovingly kissed him; and at last, with a full heavy heart, was feign to depart from him, the beholding whereof was to many of them that were present thereat so lamentable, that it made them for very sorrow thereof to mourn and weep.

The Life of Sir Thomas More

EDWARD HALL

d. 1547

41 *The End of the Krekers*

IN this busie season, the aventurers hearing what the horsemen on their parties had done, and in especial perceivyng that the English horsemen had taken good prisoners, commoned emongest themselfes, what was to be done: then one of their capitaynes said openly: Sirs, you se how long we have bene here, and wages we have none, our living riseth on the gaine of our enemies, and syth our beginnynge we have had good chaunce in all our enterprises, God be thanked: nowe the Winter draweth nere, let us now aventure to get som good botie, to make us mery with in the cold wether, and yf you wyl we shall enterpryse a thing that I truste to us shal bee profitable. Then all the compaignie cried *furthe furth*. Then wyth a banner of sainct George, they marched toward a vyllage, liyng towarde *Mustrel*, having onely xxv. light horsemen, to be their skourers, and they were not fully two hundred men. This compaigny folowing their skourers, went farre on, and had gotten a faire botie of oxen, kine, and other beastial, and were nere at their returne: and by chaunce the same day

20 *furthe furth*) *forth forth* 26 *beastial*) *live stock*

was the erle of *Dammartin*, and the captayn of *Mustrel*, with the power of the duke of *Vandosme*, goyng towarde sainct *Omers* to burne and destroy that countrey, and for that purpose thei had gathered together xv. C. horsemen, and viii. C. footmen, how be it, the footmen were a large myle behind the horsemen.

The Frenchmen on horsebacke espyed the English horsemen, which perceiving the great nomber fled, and as the said Frenchmen marched forward, they espyed the aventurers on foote, and made toward them: the Englishmen, seing the great nomber of the horsemen, studied to get some hedge or stronge place to fortifie theim, but there was no suche place in sight, and also they had no suche tyme so to do, wherefore the captayne sayed: Good felowes and brethren, we have of long time bene called aventurers, now is the tyme come of our aventure. The Frenchmen wyll not raunsome us for no thing, we be emongst them so feared: if any thing save our lyves, it must be God and our hardines, and therfore, sayd he, if you se me begin to flie, slaye me out of hande. Then every man cryed God mercie, and kneled downe and kissed the earth, and strake handes eche wyth other, in token not to depart, and then made themselfes prest to the defence.

The Frenchmen came on on every syde, the Englishmen shot their arrowes, and defended them as wel as they could. The Frenchmen perceiving that the Englishmen kept themselfes so close, caused diverse of the horse men to lyght a-fote, and so they dyd, and fought wyth their speres against the pikes, and shote wyth Crossebowes on every syde. Alas the while! for

25 *prest*) *ready*

while the Englyshmen had arrowes to shote, they were not broken, but close wythout peryl; but when their arrowes were spent, the Englyshmen fought valiauntly, and slew many Frenchmen that lyghted on foote, but in the conclusion the horsemen entered, and killed them all in maner, because there were so many of their compaignie slain, and toke fewe of them prisoners. This was the end of these compaignions, called the *Krekers* or aventurers, which were as hardie men, as ever served prince or captain.

The Lives of the Kings

SIR THOMAS ELYOT

1499 ?–1546

42 *Of Cooks and Tutors*

A GENTLEMAN, ere he take a cook in his service, he will first examine him diligently, how many sorts of meats, potages, and sauces he can perfectly make, and how well he can season them, that they may be both pleasant and nourishing. Yea, and if it be but a falconer, he will scrupulously inquire what skill he hath in feeding, called diet, and keeping of his hawk from all sickness, also how he can reclaim her and prepare her to flight. And to such a cook or falconer, whom he findeth expert, he spareth not to give much wages with other bounteous rewards. But of a schoolmaster, to whom he will commit his child to be fed with learning and instructed in virtue, whose life shall be the principal monument of his name and honour, he never maketh further inquiry but where he may have a schoolmaster, and with how little charge. And if one be perchance founden well learned, which will not take pains to teach without

18 *reclaim her) train her to come to call*

great salary, he then speaketh nothing more, or else saith, What, shall so much wages be given to a schoolmaster, which would keep me two servants? to whom may be said these words, that by his son being well learned he shall receive more commodity and also worship than by the service of a hundred cooks and falconers.

The Book named the Governor

GEORGE CAVENDISH

1500–1561

43 *The Death of Wolsey*

AFTER that he was in his confession the space of an hour. And then Master *Kingston* came to him and bid him good morrow, and asked him how he did. Sir, quoth he, I watch but God's pleasure to render up my poor soul to him. I pray you have me heartily commended unto his Royal Majesty, and beseech him on my behalf to call to his Princely remembrance all matters that have been between us from the beginning and the progress; and especially between good Queen *Katherine* and him, and then shall his Grace's Conscience know whether I have offended him or not.

He is a Prince of a most Royal carriage, and hath a Princely heart, and rather than he will miss or want any part of his will, he will endanger the one half of his Kingdom.

I do assure you I have often kneeled before him, sometimes three hours together, to perswade him from his will and appetite, but could not prevail. And, Master *Kingston*, had I but served God as diligently as I have served the King, he would not have given me over in my grey hairs. But this is the just reward that I must receive for my diligent pains and study, not regarding my service to God, but only to my Prince. Therefore let me advise you, if you be one of the Privy Council, as by your wisdom you are fit, take heed what you put in the King's head, for you can never put it out again. . . .

Master *Kingston*, farewell; I wish all things may have good success. My time draws on; I may not tarry with you. I pray you remember my words.

Now began the time to draw near, for he drew his speech at length, and his tongue began to fail him, his eyes perfectly set in his head, his sight failed him. Then we began to put him in mind of *Christ*'s passion, and caused the Yeoman of the Guard to stand by privately to see him die, and bear witness of his words and his departure, who heard all his communications.

And then presently the clock struck eight, at which time he gave up the Ghost, and thus departed he this life, one of us looking upon another, supposing he prophesied of his departure.

The Life and Death of Thomas Wolsey

JOHN KNOX

1505–1572

44 *Regiment of Women*

TO promote a woman to bear rule, superiority, dominion, or empire above any realm, nation, or city, is repugnant to nature, contumely to God, a thing most contrarious to his revealed will and approved ordinance; and finally, it is the subversion of good order, of all equity and justice.

In the probation of this proposition, I will not be so curious as to gather whatsoever may amplify, set forth, or decore the same; but I am purposed, even as I have spoken my conscience in most plain and few words, so to stand content with a simple proof of every member, bringing in for my witness God's ordinance in nature, his plain will revealed in his word, and the minds of such as be most ancient amongst godly writers.

And first, where that I affirm the empire of a woman to be a thing repugnant to nature, I mean not only that God by the order of his creation hath spoiled woman of authority and dominion, but also that man hath seen, proved and pronounced just causes why that it should be. Man, I say, in many other cases blind, doth in this behalf see very clearly. For the causes be so manifest, that they cannot be hid. For who can deny but it repugneth to nature that the blind shall be appointed to lead and conduct such as do see? That the weak, the sick, and impotent persons shall nourish and keep the whole and strong, and finally, that the foolish, mad and phrenetic shall govern the discreet and give counsel to such as be sober of mind? And such be all women, compared unto man in bearing of authority. For their sight in civil regiment is but blindness, their strength weakness, their counsel foolishness, and judgement frenzy, if it be rightly considered.

I except such as God, by singular privilege, and for certain causes known only to himself, hath exempted from the common rank of women, and do speak of women as nature and experience do this day declare them. Nature, I say, doth paint them forth to be weak, frail, impatient, feeble and foolish; and experience hath declared them to be unconstant, variable, cruel and lacking the spirit of counsel and regiment. And these notable faults have men in all ages espied in that kind, for the which not only they have removed women from rule and authority, but also some have thought that men subject to the counsel or empire of their wives were unworthy of all public office. . .

I am not ignorant that the subtle wits of carnal men (which can never be brought under the obedience of God's simple precepts to maintain this monstrous empire) have yet two vain shifts. First, they allege that, albeit women may not absolutely reign by themselves, because they may neither sit in judgement, neither pronounce sentence, neither execute any public office, yet may they do all such things by their lieutenants, deputies and judges substitute. Secondarily, say they, a woman born to rule over any realm may choose her a husband, and to him she may transfer and give her authority and right. To both I answer in few words. First, that from a corrupt and venomed fountain can spring no wholesome water. Secondarily that no person hath power to give the thing which doth not justly appertain to themselves. But the authority of a woman is a corrupted fountain, and therefore from her can never spring any lawful officer. She is not born to rule over men, and therefore she can appoint none by her gift, nor by her power (which she hath not), to the place of a lawful magistrate.

The First Blast of the Trumpet against the monstrous Regiment of Women

ROGER ASCHAM

1515–1568

45 *Seeing the Wind*

TO see the wind, with a man his eyes, it is unpossible, the nature of it is so fine, and subtle, yet this experience of the wind had I once myself, and that was in the great snow that fell four years ago: I rode in the highway betwixt *Topcliffe-upon-Swale*, and *Borowe Bridge*, the way being somewhat trodden afore, by wayfaring men. The fields on both sides were plain and lay almost yard deep with snow, the night afore had been a little frost, so that the snow was hard and crusted above. That morning the sun shone bright and clear, the wind was whistling aloft, and sharp according to the time of the year. The snow in the highway lay loose and trodden with horse feet: so as the wind blew, it took the loose snow with it, and made it so slide upon the snow in the field which was hard and crusted by reason of the frost overnight, that thereby I might see very well, the whole nature of the wind as it blew that day. And I had a great delight and pleasure to mark it, which maketh me now far better to remember it. Sometime the wind would be not past two yards broad, and so it would carry the snow as far as I could see. Another time the snow would blow over half the field at once. Sometime the snow would tumble softly, by and by it would fly wonderfull fast. And this I perceived also that the wind goeth by streams and not whole together. For I should see one stream within a score on me, then the space of two score no snow would stir, but after so much quantity of ground, another stream of snow at the same very time should

28 *score*) *twenty paces*

be carried likewise, but not equally. For the one would stand still when the other flew apace, and so continue sometime swiftlier, sometime slowlier, sometime broader, sometime narrower, as far as I could see. Nor it flew not straight, but sometime it crooked this way sometime that way, and sometime it ran round about in a compass. And sometime the snow would be lift clean from the ground up into the air, and by and by it would be all clapped to the ground as though there had been no wind at all, straightway it would rise and fly again.

And that which was the most marvel of all, at one time two drifts of snow flew, the one out of the West into the East, the other out of the North into the East: And I saw two winds by reason of the snow the one cross over the other, as it had been two highways. And again I should hear the wind blow in the air, when nothing was stirred at the ground. And when all was still where I rode, not very far from me the snow should be lifted wonderfully. This experience made me more marvel at the nature of the wind, than it made me cunning in the knowledge of the wind: but yet thereby I learned perfectly that it is no marvel at all though men in a wind lose their length in shooting, seeing so many ways the wind is so variable in blowing.

Toxophilus

46 *From the Preface to 'The Schoolmaster'*

AFTER dinner I went up to read with the Queen's Majesty. We read then together in the Greek tongue, as I well remember, that noble Oration of *Demosthenes* against *Eschines*, for his false dealing in his Embassage to King *Philip* of *Macedony*. Sir *Rich. Sackville* came up soon after, and finding me in her Majesty's privy Chamber, he took me by the hand, and carrying me to a Window, said:

'Mr. *Ascham*, I would not for a good deal of Money have been this day absent from dinner. Where, though I said nothing, yet I gave as good Ear, and do consider as well the Talk that passed, as any one did there. Mr. Secretary said very wisely, and most truly, that many young Wits be driven to hate Learning before they know what Learning is. I can be good witness to this myself; for a fond Schoolmaster, before I was fully fourteen year old, drave me so with fear of Beating from all Love of Learning, as now, when I know what difference it is to have Learning and to have little or none at all, I feel it my greatest Grief, and find it my greatest Hurt that ever came to me, that it was my so ill chance to light upon so lewd a Schoolmaster. But seeing it is but in vain to lament things past, and also Wisdom to look to things to come, surely, God willing, if God lend me Life, I will make this my mishap some Occasion of good hap to little *Robert Sackville*, my son's son. For whose bringing up I would gladly, if it so please you, use specially your good advice. I hear say you have a son much of his age; we will deal thus together. Point you out a Schoolmaster, who by your Order shall teach my Son and yours, and for all the rest I will provide, yea, though they three do cost me a couple of hundred pounds by year; and beside, you shall find me as fast a Friend to you and yours, as perchance any you have.' Which Promise the worthy Gentleman surely kept with me until his dying day.

The Schoolmaster

47 *Lady Jane Grey*

BEFORE I went into *Germany*, I came to *Brodegate* in *Leicestershire*, to take my Leave of that noble Lady *Jane Grey*, to whom I was exceeding much beholding. Her Parents, the Duke and Duchess, with all the Household, Gentlemen and Gentlewomen, were hunting in the Park. I found her in her Chamber reading *Phaedon Platonis* in Greek, and that with as much Delight as some Gentlemen would read a merry Tale in *Boccace*. After Salutation, and Duty done, with some other Talk, I asked her, why she would lose such Pastime in the Park? Smiling, she answered me:

'*I-wis, all their Sport in the Park is but a Shadow to that Pleasure that I find in* Plato. *Alas! good Folk, they never felt what true Pleasure meant. And how came you, Madam,* quoth I, *to this deep Knowledge of Pleasure? And what did chiefly allure you unto it, seeing not many Women, but very few Men, have attained thereunto? I will tell you,* quoth she, *and tell you a Truth which perchance ye will marvel at. One of the greatest Benefits that ever God gave me, is, that he sent me so sharp and severe Parents, and so gentle a Schoolmaster. For when I am in Presence either of father or mother, whether I speak, keep Silence, sit, stand, or go, eat, drink, be merry, or sad, be sewing, playing, dancing, or doing anything else, I must do it, as it were, in such Weight, Measure, and Number, even so perfectly, as God made the World; or else I am so sharply taunted, so cruelly threatened, yea, presently sometimes with Pinches, Nips, and Bobs, and other ways (which I will not name for the Honour I bear them) so without measure misordered, that I think myself in Hell, till Time come that I must go to Master* Elmer; *who teacheth me so gently, so pleasantly, with such fair Allurements to Learning, that I think all the Time nothing, while I am with him. And when I am called from him, I fall on weeping, because whatsoever I do else but Learning is full of Grief, Trouble, Fear, and whole misliking unto me. And thus my Book hath been so much my Pleasure, and bringeth daily to me more Pleasure and more, that in respect of it, all other Pleasures in very deed, be but Trifles and Troubles unto me.*

The Schoolmaster

48 *Of Translation*

I HAVE been a looker on in the Cockpit of Learning these many Years; and one Cock only have I known, which with one Wing even at this day doth pass all other, in mine Opinion, that ever I saw in any Pit in England, though they had two Wings. Yet nevertheless, to fly well with one Wing, to run fast with one Leg, be rather rare Masteries much to be marvelled at, than sure Examples safely to be followed. A Bishop that now liveth, a good man, whose Judgement in Religion I better like, than his Opinion in Perfectness in other Learning, said once unto me: 'We have no Need now of the Greek Tongue, when all things be translated into Latin.' But the good man understood not that even the best Translation is for mere Necessity but an evil imped Wing to fly withal, or a heavy Stump Leg of Wood to go withal. Such, the higher they fly, the sooner they falter and fail: the faster they run, the ofter they stumble, and sorer they fall. Such as will needs so fly, may flie at a Pie, and catch a Daw: and such Runners, as commonly they shove and shoulder to stand foremost, yet in

23 *imped*) *grafted*

the end they come behind others, and deserve but the Hopshackles, if the Masters of the Game be right Judgers.

The Schoolmaster

JOHN FOXE

1516–1587

49 *Rowland Taylor, Vicar of Hadleigh, Suffolk*

Arrested in London. Burned on Aldham Common in his own Parish, Feb. 8, 1555

NOW when the Sheriff and his company came against St. *Botolph's* Church, *Elizabeth* cried, saying, 'O my dear Father! Mother! mother! here is my father led away.' Then cried his wife, '*Rowland*, *Rowland*, where art thou?'—for it was a very dark morning, that the one could not well see the other. Dr. *Taylor* answered, 'Dear wife, I am here,' and stayed. The Sheriff's men would have led him forth, but the Sheriff said, 'Stay a little, masters, I pray you, and let him speak with his wife,' and so they stayed. Then came she to him, and he took his daughter *Mary* in his arms, and he, his wife and *Elizabeth* kneeled down and said the Lord's Prayer. At which sight the Sheriff wept apace, and so did divers other of the company. After they had prayed he rose up and kissed his wife and shook her by the hand, and said, 'Farewell, my dear wife, be of good comfort, for I am quiet in my conscience. God shall stir up a father for my children.' . . . Then said his wife, 'God be with thee, dear *Rowland*. I will with God's grace meet thee at

2 *Hopshackles*) *hobbles*

Hadleigh.' . . . All the way Dr. *Taylor* was joyful and merry as one that accounted himself going to a most pleasant banquet or bridal. . . . Coming within a two mile of *Hadleigh* he desired to light off his horse, which done he leaped and set a frisk or twain, as men commonly do in dancing. 'Why, master Doctor,' quoth the Sheriff, 'how do you now?' He answered, 'Well, God be praised, good master Sheriff, never better; for now I know I am almost at home. I lack not past two stiles to go over, and I am even at my Father's house.'

Acts and Monuments

THOMAS WILSON

1525 ?–1581

50 *'Inkhorn Terms'*

AMONG all other lessons this should first be learned, that we never affect any strange inkhorn terms, but so speak as is commonly received, neither seeking to be over fine, nor yet living over careless, using our speech as most men do, and ordering our wits as the fewest have done. Some seek so far for outlandish English, that they forget altogether their mother's language. And I dare swear this, if some of their mothers were alive, they were not able to tell what they say; and yet these fine English clerks will say, they speak in their mother-tongue if a man should charge them for counterfeiting the King's English. Some far-journeyed gentlemen at their return home, like as they love to go in foreign apparel, so they will powder their talk with oversea language. He that cometh lately out of France will talk French English and never blush at the matter. Another chops in with English

Italienated, and applieth the Italian phrase to our English speaking, the which is, as if an Orator that professeth to utter his mind in plain Latin, would needs speak Poetry, and far-fetched colours of strange antiquity. The Lawyer will store his stomach with the prating of Pedlars. The Auditor in making his accompt and reckoning, cometh in with *sise sould*, and *cater denere*, for vis. iiii*d*. The fine courtier will talk nothing but *Chaucer*. The mystical wisemen and Poetical Clerks will speak nothing but quaint Proverbs, and blind Allegories, delighting much in their own darkness, especially, when none can tell what they do say. The unlearned or foolish fantastical, that smells but of learning (such fellows as have seen learned men in their days) will so Latin their tongues, that the simple cannot but wonder at their talk, and think surely they speak by some Revelation. I know them that think *Rhetoric* to stand wholly upon dark words, and he that can catch an inkhorn term by the tail, him they count to be a fine Englishman, and a good *Rhetorician*.

The Art of Rhetorique

RALPH ROBINSON

fl. 1551

51 *Ralph Hythlodaye*

WHILES I was there abiding oftentimes among other, but which to me was more welcome than any other, did visit me one *Peter Giles*, a Citizen of *Antwerp*, a man there in his country of honest reputation, and also preferred to high promotions, worthy truely of the highest. For it is hard to say whether the young man be in learning or in honesty more excellent. For he is both of wonderfull virtuous conditions, and also singularly well learned, and towards all sorts of people exceeding gentle; but towards his friends so kind hearted, so loving, so faithful, so trusty, and of so earnest affection, that it were very hard in any place to find a man that with him in all points of friendship may be compared. No man can be more lowly or courteous. No man useth less simulation or dissimulation; in no man is more prudent simplicity. Besides this, he is in his talk and communication so merry and pleasant, yea, and that without harm, that through his gentle entertainment and his sweet and delectable communication in me was greatly abated and diminished the fervent desire that I had to see my native country, my wife, and my children; whom then I did much long and covet to see, because that at that time I had been more than iv Months from them.

Upon a certain day when I was hearing the divine service in our Ladies Church, which is the fairest, the most gorgeous and curious church of building in all the city, and also most frequented of people, and when the divine service was done, was ready to go home to my lodging, I chanced to espy this forsaid *Peter* talking with a certain Stranger, a man well stricken in age, with a black sun-burned face, a long beard, and a cloak cast homely about his shoulders; whom by his favour and apparel forthwith I judged to be a mariner. But when this *Peter* saw me, he cometh unto me and saluteth me. And as I was about to answer him: 'see you this man?' saith he (and therewith he pointed to the man that I saw him talking with before). 'I was minded,' quoth he, 'to bring him straight home to you.' 'He should have been very welcome to me,' said I, 'for your sake.' 'Nay' (quoth he), 'for his own sake, if you knew him; for there is no man this day living that can tell you of so many strange and unknown peoples and countries as this man can. And I know well that you be very desirous to hear of such news.' 'Then I conjectured not far a miss' (quoth I), 'for even at the first sight I judged him to be a mariner.' 'Nay' (quoth he), 'there ye were greatly deceived. He hath sailed indeed, not as the mariner *Palinure*, but as the expert and prudent Prince *Ulysses*; yea, rather as the ancient and sage Philosopher *Plato*.

'For this same *Raphael Hythlodaye* (for this is his name) is very well learned in the Latin tongue; but profound and excellent in the Greek tongue, wherein he ever bestowed more study than in the Latin, because he had given himself wholly to the study of Philosophy. Whereof he knew that there is nothing extant in the Latin tongue that is to any purpose, saving a few of *Seneca*'s and *Cicero*'s doings. His patrimony that he was born unto he left to his brethren (for he is a *Portugal* born); and for the desire that he had to see and know the far Countries of the world, he joined himself in company with *Amerike Vespuce*, and in the iii last voyages of those iv, that be now in print and abroad in every man's hands, he continued still in his company, saving that in the last voyage he came not home again with him. For he made such means and shift, what by entreatance and what by importune suit, that he got licence of master *Amerike* (though it were sore against his will) to be one of the xxiv which in the end of the last voyage were left in the country of *Gulike*. He was therefore left behind for his mind's sake, as one that took more thought and care for travelling than dying; having customably in his mouth these sayings: He that hath no grave is covered with the sky; and, the way to heaven out of all places is of like length and distance. Which fantasy of his (if God had not been his better friend) he had surely bought full dear.

'But after the departing of Master *Vespuce*, when he had travelled through and about many Countries, with five of his companions *Gulikians*, at the last by marvellous chance he arrived in *Taprobane*, from whence he went to *Calicut*, where he chanced to find certain of his Country ships, wherein he returned again into his Country, nothing less than looked for.'

All this when *Peter* had told me, I thanked him for his gentle kindness, that he had vouchsafed to bring me to the speech of that man, whose communication he thought should be to me pleasant and acceptable. And therewith I turned me to *Raphael*; and when we had haylsede the one the other, and had spoken these common words, that be customably spoken at the first meeting and acquaintance of strangers, we went thence to my house, and there in my garden upon a bench covered with green turfs we sat down talking togethers.

More's *Utopia*

SIR THOMAS NORTH

1535 ?–1601 ?

52 *Coriolanus at the Hearth of Aufidius*

IT was even twilight when he entered the city of Antium, and many people met him in the streets, but no man knew him. So he went directly to *Tullus*

19 *haylsede*) *hailed*

Aufidius' house, and when he came thither, he got him up straight to the chimney hearth, and sat him down, and spake not a word to any man, his face all muffled over. They of the house, spying him, wondered what he should be, and yet they durst not bid him rise. For ill-favouredly muffled and disguised as he was, yet there appeared a certain majesty in his countenance, and in his silence: whereupon they went to *Tullus*, who was at supper, to tell him of the strange disguising of this man. *Tullus* rose presently from the board, and coming towards him, asked him what he was, and wherefore he came. Then *Martius* unmuffled himself, and after he had paused a while, making no answer, he said unto him. 'If thou knowest me not yet, *Tullus*, and seeing me dost not perhaps believe me to be the man I am indeed, I must of necessity bewray myself to be that I am. I am *Caius Martius*, who hath done to thyself particularly, and to all the VOLSCES generally, great hurt and mischief, which I cannot deny for my surname of *Coriolanus* that I bear. For I never had other benefit nor recompence of all the true and painful service I have done, and the extreme dangers I have been in, but this only surname: a good memory and witness of the malice and displeasure thou shouldst bear me. Indeed the name only remaineth with me: for the rest the envy and cruelty of the people of ROME have taken from me, by the sufferance of the dastardly nobility and magistrates, who have forsaken me and let me be banished by the people. This extremity hath now driven me to come as a poor suitor to take thy chimney hearth, not of any hope I have to save my life thereby. For if I had feared death, I would not have come hither to have put my life in hazard: but pricked forward with spite and desire I have to be revenged of them that thus have banished me, whom now I do begin to be avenged on, putting my person into the hands of their enemies. Wherefore, if thou hast any heart to be wracked of the injuries thy enemies have done thee, speed thee now, and let my misery serve thy turn, and so use it, as my service may be a benefit to the VOLSCES: promising thee, that I will fight with better good-will for all you, than I did when I was against you, knowing that they fight more valiantly, who know the force of the enemy, than such as have never proved it. And if it be so that thou dare not, and that thou art weary to prove fortune any more, then am I also weary to live any longer. And it were no wisdom in thee to save the life of him, who hath been heretofore thy mortal enemy, and whose service now can nothing help nor pleasure thee.' *Tullus*, hearing what he said, was a marvellous glad man, and, taking him by the hand, he said unto him, 'Stand up, O *Martius*, and be of good cheer, for in proffering thyself unto us thou dost us great honour: and by this means thou mayest hope also of greater things at all the VOLSCES' hands.' So he feasted him for that time, and entertained him in the honourablest manner he could, talking with him in no other matters at that present.

Plutarch's Lives of the Noble Grecians and Romans

53 *Cleopatra comes to Antony*

FOR *Caesar* and *Pompey* knew her when she was but a young thing, and knew not then what the world meant: but now she went to *Antonius* at the age when a woman's beauty is at the prime, and she also of best judgement. So she furnished herself with a world of gifts, store of gold and silver, and of riches and other sumptuous ornaments, as is credible enough she might bring from so great a house, and from so wealthy and rich a realm as EGYPT was. But yet she carried nothing with her wherein she trusted more than in herself, and in the charms and enchantment of her passing beauty and grace. Therefore when she was sent unto by divers letters, both from *Antonius* himself, and also from his friends, she made so light of it and mocked *Antonius* so much, that she disdained to set forward otherwise, but to take her barge in the river of *Cydnus*; the poop whereof was of gold, the sails of purple, and the oars of silver, which kept stroke in rowing after the sound of the musicke of flutes, howboys, citherns, viols, and such other instruments as they played upon in the barge. And now for the person of herself: she was laid under a pavilion of cloth of gold of tissue, apparelled and attired like the goddess *Venus* commonly drawn in picture: and hard by her, on either hand of her, pretty fair boys apparelled as Painters do set forth god *Cupid*, with little fans in their hands, with the which they fanned wind upon her. Her Ladies and Gentlewomen also, the fairest of them were apparelled like the Nymphs *Nereids* (which are the Mermaids of the waters) and like the *Graces*, some steering the helm, others tending the tackle and ropes of the barge, out of the which there came a wonderful passing sweet savour of perfumes, that perfumed the wharf's side, pestered with innumerable multitudes of people. Some of them followed the barge all alongst the river-side: others also ran out of the city to see her coming in. So that in the end there ran such multitudes of people one after another to see her, that *Antonius* was left post alone in the market-place in his Imperial seat to give audience: and there went a rumour in the people's mouths, that the goddess *Venus* was come to play with the god *Bacchus*, for the general good of all ASIA.

Plutarch's Lives of the Noble Grecians and Romans

SIR THOMAS BODLEY

1545–1613

54 *His Letter to the Vice-Chancellor*

SIR, although you know me not, as I suppose, yet for the furthering of an offer, of evident utility, to your whole University, I will not be too scrupulous in craving your assistance. I have been always of a mind that if God, of his goodness, should make me able to do anything for the benefit of posterity, I would show some token of affection that I have evermore borne to the studies of good Learning. I know my portion is too slender to perform, for the present, any answerable act to my willing disposition: but yet, to notify some part of my desire in that behalf, I have resolved thus to deal. Where there hath been heretofore a public library in *Oxford*, which, you know, is apparent by the room itself remaining, and by your statute Records, I will take the charge and cost upon me, to reduce it again to his former use: and to make it fit, and handsome with seats, and shelves, and desks, and all that may be needful to stir up other men's benevolence to help to furnish it with books. And this I purpose to begin, as soon as timber can be gotten, to the intent that you may reap some speedy Profit of my Project. And where before, as I conceive, it was to be reputed but a store of books of diverse benefactors, because it never had any lasting allowance, for augmentation of the Number, or supply of Books decayed: whereby it came to pass that when those that were in being were either wasted or embezzled, the whole Foundation came to ruin: to meet with that inconvenience, I will so provide hereafter (if God do not hinder my present design) as you shall be still assured of a standing annual rent, to be disbursed every year in buying of books, in officers' stipends, and other pertinent occasions, with which provision, and some order for preservation of the place, and of the furniture of it, from accustomed abuses, it may perhaps in time to come prove a notable Treasure for the multitude of volumes, an excellent benefit for the use and ease of students, and a singular ornament in the University... Which is now as much as I can think on, whereunto, at your good leisure, I would request your friendly answer. And if it lie in my ability to deserve your pains in that behalf, although we be not yet acquainted, you shall find me very forward. From London, Feb. 23, 1597.

Your Affectionate friend,

THO: BODLEY.

Letter to the Vice-Chancellor of Oxon. about restoring the Public Library

WILLIAM CAMDEN

1551–1623

55 *The Lady of the Sea*

FOR the air is most temperate and wholesome, sited in the midst of the temperate Zone, subject to no storms and tempests as the more Southern and Northern are; but stored with infinite delicate fowl. For water, it is walled and guarded with the Ocean most commodious for traffick to all parts of the world, and watered with pleasant fishfull and navigable rivers, which yield safe havens and roads, and furnished with shipping and Sailors, that it may rightly be termed the *Lady of the Sea*. That I may say nothing of healthful Baths, and of Meres stored both with fish and fowl; the earth fertile of all kind of grain, manured with good husbandry, rich in mineral of coals, tin, lead, copper, not without gold and silver, abundant in pasture, replenished with cattle both tame and wild (for it hath more parks than all *Europe* besides), plentifully wooded, provided with all complete provisions of War, beautified with many populous Cities, fair Boroughs, good Towns, and well-built Villages, strong Munitions, magnificent Palaces of the Prince, stately houses of the Nobility, frequent Hospitals, beautiful Churches, fair Colleges, as well in other places, as in the two Universities, which are comparable to all the rest in Christendom, not only in antiquity, but also in learning, buildings, and endowments. As for government Ecclesiastical and Civil, which is the very soul of a kingdom, I need to say nothing, when as I write to home-born, and not to strangers. *Remaines concerning Britain*

RAPHAEL HOLINSHED

fl. 1578

56 *The Weird Sisters*

SHORTLY after happened a strange and uncouth wonder, which afterward was the cause of much trouble in the realm of Scotland, as ye shall after hear. It fortuned as *Makbeth* and *Banquho* journeyed towards *Fores*, where the king as then lay, they went sporting by the way together without other company save only themselves, passing through the woods and fields, when suddenly in the middest of a laund, there met them three women in strange and ferly apparel, resembling creatures of an elder world, whom when they attentively beheld, wondering much at the sight, the first of them spake and said :—'All hail *Makbeth*, Thane of *Glammis*' (for he had lately entered into that dignity and office by the death of his father *Sinell*). The second of them said :—'Hail *Makbeth*, Thane of *Cawder*.' But the third said :—'All hail *Makbeth*, that hereafter shalt be King of *Scotland*.'

Then *Banquho*: 'What manner of women (saith he) are you that seem so little favourable unto me, whereas to my fellow here, besides high offices, ye assign also the kingdom, appointing forth nothing for me at all?' 'Yes' (saith the first of them), 'we promise greater benefits unto thee than unto him; for he shall reign indeed, but with an unlucky end; neither shall he leave any issue behind him to succeed in his place, where contrarily thou indeed shalt not reign at all, but of thee those shall be born which shall govern the Scottish kingdom by long order of continual descent.' Herewith the foresaid women vanished immediately out of their sight. This was reputed at the first but some vain fantastical illusion by *Makbeth* and *Banquho*, insomuch that *Banquho* would call *Makbeth* in jest, king of Scotland; and *Makbeth* again would call him in sport likewise, father of many kings. But afterwards the common opinion was, that these women were either the weird sisters, that is (as ye would say) the Goddesses of destiny, or else some Nymphs or Fairies, indued with knowledge of prophecy by their Necromantical science, because everything came to pass as they had spoken.

History of Scotland

1 *laund*) *lawn, open turf* 2 *ferly*) *marvellous*

RICHARD HAKLUYT

1552 ?–1616

57 *The First Landing in Virginia*

The FIRST VOYAGE *made to the coasts of* AMERICA, *with two barks, wherein were Captains* MASTER PHILIP AMADAS, *and* MASTER ARTHUR BARLOW, *who discovered part of the country now called* VIRGINIA, *Anno* 1584.

THE second of July we found shoal water, which smelt so sweetly, and was so strong a smell, as if we had been in the midst of some delicate garden, abounding with all kinds of odoriferous flowers ; by which we were assured that the land could not be far distant. And keeping good watch and bearing but slack sail, the fourth of the same month we arrived upon the coast, which we supposed to be a continent and firm land, and we sailed along the same 120 English miles before we could find any entrance, or river issuing into the Sea. The first that appeared unto us we entered, though not without some difficulty, and cast anchor about three arquebus-shot within the haven's mouth, on the left hand of the same ; and after thanks given to God for our safe arrival thither, we manned our boats, and went to view the land next adjoining, and to take possession of the same in the right of the Queen's most excellent Majesty, as rightful Queen and Princess of the same, and after delivered the same over to your use, according to her Majesty's grant and letters patents, under her Highness's great Seal. Which being performed, according to the ceremonies used in such enterprises, we viewed the land about us, being, whereas we first landed, very sandy and low towards the water side, but so full of grapes as the very beating and surge of the sea overflowed them. Of which we found such plenty, as well there as in all places else, both on the sand and on the green soil on the hills, as in the plains, as well on every little shrub, as also climbing towards the tops of high Cedars, that I think in all the world the like abundance is not to be found: and myself having seen those parts of Europe that most abound, find such difference as were incredible to be written.

We passed from the sea side towards the tops of those hills next adjoining, being but of mean height; and from thence we beheld the Sea on both sides, to the North and to the South, finding no end any of both ways. This land lay stretching itself to the West, which after we found to be but an Island of twenty leagues long, and not above six miles broad. Under the bank or hill whereon we stood, we beheld the valleys replenished with goodly Cedar trees, and having discharged our arquebus-shot, such a flock of Cranes (the most part white) arose under us, with such a cry redoubled by many Echoes, as if an army of men had shouted all together.

This Island had many goodly woods, and full of Deer, Coneys, Hares, and Fowl, even in the midst of Summer, in incredible abundance. The woods are not such as you find in *Bohemia*, *Moscovia*, or *Hyrcania*, barren and fruitless, but the highest and reddest cedars of the world, far bettering the Cedars of the *Azores*, of the *Indias*, or of *Libanus*; Pines, Cypress, Sassafras, the Lentisk, or the tree that beareth the Mastic; the tree that beareth the rind of black Cinnamon, of which Master *Winter* brought from the Straits of *Magellan*; and many other of excellent smell and quality. We remained by the side of this Island two whole days before we saw any people of the Country. The third day we espied one small boat rowing towards us, having in it three persons. This boat came to the land's side, four arquebus-shot from our ships; and there two of the people remaining, the third came along the shore side towards us, and we being then all within board, he walked up and down upon the point of the land next unto us. Then the Master and the Pilot of the Admiral, *Simon Ferdinando*, and the Captain, *Philip Amadas*, myself, and others, rowed to the land; whose coming this fellow attended, never making any show of fear or doubt. And after he had spoken of many things not understood by us, we brought him, with his own good liking, aboard the ships, and gave him a shirt, a hat, and some other things, and made him taste of our wine and our meat, which he liked very well; and, after having viewed both barks, he departed, and went to his own boat again, which he had left in a little Cove or Creek adjoining. As soon as he was two bow-shot into the water he fell to fishing, and in less than half an hour he had laden his boat as deep as it could swim, with which he came again to the point of the land, and there he divided his fish into two parts, pointing one part to the ship and the other to the pinnace. Which, after he had as much as he might requited the former benefits received, departed out of our sight.

The next day there came unto us divers boats, and in one of them the King's brother, accompanied with forty or fifty men, very handsome and goodly people, and in their behaviour as mannerly and civil as any of Europe. His name was *Granganimeo*, and the king is called *Wingina*; the country, *Wingandacoa*, (and now by her Majesty *Virginia*). The manner of his coming was in this sort: he left his boats altogether as the first man did, a little from the ships by the shore, and came along to the place over against the ships, followed with forty men. When he came to the place, his servants spread a long mat upon the ground, on which he sat down, and at the other end of the mat four others of his company did the like; the rest of his men stood round about him somewhat afar off. When we came to the shore to him, with our weapons, he never moved from his place, nor any of the other four, nor never mistrusted any harm to be offered from us; but, sitting still, he beckoned us to come and sit by him, which we performed; and being set, he makes all signs of joy and welcome, striking on his head and his breast and afterwards on ours, to show we were all one, smiling and making show the best he could of all love and familiarity. After he had made a long speech unto us we presented him with divers things, which he received very joyfully and thankfully. None of the company durst to speak one word all the time; only the four which were at the other end spake one in the other's ear very softly.

Principall Navigations, Voiages, and Discoveries of the English Nation

58 *The Death of Thomas Doughty at Port St. Julian*

IN this port our General began to inquire diligently of the actions of Master *Thomas Doughty*, and found them not to be such as he looked for, but tending rather to contention or mutiny, or some other disorder, whereby (without redress) the success of the voyage might greatly have been hazarded. Whereupon the company was called together and made acquainted with the particulars of the cause, which were found partly by Master *Doughty's* own confession, and partly by the evidence of the fact, to be true. Which when our General saw, although his private affection to Master *Doughty* (as he then in the presence of us all sacredly protested) was great, yet the care he had of the state of the voyage, of the expectation of her Majesty, and of the honour of his country did more touch him (as indeed it ought) than the private respect of one man. So that the cause being throughly heard, and all things done in good order as near as might be to the course of our laws in *England*, it was concluded that Master *Doughty* should receive punishment according to the quality of the offence. And he, seeing no remedy but patience for himself, desired before his death to receive the Communion, which he did at the hands of Master *Fletcher*, our Minister, and our General himself accompanied him in that holy action. Which being done, and the place of execution made ready, he having embraced our General and taken his leave of all the company, with prayer for the Queen's majesty and our realm, in quiet sort laid his head to the block, where he ended his life. This being done, our General made divers speeches to the whole company, perswading us to unity, obedience, love, and regard of our voyage; and for the better confirmation thereof, willed every man the next Sunday following to prepare himself to receive the Communion as Christian brethren and friends ought to do. Which was done in very reverent sort; and so with good contentment every man went about his business.

Principall Navigations, Voiages, and Discoveries of the English Nation

JOHN FLORIO

1553?–1625

59 *Montaigne, Of his Friend*

IF a man urge me to tell wherefore I loved him, I feel it cannot be expressed, but by answering; Because it was he, because it was myself. There is beyond all my discourse, and besides what I can particularly report of it, I know not what inexplicable and fatal power, a mean and Mediatrix of this indissoluble union. We sought one another before we had seen one another, and by the reports we heard one of another; which wrought a greater violence in us, than the reason of reports may well bear; I think by some secret ordinance of the heavens we embraced one another by our names. And at our first meeting, which was by chance at a great feast, and solemn meeting of a whole township, we found ourselves so surprised, so known, so acquainted, and so combinedly bound together, that from thenceforward nothing was so near unto us as one unto another. He writ an excellent Latin Satire, since published, by which he excuseth and expoundeth the precipitation of our acquaintance, so suddenly come to her perfection; Sithence it must continue so short a time, and begun so late (for we were both grown men, and he some years older than myself) there was no time to be lost. And it was not to be modelled or directed by the pattern of regular and remiss friendship, wherein so many precautions of a long and preallable conversation are required. This hath no other *Idea* than of itself, and can have no reference but to itself. It is not one especial consideration, nor two, nor three, nor four, nor a thousand: it is I wot not what kind of quintessence of all this commixture, which having seized all my will, induced the same to plunge and lose itself in his, which likewise having seized all his will, brought it to lose and plunge itself in mine, with a mutual greediness, and with a semblable concurrence. I may truly say, lose, reserving nothing unto us that might properly be called our own, nor that was either his or mine. . .

In this noble commerce, offices and benefits (nurses of other amities) deserve not so much as to be accounted of; this confusion so full of our wills is cause of it; for, even as the friendship I bear unto myself admits no accrease by any succour I give myself in any time of need, whatsoever the Stoicks allege; and as I acknowledge no thanks unto myself for any service I do unto myself, so the union of such friends, being truely perfect, makes them lose the feeling of such duties, and hate, and expell from one another these words of division, and difference, benefit, good deed, duty, obligation, acknowledgment, prayer, thanks, and such their like.

Montaigne's Essayes

60 *Of Cruelty*

AMONGST all other vices there is none I hate more than cruelty, both by nature and judgement, as the extremest of all vices. But it is with such an yearning and faintheartedness, that if I see but a chickens neck pulled off, or a pig sticked, I cannot choose but grieve, and I cannot well endure a seely dew-bedabbled hare to groan, when she is seized upon by the hounds; although hunting be a violent sport. . .

The Cannibals and savage people do not so much offend me with roasting and eating of dead bodies, as those which torment and persecute the living. Let any man be executed by law, how deservedly soever, I cannot endure to behold the execution with an unrelenting eye. . . Even in matters of justice, *Whatsoever is beyond a simple death, I deem it to be mere cruelty*; And especially amongst us, who ought to have a regardful respect, that their souls should be sent to heaven, which cannot be, having first by intolerable tortures agitated and as it were brought them to despair. . .

I live in an age wherein we abound with incredible examples of this vice, through the licentiousness of our civil and intestine wars; And read all ancient stories, be they never so tragical, you shall find none to equal those, we daily see practised. But that hath nothing made me acquainted with it. I could hardly be perswaded, before I had seen it, that the world could have afforded so marble-hearted and savage-minded men, that for the only pleasure of murder would commit it; then cut, mangle, and hack other members in pieces; to rouse and sharpen their wits, to invent unused tortures and unheard-of torments; to devise new and unknown deaths, and that in cold blood, without any former enmity or quarrel, or without any gain or profit; and only to this end, that they may enjoy the pleasing spectacle of the languishing gestures, pitiful motions, horror-moving yellings, deep-fetched groans, and lamentable voices of a dying and drooping man. For, that is the extremest point whereunto the cruelty of man may attain. *Ut homo hominem, non iratus, non timens, tantum spectaturus occidat. That one man should kill another, neither being angry, nor afeard, but only to look on.* As for me, I could never so much as endure, without remorse and grief, to see a poor, silly, and innocent beast pursued and killed, which is harmless and void of defence, and of whom we receive no offence at all. And as it commonly happeneth, that when the Stag begins to be embossed, and finds his strength to fail him, having no other remedy left him, doth yield and bequeath himself unto us that pursue him, with tears suing to us for mercy,

> ——*questuque cruentus*
> *Atque imploranti similis:*
> With blood from throat, and tears from eyes,
> It seems that he for pity cries——

was ever a grievous spectacle unto me.

Montaigne's Essayes

'B. R.'

fl. 1581

61 *Cleobis and Bito*

THE most famous Solon, one of the City of Athens, . . . undertoke a pilgrimage into Ægipt to King Amæsis, and from thence to Sardis to the court of Crœsus, where in gentle and curteous manner beynge entertayned by the Kinge at the thirde or fourth daye after his arrivall he was lead about the treasuryes to view the welth and riches of Crœsus, beholdyng all the inestimable and blessed jewels that were contayned in them. After he had attentively beheld and with curious eye surveyed them at his pleasure, Crœsus began to borde hym on this manner. You Gentleman

7 *embossed*) *exhausted* 26 *borde*) *accost*

of Athens, for asmuch as we hearde greate good wordes of your wysdome, beyng for knowledge and experience sake a pilgrim from your countrey, wee have deemed it convenient to aske you a question, whether at any time you have seene the happiest man alive: not mistrusting, but that the lotte would have fallen to hym selfe to have exceeded all others in blessednes. Solon not mynding to double, as one altogeather unacquaynted with pleasing phrases, delivered his mynd in free speech in forme as followeth.

I have seene O King (quoth he) Tellus, one of my countriemen of Athens, a man surpassing all others in happye lyfe; wherat Crœsus wondring, earnestlye required what cause made him thinke so highlye of Tellus.

For as muche (sayde he) as in a wel ordered common wealth, hee hadde children, trayned up in unitye, and honesty, every of which hadde likewyse increase of his owne bodye, and yet all living. And having spent the course of his age, as wel as a man might, Fortune crowned his end with the perpetual renowne of a most glorious death. For the Athenians joyning in battayle with their next neighbours, Tellus comming with a fresh supplye, and putting his ennemies to flight, ended his life in the field, whom the people of Athens in the selfe same place where he had shed his bloud, caused to be entombed with immortall honour. Solon going forward in a large discourse as touching Tellus was cut of by Crœsus with a second demaunde, who asked him the second tyme, whom in conscience he thoughte next unto him, in full hope, that at the least his part had bene next: to whom he answeared in the next degree.

Most mighty Prince, I have always reputed Cleobis

and Biton, two younge menne of the Countrey of Argos, of body so strong and active, that in alle games they wonne the prize, of whom these thinges are left to memorye.

The feast of Juno beynge kept at Argos, the mother of those two young men was to bee drawne to the temple by a yoke of bullocks, which when the howre came beyng strayed and gone out of the way, the two young youthes yoked themselves, and haling the chariot forty fyve furlongs they came to the temple: which after they had done in the sight and view of the whole multitude in a lucky howre they dyed, wherby the Goddesse gave us to understand how much better it was for man to die then live. For where as the people flocking abut extolled them to the heavens: the men praising the good nature and intent of the sonnes: the women commendinge the blessed chaunce of the mother whom nature had indued with two such children: the good old mother almost out of hyr wyttes for joy, what for the kynd deede of her sonnes and the goodly speech of the people, advauncinge their virtue: as shee stoode before the ymage of Juno, besought the Goddesse with earnest prayers to rewarde the kindnes of hir children with the chiefe and most precious blessing that might happen unto man. Her prayer made, and both the sacrifyce and feast ended, they gave themselves to rest in the temple, but never after awaking, in the morning they were founde dead, whom the people of Argos by two carved monumentes placed at Delphos commended to everlastinge memory for men of rare and excellent vertue. To these men did Solon attribute the next step to perfect happiness.

Translation of Herodotus

FULKE GREVILLE, LORD BROOKE

1554–1628

62 *A Honeymoon*

WHEN you married him, I know, for your part, he was your first love; and I judge the like of him. . . . Madam, in those neere conjunctions of society, wherein death is the only honourable divorce, there is but one end, which is mutual joy in procreation; and to that end two assured ways: the one, by cherishing affection with affection: the other, by working affection, while she is yet in her pride, to a reverence, which hath more power than itself. To which are required advantage, or at least equality: art, as well as nature. For contempt is else as neere as respect; the lovingest mind being not ever the most lovely. Now though it be true that affections are relatives, and love the surest adamant of love; yet must it not be measured by the untemperate ell of itself, since prodigality yields fullness, satiety a desire of change, and change repentance: but so tempered even in trust, enjoying, and all other familiarities, that the appetites of them we would please may still be covetous, and their strengths rich. Because the decay of either is a point of ill huswifery, and they that are first bankrupt shut up their doors.

In this estate of minds, only governed by the unwritten laws of Nature, you did at the beginning live happily together.

Letter sent to an honourable Lady

SIR PHILIP SIDNEY

1554–1586

63 *Love in Arcady*

SO it is, Mistress, said he, that yesterday driving my sheep up to the stately hill, which lifts his head over the fair City of *Mantinea*, I happened upon the side of it, in a little falling of the ground which was a rampier against the Sun's rage, to perceive a young maid, truly of the finest stamp of beauty, and that which made her beauty the more admirable, there was at all no art added to the helping of it. For her apparel was but such as Shepherds' daughters are wont to wear: and as for her hair, it hung down at the free liberty of his goodly length, but that sometimes falling before the clear stars of her sight, she was forced to put it behind her ears, and so open again the treasure of her perfections, which that for a while had in part hidden. In her lap there lay a Shepherd, so wrapped up in that well-liked place, that I could discern no piece of his face; but as mine eyes were attent in that, her Angel-like voice strake mine ears with this song:

My true love hath my heart, and I have his,
By just exchange, one for the other giv'n.
I hold his dear, and mine he cannot miss:
There never was a better bargain driv'n.

His heart in me, keeps me and him in one,
My heart in him, his thoughts and senses guides:
He loves my heart, for once it was his own:
I cherish his, because in me it bides.

Arcadia

64 *With a Tale he cometh*

NOW therein of all Sciences (I speak still of humane, and according to the humane conceits) is our Poet the Monarch. For he doth not only show the way, but giveth so sweet a prospect into the way, as will entice any man to enter into it. Nay, he doth, as if your journey should lie through a fair Vineyard, at the first give you a cluster of Grapes, that, full of that taste, you may long to passe further. He beginneth not with obscure definitions, which must blur the margent with interpretations, and load the memory with doubtfulness; but he cometh to you with words set in delightful proportion, either accompanied with, or prepared for, the well enchanting skill of Musick; and with a tale forsooth he cometh unto you: with a tale which holdeth children from play, and old men from the chimney corner. And, pretending no more, doth intend the winning of the mind from wickedness to virtue: even as the child is often brought to take most wholesome things by hiding them in such other as have a pleasant taste: which, if one should begin to tell them the nature of *Aloes* or *Rhubarb* they should receive, would sooner take their Physick at their ears than at their mouth. So is it in men (most of which are childish in the best things, till they be cradled in their graves); glad they will be to hear the tales of *Hercules*, *Achilles*, *Cyrus*, and *Aeneas*; and hearing them, must needs hear the right description of wisdom, valour, and justice; which, if they had been barely, that is to say, Philosophically set out, they would swear they be brought to school again.

An Apologie for Poetrie

SIR PHILIP SIDNEY

65 *Chevy Chase*

IS it the Lyrick that most displeaseth, who with his tuned Lyre and well-accorded voice, giveth praise, the reward of virtue, to virtuous acts; who gives moral precepts and natural Problems; who sometimes raiseth up his voice to the height of the heavens, in singing the laudes of the immortal God? Certainly, I must confess my own barbarousness, I never heard the old song of *Percy* and *Duglas* that I found not my heart moved more than with a Trumpet; and yet is it sung but by some blind Crouder, with no rougher voice than rude style; which, being so evil apparelled in the dust and cobwebs of that uncivil age, what would it work trimmed in the gorgeous eloquence of *Pindar*?

An Apologie for Poetrie

JOHN LYLY

? 1554–1606

66 *Two Sisters*

THERE are also in this Island two famous Universities, the one *Oxford*, the other *Cambridge*, both for the profession of all sciences, for Divinity, Physick, Law, and all kind of learning, excelling all the Universities in Christendom.

I was myself in either of them, and like them both so well that I mean not in the way of controversy to prefer any for the better in *England*, but both for the best in the world, saving this, that Colleges in *Oxenford* are much more stately for the building, and *Cambridge* much more sumptuous for the houses in

10 *Crouder*) *fiddler*

the town; but the learning neither lieth in the free stones of the one, nor the fine streets of the other, for out of them both do daily proceed men of great wisdom to rule in the commonwealth, of learning to instruct the common people, of all singular kind of professions to do good to all. And let this suffice, not to inquire which of them is the superior, but that neither of them have their equal; neither to ask which of them is the most ancient, but whether any other be so famous.

Euphues and his England

RICHARD HOOKER

1554–1600

67 *Laws of Nature*

NOW if nature should intermit her course, and leave altogether though it were but for a while the observation of her own laws; if those principal and mother elements of the world, whereof all things in this lower world are made, should lose the qualities which now they have; if the frame of that heavenly arch erected over our heads should loosen and dissolve itself; if celestial spheres should forget their wonted motions, and by irregular volubility turn themselves any way as it might happen; if the prince of the lights of heaven, which now as a giant doth run his unwearied course, should as it were through a languishing faintness begin to stand and to rest himself; if the moon should wander from her beaten way, the times and seasons of the year blend themselves by disordered and confused mixture, the winds breathe out their last gasp, the clouds yield no rain, the earth be defeated of heavenly influence, the fruits of the earth pine away as children at the withered breasts of their mother no longer able to yield them relief: what would become of man himself, whom these things now do all serve? See we not plainly that obedience of creatures unto the law of nature is the stay of the whole world?

The Laws of Ecclesiasticall Politie

68 *Man's Ascending Search*

MAN doth seek a triple perfection: first a sensual, consisting in those things which very life itself requireth either as necessary supplements, or as beauties and ornaments thereof; then an intellectual, consisting in those things which none underneath man is either capable of or acquainted with; lastly a spiritual and divine, consisting in those things whereunto we tend by supernatural means here, but cannot here attain unto them. They that make the first of these three the scope of their whole life, are said by the Apostle to have no god but only their belly, to be earthly minded men. Unto the second they bend themselves, who seek especially to excel in all such knowledge and virtue as doth most commend men. To this branch belongeth the law of moral and civil perfection. That there is somewhat higher than either of these two, no other proof doth need than the very process of man's desire, which being natural should be frustrate, if there were not some farther thing wherein it might rest at the length contented, which in the former it cannot do. For man doth not seem to rest satisfied, either with fruition of that wherewith his life is preserved, or with performance of such actions as advance him most deservedly in estimation; but doth further covet, yea oftentimes manifestly pursue with great sedulity and earnestness, that which cannot stand him in any stead for vital use; that which exceedeth the reach of sense; yea somewhat above capacity of reason, somewhat divine and heavenly, which with hidden exultation it rather surmiseth than conceiveth; somewhat it seeketh, and what that is directly it knoweth not, yet very intentive desire thereof doth so incite it, that all other known delights and pleasures are laid aside, they give place to the search of this but only suspected desire.

The Laws of Ecclesiasticall Politie

69 *The Permanence of Government*

OF this point therefore we are to note, that sith men naturally have no full and perfect power to command whole politic multitudes of men, therefore utterly without our consent we could in such sort be at no man's commandment living. And to be commanded we do consent, when that society whereof we are part hath at any time before consented, without revoking the same after by the like universal agreement. Wherefore as any man's deed past is good as long as himself continueth; so the act of a public society of men done five hundred years sithence standeth as theirs who presently are of the same societies, because corporations are immortal; we were then alive in our Predecessors, and they in their Successors do live still.

The Laws of Ecclesiasticall Politie

THOMAS LODGE

1558–1625

70 *Alinda's Comfort to Perplexed Rosalind*

WHY, how now, *Rosalind*, dismayed with a frown of contrary fortune? Have I not oft heard thee say that high minds were discovered in fortune's contempt, and heroical seen in the depth of extremities? . . . And more, mad lass, to be melancholy, when thou hast with thee *Alinda*, a friend, who will be a faithful co-partner of all thy misfortunes, who hath left her father to follow thee, and chooseth rather to brook all extremities than to forsake thy presence? What, *Rosalind*,

Solamen miseris socios habuisse doloris?

Cheerly, woman; as we have been bed-fellows in royalty, we will be fellow-mates in poverty. I will ever be thy *Alinda*, and thou shalt ever rest to me *Rosalind*: so shall the world canonize our friendship, and speak of *Rosalind* and *Alinda*, as they did of *Pylades* and *Orestes*. And if ever fortune smile and we return to our former honour, then folding ourselves in the sweet of our friendship, we shall merrily say (calling to mind our forepast miseries)—

Olim haec meminisse juvabit.

At this *Rosalind* began to comfort her, and after she had wept a few kind tears in the bosom of her *Alinda*, she gave her hearty thanks, and then they sat them down to consult how they should travel. *Alinda* grieved at nothing but that they might have no man in their company: saying, it would be their greatest prejudice in that two women went wandering without either guide or attendant. Tush, quoth *Rosalind*, art thou a woman, and hast not a sudden shift to prevent a misfortune? I, thou seest, am of a tall stature, and would very well become the person and apparel of a page; thou shalt be my mistress, and I will play the man so properly that, trust me, in what company soever I come I will not be discovered. I will buy me a suit, and have my rapier very handsomely at my side, and if any knave offer wrong, your page will show him the point of his weapon. At this *Alinda* smiled, and upon this they agreed, and presently gathered up all their jewels, which they trussed up in a casket, and *Rosalind* in all haste provided her of robes . . . *Alinda* being called *Aliena* and *Rosalind Ganymede*.

Rosalynde

THE BIBLE, AUTHORIZED VERSION, 1611

71 *Jacob at the Ford*

AND hee rose vp that night, and tooke his two wiues, and his two women seruants, and his eleuen sonnes, and passed ouer the foord Iabbok. And he tooke them, and sent them ouer the brooke, and sent ouer that hee had.

And Iacob was left alone: and there wrestled a man with him, vntill the breaking of the day. And when he saw, that he preuailed not against him, he touched the hollow of his thigh: and the hollow of Iacobs thigh was out of ioynt, as hee wrestled with him. And he said, Let me goe, for the day breaketh: and he said, I will not let thee goe, except thou blesse me. And he said vnto him, What is thy name? and he said, Iacob. And he said, Thy name shall be called no more Iacob, but Israel: for as a prince hast thou power with God, and with men, and hast preuailed. And Iacob asked *him*, and saide, Tell me, I pray thee, thy name: and he said, Wherefore is it, that thou doest aske after my name? and he blessed him there.

Genesis xxxii. 22–9

72 *The Death of Absalom*

AND Dauid sate betweene the two gates: and the watchman went vp to the roofe ouer the gate vnto the wall, and lift vp his eyes, and looked, and behold, a man running alone. And the watchman cried, and told the King. And the king said, If he *bee* alone, *there is* tidings in his mouth. And he came apace, and drew neere. And the watchman saw another man running, and the watchman called vnto the porter, and said, Behold, *another* man running alone. And the King said, He also bringeth tidings. And the watchman said, Mee thinketh the running of the foremost is like the running of Ahimaaz the sonne of Zadok. And the King said, Hee *is* a good man, and commeth with good tidings. And Ahimaaz called, and said vnto the King, All is well. And hee fell downe to the earth vpon his face before the King, and saide, Blessed *bee* the Lord thy God which hath deliuered vp the men that lift vp their hande against my lord the King. And the king said, Is the yong man Absalom safe? And Ahimaaz answered, When Ioab sent the kings seruant, and *me* thy seruant, I saw a great tumult, but I knew not what *it was*. And the king said *vnto him*, Turne aside *and* stand here. And hee turned aside, and stood still. And behold, Cushi came, and Cushi said, Tidings my lord the king: for the Lord hath auenged thee this day of all them that rose vp against thee. And the king said vnto Cushi, Is the yong man Absalom safe? And Cushi answered, The enemies of my lord the king, and all that rise against thee to doe *thee* hurt, be as that yong man is.

And the king was much moued, and went vp to the chamber ouer the gate, and wept: and as he went, thus hee said, O my sonne Absalom, my sonne, my sonne Absalom: would God I had died for thee, O Absalom, my sonne, my sonne.

2 Samuel xviii. 24–33

73 *'Remember now Thy Creator'*

REMEMBER now thy Creatour in the dayes of thy youth, while the euil daies come not, nor the yeeres drawe nigh, when thou shalt say, I *haue* no pleasure in them: While the Sunne, or the light, or the moone, or the starres be not darkened, nor the cloudes returne after the raine: In the day when the keepers of the house shall tremble, and the strong men shall bowe themselues, and the grinders cease, because they are fewe, and those that looke out of the windowes be darkened: And the doores shal be shut in the streets, when the sound of the grinding is low, and he shall rise vp at the voice of the bird, and all the daughters of musicke shall be brought low. Also *when* they shalbe afraid of that which is high, and feares *shall bee* in the way, and the Almond tree shall flourish, and the grashopper shall be a burden, and desire shall faile: because man goeth to his long home, and the mourners goe about the streets: Or euer the siluer corde be loosed, or the golden bowle be broken, or the pitcher be broken at the fountaine, or the wheele broken at the cisterne. Then shall the dust returne to the earth as it was: and the spirit shall returne vnto God who gaue it.

Ecclesiastes xii. 1–7

74 *The Song of Solomon*

i

THE voice of my beloued! behold! hee commeth leaping vpon the mountaines, skipping vpon the hils.

My beloued is like a Roe, or a yong Hart: behold, he standeth behind our wall, he looketh foorth at the windowe, shewing himselfe through the lattesse.

My beloued spake, and said vnto me, Rise vp, my Loue, my faire one, and come away.

For loe, the winter is past, the raine is ouer, *and* gone.

The flowers appeare on the earth, the time of the singing *of birds* is come, and the voice of the turtle is heard in our land.

The fig tree putteth foorth her greene figs, and the vines *with* the tender grape giue a *good* smell. Arise, my loue, my faire one, and come away.

O my doue! *that art* in the clefts of the rocke, in the secret *places* of the staires: let me see thy countenance, let me heare thy voice, for sweet *is* thy voice, and thy countenance *is* comely.

Take vs the foxes, the litle foxes, that spoile the vines: for our vines *haue* tender grapes.

My beloued *is* mine, and I *am* his: he feedeth among the lillies.

Vntill the day breake, and the shadowes flee away: turne my beloued and be thou like a Roe, or a yong Hart, vpon the mountaines of Bether.

Song of Solomon ii. 8–17

ii

BY night on my bed I sought *him* whome my soule loueth. I sought him, but I found him not.

I will rise now, and goe about the citie in the streets, and in the broad wayes I will seeke him whom my soule loueth: I sought him, but I found him not.

The watchmen that goe about the citie, found me: *to whom I said*, Saw ye him whom my soule loueth?

It was but a litle that I passed from them, but I found him whome my soule loueth: I helde him, and would not let him goe, vntill I had brought him into my mothers house, and into the chamber of her that conceiued me.

I charge you, O ye daughters of Ierusalem, by the Roes and by the Hindes of the field, that ye stirre not vp, nor awake my loue, till he please.

Song of Solomon iii. 1–5

iii

SET mee as a seale vpon thine heart, as a seale vpon thine arme: for loue *is* strong as death, iealousie *is* cruel as the graue: the coales thereof *are* coales of fire, *which hath* a most vehement flame.

Many waters cannot quench loue, neither can the floods drowne it: if a man would giue all the substance of his house for loue, it would vtterly be contemned.

Song of Solomon viii. 6, 7

75 *Dirge for the King of Babylon*

HELL from beneath is mooued for thee to meet *thee* at thy comming: it stirreth vp the dead for thee, *euen* all the chiefe ones of the earth; it hath raised vp from their thrones, all the kings of the nations. All they shall speake and say vnto thee; Art thou also become weake as we? art thou become like vnto us? Thy pompe is brought downe to the graue, *and* the noyse of thy violes: the worme is spread vnder thee, and the wormes couer thee. How art thou fallen from heauen, O Lucifer, sonne of the morning? *how* art thou cut downe to the ground, which didst weaken the nations?

Isaiah xiv. 9–12

76 *'Thine eyes shall see the King in his beauty'*

THINE eyes shall see the king in his beauty: they shall behold the land that is very farre off. Thine heart shall meditate terrour; Where *is* the scribe? where *is* the receiuer? where *is* he that counted the towres? Thou shalt not see a fierce people, a people of a deeper speech then thou canst perceiue; of a stammering tongue, that thou canst not vnderstand. Looke vpon Zion, the city of our solemnities: thine eyes shall see Ierusalem a quiet habitation, a tabernacle that shall not be taken downe, not one of the stakes thereof shall euer be remoued, neither shall any of the coardes thereof be broken. But there the glorious Lord *will be* vnto us a place of broad riuers *and* streames; wherein shall goe no galley with oares, neither shall gallant ship passe thereby. For the Lord *is* our Iudge, the Lord *is* our Lawgiuer, the Lord *is* our King, he wil saue vs. Thy tacklings are loosed: they could not well strengthen their mast, they could not spread the saile: then is the praye of a great spoile diuided, the lame take the praye. And the inhabitant shall not say; I am sicke: the people that dwel therein shalbe forgiuen *their* iniquitie.

Isaiah xxxiii. 17–24

77 *The Wilderness*

THE wildernesse and the solitarie place shall be glad for them: and the desert shall reioyce and blossome as the rose. It shall blossome abundantly, and reioyce euen with ioy and singing: the glory of Lebanon shal be giuen vnto it, the excellencie of Carmel and Sharon: they shall see the glory of the Lord, and the excellencie of our God.

Strengthen yee the weake hands, and confirme the feeble knees. Say to them that are of a fearefull heart; Be strong, feare not: behold, your God will come *with* vengeance, *euen* God *with* a recompence, he will come and saue you. Then the eyes of the blind shall be opened, and the eares of the deafe shalbe vnstopped. Then shall the lame man leape as an Hart, and the tongue of the dumbe sing: for in the wildernesse shall waters breake out, and streames in the desert. And the parched ground shall become a poole, and the thirstie land springs of water: in the habitation of dragons, where each lay, *shalbe* grasse with reeds and rushes. And an high way *shalbe* there, and a way, and it shall be called the way of holinesse, the vncleane shall not passe ouer it, but it shall be for those: the wayfaringmen, though fooles, shall not erre *therein*. No lyon shalbe there; nor any rauenous beast shall goe vp thereon, it shall not be found there: but the redeemed shall walke *there*. And the ransomed of the LORD shall returne and come to Zion with songs, and euerlasting ioy vpon their heads: they shall obtaine ioy and gladnesse, and sorrow and sighing shall flee away.

Isaiah xxxv. 1–10

78 *Surge, illuminare!*

ARISE, shine, for thy light is come, and the glory of the LORD is risen vpon thee. For behold, the darknesse shall couer the earth, and grosse darknesse the people: but the LORD shall arise vpon thee, and his glory shall be seene vpon thee. And the Gentiles shall come to thy light, and kings to the brightnesse of thy rising. The Sunne shall be no more thy light by day, neither for brightnesse shall the moone giue light vnto thee: but the LORD shall be unto thee an euerlasting light, and thy God thy glory. Thy Sunne shall no more goe downe, neither shall thy moone withdraw it selfe: for the LORD shall bee thine euerlasting light, and the dayes of thy mourning shall be ended.

Isaiah lx. 1–3, 19–20

79 *The Vision of Dry Bones*

THE hand of the LORD was vpon mee, and caried mee out in the Spirit of the LORD, and set mee downe in the middest of the valley which *was* full of bones, And caused mee to passe by them round about, and beholde, *there were* very many in the open valley, and loe, *they were* very drie. And hee said vnto mee,

Sonne of man, can these bones liue? and I answered, O Lord God, thou knowest. Againe he said vnto me, Prophecie vpon these bones, and say vnto them; O yee drie bones, heare the word of the Lord. Thus saith the Lord God vnto these bones, Behold, I wil cause breath to enter into you, and ye shall liue. And I wil lay sinewes vpon you, and wil bring vp flesh vpon you, and couer you with skinne, and put breath in you, and ye shall liue, and ye shall know that I *am* the Lord. So I prophecied as I was commanded: and as I prophecied, there was a noise, and beholde a shaking, and the bones came together, bone to his bone. And when I beheld, loe, the sinews and the flesh came vp vpon them, and the skin couered them aboue; but *there was* no breath in them. Then said he vnto mee, Prophecie vnto the winde, prophecie sonne of man, and say to the winde, Thus saith the Lord God; Come from the foure windes, O breath, and breathe vpon these slaine, that they may liue. So I prophecied as he commanded mee, and the breath came into them, and they liued, and stood vp vpon their feet, an exceeding great armie.

Then he said vnto me, Sonne of man, these bones are the whole house of Israel: behold, they say; Our bones are dried, and our hope is lost, wee are cut off for our parts. Therefore prophecie and say vnto them, Thus saith the Lord God, Behold, O my people, I wil open your graues, and cause you to come vp out of your graues, and bring you into the land of Israel. And ye shall know that I *am* the Lord, when I haue opened your graues, O my people, and brought you vp out of your graues.

Ezekiel xxxvii. 1–13

80 *'God's purpose is eternall'*

AND he said vnto me, in the beginning when the earth was made, before the borders of the world stood, or euer the windes blew, Before it thundred and lightned, or euer the foundations of Paradise were laide, Before the faire flowers were seene, or euer the moueable powers were established, before the innumerable multitude of Angels were gathered together, Or euer the heights of the aire were lifted vp, before the measures of the firmament were named, or euer the chimnies in Sion were hot, And ere the present yeeres were sought out, and or euer the inuentions of them that now sinne were turned, before they were sealed that haue gathered faith for a treasure: Then did I consider these things, and they all were made through mee alone, and through none other: by mee also they shall be ended, & by none other.

2 *Esdras* vi. 1–6

'Let us now praise famous men, and our
81 *fathers that begat us'*

LET vs now praise famous men, and our Fathers that begat vs. The Lorde hath wrought great glory by them, through his great power from the beginning. Such as did beare rule in their kingdomes, men renowmed for their power, giuing counsell by their vnderstanding, and declaring prophecies: Leaders of the people by their counsels, and by their knowledge of learning meet for the people, wise and eloquent in their instructions. Such as found out musical tunes, and recited verses in writing. Rich men furnished with abilitie, liuing peaceably in their habitations.

All these were honoured in their generations, and were the glory of their times. There be of them, that haue left a name behind them, that their praises might be reported. And some there be, which haue no memorial, who are perished as though they had neuer bene, and are become as though they had neuer bene borne, and their children after them. But these were mercifull men, whose righteousnesse hath not beene forgotten. With their seed shall continually remaine a good inheritance, and their children are within the couenant. Their seed stands fast, and their children for their sakes. Their seed shall remaine for euer, and their glory shall not be blotted out. Their bodies are buried in peace, but their name liueth for euermore.

Ecclesiasticus xliv. 1–14

82 *The Walk to Emmaus*

AND behold, two of them went that same day to a village called Emaus, which was from Hierusalem about threescore furlongs. And they talked together of all these things which had happened. And it came to passe, that while they communed together, and reasoned, Iesus himselfe drew neere, and went with them. But their eyes were holden, that they should not know him. And he said vnto them, What manner of communications are these that yee haue one to another as yee walke, and are sad? And the one of them, whose name was Cleophas, answering, saide vnto him, Art thou onely a stranger in Hierusalem, and hast not knowen the things which are come to passe there in these dayes? And hee saide vnto them, What things? And they said vnto him, Concerning Iesus of Nazareth, which was a Prophet, mighty in deede and word before God, and all the people. And how the chiefe Priests and our rulers deliuered him to be condemned to death, and haue crucified him. But wee trusted that it had bene hee, which should have redeemed Israel: and beside all this, to day is the third day since these things were done. Yea, and certaine women also of our company made vs astonished, which were early at the Sepulchre: And when they found not his bodie, they came, saying, that they had also seene a vision of Angels, which saide that he was aliue. And certaine of them which were with vs, went to the Sepulchre, and found it euen so as the women had said, but him they saw not. Then hee saide vnto them, O fooles, and slow of heart to beleeue all that the Prophets haue spoken: Ought not Christ to haue suffered these things, and to enter into his glorie? And beginning at Moses, and all the Prophets, hee expounded vnto them in all the Scriptures, the things concerning himselfe. And they drew nigh vnto the village, whither they went, and hee made as though hee would haue gone further. But they constrained him, saying, Abide with vs, for it is towards euening, and the day is farre spent: And he went in, to tarrie with them. And it came to passe, as hee sate at meate with them, hee tooke bread, and blessed it, and brake, and gaue to them. And their eyes were opened, and they knew him, and he vanished out of their sight. And they said one vnto another, Did not our heart burne within vs, while hee talked with vs by the way, and while hee opened to vs the Scriptures? And they rose vp the same houre, and returned to Hierusalem, and found the eleuen gathered together, and them that were with them, Saying, The Lord is risen indeed, and hath appeared to Simon.

And they told what things were done in the way, & how he was knowen of them in breaking of bread.

St. Luke xxiv. 13–35

83 '*Charity*'

THOUGH I speake with the tongues of men & of Angels, and haue not charity, I am become as sounding brasse or a tinkling cymbal. And though I haue the gift of prophesie, and vnderstand all mysteries and all knowledge: and though I haue all faith, so that I could remooue mountaines, and haue no charitie, I am nothing. And though I bestowe all my goods to feede the poore, and though I giue my body to bee burned, and haue not charitie, it profiteth me nothing. Charitie suffereth long, and is kinde: charitie enuieth not: charitie vaunteth not it selfe, is not puffed vp, Doeth not behaue it selfe vnseemly, seeketh not her owne, is not easily prouoked, thinketh no euill, Reioyceth not in iniquitie, but reioyceth in the trueth: Beareth all things, beleeueth all things, hopeth all things, endureth all things. Charitie neuer faileth: but whether there be prophesies, *they* shall faile; whether there bee tongues, *they* shall cease; whether there bee knowledge, *it* shall vanish away. For we know in part, and we prophesie in part. But when that which is perfect is come, then that which is in part, shalbe done away. When I was a childe, I spake as a childe, I vnderstood as a childe, I thought as a childe: but when I became a man, I put away childish things. For now we see through a glasse, darkely: but then face to face: now I know in part, but then shall I know euen as also I am knowen. And now abideth faith, hope, charitie, these three, but the greatest of these is charitie.

1 *Corinthians* xiii. 1–13

84 *'Behold, I show you a mystery'*

BEHOLD, I shew you a mysterie: we shall not all sleepe, but wee shall all be changed, In a moment, in the twinckling of an eye, at the last trumpe, (for the trumpet shall sound, and the dead shall be raised incorruptible, and we shall be changed.) For this corruptible must put on incorruption, and this mortall must put on immortalitie. So when this corruptible shall haue put on incorruption, & this mortall shall haue put on immortality, then shall be brought to passe the saying that is written, Death is swallowed vp in victorie. O death, where is thy sting? O graue, where is thy victorie? The sting of death is sinne, and the strength of sinne is the law. But thankes bee to God, which giueth us the victorie, through our Lord Iesus Christ. Therefore my beloued brethren, be yee stedfast, vnmoveable, alwayes abounding in the worke of the Lord, forasmuch as you know that your labour is not in vaine in the Lord.

1 *Corinthians* xv. 51–8

RICHARD CAREW

1555–1620

85 *The Praise of English*

THE *Italian* is pleasant but without sinews, as too stilly fleeting water; the *French* delicate but over nice, as a woman scarce daring to open her lips for fear of marring her countenance; the *Spanish* majestical, but fulsome, running too much on the o, and terrible like the devil in a play; the *Dutch* manlike, but withal very harsh, as one ready at every word to pick a quarrel. Now we in borrowing from them give the strength of consonants to the *Italian*, the full sound of words to the *French*, the variety of terminations to the *Spanish*, and the mollifying of more vowels to the *Dutch*; and so, like bees, gather the honey of their good properties and leave the dregs to themselves. And thus, when substantialness combineth with delightfulness, fullness with fineness, seemliness with portliness, and courrantness with staidness, how can the language which consisteth of all these sound other than most full of sweetness?

Again, the long words that we borrow, being intermingled with the short of our own store, make up a perfect harmony, by culling from out which mixture (with judgement) you may frame your speech according to the matter you must work on, majestical, pleasant, delicate, or manly, more or less, in what sort you please. Add hereunto, that whatsoever grace any other language carrieth, in verse or prose, in tropes or metaphors, in echoes or agnominations, they may all be lively and exactly represented in ours. Will you have *Plato's* vein? read Sir Thomas Smith: the *Ionic*? Sir Thomas More: *Cicero's*? Ascham: *Varro*? Chaucer: *Demosthenes*? Sir John Cheke (who in his Treatise to the Rebels hath comprised all the figures of rhetoric). Will you read *Virgil*? take the Earl of Surrey: *Catullus*? Shakespeare, and Marlowe's fragment: *Ovid*? Daniel: *Lucan*? Spenser: *Martial*? Sir John Davis and others. Will you have all in all for prose and verse? take the miracle of our age, Sir Philip Sidney.

An Epistle on the Excellency of the English Tongue

JAMES MELVILLE

1556–1614

86 The Armada Castaways in Fife

TERRIBLE was the fear, piercing were the preachings, earnest, zealous, and fervent were the prayers, sounding were the sighs and sobs, and abounding were the tears at that Fast and General Assembly keipet at *Edinburgh*, when the news was credibly tauld, sometimes of their landing at *Dunbar*, sometimes at *St. Andrews*, and in *Tay*, and now and then at *Aberdeen* and *Cromarty Firth*. And in very deed, as we knew certainly soon after, the keeper of his awin Israel, was in the meantime convoying that monstrous navy about our coasts, and directing their hulks and galiates to the islands, rocks, and sands, whereupon he had destined their wreck and destruction. For within twa or three month thereafter, early in the morning, by break of day, ane of our bailyies cam to my bedside, saying (but not with fear), 'I have to tell you news, Sir. There is arrived within our harbour this morning a ship full of *Spaniards*, but not to give mercy but to ask!' And shows me that the Commanders had landit, and he had commandit them to their ship again till the Magistrates of the town had advised, and the *Spaniards* had humbly obeyit: therefore desired me to rise and hear their petition with them. Up I got with diligence, and assembling the honest men of the town, cam to the *Tolbuthe*; and after consultation taken to hear them and what answer to make, there presents us a very reverend man of big stature, and grave and stout countenance, grey-haired, and very humble like, wha, after mickle and very low courtesy, bowing down with his face near the ground, and touching my shoe with his hand, began his harangue in the Spanish tongue, whereof I understood the substance; and being about to answer in Latin, he, having only a young man with him to be his interpreter, began and tauld over again to us in good English. The sum was, that King *Philip*, his master, had rigged out a navy and army to land in *England*, for just causes to be avengit of many intolerable wrongs quhilk he had receivit of that nation; but God for their sins had been against them, and by storm of weather had driven the navy by the coast of England, and him with a certain of Captains, being the General of twenty hulks, upon an isle of Scotland, called the *Fair Isle*, where they made shipwreck, and where sae many as had escapit the merciless seas and rocks, had mair nor sax or seven weeks suffered great hunger and cauld, till conducing that bark out of Orkney, they were come hither as to their special friends and confederates to kiss the King's Majestie's hands of Scotland (and therewith bekkit even to the earth), and to find relief and comfort thereby to himself, these gentlemen Captains, and the poor soldiers, whose condition was for the present most miserable and pitiful.

I answered this mickle, in sum: That howbeit neither our friendship, quhilk could not be great, seeing their King and they were friends to the greatest enemy of *Christ*, the Pope of *Rome*, and our King and we defied him, nor yet their cause against our neighbours and special friends of England could procure any benefit at our hands, for their relief and comfort; nevertheless, they should know by experience that we were men, and sa moved by human compassion, and Christians of better religion nor they, quhilk

20 *bekkit*) *bowed*

should kythe, in the fruits and effect, plain contrary to ours. For whereas our people resorting among them in peaceable and lawful affairs of merchandise, were violently taken and cast in prison, their guids and gear confiscate, and their bodies committed to the cruel flaming fire for the cause of Religion, they should find na things among us but Christian pity and works of mercy and alms. . . . But verily all the while my heart melted within me for desire of thankfulness to God, when I rememberit the prideful and cruel natural of they people, and how they would have used us in case they had landit with their forces among us; and saw the wonderful work of God's mercy and justice in making us see them, the chief commanders of them to make sic dewgard and courtesy to poor seamen, and their soldiers so abjectly to beg alms at our doors and in our streets.

Diary

SIR WALTER RALEGH

1552 ?–1618

87 *The Last Fight of the Revenge*

ALL the powder of the *Revenge* to the last barrel was now spent, all her pikes broken, forty of her best men slain, and the most part of the rest hurt. In the beginning of the fight she had but one hundred free from sickness, and fourscore and ten sick, laid in hold upon the ballast. A small troop to man such a ship, and a weak garrison to resist so mighty an army. By those hundred all was sustained, the volleys, boardings, and enterings of fifteen ships of war, besides those which beat her at large. On the contrary, the Spanish

1 *kythe*) *appear* 15 *dewgard*) *dieu-garde* (*salutation*)

were always supplied with soldiers brought from every squadron: all manner of arms and powder at will. Unto ours there remained no comfort at all, no hope, no supply either of ships, men, or weapons; the masts all beaten overboard, all her tackle cut asunder, her upper work altogether rased, and in effect evened she was with the water, but the very foundation or bottom of a ship, nothing being left overhead either for flight or defence. Sir *Richard* finding himself in this distress, and unable any longer to make resistance, having endured in this fifteen hours' fight the assault of fifteen several Armadoes, all by turns aboard him, and by estimation eight hundred shot of great artillery, besides many assaults and entries; and that himself and the ship must needs be possessed by the enemy, who were now all cast in a ring round about him; the *Revenge* not able to move one way or other, but as she was moved with the waves and billow of the sea: commanded the master Gunner, whom he knew to be a most resolute man, to split and sink the ship; that thereby nothing might remain of glory or victory to the Spaniards, seeing in so many hours' fight, and with so great a Navy they were not able to take her, having had fifteen hours' time, fifteen thousand men, and fifty and three sail of men-of-war to perform it withal: and perswaded the company, or as many as he could induce, to yield themselves unto God, and to the mercy of none else; but as they had like valiant resolute men repulsed so many enemies, they should not now shorten the honour of their nation, by prolonging their own lives for a few hours, or a few days. The master Gunner readily condescended, and divers others; but the Captain and the Master were of another opinion, and besought Sir *Richard* to have care of them: alleging that the Spaniard would be as ready to entertain a composition as they were willing to offer the same: and that there being divers sufficient and valiant men yet living, and whose wounds were not mortal, they might do their country and prince acceptable service hereafter. And (that where Sir *Richard* had alleged that the Spaniards should never glory to have taken one ship of Her Majesty's seeing that they had so long and so notably defended themselves) they answered, that the ship had six foot water in hold, three shot under water, which were so weakly stopped as with the first working of the sea she must needs sink, and was besides so crushed and bruised as she could never be removed out of the place.

And as the matter was thus in dispute, and Sir *Richard* refusing to hearken to any of those reasons, the master of the *Revenge* (while the Captain wan unto him the greater party) was convoyed aboard the General, *Don Alfonso Bassan*. Who finding none over hasty to enter the *Revenge* again, doubting lest Sir *Richard* would have blown them up and himself, and perceiving by the report of the master of the *Revenge* his dangerous disposition: yielded that all their lives should be saved, the company sent for England, and the better sort to pay such reasonable ransom as their estate would bear, and in the mean season to be free from galley or imprisonment. To this he so much the rather condescended as well, as I have said, for fear of further loss and mischief to themselves, as also for the desire he had to recover Sir *Richard Grenville*; whom for his notable valour he seemed greatly to honour and admire.

A Report of the Truth of the Fight about the Isle of Azores betwixt the Revenge and an Armada of the King of Spain

88 *Death*

FOR the rest, if we seek a reason of the succession and continuance of this boundless ambition in mortal men, we may add to that which hath been already said; That the Kings and Princes of the world have always laid before them the actions, but not the ends, of those great Ones which preceded them. They are always transported with the glory of the one, but they never mind the misery of the other till they find the experience in themselves. They neglect the advice of *God* while they enjoy life, or hope it; but they follow the counsel of Death upon his first approach. It is he that puts into man all the wisdom of the world without speaking a word; which *God* with all the words of his Law promises, or threats, doth not infuse. *Death*, which hateth and destroyeth man, is believed; *God*, which hath made him and loves him, is always deferred. *I have considered* (saith *Solomon*) *all the works that are under the Sun, and behold, all is vanity and vexation of spirit*: but who believes it till Death tells it us? It was Death which, opening the conscience of *Charles* the fifth, made him enjoin his son *Philip* to restore *Navarre*; and King *Francis* the first of *France* to command that justice should be done upon the Murderers of the Protestants in *Merindol* and *Cabrieres*, which till then he neglected. It is therefore Death alone that can suddenly make man to know himself. He tells the proud and insolent that they are but Abjects, and humbles them at the instant; makes them cry, complain, and repent, yea, even to hate their forepassed happiness. He takes the account of the rich and proves him a beggar; a naked beggar which hath interest in nothing but in the gravel that fills his mouth. He holds a Glass before the eyes of the most beautiful, and makes them see therein their deformity and rottenness; and they acknowledge it.

O eloquent, just, and mighty Death! whom none could advise, thou hast perswaded; what none hath dared thou hast done; and whom all the world hath flattered, thou only hast cast out of the world and despised: thou hast drawn together all the far-stretched greatness, all the pride, cruelty, and ambition of man, and covered it all over with these two narrow words, *Hic jacet.*

A History of the World

89 *Letter to his Wife on the Death of his Son*

I WAS loth to write, because I know not how to comfort you; And God knows I never knew what sorrow meant till now. All that I can say to you is, that you must obey the will and providence of God, and remember that the Queen's Majesty bare the loss of the Prince Henry with a magnanimous heart, and the Lady Harrington of her only son. Comfort your heart (Deare Bess); I shall sorrow for us both: and I shall sorrow the less because I have not long to sorrow, because I have not long to live. I refer you to Mr. Secretary Winwood's Letter, who will give you a copy of it if you send for it. Therein you shall know what hath passed, what I have written by that Letter, for my brains are broken, and 'tis a torment to me to write, especially of misery. I have desired Mr. Secretary to give my Lord Carew a copy of his letter. I have cleansed my ship of sick men, and sent them home; and hope that God will send us somewhat ere we return. Commend me to all at Lothbury. You shall hear from me if I live, from new Found Land, where I mean to Clean my ship and revictual, for I have Tobacco enough to pay for it. The Lord bless you and Comfort you, that you may bear patiently the death of your most valiant son.

Your WAL. RALEIGH.

March the 22th from the Isle of St. Christophers.

FRANCIS BACON, BARON VERULAM

1561–1626

90 *The Service of the Muses*

LET thy master, Squire, offer his service to the Muses. It is long since they received any into their court. They give alms continually at their gate, that many come to live upon; but few have they ever admitted into their palace. There shall he find secrets not dangerous to know, sides and parties not factious to hold, precepts and commandments not penal to disobey. The gardens of love wherein he now playeth himself are fresh to-day and fading to-morrow, as the sun comforts them or is turned from them. But the gardens of the Muses keep the privilege of the golden age; they ever flourish and are in league with time. The monuments of wit survive the monuments of power: the verses of a poet endure without a syllable lost, while states and empires pass many periods. Let him not think he shall descend, for he is now upon a hill as a ship is mounted upon the ridge of a wave; but that hill of the Muses is above tempests, always clear and calm ; a hill of the goodliest discovery that man can have, being a prospect upon all the errors and wanderings of the present and former times. Yea, in some cliff it leadeth the eye beyond the horizon of time, and giveth no obscure divinations of times to come. So that if he will indeed lead *vitam vitalem*, a life that unites safety and dignity, pleasure and merit ; if he will win admiration without envy ; if he will be in the feast and not in the throng, in the light and not in the heat ; let him embrace the life of study and contemplation.

Essex's Device

91 *Of First and Second Causes*

IF any man shall think by view and inquiry into these sensible and material things to attain that light, whereby he may reveal unto himself the nature or will of God, then indeed is he spoiled by vain philosophy : for the contemplation of God's creatures and works produceth (having regard to the works and creatures themselves) knowledge, but having regard to God, no perfect knowledge, but wonder, which is broken knowledge. And therefore it was most aptly said by one of Plato's school, *That the sense of man carrieth a resemblance with the Sun, which (as we see) openeth and revealeth all the terrestrial Globe ; but then again it obscureth and concealeth the stars and celestial Globe: So doth the sense discover natural things, but it darkeneth and shutteth up divine.* And hence it is true that it hath proceeded, that divers great learned men have been heretical, whilst they have sought to fly up to the secrets of the Deity by the waxen wings of the senses. And as for the conceit that too much knowledge should incline a man to atheism, and that the ignorance of second causes should make a more devout dependence upon God, which is the first cause; First, it is good to ask the question which *Job* asked of his friends: *Will you lie for God, as one man will do for another, to gratify him?* For certain it is that God worketh nothing in nature but by second causes: and if they would have it otherwise believed, it is mere imposture, as it were in favour towards God; and nothing else but to offer to the Author of truth the unclean sacrifice of a lie. But further, it is an assured truth, and a conclusion of experience, that a little or superficial knowledge of Philosophy may incline the mind of Man to Atheism, but a further proceeding therein doth bring the mind back again to Religion. For in the entrance of Philosophy, when the second causes, which are next unto the senses, do offer themselves to the mind of Man, if it dwell and stay there it may induce some oblivion of the highest cause; but when a man passeth on further, and seeth the dependence of causes, and the works of Providence, then, according to the allegory of the Poets, he will easily believe that the highest link of nature's chain must needs be tied to the foot of *Jupiter's* chair. To conclude therefore, let no man upon a weak conceit of sobriety or an ill-applied moderation think or maintain, that a man can search too far, or be too well studied in the book of God's word, or in the book of God's works, Divinity or Philosophy; but rather let men endeavour an endless progress or proficience in both; only let men beware that they apply both to Charity, and not to swelling; to use, and not to ostentation; and again, that they do not unwisely mingle or confound these learnings together.

The Advancement of Learning

92 *Of Death. I*

MEN fear *Death* as children fear to go in the dark; and as that natural fear in children is increased with tales, so is the other. Certainly, the contemplation of *Death*, as the wages of sin and passage to another world, is holy and religious; but the fear of it, as a tribute due unto Nature, is weak. . . It is as natural to die as to be born; and to a little infant perhaps the one is as painful as the other. He that dies in an earnest pursuit is like one that is wounded in hot blood, who, for the time, scarce feels the hurt; and therefore a mind fixed and bent upon somewhat that is good doth avert the dolours of *Death*; but, above all, believe it, the sweetest canticle is *Nunc dimittis*, when a man hath obtained worthy ends and expectations. *Death* hath this also, that it openeth the gate to good fame, and extinguisheth envy: *Extinctus amabitur idem.*

Essays

93 *Of Death. II*

WHY should man be in love with his fetters, though of gold? Art thou drowned in security? Then I say thou art perfectly dead. For though thou movest, yet thy soul is buried within thee, and thy good angel either forsakes his guard or sleeps. There is nothing under heaven, saving a true friend (who cannot be counted within the number of movables), unto which my heart doth lean. And this dear freedom hath begotten me this peace, that I mourn not for that end which must be, nor spend one wish to have one minute added to the incertain date of my years. It was no mean apprehension of *Lucian*, who says of *Menippus*, that in his travels through hell, he knew not the Kings of the earth from other men, but only by their louder cryings and tears: which were fostered in them through the remorseful memory of the good days they had seen, and the fruitful havings which they so unwillingly left behind them: he that was well seated, looked back at his portion, and was loth to forsake his farm; and others either minding marriages, pleasures, profit, or preferment, desired to be excused from Death's banquet: they had made an appointment with earth, looking at the blessings, not the hand that enlarged them, forgetting how unclothedly they came hither, or with what naked ornaments they were arrayed.

Essay on Death

94 *Of Delays*

FORTUNE is like the market, where many times, if you can stay a little, the price will fall; and again, it is sometimes like *Sibylla's* offer, which at first offereth the commodity at full, then consumeth part and part, and still holdeth up the price; for *Occasion* (as it is in the common verse) *turneth a bald noddle after she hath presented her locks in front, and no hold taken*; or, at least, turneth the handle of the bottle first to be received, and after the belly, which is hard to clasp. There is surely no greater wisdom than well to time the beginnings and onsets of things. . . And generally it is good to commit the beginnings of all great actions to *Argus* with his hundred eyes, and the ends to *Briareus* with his hundred hands; first to watch and then to speed; for the helmet of *Pluto*, which maketh the politic man go invisible, is secrecy in the counsel, and celerity in the execution ; for when things are once come to the execution, there is no secrecy comparable to celerity ; like the motion of a bullet in the air, which flieth so swift as it outruns the eye.

Essays

95 *Of Studies*

READ not to contradict and confute, nor to believe and take for granted, nor to find talk and discourse, but to weigh and consider. Some *Books* are to be tasted, others to be swallowed, and some few to be chewed and digested ; That is, some *Books* are to be read only in parts ; others to be read but not curiously, and some few to be read wholly, and with diligence and attention. Some *Books* also may be read by deputy, and extracts made of them by others ; but that would be only in the less important arguments and the meaner sort of *Books* ; else distilled books are like common distilled waters, flashy things. Reading maketh a full man ; Conference a ready man ; and Writing an exact man ; and therefore, if a man write little he had need have a great memory ; if he confer little he had need have a present wit ; and if he read little he had need have much cunning, to seem to know that he doth not. *Histories* make men wise ; *Poets*, witty ; the *Mathematicks*, subtile ; *Natural Philosophy*, deep ; *Moral*, grave ; *Logick and Rhetorick*, able to contend : *Abeunt studia in mores.*

Essays

96 *Of Gardens*

AND because the breath of Flowers is far sweeter in the air (where it comes and goes like the warbling of Musick) than in the hand, therefore nothing is more fit for that delight than to know what be the flowers and plants that do best perfume the air. Roses, damask and red, are fast flowers of their smells; so that you may walk by a whole row of them, and find nothing of their sweetness; yea, though it be in a morning's dew. Bays likewise yield no smell as they grow, Rosemary little, nor Sweet Marjoram; that which above all others yields the sweetest smell in the air is the Violet, especially the White double Violet, which comes twice a year, about the middle of *April* and about *Bartholomew-tide*. Next to that is the Muskrose; then the Strawberry-leaves dying, with a most excellent cordial smell; then the Flower of the Vines, it is a little dust like the dust of a Bent, which grows upon the cluster in the first coming forth; then Sweet-Briar, then Wallflowers, which are very delightful to be set under a parlour or lower chamber window; then Pinks and Gilliflowers, especially the matted pink, and Clove Gilliflower; then the flowers of the Lime-tree; then the Honeysuckles, so they be somewhat afar off. Of Bean-Flowers I speak not, because they are field-Flowers; but those which perfume the air most delightfully, not passed by as the rest, but being trodden upon and crushed, are three; that is, Burnet, Wild Thyme, and Water Mints; therefore you are to set whole alleys of them, to have the pleasure when you walk or tread.

Essays

SIR HENRY MONTAGU, EARL OF MANCHESTER

1563?–1642

97 *The Soul's Excellency*

LET me ever worship the great God of this little god, my soule, *Et ne plus ultra.* For this is an inquisition, fitter for Angelical intelligence than man's shallow capacity.

Only this I know, that to no creature else God hath given a reasonable soul: of creatures, the lowest rank have no life, the next no essence, the third no reason; none but man hath grace; nor is there hope in any creature else but man, which hope is given him for the sustentation of his soul. *Anima enim non est instar Chamaeleontis, ut pascatur vento,* it cannot be fed with fancies, nor all the favours of the world. She is *ita generosa,* as nothing but that *summum bonum* will satisfy her. Saint *Augustine,* in a comparative betwixt things temporal and eternal, saith thus, We love things temporal before we have them, more than when we have them, because the soul when she hath them cannot be satisfied with them; but things eternal, when they are actually possessed, are more loved than when but desired; for neither faith could believe, nor hope expect so much as charity shall find when eternity comes in possession. There is no soul in the world, how happy soever it thinks itself here, but points its prehensions beyond what he possesses here.

Manchester Al Mondo

98 *Falstaff and the Hostess*

CHIEF JUSTICE. How comes this, Sir *John*? Fie! what man of good temper would endure this tempest of exclamation? Are you not ashamed to enforce a poor widow to so rough a course to come by her own?

Falstaff. What is the gross sum that I owe thee?

Hostess. Marry, if thou wert an honest man, thyself, and the money too. Thou didst swear to me upon a parcel-gilt Goblet, sitting in my Dolphin-chamber, at the round table, by a sea-coal fire, on Wednesday in Whitson week, when the Prince broke thy head for likening him to a singing-man of Windsor; Thou didst swear to me then, as I was washing thy wound, to marry me, and make me my Lady thy wife. Canst thou deny it? Did not goodwife *Keech* the Butcher's wife come in then and call me gossip *Quickly*? coming in to borrow a mess of Vinegar; telling us she had a good dish of Prawns; whereby thou didst desire to eat some, whereby I told thee they were ill for a green wound? And didst not thou, when she was gone down stairs, desire me to be no more familiar with such poor people; saying that ere long they should call me Madam? And didst thou not kiss me and bid me fetch thee thirty shillings? I put thee now to thy Book-oath: deny it if thou canst.

Falstaff. My Lord, this is a poor mad soul; and she says up and down the town that her eldest son is like you. She hath been in good case, and the truth is, poverty hath distracted her. But for these foolish Officers, I beseech you I may have redress against them.

Chief Justice. Sir *John*, Sir *John*, I am well acquainted with your manner of wrenching the true cause the false way. It is not a confident brow, nor the throng of words that come with such (more than impudent) sauciness from you, can thrust me from a level consideration; I know you ha' practised upon the easy-yielding spirit of this woman.

Hostess. Yes, in troth, my Lord.

Chief Justice. Prithee, peace. Pay her the debt you owe her, and unpay the villany you have done her: the one you may do with sterling money, and the other with current repentance.

Falstaff. My Lord, I will not undergo this sneap without reply. You call honourable Boldness impudent Sauciness: If a man will curtsy, and say nothing, he is virtuous. No, my Lord, my humble duty remember'd, I will not be your suitor. I say to you, I desire deliverance from these Officers, being upon hasty employment in the King's Affairs.

Chief Justice. You speak as having power to do wrong: But answer in the effect of your Reputation, and satisfy the poor woman.

Falstaff. Come hither, Hostess. (*takes her aside*).

Enter M. Gower

Chief Justice. Now, Master *Gower*! what news?

Gower. The King, my Lord, and *Henry* Prince of Wales
Are near at hand: The rest the Paper tells.

Falstaff. As I am a Gentleman.

Hostess. Nay, you said so before.

Falstaff. As I am a Gentleman. Come, no more words of it.

Hostess. By this Heavenly ground I tread on, I must be fain to pawn both my Plate and the Tapestry of my dining chambers.

Falstaff. Glasses, glasses, is the only drinking: and for thy walls, a pretty slight Drollery, or the Story of the Prodigal, or the German hunting in Water-work, is worth a thousand of these Bed-hangings and these Fly-bitten Tapestries. Let it be ten pound, if thou canst. Come, if it were not for thy humours, there is not a better Wench in England. Go, wash thy face, and draw thy Action. Come, thou must not be in this humour with me. Come, I know thou wast set on to this.

Hostess. Prithee, Sir *John*, let it be but twenty Nobles: I loathe to pawn my Plate, in good earnest la!

Falstaff. Let it alone; I'll make other shift: you'll be a fool still.

Hostess. Well, you shall have it, although I pawn my Gown. I hope you'll come to Supper. You'll pay me all together?

Falstaff. Will I live?

2 Henry IV, II. i

99 *Justice Shallow on Death*

SHALLOW. Come on, come on, come on; give me your Hand, Sir, give me your hand, Sir: an early stirrer, by the Rood! And how doth my good Cousin *Silence*?

Silence. Good morrow, good Cousin *Shallow*.

Shallow. And how doth my Cousin, your Bedfellow? and your fairest Daughter and mine, my God-daughter *Ellen*?

Silence. Alas! a black Ousel, Cousin *Shallow*!

Shallow. By yea and nay, Sir, I dare say my Cousin *William* is become a good Scholar? He is at Oxford still, is he not?

8 *draw*) *withdraw*

Silence. Indeed, Sir, to my cost.

Shallow. He must, then, to the Inns of Court shortly. I was once of *Clement's* Inn; where, I think, they will talk of mad *Shallow* yet.

Silence. You were called 'lusty *Shallow*' then, Cousin.

Shallow. I was called any thing; and I would have done any thing indeed too, and roundly too. There was I, and little *John Doit* of Staffordshire, and black *George Bare*, and *Francis Pickbone*, and *Will Squele* a Cotswold man; you had not four such swinge-bucklers in all the Inns of Court again: And, I may say to you, we knew where the *Bona-Robas* were, and had the best of them all at commandment. Then was *Jack Falstaff* (now Sir *John*) a Boy, and Page to *Thomas Mowbray*, Duke of Norfolk.

Silence. This Sir *John*, Cousin, that comes hither anon about Soldiers?

Shallow. The same Sir *John*, the very same. I saw him break *Scoggan's* Head at the Court Gate, when he was a crack not thus high: and the very same day did I fight with one *Sampson Stockfish*, a Fruiterer, behind Gray's Inn. Oh, the mad days that I have spent! and to see how many of mine old Acquaintance are dead!

Silence. We shall all follow, Cousin.

Shallow. Certain, 'tis certain; very sure, very sure: Death is certain to all; all shall die. How a good Yoke of Bullocks at Stamford Fair?

Silence. Truly, Cousin, I was not there.

Shallow. Death is certain. Is old *Double* of your town living yet?

Silence. Dead, Sir.

Shallow. Dead? See, see: he drew a good Bow; and dead? he shot a fine shoot: *John* of Gaunt loved him well, and betted much money on his head. Dead? he would have clapped in the Clout at Twelve-score, and carried you a forehand Shaft at fourteen, and fourteen and a half, that it would have done a man's heart good to see. How a score of Ewes now?

Silence. Thereafter as they be: a score of good Ewes may be worth ten pounds.

Shallow. And is old *Double* dead?

2 Henry IV, III. ii

100 *Before Agincourt*

KING HENRY. For, though I speak it to you, I think the King is but a man, as I am: the Violet smells to him as it doth to me; the Element shows to him as it doth to me; all his Senses have but human Conditions: his Ceremonies laid by, in his Nakedness he appears but a man; and though his affections are higher mounted than ours, yet when they stoop, they stoop with the like wing. Therefore when he sees reason of fears, as we do, his fears, out of doubt, be of the same relish as ours are: yet, in reason, no man should possess him with any appearance of fear, lest he, by showing it, should dishearten his Army. . . Methinks I could not die any where so contented as in the King's company, his Cause being just and his Quarrel honourable. . .

Williams. But if the Cause be not good, the King himself hath a heavy Reckoning to make; when all those Legs and Arms and Heads, chopped off in a Battle, shall join together at the latter day, and cry all, 'We died at such a place;' some swearing, some crying for a Surgeon, some upon their Wives left poor behind them, some upon the Debts they owe, some upon their Children rawly left. I am afeard there are few die well that die in a Battle ; for how can they charitably dispose of any thing when Blood is their argument ? Now, if these men do not die well, it will be a black matter for the King that led them to it, whom to disobey were against all proportion of subjection.

King Henry. So, if a Son that is by his Father sent about Merchandise do sinfully miscarry upon the Sea, the imputation of his wickedness, by your rule, should be imposed upon his Father that sent him : or if a Servant under his Master's command transporting a sum of Money, be assailed by Robbers and die in many irreconciled Iniquities, you may call the business of the Master the author of the Servant's damnation. But this is not so : The King is not bound to answer the particular endings of his Soldiers, the Father of his Son, nor the Master of his Servant ; for they purpose not their death when they purpose their services. Besides, there is no King, be his Cause never so spotless, if it come to the arbitrement of Swords, can try it out with all unspotted Soldiers. Some, peradventure, have on them the guilt of premeditated and contrived Murder ; some, of beguiling Virgins with the broken Seals of Perjury ; some, making the Wars their Bulwark, that have before gored the gentle Bosom of Peace with Pillage and Robbery. Now, if these men have defeated the Law and outrun Native punishment, though they can outstrip men, they have no wings to fly from God : War is his Beadle, War is his Vengeance ; so that here men are punished for before-breach of the King's Laws in now the King's Quarrel : where they feared the death they have borne life away, and where they would be safe they perish. Then, if they die unprovided, no more is the King guilty of their damnation than he was before guilty of those Impieties for the which they are now visited. Every Subject's Duty is the King's; but every Subject's Soul is his own. Therefore should every Soldier in the Wars do as every sick man in his Bed, wash every Mote out of his Conscience; and dying so, Death is to him advantage; or not dying, the time was blessedly lost wherein such preparation was gained: and in him that escapes, it were not sin to think, that making God so free an offer, he let him outlive that day to see his Greatness, and to teach others how they should prepare.

Henry V, IV. i

101 *Hamlet*

I HAVE of late,—but wherefore I know not,—lost all my mirth, forgone all custom of exercise; and indeed it goes so heavily with my disposition that this goodly frame, the Earth, seems to me a sterile Promontory; this most excellent Canopy, the Air, look you, this brave o'erhanging Firmament, this Majestical Roof fretted with golden fire, why, it appears no other thing to me than a foul and pestilent congregation of vapours. What a piece of work is a man! How Noble in Reason! how infinite in faculty! in form and moving, how express and admirable! in Action how like an Angel! in apprehension how like a God! the beauty of the world! the Paragon of Animals! And yet, to me, what is this Quintessence of Dust? Man delights not me; no, nor Woman neither, though, by your smiling, you seem to say so.

Hamlet, II. ii

THOMAS NASH

1567–1601

102 *A Dedication*

To The Most Honored, And Vertuous Beautified Ladie, The Ladie Elizabeth Carey: Wife to the thrice magnanimous, and noble discended Knight, Sir *George Carey*, Knight Marshall, &c.

EXCELLENT accomplisht Court-*glorifying Lady, give mee leaue*, with the sportiue Sea Porposes, preludiatelie a little to play before the storme of my Teares: to make my prayer ere I proceede to my sacrifice.

Diuine Ladie, you I must and will memorize more especially, for you recompence learning extraordinarilie. Pardon my presumption, lend patience to my prolixitie, and if any thing in all please, thinke it was compiled to please you. This I auouche, no line of it was layde downe without awfull looking backe to your frowne. To write in Diuinitie I would not have aduentured, if ought els might haue consorted with the regenerate grauitee of your iudgement. Your thoughts are all holy, holy is your life; in your hart liues no delight but of Heauen. Farre be it I should proffer to vnhallow them with any prophane papers of mine. The care I haue to worke your holy content, I hope God hath ordained, to call me home sooner vnto him.

Varro saith, the Philosophers held two hundred and eyght opinions of felicitie: two hundred and eyght felicities to me shall it bee, if I haue framed any one line to your lyking. Most resplendent Ladie, encourage mee, fauour mee, countenaunce mee in this, and something ere long I will aspire to, beyond the common mediocritie.

Your admired Ladiships most deuoted,
THO. NASHE.

Christs Teares over Jerusalem

103 *A Roman Banqueting House*

TO tell you of the rare pleasures of theyr gardens, theyr bathes, theyr vineyardes, theyr galleries, were to write a seconde part of the gorgeous Gallerie of gallant deuices. Why, you should not come into anie mannes house of account, but hee hadde fish-pondes and little orchardes on the toppe of his leads. If by raine or any other meanes those ponds were so full they need to be slust or let out, euen of their superfluities they made melodious vse, for they had great winde instruments in stead of leaden spoutes, that went duly in consort, onely with this waters rumbling discent. I sawe a summer banketting house belonging to a merchaunt, that was the meruaile of the world, & could not be matcht except God should make another paradise. It was builte round of greene marble like a Theater with-out: within there was a heauen and earth comprehended both vnder one roofe; the heauen was a cleere ouerhanging vault of christall, wherein the Sunne and Moone and each visible Starre had his true similitude, shine, scituation, and motion, and, by what enwrapped arte I cannot conceiue, these spheares in their proper orbes obserued their circular wheelinges and turnings, making a certaine kind of soft angelical murmering musicke in their often windings and going about; which musick the

12 *slust*) *sluiced*

philosophers say in the true heauen, by reason of the grosenes of our senses, we are not capable of. For the earth, it was conterfeited in that liknes that Adam lorded out it before his fall. A wide vast spacious roome it was, such as we would conceit prince Arthurs hall to be, where he feasted all his knights of the round table together euerie penticost. The flore was painted with the beautifullest flouers that euer mans eie admired; which so linealy were delineated that he that viewd them a farre off, and had not directly stood poaringly ouer them, would haue sworne they had liued in deede. The wals round about were hedgde with oliues and palme trees, and all other odoriferous fruit-bearing plants; which at anie solemne intertainment dropt mirrhe and frankensence.

O *Rome*, if thou hast in thee such soul-exalting obiects, what a thing is heauen in comparison of thee, of which *Mercators* globe is a perfecter modell than thou art? *The Life of Jacke Wilton*

WILLIAM ADLINGTON

publ. 1566

104 *Cupid and Psyche*

WHEN *Psyche* was left alone (saving that she seemed not to be alone, being stirred by so many furies) she was in a tossing mind like the waves of the sea, and although her will was obstinate, and resisted to put in execution the counsel of her Sisters, yet she was in doubtful and divers opinions touching her calamity. Sometimes she would, sometimes she would not, sometime she is bold, sometime she feares, sometime she mistrusteth, sometime she is moved, sometime she hateth the beast, sometime she loveth her husband: but at length night came, when as she prepared for her wicked intent.

Soon after her husband came, and when he had kissed and embraced her he fell asleep. Then *Psyche* (somewhat feeble in body and mind, yet moved by cruelty of fate) received boldness and brought forth the lamp, and took the razor, and so by her audacity she changed her kind: but when she took the lamp and came to the bedside, she saw the most meek and sweetest beast of all beasts, even fair *Cupid* couched fairly, at whose sight the very lamp increased his light for joy, and the razor turned his edge.

But when *Psyche* saw so glorious a body she greatly feared, and amazed in mind, with a pale countenance all trembling fell on her knees and thought to hide the razor, yea, verily in her own heart, which doubtless she had undoubtedly done, had it not (through fear of so great an enterprise) fallen out of her hand. And when she saw and beheld the beauty of this divine visage she was well recreated in her mind, she saw his hairs of gold, that yielded out a sweet savour, his neck more white than milk, his purple cheeks, his hair hanging comely behind and before, the brightness whereof darkened the light of the lamp, his tender plume feathers, dispersed upon his shoulders like shining flowers, and trembling hither and thither, and his other parts of his body so smooth and so soft, that it repented not Venus to bear such a child. At the beds feet lay his bow, quiver, and arrows, that be the weapons of so great a god: which when *Psyche* did curiously behold, she marvelled at the weapons of her

1 *hateth the beast*) *her sisters have told Psyche that her invisible husband is a serpent.*

husband, took one of the arrows out of the quiver, and pricked herself withall, wherewith she was so grievously wounded that the blood followed, and thereby of her own accord she added love upon love; then more and more broiling in the love of *Cupid* she embraced and kissed him a thousand times, fearing the measure of his sleep. But, alas, while she was in this great joy, where it were for envy, or for desire to touch this amiable body likewise, there fell out a drop of burning oil from the lamp upon the right shoulder of the god. O rash and bold lamp, the vile ministery of love, how darest thou be so bold as to burn the god of all fire? When as he invented thee, to the intent that all lovers might with more joy pass the nights in pleasure.

The god being burned in this sort, and perceiving that promise was broken, fled away without utterance of any word, from the eyes and hands of his most unhappy wife. *The Golden Ass*

GERVASE MARKHAM

c. 1568–1637

105 '*Matched in mouth like bells*'

IF you would have your Kennel for sweetness of cry, then you must compound it of some large dogs, that have deep solemn mouths, and are swift in spending, which must as it were bear the base in the consort; then a double number of roaring, and loud ringing mouths, which must bear the counter tenor; then some hollow plain sweet mouths, which must bear the mean or middle part: and so with these three parts of musick, you shall make your cry perfect. . .

8 *where*) *whether* 22 *spending*) *giving cry*

GERVASE MARKHAM

If you would have your Kennel for loudness of mouth, you shall not then choose the hollow deep mouth, but the loud clanging mouth, which spendeth freely and sharply, and as it were redoubleth in the utterance: and if you mix with them the mouth that roareth, and the mouth that whineth, the cry will be both the louder and smarter; . . . and the more equally you compound these mouths, having as many *roarers* as *spenders*, and as many *whiners* as of either of the other, the louder and pleasanter your cry will be, especially if it be in sounding tall woods, or under the echo of Rocks.

Country Contentments

SIR HENRY WOTTON

1568–1639

106 *To Mr. John Milton*

IT was a special favour when you lately bestowed upon me here the first taste of your acquaintance, though no longer than to make me know that I wanted more time to value it and to enjoy it rightly; and in truth, if I could then have imagined your farther stay in these parts, which I understood afterward by Mr. *H.*, I would have been bold, in our vulgar phrase, to mend my draught (for you left me with an extreme thirst), and to have begged your conversation again jointly with your said learned friend at a poor meal or two, that we might have banded together some good authors of the ancient time: among which I observed you to have been familiar.

Since your going you have charged me with new obligations, both for a very kind letter from you, dated the sixth of this month, and for a dainty piece of entertainment that came therewith. Wherein I should much commend the tragical part if the lyrical did not ravish me with a certain *Dorique* delicacy in your songs and odes; whereunto I must plainly confess to have seen yet nothing parallel in our language, *Ipsa mollities.* But I must not omit to tell you that I now only owe you thanks for intimating unto me (how modestly soever) the true artificer. For the work itself I had viewed some good while before with singular delight, having received it from our common friend Mr. *R.* in the very close of the late *R.'s Poems* printed at *Oxford*; whereunto is added (as I now suppose) that the accessory might help out the principal, according to the art of Stationers, and to leave the Reader *Con la bocca dolce.*

Now, Sir, concerning your travels, wherein I may challenge a little more privilege of discourse with you. I suppose you will not blanch *Paris* in your way; therefore I have been bold to trouble you with a few lines to Master *M. B.*, whom you shall easily find attending the young Lord *S.* as his governor, and you may surely receive from him good directions for the shaping of your farther journey into *Italy*, where he did reside by my choice some time for the King, after mine own recess from *Venice.*

I should think that your best line will be through the whole length of *France* to *Marseilles*, and thence by sea to *Genoa*, whence the passage into *Tuscany* is as diurnal as a *Gravesend* barge. I hasten, as you do to *Florence*, or *Siena* the rather, to tell you a short story from the interest you have given me in your safety.

At *Siena* I was tabled in the house of one *Alberto*

1 *a dainty piece*) *i.e.* '*Comus*'

Scipioni, an old Roman courtier in dangerous times, having been steward to the *Duca di Pagliano*, who with all his family were strangled, save this only man that escaped by foresight of the tempest. With him I had often much chat of those affairs, into which he took pleasure to look back from his native harbour, and at my departure toward *Rome* (which had been the centre of his experience) I had won confidence enough to beg his advice how I might carry myself securely there, without offence of others or of mine own conscience. '*Signor Arrigo mio*' (says he), '*i pensieri stretti e il viso sciolto*: (That is, *Your thoughts close, and your countenance loose*,) will go safely over the whole world.' Of which Delphian oracle (for so I have found it) your judgement doth need no commentary; and therefore, (Sir,) I will commit you with it to the best of all securities, God's dear love, remaining,

Your friend as *much at command* as *any of longer date.*

H. Wotton.

Letter concerning 'Comus' *and advice to Milton,*
13 April 1638

BEN JONSON

1573?–1637

107 *The Dignity of Speech*

SPEECH is the only benefit man hath to express his excellency of mind above other creatures. It is the Instrument of *Society*. Therefore *Mercury*, who is the President of Language, is called *Deorum hominumque interpres*. In all speech, words and sense are as the body and the soul. The sense is as the life and soul of Language, without which all words are dead. Sense is wrought out of experience, the knowledge of human life and actions, or of the liberal Arts, which the

Greeks called *'Εγκυκλοπαιδείαν*. Words are the Peoples; yet there is a choice of them to be made. For *Verborum delectus, origo est eloquentiae*. They are to be chose according to the persons we make speak, or the things we speak of. Some are of the Camp, some of the Council-board, some of the Shop, some of the Sheep-cote, some of the Pulpit, some of the Bar, &c. And herein is seen their Elegance and Propriety, when we use them fitly, and draw them forth to their just strength and nature, by way of Translation or *Metaphor*. But in this Translation we must only serve necessity (*Nam temere nihil transfertur a prudenti*) or commodity, which is a kind of necessity; that is, when we either absolutely want a word to express by, and that is necessity; or when we have not so fit a word, and that is commodity. As when we avoid loss by it, and escape obsceneness, and gain in the grace and property, which helps significance. *Metaphors* far fet hinder to be understood, and affected, lose their grace. Or when the person fetcheth his translations from a wrong place. As if a Privy Counsellor should at the Table take his *Metaphor* from a Dicing-house, or Ordinary, or a Vintners Vault; or a Justice of Peace draw his similitudes from the *Mathematicks*; or a *Divine* from a Bawdy-house or Taverns; or a Gentleman of *Northamptonshire*, *Warwickshire*, or the *Midland*, should fetch all his Illustrations to his country neighbours from shipping, and tell them of the main *sheet*, and the Boulin. *Metaphors* are thus many times deformed, as in him that said, *Castratam morte Aphricani Rempublicam*. And another, *stercus curiae Glauciam*. And *Cana nive conspuit Alpes*. All attempts that are new in this kind are dangerous, and

19 *fet*) *fetched*

somewhat hard before they be softened with use. A man coins not a new word without some peril, and less fruit; for if it happen to be received, the praise is but moderate; if refused, the scorn is assured. Yet we must adventure, for things at first, hard and rough, are by use made tender and gentle. It is an honest error that is committed, following great *Chiefs*.

Custom is the most certain Mistress of Language, as the publicke stamp makes the current money. But we must not be too frequent with the mint, every day coining. Nor fetch words from the extreme and utmost ages; since the chief virtue of a style is perspicuity, and nothing so vicious in it, as to need an Interpreter. Words borrowed of Antiquity do lend a kind of Majesty to style, and are not without their delight sometimes. For they have the Authority of years, and out of their intermission do win to themselves a kind of grace-like newness. But the eldest of the present, and newness of the past Language, is the best. For what was the ancient Language, which some men so dote upon, but the ancient Custom? Yet when I name Custom, I understand not the vulgar Custom: For that were a precept no less dangerous to Language, than life, if we should speak or live after the manners of the vulgar: But that I call Custom of speech, which is the consent of the Learned; as Custom of life, which is the consent of the good. *Virgil* was most loving of Antiquity; yet how rarely doth he insert *aquai* and *pictai*! *Lucretius* is scabrous and rough in these; he seeks 'hem: As some do *Chaucerisms* with us, which were better expung'd and banished. Some words are to be culled out for ornament and colour, as we gather flowers to straw houses, or make Garlands; but they are better when they grow to our style; as in a Meadow, where though the mere grass and greenness delights; yet the variety of flowers doth heighten and beautify. Marry, we must not play, or riot too much with them, as in *Paranomasies*: Nor use too swelling or ill-sounding words; *Quae per salebras, altaque saxa cadunt.* It is true, there is no sound but shall find some Lovers, as the bitterest confections are grateful to some palats. Our composition must be more accurate in the beginning and end than in the midst; and in the end more than in the beginning; for through the midst the stream bears us. And this is attained by Custom more than care or diligence. We must express readily, and fully, not profusely. There is difference between a liberal and a prodigal hand. As it is a great point of Art, when our matter requires it, to enlarge, and veer out all sail; so to take it in and contract it is of no less praise when the Argument doth ask it. Either of them hath their fitness in the place. A good man always profits by his endeavour, by his help; yea, when he is absent; nay, when he is dead by his example and memory. So good Authors in their style: A strict and succinct style is that, where you can take away nothing without loss, and that loss to be manifest.

Discoveries

108 *His Poverty*

AT last they upbraided my poverty; I confess she is my Domestick; sober of diet, simple of habit; frugal, painful; a good Counsellor to me; that keeps me from Cruelty, Pride, or other more delicate impertinences; which are the Nurse-children of Riches. But let them look over all the great and monstrous wickednesses, they shall never find those in poor families. They are the issue of the wealthy *Giants*, and the mighty Hunters: Whereas no great work, or worthy of praise, or memory, but came out of poor cradles. It was the ancient poverty that founded Commonweals, built Cities, invented Arts, made wholesome Laws; armed men against vices; rewarded them with their own virtues; and preserved the honour, and state of Nations, till they betrayed themselves to Riches.

Discoveries

109 *Eloquence*

ELOQUENCE is a great and diverse thing: Nor did she yet ever favour any man so much as to become wholly his. He is happy that can arrive to any degree of her grace. Yet there are, who prove themselves Masters of her, and absolute Lords: but I believe they may mistake their evidence: For it is one thing to be *eloquent* in the *Schools*, or in the *Hall*; another at the *Bar*, or in the *Pulpit*. There is a difference between *Mooting* and *Pleading*; between *Fencing* and *Fighting*. To make Arguments in my Study and confute them is easy; where I answer my self, not an Adversary. So I can see whole *volumes* dispatched by the *umbratical* Doctors on all sides: But draw these forth into the just lists; let them appear *sub dio*, and they are changed with the place, like bodies bred i' the *shade*; they cannot suffer the *Sun*, or a *Shower*; nor bear the open Air: they scarce can find themselves, that they were wont to domineer so among their Auditors: but indeed I would no more choose a *Rhetorician* for reigning in a *School* than I would a *Pilot* for rowing in a Pond.

Discoveries

110 *Of our Fellow Countryman Shakespeare*

I *REMEMBER*, the Players have often mentioned it as an honour to *Shakespeare*, that in his writing (whatsoever he penned) he never blotted out line. My answer hath been, would he had blotted a thousand. Which they thought a malevolent speech. I had not told posterity this, but for their ignorance, who choose that circumstance to commend their friend by, wherein he most faulted; And to justify mine own candour (for I loved the man, and do honour his memory (on this side Idolatry) as much as any). He was (indeed) honest, and of an open and free nature: had an excellent *Phantsie*; brave notions, and gentle expressions: wherein he flowed with that facility, that sometime it was necessary he should be stopped: *Sufflaminandus erat*; as *Augustus* said of *Haterius*. His wit was in his own power; would the rule of it had been so too. Many times he fell into those things, could not escape laughter: As when he said in the person of *Caesar*, one speaking to him; *Caesar thou dost me wrong*. He replied: *Caesar did never wrong, but with just cause*: and such like; which were ridiculous. But he redeemed his vices with his virtues. There was ever more in him to be praised than to be pardoned.

Discoveries

111 *Of Francis Bacon*

ONE, though he be excellent, and the chief, is not to be imitated alone. For never no Imitator ever grew up to his *Author*; likeness is always on this side Truth: Yet there happened, in my time, one noble *Speaker*, who was full of gravity in his speaking. His language (where he could spare, or pass by a jest) was nobly *censorious*. No man ever spake more neatly, more pressly, more weightily, or suffered less emptiness, less idleness, in what he uttered. No member of his speech but consisted of the owne graces. His hearers could not cough, or look aside from him, without loss. He commanded where he spoke; and had his Judges angry and pleased at his devotion. No man had their affections more in his power. The fear of every man that heard him, was, lest he should make an end.

Cicero is said to be the only wit that the people of *Rome* had equalled to their *Empire*. *Ingenium par imperio*. We have had many, and in their several Ages, (to take in but the former *Seculum*.) Sir *Thomas Moore*, the elder *Wiat*; *Henry*, Earl of *Surrey*; *Chaloner*, *Smith*, *Eliot*, B. *Gardiner*, were for their times admirable: and the more, because they began Eloquence with us. Sir *Nico: Bacon* was singular, and almost alone, in the beginning of Queen *Elizabeths* times. Sir *Philip Sidney* and Mr. *Hooker* (in different matter) grew great Masters of wit and language; and in whom all vigour of Invention and strength of judgement met. The Earl of *Essex*, noble and high; and Sir *Walter Rawleigh*, not to be contemned either for judgement or style. Sir *Henry Savile* grave and truly lettered; Sir *Edwin Sandes* excellent in both; Lord *Egerton*, the Chancellor, a grave and great Orator; and best, when he was provoked. But his learned and able (though unfortunate) *Successor* is he who hath filled up all numbers; and performed that in our tongue, which may be compared, or preferred, either to insolent *Greece* or haughty *Rome*. In short, within his view, and about his times, were all the wits born that could honour a language or help study. Now things daily fall: wits grow downward and *Eloquence* grows backward: So that he may be named, and stand as the *mark*, and ἀκμὴ of our language.

I have ever observed it to have been the office of a wise Patriot, among the greatest affairs of the *State*, to take care of the *Common-wealth* of Learning. For Schools, they are the *Seminaries* of State: and nothing is worthier the study of a Statesman than that part of the *Republicke* which we call the *advancement* of Letters. Witness the care of *Julius Caesar*; who, in the heat of the civil war, wrote his books of *Analogie*, and dedicated them to *Tully*. This made the late Lord S. *Albane* entitle his work, *novum Organum*. Which though by the most of superficial men, who cannot get beyond the Title of *Nominals*, it is not penetrated, nor understood; it really openeth all defects of Learning whatsoever; and is a Book

Qui longum noto scriptori porriget aevum.

My conceit of his Person was never increased toward him by his place or honours. But I have and do reverence him for the greatness that was only proper to himself, in that he seemed to me ever, by his work, one of the greatest men, and most worthy of admiration, that had been in many Ages. In his adversity I ever prayed that *God* would give him strength:

for *Greatness* he could not want. Neither could I condole in a word or syllable for him; as knowing no Accident could do harm to virtue; but rather help to make it manifest.

Discoveries

112 *Of Public Schools*

A YOUTH should not be made to hate study before he know the causes to love it: or taste the bitterness before the sweet; but called on, and allured, entreated, and praised: Yea, when he deserves it not. For which cause I wish them sent to the best school, and a publike, which I think the best. Your Lordship I fear hardly hears of that, as willing to breed them in your eye, and at home; and doubting their manners may be corrupted abroad. They are in more danger in your own Family, among ill servants (allowing, they be safe in their School-Master), than amongst a thousand boys, however immodest: would we did not spoil our own children and overthrow their manners ourselves by too much Indulgence. To breed them at home is to breed them in a shade; where in a school they have the light and heat of the Sun. They are used and accustomed to things and men. When they come forth into the Commonwealth they find nothing new or to seek. They have made their friendships and aids; some to last till their Age. They hear what is commanded to others as well as themselves. Much approved, much corrected; all which they bring to their own store and use, and learn as much as they hear. *Eloquence* would be but a poor thing if we should only converse with singulars; speak but man and man together. Therefore I like no private breeding. I would send them where their industry should be daily increased by praise; and that kindled by emulation. It is a good thing to inflame the mind: And though Ambition itself be a vice, it is often the cause of great virtue. Give me that wit, whom praise excites, glory puts on, or disgrace grieves: he is to be nourished with Ambition, pricked forward with honour, checked with Reprehension, and never to be suspected of sloth. Though he be given to play, it is a sign of spirit and liveliness; so there be a mean had of their sports and relaxations. And from the rod, or ferrule, I would have them free, as from the menace of them: for it is both deformed and servile.

Discoveries

JOHN DONNE

1573–1631

113 *Death the Leveller*

IT comes equally to us all, and makes us all equal when it comes. The ashes of an Oak in the Chimney are no Epitaph of that Oak to tell me how high or how large that was; it tells me not what flocks it sheltered while it stood, nor what men it hurt when it fell. The dust of great persons graves is speechless too, it says nothing, it distinguishes nothing: as soon the dust of a wretch whom thou wouldest not, as of a Prince thou couldest not look upon, will trouble thine eyes, if the wind blow it thither; and when a whirlwind hath blown the dust of the Churchyard into the Church, and the man sweeps out the dust of the Church into the Churchyard, who will undertake to sift those dusts again, and to pronounce, This is the Patrician, this is the noble flower, and this the yeomanly, this the Plebeian bran. So is the death of *Jesabel* (*Jesabel* was a Queen) expressed; *They shall not say, this is Jesabel*; not only not wonder that it is, nor pity that it should be, but they shall not say, they shall not know, This is *Jesabel*.

LXXX Sermons: Sermon XV

114 All Times are God's Seasons

GOD made Sun and Moon to distinguish seasons, and day, and night, and we cannot have the fruits of the earth but in their seasons: But God hath made no decree to distinguish the seasons of his mercies; In paradise, the fruits were ripe, the first minute, and in heaven it is alwaies Autumne, his mercies are ever in their maturity. We ask *panem quotidianum*, our daily bread, and God never sayes you should have come yesterday, he never sayes you must againe to morrow, but *to day if you will heare his voice*, to day he will heare you. If some King of the earth have so large an extent of Dominion, in North, and South, as that he hath Winter and Summer together in his Dominions, so large an extent East and West, as that he hath day and night together in his Dominions, much more hath God mercy and judgement together: He brought light out of darknesse, not out of a lesser light; he can bring thy Summer out of Winter, though thou have no Spring; though in the wayes of fortune, or understanding, or conscience, thou have been benighted till now, wintred and frozen, clouded and eclypsed, damped and benummed, smothered and stupefied till now, now God comes to thee, not as in the dawning of the day, not as in the bud of the spring, but as the Sun at noon to illustrate all shadows, as the sheaves in harvest, to fill all penuries, all occasions invite his mercies, and all times are his seasons.

LXXX Sermons: Sermon II.

115 *Hearts*

MY *God*, my *God*, all that thou askest of mee, is my *Heart*, *My Sonne, give mee thy heart*; Am I thy *sonne*, as long as I have but my *heart*? Wilt thou give mee an *Inheritance*, a *Filiation*, any thing for *my heart*? O thou, who saydst to Satan, *Hast thou considered my servant Job, that there is none like him upon the earth*, shall my feare, shall my zeale, shall my jealousie, have leave to say to thee, Hast thou considered *my Heart*, that there is not so perverse a *Heart* upon earth; and wouldst thou have *that*, and shall I be thy *Sonne*, thy eternal Sonne's *Coheire*, for giving that? *The Heart is deceitful above all things, and desperately wicked; who can know it?* Hee that askes that question, makes the answere, *I the Lord search the Heart.* When didst thou search mine? Dost thou thinke to finde it, as thou madest it in *Adam*? Thou hast searched since, and found all these gradations in the ill of our *Hearts*, *That every imagination of the thoughts of our hearts, is only evill continually.* Doest thou remember this, and wouldest thou have my *Heart*? *O God of all light*, I know thou knowest all; and it is *Thou*, that declarest unto man, what is his *Heart*. Without thee, *O soveraigne goodnesse*, I could not know, how ill my *heart* were. Thou hast declared unto mee, in thy Word, that for all this *deluge* of evill, that hath surrounded all *Hearts*, yet thou soughtest and *foundest a man after thine owne heart*; That *thou couldest and wouldest give thy people Pastours according to thine owne heart*; And I can gather out of thy *Word* so good testimony of the *hearts* of men, as to find *single hearts*, *docile* and *apprehensive hearts*; Hearts that *can*, Hearts that *have* learnt; *wise hearts*, in one place, and in another, in a great degree, *wise*, *perfit* hearts; *straight* hearts, no perversnesse without, and *cleane* hearts, no foulnesse within; such hearts I can find in thy Word; and if my *heart* were such a *heart*, I would give thee my *Heart*. But I find *stonie* hearts too, and I have made mine such: I have found *Hearts, that are snares*; and I have conversed with such; *hearts that burne like Ovens*; and the fuell of *Lust*, and *Envie*, and *Ambition*, hath inflamed mine. . . The first kind of heart, alas, my *God*, I have not; the last are not *Hearts* to be given to thee; What shall I do? Without that present I cannot bee thy *Sonne*, and I have it not. To those of the first kinde thou givest *joyfulnes of heart*, and I have not that; To those of the other kinde, thou givest *faintnesse of heart*: And blessed bee thou, *O God*, for that forbearance, I have not that yet. There is then a middle kinde of *Hearts*, not so perfit as to bee given, but that the very giving mends them; Not so desperate, as not to bee accepted, but that the very accepting dignifies them. This is a *melting* heart, and a *troubled* heart; and a *wounded* heart, and a *broken* heart, and a *contrite* heart; and by the powerfull working of thy piercing Spirit, such a *Heart* I have; Thy *Samuel* spake unto all the house of thy *Israel*, and sayd, *If you returne to the Lord with all your hearts, prepare your hearts unto the Lord.* If my heart bee *prepared*, it is a *returning* heart; And if thou see it upon the way, thou wilt carrie it *home* . . and the *Peace of God, which passeth all understanding, shall keepe my Heart and Minde through Christ Jesus.*

Devotions upon Emergent Occasions

116 *The Bell*

PERCHANCE hee for whom this *Bell* tolls, may be so ill, as that he knowes not it tolls for him; And perchance I may thinke my selfe so much better than I am, as that they who are about mee, and see my state, may have caused it to toll for mee, and I know not that. The *Church* is *Catholike*, *universall*, so are all her *Actions*; *All* that she does, belongs to *all*. When she *baptizes a child*, that action concernes mee; for that child is thereby connected to that *Head* which is my *Head* too, and engraffed into that *body*, whereof I am a *member*. And when she *buries a Man*, that action concernes me: . . . As therefore the *Bell* that rings to a *Sermon*, calls not upon the *Preacher* onely, but upon the *Congregation* to come; so this *Bell* calls us all: but how much more mee, who am brought so neere the *doore* by this *sicknesse*. . . The *Bell* doth toll for him that *thinkes* it doth; and though it *intermit* againe, yet from that *minute*, that that occasion wrought upon him, hee is united to *God*. Who casts not up his *Eie* to the *Sunne* when it rises? but who takes off his *Eie* from a *Comet* when that breakes out? Who bends not his *eare* to any *bell*, which upon any occasion rings? but who can remove it from that *bell*, which is passing a *peece of himselfe* out of this *world*? No man is an *Iland*, intire of it selfe; every man is a peece of the *Continent*, a part of the *maine* ; if a *Clod* bee washed away by the *Sea*, *Europe* is the lesse, as well as if a *Promontorie* were, as well as if a *Mannor* of thy *friends* or of *thine owne* were ; any mans *death* diminishes *me*, because I am involved in *Mankinde* ; And therefore never send to know for whom the *bell* tolls ; It tolls for *thee*.

Devotions upon Emergent Occasions

ROBERT BURTON

1577–1640

117 *Black Spirits and White*

WATER-devils are those *Naiades* or *Water-nymphs* which have been heretofore conversant about waters and rivers. . . *Paracelsus* hath several stories of them that have lived and been married to mortal men, and so continued for certain years with them, and after, upon some dislike, have forsaken them. Such a one was *Egeria*, with whom *Numa* was so familiar, *Diana*, *Ceres*, &c. *Olaus Magnus* hath a long narration of one *Hotherus*, a King of *Sweden*, that, having lost his company, as he was hunting one day, met with these Water-nymphs or Fairies, and was feasted by them ; and *Hector Boethius*, of *Macbeth* and *Banquo*, two Scottish Lords, that, as they were wandering in the woods, had their fortunes told them by three strange women. . . Terrestrial devils are those *Lares*, *Genii*, *Fauns*, *Satyrs*, *Wood-nymphs*, *Foliots*, *Fairies*, *Robin Goodfellows*, *Trolli*, &c., which as they are most conversant with men, so they do them most harm. . . Some put our *Fairies* into this rank, which have been in former times adored with much superstition, with sweeping their houses, and setting of a pail of clean water, good victuals, and the like, and then they should not be pinched, but find money in their shoes, and be fortunate in their enterprises. These are they that dance on heaths and greens. . . *Paracelsus* reckons up many places in *Germany* where they do usually walk in little coats some two foot long. A bigger kind there is of them, called with us *Hobgoblins* and *Robin Goodfellows*, that would in those superstitious times grind corn for a mess of milk, cut wood, or do any manner of drudgery work. . . So likewise those . . . that walk about midnight on great heaths and desert places, which . . . draw men out of the way, and lead them all night a by-way . . . we commonly call them *Pucks*. In the deserts of Lop in Asia such illusions of walking spirits are often perceived, as you may read in *Marco Polo* the *Venetian* his travels. . . Sometimes they sit by the highway side, to give men falls, and make their horses stumble and start as they ride, if you will believe the relation of that holy man *Ketellus*, in *Nubrigensis*, that had an especial grace to see devils, . . . and talk with them . . . without offence; and if a man curse or spur his horse for stumbling, they do heartily rejoice at it; with many such pretty feats.

Anatomy of Melancholy

118 *Of Change of Air*

ALTHOUGH our ordinary air be good by nature or art, yet it is not amiss, as I have said, still to alter it; no better Physick for a melancholy man, than change of air, and variety of places, to travel abroad and see fashions. *Leo Afer* speaks of many of his countrymen so cured, without all other Physick:

amongst the *Negroes, there is such an excellent air, that if any of them be sick elsewhere, and brought thither, he is instantly recovered, of which he was often an eye-witness. Lipsius, Zuinger*, and some other, add as much of ordinary travel. No man, saith *Lipsius* in an epistle to *Phil. Lanoius*, a noble friend of his, now ready to make a voyage, *can be such a stock or stone, whom that pleasant speculation of countries, cities, towns, rivers, will not affect. Seneca* the Philosopher was infinitely taken with the sight of *Scipio Africanus* house, near *Linternum*, to view those old buildings, Cisterns, Baths, Tombs, *&c.* And how was *Tully* pleased with the sight of *Athens*, to behold those ancient and fair buildings, with a remembrance of their worthy inhabitants. *Paulus Aemilius*, that renowned *Roman* Captain, after he had conquered *Perseus*, the last King of *Macedonia*, and now made an end of his tedious wars, though he had been long absent from *Rome*, and much there desired, about the beginning of Autumn (as *Livy* describes it) made a pleasant peregrination all over *Greece*, accompanied with his son *Scipio*, and *Atheneus* the brother of King *Eumenes*, leaving the charge of his army with *Sulpitius Gallus*. By *Thessaly* he went to *Delphos*, thence to *Megaris, Aulis, Athens, Argos, Lacedaemon, Megalopolis, &c.* He took great content, exceeding delight in that his voyage, as who doth not that shall attempt the like, though his travel be *ad jactationem magis quam ad usum reipublicae* (as one well observes) to crack, gaze, see fine sights and fashions, spend time, rather than for his own or publick good? (as it is to many Gallants that travel out their best days, together with their means, manners, honesty, religion) yet it availeth howsoever. For peregrination charms our senses with such unspeakable and sweet variety, that some count him unhappy that never travelled, a kind of prisoner, and pity his case, that from his cradle to his old age beholds the same still; still, still the same, the same. Insomuch that *Rhasis cont. lib.* 1, *Tract.* 2, doth not only commend, but enjoin travel, and such variety of objects to a melancholy man, *and to lie in divers Inns, to be drawn into several companies: Montaltus cap.* 36, and many Neotericks are of the same mind. *Celsus* adviseth him therefore that will continue his health, to have *varium vitae genus*, diversity of callings, occupations, to be busied about, *sometimes to live in the City, sometimes in the Country; now to study or work, to be intent, then again to hawk or hunt, swim, run, ride, or exercise himself.* A good prospect alone will ease melancholy, as *Comesius* contends, *lib.* 2, *c.* 7, *de Sale.* The Citizens of *Barcino*, saith he, otherwise penned in, melancholy, and stirring little abroad, are much delighted with that pleasant prospect their city hath into the sea, which like that of old *Athens* beside *Egina Salamina*, and many pleasant islands, had all the variety of delicious objects: so are those *Neapolitanes*, and inhabitants of *Genua*, to see the ships, boats, and passengers go by, out of their windows, their whole cities being sited on the side of an hill, like *Pera* by *Constantinople*, so that each house almost, hath a free prospect to the sea, as some part of *London* to the *Thames*: or to have a free prospect all over the city at once, as at *Granado* in *Spain*, and *Fez* in *Africk*, the river running betwixt two declining hills, the steepness causeth each house almost, as well to oversee, as to be overseen of the rest. Every country is full of such delightsome prospects, as well within land, as by sea, as *Hermon* and *Rama* in

Palestina, *Colalto* in *Italy*, the top of *Tagetus* or *Acrochorinthus*, that old decayed castle in *Corinth*, from which *Peloponesus*, *Greece*, the *Ionian* and *Aegean* seas were *semel et simul* at one view to be taken. In *Egypt* the square top of the great Pyramis 300 yards in height, and so the *Sultan's* Palace in *Grand Cairo*, the Country being plain, hath a marvellous fair prospect as well over *Nilus*, as that great City, five *Italian* miles long, and two broad, by the river side: from mount *Sion* in *Jerusalem* the holy land is of all sides to be seen: such high places are infinite: with us those of the best note are *Glassenbury* Tower, *Bever* castle, *Rodway Grange*, *Walsby* in *Lincolnshire*, where I lately received a real kindness, by the munificence of the right honorable my noble Lady and patroness, the Lady *Frances* Countess Dowager of *Exeter*: And two amongst the rest, which I may not omit for vicinities sake, *Oldbury*, in the confines of *Warwickshire*, where I have often looked about me with great delight, at the foot of which hill I was born: And *Hanbury* in *Staffordshire*, contiguous to which is *Falde* a pleasant Village, and an ancient patrimony belonging to our family, now in the possession of mine elder brother *William Burton* Esquire. *Barclay* the *Scot* commends that of *Greenwich* tower for one of the best prospects in *Europe*, to see *London* on the one side, the *Thames*, ships, and pleasant meadows on the other. There be those that say as much and more of St. *Mark's* steeple in *Venice*. Yet these are at too great a distance; some are especially affected with such objects as be near, to see passengers go by in some great Roadway, or boats in a river, *in subjectum forum despicere*, to oversee a Fair, a Market-place, or out of a pleasant window into some thoroughfare street to behold a continual concourse, a promiscuous rout, coming and going, or a multitude of spectators at a Theatre, a Mask or some such like show. But I rove: the sum is this, that variety of actions, objects, air, places, are excellent good in this infirmity and all others, good for man, good for beast. *Constantine* the Emperor, *lib.* 18, *cap.* 13, *ex Leontio*, holds it an only cure for rotten sheep, and any manner of sick cattle. *Laelius a fonte Aegubinus* that great Doctor, at the latter end of many of his consultations (as commonly he doth set down what success his Physick had) in melancholy most especially approves of this above all other remedies whatsoever, as appears *consult.* 69, *consult.* 229, *&c.* *Many other things helped, but change of air was that which wrought the cure, and did most good.*

Anatomy of Melancholy

THOMAS CORYATE

c. 1577?–1617

119 *A Theological Argument*

BUT now I will make relation of that which I promised in my treatise of *Padua*, I mean my discourse with the *Jews* about their religion. For when as walking in the Court of the *Ghetto*, I casually met with a certaine learned Jewish Rabbin that spake good Latin, I insinuated myself after some few terms of compliment into conference with him, and asked him his opinion of *Christ*, and why he did not receive him for his Messias; he made me the same answer that the *Turk* did at *Lyons*, of whom I have before spoken, that *Christ* forsooth was a great Prophet, and in that respect as highly to be esteemed as any

Prophet amongst the *Jews* that ever lived before him; but derogated altogether from his divinity, and would not acknowledge him for the *Messias* and Saviour of the world, because he came so contemptibly, and not with that pomp and majesty that beseemed the redeemer of mankind. I replied that we *Christians* do, and will even to the effusion of our vital blood confess him to be the true and only *Messias* of the world, seeing he confirmed his Doctrine while he was here on earth, with such an innumerable multitude of divine miracles, which did most infallibly testify his divinity. . . Withal I added that the predictions and sacred oracles both of *Moyses*, and all the holy Prophets of God, aimed altogether at *Christ* as their only mark, in regard he was the full consummation of the law and the Prophets, and I urged a place of *Esay* unto him concerning the name *Emanuel*, and a virgin's conceiving and bearing of a son; and at last descended to the persuasion of him to abandon and renounce his Jewish religion and to undertake the Christian faith, without the which he should be eternally damned. He again replied that we Christians do misinterpret the Prophets, and very perversly wrest them to our own sense, and for his own part he had confidently resolved to live and die in his Jewish faith, hoping to be saved by the observations of *Moyses*' Law. In the end he seemed to be somewhat exasperated against me, because I sharply taxed their superstitious ceremonies. For many of them are such refractory people that they cannot endure to hear any terms of reconciliation to the Church of Christ. . . But to shut up this narration of my conflict with the Jewish Rabbin, after there had passed many vehement speeches to and fro betwixt us, it happened that some forty or fifty Jews more flocked about me, and some of them began very insolently to swagger with me, because I durst reprehend their religion: Whereupon fearing least they would have offered me some violence, I withdrew myself by little and little towards the bridge at the entrance into the Ghetto, with an intent to fly from them, but by good fortune our noble Ambassador Sir *Henry Wotton* passing under the bridge in his Gondola at that very time, espied me somewhat earnestly bickering with them, and so incontinently sent unto me out of his boat one of his principal Gentlemen Master *Belford* his secretary, who conveyed me safely from these unchristian miscreants, which perhaps would have given me just occasion to forswear any more coming to the Ghetto.

Coryat's Crudities

SIR THOMAS OVERBURY

1581–1613

120 *A Fair and Happy Milkmaid*

IS a Country Wench, that is so far from making herself beautiful by art that one look of hers is able to put all face-physick out of countenance. She knows a fair look is but a dumb orator to commend virtue, therefore minds it not. All her excellencies stand in her so silently, as if they had stolen upon her without her knowledge. The lining of her apparel (which is herself) is far better than outsides of tissue: for though she be not arrayed in the spoil of the silk-worm, she is decked in innocency, a far better wearing. She doth not, with lying long abed, spoil both her complexion and conditions; nature hath taught her too immoderate sleep is rust to the soul: she rises therefore with *Chanticleer*, her dame's cock, and at night makes the lamb her curfew. In milking a Cow, and straining the teats through her fingers, it seems that so sweet a milk-press makes the milk the whiter or sweeter; for never came almond glove or aromatic ointment on her palm to taint it. The golden ears of corn fall and kiss her feet when she reaps them, as if they wished to be bound and led prisoners by the same hand that felled them. Her breath is her own, which scents all the year long of *June*, like a new-made haycock. She makes her hand hard with labour, and her heart soft with pity; and when winter evenings fall early (sitting at her merry wheel) she sings a defiance to the giddy *wheel of Fortune*. She doth all things with so sweet a grace, it seems *ignorance* will not suffer her to do ill, being her mind is to do well. She bestows her year's wages at next fair; and in chusing her garments counts no bravery i' th' world like decency. The garden and beehive are all her physick and chirurgery, and she lives the longer for it. She dares go alone, and unfold sheep in the night, and fears no manner of ill, because she means none: yet to say truth, she is never alone, for she is still accompanied with old songs, honest thoughts, and prayers, but short ones; yet they have their efficacy, in that they are not palled with ensuing idle cogitations. Lastly, her dreams are so chaste that she dare tell them; only a Friday's dream is all her superstition: that she conceals for fear of anger. Thus lives she, and all her care is she may die in the springtime, to have store of flowers stuck upon her winding-sheet.

Sir Thomas Overburye His Wife, &c.

121 *A Franklin*

HIS outside is an ancient Yeoman of England, though his inside may give arms (with the best gentleman) and ne'er see the herald. There is no truer servant in the house than himself. Though he be master, he says not to his servants, 'Go to field,' but, 'Let us go;' and with his own eye doth both fatten his flock and set forward all manner of husbandry. He is taught by nature to be contented with a little; his own fold yields him both food and raiment: he is pleased with any nourishment God sends, whilst curious gluttony ransacks, as it were, *Noah's Ark* for food, only to feed the riot of one meal. He is ne'er known to go to law; understanding to be law-bound among men is like to be hide-bound among his beasts; they thrive not under it: and that such men sleep as unquietly as if their pillows were stuffed with Lawyers' penknives. When he builds, no poor tenant's cottage hinders his prospect: they are indeed his Almshouses, though there be painted on them no such superscription: he never sits up late, but when he hunts the Badger, the vowed foe of his Lambs: nor uses he any cruelty, but when he hunts the hare, nor subtilty, but when he setteth snares for the Snite or pitfalls for the Blackbird; nor oppression, but when in the month of *July* he goes to the next river and shears his sheep. He allows of honest pastime, and thinks not the bones of the dead anything bruised, or the worse for it, though the country lasses dance in the churchyard after evensong. *Rock Monday*, and the Wake in Summer, Shrovings, the wakeful catches on Christmas Eve, the Hoky, or Seed-cake, these he yearly keeps, yet holds them no relics of

Popery. He is not so inquisitive after news derived from the privy closet, when the finding an aerie of Hawks in his own ground, or the foaling of a Colt come of a good strain, are tidings more pleasant, more profitable. He is lord paramount within himself, though he hold by never so mean a Tenure ; and dies the more contentedly (though he leave his heir young), in regard he leaves him not liable to a covetous Guardian. Lastly, to end him : he cares not when his end comes, he needs not fear his Audit, for his *quietus* is in heaven.

Sir Thomas Overburye His Wife, &c.

LORD HERBERT OF CHERBURY

1583–1648

122 *The Knot of Ribband*

PASSING two or three days here, it happened one evening that a daughter of the Dutchess of about 10 or 11 years of age, going one evening from the Castle to walk in the Meadows, my self with divers French Gentlemen attended her and some Gentlewomen that were with her ; this young Lady wearing a knot of Ribband on her head, a French Chevalier took it suddenly and fastned it to his hatband ; the young lady offended herewith demands her Ribband, but he refusing to restore it, the young Lady addressing herself to me, said, Monsieur, I pray get my Ribband from that gentleman ; hereupon going towards him, I courteously, with my hat in my hand, desired him to do me the honor that I may deliver the Lady her Ribband or Bouquet again ; but he roughly answering me, Do you think I will give it you, when I have refused it to her? I replyed, nay then Sir I will make you restore it by force, whereupon also putting on my hat and reaching at his, he to save himself ran away, and after a long course in the Meadow finding that I had almost overtook him, he turned short, and running to the young Lady was about to put the Ribband on her hand, when I seizing upon his arm, said to the young Lady, it was I that gave it. Pardon me, quoth she, it is he that gives it me: I said then, Madam, I will not contradict you, but if he dare say that I did not constrain him to give it, I will fight with him. The French gentleman answered nothing thereunto for the present, and so conducted the young Lady again to the Castle. The next day I desired Mr. *Aurelian Townsend* to tell the French Cavalier that either he must confess that I constrained him to restore the Ribband, or fight with me; but the gentleman seeing him unwilling to accept of this Challenge, went out from the place, whereupon I following him, some of the gentlemen that belonged to the Constable taking notice hereof acquainted him therewith, who sending for the French Cavalier, checked him well for his Sauciness, in taking the Ribband away from his grandchild, and afterwards bid him depart his house; and this was all that I ever heard of the gentleman with whom I proceeded in that manner because I thought my self obliged thereunto by the oath taken when I was made Knight of the Bath, as I formerly related upon this occasion.

Life . . . Written by Himself

JOHN SELDEN

1584–1654

123 *Pleasure*

PLEASURE is nothing else but the intermission of pain, the enjoying of something I am in great trouble for till I have it.

'Tis a wrong way to proportion other men's pleasures to ourselves. 'Tis like a Child's using a little Bird, 'O poor Bird, thou shalt sleep with me'; so lays it in his bosom, and stifles it with his hot breath; the Bird had rather be in the cold air: and yet too 'tis the most pleasing flattery to like what other men like.

'Tis most undoubtedly true that all men are equally given to their pleasure; only thus, one man's pleasure lies one way, and another's another. Pleasures are all alike, simply considered in themselves. He that hunts, or he that governs the Commonwealth, they both please themselves alike, only we commend that, whereby we ourselves receive some benefit; as if a man place his delight in things that tend to the common good. He that takes pleasure to hear sermons enjoys himself as much as he that hears plays; and could he that loves plays endeavour to love sermons possibly he might bring himself to it as well as to any other pleasure. At first it might seem harsh and tedious, but afterwards 'twould be pleasing and delightful. So it falls out in that which is the great pleasure of some men, tobacco; at first they could not abide it, and now they cannot be without it.

While you are upon Earth enjoy the good things that are here (to that end were they given), and be not melancholy, and wish yourself in heaven. If a King should give you the keeping of a castle, with all things belonging to it, orchards, gardens, &c., and bid you use them, withal promise you after twenty years to remove you to the Court, and to make you a Privy Councillor; if you should neglect your Castle, and refuse to eat of those fruits, and sit down, and whine, and wish that I was a Privy Councillor, do you think the King would be pleased with you?

Pleasures of meat, drink, clothes, &c., are forbidden those that know not how to use them; just as nurses cry, pah! when they see a knife in a child's hand; they will never say anything to a man.

Table Talk

124 *Of a King*

A KING is a thing men have made for their own sakes, for quietness' sake. Just as in a Family one man is appointed to buy the meat. If every man should buy, or if there were many buyers, they would never agree; one would buy what the other liked not, or what the other had bought before, so there would be a confusion. But that charge being committed to one, he according to his discretion pleases all. If they have not what they would have one day, they shall have it the next, or something as good.

The word King directs our eyes. Suppose it had been consul or dictator. To think all Kings alike is the same folly as if a consul of *Aleppo* or *Smyrna* should claim to himself the same power that a Consul at *Rome* had. What, am not I consul? Or a Duke of *England* should think himself like the duke of *Florence*. Nor can it be imagined that the word βασιλεὺς did signify a king the same in Greece, as the Hebrew word מלך did with the Jews. Besides, let Divines in their pulpits say what they will, they in their practice deny that all is the King's. They sue him, and so does all the nation, whereof they are a part. What matter is it then what they preach or talk in the schools?

Kings are all individuals, this or that King; there is no species of kings.

A King that claims privileges in his own kingdom, because they have them in another, is just as a cook that claims fees in one lord's house because they are allowed in another. If the master of the house will yield them, well and good.

Table Talk

WILLIAM DRUMMOND OF HAWTHORNDEN

1585–1649

125 *Animula vagula blandula, hospes comesque corporis*

THEY had their being together, Parts they are of one reasonable Creature, the harming of the one is the weakening of the working of the other. What sweet Contentments doth the Soul enjoy by the Senses? They are the Gates and Windows of its Knowledge, the Organs of its Delight. If it be tedious to an excellent Player on the Lute, to abide but a few Months the want of One, how much more must the being without such noble Tools and Engines be painful to the Soul? And if Two Pilgrims, which have wandered some few Miles together, have a hearts-grief when they are near to part, what must the Sorrow be at parting of Two so loving Friends and never-loathing Lovers, as are the Body and Soul?

The Cypresse Grove

DRUMMOND OF HAWTHORNDEN

126 *Of Dying Young*

BUT that, perhaps, which anguisheth thee most, is to have this glorious Pageant of the World removed from thee, in the Spring and most delicious Season of thy Life; for though to die be usual, to die young may appear extraordinary. If the present Fruition of these Things be unprofitable and vain, What can a long Continuance of them be? If God had made Life happier, he had also made it longer. Stranger and new Halcyon, why would thou longer nestle amidst these unconstant and stormy Waves? Hast thou not already suffered enough of this World, but thou must yet endure more? To live long, is it not to be long troubled? But number thy Years, which are now * * * and thou shalt find, that whereas Ten have outlived thee, Thousands have not attained this Age. One Year is sufficient to behold all the Magnificence of Nature, nay, even One Day and Night; for more is but the same brought again. This Sun, that Moon, these Stars, the varying Dance of the Spring, Summer, Autumn, Winter, is that very same which the Golden Age did see. They which have the longest Time lent them to live in, have almost no Part of it at all, measuring it either by the Space of Time which is past, when they were not, or by that which is to come. Why shouldst thou then care, whether thy Days be many or few, which, when prolonged to the uttermost, prove, paralleled with Eternity, as a Tear is to the Ocean? To die young, is to do that soon, and in some fewer Days, which once thou must do; it is but the giving over of a Game, that after never so many Hazards, must be lost.

The Cypresse Grove

HENRY HEXHAM

1585?–1650

127 *The Assault on Ostend, 7 January 1602*

THIS being done, Sir FRANCIS VERE went through the Sally Port, down into the False Bray. And it being twilight, called for an old soldier, a Gentleman of his company, to go out *sentinel-perdu*, and to creep out to the strand between two gabions; giving him express command that if he saw an enemy, he should come in unto him silently, without giving any alarm at all.

He crept upon his belly as far as he could; and, at last, discovered Count FARNESE, wading and put over the Old Haven, above their Pile Battery, with his 2,000 Italians, which were to fall on first: and, as they waded over, he drew them up into battalions and divisions: which this Gentleman having discovered, came silently to Sir FRANCIS VERE, as he had commanded him. Who asked him, 'What news?'

'My Lord,' says he, 'I smell good store of gold chains, buff jerkins, Spanish cassocks, and Spanish blades.'

'Ha!' says Sir FRANCIS VERE, 'sayest thou me so! I hope thou shalt have some of them anon!' and giving him a piece of gold, he went up again through the Sally Port to the top of Sand Hill. Where he gave express order to Sergeant-Major CARPENTER to go to Helmont, and every man to his charge; and not to take any alarm, or shoot off either cannon- or

4 *sentinel-perdu*) *as sentry forlorn* 18 *cassocks*) *military cloaks*

musket-shot till he himself gave the signal: and then to give fire, both with the ordnance and small shot, as fast as ever they could charge and discharge.

When the enemy had put over his 2,000 Italians; he had also a signal, to give notice thereof to the Count of *Bucquoy*, that they were ready to fall on: whose signal was the shot of a cannon from their Pile Battery into the sea towards his quarters, with a hollow-holed bullet, which made a humming noise.

When General VERE had got them under the swoop of his cannon and small shot, he poured a volley of cannon- and musket-shot upon them, raking through their battalions, and makes lanes through them upon the bare strand; which did so amaze and startle them, that they were at a *non-plus* whether they should fall on or retreat back again. Yet at last taking courage, and tumbling over the dead bodies, they rallied themselves and came under the foot of Sand Hill and along the foot of the Curtain of the Old Wall, to the very piles that were struck under the wall, where they began to make ready to send us a volley.

Which Sir FRANCIS VERE seeing they were a presenting, and ready to give fire upon us, because indeed all the breast-work and parapet was beaten down flat to the rampire that day, with their ordnance, and we standing open to the enemy's shot, commanded all the soldiers to fall flat down upon the ground, while the enemy's shot flew like a shower of hail over their heads: which, for the reasons above said, saved a great many men's lives.

This being done; our men rising, saw the enemy hasting to come up to the breach, and mounting up the wall of the Old Town. Sir FRANCIS VERE flourishing his sword, called to them in Spanish and Italian, *Vienneza!* causing the soldiers, as they climbed up, to cast and tumble down among them, the firkins of ashes, the barrels of *frize-ruyters*, the ropes, stones, and brickbats which were provided for them.

The alarm being given, it was admirable to see with what courage and resolution our men fought. Yea, the LORD did, as it were, infuse fresh courage and strength into a company of poor snakes and sick soldiers, which came running out of their huts up to the wall to fight their shares; and the women with their laps full of powder, to supply them, when they had shot away all their ammunition.

. . . . . .

The fight upon the breach and the Old Town continued, hotter and hotter, for the space of above an hour. The enemy fell on, at the same instant, upon the *Porcépic*, Helmont, the West Ravelin, and Quarriers; but were so bravely repulsed, that they could not enter a man.

The enemy fainting, and having had his belly full; those on the west side beat a doleful retreat: while the Lord of Hosts ended our dispute for the town, and crowned us with victory: and the roaring noise of our cannon rending the air and rolling along the superficies of the water, the wind being South and with us, carried that night the news thereof, to our friends in England and Holland.

General VERE perceiving the enemy to fall off, commanded me to run, as fast as ever I could, to Sergeant-Major CARPENTER and the Auditor FLEMING, who were upon Helmont, that they should presently

4 *frize-ruyters) Frisian horsemen. The barrel was a defensive appliance, armed with spikes, to receive cavalry*

open the West Sluice: out of which there ran such a stream and torrent, through the channel of the West Haven, that, upon their retreat, it carried away many of their sound and hurt men into the sea. And besides, our men fell down our walls after them, and slew a great many of their men as they retreated. They took some prisoners, pillaged and stript a great many [of the killed], and brought in gold chains, Spanish pistols, buff jerkins, Spanish cassocks, blades, swords, and targets (among the rest, one wherein was enamelled in gold, the Seven Worthies worth 700 or 800 guilders).

Among the rest, was that soldier which Sir FRANCIS VERE had sent out to discover; who came with as much booty as ever he could lug, saying, 'Sir FRANCIS VERE was now as good as his word.'

Stuart Tracts, 1603–1693 (An English Garner)

THOMAS HOBBES

1588–1679

128 *Disastrous Effects of an Afternoon Performance*

THE opinions of the world, both in ancient and later ages, concerning the cause of madness, have been two. Some, deriving them from the Passions; some, from Demons or Spirits, either good or bad, which they thought might enter into a man, possess him, and move his organs in such strange and uncouth manner as madmen use to do. The former sort therefore called such men, Mad-men: but the Later called them sometimes *Daemoniacks* (that is, possessed

10 *targets*) *shields*

with spirits); sometimes *Energumeni* (that is, agitated, or moved with spirits); and now in *Italy* they are called not only *Pazzi*, Mad-men; but also *Spiritati*, men possessed.

There was once a great conflux of people in *Abdera*, a City of the Greeks, at the acting of the Tragedy of *Andromeda*, upon an extreme hot day: whereupon a great many of the spectators falling into Fevers had this accident from the heat and from the Tragedy together, that they did nothing but pronounce Iambics, with the names of *Perseus* and *Andromeda*; which, together with the Fever, was cured by the coming on of Winter.

Leviathan

129 *Out of Civil States, there is always Warre*

HEREBY it is manifest, that during the time men live without a common Power to keep them all in awe, they are in that condition which is called War; and such a war as is of every man, against every man. For WAR consisteth not in Battle only, or the act of fighting; but in a tract of time, wherein the Will to contend by Battle is sufficiently known: and therefore the notion of *Time* is to be considered in the nature of War, as it is in the nature of Weather. For as the nature of Foul weather lieth not in a shower or two of rain, but in an inclination thereto of many days together, so the nature of war consisteth not in actual fighting, but in the known disposition thereto during all the time there is no assurance to the contrary. All other time is PEACE.

Whatsoever therefore is consequent to a time of War, where every man is Enemy to every man, the same is consequent to the time wherein men live without other security than what their own strength and their own invention shall furnish them withal. In such condition there is no place for Industry, because the fruit thereof is uncertain: and consequently no Culture of the Earth: no Navigation, nor use of the commodities that may be imported by Sea; no commodious Building; no Instruments of moving, and removing such things as require much force; no Knowledge of the face of the Earth; no account of Time; no Arts; no Letters; no Society; and, which is worst of all, continual fear and danger of violent death; and the life of man, solitary, poor, nasty, brutish, and short.

Leviathan

130 *The Papacy*

BUT after this Doctrine, *that the Church now Militant, is the Kingdom of God spoken of in the Old and New Testament*, was received in the World, the ambition, and canvassing for the Offices that belong thereunto, and especially for that great Office of being Christs Lieutenant, and the Pomp of them that obtained therein the principal Public Charges, became by degrees so evident that they lost the inward Reverence due to the Pastoral Function: insomuch as the Wisest men of them that had any power in the Civil State needed nothing but the authority of their Princes to deny them any further Obedience. For, from the time that the Bishop of Rome had gotten to be acknowledged for Bishop Universal by pretence of Succession to St. Peter, their whole Hierarchy, or

Kingdom of Darkness may be compared not unfitly to the *Kingdom of Fairies*; that is, to the old wives *Fables* in England, concerning *Ghosts* and *Spirits*, and the feats they play in the night. And if a man consider the original of this great Ecclesiastical Dominion he will easily perceive that the *Papacy* is no other than the *Ghost* of the deceased *Romane Empire*, sitting crowned upon the grave thereof: For so did the Papacy start up on a Sudden out of the Ruins of that Heathen Power.

Leviathan

IZAAK WALTON

1593–1682

131 *A Milkmaid's Song*

VENATOR. On my word, Master, this is a gallant *Trout*, what shall we do with him?

Piscator. Marry e'en eat him to supper: We'll go to my hostess, from whence we came; she told me, as I was going out of door, that my brother *Peter*, a good angler and a cheerful companion, had sent word he would lodge there to-night, and bring a friend with him. My hostess has two beds, and, I know, you and I may have the best: we'll rejoice with my brother *Peter* and his friend, tell tales, or sing Ballads, or make a catch, or find some harmless sport to content us, and pass away a little time without offence to God or man.

Venator. A match, good Master, let 's go to that house, for the linen looks white, and smells of Lavender, and I long to lie in a pair of sheets that smells so: let 's be going, good Master, for I am hungry again with fishing.

Piscator. Nay, stay a little, good Scholar. I caught

my last *Trout* with a worm, now I will put on a minnow and try a quarter of an hour about yonder trees for another, and so walk towards our lodging. Look you Scholar, thereabout we shall have a bite presently, or not at all: Have with you (Sir!) o' my word I have hold of him. Oh, it is a great loggerheaded *Chub*; come, hang him upon that willow twig, and let 's be going. But turn out of the way a little, good Scholar, towards yonder high *honeysuckle* hedge: there we'll sit and sing whilst this shower falls so gently upon the teeming earth, and gives yet a sweeter smell to the lovely flowers that adorn these verdant meadows.

Look, under that broad *Beech-tree*, I sat down, when I was last this way a-fishing, and the birds in the adjoining grove seemed to have a friendly contention with an Echo, whose dead voice seemed to live in a hollow cave, near to the brow of that Primrose-hill; there I sat viewing the silver streams glide silently towards their centre, the tempestuous sea; yet, sometimes opposed by rugged roots, and pebble stones, which broke their waves, and turned them into foam: and sometimes I beguiled time by viewing the harmless Lambs, some leaping securely in the cool shade, whilst others sported themselves in the cheerful Sun: and saw others were craving comfort from the swollen udders of their bleating Dams. As I thus sat, these and other sights had so fully possessed my soul with content, that I thought as the Poet has happily expressed it:

I was for that time lifted above earth;
And possessed joys not promised in my birth.

As I left this place, and entered into the next field, a second pleasure entertained me, 'twas a handsome Milkmaid that had not yet attained so much age and wisdom as to load her mind with any fears of many things that will never be (as too many men too often do), but she cast away all care, and sung like a *Nightingale*: her voice was good, and the Ditty fitted for it; 'twas that smooth song, which was made by *Kit. Marlow*, now at least fifty years ago: and the Milk-maid's Mother sung an answer to it, which was made by Sir *Walter Rawleigh* in his younger days.

They were old-fashioned Poetry, but choicely good, I think much better than the strong lines that are now in fashion in this critical age. Look yonder! on my word, yonder they both be a-milking again, I will give her the *Chub*, and persuade them to sing those two songs to us.

God speed you good woman, I have been a-fishing, and am going to *Bleak-Hall* to my bed, and having caught more fish than will sup myself and my friend, I will bestow this upon you and your daughter, for I use to sell none.

Milkwoman. Marry God requite you Sir, and we'll eat it cheerfully, and if you come this way a-fishing two months hence, a grace of God I'll give you a silly-bub of new verjuice, in a new made haycock, for it, and my *Maudlin* shall sing you one of her best *Ballads*; for she and I both love all *Anglers*, they be such honest, civil, quiet men. *The Compleat Angler*

132 *George Herbert's Walks to Salisbury*

HIS chiefest recreation was Musick, in which heavenly Art he was a most excellent Master, and composed many *divine Hymns and Anthems*, which he set and sung to his *Lute* or *Viol*: and though he was a lover of retiredness, yet his love of Musick was such, that he went usually twice every week, on certain appointed days, to the Cathedral Church in *Salisbury*; and at his return would say, That his time spent in prayer, and Cathedral Music, elevated his soul, and was his Heaven upon Earth. But before his return thence to Bemerton, he would usually sing and play his part at an appointed private Musick meeting; and, to justify this practice, he would often say, Religion does not banish mirth, but only moderates and sets rules to it.

And, as his desire to enjoy his Heaven upon Earth drew him twice every week to *Salisbury*, so, his walks thither were the occasion of many accidents to others; of which I will mention some few.

In one of his walks to *Salisbury* he overtook a Gentleman, that is still living in that City; and in their walk together, Mr. *Herbert* took a fair occasion to talk with him, and humbly begged to be excused, if he asked him some account of his faith; and said, I do this the rather, because though you are not of my parish, yet I receive tithe from you by the hand of your Tenant; and, Sir, I am the bolder to do it, because I know there be some Sermon-hearers that be like those fishes, that always live in salt water, and yet are always fresh.

After which expression, Mr. *Herbert* asked him some needful Questions, and having received his answer, gave him such rules for the trial of his sincerity, and for a practical piety, and in so loving and meek a manner, that the Gentleman did so fall in love with him, and his discourse, that he would often contrive to meet him in his walk to *Salisbury*, or to attend him back to *Bemerton*; and still mentions the name of Mr. *George Herbert* with veneration, and still praiseth God that he knew him.

In another walk to *Salisbury*, he saw a poor man with

a poorer horse, that was fallen under his load: they were both in distress and needed present help; which Mr. *Herbert* perceiving, put off his canonical coat, and helped the poor man to unload, and after to load his horse. The poor man blessed him for it, and he blessed the poor man; and was so like the *good Samaritan*, that he gave him money to refresh both himself and his horse; and told him, That if he loved himself, he should be merciful to his beast. Thus he left the poor man: and at his coming to his musical friends at *Salisbury*, they began to wonder that Mr. *George Herbert*, which used to be so trim and clean, came into that company so soiled and discomposed; but he told them the occasion. And when one of the company told him, He had disparaged himself by so dirty an employment, his answer was, That the thought of what he had done, would prove Musick to him at midnight; and that the omission of it would have upbraided and made discord in his conscience, whensoever he should pass by that place: for if I be bound to pray for all that be in distress, I am sure that I am bound, so far as it is in my power, to practise what I pray for. And though I do not wish for the like occasion every day, yet let me tell you, I would not willingly pass one day of my life, without comforting a sad soul, or showing mercy; and I praise God for this occasion. And now let us tune our Instruments.

Life of George Herbert

133 *Portrait of John Donne*

HE was of stature moderately tall; of a straight and equally proportioned body, to which all his words and actions gave an unexpressible addition of comeliness.

The melancholy and pleasant humour were in him so contempered, that each gave advantage to the other, and made his company one of the delights of Mankind.

His fancy was inimitably high, equalled only by his great wit; both being made useful by a commanding judgement.

His aspect was chearful, and such as gave a silent testimony of a clear knowing soul, and of a Conscience at peace with itself.

His melting eye showed that he had a soft heart, full of noble compassion; of too brave a soul to offer injuries, and too much a *Christian* not to pardon them in others.

He did much contemplate (especially after he entered into his Sacred Calling) the mercies of Almighty God, the immortality of the Soul, and the joys of heaven; and would often say in a kind of sacred ecstasy, 'Blessed be God that he is God, only and divinely like Himself.'

He was by nature highly passionate, but more apt to reluct at the excesses of it. A great lover of the offices of humanity, and of so merciful a spirit, that he never beheld the miseries of Mankind without pity and relief.

He was earnest and unwearied in the search of knowledge, with which his vigorous soul is now satisfied, and employed in a continual praise of that God that first breathed it into his active body; that body, which once was a Temple of the Holy Ghost and is now become a small quantity of Christian dust:—But I shall see it reanimated.

Life of John Donne

134 *The Judicious Hooker makes an Injudicious Marriage*

AND by this [marriage] the good man was drawn from the tranquillity of his college; from that Garden of Piety, of Pleasure, of Peace, and a sweet Conversation, into the thorny wilderness of a busy world; into those corroding cares that attend a married priest, and a Country Parsonage; which was *Drayton-Beauchamp* in *Buckinghamshire*, not far from *Aylesbury*, and in the diocese of Lincoln; to which he was presented by *John Cheney*, Esq.—then patron of it—the 9th of December 1584, where he behaved himself so as to give no occasion of evil, but as St. *Paul* adviseth a Minister of God—in much patience, in afflictions, in anguishes, in necessities, in poverty, and no doubt in long-suffering; yet troubling no man with his discontents and wants.

And in this condition he continued about a year; in which time his two Pupils, *Edwin Sandys* and *George Cranmer*, took a journey to see their tutor; where they found him with a book in his hand (it was the *Odes* of *Horace*) he being then like humble and innocent *Abel*, tending his small allotment of sheep in a common field; which he told his Pupils he was forced to do then, for that his servant had gone home to dine, and assist his Wife to do some necessary household business. But when his servant returned and released him, then his two Pupils attended him unto his house, where their best entertainment was his quiet company, which was presently denied them; for *Richard* was called to rock the cradle; and the rest of their welcome was so like this, that they stayed but till next morning, which was time enough to discover and pity their Tutor's condition; and having in that time rejoiced in the remembrance, and then paraphrased on many of the innocent recreations of their younger days, and other like diversions, and thereby given him as much present comfort as they were able, they were forced to leave him to the company of his wife *Joan*, and seek themselves a quieter Lodging for next night. But at their parting from him, Mr. *Cranmer* said, Good tutor, I am sorry your lot is fallen in no better ground, as to your Parsonage; and more sorry that your Wife proves not a more comfortable Companion, after you have wearied yourself in your restless studies. To whom the good man replied, My dear *George*, if saints have usually a double share in the miseries of this life, I, that am none, ought not to repine at what my wise Creator hath appointed for me: but labour, as indeed I do daily, to submit mine to his will, and possess my soul in patience and peace.

Life of Richard Hooker

135 *Sir Henry Wotton*

HE yearly went also to *Oxford*. But the Summer before his death he changed that for a journey to *Winchester* College, to which school he was first removed from *Bocton*. And as he returned from *Winchester* towards *Eaton* College, said to a friend, his companion in that journey: 'How useful was that advice of a holy Monk, who persuaded his friend to perform his customary devotions in a constant place, because in that place we usually meet with those very thoughts which possessed us at our last being there! And I find it thus far experimentally true, that at my now being in that School, and seeing that very place where I sat when I was a boy, occasioned me to remember those very thoughts of my youth which then possessed me; sweet thoughts indeed, that promised my growing years numerous pleasures, without mixtures of cares: and those to be enjoyed, when time (which I therefore thought slow-paced) had changed my *youth* into *manhood*. But age and experience have taught me that those were but empty hopes. And though my dayes have been many, and those mixt with more pleasures, than the sons of men do usually enjoy: yet I have always found it true, as my *Saviour* did foretell, *Sufficient for the day is the evil thereof*. Nevertheless, I saw there a succession of boys using the same recreations, and, questionless, possessed with the same thoughts that then possessed me. Thus one generation succeeds another, both in their *lives, recreations, hopes, fears, and deaths*.'

Life of Sir Henry Wotton

JAMES HOWELL

1594–1666

136 *The Pied Piper*

SIR,—I saw such prodigious things daily done these few years that I had resolved with myself to give over *wondering* at anything; yet a passage happened this week that forced me to wonder once more, because it is without parallel. It was that some odd fellows went skulking up and down *London* streets, and with Figs and Raisins allured little Children, and so purloined them away from their Parents and carried them a Shipboard for beyond Sea, where by cutting their Hair and other devices they so disguised them that their Parents could not know them. This made me think upon that miraculous passage in *Hamelen*, a town in *Germany*, which I hoped to have passed through when I was in *Hamburg*, had we returned by *Holland*; which was thus (nor would I relate it unto you were there not some ground of truth for it): The said town of *Hamelen* was annoyed with Rats and Mice; and it chanced that a Pied-coated Piper came thither who covenanted with the chief Burghers for such a reward if he could free them quite from the said Vermin, nor would he demand it till a twelve-month and a day after. The agreement being made, he began to play on his Pipes and all the Rats and the Mice followed him to a great lough hard by, where they all perished; so the Town was infected no more. At the end of the year the Pied-Piper returned for his reward; the Burghers put him off with slightings and neglect, offering him some small matter, which he refusing and staying some days in the Town, on Sunday morning at High Mass, when most people were at church, he fell to play on his Pipes, and all the children up and down followed him out of the Town to a great Hill not far off, which rent in two and opened, and let him and the children in and so closed up again. This happened a matter of 250 years since, and in that town they date their Bills and Bonds and other Instruments in law to this day from the year of the going out of their children. Besides there is a great pillar of stone at the foot of the said Hill whereon this story is engraven.

No more now, for this is enough in conscience for one time. So I am your most affectionate Servitor.

J. H.

Fleet, 1 *Octo*. 1643.

Epistolae Ho-Elianae: Familiar Letters

JOHN EARLE

1601–1665

137 *A Child*

IS a Man in a small Letter, yet the best copy of *Adam* before he tasted of *Eve* or the apple; and he is happy whose small practice in the world can only write this Character. He is nature's fresh picture newly drawn in oil, which time, and much handling, dims and defaces. His Soul is yet a white paper unscribbled with observations of the world, wherewith, at length, it becomes a blurred notebook. He is purely happy, because he knows no evil, nor hath made means by sin to be acquainted with misery. He arrives not at the mischief of being wise, nor endures evils to come, by foreseeing them. He kisses and loves all, and, when the smart of the rod is past, smiles on his beater. Nature and his Parents alike dandle him, and 'tice him on with a bait of sugar to a draught of wormwood. He plays yet, like a young Prentice the first day, and is not come to his task of melancholy. All the language he speaks yet is tears, and they serve him well enough to express his necessity. His hardest labour is his tongue, as if he were loath to use so deceitful an Organ; and he is best company with it when he can but prattle. We laugh at his foolish sports, but his game is our earnest; and his drums, rattles, and hobby-horses, but the Emblems and mocking of man's business. His father hath writ him as his own little story, wherein he reads those days of his life that he cannot remember, and sighs to see what innocence he has out-lived. The elder he grows, he is a stair lower from God; and, like his first father, much worse in his breeches. He is the Christian's example, and the old man's relapse; the one imitates his pureness, and the other falls into his simplicity. Could he put off his body with his little coat, he had got eternity without a burthen, and exchanged but one Heaven for another.

Microcosmographie

138 *A She Precise Hypocrite*

IS one in whom good Women suffer, and have their truth misinterpreted by her folly. She is one, she knows not what herself if you ask her, but she is indeed one that has taken a toy at the fashion of Religion, and is enamoured of the new fangle. She is a Nonconformist in a close stomacher and Ruff of Geneva Print, and her purity consists much in her Linen. . . . Her devotion at the Church is much in the turning up of her eye; and turning down the leaf in her Book, when she hears named Chapter and Verse. When she comes home, she commends the Sermon for the scripture, and two hours. She loves Preaching better than Praying, and of Preachers, Lecturers; and thinks the Weekday's Exercise far more edifying than the Sunday's. Her oftest Gossipings are Sabbath-day's journeys, where (though an enemy to Superstition) she will go in Pilgrimage five miles to a silenced Minister, when there is a better Sermon in her own Parish. She doubts of the Virgin Mary's Salvation, and dare not Saint her, but knows her own place in heaven as perfectly as the Pew she has a key to. She is so taken up with faith she has no room for charity, and understands no good Works but what are wrought on the Sampler. She accounts nothing Vices but Superstition and an Oath, and thinks Adultery a less sin than to swear ' by my Truly '. She rails at other Women by the names of *Jezebel* and *Delilah*; and calls her own daughters *Rebecca* and *Abigail*, and not *Ann* but *Hannah*. . . . She overflows so with the Bible, that she spills it upon every occasion, and will not cudgel her Maids without Scripture. It is a question whether she is more troubled with the Devil, or the Devil with her: she is always challenging and daring him, and her weapons are Spells no less potent than different, as being the sage Sentences of some of her own Sectaries. Nothing angers her so much as that Women cannot preach, and in this point only thinks the Brownist erroneous; but what she cannot at the Church she does at the Table, where she prattles more than any against sense and Antichrist, till a Capon's wing silence her. She expounds the priests of *Baal*, reading ministers, and thinks the salvation of that parish as desperate as the *Turks*. She is a main derider to her capacity of those that are not her Preachers, and censures all sermons but bad ones. . . . Her conscience is like others' lust, never satisfied, and you might better answer *Scotus* than her Scruples. She is one that thinks she performs all her duty to God in hearing, and shows the fruits of it in talking. She is more fiery against the Maypole than her husband, and thinks he might do a *Phineas's* Act to break the pate of the fiddler. She is an everlasting Argument; but I am weary of her.

Microcosmographie

JOHN HOLLOND

fl. 1638

139 *A Discourse of the Navy*

IF either the honour of a nation, commerce or trade with all nations, peace at home, grounded upon our enemies' fear or love of us abroad, and attended with plenty of all things necessary either for the preservation of the public weal or thy private welfare, be things worthy thy esteem (though it may be beyond

13 *reading ministers*) *ministers who use the Prayer-book*

thy shoal conceit), then next to God and the King give thy thanks for the same to the navy, as the principal instrument whereby God works these good things to thee. As for honour, who knows not (that knows anything) that in all records of late times of actions chronicled to the everlasting fame and renown of this kingdom, still the naval part is the thread that runs through the whole wooft, the burden of the song, the scope of the text? that whereby Queen Elizabeth of famous memory immortalized her name by her many great victories obtained over all her enemies, neighbours or remote dwellers; King James of ever blessed memory by almost silent commands commanded the silence, if not the love, of all neighbouring nations; and that whereby our ever blessed Charles, when his abused patience began to be slighted (as that his power on the seas and right to the seas began thereby to be questioned), hath not only by his late expeditions of 1635, 1636, 1637, and 1638, quelled foreign insolencies, regained our almost lost power and honour, silenced homebred malcontents, but also settled his kingdoms in peace, commerce, and plenty, the common attendants of so wise and honourable a government?

As for commerce and trade, go to the Custom House, inquire and satisfy thyself in the exportations and importations of this kingdom for that part, and compare them with former precedents, and see if they do not exceed by much all former collections; then ask the ground of that so great trade by the English with all nations, and by all nations with the English. It is even money that his Majesty being master of the seas is put for all other reasons, or if not, yet made a main reason among others. Know the body by the foot, and conceive thus with thyself. If it be thus much augmented in so few years at such a petty port where thou livest, what and how much is it increased in Dover, London, or the whole kingdom? Whence is it that sundry nations that are enemies amongst themselves are all friends to the English? that we can, and do, convoy all French and Dutch bottoms to their several ports, and protect them from the fear and annoyance of the Spanish party; and on the contrary, all Spanish and Dunkirk bottoms to their several ports, and protect them from the encounter of the French and Dutch parties? How comes it to pass that when both parties are under the tuition of any of his Majesty's castles or ships, neither party dare disturb the quiet of each other till they be both out of protection? What occasioned the transmission of so much Spanish coin and plate to be either new minted here, or at least transmitted hence, by and under the convoy of his Majesty's ships? I could instance in many more particulars, were it not to prove it day at noon; suffice it thus far, nothing under God, who doth all, hath brought so much, so great commerce to this kingdom as the rightly noble employments of our navy; a wheel, if truly turned, that sets to work all Christendom by its motion; a mill, if well extended, that in a sweet yet sovereign composure contracts the grist of all nations to its own dominions, and requires only the tribute of its own people, not for, but towards, its maintenance.

Mr. Hollond: His First Discourse of the Navy

OWEN FELLTHAM

1602?–1668

140 *Of Preaching*

THE excess which is in the defect of Preaching has made the pulpit slighted; I mean the much bad oratory we find it guilty of. 'Tis a wonder to me how men can preach so little, and so long : so long a time, and so little matter ; as if they thought to please by the inculcation of their vain Tautologies. I see no reason that so high a Princess as *Divinity* is should be presented to the people in the sordid rags of the tongue ; nor that he which speaks from the *Father of Languages* should deliver his embassage in an ill one. A man can never speak too well while he speaks not too obscure. Long and distended clauses are both tedious to the ear and difficult for their retaining. A Sentence well couched takes both the sense and the understanding. I love not those Cart-rope speeches that are longer than the memory of man can fathom. I see not but that *Divinity*, put into apt significants, might ravish as well as poetry. The weighty lines men find upon the Stage, I am perswaded, have been the lures to draw away the Pulpit's followers. We complain of drowziness at a Sermon ; when a Play of a doubled length leads us on still with alacrity. But the fault is not all in ourselves. If we saw *Divinity* acted, the gesture and variety would as much invigilate. But it is too high to be personated by Humanity. . .

A good orator should pierce the ear, allure the eye, and invade the mind of his hearer. And this is *Seneca's* opinion : fit words are better than fine ones : I like not those that are injudiciously made ; but such as be expressively significant, that lead the mind to something beside the naked term. And he that speaks thus must not look to speak thus every day. A *kembed* Oration will cost both sweat and the rubbing of the brain. And *kembed* I wish it, not *frizzled* nor *curled*. *Divinity* should not lasciviate.

Resolves

SIR THOMAS BROWNE

1605–1682

141 *Of Religious Civility*

I AM, I confess, naturally inclined to that which misguided zeal terms superstition; my common conversation I do acknowledge austere, my behaviour full of rigour, sometimes not without morosity; yet at my devotion I love to use the civility of my knee, my hat, and hand, with all those outward and sensible motions which may express or promote my invisible devotion. I should violate my own arm rather than a Church, nor willingly deface the memory of Saint or Martyr. At the sight of a Cross or Crucifix I can dispense with my hat, but scarce with the thought or memory of my Saviour; I cannot laugh at but rather pity the fruitless journeys of Pilgrims, or contemn the miserable condition of Friars; for though misplaced in circumstance, there is something in it of devotion: I could never hear the *Ave Marie* Bell without an elevation, or think it a sufficient warrant, because they erred in one circumstance, for me to err in all, that is in silence and dumb contempt.

Religio Medici

142 *Of Harmony*

IT is my temper, and I like it the better, to affect all harmony; and sure there is musick even in the beauty, and the silent note which *Cupid* strikes, far sweeter than the sound of an instrument. For there is a musick wherever there is a harmony, order, or proportion; and thus far we may maintain the musick of the spheres; for those well-ordered motions and regular paces, though they give no sound unto the ear, yet to the understanding they strike a note most full of harmony. Whatsoever is harmonically composed delights in harmony; which makes me much distrust the symmetry of those heads which declaim against all Church musick. For myself, not only from my obedience but my particular genius, I do embrace it; for even that vulgar and Tavern Musick, which makes one man merry, another mad, strikes in me a deep fit of devotion, and a profound contemplation of the first Composer: there is something in it of Divinity more than the ear discovers. It is an hieroglyphical and shadowed lesson of the whole world and Creatures of God, such a melody to the ear as the whole world, well understood, would afford the understanding. In brief, it is a sensible fit of that Harmony which intellectually sounds in the ears of God.

Religio Medici

143 *Sleep*

WE term sleep a death, and yet it is waking that kills us, and destroys those spirits that are the house of life. 'Tis indeed a part of life that best expresseth death, for every man truly lives so long as he acts his nature, or someway makes good the faculties of himself: *Themistocles* therefore that slew his Soldier in his sleep was a merciful executioner, 'tis a kind of punishment the mildness of no laws hath invented; I wonder the fancy of *Lucan* and *Seneca* did not discover it. It is that death by which we may be literally said to die daily, a death which *Adam* died before his mortality; a death whereby we live a middle and moderating point between life and death; in fine, so like death, I dare not trust it without my prayers, and an half adieu unto the world, and take my farewell in a Colloquy with God.

The night is come like to the day,
Depart not thou great God away.

SIR THOMAS BROWNE

Let not my sins, black as the night,
Eclipse the lustre of thy light.
Keep still in my Horizon, for to me,
The Sun makes not the day, but thee.
Thou whose nature cannot sleep,
On my temples sentry keep;
Guard me 'gainst those watchful foes,
Whose eyes are open while mine close.
Let no dreams my head infest,
But such as Jacobs *temples blest.*
While I do rest, my soul advance,
Make my sleep a holy trance
That I may, my rest being wrought,
Awake into some holy thought.
And with as active vigour run
My course, as doth the nimble Sun.
Sleep is a death, O make me try,
By sleeping what it is to die.
And as gently lay my head
On my Grave, as now my bed.
How ere I rest, great God let me
Awake again at last with thee.
And thus assur'd, behold I lie
Securely, or to wake or die.
These are my drowsy days, in vain
I do now wake to sleep again.
O come that hour, when I shall never
Sleep again, but wake for ever

This is the dormitive I take to bedward, I need no other *Laudanum* than this to make me sleep; after which I close mine eyes in security, content to take my leave of the Sun, and sleep unto the resurrection.

Religio Medici

SIR THOMAS BROWNE

144 *Pulvis et umbra sumus*

I

NOW since these dead bones have already out-lasted the living ones of *Methuselah*, and in a Yard under Ground, and thin Walls of Clay, out-worn all the strong and specious buildings above it, and quietly rested under the drums and tramplings of three Conquests; What Prince can promise such diuturnity unto his Relics, or might not gladly say,

Sic ego componi versus in ossa velim?

Time which antiquates Antiquities, and hath an art to make dust of all things, hath yet spared these *minor* Monuments. In vain we hope to be known by open and visible Conservatories, when to be unknown was the means of their continuation, and obscurity their protection.

II

What Song the *Syrens* sang, or what name *Achilles* assumed when he hid himself among Women, though puzzling Questions, are not beyond all conjecture. What time the Persons of these Ossuaries entered the *famous Nations of the dead*, and slept with Princes and Counsellors, might admit a wide solution. But who were the proprietaries of these bones, or what bodies these ashes made up, were a question above Antiquarism. Not to be resolved by Man nor easily perhaps by Spirits, except we consult the Provincial Guardians or Tutelary Observators. Had they made as good provision for their Names, as they have done for their Relics, they had not so grossly erred in the art of perpetuation. But to subsist in bones, and be but Pyramidally extant, is a fallacy in duration. Vain ashes, which in the oblivion of Names, Persons, Times, Sexes, have found unto themselves a fruitless continuation, and only arise unto late posterity as Emblems of mortal vanities; Antidotes against pride, vainglory, and madding vices.

III

But the iniquity of oblivion blindly scattereth her Poppy, and deals with the memory of Men without distinction to merit of perpetuity. Who can but pity the Founder of the Pyramids? *Herostratus* lives that burnt the Temple of *Diana*, he is almost lost that built it; Time hath spared the Epitaph of *Adrian's* Horse, confounded that of himself. In vain we compute our felicities by the advantage of our good Names since bad have equal durations; and *Thersites* is like to live as long as *Agamemnon*. Who knows whether the best of Men be known? or whether there be not more remarkable Persons forgot, than any that stand remembered in the known account of Time? Without the favour of the everlasting Register the first Man had been as unknown as the last, and *Methuselah*'s long life had been his only Chronicle.

Oblivion is not to be hired: The greater part must be content to be as though they had not been, to be found in the Register of God, not in the Record of Man. Twenty-seven Names make up the first Story, and the recorded Names ever since contain not one living Century. The number of the dead long exceedeth all that shall live. The night of Time far surpasseth the day, and who knows when was the Equinox? Every hour adds unto that current Arithmetick, which scarce stands one moment. And since death must be the *Lucina* of life, and even *Pagans* could doubt whether thus to live were to die; Since our longest Sun sets at right descensions, and makes but Winter arches, and therefore it cannot be long before we lie down in darkness, and have our light in ashes; Since the Brother of death daily haunts us with dying *Memento's*, and Time that grows old itself bids us hope no long duration: Diuturnity is a dream and folly of expectation.

IV

There is nothing strictly immortal, but immortality; whatever hath no beginning may be confident of no end. . . But Man is a Noble Animal, splendid in Ashes, and pompous in the Grave, solemnizing Nativities and Deaths with equal lustre, nor omitting Ceremonies of bravery in the infamy of his Nature. . .

To subsist in lasting Monuments, to live in their productions, to exist in their names, and predicament of *Chimera's*, was large satisfaction unto old expectations, and made one part of their *Elysiums*. But all this is nothing in the Metaphysicks of true belief. To live, indeed, is to be again ourselves, which being not only an hope but an evidence in noble Believers, 'tis all one to lie in S. *Innocent's* Churchyard, as in the Sands of *Egypt*; Ready to be anything in the ecstasy of being ever, and as content with six Foot as the Moles of *Adrianus*.

Urn Burial

145 *The Mystic as Gardener*

BUT the Quincunx of Heaven runs low, and 'tis time to close the five ports of knowledge; We are unwilling to spin out our awaking thoughts into the phantasms of sleep, which often continueth precogitations ; making Cables of Cobwebs, and Wildernesses of handsome Groves. Beside, *Hippocrates* hath spoken so little, and the Oneirocritical Masters have left such frigid Interpretations from Plants, that there is little encouragement to dream of Paradise itself. Nor will the sweetest delight of Gardens afford much comfort in sleep ; wherein the dullness of that sense shakes hands with delectable odours ; and though in the Bed of *Cleopatra* can hardly with any delight raise up the ghost of a Rose.

Night, which *Pagan* Theology could make the Daughter of *Chaos*, affords no advantage to the description of order ; Although no lower than that Mass can we derive its Genealogy. All things began in order, so shall they end, and so shall they begin again ; according to the ordainer of order and mystical Mathematicks of the City of Heaven.

Though *Somnus* in *Homer* be sent to rouse up *Agamemnon*, I find no such effects in these drowsy approaches of sleep. To keep our eyes open longer were but to act our *Antipodes*. The Huntsmen are up in *America*, and they are already past their first sleep in *Persia*. But who can be drowsy at that hour which freed us from everlasting sleep? or have slumbering thoughts at that time, when sleep itself must end, and as some conjecture all shall awake again?

The Garden of Cyrus

146 *The Heroick Mind*

THE Heroical vein of Mankind runs much in the soldiery and courageous part of the World ; and in that form we oftenest find men above men. History is full of the gallantry of that Tribe ; and when we read their notable acts, we easily find what a difference there is between a life in *Plutarch* and in *Laertius*. Where true Fortitude dwells, Loyalty, Bounty, Friendship, and Fidelity may be found. A man may confide in persons constituted for noble ends, who dare do and suffer, and who have a hand to burn for their Country and their Friend. Small and creeping things are the product of petty Souls. He is like to be mistaken, who makes choice of a covetous Man for a Friend, or relieth upon the reed of narrow and poltron Friendship. Pitiful things are only to be found in the cottages of such Breasts; but bright Thoughts, clear Deeds, Constancy, Fidelity, Bounty, and generous Honesty are the Gems of noble Minds; wherein, to derogate from none, the true Heroick English Gentleman hath no Peer.

Christian Morals

THOMAS FULLER

1608–1661

147 *The True Gentleman*

HE is extracted from ancient and worshipful parentage. When a Pippin is planted on a Pippin stock, the fruit growing thence is called a Rennet, a most delicious Apple, as both by Sire and Dam well descended. Thus his blood must needs be well purified who is gently born on both sides.

If his birth be not, at least his qualities are generous. What if he cannot with the Hevenninghams of Suffolk count five-and-twenty knights of his family, or tell sixteen knights successively with the Tilneys of Norfolk, or with the Nauntons show where their Ancestors had seven hundred pounds a year before or at the Conquest:

yet he hath endeavoured by his own deserts to ennoble himself. Thus Valour makes him son to Caesar; Learning entitles him kinsman to Tully; and piety reports him nephew to godly Constantine.

He is not in his youth possessed with the great hopes of his possession. No flatterer reads constantly in his ears a survey of the lands he is to inherit. This hath made many boy's thoughts swell so great, they could never be kept in compass afterwards. Only his Parents acquaint him that he is the next undoubted Heir to correction, if misbehaving himself; and he finds no more favour from his Schoolmaster than his Schoolmaster finds diligence in him, whose rod respects persons no more than bullets are partial in a battle.

At the University he is so studious as if he intended learning for his profession. He knows well that cunning is no burthen to carry, as paying neither porterage by land nor poundage by sea. Yea, though to have land be a good First, yet to have learning is the surest Second, which may stand to it when the other may chance to be taken away.

At the Inns of Court he applies himself to learn the Laws of the kingdom. Object not, Why should a Gentleman learn law, who if he needeth it may have it for his money, and if he have never so much of his own he must but give it away? For what a shame is it for a man of quality to be ignorant of Solon in our Athens, of Lycurgus in our Sparta? Besides, law will help him to keep his own, and bestead his neighbours.

He is courteous and affable to his neighbours. As the sword of the best-tempered metal is most flexible, so the truly generous are most pliant and courteous in their behaviour to their inferiors.

He delights to see himself and his servants well mounted: therefore he loveth good Horsemanship.

He furnisheth and prepareth himself in peace against time of war; lest it be too late to learn when his skill is to be used. He approves himself courageous when brought to the trial, as well remembering the custom which is used at the Creation of Knights of the Bath, wherein the King's Master-Cook cometh forth, and presenteth his great knife to the new-made Knights, admonishing them to be faithful and valiant, otherwise he threatens them that that very knife is prepared to cut off their spurs.

If the Commission of the Peace finds him out, he faithfully discharges it. I say, Finds him out, for a publick Office is a guest which receives the best usage from them who never invited it. And though he declined the Place, the country knew to prize his worth, who would be ignorant of his own. He compounds many petty differences betwixt his neighbours, which are easier ended in his own Porch than in Westminster Hall; for many people think if once they have fetched a warrant from a Justice, they have given earnest to follow the suit, though otherwise the matter be so mean that the next night's sleep would have bound both parties to the peace, and made them as good friends as ever before.

Yet *He connives not at the smothering of punishable faults. If chosen a member of Parliament, he is willing to do his Country service.* If he be no rhetorician to raise affections (yea, *Mercury* was a greater speaker than *Jupiter* himself), he counts it great wisdom to be the good manager of Yea and Nay. The slow pace of his judgement is recompensed by the swift following of his affections, when his judgement is once soundly informed. And here we leave him in consultation, wishing him, with the rest of his honourable Society, all happy success.

The Holy State

148 *The Good Sea Captain*

CONCEIVE him now in a Man-of-war, with his letters of mart, well armed, victualled, and appointed, and see how he acquits himself.

The more power he hath, the more careful he is not to abuse it. Indeed, a Sea Captain is a King in the Island of a ship, supreme Judge, above appeal, in causes civil and criminal, and is seldom brought to an account in Courts of Justice on land for injuries done to his own men at sea.

He is careful in observing of the Lord's day. He hath a watch in his heart, though no bells in a steeple to proclaim that day by ringing to prayers.

He is as pious and thankful when a tempest is past, as devout when it is present: not clamorous to receive mercies, and tongue-tied to return thanks.

Escaping many dangers makes him not presumptuous to run into them.

In taking a prize he most prizeth the men's lives whom he takes; though some of them may chance to be Negroes or Savages. It is the custom of some to cast them overboard, and there is an end of them: for the dumb fishes will tell no tales. But the murder is not so soon drowned as the men. What! is a brother by half-blood no kin? A Savage hath God to his father by creation, though not the Church to his mother, and God will revenge his innocent blood.

But our Captain counts the image of God nevertheless his image cut in ebony as if done in ivory, and in the blackest Moors he sees the representation of the King of heaven.

In dividing the gains he wrongs none who took pains to get them. Not shifting off his poor mariners with nothing, or giving them only the garbage of the prize, and keeping all the flesh to himself. In time of peace he quietly returns home, and turns not to the trade of Pirates, who are the worst sea-vermin, and the devil's water-rats.

His voyages are not only for profit, but some for honour and knowledge; to make discoveries of new countries, imitating the worthy *Peter Columbus*. . .

Our Sea captain is likewise ambitious to perfect what the other began. He counts it a disgrace, seeing all mankind is one family, sundry countries but several rooms, that we who dwell in the parlour (so he counts Europe) should not know the outlodgings of the same house, and the world be scarce acquainted with itself before it be dissolved from itself at the day of judgement.

He daily sees and duly considers God's wonders in the deep.

The Holy State

149 *The Good Master of a College*

HIS learning, if beneath eminency, is far above contempt. Sometimes ordinary scholars make extraordinary good Masters. Every one who can play well on Apollo's harp cannot skilfully drive his chariot, there being a peculiar mystery of Government. Yea, as a little alloy makes gold to work the better, so, perchance, some dulness in a man makes him fitter to manage secular affairs; and those who have climbed up Parnassus but half way, better behold worldly business, as lying low and nearer to their sight, than such as have climbed to the top of the mount.

He not only keeps the Statutes in his study, but observes them. For the maintaining of them will maintain him, if he be questioned.

He is principal Porter, and chief Chapel-monitor. For where the Master keeps his chamber always, the scholars will keep theirs seldom, yea, perchance, may make all the walls of the college to be gates. As for out-lodgings (like galleries, necessary evils in populous Churches) he rather tolerates than approves them.

He winds up the Tenants to make good musick, but not to break them. Sure College-lands were never given to fat the Tenants and starve the scholars, but that both might comfortably subsist. Yea, generally I hear the Muses commended for the best Landladies, and a College-lease is accounted but as the worst kind of freehold.

He disdains to nourish dissension among the members of his house. Let Machiavel's Maxim, *Divide et regnabis*, if offering to enter into a College-gate, sink through the grate and fall down with the dirt. For besides that the fomenting of such discords agrees not with a good conscience, each party will watch advantages, and Pupils will often be made to suffer for their Tutors' quarrels.

He scorneth the plot to make only dunces Fellows, to the end he may himself command in chief: as thinking that they who know nothing will do anything, and so he shall be a figure amongst cyphers, a bee amongst drones. Yet oftentimes such Masters are justly met with, and they find by experience that the dullest horses are not easiest to be reined. But our Master endeavours so to order his elections, that every scholar may be fit to make a Fellow and every Fellow a Master.

The Holy State

150 *Wycliffe's Ashes*

HITHERTO the *Corpse* of *John Wickliffe* had quietly slept in his grave about *one and fourty years* after his death, till his *body* was reduced to *bones* and his *bones* almost to *dust*. . . But now such the *Spleen* of the *Council* of *Constance* . . . as they ordered his bones (with this charitable caution, if it may be discerned from the bodies of other faithful people) to be taken out of the ground and thrown farre off from any *Christian buriall*. In obedience hereunto *Richard Fleming Bishop* of *Lincolne Diocesan* of *Lutterworth* sent his *Officers* . . . to ungrave him accordingly. To *Lutterworth* they come, Sumner, *Commissarie Official*, *Chancellour*, *Proctors*, *Doctors*, and the *Servants* (so that the *Remnant* of the body would not hold out a *bone* amongst so many *hands*) take what was left out of the grave, and burnt them to ashes, and cast them into *Swift* a Neighbouring Brook running hard by. Thus this *Brook* hath convey'd his Ashes into *Avon* ; *Avon* into *Severn* ; Severn into the *narrow* Seas ; they, into the *main Ocean*. And thus the *Ashes* of *Wickliff* are the *Emblem* of his *Doctrine*, which now is dispersed all the World over.

Church History of Britain

JOHN MILTON

1608–1674

151 *Against Fugitive and Cloistered Virtue*

GOOD and evil we know in the field of this World grow up together almost inseparably; and the knowledge of good is so involved and interwoven with the knowledge of evil and in so many cunning resemblances hardly to be discerned, that those confused seeds which were imposed on *Psyche* as an incessant labour to cull out and sort asunder were not more intermixed. It was from out the rind of one apple tasted that the knowledge of good and evil as two twins cleaving together leapt forth into the World. And perhaps this is that doom which *Adam* fell into of knowing good and evil, that is to say of knowing good by evil. As therefore the state of man now is, what wisdom can there be to choose, what continence to forbeare, without the knowledge of evil? He that can apprehend and consider vice with all her baits and seeming pleasures, and yet abstain, and yet distinguish, and yet prefer that which is truly better, he is the true warfaring Christian. I cannot praise a fugitive and cloistered virtue, unexercised and unbreathed, that never sallies out and sees her adversary, but slinks out of the race, where that immortal garland is to be run for not without dust and heat. Assuredly we bring not innocence into the world, we bring impurity much rather: that which purifies us is trial, and trial is by what is contrary.

Areopagitica

152 *The Tyranny of Licensing*

IF we think to regulate Printing, thereby to rectify manners, we must regulate all recreations and pastimes, all that is delightful to man. No musick must be heard, no song be set or sung, but what is grave and *Dorick*. There must be licensing dancers, that no gesture, motion, or deportment be taught our youth but what by their allowance shall be thought honest; for such *Plato* was provided of. It will ask more than the work of twenty licencers to examine all the lutes, the violins, and the guitars in every house; they must not be suffered to prattle as they do, but must be licensed what they may say. And who shall silence all the airs and madrigals that whisper softness in chambers? The Windows also, and the *Balconies* must be thought on; there are shrewd books with dangerous Frontispieces set to sale; who shall prohibit them? shall twenty licencers? The villages also must have their visitors to inquire what lectures the bagpipe and the rebeck reads, even to the balladry and the gamut of every *municipal* fidler, for these are the Countryman's *Arcadia's* and his *Monte Mayors*... To sequester out of the world into *Atlantick* and *Eutopian* polities, which never can be drawn into use, will not mend our condition; but to ordain wisely as in this world of evil, in the midst whereof God hath placed us unavoidably.

Areopagitica

153 *Milton in Italy*

AND lest some should persuade ye, Lords and Commons, that these arguments of learned men's discouragement at this your order, are mere flourishes and not real, I could recount what I have seen and heard in other Countries, where this kind of inquisition tyrannizes; when I have sat among their learned men, for that honour I had, and been counted happy to be born in such a place of *Philosophic* freedom as they supposed England was, while themselves did nothing but bemoan the servile condition into which learning amongst them was brought; that this was it which had damped the glory of Italian wits, that nothing had been there written now these many years but flattery and fustian. There it was that I found and visited the famous *Galileo* grown old, a prisoner to the Inquisition, for thinking in Astronomy otherwise than the Franciscan and Dominican licencers thought. And though I knew that England then was groaning loudest under the Prelatical yoke, nevertheless I took it as a pledge of future happiness, that other Nations were so persuaded of her liberty.

Areopagitica

154 *The Profit of Free Speech to a Commonwealth*

FOR as in a body, when the blood is fresh, the spirits pure and vigorous not only to vital but to rational faculties and those in the acutest and the pertest operations of wit and subtlety, it argues in what good plight and constitution the body is, so when the cheerfulness of the people is so sprightly up, as that it has not only wherewith to guard well its own freedom and safety but to spare, and to bestow upon the solidest and sublimest points of controversy and new invention, it betokens us not degenerated, nor drooping to a fatal decay, but casting off the old and wrinkled skin of corruption to outlive these pangs and wax young again, entering the glorious ways of Truth and prosperous virtue destined to become great and honourable in these latter ages. Methinks I see in my mind a noble and puissant Nation rousing herself like a strong man after sleep, and shaking her invincible locks. Methinks I see her as an Eagle mewing her mighty youth, and kindling her undazzled eyes at the full midday beam, purging and unscaling her long abused sight at the fountain itself of heavenly radiance, while the whole noise of timorous and flocking birds, with those also that love the twilight, flutter about, amazed at what she means, and in their envious gabble would prognosticate a year of sects and schisms.

Areopagitica

155 *'Long Choosing'*

I

TIME serves not now, and perhaps I might seem too profuse to give any certain account of what the mind at home in the spacious circuits of her musing hath liberty to propose to her self, though of highest hope, and hardest attempting, whether that Epick form whereof the two poems of *Homer*, and those other two of *Virgil* and *Tasso* are a diffuse, and the book of *Job* a brief model: or whether the rules of *Aristotle* herein are strictly to be kept, or nature to be follow'd, which in them that know art, and use judgement is no transgression, but an inriching of art. And lastly what King or Knight before the conquest might be chosen in whom to lay the pattern of a Christian *Heroe*. And as *Tasso* gave to a Prince of *Italy* his choice whether he would command him to write of *Godfreys* expedition against the infidels, or *Belisarius* against the Gothes, or *Charlemain* against the Lombards; if to the instinct of nature and the imboldning of art ought may be trusted, and that there be nothing advers in our climat, or the fate of this age, it haply would be no rashnesse from an equal diligence and inclination to present the like offer in our own ancient stories. Or whether those Dramatick constitutions, wherein *Sophocles* and *Euripides* raigne, shall be found more doctrinal and exemplary to a Nation, the Scripture also affords us a divine pastoral Drama in the Song of *Solomon* consisting of two persons and a double *Chorus*, as *Origen* rightly judges. And the Apocalyps of Saint *Iohn* is the majestick image of a high and stately tragedy, shutting up and intermingling her solemn Scenes and Acts with a sevenfold *Chorus* of halleluja's and harping symphonies: and this my opinion the grave autority of *Pareus* commenting that book is sufficient to confirm. Or if occasion shall lead to imitate those magnifick Odes and Hymns wherein *Pindarus* and *Callimachus* are in most things worthy, some others in their frame judicious, in their matter most and end faulty: But those frequent songs throughout the law and prophets beyond all these, not in their divine argument alone, but in the very critical art of composition may be easily made appear over all the kinds of Lyrick poesy to be incomparable.

II

Neither do I think it shame to covnant with any knowing reader, that for some few yeers yet I may go on trust with him toward the payment of what I am now indebted, as being a work not to be rays'd from the heat of youth, or the vapours of wine, like that which flows at wast from the pen of some vulgar Amorist, or the trencher fury of a riming parasite, nor to be obtain'd by the invocation of Dame Memory and her Siren daughters, but by devout prayer to that eternall Spirit who can enrich with all utterance and knowledge, and sends out his Seraphim with the hallow'd fire of his Altar to touch and purify the lips of whom he pleases: to this must be added industrious and select reading, steddy observation, insight into all seemly and generous arts and affaires, till which in some measure be compast, at mine own peril and cost I refuse not to sustain this expectation from as many as are not loath to hazard so much credulity upon the best pledges that I can give them.

Reason of Church Government

EDWARD HYDE, EARL OF CLARENDON

1609–1674

156 *A Small Cloud in the North*

OF all the Princes of *Europe*, the King of *England* alone seemed to be seated upon that pleasant Promontory, that might safely view the tragick Sufferings of all his Neighbours about him, without any other Concernment, than what arose from his own princely Heart, and christian Compassion, to see such Desolation wrought by the Pride, and Passion, and Ambition of private Persons, supported by Princes, who knew not what themselves would have. His three Kingdoms flourishing in entire Peace, and universal Plenty; in Danger of nothing but their own

Surfeits; and his Dominions every Day enlarged, by sending out Colonies upon large, and fruitful Plantations; his strong Fleets commanding all Seas; and the numerous Shipping of the Nation bringing the Trade of the World into his Ports; nor could it with unquestionable Security be carried any whither else; and all these Blessings enjoyed, under a Prince of the greatest Clemency, and Justice, and of the greatest Piety, and Devotion, and the most indulgent to his Subjects, and most solicitous for their Happiness and Prosperity.

O fortunati nimium, bona si sua norint!

In this blessed Conjuncture, when no other Prince thought He wanted any Thing, to compass what He most desired to be possessed of, but the Affection and Friendship of the King of *England*; a small, scarce discernable Cloud arose in the North; which was shortly after attended with such a Storm, that never gave over raging, till it had shaken, and even rooted up the greatest, and tallest Cedars of the three Nations; blasted all its Beauty and Fruitfulness; brought its Strength to Decay, and its Glory to Reproach, and almost to Desolation; by such a Career, and Deluge of Wickedness, and Rebellion, as by not being enough foreseen, or, in Truth, suspected, could not be prevented.

Life, Written by Himself

157 *His Tribute to Cromwell*

HE was one of those Men, *quos vituperare ne inimici quidem possunt, nisi ut simul laudent*; whom his very Enemies could not condemn without commending him at the same time: for he could never have done half that mischief without great parts of Courage, Industry, and Judgement. And he must have had a wonderful understanding in the Natures and Humours of Men, and as great a dexterity in applying them; who, from a private and obscure birth (though of a good Family) without Interest of Estate, Alliance or Friendships, could raise himself to such a height, and compound and knead such opposite and contradictory tempers, humours, and interests into a consistence, that contributed to His designs, and to their own destruction; whilst himself grew insensibly powerful enough to cut off those by whom he had climbed, in the instant that they projected to demolish their own building. What Velleius Paterculus said of *Cinna* may very justly be said of Him, *ausum eum, quae nemo auderet bonus; perfecisse, quae a nullo, nisi fortissimo, perfici possent,* He attempted those things which no good Man durst have ventured on; and achieved those in which none but a valiant and great Man could have succeeded. Without doubt, no Man with more wickedness ever attempted anything, or brought to pass what he desired more wickedly, more in the face and contempt of Religion, and moral Honesty; yet wickedness as great as his could never have accomplish'd those trophies, without the assistance of a great Spirit, an admirable circumspection, and sagacity, and a most magnanimous resolution.

When he appeared first in the Parliament he seemed to have a Person in no degree gracious, no ornament of discourse, none of those Talents which use to reconcile the Affections of the Standers by: yet as he grew into Place and Authority, his parts seemed to be renewed, as if he had concealed Faculties, till he had occasion to use them; and when he was to act the part of a great Man, he did it without any indecency through the want of Custom.

A History of the Rebellion

158 *The Battle of Stamford Hill*

ON *Tuesday* the sixteenth of *May*, about five of the Clock in the Morning, they disposed themselves to their Work; having stood in their Armes all the Night. The Number of the Foot was about two thousand four hundred, which they divided into four Parts, and agreed on their several Provinces. The first was Commanded by the Lord *Mohun*, and Sir *Ralph Hopton*; who undertook to Assault the Camp on the South side. Next them, on the left hand, Sir *John Berkley*, and Sir *Bevil Greenvil* were to force their way. Sir *Nicholas Slanning*, and Colonel *Trevannion* were to Assault the North side; and, on the left hand, Colonel *Thomas Basset*, who was Major General of their Foot, and Colonel *William Godolphin* were to advance with Their Party; each Party having two pieces of Cannon to dispose as they found necessary: Colonel *John Digby* Commanding the Horse and Dragoons, being about five hundred, and stood upon a Sandy Common which had a way to the Camp, to take any advantage he could on the Enemy, if they Charged; otherwise, to be firm as a Reserve.

In this manner the Fight begun; the King's Forces pressing, with their utmost vigour, those four ways up the Hill, and the Enemies as obstinately defending their ground. The Fight continued with very doubtful success, till towards three of the Clock in the Afternoon; when word was brought to the Chief

Officers of the *Cornish*, that their Ammunition was spent to less than four Barrels of Powder; which (concealing the defect from the Soldiers) they resolved could only be supplied with Courage: and therefore, by Messengers to one another, they agreed to advance with their full Bodies, without making any more shot, till they reached the top of the Hill, and so might be upon even ground with the Enemy; wherein the Officers' Courage, and Resolution, was so well seconded by the Soldier, that they begun to get ground in all places; and the Enemy, in wonder of the Men, who out faced their shot with their Swords, to quit their Post. Major General *Chudleigh*, who ordered the Battle, failed in no part of a Soldier; and when he saw his Men recoile from less Numbers, and the Enemy in all places gaining the Hill upon him, himself advanced, with a good stand of Pikes, upon that Party which was led by Sir *John Berkley*, and Sir *Bevil Greenvil*; and Charged them so smartly, that he put them into disorder; Sir *Bevil Greenvil*, in the shock, being borne to the Ground, but quickly relieved by his Companion; they so reinforced the Charge, that having killed most of the Assailants, and dispersed the rest, they took the Major General Prisoner, after he had behaved himself with as much Courage, as a Man could do. Then the Enemy gave ground apace, insomuch as the four Parties, growing nearer and nearer as they ascended the Hill, between three and four of the Clock, they all met together upon one ground near the top of the Hill; where they embraced with unspeakable joy, each congratulating the others success, and all acknowledging the wonderful blessing of God; and being there possessed of some of the Enemies Cannon, they turned them upon the Camp, and advanced together to perfect their Victory. But the Enemy no sooner understood the loss of their Major General, but their hearts failed them; and being so resolutely pressed, and their ground lost, upon the security and advantage whereof they wholely depended, some of them threw down their Armes, and Others fled; dispersing themselves, and every Man shifting for himself: Their General, the Earl of *Stamford*, giving the example, who (having stood at a safe distance all the time of the Battle, environed with all the Horse, which in small Parties, though it is true their whole Number was not above six or seven score, might have done great mischief to the several Parties of Foot, who with so much difficulty scaled the steep Hill) as soon as he saw the day lost, and some said sooner, made all imaginable hast to *Exeter*, to prepare them for the condition they were shortly to expect.

A History of the Rebellion

159 *Character of Lord Falkland*

AS he was of a most incomparable gentleness, application, and even a demissness and submission to good, and worthy, and entire Men, so he was naturally (which could not but be more evident in his Place, which objected him to another conversation and intermixture, than his own election had done) *adversus malos injucundus*; and was so ill a dissembler of his dislike and disinclination to ill Men, that it was not possible for Such not to discern it. There was once, in the House of Commons, such a declared acceptation of the good Service an eminent Member had done to Them, and, as they said, to the whole

Kingdom, that it was moved, he being present, 'that the Speaker might, in the name of the whole House, give him thanks; and then, that every Member might, as a testimony of his particular acknowledgement, stir or move his hat towards him'; the which (though not ordered) when very many did, the Lord *Falkland* (who believed the Service itself not to be of that moment, and that an honorable and generous Person could not have stooped to it for any recompence) instead of moving his hat, stretched both his Arms out, and clasped his hands together upon the Crown of his hat, and held it close down to his head; that all Men might see how odious that flattery was to him, and the very approbation of the Person, though at that time most popular.

When there was any Overture, or hope of Peace, he would be more erect and vigorous, and exceedingly sollicitous to press anything which he thought might promote it; and sitting amongst his Friends, often, after a deep silence and frequent sighs, would, with a shrill and sad accent, ingeminate the word *Peace, Peace*; and would passionately profess, 'that the very agony of the War, and the view of the calamities and desolation the Kingdom did, and must endure, took his sleep from him, and would shortly break his heart'. This made some think, or pretend to think, 'that he was so much enamoured on Peace, that he would have been glad, the King should have bought it at any price', which was a most unreasonable Calumny. As if a Man that was himself the most punctual and precise in every circumstance that might reflect upon Conscience or Honour, could have wished the King to have committed a trespass against either.

A History of the Rebellion

JAMES HARRINGTON

1611–1677

160 *Oceana*

TO speak of the People in each of these Countries, this of *Oceana*, for so soft a one, is the most martial in the whole World. *Let States that aim at Greatness* (says VERULAMIUS) *take heed how their Nobility and Gentlemen multiply too fast, for that makes the common Subject grow to be a Peasant and base Swain driven out of heart, and in effect but a Gentleman's Labourer; just as you may see in Coppice Woods, if you leave the Staddels too thick, you shall never have clean Underwood, but Shrubs and Bushes: So in Countries if the Gentlemen be too many, the Commons will be base; and you will bring it to that at last, that not the hundredth Poll will be fit for a Helmet, specially as to the Infantry, which is the nerve of an Army, and so there will be great Population and little Strength. This of which I speak has been nowhere better seen than by comparing of* Oceana *and* France, *whereof* Oceana, *though far less in Territory and Population, has been nevertheless an overmatch, in regard the middle People of* Oceana *make good Soldiers, which the Peasants in* France *do not.* In which words VERULAMIUS (as MACHIAVEL has done before him) harps much upon a string which he has not perfectly tuned, and that is the *balance of Dominion or Property*: as it follows more plainly in his praise *of the profound and admirable device of* PANURGUS, *King of* Oceana, *in making Farms and Houses of Husbandry of a Standard; that is, maintained with such a proportion of Land to them, as may breed a Subject to live in convenient plenty, and no servile condition, and to keep the Plow in the hand of the owners, and not mere hirelings. And thus indeed*

9 *Staddels*) *trees left standing*

(says he) *you shall attain to* Virgil's *Character which he gives of ancient* Italy:

Terra potens armis atque ubere glebae.

But the Tillage bringing up a good Soldiery, brings up a good Commonwealth; which the Author in the praise of Panurgus did not mind, nor Panurgus in deserving that praise: for where the owner of the Plow comes to have the Sword too, he will use it in defence of his own; whence it has happened that the People of *Oceana* in proportion to their property have been always free. And the Genius of this Nation has ever had some resemblance with that of ancient *Italy*, which was wholly addicted to Commonwealths, and where *Rome* came to make the greatest account of her rustic Tribes, and to call her Consuls from the Plow; for in the way of Parliaments, which was the Government of this Realm, men of Country-lives have been still entrusted with the greatest Affairs, and the People have constantly had an aversion to the ways of the Court. Ambition loving to be gay, and to fawn, has been a Gallantry looked upon as having something in it of the Livery; and Husbandry, or the country way of Life, though of a grosser spinning, as the best stuff of a Commonwealth, according to Aristotle, such a one being the most obstinate Assertress of her Liberty, and the least subject to Innovation or Turbulency. Wherefore till the Foundations (as will be hereafter showed) were removed, this People was observed to be the least subject to Shakings and Turbulency of any: Whereas Commonwealths, upon which the City Life has had the stronger influence, as *Athens*, have seldom or never been quiet; but at the best are found to have injured their own business by over-doing it. Whence the Urban Tribes of *Rome*, consisting of the *Turba forensis*, and *Libertins* that had received their Freedom by manumission, were of no reputation in comparison of the Rustics. It is true, that with *Venice* it may seem to be otherwise, in regard the Gentlemen (for so are all such called as have a right to that Government) are wholly addicted to the City Life: but then the *Turba forensis*, the Secretaries, *Cittadini*, with the rest of the Populace, are wholly excluded. Otherwise a Commonwealth, consisting but of one City, would doubtless be stormy, in regard that Ambition would be every man's trade: but where it consists of a Country, the Plow in the hands of the owner finds him a better calling, and produces the most innocent and steady Genius of a Commonwealth, such as is that of *Oceana*.

Oceana

SIR THOMAS URQUHART

1611–1660

161 *Fay ce que Voudras*

ALL their life was spent not in lawes, statutes or rules, but according to their own free will and pleasure. They rose out of their beds, when they thought good: they did eat, drink, labour, sleep, when they had a minde to it, and were disposed for it. None did awake them, none did offer to constrain them to eat, drink, nor to do any other thing; for so had Gargantua established it. In all their rule, and strictest tie of their order, there was but this one clause to be observed,

DO WHAT THOU WILT.

Because men that are free, well-borne, well-bred, and conversant in honest companies, have naturally an instinct and spurre that prompteth them unto vertuous actions, and withdraws them from vice, which is called honour.

Translation of Rabelais, *Gargantua and Pantagruel*

162 *Gargantua to his Son, at Paris University*

BUT although my deceased father of happy memory Grangousier, had bent his best endeavours to make me profit in all perfection and Political knowledge, and that my labour and study was fully correspondent to, yea, went beyond his desire: neverthelesse, as thou mayest well understand, the time then was not so proper and fit for learning as it is at present, neither had I plenty of good masters such as thou hast had; for that time was darksome, obscured with clouds of ignorance, and savouring a little of the infelicity and calamity of the Gothes, who, whereever they set footing, destroyed all good literature, which in my age hath by the divine goodnesse been restored unto its former light and dignity, and that with such amendment and increase of the knowledge, that now hardly should I be admitted unto the first forme of the little Grammar-school-boyes: I say, I, who in my youthful dayes was (and that justly) reputed the most learned of that age; which I do not speak in vain boasting, although I might lawfully do it in writing unto thee, in verification whereof thou hast the authority of Marcus Tullius in his book of old age, and the sentence of Plutarch, in the book intituled, how a man may praise himself without envie: but to give thee an emulous encouragement to strive yet further.

Now is it that the mindes of men are qualified with all manner of discipline, and the old sciences revived, which for many ages were extinct : now it is, that the learned languages are to their pristine purity restored, viz. Greek (without which a man may be ashamed to account himself a scholar) Hebrew, Arabick, Chaldaean and Latine. Printing likewise is now in use, so elegant, and so correct, that better cannot be imagined, although it was found out but in my time by divine inspiration, as by a diabolical suggestion on the other side was the invention of Ordnance. All the world is full of knowing men, of most learned Schoolmasters, and vast Libraries : and it appears to me as a truth, that neither in Plato's time, nor Cicero's, nor Papinian's, there was ever such conveniency for studying, as we see at this day there is : nor must any adventure henceforward to come in publick, or present himself in company, that hath not been pretty well polished in the shop of Minerva : I see robbers, hangmen, free-booters, tapsters, ostlers, and such like, of the very rubbish of the people, more learned now, then the Doctors and Preachers were in my time.

What shall I say? the very women and children have aspired to this praise and celestial Manna of good learning.

Translation of Rabelais, *Gargantua and Pantagruel*

JEREMY TAYLOR, BISHOP OF DOWN AND CONNOR

1613–1667

163 *Against Bitterness of Zeal*

ANY Zeal is proper for Religion, but the zeal of the Sword and the Zeal of Anger ; this is *the Bitterness of Zeal*, and it is a certain Temptation to every

Man against his Duty ; for if the Sword turns Preacher, and dictates Propositions by Empire instead of Arguments, and engraves them in Men's Hearts with a Poignard, that it shall be Death to believe what I innocently and ignorantly am persuaded of, it must needs be unsafe to *try the Spirits*, to *try all Things*, to make inquiry ; and yet, without this Liberty, no Man can justify himself before *God* or Man, nor confidently say that his Religion is best ; since he cannot without a final Danger make himself to give a right Sentence, and to follow that which he finds to be best. This may ruin Souls by making Hypocrites, or careless and compliant against Conscience or without it ; but it does not save Souls, though peradventure it should force them to a good Opinion. This is *Inordination of Zeal* ; for Christ, by reproving St. Peter drawing his Sword even in the Cause of *Christ*, for his sacred and yet injured Person, saith *Theophylact*, 'teaches us not to use the Sword, though in the cause of *God* or for *God* himself'. . .

When *Abraham* sat at his Tent Door, according to his custom, waiting to entertain Strangers, he espied an old Man, stooping and leaning on his Staff, weary with Age and Travel, coming towards him, who was a hundred years of Age. He received him kindly, washed his Feet, provided Supper, caused him to sit down ; but observing that the Old man Eat and prayed not nor begged a Blessing on his Meat, he asked him why he did not worship the *God* of Heaven. The old man told him that he worshipped the Fire only, and acknowledged no other *God*. At which answer *Abraham* grew so zealously angry that he thrust the old Man out of his Tent, and exposed him to all the Evils of the Night and an unguarded Condition. When the old Man was gone, *God* called to *Abraham* and asked him where the Stranger was? He replied, I thrust him away because he did not worship thee. *God* answered him, 'I have suffered him these hundred Years, although he dishonoured me: and couldst not thou endure him one Night?'

Sermons

164 *Vicisti, Galilæe!*

THAT such a Religion, in such a Time, by the Sermons and Conduct of Fishermen, Men of mean breeding and illiberal Arts, should so speedily triumph over the Philosophy of the World, and the Arguments of the Subtle, and the Sermons of the Eloquent; the Power of Princes and the Interests of States, the Inclinations of Nature and the Blindness of Zeal, the Force of Custom and the Solicitation of Passions, the Pleasures of Sin and the busy Arts of the Devil; that is against Wit and Power, Superstition and Wilfulness, Fame and Money, Nature and Empire, which are all the causes in this World that can make a Thing impossible; this, this is to be ascribed to the Power of *God*, and is the great Demonstration of the Resurrection of *Jesus*. Every thing was an Argument for it, and improved it: no objection could hinder it, no Enemies destroy it, whatsoever was for them, it made the Religion to increase; whatsoever was against them, made it to increase; Sun-shine and Storms, fair Weather or foul, it was all one as to the event of Things: for they were Instruments in the Hands of *God*, who could make what himself should choose to be the product of any cause; so that if the *Christians* had Peace, they went abroad and brought in Converts;

if they had no Peace, but Persecution, the Converts came in to them. In prosperity they allured and enticed the World by the Beauty of Holiness; in Affliction and Trouble they amazed all Men with the splendour of their Innocence and the Glories of their Patience; and quickly it was that the world became Disciple to the glorious Nazarene, and men could no longer doubt of the Resurrection of Jesus, when it became so demonstrated by the certainty of them that saw it, and the Courage of them that died for it, and the Multitude of them that believed it.

Sermon preached at the Funeral of the Lord Primate

165 *How Amiable are Thy Tabernacles*

WE have not only felt the Evils of an intestine War, but *God* hath smitten us in our Spirit. But I delight not to observe the Correspondencies of such sad Accidents. . . I will therefore deny leave to my own Affections to ease themselves by complaining of Others; I shall only crave leave that I may remember *Jerusalem*, and call to Mind the Pleasures of the Temple, the Order of her Services, the Beauty of her Buildings, the Sweetness of her Songs, the Decency of her Ministrations, the Assiduity and Economy of her Priests and Levites, the Daily Sacrifice, and that Eternal Fire of Devotion that went not out by Day nor by Night; these were the Pleasures of our Peace; and there is a remanent Felicity in the very Memory of those spiritual Delights which we then enjoyed as Antepasts of Heaven, and consignations to an Immortality of Joys. And it may be so again when it shall please *God*, who hath the Hearts of all Princes in his Hand, and turneth them as the Rivers of Waters; and when Men will consider the invaluable Loss that is consequent, and the Danger of Sin that is appendant, to the destroying such Forms of Discipline and Devotion in which *God* was purely worshipped, and the Church was edified, and the People instructed to great Degrees of Piety, Knowledge and Devotion.

Polemical Discourses

166 *Marriage*

MARRIAGE is a School and Exercise of Virtue; and though Marriage hath Cares, yet the Single Life hath Desires, which are more troublesome and more dangerous, and often end in Sin; while the Cares are but Instances of Duty, and Exercises of Piety; and therefore if Single Life hath more Privacy of Devotion, yet Marriage hath more Necessities and more Variety of it, and is an Exercise of more Graces.

Marriage is the proper Scene of Piety and Patience, of the Duty of Parents and the Charity of Relations; here Kindness is spread Abroad, and Love is united and made firm as a Centre; Marriage is the Nursery of Heaven. The Virgin sends Prayers to *God*; but she carries but one soul to him: but the State of Marriage fills up the Number of the Elect, and hath in it the Labour of Love, and the Delicacies of Friendship, the Blessing of Society, and the Union of Hands and Hearts. It hath in it less of Beauty, but more of Safety than the Single Life; it hath more Care, but less Danger; it is more Merry, and more Sad; is fuller of Sorrows, and fuller of Joys: it lies under more Burdens, but is supported by all the Strengths of Love and Charity, and those Burdens are delightful.

Sermons: The Marriage Ring

167 *The Husband*

THERE is nothing can please a Man without Love; and if a Man be weary of the Wise discourses of the Apostles, and of the Innocency of an even and private Fortune, or hates Peace or a Fruitful Year, he hath reaped Thorns and Thistles from the choicest Flowers of *Paradise*: for nothing can sweeten Felicity itself but Love. No Man can tell but he that loves his Children how many delicious Accents makes a Man's Heart dance in the pretty Conversation of those dear Pledges: their Childishness, their Stammering, their little Angers, their Innocence, their Imperfections, their Necessities, are so many Emanations of Joy and Comfort to him that delights in their Persons and Society; but he that loves not his Wife and Children feeds a Lioness at Home, and broods a Nest of Sorrows; and Blessing itself cannot make him happy: so that all the Commandments of *God* enjoining a Man to love his Wife are nothing but so many Necessities and Capacities of Joy. She that is loved is safe, and he that loves is joyful.

Sermons: The Marriage Ring

ROBERT LEIGHTON, ARCHBISHOP OF GLASGOW

1611–1684

168 *Quia omnis caro ut foenum*

THERE is indeed a great deal of seeming difference betwixt the outward conditions of life amongst men. Shall the rich and honourable and beautiful and healthful go in together, under the same name, with the baser and unhappier part, the poor, wretched sort of the world, who seem to be born for nothing but sufferings and miseries? At least, hath the wise no advantage beyond the fools? Is all grass? Make you no distinction? No; *all is grass*, or, if you will have some other name, be it so, once this is true, that all flesh is grass; and if that glory which shines so much in your eyes must have a difference, then this is all it can have—it is but *the flower* of that same grass; somewhat above the common grass in gayness, a little comelier, and better apparelled than it, but partaker of its frail and fading nature; it hath no privilege nor immunity that way; yea, of the two, it is the less durable, and usually shorter lived; at the best it decays with it: *The grass withereth, and the flower thereof falleth away.*

Commentary on the First Epistle of St. Peter

GEORGE THORNLEY

b. 1614

169 *The Grasshopper*

WHILE he was muttering this passion, a grasshopper that fled from a swallow took sanctuary in *Chloe's* bosom. And the pursuer could not take her, but her wing by reason of her close pursuit slapped the girl upon the cheek. And she not knowing what was done cried out, and started from her sleep. But when she saw the swallow flying near by and *Daphnis* laughing at her fear, she began to give it over and rub her eyes that yet would be sleeping. The grasshopper sang out of her bosom, as if her suppliant were now giving thanks for the protection. Therefore *Chloe* again squeaked out; but *Daphnis* could not hold laughing, nor pass the opportunity to put his hand into her bosom and draw forth friend Grasshopper, which still did sing even in his hand. When *Chloe* saw it she was pleased and kissed it, and took and put it in her bosom again, and it prattled all the way.

Translation of Longus, *Daphnis and Chloe*

170 *The Nightingales*

IT was now the beginning of spring, the snow melting, the earth uncovering herself, and the grass growing green, when the other shepherds drove out their flocks to pasture, and *Chloe* and *Daphnis* before the rest, as being servants to a greater shepherd. And forthwith they took their course up to the *Nymphs* and that cave, and thence to *Pan* and his pine; afterwards to their own oak, where they sat down to look to their flocks and kiss each other. They sought about for flowers too to crown the statues of the Gods. The soft breath of Zephyrus, and the warm Sun, had but now brought them forth; but there were then to be found the violet, the daffodil, the anagall, with the other primes and dawnings of the spring. And when they had crowned the statues of the Gods with them, they made a libation with new milk, *Chloe* from the sheep and *Daphnis* from the goats. They paid too the first-fruits of the pipe, as it were to provoke and challenge the nightingales with their music and song. The nightingales answered softly from the groves, and as if they remembered their long intermitted song, began by little and little to jug and warble their *Tereus* and *Itys* again.

Translation of Longus, *Daphnis and Chloe*

18 *anagall*) *pimpernel*

HENRY MORE

1614–1687

171 *The World-Comedy*

THE Affairs of this World are like a curious, but intricately contrived Comedy; and we cannot judge of the Tendency of what is Past, or acting at Present, before the Entrance of the last Act, which shall bring in *Righteousness* in triumph; who, though she hath abided many a Brunt, and has been very cruelly and despitefully used hitherto in the World, yet at last, according to our Desires, we shall see the Knight overcome the Giant. For what is the Reason we are so much pleased with the reading Romances and the Fictions of the Poets, but that here, as *Aristotle* says, Things are set down as they should be; but in the true History hitherto of the World, Things are recorded indeed as they are, but it is but a Testimony, that they have not been as they should be? Wherefore, in the Upshot of all, when we shall see that come to pass that so mightily pleases us in the reading the most ingenious Plays and heroick Poems, that long afflicted Virtue at last comes to the Crown, the Mouth of all Unbelievers must be for ever stopped. And for my own Part, I doubt not but that it shall so come to pass in the Close of the World. But impatiently to call for Vengeance upon every Enormity before that Time, is rudely to overturn the Stage before the entrance into the fifth Act, out of Ignorance of the Plot of the Comedy; and to prevent the Solemnity of the general Judgement by more paltry and particular Executions.

Divine Dialogues

EDMUND LUDLOW

1617–1692

172 *The Lying-in-State of Oliver Cromwell*

ONE of the first acts of the new Government was to order the funeral of the late usurper; and the Council having resolved that it should be very magnificent, the care of it was referred to a Committee of them, who, sending for Mr. *Kinnersly*, master of the Wardrobe, desired him to find out some precedent by which they might govern themselves in this important affair. After examination of his books and papers Mr. *Kinnersly*, who was suspected to be inclined to Popery, recommended to them the solemnities used upon the like occasion for *Philip* the Second, King of *Spain*, who had been represented to be in Purgatory for about two months. In the like manner was the body of this great Reformer laid in *Somerset-house*: the apartment was hung with black, the daylight was excluded, and no other but that of wax tapers to be seen. This scene of Purgatory continued till the first of *November*, which being the day preceding that commonly called *All Souls*, he was removed into the great Hall of the said House, and represented in *effigy*, standing on a bed of crimson velvet covered with a gown of the like coloured velvet, a sceptre in his hand, and a crown on his head. That part of the Hall wherein the Bed stood was railed in, and the rails and ground within them covered with crimson velvet. Four or five hundred candles set in flat shining candlesticks were so placed round near the roof of the hall that the light they gave seemed like the rays of the Sun: by all which he was represented to be now in a state of glory. This folly and profusion so far provoked the

People that they threw dirt in the night on his Escutcheon, that was placed over the great gate of *Somerset-house*. I purposely omit the rest of the Pageantry, the great number of persons that attended on the body, the procession to *Westminster*, the vast expense in Mourning, the state and magnificence of the Monument erected for him, with many other things that I care not to remember.

Memoirs

ABRAHAM COWLEY

1618–1667

173 *Of Solitude*

THE truth of the matter is, that neither he who is a Fop in the world, is a fit man to be alone; nor he who has set his heart much upon the world, though he have never so much understanding; so that Solitude can be well fitted and set right but upon a very few persons. They must have enough knowledge of the World to see the vanity of it, and enough Virtue to despise all Vanity; if the Mind be possessed with any Lust or Passions a man had better be in a Fair than in a Wood alone. They may, like petty Thieves, cheat us perhaps, and pick our pockets in the midst of company, but like Robbers they use to strip and bind, or murder us when they catch us alone. This is but to retreat from Men, and fall into the hands of Devils. 'Tis like the punishment of Parricides among the *Romans*, to be sowed into a Bag with an Ape, a Dog, and a Serpent. The first work therefore that a man must do to make himself capable of the good of Solitude is the very Eradication of all Lusts, for how is it possible for a Man to enjoy himself while his Affections are tied to things without Himself? In the second place, he must learn the Art and get the Habit of Thinking; for this, too, no less than well speaking, depends upon much practice, and Cogitation is the thing which distinguishes the Solitude of a God from a wild Beast. Now because the soul of Man is not by its own Nature or observation furnished with sufficient Materials to work upon, it is necessary for it to have continual recourse to Learning and Books for fresh supplies, so that the solitary Life will grow indigent, and be ready to starve without them; but if once we be throughly engaged in the Love of Letters, instead of being wearied with the length of any day we shall only complain of the shortness of our whole Life.

O vita, stulto longa, sapienti brevis!

O Life, long to the Fool, short to the Wise!

The first Minister of State has not so much business in public as a wise man has in private; if the one have little leisure to be alone, the other has less leisure to be in company; the one has but part of the affairs of one Nation, the other all the works of God and Nature under his consideration. There is no saying shocks me so much as that which I hear very often, That a man does not know how to pass his Time. 'Twould have been but ill-spoken by *Methusalem* in the Nine hundred sixty-ninth year of his Life; so far it is from us, who have not time enough to attain to the utmost perfection of any part of any Science, to have cause to complain that we are forced to be idle for want of work. But this, you'll say, is work only for the Learned; others are not capable either of the employments or divertisements that arrive from

Letters. I know they are not, and therefore cannot much recommend Solitude to a man totally illiterate.

Essays

174 *Of Himself*

As far as my Memory can return back into my past Life, before I knew, or was capable of guessing what the world, or glories, or business of it were, the natural affections of my soul gave me a secret bent of aversion from them, as some Plants are said to turn away from others, by an Antipathy imperceptible to themselves and inscrutable to man's understanding. Even when I was a very young Boy at School, instead of running about on Holidays and playing with my fellows, I was wont to steal from them, and walk into the fields, either alone with a Book, or with some one Companion, if I could find any of the same temper. I was then, too, so much an Enemy to all constraint, that my Masters could never prevail on me, by any perswasions or encouragements, to learn without Book the common rules of Grammar, in which they dispensed with me alone, because they found I made a shift to do the usual exercise out of my own reading and observation. That I was then of the same mind as I am now (which I confess, I wonder at myself) may appear by the latter end of an Ode, which I made when I was but thirteen years old, and which was then printed with many other Verses. . .

You may see by it I was even then acquainted with the Poets (for the Conclusion is taken out of *Horace*); and perhaps it was the immature and immoderate love of them which stamped first, or rather engraved, these Characters in me. They were like Letters cut into the Bark of a young Tree, which with the Tree still grow proportionably. But how this love came to be produced in me so early is a hard question. I believe I can tell the particular little chance that filled my head first with such Chimes of Verse, as have never since left ringing there: for I remember when I began to read, and to take some pleasure in it, there was wont to lie in my Mother's Parlour (I know not by what accident, for she herself never in her life read any Book but of Devotion), but there was wont to lie *Spencers* Works; this I happened to fall upon, and was infinitely delighted with the Stories of the Knights, and Giants, and Monsters, and brave Houses, which I found everywhere there (though my understanding had little to do with all this), and by degrees with the tinkling of the Rhyme and Dance of the Numbers, so that I think I had read him all over before I was twelve years old, and was thus made a Poet as irremediably as a Child is made an Eunuch.

Essays

175 *Fallentis semita vitae*

I LOVE and commend a true good Fame, because it is the shadow of Virtue; not that it doeth any good to the Body which it accompanies, but 'tis an efficacious shadow, and like that of St. *Peter* cures the Diseases of others. The best kind of Glory, no doubt, is that which is reflected from Honesty, such as was the Glory of *Cato* and *Aristides*, but it was harmful to them both, and is seldom beneficial to any man whilst he lives; what it is to him after his death I cannot say, because I love not *Philosophy* merely notional and conjectural, and no man who has made the Experiment has been so kind as to come back to inform us. Upon the whole matter, I account a person who has a moderate Mind and Fortune, and lives in the conversation of two or three agreeable friends, with little commerce in the world besides, who is esteemed well enough by his few neighbours that know him, and is truly irreproachable by anybody, and so after a healthful quiet life, before the great inconveniences of old age, goes more silently out of it than he came in (for I would not have him so much as Cry in the *Exit*), this Innocent Deceiver of the world, as *Horace* calls him, this *Muta persona*, I take to have been more happy in his Part than the greatest Actors that fill the Stage with show and noise, nay, even than *Augustus* himself, who asked with his last breath, Whether he had not played his *Farce* very well.

Essays

JOHN EVELYN

1620–1706

176 *On his Plan of a Garden Book*

Co. Garden, Lond. 28 Jan. [1657–8].

SIR, I return you a thousand acknowledgements for the papers which you transmitted me, and I will render you this account of my present undertaking. The truth is, that which imported me to discourse on this subject after this sort was the many defects which I encountered in books and in gardens, wherein neither words nor cost had been wanting, but judgement very much; and though I cannot boast of my science in this kind, as both unbecoming my years and my small experience, yet I esteemed it pardonable at least, if in doing my endeavour to rectify some mistakes, and advancing so useful and innocent a divertisement, I made some essay, and cast in my symbol with the rest. . . . The model, which I perceive you have seen, will abundantly testify my abhorrency of those painted and formal projections of our cockney gardens and plots, which appear like gardens of paste-board and marchpane, and smell more of paint than of flowers and verdure: our drift is a noble, princely, and universal *Elysium*, capable of all the amenities that can naturally be introduced into gardens of pleasure, and such as may stand in competition with all the august designs and stories of this nature, either of ancient or modern times; yet so as to become useful and significant to the least pretences and faculties. We will endeavour to show how the air and genius of gardens operate upon human spirits towards virtue and sanctity, I mean in a remote, preparatory, and instrumental working. How caves, grots, mounts, and irregular ornaments of gardens do contribute to contemplative and philosophical enthusiasm; how *elysium*, *antrum*, *nemus*, *paradysus*, *hortus*, *lucus*, &c., signify all of them *rem sacram et divinam*; for these expedients do influence the soul and spirits of man, and prepare them for converse with good angels; besides which, they contribute to the less abstracted pleasures, philosophy natural and longevity; and I would have not only the eulogies and effigy of the ancient and famous garden heroes, but a society of the *paradisi cultores*, persons of ancient simplicity, Paradisean and Hortulan saints, to be a society of learned and ingenuous men, such as Dr. *Browne*, by whom we might hope to redeem the time that has been lost in pursuing *Vulgar Errours* and still propagating them, as so many bold men do yet presume to do. Were it to be hoped, *inter hos armorum strepitus*, and in so general a catalysis of integrity, interruption of peace and propriety, the hortulan pleasures, these innocent, pure, and useful diversions might enjoy the least encouragement, whilst brutish and ambitious persons seek themselves in the ruins of our miserable yet dearest country, *quis talia fando*—?

Letter to Sir Thomas Browne

177 *Galley-Slaves*

WE went to visit the Galleys, being about twenty-five; the Captain of the *Galley Royal* gave us most courteous entertainment in his cabin, the slaves in the interim playing both loud and soft music very rarely. Then he showed us how he commanded their motions with a nod and his whistle, making them row out. The spectacle was to me new and strange, to see so many hundreds of miserably naked persons, having their heads shaven close and having only high red bonnets, a pair of coarse canvas drawers, their whole backs and legs naked, doubly chained about their middle and legs, in couples, and made fast to their seats, and all commanded in a trice by an imperious and cruel seaman. One Turk he much favoured, who waited on him in his cabin, but with no other dress than the rest, and a chain locked about his leg but not coupled. This galley was richly carved and gilded, and most of the rest were very beautiful. After bestowing something on the slaves, the captain sent a band of them to give us music at dinner where we lodged. I was amazed to contemplate how these miserable catiffs lie in their galley crowded together, yet there was hardly one but had some occupation by which, as leisure and calms permitted, they get some little money, insomuch as some of them have, after many years of cruel servitude, been able to purchase their liberty. Their rising forward and falling back at their oar is a miserable spectacle, and the noise of their chains with the roaring of the beaten waters has something of strange and fearful to one unaccustomed to it. They are ruled and chastised by strokes on their backs and soles of their feet on the least disorder, and without the least humanity; yet are they cheerful and full of knavery.

Diary

178 *The Great Fire*

SEPT. 7. I went this morning on foot from *Whitehall* as far as *London Bridge*, through the late *Fleet Street*, *Ludgate Hill*, by *St. Paul's*, *Cheapside*, *Exchange*, *Bishopsgate*, *Aldersgate*, and out to *Moorfields*, thence through *Cornhill*, &c., with extraordinary difficulty, clambering over heaps of yet smoking rubbish, and frequently mistaking where I was. The ground under my feet so hot, that it even burnt the soles of my shoes. In the meantime his Majesty got to the *Tower* by water, to demolish the houses about the graff, which being built entirely about it, had they taken fire and attacked the *White Tower* where the magazine of powder lay, would undoubtedly not only have beaten down and destroyed all the bridge, but sunk and torn the vessels in the river, and rendered the demolition beyond all expression for several miles about the country.

At my return I was infinitely concerned to find that goodly Church *St. Paul's* now a sad ruin, and that

22 *graff)* *wharf*

beautiful portico (for structure comparable to any in Europe, as not long before repaired by the late King) now rent in pieces, flakes of vast stone split asunder, and nothing remaining entire but the inscription in the architrave, showing by whom it was built, which had not one letter of it defaced. It was astonishing to see what immense stones the heat had in a manner calcined, so that all the ornaments, columns, freizes, capitals, and projectures of massy *Portland* stone flew off, even to the very roof, where a sheet of lead covering a great space (no less than 6 acres by measure) was totally melted; the ruins of the vaulted roof falling broke into *St. Faith's*, which being filled with the magazines of books belonging to the *Stationers*, and carried thither for safety, they were all consumed, burning for a week following. It is also observable that the lead over the altar at the East end was untouched, and among the divers monuments, the body of one Bishop remained entire.

Thus lay in ashes that most venerable Church, one of the most ancient pieces of early piety in the Christian world, besides near 100 more. The lead, iron-work, bells, plate, &c., melted; the exquisitely wrought *Mercers' Chapel*, the sumptuous *Exchange*, the august fabric of *Christ Church*, all the rest of the *Companies' Halls*, splendid buildings, arches, entries, all in dust; the fountains dried up and ruined, whilst the very waters remained boiling; the voragos of subterranean cellars, wells, and dungeons, formerly warehouses, still burning in stench and dark clouds of smoke, so that in five or six miles traversing about, I did not see one load of timber unconsumed, nor many stones but what were calcined white as snow. The people who now walked about the ruins appeared like men in some dismal desert, or rather in some great City laid waste by a cruel enemy; to which was added the stench that came from some poor creatures bodies, beds, and other combustible goods. Sir *Tho. Gressham's* statue, though fallen from its nich in the *Royal Exchange*, remained entire, when all those of the Kings since the Conquest were broken to pieces; also the standard in *Cornhill*, and *Queen Elizabeth's* effigies, with some arms on *Ludgate*, continued with but little detriment, whilst the vast iron chains of the *City* streets, hinges, bars and gates of prisons were many of them melted and reduced to cinders by the vehement heat.

Nor was I yet able to pass through any of the narrower streets, but kept the widest; the ground and air, smoke and fiery vapour, continued so intense that my hair was almost singed, and my feet unsufferably surbated. The by-lanes and narrower streets were quite filled up with rubbish, nor could one have possibly known where he was, but by the ruins of some Church or Hall, that had some remarkable tower or pinnacle remaining. I then went towards Islington and *Highgate*, where one might have seen 200,000 people of all ranks and degrees dispersed and lying along by their heaps of what they could save from the fire, deploring their loss, and though ready to perish for hunger and destitution, yet not asking one penny for relief, which to me appeared a stranger sight than any I had yet beheld. His Majesty and Council indeed took all imaginable care for their relief by proclamation for the country to come in and refresh them with provisions.

Diary

17 *surbated*) *made sore*

LUCY HUTCHINSON

b. 1620

179 *A Puritan Courtship*

HE therefore went to Richmond, where he found a great deal of good young company, and many ingenuous persons that, by reason of the court, where the young princes were bred, entertained themselves in that place, and had frequent resort to the house where Mr. *Hutchinson* tabled. . . In the same house with him there was a younger daughter of Sir *Allen Apsley*, late lieutenant of the *Tower*, tabled for the practice of her lute, till the return of her mother, who was gone into *Wiltshire* for the accomplishment of a treaty that had been made some progress in, about the marriage of her elder daughter with a gentleman of that country, out of which my lady herself came, and where her brothers, Sir *John St. John* and Sir *Edward Hungerford*, living in great honour and reputation, had invited her to a visit of them. This gentlewoman, that was left in the house with Mr. *Hutchinson*, was a very child, her elder sister being at that time scarcely past it; but a child of such pleasantness and vivacity of spirit, and ingenuity in the quality she practised, that Mr. *Hutchinson* took pleasure in hearing her practise, and would fall in discourse with her. She having the keys of her mother's house, some half a mile distant, would sometimes ask Mr. *Hutchinson*, when she went over, to walk along with her. One day when he was there, looking upon an odd by-shelf in her sister's closet, he found a few Latin books; asking whose they were, he was told they were her elder sister's; whereupon, inquiring more after her, he began first to be sorry she was gone, before he had seen her, and gone upon such an account that he was not likely to see her. Then he grew to love to hear mention of her, and the other gentlewomen who had been her companions used to talk much to him of her, telling him how reserved and studious she was, and other things which they esteemed no advantage. But it so much inflamed Mr. *Hutchinson's* desire of seeing her, that he began to wonder at himself, that his heart, which had ever had so much indifferency for the most excellent of womankind, should have such strong impulses towards a stranger he never saw; and certainly it was of the Lord (though he perceived it not), who had ordained him, through so many various providences, to be yoked with her in whom he found so much satisfaction. There scarcely passed any day but some accident or some discourse still kept alive his desire of seeing this gentlewoman; although the mention of her, for the most part, was inquiries whether she had yet accomplished the marriage that was in treaty. . .

One day, having been invited by one of the ladies of that neighbourhood to a noble treatment at *Sion Garden*, which a courtier, that was her servant, had made for her and whom she would bring, Mr. *Hutchinson*, Mrs. *Apsley*, and Mr. *Coleman's* daughter were of the party, and having spent the day in several pleasant divertisements, at evening when they were at supper, a messenger came to tell Mrs. *Apsley* her mother was come. She would immediately have gone, but Mr. *Hutchinson*, pretending civility to conduct her home, made her stay till the supper was ended, of which he ate no more, now only longing for that sight which he had with such perplexity expected. This at length he obtained; but his heart, being prepossessed with his own fancy, was not free to discern how little there was in her to answer so great an expectation. She was not ugly in a careless riding-habit, she had a melancholy negligence both of herself and others, as if she neither affected to please others, nor took notice of anything before her; yet, in spite of all her indifferency, she was surprised with some unusual liking in her soul when she saw this gentleman, who had hair, eyes, shape, and countenance enough to beget love in any one at the first, and these set off with a graceful and generous mien, which promised an extraordinary person. He was at that time, and indeed always very neatly habited, for he wore good and rich clothes, and had a variety of them, and had them well suited and every way answerable; in that little thing, showing both good judgment and great generosity, he equally becoming them and they him, which he wore with such unaffectedness and such neatness as do not often meet in one.

Although he had but an evening sight of her he had so long desired, and that at disadvantage enough for her; yet the prevailing sympathy of his soul made him think all his pains well paid, and this first did whet his desire to a second sight, which he had by accident the next day, and to his joy found that she was wholly disengaged from that treaty, which he so much feared had been accomplished; he found withal, that though she was modest, she was accostable, and willing to entertain his acquaintance. This soon passed into a mutual friendship between them, and though she innocently thought nothing of love, yet was she glad to have acquired such a friend, who had wisdom and virtue enough to be trusted with her councils, for she was then much perplexed in mind. Her mother and friends had a great desire she should marry, and were displeased that she refused many offers which they thought advantageous enough ; she was obedient, loth to displease them, but more herself, in marrying such as she could find no inclination to. . . Mr. *Hutchinson*, on the other side, having been told, and seeing how she shunned all other men, and how civilly she entertained him, believed that a secret power had wrought a mutual inclination between them, and daily frequented her mother's house, and had the opportunity of conversing with her in those pleasant walks, which, at that sweet season of the spring, invited all the neighbouring inhabitants to seek their joys ; where, though they were never alone, yet they had every day opportunity for converse with each other, which the rest shared not in, while every one minded their own delights. . .

He, in the meanwhile, prosecuted his love with so much discretion, duty, and honour, that at the length, through many difficulties, he accomplished his design. I shall pass by all the little amorous relations, which, if I would take the pains to relate, would make a true history of a more handsome management of love than the best romances describe ; but these are to be forgotten as the vanities of youth, not worthy of mention among the greater transactions of his life. There is this only to be recorded, that never was there a passion more ardent and less idolatrous ; he loved her better than his life, with inexpressible tenderness and kindness, had a most high obliging esteem of her, yet still considered honour, religion, and duty above her, nor ever suffered the intrusion of such a dotage as should blind him from marking her imperfections. . . and thus indeed he soon made her more equal to him than he found her; for she was a very faithful mirror, reflecting truly, though but dimly, his own glories upon him, so long as he was present; but she, that was nothing before his inspection gave her a fair figure, when he was removed, was only filled with a dark mist, and never could again take in any delightful object, nor return any shining representation. The greatest excellency she had was the power of apprehending and the virtue of loving his; so as his shadow she waited on him everywhere, till he was taken into that region of light which admits of none, and then she vanished into nothing.

Memoirs of Colonel Hutchinson

HENRY VAUGHAN

1622–1695

180 *Finis rerum*

WHAT is become now of these great *Merchants of the earth*, and where is the fruit *of all their labours under the Sun*? Why, truly they are *taken out of the way as all others, and they are cut off as the tops of the eares of corn.* Their dwelling is in the dust, and as for their place here, it lies waste, and is not known: *Nettles and Brambles come up in it, and the Owl and the Raven dwell in it.* But if you will visit them at their *long homes*, and knock at those *desolate doors*, you shall find some remains of them, a heap of loathsomeness and corruption. O miserable and sad mutations! Where is now their *pompous* and *shining train*? Where are their *triumphs*, *fireworks*, *and feasts*, with all the *ridiculous tumults* of a *popular, prodigious pride*? Where is their *purple* and *fine linen*, their chains of *massie gold*, and sparkling ornaments of *pearls*? Where are their *Cooks* and *Carvers*, their *fowlers* and *fishers*? Where are their curious *Utensils*, their *Cups* of *Agate*, *Crystal*, and *China-earth*? Where are their sumptuous *Chambers*, where they enclosed themselves in *Cedar*, *Ivory*, and *Ebony*? Where is their *Musick*, their *soft* and *delicate dressings*, *pleasing motions*, and *excellency of looks*? Where are their rich *perfumes*, costly *Conserves*, with their precious and various store of *foreign* and *domestick* wines? Where are their *sons* and their *daughters* fair as the *flowers*, straight as the *Palm-trees*, and *polished as the corners of the Temple*? O pitiful and astonishing transformations! all is gone, all is dust, deformity, and desolation. *Their bones are scattered in the pit, and instead of well-set hair, there is baldness and loathsomeness instead of beauty.* This is the state of their *bodies*, and (O blessed *Jesus*!) who knows the state of their *souls*?

The Mount of Olives

ANTHONY ASHLEY COOPER, EARL OF SHAFTESBURY

1621–1683

181 *Character of Henry Hastings*

MR. HASTINGS, by his quality, being the son, brother, and uncle to the Earls of Huntingdon, and his way of living, had the first place amongst us. He was peradventure an original in our age, or rather the copy of our nobility in ancient days in hunting and not warlike times; he was low, very strong and very active, of a reddish flaxen hair, his clothes always green cloth, and never all worth when new five pounds. His house was perfectly of the old fashion, in the midst of a large park well stocked with deer, and near the house rabbits to serve his kitchen, many fish-ponds, and great store of wood and timber; a bowling-green in it, long but narrow, full of high ridges, it being never levelled since it was ploughed; they used round sand bowls, and it had a banqueting-house like a stand, a large one built in a tree. He kept all manner of sport-hounds that ran buck, fox, hare, otter, and badger, and hawks long and short winged; he had all sorts of nets for fishing: he had a walk in the New Forest and the manor of Christ Church. This last supplied him with red deer, sea and river fish; and indeed all his neighbours' grounds and royalties were free to him, who bestowed all his time in such sports, but what he borrowed to caress his neighbours' wives and daughters, there being not a woman in all his walks of the degree of a yeoman's wife or under, and under the age of forty, but it was extremely her fault if he were not intimately acquainted with her. This made him very popular, always speaking kindly to the husband, brother, or father, who was to boot very welcome to his house whenever he came. There he found beef pudding and small beer in great plenty, a house not so neatly kept as to shame him or his dirty shoes, the great hall strewed with marrow bones, full of hawks' perches, hounds, spaniels, and terriers, the upper sides of the hall hung with the fox-skins of this and the last year's skinning, here and there a polecat intermixed, guns and keepers' and huntsmen's poles in abundance. The parlour was a large long room, as properly furnished; on a great hearth paved with brick lay some terriers and the choicest hounds and spaniels; seldom but two of the great chairs had litters of young cats in them, which were not to be disturbed, he having always three or four attending him at dinner, and a little white round stick of fourteen inches long lying by his trencher, that he might defend such meat as he had no mind to part with to them. The windows, which were very large, served for places to lay his arrows, crossbows, stonebows, and other such like accoutrements; the corners of the room full of the best chose hunting and hawking poles; an oyster-table at the lower end, which was of constant use twice a day all the year round, for he never failed to eat oysters before dinner and supper through all seasons: the neighbouring town of Poole supplied him with them. The upper part of this room had two small tables and a desk, on the one side of which was a church Bible, on the other the Book of Martyrs; on the tables were hawks' hoods, bells, and such like, two or three old green hats with their crowns thrust in so as to hold ten or a dozen eggs, which were of a pheasant kind of poultry he took much care of and fed himself; tables, dice, cards, and boxes were not wanting. In the hole of the desk were store of tobacco-pipes that had been used. On one side of this end of the room was the door of a closet, wherein stood the strong beer and the wine, which never came thence but in single glasses, that being the rule of the house exactly observed, for he never exceeded in drink or permitted it. On the other side was a door into an old chapel not used for devotion; the pulpit, as the safest place, was never wanting of a cold chine of beef, pasty of venison, gammon of bacon, or great apple-pie, with thick crust extremely baked. His table cost him not much, though it was very good to eat at, his sports supplying all but beef and mutton, except Friday, when he had the best sea-fish as well as other fish he could get, and was the day that his neighbours of best quality most visited him. He never wanted a London pudding, and always sung it in with 'my part lies therein-a.' He drank a glass of wine or two at meals, very often syrrup of gilliflower in his sack, and had always a tun glass without feet stood by him holding a pint of small beer, which he often stirred with a great sprig of rosemary. He was well natured, but soon angry, calling his servants bastard and cuckoldy knaves, in one of which he often spoke truth to his own knowledge, and sometimes in both, though of the same man. He lived to a hundred, never lost his eyesight, but always writ and read without spectacles, and got to horse without help. Until past fourscore he rode to the death of a stag as well as any.

Fragment of Autobiography

ALGERNON SIDNEY

1622–1683

182 *The Sanction of Government*

NO man can be my Judge, unless he be my Superior; and he cannot be my Superior, who is not so by my consent, nor to any other purpose than I consent to. This cannot be the case of a Nation, which can have no equal within itself. Controversies may arise with other Nations, the decision of which may be left to Judges chosen by mutual agreement; but this relates not to our question. A Nation, and most especially one that is powerful, cannot recede from its own right, as a private man from the knowledge of his own weakness and inability to defend himself, must come under the protection of a greater Power than his own. The strength of a Nation is not in the Magistrate, but the strength of the Magistrate is in the Nation. The wisdom, industry, and valour of a Prince may add to the glory and greatness of a Nation, but the foundation and substance will always be in itself. . . . The people therefore cannot be deprived of their natural rights upon a frivolous pretence to that which never was and never can be. They who create Magistracies, and give to them such name, form, and power as they think fit, do only know, whether the end for which they were created, be performed or not. They who give a being to the power which had none, can only judge whether it be employed to their welfare, or turned to their ruin. They do not set up one or a few men, that they and their posterity may live in splendor and greatness, but that Justice may be administered, Virtue established, and provision made for the publick safety. No wise man will think this can be done, if those who set themselves to overthrow the Law, are to be their own Judges. *A Discourse on Government*

GEORGE FOX

1624–1690

183 *The Cloud*

ONE morning, as I was sitting by the fire, a great cloud came over me, and a temptation beset me, and I sate still. And it was said, All things come by nature; and the Elements and Stars came over me, so that I was in a moment quite clouded with it; but, inasmuch as I sate still and said nothing, the people of the house perceived nothing. And as I sate still under it and let it alone, a living hope rose in me, and a true voice arose in me which cried: There is a living God who made all things. And immediately the cloud and temptation vanished away, and the life rose over it all, and my heart was glad, and I praised the living God. *Journal of George Fox*

JOHN BUNYAN

1628–1688

184 *He Plays Tip Cat on Sunday*

BUT one day, amongst all the Sermons our Parson made, his Subject was, to treat of the Sabbath-day, and of the Evil of breaking that, either with Labour, Sports, or otherwise. (Now I was, notwithstanding my Religion, one that took much delight in all manner of Vice, and especially that was the day that I did solace myself therewith.) Wherefore I fell in my Conscience under his Sermon, thinking and believing that he made that Sermon on purpose to show me my evil doing. And at that time I felt what guilt was, though never before, that I can remember. But then I was, for the present, greatly loaden therewith, and so went home when the Sermon was ended, with a great burden upon my Spirit.

This, for that instant, did benumb the Sinews of my best Delights, and did embitter my former Pleasures to me. But behold, it lasted not, for before I had well dined, the Trouble began to go off my Mind, and my Heart returned to its old Course. But oh! How glad was I, that this Trouble was gone from me, and that the Fire was put out, that I might sin again without control! Wherefore, when I had satisfied Nature with my Food, I shook the Sermon out of my Mind, and to my old Custom of Sports and Gaming I returned with great Delight.

But the same day, as I was in the midst of a game at Cat, and having struck it one blow from the Hole, just as I was about to strike it the second time, a Voice did suddenly dart from Heaven into my Soul, which said, *Wilt thou leave thy sins and go to Heaven, or have thy sins and go to Hell?* At this I was put to an exceeding Maze. Wherefore, leaving my Cat upon the ground, I looked up to Heaven, and was as if I had, with the Eyes of my understanding, seen the Lord Jesus looking down upon me, as being very hotly displeased with me, and as if he did severely threaten me with some grievous Punishment for these and other my ungodly Practices.

I had no sooner thus conceived in my Mind, but suddenly this conclusion was fastened on my Spirit (for the former hint did set my sins again before my Face), *That I had been a great and grievous sinner, and that it was now too late for me to look after Heaven; for Christ would not forgive me, nor pardon my Transgressions.* Then I fell to musing upon this also. And while I was thinking on it and fearing lest it should be so, I felt my Heart sink in Despair, concluding it was too late; and therefore I resolved in my Mind I would go on in sin. For, thought I, if the Case be thus, my State is surely miserable. Miserable if I leave my Sins, and but miserable if I follow them. I can but be damned, and if I must be so, I had as good be damned for many sins as be damned for few.

Thus I stood in the midst of my Play, before all that then were present; but yet I told them nothing. But I say, I having made this conclusion, I returned desperately to my sport again; and I well remember, that presently this kind of Despair did so possess my Soul, that I was perswaded, I could never attain to other Comfort than what I should get in sin; for Heaven was gone already, so that on that I must not think.

Grace Abounding

185 *Christian and Faithful come to Vanity Fair*

THEN I saw in my Dream, that when they were got out of the Wilderness, they presently saw a Town before them, and the name of that Town is *Vanity*; and at the Town there is a *Fair* kept, called *Vanity-Fair*. It is kept all the Year long: it beareth the name of *Vanity-Fair*, because the Town where it is kept, *is lighter than* Vanity; and also, because all that is there sold, or that cometh thither, is *Vanity*. As is the saying of the wise, *All that cometh is Vanity*.

This Fair is no new erected business, but a thing of ancient standing; I will show you the original of it.

Almost five thousand years agone, there were Pilgrims walking to the Celestial City, as these two honest persons are; and *Beelzebub*, *Apollyon*, and *Legion*, with their Companions, perceiving by the Path that the Pilgrims made, that their way to the City lay through this *Town* of *Vanity*, they contrived here to set up a Fair; a Fair wherein should be sold of *all sorts of Vanity*, and that it should last all the year long. Therefore at this *Fair* are all such Merchandize sold, as Houses, Lands, Trades, Places, Honours, Preferments, Titles, Countries, Kingdoms, Lusts, Pleasures, and Delights of all sorts, as Whores, Bawds, Wives, Husbands, Children, Masters, Servants, Lives, Blood, Bodies, Souls, Silver, Gold, Pearls, Precious Stones, and what not.

And moreover, at this Fair there is at all times to be seen Jugglings, Cheats, Games, Plays, Fools, Apes, Knaves, and Rogues, and that of every kind.

Here are to be seen too, and that for nothing,

Thefts, Murders, Adulteries, False-swearers, and that of a blood-red colour.

And as in other Fairs of less moment, there are the several Rows and Streets, under their proper names, where such and such Wares are vended: So here likewise, you have the proper Places, Rows, Streets (*viz.* Countrys and Kingdoms), where the Wares of this Fair are soonest to be found: Here is the *Britain* Row, the *French* Row, the *Italian* Row, the *Spanish* Row, the *German* Row, where several sorts of Vanities are to be sold. But as in other Fairs, some one Commodity is as the chief of all the *Fair*, so the Ware of *Rome* and her Merchandize is greatly promoted in this *Fair*: Only our *English* Nation, with some others, have taken a dislike thereat.

Now, as I said, the way to the Celestial City lies just through this *Town*, where this lusty Fair is kept; and he that will go to the City, and yet not go through this Town, must needs *go out of the World*. The Prince of Princes himself, when here, went through this *Town* to his own Country, and that upon a *Fair-day* too: Yea, and as I think, it was *Beelzebub*, the chief Lord of this *Fair*, that invited him to buy of his *Vanities*; yea, would have made him Lord of the *Fair*, would he but have done him Reverence as he went through the *Town*. Yea, because he was such a person of Honour, *Beelzebub* had him from *Street* to *Street*, and showed him all the Kingdoms of the World in a little time, that he might, if possible, allure that Blessed One, to cheapen and buy some of his *Vanities*. But he had no mind to the Merchandize, and therefore left the *Town*, without laying out so much as one Farthing upon these *Vanities*. This *Fair* therefore is an ancient thing, of long standing, and a very great *Fair*.

Now these Pilgrims, as I said, must needs go through this *Fair*. Well, so they did; but behold, even as they entered into the *Fair*, all the people in the *Fair* were moved, and the Town itself as it were in a Hubbub about them; and that for several reasons: For,

First, The Pilgrims were cloathed with such kind of Raiment as was diverse from the Raiment of any that Traded in that *Fair*. The people therefore of the *Fair* made a great gazing upon them. Some said they were Fools, some they were Bedlams, and some they are Outlandish-men.

Secondly, And as they wondered at their *Apparel*, so they did likewise at their *Speech*, for few could understand what they said; they naturally spoke the Language of *Canaan*, but they that kept the *Fair*, were the men of this World: so that from one end of the *Fair* to the other, they seemed *Barbarians* each to the other.

Thirdly, But that which did not a little amuse the Merchandizers, was, that these Pilgrims set very light by all their Wares.

The Pilgrim's Progress

186 *The Valley of Humiliation*

BUT we will come again to this Valley of *Humiliation*. It is the best, and most fruitful piece of Ground in all those parts. It is fat Ground, and as you see consisteth much in Meadows; and if a Man was to come here in the Summer-time as we do now, if he knew not anything before thereof, and if he also delighted himself in the sight of his Eyes, he might see that that would be delightful to him. Behold, how green this Valley is, also how beautified with *Lilies*. I have also known many labouring men that have got good Estates in this Valley of *Humiliation.* (For God resisteth the Proud; but gives *more, more* Grace to the Humble) for indeed it is a very fruitful Soil, and doth bring forth by handfuls. Some also have wished that the next way to their Father's House were here, that they might be troubled no more with either Hills or Mountains to go over; but the way is the way, and there 's an end.

Now as they were going along and talking, they espied a Boy feeding his Father's Sheep. The Boy was in very mean Cloathes, but of a very fresh and well-favoured Countenance, and as he sat by himself he sung. Hark, said Mr. *Greatheart*, to what the Shepherd's Boy saith. So they hearkened, and he said,

He that is down, needs fear no fall,
He that is low, no Pride:
He that is humble, ever shall
Have God to be his Guide.
I am content with what I have,
Little be it, or much:
And, Lord, contentment still I crave,
Because thou savest such.
Fullness to such a burden is
That go on Pilgrimage:
Here little, and hereafter Bliss,
Is best from Age to Age.

Then said the *Guide*, Do you hear him? I will dare to say, that this Boy lives a merrier Life, and wears more of that Herb called *Hearts-ease* in his Bosom, than he that is clad in Silk and Velvet; but we will proceed in our Discourse.

The Pilgrim's Progress

JOHN BUNYAN

187 *Mr. Valiant-for-truth Crosses the River*

AFTER this, it was noised abroad that Mr. *Valiant-for-truth* was taken with a Summons, by the same *Post* as the other, and had this for a Token that the Summons was true, *That his Pitcher was broken at the Fountain.* When he understood it, he called for his Friends, and told them of it. Then said he, I am going to my Fathers, and though with great difficulty I am got hither, yet now I do not repent me of all the Trouble I have been at to arrive where I am. *My Sword*, I give to him that shall succeed me in my Pilgrimage, and my *Courage* and *Skill*, to him that can get it. My *Marks* and *Scars* I carry with me, to be a Witness for me, that I have fought his Battles who now will be my Rewarder. When the Day that he must go hence, was come, many accompanied him to the River side, into which, as he went, he said, *Death, where is thy Sting?* And as he went down deeper, he said, *Grave, where is thy Victory?* So he passed over, and the Trumpets sounded for him on the other side.

The Pilgrim's Progress

SIR WILLIAM TEMPLE

1628–1699

188 *Of Poetry*

WHETHER it be that the Fierceness of the *Gothick* Humors, or Noise of their perpetual Wars, frighted it away, or that the unequal mixture of the modern Languages would not bear it, certain it is, that the great Heighths and Excellency both of

Poetry and Musick fell with the *Roman* Learning and Empire, and have never since recovered the Admiration and Applauses that before attended them. Yet such as they are amongst us, they must be confessed to be the softest and sweetest, the most general and most innocent Amusements of common Time and Life. They still find Room in the Courts of Princes and the Cottages of Shepherds. They serve to revive and animate the dead Calm of poor or idle Lives, and to allay or divert the violent Passions and Perturbations of the greatest and the busiest Men. And both these Effects are of equal use to Humane Life; for the Mind of Man is like the Sea, which is neither agreeable to the Beholder nor the Voyager in a Calm or in a Storm, but is so to both when a little agitated by gentle Gales; and so the Mind, when moved by soft and easy Passions or Affections. I know very well that many, who pretend to be Wise by the Forms of being Grave, are apt to despise both Poetry and Musick as Toys and Trifles too light for the Use or Entertainment of serious Men. But whoever find themselves wholly insensible to these Charms would, I think, do well to keep their own Counsel, for fear of reproaching their own Temper, and bringing the Goodness of their Natures, if not of their Understandings, into Question. It may be thought at least an ill Sign, if not an ill Constitution, since some of the Fathers went so far as to esteem the Love of Musick a Sign of Predestination, as a thing Divine, and reserved for the Felicities of Heaven itself. While this World lasts, I doubt not but the Pleasure and Request of these two Entertainments will do so too; and happy those that content themselves with these or any other so easy and so innocent, and do not trouble the World or other Men, because they cannot be quiet themselves, though no Body hurts them!

When all is done, Human Life is, at the greatest and the best, but like a froward Child, that must be played with and humoured a little to keep it quiet till it falls asleep, and then the Care is over.

Essays

189 *On his Retirement from Public Life*

FOR the Ease of my own Life, if I know myself, it will be infinitely more in the retired, than it has been in the busy Scene: for no good Man can, with any Satisfaction, take part in the Divisions of his Country that knows and considers, as I do, what they have cost *Athens*, *Rome*, *Constantinople*, *Florence*, *Germany*, *France*, and *England*: nor can the wisest Man foresee how ours will end, or what they are like to cost the rest of Christendom as well as ourselves. I never had but two aims in publick Affairs; one, to see the King great as he may be by the Hearts of his People, without which I know not how he can be great by the Constitutions of this Kingdom: The other, in case our Factions must last, yet to see a Revenue established for the constant maintaining a Fleet of fifty men of War, at Sea or in Harbour, and the Seamen in constant Pay; which would be at least our Safety from abroad, and make the Crown still considered in any foreign Alliances, whether the King and his Parliaments should agree or not in undertaking any great or National War. And such an Establishment I was in Hopes the last Parliament at *Westminster* might have agreed in with the King, by adding so much of a new Fund to Three Hundred Thousand

Pounds a Year out of the present Customs. But these have both failed, and I am content to have failed with them.

Memoirs

190 *On Gardens*

IN every Garden four things are necessary to be provided for, Flowers, Fruit, Shade, and Water; and whoever lays out a Garden without all these, must not pretend it in any Perfection. It ought to lie to the best Parts of the House, or to those of the Master's commonest use, so as to be but like one of the Rooms out of which you step into another. The part of your Garden next your House (besides the Walks that go round it), should be a Parterre for Flowers, or Grass-plots bordered with Flowers; or if, according to the newest Mode, it be cast all into Grass-plots and Gravel Walks, the dryness of these should be relieved with Fountains, and the plainness of those with Statues; otherwise, if large, they have an ill effect upon the Eye. However, the part next the House should be open, and no other Fruit but upon the Walls. If this take up one half of the Garden, the other should be Fruit-trees, unless some Grove for shade lie in the middle. If it take up a third part only, then the next third may be Dwarf-trees, and the last Standard-fruit; or else the second part Fruit-trees, and the third all sorts of Winter-Greens, which provide for all Seasons of the Year. . .

The best Figure of a Garden is either a Square or an Oblong, and either upon a Flat or a Descent; they have all their Beauties, but the best I esteem an Oblong upon a Descent. The Beauty, the Air, the View makes amends for the Expense, which is very great in finishing and supporting the Terrace-walks, in levelling the Parterres, and in the Stone-stairs that are necessary from one to the other.

Upon the Gardens of Epicurus

CHARLES COTTON

1630–1687

191 *The Fishing-house*

PISCATOR. Good morrow, *Sir*: what! up and dressed, so early?

Viator. Yes, *Sir*, I have been dressed this half-hour: for I rested so well, and have so great a mind either to take, or to see a Trout taken in your fine River, that I could no longer lie a-bed.

Piscator. I am glad to see you so brisk this morning, and so eager of sport: though I must tell you this day proves so calm, and the Sun rises so bright, as promises no great success to the Angler: but, however, we'll try, and, one way or other, we shall, sure, do something. What will you have to your breakfast, or what will you drink this Morning?

Viator. For Breakfast I never eat any, and for Drink am very indifferent; but if you please to call for a glass of Ale, I'm for you; and let it be quickly if you please, for I long to see the little Fishing-house you spoke of, and to be at my lesson.

Piscator. Well, *Sir*, you see the Ale is come without calling: for though I do not know yours, my people know my diet, which is always one Glass so soon as I am dressed, and no more till Dinner: and so my Servants have served you.

Viator. My thanks. And now, if you please, let us look out this fine morning.

Piscator. With all my heart. Boy, take the Key of my Fishing-house, and carry down those two angle-Rods in the Hall window, thither, with my Fish-pannier, Pouch, and Landing-net; and stay you there till we come. Come, *Sir*, we'll walk after, where, by the way, I expect you should raise all the exceptions against our Country you can.

Viator. Nay, *Sir*, do not think me so ill-natured, nor so uncivil: I only made a little bold with it last night to divert you, and was only in jest.

[*Piscator.*] You were then in as good earnest as I am now with you: but had you been really angry at it, I could not blame you; for, to say the truth, it is not very taking at first sight. But look you, Sir, now you are abroad, does not the sun shine as bright here as in *Essex*, *Middlesex*, or *Kent*, or any of your southern countries?

Viator. 'Tis a delicate Morning indeed, and I now think this a marvellous pretty place.

Piscator. Whether you think so or no, you cannot oblige me more than to say so: and those of my friends who know my humour, and are so kind as to comply with it, usually flatter me that way. But look you, *Sir*, now you are at the brink of the Hill, how do you like my River, the Vale it winds through like a snake, and the situation of my little Fishing-house?

Viator. Trust me, 'tis all very fine; and the house seems, at this distance, a neat building.

Piscator. Good enough for that purpose. And here is a bowling Green too, close by it; so, though I am myself no very good bowler, I am not totally devoted to my own pleasure, but that I have also some regard to other men's. And now, *Sir*, you are come to the door; pray walk in, and there we will sit, and talk as long as you please.

Viator. Stay, what 's here over the door? *Piscatoribus Sacrum*. Why then, I perceive I have some Title here; for I am one of them, though one of the worst. And here, below it, is the Cipher too you spoke of; and 'tis prettily contrived. Has my master Walton ever been here to see it; for it seems new built?

Piscator. Yes, he saw it cut in the stone before it was set up; but never in the posture it now stands: for the house was but building when he was last here, and not raised so high as the Arch of the door. And I am afraid he will not see it yet: for he has lately writ me word, he doubts his coming down this Summer; which, I do assure you, was the worst news he could possibly have sent me.

Viator. Men must sometimes mind their affairs to make more room for their pleasures. And 'tis odds he is as much displeased with the business that keeps him from you, as you are that he comes not. But I am the most pleased with this little house of anything I ever saw: it stands in a kind of *Peninsula* too, with a delicate clear River about it. I dare hardly go in, lest I should not like it so well within as without: but by your leave, I'll try. Why, this is better and better, fine lights, finely wainscoted, and all exceeding neat, with a Marble Table and all in the middle!

Piscator. Enough, *Sir*, enough, I have laid open to you the part where I can worst defend myself, and now you attack me there. Come, Boy, set two Chairs; and whilst I am taking a Pipe of Tobacco, which is always my Breakfast, we will, if you please, talk of some other Subject.

Viator. None fitter, then, *Sir*, for the time and place, than those instructions you promised.

The Compleat Angler, Part II

JOHN TILLOTSON, ARCHBISHOP OF CANTERBURY

1630–1694

192 *Of Feasts*

ONE would be apt to wonder, that *Nehemiah* (Chap. v, Verses 16, 17, 18) should reckon a huge bill of fare, and a vast number of promiscuous guests amongst his virtues and good deeds, for which he desires God to remember him. But, upon better consideration, besides the bounty, and sometimes charity, of a great table (provided there be nothing of vanity or ostentation in it) there may be exercised two very considerable virtues; one is *temperance*, and the other *self-denial*, in a man's being contented, for the sake of the public, to deny himself so much, as to sit down every day to a feast, and to eat continually in a crowd, and almost never to be alone, especially when, as it often happens, a great part of the company that a man must have is the company that a man would not have. I doubt it will prove but a melancholy business, when a man comes to die, to have made a great noise and bustle in the world, and to have been known far and near, but all this while to have been hid and concealed from himself. It is a very odd and fantastical sort of life for a man to be continually from home, and most of all a stranger at his own house.

It is surely an uneasy thing, to sit always in a frame,

and to be perpetually upon a man's guard; not to be able to speak a careless word, or to use a negligent posture, without observation and censure.

Men are apt to think, that they, who are in highest places, and have the most power, have most liberty to say and do what they please. But it is quite otherwise; for they have the least liberty, because they are most observed. It is not mine own observation; a much wiser man (I mean TULLY) says, *In maxima quaque fortuna minimum licere*. They, that are in the highest and greatest condition, have of all others the least liberty.

Reflections

JOHN DRYDEN

1631–1700

193 *June 3rd, 1665*

IT was that memorable day, in the first summer of the late War, when our Navy engaged the Dutch; a day wherein the two most mighty and best-appointed Fleets which any age had ever seen, disputed the command of the greater half of the Globe, the commerce of nations, and the riches of the Universe. While these vast floating bodies, on either side, moved against each other in parallel lines, and our Countrymen, under the happy conduct of his Royal Highness, went breaking, by little and little, into the line of the Enemies; the noise of the Cannon from both Navies reached our ears about the City, so that all men being alarmed with it, and in a dreadful suspense of the event which we knew was then deciding, every one went following the sound as his fancy led him; and leaving the Town almost empty, some took towards the Park, some cross the River, others down it; all seeking the noise in the depth of silence.

Among the rest it was the fortune of *Eugenius*, *Crites*, *Lisideius*, and *Neander*, to be in company together; three of them persons whom their wit and Quality have made known to all the Town; and whom I have chose to hide under these borrowed names that they may not suffer by so ill a relation as I am going to make of their discourse.

Taking then a Barge which a servant of *Lisideius* had provided for them, they made haste to shoot the Bridge, and left behind them that great fall of waters which hindered them from hearing what they desired: after which, having disengaged themselves from many Vessels which rode at anchor in the *Thames* and almost blocked up the passage towards *Greenwich*, they ordered the Watermen to let fall their oars more gently; and then, every one favouring his own curiosity with a strict silence, it was not long ere they perceived the Air break about them like the noise of distant Thunder, or of swallows in a Chimney: those little undulations of sound, though almost vanishing before they reached them, yet still seeming to retain somewhat of their first horror which they had betwixt the Fleets. After they had attentively listened till such time as the sound by little and little went from them, *Eugenius*, lifting up his head, and taking notice of it, was the first who congratulated to the rest that happy Omen of our Nation's Victory: adding, we had but this to desire in confirmation of it, that we might hear no more of that noise which was now leaving the English Coast.

Essay of Dramatic Poesy

194 *Shakespeare and Ben Jonson*

To begin, then, with *Shakespeare*. He was the man who of all Modern, and perhaps Ancient Poets, had the largest and most comprehensive soul. All the Images of Nature were still present to him, and he drew them, not laboriously, but luckily; when he describes anything you more than see it, you feel it too. Those who accuse him to have wanted learning give him the greater commendation: he was naturally learned; he needed not the spectacles of Books to read Nature; he looked inwards, and found her there. I cannot say he is everywhere alike; were he so, I should do him injury to compare him with the greatest of Mankind. He is many times flat, insipid; his Comick wit degenerating into clenches, his serious swelling into Bombast. But he is always great when some great occasion is presented to him; no man can say he ever had a fit subject for his wit and did not then raise himself as high above the rest of poets,

Quantum lenta solent inter viburna cupressi.

The consideration of this made Mr. *Hales* of *Eaton* say, that there was no subject of which any poet ever writ but he would produce it much better treated of in *Shakespeare*; and however others are now generally preferred before him, yet the age wherein he lived, which had contemporaries with him *Fletcher* and *Johnson*, never equalled them to him in their esteem: and in the last King's court, when *Ben's* reputation was at highest, Sir *John Suckling*, and with him the greater part of the Courtiers, set our *Shakespeare* far above him. . .

As for *Johnson*, to whose Character I am now arrived,

if we look upon him while he was himself (for his last Plays were but his dotages), I think him the most learned and judicious Writer which any Theatre ever had. He was a most severe Judge of himself, as well as others. One cannot say he wanted wit, but rather that he was frugal of it. In his works you find little to retrench or alter. Wit and Language and Humour also in some measure, we had before him ; but something of Art was wanting to the *Drama* till he came. He managed his strength to more advantage than any who preceded him. You seldom find him making Love in any of his Scenes, or endeavouring to move the Passions ; his genius was too sullen and saturnine to do it gracefully, especially when he knew he came after those who had performed both to such an height. Humour was his proper Sphere ; and in that he delighted most to represent Mechanick people. He was deeply conversant in the Ancients, both Greek and Latin, and he borrowed boldly from them : there is scarce a Poet or Historian among the Roman Authors of those times whom he has not translated in *Sejanus* and *Catiline*. But he has done his Robberies so openly that one may see he fears not to be taxed by any Law. He invades Authors like a Monarch ; and what would be theft in other Poets is only victory in him. With the spoils of these Writers he so represents old *Rome* to us, in its Rites, Ceremonies, and Customs, that if one of their Poets had written either of his Tragedies we had seen less of it than in him. If there was any fault in his Language 'twas that he weaved it too closely and laboriously in his serious Plays : perhaps, too, he did a little too much Romanize our Tongue, leaving the words which he translated almost as much Latin as he found them : wherein, though he learnedly followed the Idiom of their language, he did not enough comply with ours. If I would compare him with *Shakespeare*, I must acknowledge him the more correct poet, but *Shakespeare* the greater wit. *Shakespeare* was the *Homer*, or father of our Dramatick Poets; *Johnson* was the *Virgil*, the pattern of elaborate writing; I admire him, but I love *Shakespeare*.

Essay of Dramatic Poesy

195 *Chaucer*

HE must have been a Man of a most wonderful comprehensive Nature, because, as it has been truly observed of him, he has taken into the compass of his *Canterbury Tales* the various Manners and Humours (as we now call them) of the whole *English* Nation, in his Age. Not a single Character has escaped him. All his Pilgrims are severally distinguished from each other; and not only in their inclinations, but in their very physiognomies and persons. *Baptista Porta* could not have described their natures better than by the marks which the Poet gives them. The Matter and Manner of their Tales, and of their Telling, are so suited to their different Educations, Humours, and Callings, that each of them would be improper in any other mouth. Even the grave and serious Characters are distinguished by their several sorts of Gravity: their Discourses are such as belong to their Age, their Calling, and their Breeding; such as are becoming of them, and of them only. Some of his Persons are Vicious, and some Vertuous; some are unlearned, or (as *Chaucer* calls them) lewd, and some are learned. Even the ribaldry of the Low Characters is different: the *Reeve*, the *Miller*, and the *Cook*, are several men, and distinguished from each other as much as the mincing *Lady-Prioress* and the broad-speaking, gap-toothed Wife of *Bath*. But enough of this; there is such a variety of Game springing up before me, that I am distracted in my Choice, and know not which to follow. 'Tis sufficient to say, according to the Proverb, that *here is God's plenty*.

Preface to the Fables

196 *Dryden Grown Old*

I HAVE added some Original Papers of my own, which whether they are equal or inferior to my other Poems, an Author is the most improper Judge; and therefore I leave them wholly to the Mercy of the Reader. I will hope the best, that they will not be condemned; but if they should, I have the Excuse of an old Gentleman, who, mounting on Horseback before some Ladies, when I was present, got up somewhat heavily, but desired of the Fair Spectators that they would count Fourscore and eight before they judged him. By the Mercy of God, I am already come within Twenty Years of his Number, a Cripple in my Limbs; but what Decays are in my Mind, the Reader must determine. I think my self as vigorous as ever in the Faculties of my Soul, excepting only my Memory, which is not impaired to any great degree; and if I lose not more of it, I have no great reason to complain. What Judgment I had, increases rather than diminishes; and Thoughts, such as they are, come crowding in so fast upon me, that my only Difficulty is to chuse or to reject; to run them into Verse or to give them the other harmony of Prose: I have so long studied and practised both, that they are grown into a Habit, and become familiar to me. In short, though I may lawfully plead some part of the old Gentleman's Excuse, yet I will reserve it till I think I have greater need, and ask no Grains of Allowance for the Faults of this my present Work, but those which are given of course to Humane Frailty.

Preface to the Fables

JOHN LOCKE

1632–1704

197 *On the Teaching of English*

TO write and speak correctly gives a Grace, and gains a favourable attention to what one has to say; and, since it is *English* that an *English* Gentleman will have constant use of, that is the Language he should chiefly cultivate, and wherein most care should be taken to polish and perfect his Style. To speak or write better Latin than English may make a man be talked of; but he would find it more to his purpose to express himself well in his own tongue, that he uses every moment, than to have the vain commendation of others for a very insignificant quality. This I find universally neglected, and no care taken anywhere to improve Young Men in their own Language, that they may thoroughly understand and be Masters of it. If any one among us have a facility or purity more than ordinary in his Mother Tongue, it is owing to Chance, or his Genius, or anything, rather than to his Education, or any care of his Teacher. To mind what *English* his Pupil speaks or writes is below the dignity of one bred up amongst *Greek* and *Latin*, though he have but little of them himself. These are the learned Languages, fit only for learned Men to meddle with and teach ; *English* is the language of the illiterate Vulgar, though yet we see the policy of some of our neighbours hath not thought it beneath the public care to promote and reward the improvement of their own Language. Polishing and enriching their Tongue is no small Business amongst them : it hath colleges and stipends appointed it, and there is raised amongst them a great Ambition and Emulation of writing correctly ; and we see what they are come to by it, and how far they have spread one of the worst Languages, possibly, in this part of the World ; if we look upon it as it was in some few Reigns backwards, whatever it be now. The great Men amongst the *Romans* were daily exercising themselves in their own language ; and we find yet upon record the Names of Orators who taught some of their emperors *Latin*, though it were their Mother Tongue.

It is plain the *Greeks* were yet more nice in theirs ; all other Speech was barbarous to them but their own, and no Foreign Language appears to have been studied or valued amongst that learned and acute People ; though it be past doubt, that they borrowed their Learning and Philosophy from abroad.

I am not here speaking against *Greek* and *Latin* ; I think they ought to be studied, and the *Latin*, at least, understood well, by every Gentleman. But whatever foreign Languages a Young Man meddles with (and the more he knows the better), that which he should critically study and labour to get a facility, clearness, and elegancy to express himself in, should be his own, and to this purpose he should daily be exercised in it.

Some Thoughts concerning Education

SAMUEL PEPYS

1633–1703

198 *A Jaunt into the Country*

JULY 14, 1667. (Lord's day.) Up, and my wife, a little before four, and to make us ready; and by and by Mrs. Turner come to us by agreement, and she and I stayed talking below while my wife dressed herself, which vexed me that she was so long about it, keeping us till past five o'clock before she was ready. She ready; and taking some bottles of wine, and beer, and some cold fowl with us into the coach, we took coach and four horses, which I had provided last night, and so away. A very fine day, and so towards Epsom, talking all the way pleasantly, and particularly of the pride and ignorance of Mrs. Lowther, in having of her train carried up. The country very fine, only the way very dusty. To Epsom, by eight o'clock, to the well; where much company, and I drank the water: they did not, but I did drink four pints. And to the town, to the King's Head; and hear that my Lord Buckhurst and Nelly are lodged at the next house, and Sir Charles Sedley with them; and keep a merry house. Poor girl! I pity her; but more the loss of her at the King's house. W. Hewer rode with us, and I left him and the women, and myself walked to church, where few people to what I expected, and none I knew, but all the Houblons, brothers, and them after sermon I did salute, and walk with towards my inn. James did tell me that I was the only happy man of the Navy, of whom, he says, during all this freedom the people hath taken to speaking treason, he hath not heard one bad word of me, which is a great joy to me; for I hear the same of others, but do know that I have deserved as well as most. We parted to meet anon, and I to my women into a better room, which the people of the house borrowed for us, and there to a good dinner, and were merry, and Pembleton come to us, who happened to be in the house, and there talked and were merry.

After dinner, he gone, we all lay down (the day being wonderful hot) to sleep, and each of us took a good nap, and then rose . . . and we took coach and to take the air, there being a fine breeze abroad; and I carried them to the well, and there filled some bottles of water to carry home with me; and there I talked with the two women that farm the well, at £12 per annum, of the lord of the manor. . . Here W. Hewer's horse broke loose, and we had the sport to see him taken again. Then I carried them to see my cousin Pepys's house, and 'light, and walked round about it, and they like it, as indeed it deserves, very well, and is a pretty place; and then I walked them to the wood hard by, and there got them in the thickets till they lost themselves, and I could not find the way into any of the walks in the wood, which indeed are very pleasant, if I could have found them. At last got out of the wood again; and I, by leaping down the little bank, coming out of the wood, did sprain my right foot, which brought me great present pain, but presently, with walking, it went away for the present, and so the women and W. Hewer and I walked upon the Downes, where a flock of sheep was; and the most pleasant and innocent sight that ever I saw in my life. We found a shepherd and his little boy reading, far from any houses or sight of people, the Bible to him; so I made the boy read to me, which he did, with the forced tone that children do usually read, that was mighty pretty, and then I did give him something, and went to the father, and talked with him; and I find he had been a servant in my cousin Pepys's house, and told me what was become of their old servants. He did content himself mightily in my liking his boy's reading, and did bless God for him, the most like one of the old patriarchs that ever I saw in my life, and it brought those thoughts of the old age of the world in my mind for two or three days after. We took notice of his woollen knit stockings of two colours mixed, and of his shoes shod with iron, both at the toe and heels, and with great nails in the soles of his feet, which was mighty pretty; and, taking notice of them, 'why,' says the poor man, 'the downes, you see, are full of stones, and we are fain to shoe ourselves thus; and these,' says he, 'will make the stones fly till they ring before me.' I did give the poor man something, for which he was mighty thankful, and I tried to cast stones with his horn crook. He values his dog mightily, that would turn a sheep any way which he would have him, when he goes to fold them: told me there was about eighteen score sheep in his flock, and that he hath four shillings a-week the year round for keeping of them: and Mrs. Turner, in the common fields here, did gather one of the prettiest nosegays that ever I saw in my life.

So to our coach, and through Mr. Minnes's wood, and looked upon Mr. Evelyn's house; and so over the common, and through Epsom town to our inn, in the way stopping a poor woman with her milk-pail, and in one of my gilt tumblers did drink our bellyfuls of milk, better than any cream; and so to our inn, and there had a dish of cream, but it was sour, and so had no pleasure in it; and so paid our reckoning, and took coach, it being about seven at night, and passed and saw the people walking with their wives and children to take the air, and we set out for home, the sun by and by going down, and we in the cool of the evening all the way with much pleasure home, talking and pleasing ourselves with the pleasure of this day's work. Mrs. Turner mightily pleased with my resolution, which, I tell her, is never to keep a country-house, but to keep a coach, and with my wife on the Saturday to go sometimes for a day to this place, and then quit to another place; and there is more variety and as little charge, and no trouble, as there is in a country-house. Anon it grew dark, and we had the pleasure to see several glow-worms, which was mighty pretty, but my foot begins more and more to pain me, which Mrs. Turner, by keeping her warm hand upon it, did much ease: but so that when we come home, which was just at eleven at night, I was not able to walk from the lane's end to my house without being helped. So to bed, and there had a cere-cloth laid to my foot, but in great pain all night long.

Diary

199 *Amantium irae*

JAN. 12, 1668–9. This evening I observed my wife mighty dull, and I myself was not mighty fond, because of some hard words she did give me at noon, out of a jealousy at my being abroad this morning, which, God knows, it was upon the business of the Office unexpectedly; but I to bed, not thinking but she would come after me. But waking by and by, out of a slumber, which I usually fall into presently after my coming into the bed, I found she did not prepare to come to bed, but got fresh candles, and more wood for her fire, it being mighty cold, too. At this being troubled, I after a while prayed her to come to bed; so, after an hour or two, she silent, and I now and then praying her to come to bed, she fell into a fury, that I was a rogue, and false to her. I did, as I might truly, deny it, and was mightily troubled, but all would not serve. At last, about one o'clock, she came to my side of the bed, and drew my curtain open, and with the tongs red hot at the ends, made as if she did design to pinch me with them, at which, in dismay, I rose up, and with a few words she laid them down; and did by little and little, very sillily, let all the discourse fall; and about two, but with much seeming difficulty, come to bed, and there lay well all night, and long in bed talking together, with much pleasure, it being, I know, nothing but her doubt of my going out yesterday, without telling her of my going, which did vex her, poor wretch! last night, and I cannot blame her jealousy, though it do vex me to the heart.

Diary

SIR GEORGE SAVILE, MARQUIS OF HALIFAX

1633–1695

200 *Charles II*

WHEN once the Aversion to bear Uneasiness taketh place in a Man's Mind it doth so check all the Passions that they are damped into a kind of Indifference; they grow faint and languishing, and come to be subordinate to that fundamental Maxim of not purchasing anything at the price of a Difficulty.

This made that he had as little Eagerness to oblige as he had to hurt Men; the Motive of his giving Bounties was rather to make Men less uneasy to him than more easy to themselves; and yet no ill-nature all this while. He would slide from an asking Face, and could guess very well. It was throwing a Man off from his Shoulders that leaned upon them with his whole weight, so that the Party was not gladder to receive than he was to give. . .

That Men have the less Ease for their loving it so much is so far from a wonder that it is a natural Consequence, especially in the case of a Prince. Ease is seldom got without some pains, but it is yet seldomer kept without them. He thought giving would make Men more easy to him, whereas he might have known it would certainly make them more troublesome.

When Men receive Benefits from Princes they attribute less to his Generosity than to their own Deserts; so that in their own Opinion their Merit cannot be bounded; by that mistaken Rule it can as little be satisfied. They would take it for a diminution to have it circumscribed. Merit hath a Thirst upon it that can never be quenched by golden Showers. It is not only still ready, but greedy to receive more. This King *Charles* found in as many Instances as any Prince that ever reigned, because the Easiness of Access introducing the good Success of their first Request, they were the more encouraged to repeat those Importunities, which had been more effectually stopped in the Beginning by a short and resolute Denial. But his Nature did not dispose him to that Method; it directed him rather to put off the troublesome Minute for the time, and that being his Inclination he did not care to struggle with it. . .

It must be allowed he had a little Over-balance on the well-natured Side—not Vigour enough to be earnest to do a kind Thing, much less to do a harsh one; but if a hard thing was done to another Man he did not eat his Supper the worse for it.

A Character of King Charles the Second

201 *Look to your Moat*

I WILL make no other Introduction to the following Discourse, than that as the Importance of our being strong at Sea was ever very great, so in our present Circumstances it is grown to be much greater; because, as formerly our Force in Shipping contributed greatly to our Trade and Safety, so now it is become indispensably necessary to our very being.

It may be said now to *England*, Martha, Martha, *thou art busy about many things*, *but one thing* is necessary. To the question, What shall we do to be saved in this World? there is no other answer but this, Look to your *Moat*.

The first Article of an Englishman's Political Creed must be, That he believeth in the Sea, &c., without that there needeth no General Council to pronounce him incapable of Salvation here.

We are in an Island, confined to it by God Almighty, not as a Penalty but a Grace, and one of the greatest that can be given to Mankind. Happy confinement, that hath made us Free, Rich, and Quiet; a fair Portion in this World, and very well worth the preserving; a Figure that ever hath been envied, and could never be imitated by our Neighbours. Our Situation hath made Greatness abroad by Land Conquests unnatural things to us. It is true, we have made Excursions, and glorious ones too, which make our Names great in History, but they did not last.

A Rough Draft of a New Model at Sea

ROBERT SOUTH

1634–1716

202 *Hypocrites*

BODILY Abstinence, joined with a demure, affected countenance, is often called and accounted *Piety* and *Mortification.* Suppose a Man infinitely ambitious, and equally spiteful and malicious; one who poisons the ears of great men by venomous Whispers, and rises by the fall of better Men than himself; yet if he steps forth with a Friday-look and a Lenten face, with a *blessed Jesu!* and a mournful Ditty for the Vices of the times, oh! then he is a Saint upon Earth; an *Ambrose* or an *Augustine*; I mean not for that earthly trash of book-learning; for, alas! such are above that, or at least that 's above them; but for Zeal, and for Fasting, for a devout Elevation of the Eyes, and an holy Rage against other Men's Sins. And happy those Ladies and religious Dames, characterized in 2 *Tim.* iii. 6, who can have such self-denying, thriving, able Men for their Confessors! and thrice happy those Families, where they vouchsafe to take their Friday-Night's Refreshments! and thereby demonstrate to the world what Christian Abstinence, and what primitive, self-mortifying Rigour there is in forbearing a Dinner, that they may have the better Stomach to their Supper.

In fine, the whole World stands in Admiration of them; Fools are fond of them, and wise Men are afraid of them; they are talked of, they are pointed at; and as they order the matter, they draw the Eyes of all Men after them, and generally something else.

But as it is observed in Greyhounds, that the thinness of their Jaws does not at all allay the ravening fury of their Appetite, there being no Creature whose teeth are sharper, and whose feet are swifter when they are in pursuit of their Prey; so woe be to that Man who stands in the way of a meagre, mortified, fasting, sharp-set Zeal, when it is in full chase of its spiritual Game. And therefore, as the Apostle admonishes the *Philippians*, *Phil.* iii. 2, *To beware of Dogs*, so his advice cannot be too frequently remembered, nor too warily observed, when we have to deal with those who are always fawning upon some and biting others, as shall best serve their Occasions.

Sermon: On the Mischievous Influence of Words and Names falsely applied

THOMAS BURNET

1635?–1715

203 *Dies irae, dies illa*

WHERE are now the great Empires of the World, and their great Imperial Cities? Their Pillars, Trophies, and Monuments of Glory? Show me where they stood, read the Inscription, tell me the Victor's Name. What Remains, what Impressions, what Difference or Distinction do you see in this Mass of Fire?

Rome itself, *Eternal Rome*, the Great City, the Empress of the World, whose domination and superstition, antient and modern, make a great part of the History of this Earth, what is become of her now? She laid her Foundations deep, and her Palaces were strong and sumptuous; *She glorified herself and lived deliciously; and said in her heart, I sit a Queen, and shall see no sorrow.* But her hour is come, she is wiped away from the face of the Earth, and buried in perpetual oblivion. But 'tis not Cities only, and works of men's hands, but the everlasting Hills, the Mountains and Rocks of the Earth are melted as wax before the Sun; and *their place is nowhere found.*

Here stood the *Alps*, a prodigious range of stone, the Load of the Earth, that covered many Countries, and reached their arms from the Ocean to the *Black Sea*; this huge mass of Stone is softened and dissolved, as a tender Cloud into Rain. Here stood the *African* Mountains, and *Atlas* with his Top above the Clouds. There was frozen *Caucasus*, and *Taurus*, and *Imaus*, and the Mountains of *Asia*. And yonder towards the North, stood the *Riphaean Hills*, clothed in Ice and Snow. All these are vanished, dropped away as the Snow upon their Heads, and swallowed up in a Red Sea of Fire.

A Sacred Theory of the Earth

THOMAS SPRAT, BISHOP OF ROCHESTER

1635–1713

204 *The Philosophy of the Primitive Church*

THIS was the Condition of Philosophy when the Christian Religion came into the World. That maintained itself in its first Age by the Innocence, and Miracles, and Sufferings of its Founder and his Apostles. But after their Deaths, when Christianity began to spread into the farthest Nations, and when the Power of Working Wonders had ceased, it was thought necessary for its Increase that its Professors should be able to defend it against the Subtilities of the Heathens by those same ways of Arguing which were then in use among the Heathen Philosophers. It was therefore on this Account that the Fathers and chief Doctors of our Church applied themselves to the Peripatetick and Platonick Sects; but chiefly to the Platonick, because that seemed to speak plainer about the Divine Nature; and also because the Sweetness and Powerfulness of *Plato's* Writings did serve as well to make them popular Speakers as Disputers. Having thus provided themselves against their Adversaries they easily got the Victory over them. And though the idolatrous Gentiles had kept the Instruments of disputing in their own Hands so many hundred Years, yet they soon convinced them of the Ridiculousness of their Worship, and the Purity and Reasonableness of ours.

But now the Christians having had so good Success against the Religions of the Heathens by their own Weapons, instead of laying them down when they had done, unfortunately fell to manage them one against another. So many subtile Brains having been set on work and warmed against a Foreign Enemy, when that was over, and they had nothing else to do (like an Army that returns victorious and is not presently disbanded) they began to spoil and quarrel amongst themselves. Hence that Religion, which at first appeared so innocent and peaceable, and fitted for the benefit of human Society, which consisted in the plain and direct Rules of good Life and Charity, and the Belief in a Redemption by one Saviour, was miserably divided into a thousand intricate Questions, which neither advance true Piety nor good Manners.

The History of the Royal Society

205 *The Plague*

THE *Plague* was indeed an irreparable Damage to the whole Kingdom; but that which chiefly added to the Misery was the *Time* wherein it happened. For what could be a more deplorable Accident than that so many *brave Men* should be cut off by the *Arrow that flies in the dark*, when our Country was engaged in a *foreign War*, and when their Lives might have been honourably ventured on a glorious Theatre in its Defence? And we had scarce recovered this *first Misfortune* when we received a *second* and a deeper Wound; which cannot be equalled in all *History*, if either we consider the Obscurity of its *Beginning*, the irresistible Violence of its Progress, the Horror of its *Appearance*, or the Wideness of the Ruin it made, in one of the most renowned *Cities* of the World.

Yet when, on the one side, I remember what *Desolation* these Scourges of Mankind have left behind them; and on the other, when I reflect on the *Magnanimity* wherewith the English Nation did support the Mischiefs; I find that I have not more Reason to *bewail* the one than to *admire* the other.

Upon our Return after the abating of the *Plague*, what else could we expect but to see the *Streets* unfrequented, the *River* forsaken, the *Fields* deformed with the *Graves* of the *Dead*, and the *Terrors* of *Death* still abiding on the Faces of the living? But instead of such dismal Sights there appeared almost the same Throngs in all publick Places, the same Noise of *Business*, the same Freedom of Converse, and, with the Return of the *King*, the same Cheerfulness returning on the Minds of the *People* as before.

Nor was their *Courage* less in sustaining the *second Calamity*, which destroyed their *Houses* and *Estates*. This the greatest Losers endured with such undaunted Firmness of Mind that their Example may incline us to believe that not only the best *Natural*, but the best *Moral* Philosophy too, may be learned from the Shops of *Mechanicks*. It was indeed an admirable Thing to behold with what *Constancy* the meanest Artificers saw all the *Labours* of their *Lives* and the *Support* of their *Families* devoured in an instant. The Affliction, 'tis true, was widely spread over the whole Nation; every Place was filled with Signs of *Pity* and *Commiseration*; but those who had suffered most seemed the least affected with the Loss: no *unmanly Bewailings* were heard in the few *Streets* that were preserved; they beheld the Ashes of their *Houses* and *Gates* and *Temples* without the least Expression of Pusillanimity. If *Philosophers* had done this it had well become their Profession of Wisdom; if *Gentlemen*, the Nobleness of their *Breeding* and *Blood* would have required it: but that such Greatness of Heart should be found amongst the poor *Artizans* and the obscure *Multitude* is no doubt one of the most honourable Events that ever happened. Yet still there is one *Circumstance* behind which may raise our *Wonder* higher; and that is, that amidst such horrible *Ruins* they still prosecuted the *War* with the same *Vigour* and *Courage* against three of the most powerful

States of all *Europe.* What Records of Time, or Memory of past Ages, can show us a greater Testimony of an invincible and heroick *Genius* than this of which I now speak? that the Sound of the *Heralds* proclaiming new *Wars* should be pleasant to the People, when the sad Voice of the *Bell-man* was scarce yet gone out of their Ears? That the Increase of their Adversaries *Confederates*, and of their own *Calamities*, should be so far from affrighting them, that they rather seemed to receive from thence a *new Vigour* and *Resolution*? and that they should still be eager upon *Victories* and *Triumphs* when they were thought almost quite exhausted by so great Destructions?

The History of the Royal Society

EDWARD STILLINGFLEET, BISHOP OF WORCESTER

1635–1699

206 *London's Judgement by Fire*

LOOK now upon me, you who so lately admired the greatness of my trade, the riches of my merchants, the number of my people, the conveniency of my *Churches*, the multitude of my Streets, and see what desolations sin hath made in the earth. Look upon me, and then tell me whether it be nothing to dally with Heaven, to make a mock at sin, to slight the judgements of *God*, and abuse his mercies, and after all the attempts of Heaven to reclaim a people from their sins, to remain still the same that ever they were? Was there no way to expiate your guilt but by my misery? Had the *leprosy* of your sins so fretted into my walls, that there was no cleansing them, but by the flames which consume them? Must I mourn in *my dust and ashes* for your iniquities, while you are so ready to return to the practice of them? Have I suffered so much by reason of *them*, and do you think to escape yourselves? Can you then look upon my ruins with hearts as hard and unconcerned as the *stones* which lie in them? If you have any kindness for me, or for yourselves; if you ever hope to see my breaches repaired, my beauty restored, my glory advanced, look on *London's* ruins and *repent*. Thus would she bid her inhabitants not weep for her miseries, but for their own sins; for if *never any sorrow were like to her sorrow*, it is because never any sins were like to their sins. Not as though they were only the sins of the City which have brought this evil upon her; no, but as far as the judgement reaches, so great hath the compass of the sins been, which have provoked *God* to make her an example of his justice. And I fear the effects of *London's* calamity will be felt all the Nation over. For, considering the present languishing condition of this Nation, it will be no easy matter to recover the *blood* and *spirits* which have been lost by this *Fire*.

Sermon preached after the Great Fire of London

JOSEPH GLANVILL

1636–1680

207 *The Scholar Gipsy*

THERE was very lately a Lad in the *University* of *Oxford*, who being of very pregnant and ready parts, and yet wanting the encouragement of preferment; was by his poverty forced to leave his studies there, and to cast himself upon the wide world for a livelihood. Now, his necessities growing daily on him, and wanting the help of friends to relieve him; he was at last forced to joyn himself to a company of *Vagabond Gypsies*, whom occasionally he met with, and to follow their Trade for a maintenance. Among these extravagant people, by the insinuating subtilty of his carriage, he quickly got so much of their love, and esteem; as that they discovered to him their *Mystery*: in the practice of which, by the pregnancy of his wit and parts he soon grew so good a proficient, as to be able to out-do his Instructours. After he had been a pretty well while exercised in the Trade; there chanced to ride by a couple of *Scholars* who had formerly bin of his acquaintance. The *Scholars* had quickly spied out their old friend, among the *Gypsies*; and their amazement to see him among such society, had well-nigh discovered him: but by a sign he prevented their owning him before that Crew: and taking one of them aside privately, desired him with his friend to go to an *Inn*, not far distant thence, promising there to come to them. They accordingly went thither, and he follows: after their first salutations, his friends enquire how he came to lead so odd a life as that was, and to join himself with such a *cheating beggerly* company. The *Scholar-Gypsy* having given them an account of the necessity, which drove him to that kind of life; told them, that the people he went with were not such *Impostors* as they were taken for, but that they had a *traditional* kind of *learning* among them, and could do wonders by the power of *Imagination*, and that himself had learnt much of their Art, and improved it further then themselves could. And to evince the truth of what he told them, he said, he'd remove into another room, leaving them to discourse together; and upon his return tell them the sum of what they had talked of: which accordingly he performed, giving them a full account of what had passed between them in his absence. *The Scholars* being amazed at so unexpected a discovery, earnestly desired him to unriddle the *mystery*. In which he gave them satisfaction, by telling them, that what he did was by the power of *Imagination*, his Phancy binding theirs; and that himself had dictated to them the discourse they held together, while he was from them: That there were warrantable wayes of heightening the *Imagination* to that pitch, as to bind another's; and that when he had compassed the whole *secret*, some parts of which he said he was yet ignorant of, he intended to leave their company, and give the world an account of what he had learned.

The Vanity of Dogmatizing

THOMAS TRAHERNE

1636?–1674

208 *The Heir of All Things*

YOU never enjoy the world aright, till the Sea itself floweth in your veins, till you are clothed with the heavens, and crowned with the stars: and perceive yourself to be the sole heir of the whole world, and more than so, because men are in it who are every one sole heirs as well as you. Till you can sing and rejoice and delight in God, as misers do in gold, and Kings in sceptres, you never enjoy the world.

Till your spirit filleth the whole world, and the stars are your jewels; till you are as familiar with the ways of God in all Ages as with your walk and table: till you are intimately acquainted with that shady nothing out of which the world was made: till you love men so as to desire their happiness, with a thirst equal to the zeal of your own: till you delight in God for being good to all: you never enjoy the world. Till you more feel it than your private estate, and are more present in the hemisphere, considering the glories and the beauties there, than in your own house: Till you remember how lately you were made, and how wonderful it was when you came into it: and more rejoice in the palace of your glory, than if it had been made but to-day morning.

Centuries of Meditations

209 *A Child's Vision of the World*

WILL you see the infancy of this sublime and celestial greatness? Those pure and virgin apprehensions I had from the womb, and that divine light wherewith I was born are the best unto this day, wherein I can see the Universe. By the Gift of God they attended me into the world, and by His special favour I remember them till now. Verily they seem the greatest gifts His wisdom could bestow, for without them all other gifts had been dead and vain. They are unattainable by book, and therefore I will teach them by experience. Pray for them earnestly: for they will make you angelical, and wholly celestial. Certainly Adam in Paradise had not more sweet and curious apprehensions of the world, than I when I was a child.

All appeared new, and strange at first, inexpressibly rare and delightful and beautiful. I was a little stranger, which at my entrance into the world was saluted and surrounded with innumerable joys. My knowledge was Divine. I knew by intuition those things which since my Apostasy, I collected again by the highest reason. My very ignorance was advantageous. I seemed as one brought into the Estate of Innocence. All things were spotless and pure and glorious: yea, and infinitely mine, and joyful and precious. I knew not that there were any sins, or complaints or laws. I dreamed not of poverties, contentions, or vices. All tears and quarrels were hidden from mine eyes. Everything was at rest, free and immortal. I knew nothing of sickness or death or rents or exaction, either for tribute or bread. In the absence of these I was entertained like an Angel with the works of God in their splendour and glory, I saw all in the peace of Eden; Heaven and Earth did sing my Creator's praises, and could not make more melody to Adam, than to me. All Time was Eternity, and a perpetual Sabbath. Is it not strange, that an infant should be heir of the whole World, and see those mysteries which the books of the learned never unfold?

The corn was orient and immortal wheat, which never should be reaped, nor was ever sown. I thought it had stood from everlasting to everlasting. The dust and stones of the street were as precious as gold: the gates were at first the end of the world. The green trees when I saw them first through one of the gates transported and ravished me, their sweetness and unusual beauty made my heart to leap, and almost mad with ecstasy, they were such strange and wonderful things. The Men! O what venerable and reverend creatures did the aged seem! Immortal Cherubims! And young men glittering and sparkling Angels, and maids strange seraphic pieces of life and beauty! Boys and girls tumbling in the street, and playing, were moving jewels. I knew not that they were born or should die; But all things abided eternally as they were in their proper places. Eternity was manifest in the Light of the Day, and something infinite behind everything appeared: which talked with my expectation and moved my desire. The city seemed to stand in Eden, or to be built in Heaven. The streets were mine, the temple was mine, the people were mine, their clothes and gold and silver were mine, as much as their sparkling eyes, fair skins, and ruddy faces. The skies were mine, and so were the sun and moon and stars, and all the World was mine; and I the only spectator and enjoyer of it.

Centuries of Meditations

210 *Love a Trinity*

IN all Love there is a love begetting, and a love begotten, and a love proceeding. Which though they are one in essence subsist nevertheless in three several manners. For love is benevolent affection to another: Which is of itself, and by itself relateth to its object. It floweth from itself and resteth in its object. Love proceedeth of necessity from itself, for unless it be of itself it is not Love. Constraint is destructive and opposite to its nature. The Love from which it floweth is the fountain of Love. The Love which streameth from it, is the communication of Love, or Love communicated. The Love which resteth in the object is the Love which streameth to it. So that in all Love, the Trinity is clear. By secret passages without stirring it proceedeth to its object, and is as powerfully present as if it did not proceed at all. The Love that lieth in the bosom of the Lover, being the love that is perceived in the spirit of the Beloved: that is, the same in substance, though in the manner of substance, or subsistence, different. Love in the bosom is the parent of Love, Love in the stream is the effect of Love, Love seen, or dwelling in the object proceedeth from both. Yet are all these, one and the self-same Love: though three Loves.

Centuries of Meditations

GILBERT BURNET, BISHOP OF SALISBURY

1643–1715

211 *The Battle of Dunbar*

THE army was indeed one of the best that ever *Scotland* had brought together, but it was ill commanded: for all that had made defection from their cause, or that were thought indifferent as to either side, which they called detestable neutrality, were put out of commission. The preachers thought it an army of saints, and seemed well assured of success. They drew near *Cromwell*, who being pressed by them retired towards *Dunbar*, where his ships and provisions lay. The *Scots* followed him, and were posted on a hill about a mile from thence, where there was no attacking them. *Cromwell* was then in great distress, and looked on himself as undone. There was no marching towards *Berwick*, the ground was too narrow: Nor could he come back into the country without being separated from his ships, and starving his army. The least evil seemed to be to kill his horses, and put his army on board, and sail back to *Newcastle*; which, in the disposition that *England* was in at that time, would have been all their destruction, for it would have occasioned an universal insurrection for the King. They had not above three days' forage for their horses. So *Cromwell* called his officers to a day of seeking the Lord, in their style. He loved to talk much of that matter all his life long afterwards: He said he felt such an enlargement of heart in prayer, and such quiet upon it, that he bade all about him take heart, for God had certainly heard them, and would appear for them. After prayer they walked in the Earl of *Roxburgh's* gardens, that lie under the hill: And by prospective glasses they discerned a great motion in the *Scotish* Camp: upon which *Cromwell* said, 'God is delivering them into our hands, they are coming down to us.' *Leslie* was in the chief command: but he had a committee of the States with him to give him his orders, among whom *Warriston* was one. These were weary of lying in the fields, and thought that *Leslie* made not haste enough to destroy those Sectaries; for so they loved to call them. He told them, by lying there all was sure, but that by engaging into action with gallant and desperate men all might be lost: Yet they still called on him to fall on. Many have thought that all this was treachery, done on design to deliver up our army to *Cromwell*; some laying it upon *Leslie*, and others upon my uncle. I am persuaded there was no treachery in it: only *Warriston* was too hot, and Leslie was too cold, and yielded too easily to their humours, which he ought not to have done. They were all the night employed in coming down the hill: And in the morning, before they were put in order, *Cromwell* fell upon them. Two regiments stood their ground, and were almost all killed in their ranks: The rest did run in a most shameful manner: So that both their artillery and baggage, and with these a great many prisoners, were taken, some thousands in all.

A History of His Own Time

212 *The Conclusion of the Whole Matter*

SO that by Religion I mean, such a Sense of divine Truth, as enters into a Man, and becomes a Spring of a new Nature within him; reforming his Thoughts and Designs, purifying his Heart, and sanctifying him, and governing his whole Deportment, his Words as well as his Actions; convincing him that, it is not enough, not to be scandalously vicious, or to be innocent in his Conversation, but that he must be entirely, uniformly and constantly pure and Virtuous, animating him with a Zeal, to be still better and better, more eminently good and exemplary, using Prayers and all outward Devotions, as solemn Acts testifying what he is inwardly and at heart, and as Methods instituted by God, to be still advancing in the use of them further and further, into a more refined and spiritual Sense of divine Matters. This is true Religion, which is the Perfection of Human Nature, and the Joy and Delight of every one, that feels it active and strong within him; it is true this is not arrived at all at once; and it will have an unhappy allay, hanging long even about a good Man: But, as those ill Mixtures are the perpetual Grief of his Soul, so it is his chief Care to watch over and to mortify them; he will be in a continual Progress, still gaining ground upon himself: and, as he attains to a good degree of purity, he will find a noble Flame of Life and Joy growing upon him. Of this I write with the more concern and Emotion, because I have felt this the true and indeed the only Joy, which runs through a Man's Heart and Life: It is that which has been for many Years my greatest Support; I rejoice daily in it; I feel from it the Earnest of that supreme Joy, which I pant and long for; I am sure there is nothing else can afford any true or complete Happiness. I have, considering my Sphere, seen a great deal of all that is most shining and tempting in this World: The Pleasures of Sense I did soon nauseate; Intrigues of State, and the Conduct of Affairs have something in them that is more specious; and I was, for some Years, deeply immersed in these, but still with Hopes of reforming the World, and of making Mankind wiser and better: But I have found, *That which is crooked cannot be made straight.* I acquainted myself with Knowledge and Learning, and that in a great Variety, and with more Compass than depth: but though *wisdom excelleth Folly, as much as Light does Darkness*; yet, as it is a *sore Travail*, so it is so very defective, that what is *wanting* to complete it, *cannot be numbered.* I have seen that *two were better than one*, and that a *threefold Cord is not easily loosed*; and have therefore cultivated Friendship with much Zeal and a disinterested Tenderness; but I have found this was also Vanity and Vexation of Spirit, though it be of the best and noblest sort. So that, upon great and long Experience, I could enlarge on the Preacher's Text, *Vanity of Vanities, and all is Vanity*; but I must also conclude with him; *Fear God, and keep his Commandments, for this is the All of Man*, the Whole both of his Duty, and of his Happiness.

A History of His Own Time

WILLIAM PENN

1644–1718

213 *The Comfort of Friends*

THEY that love beyond the world cannot be separated by it.

Death cannot kill what never dies.

Nor can spirits ever be divided, that love and live in the same divine principle, the root and record of their friendship.

If absence be not death, neither is theirs.

Death is but crossing the world, as friends do the seas; they live in one another still.

For they must needs be present, that love and live in that which is omnipresent.

In this divine glass they see face to face; and their converse is free, as well as pure.

This is the comfort of friends, that though they may be said to die, yet their friendship and society are, in the best sense, ever present, because immortal.

Fruits of Solitude

ROGER NORTH

1653–1734

214 *Judge Jeffries*

AND since nothing historical is amiss in a design like this, I will subjoin what I have personally noted of that man, and some things of indubitable report concerning him. His friendship and conversation lay much among the good fellows and humorists; and his delights were accordingly drinking, laughing, singing, and all the extravagances of the bottle. He had a set of banterers for the most part near him, as in old time great men kept fools to make them merry.

And these fellows abusing one another and their betters were a regale to him. And no friendship or dearness could be so great in private, which he would not use ill, and to an extravagant degree, in public. No one that had any expectation from him was safe from his public contempt and derision, which some of his minions at the bar bitterly felt. Those above or that could hurt or benefit him, and none else, might depend on fair quarter at his hands. When he was in temper, and matter indifferent came before him, he became his seat of justice better than any I ever saw in his place. He had extraordinary natural abilities, but little acquired, beyond what practice in affairs had supplied. He talked fluently and with spirit; and his weakness was that he could not reprehend without scolding, and in such *Billingsgate* language as should not come out of the mouth of any man. He called it 'Giving a lick with the rough side of his tongue'.

Life of the Lord Keeper Guilford

215 *Recreations of a College Don*

THE doctor had no favourite diversion, or manual exercise, to rest his mind a little, which he held bent with continual thinking. His parents, who were much addicted to music, recommended that to him for a diversion, and particularly the noble organ, as the fullest, and not only a complete solitary concert, but most proper for an ecclesiastic. And indeed, if study had not had the upper hand of all his intendments, he must of course have taken up in that way, his parents themselves being so fond of it. For after the care of prayers and meals, nothing was more constant and solemn than music was in that family.

He was sensible the advice was very good, and accordingly got a small organ into his chamber at *Jesus College*, and suffered himself to be taught a lesson or two, which he practised over when he had a mind to be unbent; but he made no manner of advance, and one accident put him out of all manner of conceit of it. His under neighbour was a morose and importune master of arts; and one night the doctor could not sleep; and thought to fit himself for it by playing upon his organ. The bellows knocking on the floor, and the hum of the pipes, made a strange din at midnight, and the gentleman below, that never heard it so before, could not tell what to make of it; but, at length, he found it out to be his neighbour's organ. And thereupon, to retaliate this night's work, got out of his bed, and, with his two couple of bowls, went to bowls by himself. This made a much louder noise than the organ, and the doctor was as much at a loss to know what that meant, but, suspecting how the case stood, he left off, and scarce ever touched his organ after. The pleasure of music is like that of books, never true and good, unless easily and familiarly read, and performed; and then nothing is more medicinal to a crazy and fatigued mind than that.

Life of the Hon. and Rev. Dr. John North

DANIEL DEFOE

1661–1731

216 *Crusoe visits the Wreck*

A LITTLE after noon I found the sea very calm, and the tide ebbed so far out, that I could come within a quarter of a mile of the ship; and here I found a fresh renewing of my grief, for I saw evidently, that if we had kept on board we had been all safe, that is to say, we had all got safe on shore, and I had not been so miserable as to be left entirely destitute of all comfort and company, as I now was. This forced tears from my eyes again; but as there was little relief in that, I resolved, if possible, to get to the ship; so I pulled off my cloaths, for the weather was hot to extremity, and took the water. But when I came to the ship, my difficulty was still greater to know how to get on board; for as she lay aground, and high out of the water, there was nothing within my reach to lay hold of. I swam round her twice, and the second time I spied a small piece of a rope, which I wondered I did not see at first, hang down by the fore-chains so low, as that with great difficulty I got hold of it, and by the help of that rope got up into the forecastle of the ship. Here I found that the ship was bilged, and had a great deal of water in her hold, but that she lay so on the side of a bank of hard sand, or rather earth, that her stern lay lifted up upon the bank, and her head low almost to the water. By this means all her quarter was free, and all that was in that part was dry; for you may be sure my first work was to search and to see what was spoiled and what was free. And first I found that all the ship's provisions were dry and untouched by the water; and being very well disposed to eat, I went to the bread-room and filled my pockets with biscuit, and eat it as I went about other things, for I had no time to lose. I also found some rum in the great cabin, of which I took a large dram, and which I had indeed need enough of to spirit me for what was before me. Now I wanted nothing but a boat, to furnish myself with many things which I foresaw would be very necessary to me.

It was in vain to sit still and wish for what was not to be had, and this extremity roused my application. We had several spare yards, and two or three large spars of wood, and a spare top-mast or two in the ship. I resolved to fall to work with these, and flung as many of them overboard as I could manage for their weight, tying every one with a rope, that they might not drive away. When this was done I went down the ship's side, and, pulling them to me, I tied four of them fast together at both ends as well as I could, in the form of a raft; and laying two or three short pieces of plank upon them crossways, I found I could walk upon it very well, but that it was not able to bear any great weight, the pieces being too light. So I went to work, and with the carpenter's saw I cut a spare top-mast into three lengths, and added them to my raft, with a great deal of labour and pains; but hope of furnishing myself with necessaries encouraged me to go beyond what I should have been able to have done upon another occasion.

My raft was now strong enough to bear any reasonable weight. My next care was what to load it with, and how to preserve what I laid upon it from the surf of the sea; but I was not long considering this. I first laid all the planks or boards upon it that I could get, and having considered well what I most wanted, I first got three of the seamen's chests, which I had broken open and emptied, and lowered them down upon my raft. The first of these I filled with provisions, viz., bread, rice, three *Dutch* cheeses, five pieces of dried goat's flesh, which we lived much upon, and a little remainder of *European* corn, which had been laid by for some fowls which we brought to sea with us, but the fowls were killed. There had been some barley and wheat together, but, to my great disappointment, I found afterwards that the rats had eaten or spoiled it all. As for liquors, I found several cases of bottles belonging to our skipper, in which were some cordial waters, and, in all, about five or six gallons of rack. These I stowed by themselves, there being no need to put them into the chest, nor no room for them. While I was doing this, I found the tide began to flow, though very calm, and I had the mortification to see my coat, shirt, and waistcoat, which I had left on shore upon the sand, swim away; as for my breeches, which were only linen, and open-kneed, I swam on board in them, and my stockings. However, this put me upon rummaging for clothes, of which I found enough, but took no more than I wanted for present use; for I had other things which my eye was more upon, as first tools to work with on shore; and it was after long searching that I found out the carpenter's chest, which was indeed a very useful prize to me, and much more valuable than a ship-loading of gold would have been at that time. I got it down to my raft, even whole as it was, without losing time to look into it, for I knew in general what it contained.

My next care was for some ammunition and arms; there were two very good fowling-pieces in the great cabin, and two pistols; these I secured first, with some powder-horns, and a small bag of shot, and two old rusty swords. I knew there were three barrels of powder in the ship, but knew not where our gunner had stowed them; but with much search I found them, two of them dry and good, the third had taken water; those two I got to my raft with the arms. And now I thought myself pretty well freighted, and began to think how I should get to shore with them, having neither sail, oar, or rudder; and the least capful of wind would have overset all my navigation.

I had three encouragements. 1. A smooth, calm sea. 2. The tide rising and setting in to the shore. 3. What little wind there was blew me towards the land. And thus, having found two or three broken oars belonging to the boat, and besides the tools which were in the chest, I found two saws, an axe, and a hammer, and with this cargo I put to sea. For a mile or thereabouts my raft went very well, only that I found it drive a little distant from the place where I had landed before, by which I perceived that there was some indraft of the water, and consequently I hoped to find some creek or river there, which I might make use of as a port to get to land with my cargo.

Robinson Crusoe

217 *The Footprint*

IT happened one day, about noon, going towards my boat, I was exceedingly surprised with the print of a man's naked foot on the shore, which was very plain to be seen in the sand. I stood like one thunder-struck, or as if I had seen an apparition. I listened, I looked round me, I could hear nothing, nor see anything. I went up to a rising ground, to look farther. I went up the shore, and down the shore, but it was all one; I could see no other impression but that one. I went to it again to see if there were any more, and to observe if it might not be my fancy; but there was no room for that, for there was exactly the very print of a foot—toes, heel, and every part of a foot. How it came thither I knew not, nor could in the least imagine. But after innumerable fluttering thoughts, like a man perfectly confused and out of myself, I came home to my fortification, not feeling, as we say, the ground I went on, but terrified to the last degree, looking behind me at every two or three steps, mistaking every bush and tree, and fancying every stump at a distance to be a man ; nor is it possible to describe how many various shapes affrighted imagination represented things to me in, how many wild ideas were found every moment in my fancy, and what strange, unaccountable whimsies came into my thoughts by the way.

When I came to my castle, for so I think I called it ever after this, I fled into it like one pursued. Whether I went over by the ladder, as first contrived, or went in at the hole in the rock, which I called a door, I cannot remember ; no, nor could I remember the next morning, for never frighted hare fled to cover, or fox to earth, with more terror of mind than I to this retreat.

Robinson Crusoe

218 *London in Plague Time*

DURING the month of July, and while, as I have observed, our part of the town seemed to be spared in comparison of the west part, I went ordinarily about the streets, as my business required, and particularly went generally once in a day, or in two days, into the city, to my brother's house, which he had given me charge of, and to see if it was safe ; and having the key in my pocket, I used to go into the house, and over most of the rooms, to see that all was well ; for though it be something wonderful to tell, that any should have hearts so hardened, in the midst of such a calamity, as to rob and steal; yet certain it is, that all sorts of villanies, and even levities and debaucheries, were then practised in the town, as openly as ever, I will not say quite as frequently, because the numbers of people were many ways lessened.

But the city itself began now to be visited too, I mean within the walls; but the number of people there were, indeed, extremely lessened, by so great a multitude having been gone into the country; and even all this month of July, they continued to flee, though not in such multitudes as formerly. In August, indeed, they fled in such a manner, that I began to think there would be really none but magistrates and servants left in the city. . . The face of London was now indeed strangely altered, I mean the whole mass of buildings, city, liberties, suburbs, Westminster, Southwark, and altogether; for, as to the particular part called the city, or within the walls, that was not yet much infected; but in the whole, the face of things, I say, was much altered; sorrow and sadness sat upon every face, and though some part were not yet overwhelmed, yet all looked deeply concerned; and as we saw it apparently coming on, so every one looked on himself, and his family, as in the utmost danger: were it possible to represent those times exactly, to those that did not see them, and give the reader due ideas of the horror that everywhere presented itself, it must make just impressions upon their minds, and fill them with surprise. London might well be said to be all in tears! the mourners did not go about the streets indeed, for nobody put on black, or made a formal dress of mourning for their nearest friends; but the voice of mourning was truly heard in the streets; the shrieks of women and children at the windows and doors of their houses, where their dearest relations were, perhaps dying, or just dead, were so frequent to be heard, as we passed the streets, that it was enough to pierce the stoutest heart in the world to hear them. Tears and lamentations were seen almost in every house, especially in the first part of the visitation; for towards the latter end, men's hearts were hardened, and death was so always before their eyes, that they did not so much concern themselves for the loss of their friends, expecting that themselves should be summoned the next hour.

Business led me out sometimes to the other end of the town, even when the sickness was chiefly there; and as the thing was new to me, as well as to everybody else, it was a most surprising thing to see those streets, which were usually so thronged, now grown desolate, and so few people to be seen in them, that if I had been a stranger, and at a loss for my way, I might sometimes have gone the length of a whole street, I mean of the by-streets, and see nobody to direct me, except watchmen set at the doors of such houses as were shut up; of which I shall speak presently.

One day, being at that part of the town, on some special business, curiosity led me to observe things more than usually; and indeed I walked a great way where I had no business; I went up Holborn, and there the street was full of people; but they walked in the middle of the great street, neither on one side or other, because, as I suppose, they would not mingle with anybody that came out of the houses, or meet with smells and scents from houses that might be infected.

The inns of court were all shut up, nor were very

many of the lawyers in the Temple, or Lincoln's-Inn, or Gray's-Inn, to be seen there. Everybody was at peace, there was no occasion for lawyers; besides, it being in the time of the vacation too, they were generally gone into the country. Whole rows of houses in some places, were shut close up, the inhabitants all fled, and only a watchman or two left.

A Journal of the Plague Year

219 *A Young Thief*

I

NOTHING could be more perplexing than this money was to me all that night. I carried it in my hand a good while, for it was in gold, all but 14*s.*; and that is to say, it was in four guineas, and that 14*s.* was more difficult to carry than the four guineas; at last I sat down, and pulled off one of my shoes, and put the four guineas into that; but after I had gone a while, my shoe hurt me so I could not go, so I was fain to sit down again, and take it out of my shoe, and carry it in my hand; then I found a dirty linen rag in the street, and I took that up, and wrapped it all together, and carried it in that a good way. I have often since heard people say, when they have been talking of money that they could not get in, 'I wish I had it in a foul clout:' in truth, I had mine in a foul clout; for it was foul, according to the letter of that saying, but it served me till I came to a convenient place, and then I sat down and washed the cloth in the kennel, and so then put my money in again.

Well, I carried it home with me to my lodging in the glass-house, and when I went to go to sleep, I knew not what to do with it; if I had let any of the black crew I was with know of it, I should have been smothered in the ashes for it, or robbed of it, or some trick or other put upon me for it; so I knew not what to do, but lay with it in my hand, and my hand in my bosom, but then sleep went from my eyes. . . Every now and then dropping asleep, I should dream that my money was lost, and start like one frighted; then, finding it fast in my hand, try to go to sleep again, but could not for a long while, then drop and start again. At last a fancy came into my head that if I fell asleep, I should dream of the money and talk of it in my sleep, and tell that I had money, which if I should do, and one of the rogues should hear me, they would pick it out of my bosom, and of my hand too, without waking me; and after that thought I could not sleep a wink more. . . As soon as it was day, I got out of the hole we lay in, and rambled abroad into the fields towards Stepney, and there I mused and considered what I should do with this money, and many a time I wished that I had not had it; for, after all my ruminating upon it, and what course I should take with it, or where I should put it, I could not hit upon any one thing, or any possible method to secure it. . . At last it came into my head, that I would look out for some hole in a tree, and see to hide it there till I should have occasion for it. Big with this discovery, as I then thought it, I began to look about me for a tree; but there were no trees in the fields about Stepney or Mile-End, that looked fit for my purpose; and if there were any, that I began to look narrowly at, the fields were so full of people, that they would see if I went to hide anything there, and I thought the people eyed me as it was, and that two men in particular followed me to see what I intended to do.

This drove me farther off, and I crossed the road at Mile-End, and in the middle of the town went down a lane that goes away to the 'Blind Beggars', at Bethnal-Green; when I came a little way in the lane, I found a footpath over the fields, and in those fields several trees for my turn, as I thought; at last, one tree had a little hole in it, pretty high out of my reach, and I climbed up the tree to get to it, and when I came there, I put my hand in, and found (as I thought) a place very fit, so I placed my treasure there, and was mighty well satisfied with it; but, behold, putting my hand in again to lay it more commodiously, as I thought, of a sudden it slipped away from me, and I found the tree was hollow, and my little parcel was fallen in quite out of my reach, and how far it might go in I knew not; so that, in a word, my money was quite gone, irrecoverably lost; there could be no room so much as to hope ever to see it again, for it was a vast great tree.

As young as I was, I was now sensible what a fool I was before, that I could not think of ways to keep my money, but I must come thus far to throw it into a hole where I could not reach it. Well, I thrust my hand quite up to my elbow, but no bottom was to be found, or any end of the hole or cavity; I got a stick off of the tree, and thrust it in a great way, but all was one; then I cried, nay, I roared out, I was in such a passion; then I got down the tree again, then up again, and thrust in my hand again till I scratched my arm and made it bleed, and cried all the while most violently... The last time I had gotten up the tree I happened to come down not on the same side that I went up and came down before, but on the other side of the tree, and on the other side of the bank also; and, behold, the tree had a great open place, in the side of it close to the ground, as old hollow trees often have; and looking into the open place, to my inexpressible joy, there lay my money and my linen rag, all wrapped up just as I had put it into the hole; for the tree being hollow all the way up, there had been some moss or light stuff, which I had not judgement enough to know was not firm, and had given way when it came to drop out of my hand, and so it had slipped quite down at once.

I was but a child, and I rejoiced like a child, for I holloaed quite out aloud when I saw it; then I run to it, and snatched it up, hugged and kissed the dirty rag a hundred times; then danced and jumped about, run from one end of the field to the other, and, in short, I knew not what, much less do I know now what I did, though I shall never forget the thing, either what a sinking grief it was to my heart, when I thought I had lost it, or what a flood of joy overwhelmed me when I had got it again.

II

Well, I came away with my money, and, having taken sixpence out of it, before I made it up again, I went to a chandler's shop in Mile-End, and bought a half-penny roll and a half-pennyworth of cheese, and sat down at the door after I bought it, and ate it very heartily, and begged some beer to drink with it, which the good woman gave me very freely.

Away I went then for the town, to see if I could find any of my companions, and resolved I would try no more hollow trees for my treasure. As I came along

Whitechapel, I came by a broker's shop, over against the church, where they sold old clothes, for I had nothing on but the worst of rags; so I stopped at the shop, and stood looking at the clothes which hung at door.

'Well, young gentleman,' says a man that stood at the door, 'you look wishly; do you see anything you like, and will your pocket compass a good coat now, for you look as if you belonged to the ragged regiment?' I was affronted at the fellow. 'What 's that to you,' said I, 'how ragged I am? if I had seen anything I liked, I have money to pay for it; but I can go where I shan't be huffed at for looking.'

While I said thus, pretty boldly to the fellow, comes a woman out, 'What ails you,' says she to the man, 'to bully away our customers so? a poor boy's money is as good as my lord mayor's; if poor people did not buy old clothes, what would become of our business?' and then, turning to me, 'Come hither, child,' says she, 'if thou hast a mind to anything I have, you shan't be hectored by him; the boy is a pretty boy, I assure you,' says she, to another woman that was by this time come to her. 'Aye,' says t'other, 'so he is, a very well-looking child, if he was clean and well dressed, and may be as good a gentleman's son for anything we know, as any of those that are well dressed. Come, my dear,' says she, 'tell me what is it you would have?' She pleased me mightily to hear her talk of my being a gentleman's son, and it brought former things to mind; but when she talked of my being not clean, and in rags, then I cried.

She pressed me to tell her if I saw anything that I wanted; I told her no, all the clothes I saw there were too big for me. 'Come, child,' says she, 'I have two things here that will fit you, and I am sure you want them both ; that is, first, a little hat, and there,' says she (tossing it to me), 'I'll give you that for nothing ; and here is a good warm pair of breeches ; I dare say,' says she, 'they will fit you ; and they are very tight and good ; and,' says she, 'if you should ever come to have so much money that you don't know what to do with it, here are excellent good pockets,' says she, 'and a little fob to put your gold in, or your watch in, when you get it.'

It struck me with a strange kind of joy that I should have a place to put my money in, and need not go to hide it again in a hollow tree ; that I was ready to snatch the breeches out of her hands, and wondered that I should be such a fool never to think of buying me a pair of breeches before, that I might have a pocket to put my money in, and not carry it about two days together in my hand, and in my shoe, and I knew not how ; so, in a word, I gave her two shillings for the breeches, and went over into the churchyard, and put them on, put my money into my new pockets, and was as pleased as a prince is with his coach and six horses.

The Life of Colonel Jack

FRANCIS ATTERBURY, BISHOP OF ROCHESTER

1662–1732

220 *To his sick Daughter, about to rejoin him in his Exile*

Montpelier, Sept. 3, 1729.

MY DEAR HEART,

I have so much to say to you, that I can hardly say any thing to you till I see you. My heart is full ; but it is in vain to begin upon paper what I can never end. I have a thousand desires to see you, which are checked by a thousand fears lest any ill accident should happen to you in the journey. God preserve you in every step of it, and send you safe hither ! And I will endeavour, by his blessing and assistance, to send you well back again, and to accompany you in the journey, as far as the law of England will suffer me. I stay here only to receive and take care of you (for no other view should have hindered my coming into the North of France this autumn) ; and I live only to help towards lengthening your life, and rendering it, if I can, more agreeable to you : for I see not of what use I am, or can be, in other respects. I shall be impatient till I hear you are safely landed, and as impatient after that till you are safely arrived in your winter quarters. God, I hope, will favour you with good weather, and all manner of good accidents on the way ; and I will take care, my dear love, to make you as easy and happy as I can at the end of your journey.

I have written to Mr. Morice about every thing I can think of relating to your accommodation on the road, and shall not therefore repeat any part of it in this letter, which is intended only to acknowledge a mistake under which I find myself. I thought I loved you before as much as I could possibly. But I feel such new degrees of tenderness arising in me upon this terrible long journey, as I was never before acquainted with. God will reward you, I hope, for your piety to me, which had, I doubt not, its share in producing this resolution, and will in rewarding you reward me also ; that being the chief thing I have to beg of him.

Adieu, my dear heart, till I see you! and till then satisfy yourself, that, whatever uneasiness your journey may give you, my expectation of you, and concern for you, will give me more. I am got to another page, and must do violence to myself to stop here—But I will—and abruptly bid you, my dear heart, adieu, till I bid you welcome to Montpelier.

A line, under your own hand, pray, by the post that first sets out after you land at Bourdeaux.

FR. ROFFEN.

Epistolary Correspondence

MATTHEW PRIOR

1664–1721

221 *The Vicar of Bray and Sir Thomas More*

MORE. And yet Vicar, Cicero himself was beheaded as well as I.

Vicar. Why that is just the thing I have often taken into my consideration, he lost his life when he forsook his Maxim, to say the truth on't his Case in some respect was not unlike yours. He had his head cutt off because he would be running it [too] far into Affairs, from which he had better to have receeded. He spoke so violently against Anthony that he could never hope in Prudence to be forgiven by Him, tho Anthony had good Nature enough, and you contradicted Henry, who as to his temper was inflexible, and in his Anger never forgave any Man.

More. But did not Anthony deserve that and more from Cicero? And as to my Case, if the King—

Vicar. Alas, Sir, let People deserve or not deserve,

that is not six pence matter. Have they power or have they not? There's the Question. If they have, never provoke them; let me tell you, my late Lord Chancellor, as there are an Hundred old Womens Receipts of more real use than any that the Physitians can prescribe; by which the Vulgar live, while the Learned laugh at them: there are as many common rules by which we Ordinary People are directed, which you wise Men (as you think your selves) either do not know, or at least never Practice; if You did it would be better for You. . . .

More. But what did you think was your Business in the World, for what Cause did You live?

Vicar. Why to teach my Parish and to receive my Tythes.

More. Oh, as to receiving your Tythes I have no Scruple, but what did you teach your Parish?

Vicar. What a Question is That, Why Religion.

More. What Religion?

Vicar. Again, sometimes the Antient Roman Catholick, some times that of the Reformed Church of England.

More. How came you to teach them the first?

Vicar. Why my Canonical Obedience, the order of my Diocessan Bishop, the Missal and Breviary all enjoyned it.

More. How happened it then you taught the t'other?

Vicar. Why New Acts of Parliament were made for the Reformation of Popery. My Bishop was put into the Tower for Disobeying them, and our Missals and Breviarys were burnt. You are not going to Catachise me, Are you?

More. And You continued stil in your Vicarage of Bray?

Vicar. Where would you have had me been? in Foxes Book of Martyrs?

More. Soft and fair, Vicar, only one word more. Did you make all those leaps and Changes without any previous Examination, as to the Essential good or ill of them?

Vicar. Why, what should I have done? The King had a mind to fall out with the Pope. Would you have a single Man oppose either of these mighty Potentates? His Highness upon the Quarrel bids me read the Mass in English, and I do so. His Son Edward enjoins the same thing, and I continue my Obedience. Queen Mary is [in] Communion with the Church of Rome, and She commands me to turn my English Mass again into Latin. Why then things are just as they were when first I took Orders. Elizabeth will have it Translated back into English. Why then matters stand as they did when I first reformed. You see, Sir, it was the Opinion of the Church of which I was a Member, that Changed, but the Vicar of Bray remained always the same Man.

Dialogues of the Dead

JOHN ARBUTHNOT

1667–1735

222 The Christening of Martin Scriblerus

THE day of the Christening being come, and the house filled with Gossips, the Levity of whose Conversation suited but ill with the Gravity of Dr. Cornelius, he cast about how to pass this day more agreeably to his Character; that is to say, not without some *Profitable Conference*, nor wholly without observance of some *Ancient Custom.*

He remembered to have read in Theocritus, that the Cradle of Hercules was a Shield; and being possessed of an antique *Buckler*, which he held as a most inestimable Relick, he determined to have the infant laid therein, and in that manner brought into the Study, to be shown to certain learned men of his acquaintance.

The regard he had for this Shield had caused him formerly to compile a Dissertation concerning it, proving from the several properties, and particularly the colour of the Rust, the exact chronology thereof.

With this Treatise, and a moderate supper, he proposed to entertain his Guests; though he had also another design, to have their assistance in the calculation of his Son's *Nativity*.

He therefore took the Buckler out of a Case (in which he always kept it, lest it might contract any modern rust), and entrusted it to his House-maid, with orders that, when the company was come, she should lay the Child carefully in it, covered with a mantle of blue Satin.

The Guests were no sooner seated, but they entered into a warm Debate about the *Triclinium*, and the manner of *Decubitus* of the Ancients, which Cornelius broke off in this manner:—

'This day, my Friends, I purpose to exhibit my son before you; a Child not wholly unworthy of Inspection, as he is descended from a Race of Virtuosi. Let the Physiognomists examine his features; let the Chirographists behold his Palm; but above all, let us consult for the calculation of his Nativity. To this end, as the child is not vulgar, I will not present him unto you in a vulgar manner. He shall be cradled in my Ancient Shield, so famous through the Universities of Europe. You all know how I purchased that invaluable piece of Antiquity, at the great (though indeed inadequate) expence of all the Plate of our family, how happily I carried it off, and how triumphantly I transported it hither, to the inexpressible grief of all Germany. Happy in every circumstance, but that it broke the heart of the great Melchior Insipidus!'

Here he stopped his Speech, upon the sight of the Maid, who entered the room with the Child; He took it in his arms, and proceeded.

'Behold then my Child, but first behold the Shield; Behold this Rust,—or rather let me call it this precious Ærugo,—behold this beautiful Varnish of Time,—this venerable Verdure of so many Ages—'

In speaking these words, he slowly lifted up the Mantle which covered it, inch by inch; but at every inch he uncovered his cheeks grew paler, his hand trembled, his nerves failed, till on sight of the whole, the Tremor became universal; the Shield and the Infant both dropped to the ground, and he had only strength enough to cry out, 'O God! my Shield, my Shield!'

The Truth was, the Maid (extreamly concerned for the reputation of her own cleanliness, and her young master's honour) had scoured it as clean as her Andirons.

Cornelius sunk back on a chair, the guests stood astonished, the infant squawled, the maid ran in, snatched it up again in her arms, flew into her mistress's room, and told what had happened. Down stairs in an instant hurried all the Gossips, where they found the Doctor in a Trance. . . .

As soon as Cornelius awaked, he raised himself on his elbow, and casting his eye on Mrs. Scriblerus, spoke as follows: 'Wisely was it said by Homer, that in the

Cellar of Jupiter are two barrels, the one of good, the other of evil, which he never bestows on mortals separately, but constantly mingles them together. Thus at the same time hath Heaven blessed me with the birth of a Son, and afflicted me with the scouring of my Shield. Yet let us not repine at his Dispensations, who gives and who takes away; but rather join in prayer, that the Rust of Antiquity which he hath been pleased to take from my Shield may be added to my Son; and that so much of it as it is my purpose he shall contract in his Education may never be destroyed by any Modern Polishing.'

Memoirs of Martin Scriblerus

JONATHAN SWIFT

1667–1745

223 *Stella goes Riding*

NOW, madam Stella, what say you? you ride every day; I know that already, sirrah; and if you ride every day for a twelvemonth, you would be still better and better. No, I hope Parvisol will not have the impudence to make you stay an hour for the money; if he does, I'll un-Parvisol him; pray let me know. O Lord, how hasty we are; Stella can't stay writing and writing; she must ride and go a cockhorse, pray now. Well, but the horses are not come to the door; the fellow can't find the bridle; your stirrup is broken; where did you put the whips, Dingley? Marget, where have you laid Mrs. Johnson's riband to tie about her? reach me my mask: sup up this before you go. So, so, a gallop, a gallop: sit fast, sirrah, and don't ride hard upon the stones. Well, now Stella is gone, tell me, Dingley, is she a good girl? and what news is that you are to tell me? . . . O madam Stella, welcome home; was it pleasant riding? did your horse stumble? how often did the man light to settle your stirrup? ride nine miles? faith, you have galloped indeed. Well, but where 's the fine thing you promised me? I have been a good boy, ask Dingley else. I believe you did not meet the fine-thing-man: faith, you are a cheat. So you'll see Raymond and his wife in town. Faith, that riding to Laracor gives me short sighs, as well as you. All the days I have passed here, have been dirt to those. I have been gaining enemies by the score, and friends by the couples; which is against the rules of wisdom, because they say one enemy can do more hurt than ten friends can do good. But I have had my revenge at least, if I get nothing else. And so let fate govern.

Journal to Stella

224 *A Standard for English*

IF it were not for the *Bible* and *Common Prayer Book* in the Vulgar Tongue, we should hardly be able to understand anything that was written among us an hundred years ago; which is certainly true: for those books, being perpetually read in Churches, have proved a kind of standard for language, especially to the common people. And I doubt whether the alterations since introduced have added much to the beauty or strength of the *English* Tongue, though they have taken off a great deal from that *Simplicity* which is one of the greatest perfections in any language. You, my Lord, who are so conversant in the sacred writings, and so great a judge of them in their originals, will agree, that no Translation our Country ever yet produced, has come up to that of the *Old* and *New Testament*: And by the many beautiful passages which I have often had the honour to hear your Lordship cite from thence, I am persuaded that the Translators of the *Bible* were Masters of an *English* style much fitter for that work than any we see in our present writings; which I take to be owing to the *Simplicity* that runs through the whole. Then, as to the greatest part of our *Liturgy*, compiled long before the Translation of the *Bible* now in use, and little altered since, there seem to be in it as great strains of true sublime eloquence as are anywhere to be found in our language; which every man of good Taste will observe in the *Communion Service*, that of *Burial*, and other parts.

Letter Dedicatory to the Earl of Oxford

225 *Gulliver Captures the Fleet of Blefuscu*

THE Empire of *Blefuscu* is an Island situated to the North North-East side of *Lilliput*, from whence it is parted only by a Channel of eight hundred Yards wide. I had not yet seen it, and upon this Notice of an intended Invasion, I avoided appearing on that side of the Coast, for fear of being discovered by some of the Enemy's Ships, who had received no Intelligence of me, all Intercourse between the two Empires having been strictly forbidden during the War, upon pain of Death, and an Embargo laid by our Emperor upon all Vessels whatsoever. I communicated to his Majesty a Project I had formed of seizing the Enemy's whole Fleet: which, as our Scouts assured us, lay at Anchor in the Harbour ready to sail with the first fair Wind. I consulted the most experienced Seamen, upon the depth of the Channel, which they had often plumbed, who told me, that in the middle at high Water it was seventy *Glumgluffs* deep, which is about six foot of *European* Measure ; and the rest of it fifty *Glumgluffs* at most. I walked towards the North-East Coast over against *Blefuscu* ; and lying down behind a Hillock, took out my small Pocket Perspective-Glass, and viewed the Enemy's Fleet at Anchor, consisting of about fifty Men of War, and a great Number of Transports : I then came back to my House, and gave Order (for which I had a Warrant) for a great Quantity of the strongest Cable and Bars of Iron. The Cable was about as thick as Packthread, and the Bars of the length and size of a Knitting-Needle. I trebled the Cable to make it stronger, and for the same reason I twisted three of the Iron Bars together, binding the Extremities into a Hook. Having thus fixed fifty Hooks to as many Cables, I went back to the North-East Coast, and putting off my Coat, Shoes, and Stockings, walked into the Sea in my Leathern Jerkin, about half an hour before high Water. I waded with what Haste I could, and swam in the middle about thirty Yards till I felt ground ; I arrived at the Fleet in less than half an hour. The Enemy was so frighted when they saw me, that they leaped out of their Ships, and swam to shore, where there could not be fewer than thirty thousand Souls. I then took my Tackling, and fastening a Hook to the hole at the Prow of each, I tied all the Cords together at the End. While I was thus employed, the Enemy discharged several thousand Arrows, many of which stuck in my Hands and Face ; and besides the excessive smart, gave me much disturbance in my Work. My greatest Apprehension was for my Eyes, which I should have infallibly lost, if I had not suddenly thought of an Expedient. I kept among other little Necessaries a pair of Spectacles in a private Pocket, which, as I observed before, had scaped the Emperor's Searchers. These I took out and fastened as strongly as I could upon my Nose, and thus armed went on boldly with my Work in spite of the Enemy's Arrows, many of which struck against the Glasses of my Spectacles, but without any other Effect, further than a little to discompose them. I had now fastened all the Hooks, and taking the Knot in my Hand, began to pull; but not a Ship would stir, for they were all too fast held by their Anchors, so that the boldest part of my Enterprise remained. I therefore let go the Cord, and leaving the Hooks fixed to the Ships, I resolutely cut with my Knife the Cables that fastened the Anchors, receiving above two hundred Shots in my Face and Hands; then I took up the knotted End of the Cables, to which my Hooks were tied, and with great ease drew fifty of the Enemy's largest Men of War after me.

The *Blefuscudians*, who had not the least Imagination of what I intended, were at first confounded with Astonishment. They had seen me cut the Cables, and thought my Design was only to let the Ships run a-drift, or fall foul on each other: but when they perceived the whole Fleet moving in Order, and saw me pulling at the End, they set up such a scream of Grief and Despair that it is almost impossible to describe or conceive. When I had got out of danger, I stopped awhile to pick out the Arrows that stuck in my Hands and Face; and rubbed on some of the same Ointment that was given me at my first arrival, as

I have formerly mentioned. I then took off my Spectacles, and waiting about an Hour, till the Tide was a little fallen, I waded through the middle with my Cargo, and arrived safe at the Royal Port of *Lilliput.*

A Voyage to Lilliput

226 *The Academy of Projectors*

I WAS received very kindly by the Warden, and went for many Days to the Academy. Every Room hath in it one or more Projectors, and I believe I could not be in fewer than five Hundred Rooms.

The first Man I saw was of a meagre Aspect, with sooty Hands and Face, his Hair and Beard long, ragged and singed in several places. His Clothes, Shirt, and Skin, were all of the same Colour. He had been eight Years upon a Project for extracting Sun-Beams out of Cucumbers, which were to be put into Vials hermetically Sealed, and let out to warm the Air in raw inclement Summers. He told me, he did not doubt, in eight Years more, he should be able to supply the Governor's Gardens with Sunshine at a reasonable Rate ; but he complained that his Stock was low, and entreated me to give him something as an Encouragement to Ingenuity, especially since this had been a very dear Season for Cucumbers. I made him a small Present, for my Lord had furnished me with Money on purpose, because he knew their Practice of begging from all who go to see them.

A Voyage to Laputa

227 *A Dedication to Prince Posterity*

I PROFESS to *Your Highness*, in the Integrity of my Heart, that what I am going to say is literally true this Minute I am writing; What Revolutions may happen before it shall be ready for your Perusal, I can by no means warrant; However I beg You to accept it as a Specimen of our Learning, our Politeness and our Wit. I do therefore affirm upon the Word of a sincere Man, that there is now actually in being, a certain Poet called *John Dryden*, whose Translation of *Virgil* was lately printed in a large Folio, well bound, and if diligent search were made, for ought I know, is yet to be seen. There is another call'd *Nahum Tate*, who is ready to make Oath that he has caused many Rheams of Verse to be published, whereof both himself and his Bookseller (if lawfully required) can still produce authentick Copies, and therefore wonders why the World is pleased to make such a Secret of it. There is a Third, known by the Name of *Tom Durfey*, a Poet of a vast Comprehension, an universal Genius, and most profound Learning. There are also one Mr. *Rymer*, and one Mr. *Dennis*, most profound Criticks. There is a Person styl'd Dr. *B–tl–y*, who has wrote near a thousand Pages of immense Erudition, *giving a full and true Account* of a certain *Squable* of wonderful Importance between himself and a Bookseller: He is a Writer of Infinite Wit and Humour; no Man raillyes with a better Grace, and in more sprightly Turns. Farther, I avow to *Your Highness*, that with these Eyes I have beheld the Person of *William W–tt–n*, B.D. who has written a good sizeable Volume against a *Friend of Your*

Governor (from whom, alas! he must therefore look for little Favour) in a most gentlemanly Style, adorned with utmost Politeness and Civility; replete with Discoveries equally valuable for their Novelty and Use: and embellish'd with *Traits* of Wit so poignant and so apposite, that he is a worthy Yokemate to his forementioned *Friend*. *The Tale of a Tub*

JOSEPH ADDISON

1672–1719

228 *Mr. Shapely*

'MR. SPECTATOR,

Now, Sir, the thing is this: Mr. *Shapely* is the prettiest Gentleman about Town. He is very tall, but not too tall neither. He dances like an Angel. His Mouth is made I don't know how, but 'tis the prettiest that I ever saw in my Life. He is always laughing, for he has an infinite deal of Wit. If you did but see how he rolls his Stockings! He has a thousand pretty Fancies, and I am sure, if you saw him, you would like him. He is a very good Scholar, and can talk *Latin* as fast as *English*. I wish you could but see him dance. Now you must understand poor Mr. *Shapely* has no Estate; but how can he help that, you know? And yet my Friends are so unreasonable as to be always teazing me about him, because he has no Estate. But, I am sure, he has that that is better than an Estate; for he is a Good-natured, Ingenious, Modest, Civil, Tall, Well-bred, handsome Man, and I am obliged to him for his Civilities ever since I saw him. I forgot to tell you that he has black Eyes, and looks upon me now and then as if he had Tears in

1 *Your Governor*) i.e. *Time*

them. And yet my Friends are so unreasonable, that they would have me be uncivil to him. I have a good Portion which they cannot hinder me of, and I shall be Fourteen on the 29th Day of *August* next, and am therefore willing to settle in the World as soon as I can, and so is Mr. *Shapely*. But every Body I advise with here is poor Mr. *Shapely*'s Enemy. I desire therefore you will give me your Advice, for I know you are a wise Man, and if you advise me well, I am resolved to follow it. I heartily wish you could see him dance, and am,

SIR,

Your most humble Servant,

B. D.

He loves your *Spectators* mightily.'

The Spectator, No. 475

229 *Will Wimble*

AS I was Yesterday Morning walking with Sir Roger before his House, a Country-Fellow brought him a huge Fish, which, he told him, Mr. *William Wimble* had caught that very Morning; and that he presented it, with his Service, to him, and intended to come and dine with him. At the same Time he delivered a Letter, which my Friend read to me as soon as the Messenger left him.

'*Sir* Roger,

I Desire you to accept of a Jack, which is the best I have caught this Season. I intend to come and stay with you a Week, and see how the Perch bite in the *Black River*. I observed, with some Concern, the last Time I saw you upon the Bowling-Green, that your Whip wanted a Lash to it: I will bring half a Dozen with me that I twisted last Week, which I hope will serve you all the Time you are in the Country. I have not been out of the Saddle for six Days last past, having been at *Eaton* with Sir *John*'s eldest Son. He takes to his Learning hugely. I am,

SIR,

Your humble Servant,

Will. Wimble.'

This extraordinary Letter, and Message that accompanied it, made me very curious to know the Character and Quality of the Gentleman who sent them; which I found to be as follows; *Will. Wimble* is younger Brother to a Baronet, and descended of the ancient Family of the *Wimbles*. He is now between Forty and Fifty; but being bred to no Business and born to no Estate, he generally lives with his elder Brother as Superintendant of his Game. He hunts a Pack of Dogs better than any Man in the Country, and is very famous for finding out a Hare. He is extremely well versed in all the little Handicrafts of an idle Man: He makes a *May*-fly to a Miracle; and furnishes the whole Country with Angle-Rods. As he is a good-natur'd officious Fellow, and very much esteemed upon Account of his Family, he is a welcome Guest at every House, and keeps up a good Correspondence among all the Gentlemen about him. He carries a Tulip-Root in his Pocket from one to another, or exchanges a Puppy between a couple of Friends that live perhaps in the opposite Sides of the County. *Will.* is a particular Favourite of all the young Heirs, whom he frequently obliges with a Net that he has weaved, or a Setting-dog that he has *made* himself: He now and then presents a Pair of Garters of his own knitting to their Mothers or Sisters ; and raises a great deal of Mirth among them, by enquiring as often as he meets them *how they wear?* These Gentlemen-like Manufactures and obliging little Humours, make *Will.* the Darling of the Country.

The Spectator, No. 108

230 *Sir Roger at Church*

I AM always very well pleased with a Country *Sunday*; and think, if keeping holy the Seventh Day were only a human Institution, it would be the best Method that could have been thought of for the polishing and civilizing of Mankind. It is certain the Country-People would soon degenerate into a kind of Savages and Barbarians, were there not such frequent Returns of a stated Time, in which the whole Village meet together with their best Faces, and in their cleanliest Habits, to converse with one another upon indifferent Subjects, hear their Duties explained to them, and join together in Adoration of the Supreme Being. *Sunday* clears away the Rust of the whole Week, not only as it refreshes in their Minds the Notions of Religion, but as it puts both the Sexes upon appearing in their most agreeable Forms, and exerting all such Qualities as are apt to give them a Figure in the Eye of the Village. A Country-Fellow distinguishes himself as much in the *Church-yard*, as a Citizen does upon the *Change*; the whole Parish-Politicks being generally discuss'd in that Place either after Sermon or before the Bell rings.

My Friend Sir Roger being a good Church-man, has beautified the Inside of his Church with several Texts of his own chusing: He has likewise given a handsome Pulpit-Cloth, and railed in the Communion-Table at his own Expence. He has often told me, that at his coming to his Estate he found his Parishioners very irregular; and that in order to make them kneel and join in the Responses, he gave every one of them a Hassock and a Common-prayer Book: and at the same Time employed an itinerant Singing-Master, who goes about the Country for that Purpose, to instruct them rightly in the Tunes of the Psalms; upon which they now very much value themselves, and indeed out-do most of the Country Churches that I have ever heard.

As Sir ROGER is Landlord to the whole Congregation, he keeps them in very good Order, and will suffer no Body to sleep in it besides himself; for if by Chance he has been surprized into a short Nap at Sermon, upon recovering out of it he stands up and looks about him, and if he sees any Body else nodding, either wakes them himself, or sends his Servants to them. Several other of the old Knight's Particularities break out upon these Occasions: Sometimes he will be lengthening out a Verse in the Singing-Psalms, half a Minute after the rest of the Congregation have done with it; sometimes, when he is pleased with the Matter of his Devotion, he pronounces *Amen* three or four times to the same Prayer; and sometimes stands up when every Body else is upon their Knees, to count the Congregation, or see if any of his Tenants are missing.

I was Yesterday very much surprized to hear my old Friend, in the Midst of the Service, calling out to one *John Matthews* to mind what he was about, and not disturb the Congregation. This *John Matthews* it seems is remarkable for being an idle Fellow, and at that Time was kicking his Heels for his Diversion. This Authority of the Knight, though exerted in that odd Manner which accompanies him in all Circumstances of Life, has a very good Effect upon the Parish, who are not polite enough to see any thing ridiculous in his Behaviour; besides that, the general good Sense and Worthiness of his Character, make his Friends observe these little Singularities as Foils that rather set off than blemish his good Qualities.

As soon as the Sermon is finished, no Body presumes to stir till Sir Roger is gone out of the Church. The Knight walks down from his Seat in the Chancel between a double Row of his Tenants, that stand bowing to him on each Side; and every now and then enquires how such an one's Wife, or Mother, or Son, or Father do whom he does not see at Church; which is understood as a secret Reprimand to the Person that is absent.

The Spectator, No. 112

231 *Sir Roger goes to Spring Garden*

As I was sitting in my Chamber, and thinking on a Subject for my next *Spectator*, I heard two or three irregular Bounces at my Landlady's Door, and upon the opening of it, a loud chearful Voice enquiring whether the Philosopher was at home. The Child who went to the Door answered very innocently, that he did not lodge there. I immediately recollected that it was my good Friend Sir Roger's Voice: and that I had promised to go with him on the Water to *Spring-Garden*, in case it proved a good Evening. The Knight put me in mind of my Promise from the bottom of the Stair-Case, but told me that if I was speculating he would stay below till I had done.

Upon my coming down I found all the Children of the Family got about my old Friend, and my Landlady herself, who is a notable prating Gossip, engaged in a Conference with him, being mightily pleased with his stroaking her little Boy upon the Head, and bidding him be a good Child, and mind his Book.

We were no sooner come to the *Temple* Stairs, but we were surrounded with a crowd of Water-men, offering us their respective Services. Sir ROGER, after having looked about him very attentively, spied one with a Wooden-Leg, and immediately gave him Orders to get his Boat ready. As we were walking towards it, *You must know*, says Sir ROGER, *I never make use of any Body to row me that has not either lost a Leg or an Arm. I wou'd rather bate him a few Strokes of his Oar, than not employ an honest Man that has been wounded in the Queen's Service. If I was a Lord or a Bishop, and kept a Barge, I would not put a Fellow in my Livery that had not a Wooden-Leg.*

My old Friend, after having seated himself, and trimmed the Boat with his Coachman, who, being a very sober Man, always serves for Ballast on these Occasions, we made the best of our way for *Fox-Hall.* Sir ROGER obliged the Waterman to give us the History of his right Leg, and hearing that he had left it at *La Hogue*, with many Particulars which passed in that glorious Action, the Knight in the Triumph of his Heart made several Reflections on the Greatness of the *British* Nation ; as, that one *Englishman* could beat three *Frenchmen* ; that we cou'd never be in Danger of Popery so long as we took care of our Fleet ; that the *Thames* was the noblest River in *Europe* ; that *London-Bridge* was a greater Piece of Work than any of the seven Wonders of the World ; with many other honest Prejudices which naturally cleave to the Heart of a true *Englishman.*

After some short Pause, the old Knight turning about his Head twice or thrice, to take a Survey of this great Metropolis, bid me observe how thick the City was set with Churches, and that there was scarce a single Steeple on this side *Temple-Bar. A most Heathenish Sight!* says Sir Roger: *There is no Religion at this End of the Town. The fifty new Churches will very much mend the Prospect; but Church-work is slow, Church-work is slow!*. .

We were now arrived at *Spring-Garden*, which is exquisitely pleasant at this time of the Year. When I considered the Fragrancy of the Walks and Bowers, with the Choirs of Birds that sung upon the Trees, and the loose Tribe of People that walk'd under their Shades, I could not but look upon the Place as a kind of *Mahometan* Paradise. Sir Roger told me it put him in mind of a little Coppice by his House in the Country, which his Chaplain used to call an Aviary of Nightingales. *You must understand*, says the Knight, *there is nothing in the World that pleases a Man in Love so much as your Nightingale. Ah, Mr.* Spectator! *The many Moonlight Nights that I have walked by my self, and thought on the Widow by the Musick of the Nightingale!* Here he fetch'd a deep Sigh, and was falling into a Fit of musing, when a Mask, who came behind him, gave him a gentle Tap upon the Shoulder, and asked him if he would drink a Bottle of Mead with her? But the Knight being startled at so unexpected a Familiarity, and displeased to be interrupted in his Thoughts of the Widow, told her, *She was a wanton Baggage*, and bid her go about her Business.

We concluded our Walk with a Glass of *Burton*-Ale, and a Slice of Hung-Beef. When we had done eating our selves, the Knight called a Waiter to him, and bid him carry the remainder to the Waterman that had but one Leg. I perceived the Fellow stared upon him at the oddness of the Message, and was going to be saucy; upon which I ratified the Knight's Commands with a peremptory Look.

As we were going out of the Garden, my old Friend thinking himself obliged, as a Member of the *Quorum*, to animadvert upon the Morals of the Place, told the Mistress of the House, who sat at the Bar, That he should be a better Customer to her Garden, if there were more Nightingales, and fewer Strumpets.

The Spectator, No. 383

232 *The Royal Exchange*

THERE is no Place in the Town which I so much love to frequent as the *Royal Exchange*. It gives me a secret Satisfaction, and, in some measure, gratifies my Vanity, as I am an *Englishman*, to see so rich an Assembly of Country-men and Foreigners consulting together upon the private Business of Mankind, and making this Metropolis a kind of *Emporium* for the whole Earth. I must confess I look upon High-Change to be a great Council, in which all considerable Nations have their Representatives. Factors in the Trading World are what Ambassadors are in the Politick World; they negotiate Affairs, conclude Treaties, and maintain a good Correspondence between those wealthy Societies of Men that are divided from one another by Seas and Oceans, or live on the different Extremities of a Continent. I have often been pleased to hear Disputes adjusted between an Inhabitant of

Japan and an Alderman of *London*, or to see a Subject of the *Great Mogul* entering into a League with one of the *Czar* of *Muscovy*. I am infinitely delighted in mixing with these several Ministers of Commerce, as they are distinguished by their different Walks and different Languages: Sometimes I am justled among a Body of *Armenians*: Sometimes I am lost in a Crowd of *Jews*; and sometimes make one in a Groupe of *Dutch-men*. I am a *Dane*, *Swede*, or *Frenchman* at different times; or rather fancy my self like the old Philosopher, who upon being asked what Countryman he was, replied, That he was a Citizen of the World. . .

Nature seems to have taken a particular Care to disseminate her Blessings among the different Regions of the World, with an Eye to this mutual Intercourse and Traffick among Mankind, that the Natives of the several Parts of the Globe might have a kind of Dependance upon one another, and be united together by their common Interest. Almost every *Degree* produces something peculiar to it. The Food often grows in one Country, and the Sauce in another. The Fruits of *Portugal* are corrected by the Products of *Barbadoes*: The Infusion of a *China* Plant sweetned with the Pith of an *Indian* Cane. The *Philippick* Islands give a Flavour to our *European* Bowls. The single Dress of a Woman of Quality is often the Product of an Hundred Climates. The Muff and the Fan come together from the different Ends of the Earth. The Scarf is sent from the Torrid Zone, and the Tippet from beneath the Pole. The Brocade Petticoat rises out of the Mines of *Peru*, and the Diamond Necklace out of the Bowels of *Indostan*. . .

Our Ships are laden with the Harvest of every Climate: Our Tables are stored with Spices, and Oils, and Wines: Our Rooms are filled with Pyramids of *China*, and adorned with the Workmanship of *Japan*: Our Morning's-Draught comes to us from the remotest Corners of the Earth: We repair our Bodies by the Drugs of *America*, and repose our selves under *Indian* Canopies. . .

For these Reasons there are not more useful Members in a Commonwealth than Merchants. They knit Mankind together in a mutual Intercourse of good Offices, distribute the Gifts of Nature, find Work for the Poor, add Wealth to the Rich, and Magnificence to the Great. Our *English* Merchant converts the Tin of his own Country into Gold, and exchanges his Wooll for Rubies. The *Mahometans* are cloathed in our *British* Manufacture, and the Inhabitants of the Frozen Zone warmed with the Fleeces of our Sheep.

When I have been upon the '*Change*, I have often fancied one of our old Kings standing in Person, where he is represented in Effigy, and looking down upon the wealthy Concourse of People with which that Place is every Day filled. In this Case, how would he be surprized to hear all the Languages of *Europe* spoken in this little spot of his former Dominions, and to see so many private Men, who in his Time would have been the Vassals of some powerful Baron, Negotiating like Princes for greater Sums of Money than were formerly to be met with in the Royal Treasury! Trade, without enlarging the *British* Territories, has given us a kind of additional Empire: It has multiplied the Number of the Rich, made our Landed Estates infinitely more Valuable than they were formerly, and added to them an Accession of other Estates as Valuable as the Lands themselves.

The Spectator, No. 69

233 *Westminster Abbey*

WHEN I am in a serious Humour, I very often walk by my self in *Westminster* Abbey; where the Gloominess of the Place, and the Use to which it is applied, with the Solemnity of the Building, and the Condition of the People who lye in it, are apt to fill the Mind with a kind of Melancholy, or rather Thoughtfulness, that is not disagreeable. . .

For my own part, though I am always serious, I do not know what it is to be melancholy; and can therefore take a View of Nature in her deep and solemn Scenes, with the same Pleasure as in her most gay and delightful ones. By this means I can improve my self with those Objects, which others consider with Terror. When I look upon the Tombs of the Great, every Emotion of Envy dies in me; when I read the Epitaphs of the Beautiful, every inordinate Desire goes out; when I meet with the Grief of Parents upon a Tomb-stone, my Heart melts with Compassion; when I see the Tomb of the Parents themselves, I consider the Vanity of grieving for those whom we must quickly follow: When I see Kings lying by those who deposed them, when I consider rival Wits placed Side by Side, or the holy Men that divided the World with their Contests and Disputes, I reflect with Sorrow and Astonishment on the little Competitions, Factions, and Debates of Mankind. When I read the several Dates of the Tombs of some that died Yesterday, and some six hundred Years ago, I consider that great Day when we shall all of us be Contemporaries, and make our Appearance together.

The Spectator, No. 26

234 *The Vision of Mirza*

HE then led me to the highest Pinnacle of the Rock, and placing me on the Top of it, Cast thy Eyes Eastward, said he, and tell me what thou seest. I see, said I, a huge Valley and a prodigious Tide of Water rolling through it. The Valley that thou seest, said he, is the Vale of Misery, and the Tide of Water that thou seest is part of the great Tide of Eternity. What is the Reason, said I, that the Tide I see rises out of a thick Mist at one End, and again loses it self in a thick Mist at the other? What thou seest, said he, is that Portion of Eternity which is called Time, measured out by the Sun, and reaching from the Beginning of the World to its Consummation. Examine now, said he, this Sea that is thus bounded with Darkness at both Ends, and tell me what thou discoverest in it. I see a Bridge, said I, standing in the Midst of the Tide. The Bridge thou seest, said he, is humane Life; consider it attentively. Upon a more leisurely Survey of it, I found that it consisted of threescore and ten entire Arches, with several broken Arches, which added to those that were entire, made up the Number about an hundred. As I was counting the Arches, the Genius told me that this Bridge consisted at first of a thousand Arches; but that a great Flood swept away the rest, and left the Bridge in the ruinous Condition I now beheld it. But tell me further, said he, what thou discoverest on it. I see Multitudes of People passing over it, said I, and a black Cloud hanging on each End of it. As I looked more attentively, I saw several of the Passengers dropping thro' the Bridge, into the great Tide that flowed underneath it; and upon further Examination, perceived there were innumerable Trap-doors that lay concealed in the Bridge, which the Passengers no sooner trod upon, but they fell through them into the Tide and immediately disappeared. These hidden Pit-falls were set very thick at the Entrance of the Bridge, so that Throngs of People no sooner broke through the Cloud, but many of them fell into them. They grew thinner towards the Middle, but multiplied and lay closer together towards the End of the Arches that were entire.

The Spectator, No. 159

235 *My Garden*

'SIR,

Having lately read your Essay on the Pleasures of the Imagination, I was so taken with your Thoughts upon some of our *English* Gardens, that I cannot forbear troubling you with a Letter upon that Subject. I am one, you must know, who am looked upon as a Humorist in Gardening. I have several Acres about my House, which I call my Garden, and which a skillful Gardener would not know what to call. It is a Confusion of Kitchen and Parterre, Orchard and Flower Garden, which lie so mixt and interwoven with one another, that if a Foreigner who had seen nothing of our Country should be conveyed into my Garden at his first landing, he would look upon it as a natural Wilderness, and one of the uncultivated Parts of our Country. My Flowers grow up in several Parts of the Garden in the greatest Luxuriancy and Profusion. I am so far from being fond of any particular one, by reason of its Rarity, that if I meet with any one in a Field which pleases me, I give it a Place in my Garden. By this Means, when a Stranger walks with me, he is surprized to see several large Spots of Ground covered with ten thousand different Colours, and has often singled out Flowers that he might have met with under a common Hedge, in a Field, or in a Meadow, as some of the greatest Beauties of the Place. The only Method I observe in this Particular, is to range in the same Quarter the Products of the same Season, that they may make their Appearance together, and compose a Picture of the greatest Variety. There is the same Irregularity in my Plantations, which run into as great a Wildness as their Natures will permit. I take in none that do not naturally rejoyce in the Soil, and am pleased when I am walking in a Labyrinth of my own raising, not to know whether the next Tree I shall meet with is an Apple or an Oak, an Elm or a Pear-tree. My Kitchen has likewise its particular Quarters assigned it; for besides the wholsome Luxury which that Place abounds with, I have always thought a Kitchen-garden a more pleasant Sight than the finest Orangerie, or artificial Green-house. I love to see every thing in its perfection, and am more pleased to survey my Rows of Coleworts and Cabbages, with a thousand nameless Pot-herbs, springing up in their full Fragrancy and Verdure, than to see the tender Plants of Foreign Countries kept alive by artificial Heats, or withering in an Air and Soil that are not adapted to them. I must not omit, that there is a Fountain rising in the upper Part of my Garden, which forms a little wandring Rill, and administers to the Pleasure as well as the Plenty of the Place. I have so conducted it, that it visits most of my Plantations, and have taken particular Care to let it run in the same Manner as it would do in an open Field, so that it generally passes through Banks of Violets and Primroses, Plats of Willow, or other Plants, that seem to be of its own producing.'

The Spectator, No. 477

SIR RICHARD STEELE

1672–1729

236 *His First Grief*

THE first Sense of Sorrow I ever knew was upon the Death of my Father, at which Time I was not quite Five Years of Age; but was rather amazed at what all the House meant, than possessed with a real Understanding why no Body was willing to play with me. I remember I went into the Room where his Body lay, and my Mother sat weeping alone by it. I had my Battledore in my Hand, and fell a beating the Coffin, and calling Papa; for, I know not how, I had some slight Idea that he was locked up there. My Mother catched me in her Arms, and, transported beyond all Patience of the silent Grief she was before in, she almost smothered me in her Embraces; and told me in a Flood of Tears, Papa could not hear me, and would play with me no more, for they were going to put him under Ground, where he could never come to us again. She was a very beautiful Woman, of a noble Spirit, and there was a Dignity in her Grief amidst all the Wildness of her Transport; which, methought, struck me with an Instinct of Sorrow, that, before I was sensible of what it was to grieve, seized my very Soul, and has made Pity the Weakness of my Heart ever since. The Mind in Infancy is, methinks, like the Body in Embryo; and receives Impressions so forcible, that they are as hard to be removed by Reason, as any Mark, with which a Child is born, is to be taken away by any future Application. Hence it is, that Good-nature in me is no Merit; but having been so frequently overwhelmed with her Tears before I knew the Cause of any Affliction, or could draw Defences from my own Judgment, I imbibed Commiseration, Remorse, and an unmanly Gentleness of Mind, which has since insnared me into Ten Thousand Calamities; and from whence I can reap no Advantage, except it be, that, in such a Humour as I am now in, I can the better indulge myself in the Softnesses of Humanity, and enjoy that sweet Anxiety which arises from the Memory of past Afflictions.

The Tatler, No. 181

237 *Mr. Bickerstaff visits a Friend*

THERE are several Persons who have many Pleasures and Entertainments in their Possession, which they do not enjoy. It is therefore a kind and good Office to acquaint them with their own Happiness, and turn their Attention to such Instances of their good Fortune as they are apt to overlook. Persons in the married State often want such a Monitor; and pine away their Days, by looking upon the same Condition in Anguish and Murmur, which carries with it in the Opinion of others a Complication of all the Pleasures of Life, and a Retreat from its Inquietudes.

I am led into this Thought by a Visit I made an old Friend, who was formerly my School-Fellow. He came to Town last Week with his Family for the Winter, and yesterday Morning sent me Word his Wife expected me to Dinner. I am as it were at Home at that House, and every Member of it knows me for their Well-wisher. I cannot indeed express the Pleasure it is, to be met by the Children with so much Joy as I am when I go thither: The Boys and Girls strive who shall come first, when they think it is I that am knocking at the Door; and that Child which loses the Race to me, runs back again to tell the Father it is Mr. *Bickerstaff*. This Day I was led in by a Pretty Girl that we all thought must have forgot me; for the Family has been out of Town these two Years. Her knowing me again was a mighty Subject with us, and took up our Discourse at the first Entrance. After which, they began to rally me upon a thousand little Stories they heard in the Country, about my Marriage to one of my Neighbour's Daughters: Upon which the Gentleman, my Friend, said, 'Nay, if Mr. *Bickerstaff* marries a Child of any of his old Companions, I hope mine shall have the Preference; there is Mrs. *Mary* is now Sixteen, and would make him as fine a Widow as the best of them: But I know him too well; he is so enamoured with the very Memory of those who flourished in our Youth, that he will not so much as look upon the modern Beauties. I remember, old Gentleman, how often you went Home in a Day to refresh your Countenance and Dress, when *Teraminta* reigned in your Heart. As we came up in the Coach, I repeated to my Wife some of your Verses on her.' With such Reflections on little Passages which happened long ago, we passed our Time during a chearful and elegant Meal. After Dinner, his Lady left the room, as did also the Children. As soon as we were alone, he took me by the Hand; Well, my good Friend, says he, I am heartily glad to see thee; I was afraid you would never have seen all the Company that dined with you to Day again. Do not you think the good Woman of the House a little altered since you followed her from the Playhouse, to find out who she was for me? I perceived a Tear fall down his Cheek as he spoke, which moved me not a little. But to turn the Discourse, I said, She is not indeed quite that

Creature she was when she returned me the Letter I carried from you ; and told me, she hoped, as I was a Gentleman, I would be employed no more to trouble her, who had never offended me ; but would be so much the Gentleman's Friend as to disswade him from a Pursuit which he could never succeed in. You may remember, I thought her in earnest ; and you were forced to employ your Cousin *Will*, who made his Sister get acquainted with her for you. You cannot expect her to be for ever Fifteen. Fifteen ! replied my good Friend : Ah ! you little understand, you that have lived a Bachelor, how great, how exquisite a Pleasure there is in being really beloved ! It is impossible that the most beauteous Face in Nature should raise in me such pleasing Ideas, as when I look upon that excellent Woman. That Fading in her Countenance is chiefly caused by her watching with me in my Fever. This was followed by a Fit of Sickness, which had like to have carried her off last Winter. . . Her Face is to me much more beautiful than when I first saw it ; there is no Decay in any Feature, which I cannot trace from the very Instant it was occasioned by some anxious Concern for my Welfare and Interests. . . Oh ! she is an inestimable Jewel. In her Examination of her Houshold Affairs, she shews a certain Fearfulness to find a Fault, which makes her Servants obey her like Children ; and the meanest we have has an ingenuous Shame for an Offence, not always to be seen in Children in other Families. I speak freely to you, my old Friend ; ever since her Sickness, Things that gave me the quickest Joy before, turn now to a certain Anxiety.

He would have gone on in this tender Way, when the good Lady entered, and with an inexpressible

Sweetness in her Countenance told us, she had been searching her Closet for something very good, to treat such an old Friend as I was. Her Husband's Eyes sparkled with Pleasure at the Chearfulness of her Countenance; and I saw all his Fears vanish in an Instant. The Lady observing something in our Looks which shewed we had been more serious than ordinary, and seeing her Husband receive her with great Concern under a forced Chearfulness, immediately guessed at what we had been talking of; and applying herself to me, said, with a Smile, Mr. *Bickerstaff*, don't believe a Word of what he tells you, I shall still live to have you for my Second, as I have often promised you, unless he takes more care of Himself than he has done since his coming to Town. You must know, he tells me, That he finds *London* is a much more healthy Place than the Country; for he sees several of his old Acquaintance and School-fellows are here young Fellows with fair full-bottomed Periwigs. I could scarce keep him this Morning from going out open-breasted. My Friend, who is always extremely delighted with her agreeable Humour, made her sit down with us. She did it with that Easiness which is peculiar to Women of Sense; and to keep up the good Humour she had brought in with her, turned her Raillery upon me: Mr. *Bickerstaff*, you remember you followed me one Night from the Playhouse; Supposing you should carry me thither to Morrow Night, and lead me into the Front-Box. This put us into a long Field of Discourse about the Beauties, who were Mothers to the present, and shined in the Boxes twenty Years ago. I told her, I was glad she had transferred so many of her Charms, and I did not question but her eldest Daughter was within Half a Year of being a Toast.

We were pleasing ourselves with this fantastical Preferment of the young Lady, when on a sudden we were alarmed with the Noise of a Drum, and immediately entered my little Godson to give me a Point of War. His Mother, between Laughing and Chiding, would have put him out of the Room; but I would not part with him so. I found upon Conversation with him, though he was a little noisy in his Mirth, that the Child had excellent Parts, and was a great Master of all the Learning on t'other Side Eight Years old. I perceived him a very great Historian in *Æsop's* Fables: But he frankly declared to me his Mind, that he did not delight in that Learning, because he did not believe they were true; for which Reason I found he had very much turned his Studies, for about a Twelve month past, into the Lives and Adventures of Don *Belianis* of *Greece*, *Guy* of *Warwick*, the *Seven Champions*, and other Historians of that Age. . . . I was extolling his Accomplishments, when the Mother told me, That the little Girl who led me in this Morning, was in her Way a better Scholar than he: *Betty*, (said she,) deals chiefly in Fairies and Sprights; and sometimes in a Winter-Night will terrify the Maids with her Accounts, until they are afraid to go up to Bed.

I sat with them until it was very late, sometimes in merry, sometimes in serious Discourse, with this particular Pleasure, which gives the only true Relish to all Conversation, a Sense that every one of us liked each other. I went Home, considering the different Conditions of a married Life and that of a Bachelor; and I must confess it struck me with a secret Concern, to reflect, that whenever I go off, I shall leave no Traces behind me. In this pensive Mood I returned to my Family; that is to say, to my Maid, my Dog, and my Cat, who only can be the better or worse for what happens to me.

The Tatler, No. 95

238 *A Dream after Reading in Bed*

AFTER the Lassitude of a Day, spent in the strolling Manner, which is usual with Men of Pleasure in this Town, and with a Head full of a Million of Impertinencies, which had danced round it for ten Hours together, I came to my Lodging, and hastened to bed. My *Valet de Chambre* knows my University-Trick of reading there; and he, being a good Scholar for a Gentleman, ran over the Names of *Horace*, *Tibullus*, *Ovid*, and others, to know which I would have. Bring *Virgil*, said I; and, if I fall asleep, take care of the Candle. I read the Sixth Book over with the most exquisite Delight, and had gone half through it a second time, when the pleasant Ideas of *Elysian* Fields, deceased Worthies walking in them, sincere Lovers enjoying their Languishment without Pain, Compassion for the unhappy Spirits who had mispent their short Day-light, and were exiled from the Seats of Bliss for ever; I say, I was deep again in my Reading, when this Mixture of Images had taken place of all others in my Imagination before, and lulled me into a Dream, from which I am just awake, to my great Disadvantage. The happy Mansions of *Elysium*, by degrees, seemed to be wafted from me, and the very Traces of my late waking Thoughts began to fade away, when I was cast by a sudden Whirlwind upon an Island, encompassed with a roaring and troubled Sea, which shaked its very Centre, and rocked its Inhabitants as in a Cradle. The Islanders lay on their Faces without offering to look up, or hope for Preservation; all her Harbours were crowded with Mariners, and tall Vessels of War lay in Danger of being driven to pieces on her Shores. Bless me! said I, why have I lived in such a Manner, that the Convulsion of Nature should be so terrible to me, when I feel in myself that the better Part of me is to survive it? Oh! may that be in Happiness.

The Tatler, No. 8

239 *A True Magistrate*

IT would become all Men, as well as me, to lay before them the noble Character of *Verus* the Magistrate, who always sat in Triumph over, and Contempt of, Vice: He never searched after it, or spared it when it came before him: At the same time, he could see through the Hypocrisy and Disguise of those, who have no Pretence to Virtue themselves, but by their Severity to the Vicious. The same *Verus* was, in Times long past, Chief Justice (as we call it amongst us) in *Felicia*. He was a Man of profound Knowledge of the Laws of his Country, and as just an Observer of them in his own Person. He considered Justice as a Cardinal Virtue, not as a Trade for Maintenance. Wherever he was Judge, he never forgot that he was also Counsel. The Criminal before him was always sure he stood before his Country, and, in a sort, a Parent of it. The Prisoner knew, that though his Spirit was broken with Guilt, and incapable of Language to defend itself, all would be gathered from him which could conduce to his Safety; and that his Judge would wrest no Law to destroy him, nor conceal any that could save him. In his Time there was a Nest of

Pretenders to Justice, who happened to be employed, to put Things in a Method for being examined before him at his usual Sessions: These Animals were to *Verus*, as Monkies are to Men, so like, that you can hardly disown them; but so base, that you are ashamed of their Fraternity. It grew a phrase, *Who would do Justice on the Justices?* That certainly would *Verus*.

The Tatler, No. 14

240 *Satire*

THE ordinary Subjects for Satire are such as incite the greatest Indignation in the best Tempers, and consequently Men of such a make are the best qualified for speaking of the Offences in Human Life. These Men can behold Vice and Folly, when they injure Persons to whom they are wholly unacquainted, with the same severity as others resent the Ills they do to themselves. A good-natured Man cannot see an over-bearing Fellow put a bashful Man of Merit out of Countenance, or out-strip him in the pursuit of any Advantage, but he is on Fire to succour the oppressed, to produce the Merit of the One, and confront the Impudence of the Other. . .

There is a certain Impartiality necessary to make what a Man says bear any Weight with those he speaks to. This Quality, with respect to Men's Errors and Vices, is never seen but in good-natured Men. They have ever such a Frankness of Mind, and Benevolence to all Men, that they cannot receive Impressions of Unkindness without mature Deliberation; and writing or speaking ill of a man upon personal Considerations, is so irreparable and mean an Injury, that no one possessed of this quality is capable of doing it: but in all Ages there have been Interpreters to Authors when living, of the same Genius with the Commentators into whose Hands they fall when dead. I dare say it is impossible for any Man of more Wit than one of these to take any of the four-and-twenty Letters, and form out of them a name to describe the Character of a vicious Man with greater Life, but one of these would immediately cry, 'Mr. *Such-a-one* is meant in that Place.' But the Truth of it is, Satirists describe the Age, and Backbiters assign their Descriptions to private Men.

The Tatler, No. 242

HENRY ST. JOHN, VISCOUNT BOLINGBROKE

1678–1751

241 *The Statesman and the Charlatan*

WE may observe much the same difference between wisdom and cunning, both as to the objects they propose and to the means they employ, as we observe between the visual powers of different men. One sees distinctly the objects that are near to him, their immediate relations, and their direct tendencies : and a sight like this serves well enough the purpose of those who concern themselves no further. The cunning minister is one of those : he neither sees, nor is concerned to see, any further than his personal interests, and the support of his administration, require. If such a man overcomes any actual difficulty, avoids any immediate distress, or, without doing either of these effectually, gains a little time by all the low artifice which cunning is ready to suggest and baseness of mind to employ, he triumphs, and is flattered by his mercenary train, on the great event; which amounts often to no more than this, that he got into distress by one series of faults, and out of it by another. The wise minister sees, and is concerned to see further, because government has a further concern: he sees the objects that are distant as well as those that are near, and all their remote relations, and even their indirect tendencies. He thinks of fame as well as of applause, and prefers that, which to be enjoyed must be given, to that which may be bought. He considers his administration as a single day in the great year of government; but as a day that is affected by those which went before, and that must affect those which are to follow. He combines, therefore, and compares all these objects, relations, and tendencies: and the judgement he makes, on an entire not a partial survey of them, is the rule of his conduct. That scheme of the reason of state, which lies open before a wise minister, contains all the great principles of government, and all the great interests of his country: so that, as he prepares some events, he prepares against others, whether they be likely to happen during his administration, or in some future time.

Idea of a Patriot King

242 *The Sea our Element*

'ARE we never to be soldiers?' it will be said. Yes, constantly, in such proportion as is necessary for the defence of good government. To establish such a military force as none but bad governors can want, is to establish tyrannical power in the king or in the ministers; and may be wanted by the latter, when the former would be secure without his army, if he broke his minister. Occasionally too we must be soldiers, and for offence as well as defence; but in proportion to the nature of the conjuncture, considered always relatively to the difference here insisted upon between our situation, our interest, and the nature of our strength, compared with those of the other powers of *Europe*; and not in proportion to the desires, or even to the wants, of the nations with whom we are confederated. Like other amphibious animals, we must come occasionally on shore: but the water is more properly our element, and in it, like them, as we find our greatest security, so we exert our greatest force.

Idea of a Patriot King

CONYERS MIDDLETON

1683–1750

243 *The Political Character of Cicero*

HE made a just distinction, between *bearing what we cannot help, and approving what we ought to condemn*; and submitted therefore, yet never consented to those usurpations; and when he was forced to comply with them, did it always with a reluctance, that he expresses very keenly in his letters to his friends. But whenever that force was removed, and he was at liberty to pursue his principles, and act without controul, as in his *Consulship*, in his *Province*, and after CAESAR's *death*; the onely periods of his life, in which he was truly Master of himself; there we see him shining out in his genuine character, of an excellent Citizen; a great Magistrate; a glorious Patriot: there we see the man, who could declare of himself with truth, in an appeal to ATTICUS, as to the best witness of his conscience, *that he had always done the greatest services to his country, when it was in his power; or when it was not, had never harboured a thought of it, but what was divine.*

Life of Cicero

GEORGE BERKELEY, BISHOP OF CLOYNE

1685–1753

244 *Matter for a May Morning*

PHILONOUS. Good Morrow, *Hylas*: I did not expect to find you abroad so early.

Hylas. It is indeed something unusual; but my Thoughts were so taken up with a Subject I was discoursing of last Night, that finding I could not sleep, I resolved to rise and take a turn in the Garden.

Philonous. It happened well, to let you see what innocent and agreeable Pleasures you lose every Morning. Can there be a pleasanter time of the Day, or a more delightful Season of the Year? That purple Sky, those wild but sweet Notes of Birds, the fragrant Bloom upon the Trees and Flowers, the gentle Influence of the rising Sun, these and a thousand nameless Beauties of Nature inspire the Soul with secret Transports; its Faculties too being at this time fresh and lively, are fit for those Meditations, which the Solitude of a Garden and Tranquillity of the Morning naturally dispose us to. But I am afraid I interrupt your Thoughts: for you seemed very intent on something.

Hylas. It is true, I was, and shall be obliged to you if you will permit me to go on in the same Vein; not that I would by any means deprive myself of your Company, for my Thoughts always flow more easily in

Conversation with a Friend, than when I am alone: but my Request is, that you would suffer me to impart my Reflexions to you.

Philonous. With all my Heart, it is what I should have requested myself if you had not prevented me.

Hylas. I was considering the odd Fate of those Men who have in all Ages, through an Affectation of being distinguished from the Vulgar, or some unaccountable Turn of Thought, pretended either to believe nothing at all, or to believe the most extravagant Things in the World. This however might be borne, if their Paradoxes and Scepticism did not draw after them some Consequences of general Disadvantage to Mankind. But the Mischief lieth here; that when Men of less Leisure see them who are supposed to have spent their whole time in the Pursuits of Knowledge professing an entire Ignorance of all Things, or advancing such Notions as are repugnant to plain and commonly received Principles, they will be tempted to entertain Suspicions concerning the most important Truths, which they had hitherto held sacred and unquestionable.

Philonous. I entirely agree with you, as to the ill Tendency of the affected Doubts of some Philosophers, and fantastical Conceits of others. I am even so far gone of late in this way of Thinking, that I have quitted several of the sublime Notions I had got in their Schools for vulgar Opinions. And I give it you on my Word; since this Revolt from Metaphysical Notions to the plain Dictates of Nature and common Sense, I find my Understanding strangely enlightened, so that I can now easily comprehend a great many Things which before were all Mystery and Riddle.

. . . .

Hylas. I agree with you. *Material Substance* was no

more than an Hypothesis ; and a false and groundless one too. I will no longer spend my Breath in Defence of it. But whatever Hypothesis you advance, or whatsoever Scheme of Things you introduce in its stead, I doubt not it will appear every whit as false : Let me but be allowed to question you upon it. . .

Philonous. I assure you, *Hylas*, I do not pretend to frame any Hypothesis at all. I am of a vulgar Cast, simple enough to believe my Senses, and leave Things as I find them.

Three Dialogues between Hylas and Philonous

245 *Anodynes for the Spleen*

LYSICLES. Play is a serious amusement, that comes to the relief of a Man of pleasure after the more lively and affecting enjoyments of Sense. It kills time beyond anything ; and is a most admirable Anodyne to divert or prevent thought, which might otherwise prey upon the mind.

Crito. I can easily comprehend that no Man upon Earth ought to prize Anodynes for the Spleen more than a Man of fashion and pleasure. An ancient Sage, speaking of one of that character, saith he is made wretched by disappointments and appetites, *λυπεῖται ἀποτυγχάνων καὶ ἐπιθυμῶν*. And if this was true of the *Greeks*, who lived in the Sun, and had so much Spirit, I am apt to think it is still more so of our modern *English*. Something there is in our climate and complexion that makes idleness nowhere so much its own punishment as in *England*, where an uneducated fine Gentleman pays for his momentary pleasures, with long and cruel intervals of Spleen : for relief of which he is driven into sensual excesses, that produce a proportionable depression of Spirits, which, as it createth a greater want of pleasures, so it lessens the ability to enjoy them. There is a cast of Thought in the Complexion of an *Englishman*, which renders him the most unsuccessful Rake in the World. He is (as *Aristotle* expresseth it) at variance with himself. He is neither Brute enough to enjoy his appetites, nor Man enough to govern them.

Alciphron

246 *The Fox-hunters*

WE amused ourselves next Day every one to his Fancy till Nine of the Clock, when Word was brought that the Tea-table was set in the Library, which is a Gallery on a Ground-floor, with an arched Door at one End opening into a Walk of Limes; where, as soon as we had drunk Tea, we were tempted by fine Weather to take a Walk which led us to a small Mount of easy Ascent, on the Top whereof we found a Seat under a spreading Tree. Here we had a Prospect on one hand of a narrow Bay or Creek of the Sea, enclosed on either Side by a Coast beautified with Rocks and Woods, and green Banks and Farm-houses. At the End of the Bay was a small Town, placed upon the Slope of a Hill, which, from the Advantage of its Situation, made a considerable Figure. Several Fishing-boats and Lighters, gliding up and down on a Surface as smooth and bright as Glass, enlivened the Prospect. On the other Side, we looked down on green Pastures, Flocks, and Herds basking beneath in Sunshine, while we, in our superior Situation, enjoyed the Freshness of Air and Shade.

Here we felt that sort of joyful Instinct which a rural Scene and fine Weather inspire ; and proposed no small Pleasure in resuming and continuing our Conference without Interruption till Dinner. But we had hardly seated ourselves and looked about us when we saw a Fox run by the Foot of our Mount into an adjacent Thicket. A few Minutes after, we heard a confused Noise of the opening of Hounds, the winding of Horns, and the roaring of Country Squires. While our Attention was suspended by this Event, a Servant came running, out of Breath, and told *Crito* that his Neighbour *Ctesippus*, a Squire of Note, was fallen from his Horse, attempting to leap over a Hedge, and brought into the Hall, where he lay for dead. Upon which we all rose, and walked hastily to the House, where we found *Ctesippus* just come to himself, in the midst of half-a-dozen Sun-burnt Squires, in Frocks, and short Wigs, and Jockey-Boots. Being asked how he did, he answered it was only a broken Rib. With some Difficulty *Crito* persuaded him to lie on a Bed till the Chirurgeon came. These Fox-hunters, having been up early at their Sport, were eager for Dinner, which was accordingly hastened. They passed the Afternoon in a loud rustic Mirth, gave Proof of their Religion and Loyalty by the Healths they drank, talked of Hounds, and Horses, and Elections, and Country Affairs, till the Chirurgeon, who had been employed about *Ctesippus*, desired he might be put into *Crito's* Coach, and sent home, having refused to stay all Night.

Our Guests being gone, we reposed ourselves after the Fatigue of this tumultuous Visit, and next Morning assembled again at the Seat on the Mount.

Now *Lysicles*, being a nice Man and a *bel esprit*, had an infinite Contempt for the rough Manners and

Conversation of Fox-hunters, and could not reflect with Patience that he had lost, as he called it, so many Hours in their Company. I flattered myself, said he, that there had been none of this Species remaining among us: Strange that Men should be diverted with such uncouth Noise and Hurry, or find Pleasure in the Society of Dogs and Horses! How much more elegant are the Diversions of the Town!

There seems, replied *Euphranor*, to be some Resemblance between Fox-hunters and Free-thinkers; the former exerting their animal Faculties in pursuit of Game, as you Gentlemen employ your Intellectuals in the pursuit of Truth. The kind of Amusement is the same, although the Object be different.

Alciphron

ALEXANDER POPE

1688–1744

247 *On Translating the Classics*

IT is certain no literal Translation can be just to an excellent Original in a superior Language: but it is a great Mistake to imagine (as many have done) that a rash Paraphrase can make amends for this general Defect; which is no less in danger to lose the Spirit of an Ancient, by deviating into the modern Manners of Expression. If there be sometimes a *Darkness*, there is often a *Light* in Antiquity, which nothing better preserves than a Version almost literal. I know no Liberties one ought to take, but those which are necessary for transfusing the Spirit of the Original, and supporting the Poetical Style of the Translation: and I will venture to say, there have not been more Men misled in former times by a servile dull Adherence to the Letter, than have been deluded in ours by a chimerical insolent Hope of raising and improving their Author. It is not to be doubted that the *Fire* of the Poem is what a Translator should principally regard, as it is most likely to expire in his managing: However it is his safest way to be content with preserving this to his utmost in the Whole, without endeavouring to be more than he finds his Author is, in any particular Place. 'Tis a great Secret in Writing to know when to be plain, and when poetical and figurative; and it is what *Homer* will teach us if we will but follow modestly in his Footsteps. Where his Diction is bold and lofty, let us raise ours as high as we can; but where his is plain and humble, we ought not to be deterr'd from imitating him by the fear of incurring the Censure of a meer *English* Critick. Nothing that belongs to *Homer* seems to have been more commonly mistaken than the just Pitch of his Style: Some of his Translators having swell'd into Fustian in a proud Confidence of the *Sublime*; others sunk into Flatness in a cold and timorous Notion of *Simplicity*. Methinks I see these different Followers of *Homer*, some sweating and straining after him by violent Leaps and Bounds, (the certain Signs of false Mettle) others slowly and servilely creeping in his Train, while the Poet himself is all the time proceeding with an unaffected and equal Majesty before them. However of the two Extreams one could sooner pardon Frenzy than Frigidity: No Author is to be envy'd for such Commendations as he may gain by that Character of Style, which his Friends must agree together to call *Simplicity*, and the rest of the World will call *Dulness*. There is a *graceful* and *dignify'd* Simplicity, as well as a *bald* and *sordid* one, which differ as much from each other as the Air of a *plain* Man from that of a *Sloven*: 'Tis one thing to be tricked up, and another not to be dress'd at all. Simplicity is the Mean between Ostentation and Rusticity.

Preface to the 'Iliad'

248 *An Ancient Country Seat*

YOU must expect nothing regular in my description of a house that seems to be built before rules were in fashion; the whole is so disjointed and the parts so detached from each other and yet so joining again one cannot tell how, that (in a poetical fit) you would imagine it had been a village in Amphion's time, where twenty cottages had taken a dance together, were all out, and stood still in amazement ever since. A stranger would be grievously disappointed who should ever think to get into this house the right way; one would expect after entering through the porch to be let into the hall; alas! nothing less; you find yourself in a brewhouse. From the parlour you think to step into the drawing-room; but upon opening the iron-nailed door, you are convinced by a flight of birds about your ears, and a cloud of dust in your eyes, that it is the pigeon-house. On each side our porch are two chimneys, that wear their greens on the outside, which would do as well within, for whenever we make a fire, we let the smoke out of the windows. Over the parlour window hangs a sloping balcony, which time has turned to a very convenient pent-house. The top is crowned with a very venerable tower, so like that of the church just by, that the jackdaws build in it as if it were the true steeple.

The great hall is high and spacious, flanked with long tables, images of ancient hospitality; ornamented with monstrous horns, about twenty broken pikes, and a match-lock musquet or two, which they say were used in the civil wars. . .

Our best room above is very long and low, of the exact proportion of a bandbox: it has hangings of the finest work in the world, those, I mean, which Arachne spins out of her own bowels; indeed the roof is so decayed, that after a favourable shower of rain, we may (with God's blessing) expect a crop of mushrooms between the chinks of the floors.

All this upper story has for many years had no other inhabitants than certain rats, whose very age renders them worthy of this venerable mansion, for the very rats of this ancient seat are grey. Since these had not quitted it, we hope at least this house may stand during the small remainder of days these poor animals have to live, who are now too infirm to remove to another: they have still a small subsistence left them in the few remaining books of the library.

I had never seen half what I have described, but for an old starched greyheaded steward, who is as much an antiquity as any in the place, and looks like an old family picture walked out of its frame. He failed not, as we passed from room to room, to relate several memoirs of the family, but his observations were particularly curious in the cellar: he showed where stood the triple rows of butts of sack, and where were ranged the bottles of tent for toasts in the morning: he pointed to the stands that supported the iron-hooped hogsheads of strong beer; then stepping to a corner, he lugged out the tattered fragment of an unframed picture: 'This (says he, with tears in his eyes) was poor Sir Thomas, once master of the drink I told you of: he had two sons (poor young masters!) that never arrived to the age of this beer; they both fell ill in this very cellar, and never went out upon their own legs.'

Letter from Stanton Harcourt

249 *A Tragic Pastoral*

I HAVE a mind to fill the rest of this paper with an accident that happened just under my eyes, and has made a great impression upon me. I have just passed part of this summer at an old romantic seat of my Lord Harcourt's, which he lent me. It overlooks a common-field, where, under the shade of a haycock, sat two lovers, as constant as ever were found in romance, beneath a spreading beech. The name of the one (let it sound as it will) was John Hewet; of the other, Sarah Drew. John was a well set man about five and twenty, Sarah a brown woman of eighteen. John had for several months borne the labour of the day in the same field with Sarah; when she milked, it was his morning and evening charge to bring the cows to her pail. Their love was the talk, but not the scandal, of the whole neighbourhood; for all they aimed at was the blameless possession of each other in marriage. It was but this very morning that he had obtained her parents' consent, and it was but till the next week that they were to wait to be happy. Perhaps this very day, in the intervals of their work, they were talking of their wedding clothes; and John was now matching several kinds of poppies and field-flowers to her complexion, to make her a present of knots for the day. While they were thus employed (it was on the last of July,) a terrible storm of thunder and lightning arose, that drove the labourers to what shelter the trees or hedges afforded. Sarah, frighted and out of breath, sunk on a haycock, and John (who never separated from her) sate by her side, having raked two or three heaps together to secure her. Immediately there was heard so loud a crack as if heaven had burst asunder. The labourers, all solicitous for each other's safety, called to one another: those that were nearest our lovers, hearing no answer, stepped to the place where they lay: they first saw a little smoke, and after, this faithful pair;—John with one arm about his Sarah's neck, and the other held over her face, as if to screen her from the lightning. They were struck dead, and already grown stiff and cold in this tender posture. There was no mark or discolouring on their bodies, only that Sarah's eyebrow was a little singed, and a small spot between her breasts. They were buried the next day in one grave, in the parish of Stanton Harcourt in Oxfordshire; where my Lord Harcourt, at my request, has erected a monument over them.

Letter to Lady Mary Montagu, 1 September, 1718

LADY MARY WORTLEY MONTAGU

1689–1762

250 *To Mr. Pope, from Adrianople*

I AM at this present moment writing in a house situated on the banks of the Hebrus, which runs under my chamber window. My garden is full of tall cypress-trees, upon the branches of which several couple of true turtles are saying soft things to one another from morning till night. How naturally do *boughs* and *vows* come into my mind at this minute! And must not you confess, to my praise, that 'tis more than an ordinary discretion that can resist the wicked suggestions of poetry, in a place where truth, for once, furnishes all the ideas of pastoral? The summer is already far advanced in this part of the world; and, for some miles round Adrianople, the whole ground is laid out in gardens, and the banks of the rivers are set with rows of fruit trees, under which all the most considerable Turks divert themselves every evening; not with walking, that is not one of their pleasures, but a set party of them choose out a green spot, where the shade is very thick, and there they spread a carpet, on which they sit drinking their coffee, and are generally attended by some slave with a fine voice, or that plays on some instrument. Every twenty paces you may see one of these little companies listening to the dashing of the river; and this taste is so universal, that the very gardeners are not without it. . . The young lads generally divert themselves with making garlands for their favourite lambs, which I have often seen painted and adorned with flowers, lying at their feet while they sung or played. It is not that they ever read Romances, but these are the ancient amusements here, and as natural to them as cudgel-playing and foot-ball to our British swains; the softness and warmth of the climate forbidding all rough exercises, which were never so much as heard of amongst them, and naturally inspiring a laziness and aversion to labour, which the great plenty indulges.

These gardeners are the only happy race of country people in Turkey. They furnish all the city with fruits and herbs, and seem to live very easily. They are most of them Greeks, and have little houses in the midst of their gardens, where their wives and daughters take a liberty not permitted in the town, I mean, to go unveiled. These wenches are very neat and handsome, and pass their time at their looms under the shade of the trees.

Letters

SAMUEL RICHARDSON

1689–1761

251 *A Filial Victim*

Miss Clarissa Harlowe, *to Miss* Howe

Friday, March 3.

O MY dear friend, I have had a sad conflict! trial upon trial; conference upon conference!—But what law, what ceremony, can give a man a right to a heart which abhors him more than it does any of God Almighty's creatures?

I hope my mamma will be able to prevail for me. —But I will recount all, tho' I sit up the whole night to do it; for I have a vast deal to write; and will be as minute as you wish me to be.

In my last, I told you, in a fright, my apprehensions; which were grounded upon a conversation that passed between my mamma and my aunt, part of which Hannah overheard. I need not give you the further particulars; since what I have to relate to you from different conversations that have passed between my mamma and me in the space of a very few hours, will include them all. I will begin then.

I went down this morning, when breakfast was ready, with a very uneasy heart, from what Hannah had told me yesterday afternoon; wishing for an opportunity, however, to appeal to my mamma, in hopes to engage her interest in my behalf, and purposing to try to find one, when she retired to her own apartment after breakfast:—But, unluckily, there was the odious Solmes sitting asquat between my mamma and sister, with *so much* assurance in his looks!—But you know, my dear, that those we love not, cannot do any-thing to please us.

Had the wretch kept his seat, it might have been well enough: But the bent and broad-shoulder'd creature must needs rise, and stalk towards a chair, which was just by that which was set for me.

I removed it at a distance, as if to make way to my own: And down I sat, abruptly I believe; what I had heard, all in my head.

But this was not enough to daunt him: The man is a very confident, he is a very bold, staring man! Indeed, my dear, the man is very confident.

He took the removed chair, and drew it so near mine, squatting in it with his ugly weight, that he press'd upon my hoop.—I was so offended (all I had heard, as I said, in my head), that I removed to another chair. I own I had too little command of myself: It gave my brother and sister too much advantage; I dare say they took it:—But I did it involuntarily, I think: I could not help it.—I knew not what I did.

I saw my papa was excessively displeased. When

angry, no man's countenance ever shew'd it so much as my papa's. Clarissa Harlowe! said he, with a big voice; and there he stopp'd.—Sir! said I, and courtesy'd.—I trembled; and put my chair nearer the wretch, and sat down; my face I could feel all in a glow.

Make tea, child, said my kind mamma: Sit by me, love; and make tea.

I removed with pleasure to the seat the man had quitted; and being thus indulgently put into employment, soon recover'd myself; and in the course of the breakfasting officiously asked two or three questions of Mr. Solmes, which I would not have done, but to make up with my papa.—*Proud spirits may be brought to*; whisperingly spoke my sister to me, over her shoulder, with an air of triumph and scorn: But I did not mind her.

My mamma was all kindness and condescension. I asked her once, if she were pleased with the tea? She said, softly, and again called me *dear*, she was pleased with all I did. I was very proud of this encouraging goodness: And all blew over, as I hoped, between my papa and me; for he also spoke kindly to me two or three times.

Small incidents these, my dear, to trouble you with; only as they lead to greater; as you shall hear.

Before the usual breakfast-time was over, my papa withdrew with my mamma, telling her he wanted to speak to her. My sister, and my aunt, who was with us, next dropt away.

My brother gave himself some airs of insult, that I understood well enough; but which Mr. Solmes could make nothing of:—And at last he arose from his seat—Sister, said he, I have a curiosity to shew you: I will fetch it: And away he went; shutting the door close after him.

I saw what all this was for. I arose; the man hemming up for a speech, rising, and beginning to set his splay-feet (indeed, my dear, the man in all his ways is hateful to me) in an approaching posture.—I will save my brother the trouble of bringing to me his curiosity, said I.—I courtesy'd—Your servant, Sir—The man cry'd, Madam, Madam, twice, and look'd like a fool.—But away I went—to find my brother, to save my word.—But my brother was gone, indifferent as the weather was, to walk in the garden with my sister. A plain case, that he had left his curiosity with me, and design'd to shew me no other.

I had but just got into my own apartment, and began to think of sending Hannah to beg an audience of my mamma (the more encouraged by her condescending goodness at breakfast), when Shorey, her woman, brought me her commands to attend her in her closet.

My papa, Hannah told me, had just gone out of it with a positive, angry countenance. Then I as much dreaded the audience, as I had wished for it before.

I went down, however; but, apprehending the subject, approached her trembling, and my heart in visible palpitations.

She saw my concern. Holding out her kind arms, as she sat, Come kiss me, my dear, said she, with a smile like a sun-beam breaking thro' the cloud that overshadowed her naturally benign aspect. Why flutters my jewel so?

This preparative sweetness, with her goodness just before, confirmed my apprehensions. My mamma saw the bitter pill wanting gilding.

O my mamma! was all I could say; and I clasp'd

my arms round her neck, and my face sunk into her bosom.

My child! my child! restrain, said she, your powers of moving!—I dare not else trust myself with you.—And my tears trickled down her bosom, as hers bedew'd my neck.

O the words of kindness, all to be express'd in vain, that flow'd from her lips!

Lift up your sweet face, my best child, my own Clarissa Harlowe!—O my daughter, best-beloved of my heart, lift up a face so ever-amiable to me!—Why these sobs?—Is an apprehended duty so affecting a thing, that before I can speak—But I am glad, my love, you can guess at what I have to say to you. I am spared the pains of breaking to you what was a task upon me reluctantly enough undertaken to break to you.

Then rising, she drew a chair near her own, and made me sit down by her, overwhelm'd as I was with tears of apprehension of what she had to say, and of gratitude for her truly maternal goodness to me; sobs still my only language.

And drawing her chair still nearer to mine, she put her arms round my neck, and my glowing cheek, wet with my tears, close to her own: Let me talk to you, my child; since silence is your choice, hearken to me, and *be* silent.

You know, my dear, what I every day forego, and undergo, for the sake of peace: Your papa is a very good man, and means well; but he will not be controuled; nor yet persuaded. You have seem'd to pity *me* sometimes, that I am obliged to give up every point. Poor man! *his* reputation the less for it; *mine* the greater; yet would I not have this credit, if I could help it, at so dear a rate to *him* and to *myself*. You are a dutiful, a prudent, and a *wise* child, she was pleased to say (in hope, no doubt, to make me so): You would not add, I am sure, to my trouble: You would not wilfully break that peace which costs your mamma so much to preserve. Obedience is better than sacrifice. O my Clary Harlowe, rejoice my heart, by telling me I have apprehended too much! —I see your concern! I see your perplexity! I see your conflict (loosing her arm, and rising, not willing I should see how much she herself was affected). I will leave you a moment.—Answer me not (for I was essaying to speak, and had, as soon as she took her dear cheek from mine, dropt down on my knees, my hands clasped and lifted up in a supplicating manner): I am not prepared for your irresistible expostulation, she was pleased to say.—I will leave you to recollection: And I charge you, on my blessing, that all this my truly maternal tenderness be not thrown away upon you.

And then she withdrew into the next apartment; wiping her eyes, as she went from me; as mine overflow'd.

Clarissa; or, The History of a Young Lady

PHILIP DORMER STANHOPE, EARL OF CHESTERFIELD

1694–1773

252 The Art of Pleasing

London, October the 16th, O.S. 1747.

DEAR BOY,

The art of pleasing is a very necessary one to possess; but a very difficult one to acquire. It can hardly be reduced to rules; and your own good sense and observation will teach you more of it than I can.

Do as you would be done by, is the surest method that I know of pleasing. Observe carefully what pleases you in others, and probably the same things in you will please others. If you are pleased with the complaisance and attention of others to your humours, your tastes, or your weaknesses, depend upon it, the same complaisance and attention, on your part, to theirs, will equally please them. Take the tone of the company, that you are in, and do not pretend to give it; be serious, gay, or even trifling, as you find the present humour of the company: this is an attention due from every individual to the majority. Do not tell stories in company; there is nothing more tedious and disagreeable: if by chance you know a very short story, and exceedingly applicable to the present subject of conversation, tell it in as few words as possible; and even then, throw out that you do not love to tell stories; but that the shortness of it tempted you. Of all things, banish the egotism out of your conversation, and never think of entertaining people with your own personal concerns, or private affairs; though they are interesting to you, they are tedious and impertinent to every body else: besides that, one cannot keep one's own private affairs too secret. Whatever you think your own excellencies may be, do not affectedly display them in company; nor labour, as many people do, to give that turn to the conversation, which may supply you with an opportunity of exhibiting them. If they are real, they will infallibly be discovered, without your pointing them out yourself, and with much more advantage. Never maintain an argument with heat and clamour, though you think or know yourself to be in the right; but give your opinion modestly and coolly, which is the only way to convince; and, if that does not do, try to change the conversation, by saying, with good humour, 'We shall hardly convince one another, nor is it necessary that we should, so let us talk of something else.'

Letters to his Son

253 *Dissimulation*

London, May the 22nd, O.S. 1749.

IT may be objected, that I am now recommending dissimulation to you; I both own and justify it. It has been long said, *Qui nescit dissimulare nescit regnare*: I go still farther, and say, that without some dissimulation no business can be carried on at all. It is *simulation* that is false, mean, and criminal: that is the cunning which Lord Bacon calls, crooked or left-handed wisdom, and which is never made use of but by those who have not true wisdom. And the same great man says, that dissimulation is only to hide our own cards; whereas simulation is put on in order to look into other people's. Lord Bolingbroke, in his 'Idea of a patriot King,' which he has lately published, and which I will send you by the first opportunity, says, very justly, that simulation is a *stiletto*; not only an unjust but an unlawful weapon, and the use of it very rarely to be excused, never justified. Whereas dissimulation is a shield, as secrecy is armour; and it is no more possible to preserve secrecy in business, without some degree of dissimulation, than it is to succeed in business without secrecy. He goes on, and says, that those two arts, of dissimulation and secrecy, are like the alloy mingled with pure ore: a little is necessary, and will not debase the coin below its proper standard; but if more than that little be employed (that is, simulation and cunning) the coin loses its currency, and the coiner his credit.

Letters to his Son

254 *A Collateral Security*

London, January the 8th, O.S. 1750.

DEAR BOY,

I have seldom or never written to you upon the subject of Religion and Morality: your own reason, I am persuaded, has given you true notions of both; they speak best for themselves; but, if they wanted assistance, you have Mr. Harte at hand, both for precept and example: to your own reason, therefore, and to Mr. Harte, shall I refer you, for the Reality of both; and confine myself, in this letter, to the decency, the utility, and the necessity, of scrupulously preserving the Appearances of both. When I say the Appearances of religion, I do not mean that you should talk or act like a Missionary, or an Enthusiast, nor that you should take up a controversial cudgel, against whoever attacks the sect you are of; this would be both useless, and unbecoming your age: but I mean that you should by no means seem to approve, encourage, or applaud, those libertine notions, which strike at religions equally, and which are the poor thread-bare topics of half Wits, and minute Philosophers. Even those who are silly enough to laugh at their jokes, are still wise enough to distrust and detest their characters: for, putting moral virtues at the highest, and religion at the lowest, religion must still be allowed to be a collateral security, at least, to Virtue; and every prudent man will sooner trust to two securities than to one.

Letters to his Son

HENRY FIELDING

1707–1754

255 *Mr. Allworthy and the Foundling*

MR. *ALLWORTHY* had been absent a full Quarter of a Year in *London*, on some very particular Business, though I know not what it was; but judge of its Importance, by its having detained him so long from home, whence he had not been absent a Month at a Time during the Space of many Years. He came to his House very late in the Evening, and after a short Supper with his Sister, retired much fatigued to his Chamber. Here, having spent some Minutes on his Knees, a Custom which he never broke through on any Account, he was preparing to step into Bed, when, upon opening the Cloaths, to his great Surprize, he beheld an Infant, wrapt up in some coarse Linnen, in a sweet and profound Sleep, between his Sheets. He stood some Time lost in Astonishment at this Sight; but, as Good-nature was always the Ascendant in his Mind, he soon began to be touched with Sentiments of Compassion for the little Wretch before him. He then rang his Bell, and ordered an elderly Woman Servant to rise immediately and come to him, and in the mean Time was so eager in contemplating the Beauty of Innocence, appearing in those lively Colours with which Infancy and Sleep always display it, that his Thoughts were too much engaged to reflect that he was in his Shirt, when the Matron came in. She had indeed given her Master sufficient Time to dress himself; for out of Respect to him, and Regard to Decency, she had spent many Minutes in adjusting her Hair at the Looking-glass, notwithstanding all the Hurry in which she had been summoned by the Servant, and tho' her Master, for ought she knew, lay expiring in an Apoplexy, or in some other Fit.

It will not be wondered at, that a Creature, who had so strict a Regard to Decency in her own Person, should be shocked at the least Deviation from it in another. She therefore no sooner opened the Door, and saw her Master standing by the Bed-side in his Shirt, with a Candle in his Hand, than she started back in a most terrible Fright, and might perhaps have swooned away, had he not now recollected his being undrest, and put an End to her Terrors, by desiring her to stay without the Door, till he had thrown some Cloaths over his Back, and was become incapable of shocking the pure Eyes of Mrs. *Deborah Wilkins*, who, tho' in the 52d Year of her Age, vowed she had never beheld a Man without his Coat. Sneerers and prophane Wits may perhaps laugh at her first Fright; yet my graver Reader, when he considers the Time of Night, the Summons from her Bed, and the Situation in which she found her Master, will highly justify and applaud her Conduct; unless the Prudence, which must be supposed to attend Maidens at that Period of Life at which Mrs. *Deborah* had arrived, should a little lessen his Admiration.

When Mrs. *Deborah* returned into the Room, and was acquainted by her Master with the finding the little Infant, her Consternation was rather greater than his had been; nor could she refrain from crying out, with great Horror of Accent as well as Look, 'My good Sir! what 's to be done?' Mr. *Allworthy* answered, She must take care of the Child that Evening, and in the Morning he would give Orders to provide it a Nurse. 'Yes, Sir,' says she, 'and I hope your Worship will send out your Warrant to take up the Hussy its Mother (for she must be one of the Neighbourhood) and I should be glad to see her committed to *Bridewel*, and whipt at the Cart's Tail. Indeed, such wicked Sluts cannot be too severely punished. I'll warrant 'tis not her first, by her Impudence in laying it to your Worship.' 'In laying it to me, *Deborah*,' answered *Allworthy*, 'I can't think she hath any such Design. I suppose she hath only taken this Method to provide for her Child; and truly I am glad she hath not done worse.'

Tom Jones

256 *London River*

THE Morning was fair and bright, and we had a Passage thither [to Gravesend], I think, as pleasant as can be conceiv'd; for, take it with all its Advantages, particularly the number of fine Ships you are always sure of seeing by the Way, there is nothing to equal it in all the Rivers of the World. The yards of *Deptford* and of *Woolwich* are noble Sights; and give us a just idea of the great Perfection to which we are arrived in building those Floating Castles, and the Figure which we may always make in Europe among the other Maritime Powers. That of Woolwich, at least, very strongly imprinted this idea on my Mind; for, there was now on the Stocks there the *Royal Anne*, supposed to be the largest Ship ever built, and which contains ten Carriage Guns more than had ever yet equipped a First-rate.

It is true, perhaps, that there is more of Ostentation than of real Utility, in ships of this vast and unwieldy Burthen, which are rarely capable of acting against an

Enemy; but if the building such contributes to preserve, among other nations, the Notion of the *British* superiority in Naval Affairs, the expence, though very great, is well incurred, and the Ostentation is laudable and truly political. Indeed I should be sorry to allow that *Holland*, *France* or *Spain*, possessed a Vessel larger and more beautiful than the largest and most Beautiful of ours; for this Honour I would always administer to the Pride of our Sailors, who should challenge it from all their Neighbours with Truth and Success. And sure I am, that not our honest Tars alone, but every Inhabitant of this Island, may exult in the Comparison, when he considers the King of *Great-Britain* as a Maritime Prince, in opposition to any other Prince in *Europe*; but I am not so certain that the same idea of superiority will result from comparing our Land-forces with those of many other Crowned Heads. In Numbers, they all far exceed us, and in the Goodness and splendor of their troops, many Nations, particularly the *Germans* and *French*, and perhaps the *Dutch*, cast us at a Distance. . .

In our Marine the case is entirely the reverse, and it must be our own Fault if it doth not continue so; for continue so it will, as long as the flourishing State of our Trade shall support it; and this support it can never want, till our Legislature shall cease to give sufficient attention to the Protection of our Trade, and our Magistrates want sufficient Power, Ability, and Honesty to execute the Laws: a circumstance not to be apprehended, as it cannot happen, till our Senates and our Benches shall be filled with the blindest Ignorance, or with the blackest Corruption. . .

We saw likewise several *Indiamen* just returned from their Voyage. These are, I believe, the largest and finest Vessels which are any where employed in Commercial Affairs. The Colliers, likewise, which are very numerous, and even assemble in Fleets, are Ships of great bulk; and, if we descend to those used in the *American*, *African*, and *European* Trades, and pass through those which visit our own Coasts, to the small Craft that lye between Chatham and the Tower, the whole forms a most pleasing Object to the Eye, as well as highly warming to the Heart of an *Englishman*, who has any Degree of Love for his Country, or can recognize any effect of the Patriot in his Constitution.

Journal of a Voyage to Lisbon

257 *Cat Overboard!*

A MOST tragical Incident fell out this day at Sea. While the Ship was under Sail, but making, as will appear, no great Way, a Kitten, one of four of the Feline Inhabitants of the Cabin, fell from the Window into the Water: an Alarm was immediately given to the Captain, who was then upon Deck, and received it with the utmost Concern. He immediately gave Orders to the Steersman in favour of the poor Thing, as he called it; the Sails were instantly slackened, and all Hands, as the Phrase is, employed to recover the poor Animal. I was, I own, extremely surprised at all this; less, indeed, at the Captain's extreme Tenderness, than at his conceiving any Possibility of Success; for, if Puss had had nine thousand, instead of nine Lives, I concluded they had been all lost. The Boatswain, however, had more sanguine Hopes; for, having stript himself of his Jacket, Breeches, and Shirt, he leapt boldly into the Water, and, to my great Astonishment, in a few Minutes, returned to the Ship, bearing the motionless Animal in his Mouth. Nor was this, I observed, a Matter of such great Difficulty as it appeared to my Ignorance, and possibly may seem to that of my Fresh-water Reader: the Kitten was now exposed to Air and Sun on the Deck, where its Life, of which it retained no Symptoms, was despaired of by all.

The Captain's humanity, if I may so call it, did not so totally destroy his Philosophy, as to make him yield himself up to affliction on this melancholy Occasion. Having felt his Loss like a Man, he resolved to shew he could bear it like one; and, having declared, he had rather have lost a Cask of Rum or Brandy, betook himself to threshing at Backgammon with the *Portuguese* Friar, in which innocent Amusement they passed their leisure hours.

But as I have, perhaps, a little too wantonly endeavoured to raise the tender Passions of my Readers, in this Narrative, I should think myself unpardonable if I concluded it, without giving them the Satisfaction of hearing that the Kitten at last recovered, to the great Joy of the good Captain.

Journal of a Voyage to Lisbon

WILLIAM PITT, EARL OF CHATHAM

1708–1778

258 *On the Employment of Red Indians in the American War*

I CALL upon that right reverend bench, those holy ministers of the Gospel, and pious pastors of our Church—I conjure them to join in the holy work, and vindicate the religion of their God. I appeal to the wisdom and the law of this learned bench to defend and support the justice of their country. I call upon the bishops to interpose the unsullied sanctity of their lawn; upon the learned judges to interpose the purity of their ermine, to save us from this pollution. I call upon the honour of your lordships to reverence the dignity of your ancestors, and to maintain your own. I call upon the spirit and humanity of my country to vindicate the national character. I invoke the genius of the Constitution. From the tapestry that adorns these walls the immortal ancestor of this noble lord [Lord Suffolk] frowns with indignation at the disgrace of his country. In vain he led your victorious fleets against the boasted Armada of Spain; in vain he defended and established the honour, the liberties, the religion—the *Protestant religion*—of this country, against the arbitrary cruelties of Popery and the Inquisition, if these more than Popish cruelties and inquisitorial practices are let loose among us—to turn forth into our settlements, among our ancient connexions, friends, and relations, the merciless cannibal, thirsting for the blood of man, woman, and child! to send forth the infidel savage—against whom? against your Protestant brethren; to lay waste their country, to desolate their dwellings, and extirpate their race and name with these horrible hell-hounds of savage war!—hell-hounds, I say, of savage war! Spain armed herself with blood-hounds to extirpate the wretched natives of America, and we improve on the inhuman example even of Spanish cruelty; we turn loose these savage hell-hounds against our brethren and countrymen in America, of the same language, laws, liberties, and religion, endeared to us by every tie that should sanctify humanity. . .

My lords, I am old and weak, and at present unable to say more; but my feelings and indignation were too strong to have said less. I could not have slept this night in my bed, nor reposed my head on my pillow, without giving this vent to my eternal abhorrence of such preposterous and enormous principles.

Speech in the House of Lords, 20 November, 1777

SAMUEL JOHNSON

1709–1784

259 *The Last 'Idler'*

Saturday, April 5 [1760]

MUCH of the Pain and Pleasure of mankind arises from the conjectures which every one makes of the thoughts of others; we all enjoy praise which we do not hear, and resent contempt which we do not see. The *Idler* may therefore be forgiven, if he suffers his Imagination to represent to him what his readers will say or think when they are informed that they have now his last paper in their hands.

Value is more frequently raised by scarcity than by use. That which lay neglected when it was common, rises in estimation as its quantity becomes less. We seldom learn the true want of what we have till it is discovered that we can have no more.

This essay will, perhaps, be read with care even by those who have not yet attended to any other; and he that finds this late attention recompensed, will not forbear to wish that he had bestowed it sooner.

Though the *Idler* and his readers have contracted

no close friendship they are perhaps both unwilling to part. There are few things not purely evil, of which we can say, without some emotion of uneasiness, *this is the last.* Those who never could agree together, shed tears when mutual discontent has determined them to final separation; of a place which has been frequently visited, tho' without pleasure, the last look is taken with heaviness of heart; and the *Idler*, with all his chilness of tranquillity, is not wholly unaffected by the thought that his last essay is now before him.

This secret horrour of the last is inseparable from a thinking being whose life is limited, and to whom death is dreadful. We always make a secret comparison between a part and the whole; the termination of any period of life reminds us that life itself has likewise its termination; when we have done any thing for the last time, we involuntarily reflect that a part of the days allotted us is past, and that as more is past there is less remaining.

It is very happily and kindly provided, that in every life there are certain pauses and interruptions, which force consideration upon the careless, and seriousness upon the light; points of time where one course of action ends and another begins; and by vicissitude of fortune, or alteration of employment, by change of place, or loss of friendship, we are forced to say of something, *this is the last.*

An even and unvaried tenour of life always hides from our apprehension the approach of its end. Succession is not perceived but by variation; he that lives to day as he lived yesterday, and expects that, as the present day is, such will be the morrow, easily conceives time as running in a circle and returning to itself. The uncertainty of our duration is impressed commonly by dissimilitude of condition ; it is only by finding life changeable that we are reminded of its shortness.

This conviction, however forcible at every new impression, is every moment fading from the mind ; and partly by the inevitable incursion of new images, and partly by voluntary exclusion of unwelcome thoughts, we are again exposed to the universal fallacy ; and we must do another thing for the last time, before we consider that the time is nigh when we shall do no more. . .

The Idler, No. 103

260 *The Aviator*

AMONG the artists that had been allured into the happy valley, to labour for the accommodation and pleasure of its inhabitants, was a man eminent for his knowledge of the mechanick powers, who had contrived many engines both of use and recreation. . .

This artist was sometimes visited by Rasselas, who was pleased with every kind of knowledge, imagining that the time would come when all his acquisitions should be of use to him in the open world. He came one day to amuse himself in his usual manner, and found the master busy in building a sailing chariot : he saw that the design was practicable upon a level surface, and with expressions of great esteem solicited its completion. The workman was pleased to find himself so much regarded by the prince, and resolved to gain yet higher honours. ‘ Sir, said he, you have seen but a small part of what the mechanick sciences can perform. I have been long of opinion, that, instead of the tardy conveyance of ships and chariots, man might use the swifter migration of wings ; that the fields of air are open to knowledge, and that only ignorance and idleness need crawl upon the ground.'

This hint rekindled the prince's desire of passing the mountains ; having seen what the mechanist had already performed, he was willing to fancy that he could do more ; yet resolved to enquire further before he suffered hope to afflict him by disappointment. 'I am afraid, said he to the artist, that your imagination prevails over your skill, and that you now tell me rather what you wish than what you know. Every animal has his element assigned him ; the birds have the air, and man and beasts the earth.' 'So, replied the mechanist, fishes have the water, in which yet beasts can swim by nature, and men by art. He that can swim needs not despair to fly : to swim is to fly in a grosser fluid, and to fly is to swim in a subtler. We are only to proportion our power of resistance to the different density of matter through which we are to pass. You will be necessarily upborn by the air, if you can renew any impulse upon it, faster than the air can recede from the pressure.'

'But the exercise of swimming, said the prince, is very laborious ; the strongest limbs are soon wearied ; I am afraid the act of flying will be yet more violent, and wings will be of no great use, unless we can fly further than we can swim.'

'Nothing, replied the artist, will ever be attempted, if all possible objections must be first overcome. If you will favour my project I will try the first flight at my own hazard. I have considered the structure of all volant animals, and find the folding continuity of the bat's wings most easily accommodated to the human form. Upon this model I shall begin my task to morrow, and in a year expect to tower into the air beyond the malice or pursuit of man. But I will work only on this condition, that the art shall not be divulged, and that you shall not require me to make wings for any but ourselves.'

'Why, said Rasselas, should you envy others so great an advantage? All skill ought to be exerted for universal good; every man has owed much to others, and ought to repay the kindness that he has received.'

'If men were all virtuous, returned the artist, I should with great alacrity teach them all to fly. But what would be the security of the good, if the bad could at pleasure invade them from the sky? Against an army sailing through the clouds neither walls, nor mountains, nor seas, could afford any security. A flight of northern savages might hover in the wind, and light at once with irresistible violence upon the capital of a fruitful region that was rolling under them. Even this valley, the retreat of princes, the abode of happiness, might be violated by the sudden descent of some of the naked nations that swarm on the coast of the southern sea.'

The prince promised secrecy, and waited for the performance, not wholly hopeless of success. He visited the work from time to time, observed its progress, and remarked many ingenious contrivances to facilitate motion, and unite levity with strength. The artist was every day more certain that he should leave vultures and eagles behind him, and the contagion of his confidence seized upon the prince.

In a year the wings were finished, and, on a morning appointed, the maker appeared furnished for flight on a little promontory: he waved his pinions a while to gather air, then leaped from his stand, and in an instant dropped into the lake. His wings, which were of no use in the air, sustained him in the water, and the prince drew him to land, half dead with terrour and vexation.

Rasselas

261 *Pope and Dryden*

HE professed to have learned his poetry from Dryden, whom, whenever an opportunity was presented, he praised through his whole life with unvaried liberality; and perhaps his character may receive some illustration if he be compared with his master.

Integrity of understanding and nicety of discernment were not allotted in a less proportion to Dryden than to Pope. The rectitude of Dryden's mind was sufficiently shewn by the dismission of his poetical prejudices, and the rejection of unnatural thoughts and rugged numbers. But Dryden never desired to apply all the judgement that he had. He wrote, and professed to write, merely for the people; and when he pleased others, he contented himself. He spent no time in struggles to rouse latent powers; he never attempted to make that better which was already good, nor often to mend what he must have known to be faulty. He wrote, as he tells us, with very little consideration; when occasion or necessity called upon him, he poured out what the present moment happened to supply, and, when once it had passed the press, ejected it from his mind; for when he had no pecuniary interest, he had no further solicitude.

Pope was not content to satisfy; he desired to excel, and therefore always endeavoured to do his best: he did not court the candour, but dared the judgement of his reader, and, expecting no indulgence from others, he shewed none to himself. He examined lines and words with minute and punctilious observation, and retouched every part with indefatigable diligence, till he had left nothing to be forgiven. . .

Of genius, that power which constitutes a poet; that quality without which judgement is cold and knowledge is inert; that energy which collects, combines, amplifies, and animates—the superiority must, with some hesitation, be allowed to Dryden. It is not to be inferred that of this poetical vigour Pope had only a little, because Dryden had more; for every other writer since Milton must give place to Pope; and even of Dryden it must be said that if he has brighter paragraphs, he has not better poems. Dryden's performances were always hasty, either excited by some external occasion, or extorted by domestick necessity; he composed without consideration, and published without correction. What his mind could supply at call, or gather in one excursion, was all that he sought, and all that he gave. The dilatory caution of Pope enabled him to condense his sentiments, to multiply his images, and to accumulate all that study might produce, or chance might supply. If the flights of Dryden therefore are higher, Pope continues longer on the wing. If of Dryden's fire the blaze is brighter, of Pope's the heat is more regular and constant. Dryden often surpasses expectation, and Pope never falls below it. Dryden is read with frequent astonishment, and Pope with perpetual delight.

Lives of the Poets

262 *William Collins*

HE now (about 1744) came to London a literary adventurer, with many projects in his head, and very little money in his pocket. He designed many works, but his great fault was irresolution, or the frequent calls of immediate necessity broke his schemes, and suffered him to pursue no settled purpose. A man, doubtful of his dinner, or trembling at a creditor, is not much disposed to abstracted meditation or remote enquiries. He published proposals for a *History of the Revival of Learning*, and I have heard him speak with great kindness of Leo the Tenth, and with keen resentment of his tasteless successor. But probably not a page of the *History* was ever written. He planned several tragedies, but he only planned them. He wrote now and then odes and other poems, and did something, however little.

About this time I fell into his company. His appearance was decent and manly; his knowledge considerable, his views extensive, his conversation elegant, and his disposition chearful. By degrees I gained his confidence; and one day was admitted to him when he was immured by a bailiff that was prowling in the street. On this occasion recourse was had to the booksellers, who, on the credit of a translation of Aristotle's *Poeticks*, which he engaged to write with a large commentary, advanced as much money as enabled him to escape into the country. He shewed me the guineas safe in his hand. Soon afterwards his uncle, Mr. Martin, a lieutenant-colonel, left him about two thousand pounds; a sum which Collins could scarcely think exhaustible, and which he did not live to exhaust. The guineas were then repaid, and the translation neglected.

But man is not born for happiness. Collins, who, while he *studied to live*, felt no evil but poverty, no sooner *lived to study* than his life was assailed by more dreadful calamities, disease and insanity. . .

Such was the fate of Collins, with whom I once delighted to converse, and whom I yet remember with tenderness.

Lives of the Poets

263 *Congregational Music*

AS we sat at Sir Alexander's table, we were entertained, according to the ancient usage of the North, with the melody of the bagpipe. Every thing in these countries has its history. As the bagpiper was playing, an elderly Gentleman informed us, that in some remote time, the *Macdonalds* of Glengary having been injured, or offended by the inhabitants of *Culloden*, and resolving to have justice or vengeance, came to *Culloden* on a Sunday, where finding their enemies at worship, they shut them up in the church, which they set on fire ; and this, said he, is the tune that the piper played while they were burning.

Narrations like this, however uncertain, deserve the notice of a traveller, because they are the only records of a nation that has no historians, and afford the most genuine representation of the life and character of the ancient Highlanders.

Journey to the Western Islands

264 *On his Dictionary*

IN hope of giving longevity to that which its own nature forbids to be immortal, I have devoted this book, the labour of years, to the honour of my country, that we may no longer yield the palm of philology, without a contest, to the nations of the continent. The chief glory of every people arises from its authours: whether I shall add any thing by my own writings to the reputation of *English* literature, must be left to time: much of my life has been lost under the pressures of disease; much has been trifled away; and much has always been spent in provision for the day that was passing over me; but I shall not think my employment useless or ignoble, if by my assistance foreign nations, and distant ages, gain access to the propagators of knowledge, and understand the teachers of truth; if my labours afford light to the repositories of science, and add celebrity to *Bacon*, to *Hooker*, to *Milton*, and to *Boyle*.

When I am animated by this wish, I look with pleasure on my book, however defective, and deliver it to the world with the spirit of a man that has endeavoured well. That it will immediately become popular I have not promised to myself: a few wild blunders, and risible absurdities, from which no work of such multiplicity was ever free, may for a time furnish folly with laughter, and harden ignorance in contempt; but useful diligence will at last prevail, and there never can be wanting some who distinguish desert; who will consider that no dictionary of a living tongue ever can be perfect, since, while it is hastening to publication, some words are budding, and some falling away; that a whole life cannot be spent upon syntax and etymology, and that even a whole life would not be sufficient; that he, whose design includes whatever language can express, must often speak of what he does not understand; that a writer will sometimes be hurried by eagerness to the end, and sometimes faint with weariness under a task, which *Scaliger* compares to the labours of the anvil and the mine; that what is obvious is not always known, and what is known is not always present; that sudden fits of inadvertency will surprize vigilance, slight avocations will seduce attention, and casual eclipses of the mind will darken learning; and that the writer shall often in vain trace his memory at the moment of need, for that which yesterday he knew with intuitive readiness, and which will come uncalled into his thoughts to-morrow.

In this work, when it shall be found that much is omitted, let it not be forgotten that much likewise is performed; and though no book was ever spared out of tenderness to the authour, and the world is little solicitous to know whence proceeded the faults of that which it condemns; yet it may gratify curiosity to inform it, that the *English Dictionary* was written with little assistance of the learned, and without any patronage of the great; not in the soft obscurities of retirement, or under the shelter of academick bowers, but amidst inconvenience and distraction, in sickness and in sorrow. It may repress the triumph of malignant criticism to observe, that if our language is not here fully displayed, I have only failed in an attempt which no human powers have hitherto completed. If the lexicons of ancient tongues, now immutably fixed, and comprised in a few volumes, be yet, after the toil of successive ages, inadequate and delusive; if the aggregated knowledge, and co-operating diligence of the *Italian* academicians, did not secure them from the censure of *Beni*; if the embodied criticks of *France*, when fifty years had been spent upon their work, were obliged to change its œconomy, and give their second edition another form, I may surely be contented without the praise of perfection, which, if I could obtain, in this gloom of solitude, what would it avail me? I have protracted my work till most of those whom I wished to please have sunk into the grave, and success and miscarriage are empty sounds: I therefore dismiss it with frigid tranquillity, having little to fear or hope from censure or from praise.

Preface to the English Dictionary

265 *Letter to Lord Chesterfield*

To the Right Honourable the Earl of Chesterfield.

MY LORD, February 7, 1755.

I HAVE been lately informed, by the proprietor of the World, that two papers, in which my Dictionary is recommended to the publick, were written by your Lordship. To be so distinguished, is an honour, which, being very little accustomed to favours from the great, I know not well how to receive, or in what terms to acknowledge.

When, upon some slight encouragement, I first visited your Lordship, I was overpowered, like the rest of mankind, by the enchantment of your address;

and could not forbear to wish that I might boast myself *Le vainqueur du vainqueur de la terre* ;—that I might obtain that regard for which I saw the world contending ; but I found my attendance so little encouraged, that neither pride nor modesty would suffer me to continue it. When I had once addressed your Lordship in publick, I had exhausted all the art of pleasing which a retired and uncourtly scholar can possess. I had done all that I could ; and no man is well pleased to have his all neglected, be it ever so little.

Seven years, my Lord, have now past, since I waited in your outward rooms, or was repulsed from your door ; during which time I have been pushing on my work through difficulties, of which it is useless to complain, and have brought it, at last, to the verge of publication, without one act of assistance, one word of encouragement, or one smile of favour. Such treatment I did not expect, for I never had a Patron before.

The shepherd in Virgil grew at last acquainted with Love, and found him a native of the rocks.

Is not a Patron, my Lord, one who looks with unconcern on a man struggling for life in the water, and, when he has reached ground, encumbers him with help ? The notice which you have been pleased to take of my labours, had it been early, had been kind ; but it has been delayed till I am indifferent, and cannot enjoy it ; till I am solitary, and cannot impart it ; till I am known, and do not want it. I hope it is no very cynical asperity not to confess obligations where no benefit has been received, or to be unwilling that the publick should consider me as owing that to a Patron, which Providence has enabled me to do for myself.

Having carried on my work thus far with so little obligation to any favourer of learning, I shall not be disappointed though I should conclude it, if less be possible, with less; for I have been long wakened from that dream of hope, in which I once boasted myself with so much exultation,

My Lord,

Your Lordship's most humble,

Most obedient servant,

SAM. JOHNSON.

WILLIAM MELMOTH

1710–1799

266 *The Source of the Clitumnus*

(*Pliny to Romanus*)

HAVE you ever seen the source of the river Clitumnus? As I never heard you mention it, I imagine not; let me therefore advise you to do so immediately. It is but lately indeed I had that pleasure, and I condemn myself for not having seen it sooner. At the foot of a little hill, covered with venerable and shady cypress-trees, a spring issues out, which gushing in different and unequal streams, forms itself, after several windings, into a spacious bason, so extremely clear, that you may see the pebbles, and the little pieces of money which are thrown into it, as they lie at the bottom. From thence it is carried off not so much by the declivity of the ground, as by its own strength and fulness. It is navigable almost as soon as it has quitted its source, and wide enough to admit a free passage for ships to pass by each other, as they sail with or against the stream. The current runs so strong, tho' the ground is level, that the vessels which go down the river have no occasion to make use of their oars ; while those which ascend, find it difficult to advance, even with the assistance of oars and poles : and this vicissitude of labor and ease, is exceedingly amusing when one sails up and down merely for pleasure. The banks on each side are shaded with the verdure of great numbers of ash and poplar trees, as clearly and distinctly seen in the stream, as if they were actually sunk in it. The water is cold as snow, and as white too. Near it stands an antient and venerable temple, wherein is placed the river-god Clitumnus cloathed in a robe, whose immediate presence the prophetic oracles here delivered, sufficiently testify. Several little chapels are scattered round, dedicated to particular gods distinguished by different names, and some of them too presiding over different fountains. For, besides the principal one, which is, as it were, the parent of all the rest, there are several other lesser streams, which, taking their rise from various sources, lose themselves in the river ; over which a bridge is built, that separates the sacred part from that which lies open to common use. Vessels are allowed to come over this bridge, but no person is permitted to swim, except below it. The Hispellates, to whom Augustus gave this place, furnish a public bath and likewise entertain all strangers, at their own expence. Several villas, attracted by the beauty of this river, are situated upon its borders. In short, every object that presents itself will afford you entertainment. You may also amuse yourself with numberless inscriptions, that are fixed upon the pillars and walls by different persons, celebrating the virtues of the fountain, and the divinity that presides over it. There are many of them you will greatly admire, as there are some that will make you laugh: but I must correct myself when I say so; you are too humane, I know, to laugh upon such an occasion. Farewel.

Translation of Pliny's Letters

DAVID HUME

1711–1776

267 *Delicacy of Taste and Delicacy of Passion*

THERE is a certain *Delicacy* of *Passion* to which some People are subject that makes them extremely sensible to all the Accidents of Life, and gives them a lively Joy upon every prosperous Event, as well as a piercing Grief when they meet with Crosses and Adversity. Favours and Good offices easily engage their Friendship, while the smallest Injury provokes their Resentment. Any Honour or Mark of Distinction elevates them above Measure; but they are as sensibly touched with Contempt. People of this Character have, no doubt, more lively Enjoyments, as well as more pungent Sorrows, than Men of more cool and sedate Tempers. But, I believe, when every Thing is balanced, there is no one that would not rather chuse to be of the latter Character, were he entirely Master of his own Disposition. Good or ill Fortune is very little at our Disposal: And when a Person that has this Sensibility of Temper meets with any Misfortune, his Sorrow or Resentment takes entire Possession of him, and deprives him of all Relish in the common Occurrences of Life, the right Enjoyment of which forms the greatest Part of our Happiness. Great Pleasures are much less frequent than great Pains, so that a sensible Temper must meet with fewer Trials in the former Way than in the latter. Not to mention, that Men of such lively Passions are apt to be transported beyond all Bounds of Prudence and Discretion, and take false Steps in the Conduct of Life, which are often irretrievable.

There is a *Delicacy* of *Taste* observable in some Men, which very much resembles this *Delicacy* of *Passion*, and produces the same Sensibility to Beauty and Deformity of every Kind, as that does to Prosperity and Adversity, Obligations and Injuries. When you present a Poem or a Picture to a Man possessed of this Talent, the Delicacy of his Feeling or Sentiments makes him be touched very sensibly by every Part of it; nor are the masterly Strokes perceived with a more exquisite Relish and Satisfaction, than the Negligences or Absurdities with Disgust and Uneasiness. A polite and judicious Conversation affords him the highest Entertainment. Rudeness or Impertinence is as great a Punishment to him. In short, Delicacy of Taste has the same Effect as Delicacy of Passion: It enlarges the Sphere both of our Happiness and Misery, and makes us sensible of Pains as well as Pleasures that escape the rest of Mankind.

I believe, however, there is no one who will not agree with me, that notwithstanding this Resemblance, a Delicacy of Taste is as much to be desired and cultivated, as a Delicacy of Passion is to be lamented, and to be remedied, if possible. The good or ill Accidents of Life are very little at our Disposal: But we are pretty much Masters what Books we shall read, what Diversions we shall partake of, and what Company we shall keep. The ancient Philosophers endeavoured to render Happiness entirely independent of every Thing external. That is impossible to be *attained*: But every wise Man will endeavour to place his Happiness on such Objects as depend most upon himself; And *that* is not to be *attained* so much by any other Means as by this Delicacy of Sentiment. When a Man is possessed of that Talent, he is more happy by what pleases his Taste, than by what gratifies his Appetites, and receives more Enjoyment from a Poem, or a Piece of Reasoning, than the most expensive Luxury can afford.

Essays

268 *Foreign Trade*

IF we consult history, we shall find, that in most nations foreign trade has preceded any refinement in home manufactures, and given birth to domestic luxury. The temptation is stronger to make use of foreign commodities which are ready for use, and which are entirely new to us, than to make improvements on any domestic commodity, which always advance by slow degrees, and never affect us by their novelty. The profit is also very great in exporting what is superfluous at home, and what bears no price, to foreign nations whose soil or climate is not favourable to that commodity. Thus men become acquainted with the *pleasures* of luxury, and the *profits* of commerce ; and their *delicacy* and *industry* being once awakened, carry them on to farther improvements in every branch of domestic as well as foreign trade ; and this perhaps is the chief advantage which arises from a commerce with strangers. It rouses men from their indolence ; and, presenting the gayer and more opulent part of the nation with objects of luxury which they never before dreamed of, raises in them a desire of a more splendid way of life than what their ancestors enjoyed. And at the same time, the few merchants who possess the secret of this importation and exportation, make great profits ; and, becoming rivals in wealth to the ancient nobility, tempt other adventurers to become their rivals in commerce. Imitation soon diffuses all those arts, while domestic manufacturers emulate the foreign in their improvements, and work up every home commodity to the utmost perfection of which it is susceptible. Their own steel and iron, in such laborious hands, become equal to the gold and rubies of the *Indies*.

Essays

LAURENCE STERNE

1713–1768

269 *Consolations of Philosophy*

NOW let us go back to my brother's death.

Philosophy has a fine saying for every thing.—For *Death* it has an entire set ; the misery was, they all at once rushed into my father's head, that 'twas difficult to string them together, so as to make any thing of a consistent show out of them.—He took them as they came.

''Tis an inevitable chance—the first statute in

Magna Charta—it is an everlasting act of parliament, my dear brother,—*All must die.*

'If my son could not have died, it had been matter of wonder,—not that he is dead.

'Monarchs and princes dance in the same ring with us.

'—*To die*, is the great debt and tribute due unto nature: tombs and monuments, which should perpetuate our memories, pay it themselves; and the proudest pyramid of them all, which wealth and science have erected, has lost its apex, and stands obtruncated in the traveller's horizon.' (My father found he got great ease, and went on)—' Kingdoms and provinces, and towns and cities, have they not their periods? and when those principles and powers, which at first cemented and put them together, have performed their several evolutions, they fall back.'—Brother *Shandy*, said my uncle *Toby*, laying down his pipe at the word *evolutions*—Revolutions, I meant, quoth my father,—by heaven! I meant revolutions, brother *Toby*—evolutions is nonsense.—'Tis not nonsense—said my uncle *Toby*.—But is it not nonsense to break the thread of such a discourse upon such an occasion? cried my father—do not—dear *Toby*, continued he, taking him by the hand, do not—do not, I beseech thee, interrupt me at this crisis.—My uncle *Toby* put his pipe into his mouth.

'Where is *Troy* and *Mycenae*, and *Thebes* and *Delos*, and *Persepolis* and *Agrigentum*?'—continued my father, taking up his book of post-roads, which he had laid down.—' What is become, brother *Toby*, of *Nineveh* and *Babylon*, of *Cizicum* and *Mitylenae*? The fairest towns that ever the sun rose upon, are now no more; the names only are left, and those (for many of them are wrong spelt) are falling themselves by piece-meals to decay, and in length of time will be forgotten, and involved with every thing in a perpetual night: the world itself, brother *Toby*, must—must come to an end.

'Returning out of *Asia*, when I sailed from *Aegina* towards *Megara*,' (*when can this have been? thought my uncle Toby*) 'I began to view the country round about. *Aegina* was behind me, *Megara* was before, *Pyraeus* on the right hand, *Corinth* on the left.—What flourishing towns now prostrate upon the earth! Alas! alas! said I to myself, that man should disturb his soul for the loss of a child, when so much as this lies awfully buried in his presence—Remember, said I to myself again—remember thou art a man.'—

Now my uncle *Toby* knew not that this last paragraph was an extract of *Servius Sulpicius's* consolatory letter to *Tully*.—He had as little skill, honest man, in the fragments, as he had in the whole pieces of antiquity.—And as my father, whilst he was concerned in the *Turkey* trade, had been three or four different times in the *Levant*, in one of which he had stayed a whole year and an half at *Zant*, my uncle *Toby* naturally concluded, that, in some one of these periods, he had taken a trip across the *Archipelago*, into *Asia*; and that all this sailing affair with *Aegina* behind, and *Megara* before, and *Pyraeus* on the right hand, etc. etc., was nothing more than the true course of my father's voyage and reflections.—'Twas certainly in his *manner*, and many an undertaking critick would have built two stories higher upon worse foundations. —And pray, brother, quoth my uncle *Toby*, laying the end of his pipe upon my father's hand in a kindly way of interruption—but waiting till he finished the account—what year of our Lord was this?—'Twas no year of our Lord, replied my father.—That 's impossible, cried my uncle *Toby*.—Simpleton! said my father,—'twas forty years before Christ was born.

My uncle *Toby* had but two things for it; either to suppose his brother to be the wandering *Jew*, or that his misfortunes had disordered his brain.—'May the Lord God of heaven and earth protect him and restore him,' said my uncle *Toby*, praying silently for my father, and with tears in his eyes.

—My father placed the tears to a proper account, and went on with his harangue with great spirit.

Tristram Shandy

270 *Trim's Hat*

MY young master in *London* is dead! said *Obadiah*.—

——A green sattin night-gown of my mother's, which had been twice scoured, was the first idea which *Obadiah's* exclamation brought into *Susannah's* head. —Well might *Locke* write a chapter upon the imperfections of words.—Then, quoth *Susannah*, we must all go into mourning.—But note a second time: the word *mourning*, notwithstanding *Susannah* made use of it herself—failed also of doing its office; it excited not one single idea, tinged either with grey or black, —all was green.—The green sattin night-gown hung there still.

—O! 'twill be the death of my poor mistress, cried *Susannah*.—My mother's whole wardrobe followed. —What a procession! her red damask,—her orange tawny,—her white and yellow lute strings,—her brown taffata,—her bone-laced caps, her bed-gowns, and comfortable under-petticoats.—Not a rag was left behind.—'*No,—she will never look up again*,' said *Susannah*.

We had a fat, foolish scullion—my father, I think, kept her for her simplicity;—she had been all autumn struggling with a dropsy.—He is dead, said *Obadiah*,—he is certainly dead!—So am not I, said the foolish scullion.

—Here is sad news, *Trim*! cried *Susannah*, wiping her eyes as *Trim* stepped into the kitchen,—master *Bobby* is dead and *buried*—the funeral was an interpolation of *Susannah's*—we shall have all to go into mourning, said *Susannah*.

I hope not, said *Trim*.—You hope not! cried *Susannah* earnestly.—The mourning ran not in *Trim's* head, whatever it did in *Susannah's*.—I hope—said *Trim*, explaining himself, I hope in God the news is not true.—I heard the letter read with my own ears, answered *Obadiah*; and we shall have a terrible piece of work of it in stubbing the ox-moor.—Oh! he's dead, said *Susannah*.—As sure, said the scullion, as I'm alive.

I lament for him from my heart and my soul, said *Trim*, fetching a sigh.—Poor creature!—poor boy!—poor gentleman!

—He was alive last *Whitsuntide*! said the coachman.—*Whitsuntide*! alas! cried *Trim*, extending his right arm, and falling instantly into the same attitude in which he read the sermon,—What is *Whitsuntide*, *Jonathan* (for that was the coachman's name), or *Shrovetide*, or any tide or time past, to this? Are we not here now, continued the corporal (striking the end of his stick perpendicularly upon the floor, so as to give an idea of health and stability)—and are we not—

(dropping his hat upon the ground) gone! in a moment! —'Twas infinitely striking! *Susannah* burst into a flood of tears.—We are not stocks and stones.—*Jonathan*, *Obadiah*, the cook-maid, all melted.—The foolish fat scullion herself, who was scouring a fish-kettle upon her knees, was roused with it.—The whole kitchen crowded about the corporal. . .

There was nothing in the sentence—'twas one of your self-evident truths we have the advantage of hearing every day; and if *Trim* had not trusted more to his hat than his head—he had made nothing at all of it.

——'Are we not here now;' continued the corporal, 'and are we not'—(dropping his hat plumb upon the ground—and pausing before he pronounced the word)—'gone! in a moment?' The descent of the hat was as if a heavy lump of clay had been kneaded into the crown of it.—Nothing could have expressed the sentiment of mortality, of which it was the type and forerunner, like it,—his hand seemed to vanish from under it,—it fell dead,—the corporal's eye fixed upon it, as upon a corpse,—and *Susannah* burst into a flood of tears.

Now—Ten thousand, and ten thousand times ten thousand (for matter and motion are infinite) are the ways by which a hat may be dropped upon the ground, without any effect.—Had he flung it, or thrown it, or cast it, or skimmed it, or squirted it, or let it slip or fall in any possible direction under heaven,—or in the best direction that could be given to it,—had he dropped it like a goose—like a puppy—like an ass—or in doing it, or even after he had done, had he looked like a fool—like a ninny—like a nincompoop—it had failed, and the effect upon the heart had been lost.

Ye who govern this mighty world and its mighty concerns with the *engines* of eloquence,—who heat it, and cool it, and melt it, and mollify it,—and then harden it again to *your purpose*—

Ye who wind and turn the passions with this great windlass, and, having done it, lead the owners of them, whither ye think meet—

Ye, lastly, who drive—and why not, Ye also who are driven, like turkeys to market with a stick and a red clout—meditate—meditate, I beseech you, upon *Trim's* hat.

Tristram Shandy

271 *Death of Le Fever*

THE sun looked bright the morning after, to every eye in the village but *Le Fever's* and his afflicted son's; the hand of death pressed heavy upon his eye-lids,—and hardly could the wheel at the cistern turn round its circle,—when my uncle *Toby*, who had rose up an hour before his wonted time, entered the lieutenant's room, and without preface or apology, sat himself down upon the chair by the bed-side, and, independently of all modes and customs, opened the curtain in the manner an old friend and brother officer would have done it, and asked him how he did,—how he had rested in the night,—what was his complaint,—where was his pain,—and what he could do to help him:—and without giving him time to answer any one of the enquiries, went on, and told him of the little plan which he had been concerting with the corporal the night before for him.—

—You shall go home directly, *Le Fever*, said my uncle *Toby*, to my house,—and we'll send for a doctor to see what 's the matter,—and we'll have an apothecary,—and the corporal shall be your nurse;—and I'll be your servant, *Le Fever*.

There was a frankness in my uncle *Toby*,—not the *effect* of familiarity,—but the *cause* of it,—which let you at once into his soul, and shewed you the goodness of his nature; to this, there was something in his looks, and voice, and manner, superadded, which eternally beckoned to the unfortunate to come and take shelter under him; so that before my uncle *Toby* had half finished the kind offers he was making to the father, had the son insensibly pressed up close to his knees, and had taken hold of the breast of his coat, and was pulling it towards him.—The blood and spirits of *Le Fever*, which were waxing cold and slow within him, and were retreating to their last citadel, the heart—rallied back,—the film forsook his eyes for a moment, —he looked up wishfully in my uncle *Toby's* face,—then cast a look upon his boy,—and that *ligament*, fine as it was,—was never broken.

Tristram Shandy

272 *Nannette*

'TWAS in the road betwixt Nismes and Lunel, where there is the best Muscatto wine in all France, and which by the bye belongs to the honest canons of MONTPELLIER—and foul befall the man who has drank it at their table, who grudges them a drop of it.

—The sun was set—they had done their work; the nymphs had tied up their hair afresh—and the swains were preparing for a carousal—My mule made a dead point—'Tis the fife and tabourin, said I—I'm frightened to death, quoth he. . . 'Tis very well, sir, said I—I never will argue a point with one of your family, as long as I live; so leaping off his back, and kicking off one boot into this ditch, and t'other into that—I'll take a dance, said I—so stay you here.

A sun-burnt daughter of Labour rose up from the groupe to meet me, as I advanced towards them; her hair, which was a dark chestnut approaching rather to a black, was tied up in a knot, all but a single tress.

We want a cavalier, said she, holding out both her hands, as if to offer them—And a cavalier ye shall have; said I, taking hold of both of them.

Hadst thou, Nannette, been arrayed like a duchess!—But that cursed slit in thy petticoat!

Nannette cared not for it.

We could not have done without you, said she, letting go one hand, with self-taught politeness, leading me up with the other.

A lame youth, whom Apollo had recompenced with a pipe, and to which he had added a tabourin of his own accord, ran sweetly over the prelude, as he sat upon the bank—Tie me up this tress instantly, said Nannette, putting a piece of string into my hand—It taught me to forget I was a stranger—The whole knot fell down—We had been seven years acquainted.

The youth struck the note upon the tabourin—his pipe followed, and off we bounded—'the deuce take that slit!'

The sister of the youth, who had stolen her voice from heaven, sung alternately with her brother—'twas a Gascoigne roundelay.

VIVA LA JOIA!
FIDON LA TRISTESSA!

The nymphs joined in unison, and their swains an octave below them—

I would have given a crown to have it sewed up—Nannette would not have given a sous—*Vive la joia!* was in her lips—*Vive la joia!* was in her eyes. A transient spark of amity shot across the space betwixt us—She looked amiable!—Why could I not live, and end my days thus? Just disposer of our joys and sorrows, cried I, why could not a man sit down in the lap of content here—and dance, and sing, and say his prayers, and go to heaven with this nut-brown maid?

Tristram Shandy

273 *The Monk*

THE monk, as I judged from the break in his tonsure, a few scattered white hairs upon his temples being all that remained of it, might be about seventy—but from his eyes, and that sort of fire which was in them, which seemed more tempered by courtesy than years, could be no more than sixty—Truth might lie between—He was certainly sixty-five; and the general air of his countenance, notwithstanding something seemed to have been planting wrinkles in it before their time, agreed to the account.

It was one of those heads which Guido has often painted—mild, pale—penetrating, free from all common-place ideas of fat contented ignorance looking downwards upon the earth—it looked forwards; but looked, as if it looked at something beyond this world. How one of his order came by it, heaven above, who let it fall upon a monk's shoulders, best knows; but it would have suited a Bramin, and had I met it upon the plains of Indostan, I had reverenced it. . .

When he had entered the room three paces, he stood still; and laying his left hand upon his breast (a slender white staff with which he journeyed being in his right)—when I had got close up to him, he introduced himself with the little story of the wants of his convent, and the poverty of his order—and did it with so simple a grace—and such an air of deprecation was there in the whole cast of his look and figure—I was bewitched not to have been struck with it—

—A better reason was, I had predetermined not to give him a single sous. . .

My heart smote me the moment he shut the door—Psha! said I, with an air of carelessness, three several times—but it would not do: every ungracious syllable I had uttered, crowded back into my imagination: I reflected, I had no right over the poor Franciscan, but to deny him; and that the punishment of that was enough to the disappointed, without the addition of unkind language—I considered his grey hairs—his courteous figure seemed to re-enter and gently ask me what injury he had done me?—and why I could use him thus?—I would have given twenty livres for an advocate—I have behaved very ill, said I within myself; but I have only just set out upon my travels; and shall learn better manners as I get along.

A Sentimental Journey

THOMAS GRAY

1716–1771

274 *Netley Abbey*

To the Rev. N. Nicholls, Monday, 19 November 1764.

SIR,

I received your letter at Southampton, and, as I would wish to treat everybody according to their own rule and measure of good-breeding, have against my inclination waited till now, before I answered it, purely out of fear and respect, and an ingenuous diffidence of my own abilities. If you will not take this as an excuse, accept it at least as a well-turned period, which is always my principal concern.

So I proceed to tell you, that my health is much improved by the sea; not that I drank it, or bathed in it, as the *common people* do: no! I only walked by it, and looked upon it. The climate is remarkably mild, even in October and November. No snow has been seen to lie there for these thirty years past, the myrtles grow in the ground against the houses, and Guernsey-Lillies bloom in every window. The Town, clean and well built, surrounded by its old stone-walls with their towers and gateways, stands at the point of a peninsula, and opens full south to an arm of the sea, which, having formed two beautiful bays on each hand of it stretches away in direct view till it joins the British Channel. It is skirted on either side with gently-rising grounds cloathed with thick wood, and directly cross its mouth rise the high lands of the Isle of Wight at distance, but distinctly seen. In the bosom of the woods (concealed from profane eyes) lie hid the ruins of Netteley-abbey. There may be richer and greater houses of religion, but the Abbot is content with his situation. See there, at the top of that hanging meadow under the shade of those old trees, that bend into a half-circle about it, he is walking slowly (good Man!) and bidding his beads for the souls of his Benefactors, interred in that venerable pile, that lies beneath him. Beyond it (the meadow still descending) nods a thicket of oaks, that mask the building, and have excluded a view too garish, and too luxuriant for a holy eye, only on either hand they leave an opening to the blew glittering sea. Did not you observe how, as that white sail shot by and was lost, he turned and crossed himself, to drive the Tempter from him, that had thrown that distraction in his way. I should tell you, that the Ferryman, who rowed me, a lusty young Fellow, told me that he would not for all the world pass a night at the Abbey (there were such things seen near it), though there was a power of money hid there. From thence I went to Salisbury, Wilton, and Stone-Henge, but of these things I say no more: they will be published at the University-Press.

Letters

275 *To H. Walpole, with a Copy of his Elegy*

DEAR SIR,

As I live in a place, where even the ordinary tattle of the town arrives not till it is stale, and which produces no events of its own, you will not desire any excuse from me for writing so seldom, especially as of all people living I know you are the least a friend to letters spun out of one's brains, with all the toil and constraint that accompanies sentimental productions. I have been here at Stoke a few days (where I shall continue good part of the summer); and having put an end to a thing, whose beginning you have seen long ago, I immediately send it you. You will, I hope, look upon it in the light of a *thing with an end to it*; a merit that most of my writings have wanted, and are like to want, but which this epistle I am determined shall not want, when it tells you that I am ever

Yours,

T. GRAY.

Letters

HORACE WALPOLE

1717–1797

276 *Strawberry Hill*

Twickenham, June 8, 1747.

YOU perceive by my date that I am got into a new camp, and have left my tub at Windsor. It is a little plaything-house that I got out of Mrs. Chenevix's shop, and is the prettiest bauble you ever saw. It is set in enamelled meadows, with filigree hedges:

> A small Euphrates through the piece is roll'd,
> And little finches wave their wings in gold.

Two delightful roads, that you would call dusty, supply me continually with coaches and chaises: barges as solemn as Barons of the Exchequer move under my window; Richmond Hill and Ham Walks bound my prospect; but, thank God! the Thames is between me and the Duchess of Queensberry. Dowagers as plenty as flounders inhabit all around, and Pope's ghost is just now skimming under my window by a most poetical moonlight. I have about land enough to keep such a farm as Noah's, when he set up in the ark with a pair of each kind; but my cottage is rather cleaner than I believe his was after they had been cooped up together forty days. The Chenevixes had tricked it out for themselves: up two pair of stairs is what they call Mr. Chenevix's library, furnished with three maps, one shelf, a bust of Sir Isaac Newton, and a lame telescope without any glasses. Lord John Sackville *predecessed* me here, and instituted certain games called *cricketalia*, which have been celebrated this very evening in honour of him in a neighbouring meadow.

Letter to H. S. Conway

277 *Funeral of George II*

Arlington Street, Nov. 13, 1760.

DO you know, I had the curiosity to go to the burying t'other night; I had never seen a royal funeral; nay, I walked as a rag of quality, which I found would be, and so it was, the easiest way of seeing it. It is absolutely a noble sight. The Prince's Chamber, hung with purple, and a quantity of silver lamps, the coffin under a canopy of purple velvet, and six vast chandeliers of silver on high stands, had a very good effect. The Ambassador from Tripoli and his son were carried to see that chamber. The procession through a line of foot-guards, every seventh man bearing a torch, the horse-guards lining the outside, their officers with drawn sabres and crape sashes on horseback, the drums muffled, the fifes, bells tolling, and minute guns, all this was very solemn. But the charm was the entrance of the Abbey, where we were received by the Dean and Chapter in rich robes, the choir and almsmen all bearing torches; the whole Abbey so illuminated, that one saw it to greater advantage than by day; the tombs, long aisles, and fretted roof, all appearing distinctly, and with the happiest chiaroscuro. There wanted nothing but incense, and little chapels here and there, with priests saying mass for the repose of the defunct—yet one could not complain of its not being catholic enough. I had been in dread of being coupled with some boy of ten years old—but the heralds were not very accurate, and I walked with George Grenville, taller and older enough to keep me in countenance. When we came to the chapel of Henry the Seventh, all solemnity and decorum ceased—no order was observed, people set or stood where they could or would, the yeomen of the guard were crying out for help, oppressed by the immense weight of the coffin, the Bishop read sadly, and blundered in the prayers, the fine chapter, *Man that is born of a woman*, was chanted, not read, and the anthem, besides being unmeasurably tedious, would have served as well for a nuptial. The real serious part was the figure of the Duke of Cumberland, heightened by a thousand melancholy circumstances. He had a dark brown adonis, and a cloak of black cloth, with a train of five yards. Attending the funeral of a father, however little reason he had so to love him, could not be pleasant. His leg extremely bad, yet forced to stand upon it near two hours, his face bloated and distorted with his late paralytic stroke, which has affected, too, one of his eyes, and placed over the mouth of the vault, into which, in all probability, he must himself so soon descend—think how unpleasant a situation! He bore it all with a firm and unaffected countenance. This grave scene was fully contrasted by the burlesque Duke of Newcastle. He fell into a fit of crying the moment he came into the chapel, and flung himself back in a stall, the Archbishop hovering over him with a smelling-bottle—but in two minutes his curiosity got the better of his hypocrisy, and he ran about the chapel with his glass to spy who was or was not there, spying with one hand, and mopping his eyes with t'other. Then returned the fear of catching cold, and the Duke of Cumberland, who was sinking with heat, felt himself weighed down, and turning round, found it was the Duke of Newcastle standing upon his train to avoid the chill of the marble. It was very theatric to look down into the vault, where the coffin lay, attended by mourners with lights. Clavering, the Groom of the Bedchamber, refused to sit up with the body, and was dismissed by the King's order.

Letter to George Montagu

GILBERT WHITE

1720–1793

278 *The Red Deer of Wolmer Forest*

i

NOR does the loss of our black game prove the only gap in the *Fauna Selborniensis*; for another beautiful link in the chain of beings is wanting,—I mean the *red deer*, which, toward the beginning of this century, amounted to about five hundred head, and made a stately appearance. There is an old keeper, now alive, named *Adams*, whose great grandfather (mentioned in a perambulation taken in 1635), grandfather, father, and self, enjoyed the head keepership of *Wolmer-forest* in succession for more than a hundred years. This person assures me that his father has often told him that Queen *Anne*, as she was journeying on the *Portsmouth* road, did not think the forest of *Wolmer* beneath her royal regard. For she came out of the great road at *Lippock*, which is just by, and reposing herself on a bank, smoothed for that purpose, lying about half a mile to the east of *Wolmer-pond*, and still called *Queen's-bank*, saw with great complacency and satisfaction the whole herd of red deer brought by the keepers along the vale before her, consisting then of about five hundred head. A sight this, worthy the attention of the greatest sovereign! But he farther adds, that, by means of the *Waltham blacks*, or, to use his own expression, as soon as they began *blacking*, they were reduced to about fifty head, and so continued decreasing till the time of the late Duke of *Cumberland*. It is now more than thirty years ago that his highness sent down an huntsman, and six yeoman-prickers, in scarlet jackets laced with gold, attended by the stag-hounds, ordering them to take every deer in this forest alive, and to convey them in carts to *Windsor*. In the course of the summer they caught every stag, some of which showed extraordinary diversion; but, in the following winter, when the hinds were also carried off, such fine chases were exhibited as served the country people for matter of talk and wonder for years afterwards. I saw myself one of the yeoman-prickers single out a stag from the herd, and must confess that it was the most curious feat of activity I ever beheld,—superior to anything in Mr. *Astley's* riding-school. The exertions made by the horse and deer much exceeded all my expectations, though the former greatly excelled the latter in speed. When the devoted deer was separated from his companions, they gave him, by their watches, law, as they called it, for twenty minutes; when, sounding their horns, the stop-dogs were permitted to pursue, and a most gallant scene ensued.

ii

Though large herds of deer do much harm to the neighbourhood, yet the injury to the morals of the people is of more moment than the loss of their crops. The temptation is irresistible; for most men are sportsmen by constitution: and there is such an inherent spirit for hunting in human nature, as scarce any inhibitions can restrain. Hence, towards the beginning of this century, all this country was wild about deer-stealing. Unless he was a *hunter*, as they affected to call themselves, no young person was allowed to be possessed of manhood or gallantry. The

Waltham blacks at length committed such enormities, that government was forced to interfere with that severe and sanguinary act called the *black act*, which now comprehends more felonies than any law that ever was framed before; and, therefore, a late bishop of *Winchester*, when urged to re-stock *Waltham-chase*, refused, from a motive worthy of a prelate, replying, that 'it had done mischief enough already.'

Our old race of deer-stealers are hardly extinct yet. It was but a little while ago that, over their ale, they used to recount the exploits of their youth; such as watching the pregnant hind to her lair, and when the calf was dropped, paring its feet with a penknife to the quick, to prevent its escape, till it was large and fat enough to be killed; the shooting at one of their neighbours with a bullet, in a turnip-field, by moonshine, mistaking him for a deer; and the losing a dog in the following extraordinary manner:—Some fellows, suspecting that a calf new-fallen was deposited in a certain spot of thick fern, went with a lurcher to surprise it; when the parent hind rushed out of the brake, and taking a vast spring, with all her feet close together, pitched upon the neck of the dog, and broke it short in two.

Natural History of Selborne

279 *The Bat*

I WAS much entertained last summer with a tame bat, which would take flies out of a person's hand. If you gave it anything to eat, it brought its wings round before the mouth, hovering and hiding its head in the manner of birds of prey when they feed. The adroitness it showed in shearing off the wings of the flies, which were always rejected, was worthy of observation and pleased me much. Insects seemed to be most acceptable, though it did not refuse raw flesh when offered; so that the notion that bats go down chimneys and gnaw men's bacon seems no improbable story. While I amused myself with this wonderful quadruped, I saw it several times confute the vulgar opinion, that bats, when down on a flat surface, cannot get on the wing again, by rising with great ease from the floor. It ran, I observed, with more despatch than I was aware of; but in a most ridiculous and grotesque manner.

Bats drink on the wing, like swallows, by sipping the surface, as they play over pools and streams. They love to frequent waters, not only for the sake of drinking, but on account of insects, which are found over them in the greatest plenty. As I was going some years ago, pretty late, in a boat from *Richmond* to *Sunbury*, on a warm summer's evening, I think I saw myriads of bats between the two places; the air swarmed with them all along the *Thames*, so that hundreds were in sight at a time.

Natural History of Selborne

280 *The Sussex Downs*

THOUGH I have now travelled the *Sussex-downs* upwards of thirty years, yet I still investigate that chain of majestic mountains with fresh admiration year by year; and I think I see new beauties every time I traverse it. The range, which runs from *Chichester* eastward as far as *East-Bourn*, is about sixty miles in length, and is called *The South Downs*, properly speaking, only round *Lewes*. As you pass along, you command a noble view of the wild, or weald, on one hand, and the broad downs and sea on the other. Mr. *Ray* used to visit a family just at the foot of these hills, and was so ravished with the prospect from *Plumpton-plain*, near *Lewes*, that he mentions those scapes in his 'Wisdom of God in the Works of the Creation,' with the utmost satisfaction, and thinks them equal to any thing he had seen in the finest parts of Europe.

For my own part, I think there is somewhat peculiarly sweet and amusing in the shapely figured aspect of chalk-hills, in preference to those of stone, which are rugged, broken, abrupt, and shapeless.

Perhaps I may be singular in my opinion, and not so happy as to convey to you the same idea, but I never contemplate these mountains without thinking I perceive somewhat analogous to growth in their gentle swellings and smooth fungus-like protuberances, their fluted sides, and regular hollows and slopes, that carry at once the air of vegetative dilatation and expansion. . .[1] Or was there ever a time when these immense masses of calcareous matter were thrown into fermentation by some adventitious moisture,—were raised and leavened into such shapes by some plastic power, and so made to swell and heave their broad backs into the sky, so much above the less animated clay of the wild below?

Natural History of Selborne

281 *Rooks*

THE evening proceedings and manœuvres of the rooks are curious and amusing in the autumn. Just before dusk they return in long strings from the foraging of the day, and rendezvous by thousands over *Selborne-down*, where they wheel round in the air,

[1] So in original: no omission.

and sport and dive in a playful manner, all the while exerting their voices, and making a loud cawing, which, being blended and softened by the distance that we at the village are below them, becomes a confused noise or chiding; or rather a pleasing murmur, very engaging to the imagination, and not unlike the cry of a pack of hounds in hollow echoing woods, or the rushing of the wind in tall trees, or the tumbling of the tide upon a pebbly shore. When this ceremony is over, with the last gleam of day, they retire for the night to the deep beechen woods of *Tisted* and *Ropley*. We remember a little girl who, as she was going to bed, used to remark on such an occurrence, in the true spirit of *physico-theology*, that the rooks were saying their prayers; and yet this child was much too young to be aware that the scriptures have said of the Deity, that ‘he feedeth the ravens who call upon Him’.

Natural History of Selborne

WILLIAM ROBERTSON

1721–1793

282 *The Murder of Rizio*

NOTHING now remained but to concert the plan of operation, to chuse the actors, and to assign them their parts in perpetrating this detestable crime. Every circumstance here paints and characterises the manners and men of that age, and fills us with horror at both. The place chosen for committing such a deed was the Queen's bedchamber. Though Mary was now in the sixth month of her pregnancy, and though Rizio might have been seized elsewhere without any difficulty, the King pitched upon this place, that he might enjoy the malicious pleasure of reproaching Rizio with his crimes before the Queen's face. The Earl of Morton, the Lord High Chancellor of the kingdom, undertook to direct an enterprize, carried on in defiance of all the laws of which he was bound to be guardian. The Lord Ruthven, who had been confined to his bed for three months by a very dangerous distemper, and who was still so feeble that he could scarce walk, or bear the weight of his own armour, was entrusted with the executive part; and while he himself needed to be supported by two men, he came abroad to commit a murder in the presence of his sovereign.

On the 9th of March, Morton entered the court of the palace with an hundred and sixty men; and without noise, or meeting with any resistance, seized all the gates. While the Queen was at supper with the Countess of Argyll, Rizio, and a few domestics, the King suddenly entered the apartment by a private passage. At his back was Ruthven, clad in complete armour, and with that ghastly and horrid look which long sickness had given him. Three or four of his most trusty accomplices followed him. Such an unusual appearance alarmed those who were present. Rizio instantly apprehended that he was the victim at whom the blow was aimed; and in the utmost consternation retired behind the Queen, of whom he laid hold, hoping that the reverence due to her person might prove some protection to him. The conspirators had proceeded too far to be restrained by any considerations of that kind. Numbers of armed men rushed into the chamber. Ruthven drew his dagger, and with a furious mien and voice commanded Rizio to leave a place of which he was unworthy, and which he had occupied too long. Mary employed tears, and entreaties, and threatenings, to save her favourite. But, notwithstanding all these, he was torn from her by violence, and before he could be dragged through the next apartment, the rage of his enemies put an end to his life, piercing his body with fifty-six wounds.

History of Scotland

TOBIAS SMOLLETT

1721–1771

283 *Trunnion's Wedding*

THE fame of this extraordinary conjunction spread all over the county; and on the day appointed for their spousals, the church was surrounded by an inconceivable multitude. The commodore, to give a specimen of his gallantry, by the advice of his friend Hatchway, resolved to appear on horseback on the grand occasion, at the head of all his male attendants, whom he had rigged with the white shirts and black caps formerly belonging to his barge's crew; and he bought a couple of hunters for the accommodation of himself and his lieutenant. With this equipage then he set out from the garrison for the church, after having dispatched a messenger to apprize the bride that he and his company were mounted; whereupon she got immediately into the coach, accompanied by her brother and his wife, and drove directly to the place of assignation, where several pews were demolished, and divers persons almost pressed to death, by the eagerness of the crowd that broke in to see the ceremony performed. Thus arrived at the altar, and the priest in attendance, they waited a whole half hour for the commodore, at whose slowness they began to be under some apprehension, and accordingly dismissed a servant to quicken his pace. The valet having rode something more than a mile, espied the whole troop disposed in a long field, crossing the road obliquely, and headed by the bridegroom and his friend Hatchway, who, finding himself hindered by a hedge from proceeding farther in the same direction, fired a pistol, and stood over to the other side, making an obtuse angle with the line of his former course; and the rest of the squadron followed his example, keeping always in the rear of each other, like a flight of wild geese.

Surprized at this strange method of journeying, the messenger came up, and told the commodore that his lady and her company expected him in the church, where they had tarried a considerable time, and were beginning to be very uneasy at his delay; and therefore desired he would proceed with more expedition. To this message Mr. Trunnion replied, 'Hark ye, brother, don't you see we make all possible speed? go back, and tell those who sent you, that the wind has shifted since we weighed anchor, and that we are obliged to make very short trips in tacking, by reason of the narrowness of the channel; and that, as we lie within six points of the wind, they must make some allowance for variation and leeway.' 'Lord, sir!' said the valet, 'what occasion have you to go zigzag in that manner? Do but clap spurs to your horses, and ride straight forward, and I'll engage you shall be at the church porch in less than a quarter of an hour.' 'What! right in the wind's eye?' answered the commander, 'ahey! brother, where did you learn your navigation? Hawser Trunnion is not to be taught at this time of day how to lie his course, or keep his own reckoning. And as for you, brother, you know best the trim of your own frigate.' The courier finding he had to do with people who would not be easily persuaded out of their own opinions, returned to the temple, and made a report of what he had seen and heard, to the no small consolation of the bride, who had begun to discover some signs of disquiet. Composed, however, by this piece of intelligence, she exerted her patience for the space of another half hour, during which period, seeing no bridegroom arrive, she was exceedingly alarmed; so that all the spectators could easily perceive her perturbation, which manifested itself in frequent palpitations, heart-heavings, and alterations of countenance, in spite of the assistance of a smelling-bottle, which she incessantly applied to her nostrils.

Various were the conjectures of the company on this occasion. Some imagined he had mistaken the place of rendezvous, as he had never been at church since he first settled in that parish; others believed he had met with some accident, in consequence of which his attendants had carried him back to his own house; and a third set, in which the bride herself was thought to be comprehended, could not help suspecting that the commodore had changed his mind. But all these suppositions, ingenious as they were, happened to be wide of the true cause that detained him, which was no other than this: the commodore and his crew had, by dint of turning, almost weathered the parson's house that stood to windward of the church, when the notes of a pack of hounds unluckily reached the ears of the two hunters which Trunnion and the lieutenant bestrode. These fleet animals no sooner heard the enlivening sound, than, eager for the chace, they sprung away all of a sudden, and straining every nerve to partake of the sport, flew across the fields with incredible speed, overleaped hedges and ditches, and everything in their way, without the least regard to their unfortunate riders. The lieutenant, whose steed had got the heels of the other, finding it would be great folly and presumption in him to pretend to keep the saddle with his wooden leg, very wisely took the opportunity of throwing himself off in his passage through a field of rich clover, among which he lay at his ease; and seeing his captain advancing at full gallop, hailed him with the salutation of 'What chear? ho!' The commodore, who was in infinite distress, eyeing him askance, as he passed, replied with a faultering voice, 'O damn ye! you are safe at an anchor; I wish to God I were as fast moored.' Nevertheless, conscious of his disabled heel, he would not venture to try the same experiment which had succeeded so well with Hatchway, but resolved to stick as close as possible to his horse's back, until providence should interpose in his behalf. With this view he dropped his whip, and with his right hand laid fast hold on the pummel, contracting every muscle in his body to secure himself in the seat, and grinning most formidably, in consequence of this exertion. In this attitude he was hurried on a considerable way, when all of a sudden his view was comforted by a five bar gate that appeared before him, as he never doubted that there the career of his hunter must necessarily end. But, alas! he reckoned without his host; far from halting at this obstruction, the horse sprung over it with amazing agility, to the utter confusion and disorder of his owner, who lost his hat and periwig in the leap, and now began to think in good earnest that he was actually mounted on the back of the devil. He recommended himself to God, his reflection forsook him, his eye-sight and all his other senses failed, he quitted the reins, and, fastening by instinct on the mane, was in this condition conveyed into the midst of the sportsmen, who were astonished at the sight of such an apparition. Neither was their surprize to be wondered at, if we reflect on the figure that presented itself to their view. The commodore's person was at all times an object of admiration; much more so on this occasion, when every singularity was aggravated by the circumstances of his dress and disaster.

He had put on, in honour of his nuptials, his best coat of blue broad cloth, cut by a taylor of Ramsgate, and trimmed with five dozen of brass buttons, large and small; his breeches were of the same piece, fastened at the knees with large bunches of tape; his waistcoat was of red plush, lapelled with green velvet, and garnished with vellum holes; his boots bore an intimate resemblance, both in colour and shape, to a pair of leather buckets; his shoulder was graced with a broad buff belt, from whence depended a huge hanger with a hilt like that of a backsword; and on each side of his pummel appeared a rusty pistol, rammed in a case covered with a bear-skin. The loss of his tye-periwig and laced hat, which were curiosities of the kind, did not at all contribute to the improvement of the picture, but, on the contrary, by exhibiting his bald pate, and the natural extension of his lanthorn jaws, added to the peculiarity and extravagance of the whole. Such a spectacle could not have failed of diverting the whole company from the chace, had his horse thought proper to pursue a different route, but the beast was too keen a sporter to choose any other way than that which the stag followed ; and, therefore, without stopping to gratify the curiosity of the spectators, he, in a few minutes, outstripped every hunter in the field ; and there being a deep hollow way betwixt him and the hounds, rather than ride round about the length of a furlong to a path that crossed the lane, he transported himself, at one jump, to the unspeakable astonishment and terror of a waggoner who chanced to be underneath, and saw this phenomenon fly over his carriage. This was not the only adventure he achieved. The stag having taken a deep river that lay in his way, every man directed his course to a bridge in the neighbourhood ; but our bridegroom's courser, despising all such conveniences, plunged into the stream without hesitation, and swam in a twinkling to the opposite shore. This sudden immersion into an element, of which Trunnion was properly a native, in all probability helped to recruit the exhausted spirits of his rider, who, at his landing on the other side, gave some tokens of sensation, by hollowing aloud for assistance, which he could not possibly receive, because his horse still maintained the advantage he had gained, and would not allow himself to be overtaken.

In short, after a long chace that lasted several hours, and extended to a dozen miles at least, he was the first in at the death of the deer, being seconded by the lieutenant's gelding, which, actuated by the same spirit, had, without a rider, followed his companion's example.

Peregrine Pickle

SIR JOSHUA REYNOLDS

1723–1792

284 *The Contemplation of Excellence*

WHOEVER has so far formed his taste, as to be able to relish and feel the beauties of the great masters, has gone a great way in his study; for, merely from a consciousness of this relish of the right, the mind swells with an inward pride, and is almost as powerfully affected, as if it had itself produced what it admires. Our hearts, frequently warmed in this manner by the contact of those whom we wish to resemble, will undoubtedly catch something of their way of thinking; and we shall receive in our own bosoms some radiation at least of their fire and splendour. That disposition, which is so strong in children, still continues with us, of catching involuntarily the general air and manner of those with whom we are most conversant; with this difference only, that a young mind is naturally pliable and imitative; but in a more advanced state it grows rigid, and must be warmed and softened before it will receive a deep impression.

From these considerations, which a little of your own reflection will carry a great way further, it appears, of what great consequence it is, that our minds should be habituated to the contemplation of excellence; and that, far from being contented to make such habits the discipline of our youth only, we should, to the last moment of our lives, continue a settled intercourse with all the true examples of grandeur. Their inventions are not only the food of our infancy, but the substance which supplies the fullest maturity of our vigour. . .

Nor, whilst I recommend studying the Art from Artists, can I be supposed to mean that Nature is to be neglected; I take this study in aid, and not in exclusion of the other. Nature is and must be the fountain which alone is inexhaustible, and from which all excellencies must originally flow.

The great use of studying our predecessors is, to open the mind, to shorten our labour, and to give us the result of the selection made by those great minds of what is grand or beautiful in Nature; her rich stores are all spread out before us; but it is an art, and no easy art, to know how or what to choose, and how to attain and secure the object of our choice.

Thus the highest beauty of form must be taken from nature; but it is an art of long deduction and great experience to know how to find it.

We must not content ourselves with merely admiring and relishing; we must enter into the principles on which the work is wrought: these do not swim on the superficies, and consequently are not open to superficial observers.

Art in its perfection is not ostentatious; it lies hid and works its effect, itself unseen. It is the proper study and labour of an artist to uncover and find out the latent cause of conspicuous beauties, and from thence form principles for his own conduct; such an examination is a continual exertion of the mind; as great, perhaps, as that of the Artist whose works he is thus studying.

Sixth Discourse

ADAM SMITH

1723–1790

285 *The Rewards of the Professions*

FIFTHLY, The wages of labour in different employments vary according to the probability or improbability of success in them.

The probability that any particular person should ever be qualified for the employment to which he is educated, is very different in different occupations. In the greater part of mechanick trades, success is almost certain; but very uncertain in the liberal professions. Put your son apprentice to a shoemaker, there is little doubt of his learning to make a pair of shoes: But send him to study the law, it is at least twenty to one if ever he makes such a proficiency as will enable him to live by the business. In a perfectly fair lottery, those who draw the prizes ought to gain all that is lost by those who draw the blanks. In a profession where twenty fail for one that succeeds, that one ought to gain all that should have been gained by the unsuccessful twenty. The counsellor at law, who, perhaps, at near forty years of age, begins to make something by his profession, ought to receive the retribution, not only of his own so tedious and expensive education, but of that of more than twenty others who are never likely to make anything by it. How extravagant soever the fees of counsellors at law may sometimes appear, their real retribution is never equal to this. Compute in any particular place, what is likely to be annually gained, and what is likely to be annually spent, by all the different workmen in any common trade, such as that of shoemakers or weavers, and you will find that the former sum will generally exceed the latter. But make the same computation with regard to all the counsellors and students of law, in all the different inns of court, and you will find that their annual gains bear but a very small proportion to their annual expence, even though you rate the former as high, and the latter as low, as can well be done. The lottery of the law, therefore, is very far from being a perfectly fair lottery; and that, as well as many other liberal and honourable professions, are, in point of pecuniary gain, evidently under-recompenced.

Those professions keep their level, however, with other occupations, and, notwithstanding these discouragements, all the most generous and liberal spirits are eager to crowd into them. Two different causes contribute to recommend them. First, the desire of the reputation which attends upon superior excellence in any of them; and, secondly, the natural confidence which every man has, more or less, not only in his own abilities, but in his own good fortune.

To excel in any profession, in which but few arrive at mediocrity, is the most decisive mark of what is called genius or superior talents. The publick admiration which attends upon such distinguished abilities, makes always a part of their reward; a greater or smaller in proportion as it is higher or lower in degree. It makes a considerable part of it in the profession of physick; a still greater perhaps in that of law; in poetry and philosophy it makes almost the whole.

Wealth of Nations

OLIVER GOLDSMITH

1728–1774

286 *A Party at Vauxhall*

THE People of *London* are as fond of walking, as our friends at *Pekin* of riding; one of the principal entertainments of the citizens here in summer, is to repair about nightfall to a garden not far from town, where they walk about, shew their best cloaths and best faces, and listen to a concert provided for the occasion.

I accepted an invitation a few evenings ago from my old friend, the man in black, to be one of a party that was to sup there, and at the appointed hour waited upon him at his lodgings. There I found the company assembled and expecting my arrival. Our party consisted of my friend in superlative finery, his stockings rolled, a black velvet waistcoat, which was formerly new, and his grey wig combed down in imitation of hair. A pawn-broker's widow, of whom, by the bye, my friend was a professed admirer, dressed out in green damask, with three gold rings on every finger. Mr. *Tibbs*, the second-rate beau, I have formerly described, together with his lady, in flimsy silk, dirty gauze instead of linnen, and an hat as big as an umbrello. . .

The illuminations began before we arrived, and I must confess, that upon entring the gardens, I found every sense overpaid with more than expected pleasure; the lights every where glimmering through the scarcely moving trees; the full-bodied concert bursting on the stillness of the night, the natural concert of the birds in the more retired part of the grove, vying with that which was formed by art; the company gayly dressed, looking satisfaction, and the tables spread with various delicacies, all conspired to fill my imagination with the visionary happiness of the *Arabian* lawgiver, and lifted me into an extasy of admiration. Head of *Confucius*, cried I to my friend, this is fine! this unites rural beauty with courtly magnificence; if we except the virgins of immortality that hang on every tree, and may be plucked at every desire, I don't see how this falls short of *Mahomet's Paradise!* As for virgins, cries my friend, it is true they are a fruit that don't much abound in our gardens here; but if ladies as plenty as apples in autumn, and as complying as any *hoüry* of them all, can content you, I fancy we have no need to go to heaven for Paradise.

I was going to second his remarks, when we were called to a consultation by Mr. *Tibbs* and the rest of the company, to know in what manner we were to lay out the evening to the greatest advantage. Mrs. *Tibbs* was for keeping the genteel walk of the garden, where she observed there was always the very best company; the widow, on the contrary, who came but once a season, was for securing a good standing-place to see the water-works, which she assured us would begin in less than an hour at farthest; a dispute therefore began, and as it was managed between two of very opposite characters, it threatened to grow more bitter at every reply. Mrs. *Tibbs* wondered how people could pretend to know the polite world, who had received all their rudiments of breeding behind a compter; to which the other replied, that tho' some people sat behind compters, yet they could sit at the head of their own tables too, and carve three good dishes of hot meat whenever they thought proper, which was more than some people could say for themselves, that hardly knew a rabbet and onions from a green goose and gooseberries.

It is hard to say where this might have ended, had not the husband, who probably knew the impetuosity of his wife's disposition, proposed to end the dispute by adjourning to a box, and try if there was any thing to be had for supper that was supportable. . .

Mr. *Tibbs* now willing to prove that his wife's pretensions to music were just, entreated her to favour the company with a song; but to this she gave a positive denial, for you know very well, my dear, says she, that I am not in voice to day, and when one's voice is not equal to one's judgment, what signifies singing; besides, as there is no accompanyment, it would be but spoiling music. All these excuses however were overruled by the rest of the company, who though one would think they already had music enough, joined in the intreaty. But particularly the widow, now willing to convince the company of her breeding, pressed so warmly, that she seemed determined to take no refusal. At last, then, the lady complied, and after humming for some minutes, began with such a voice and such affectation, as, I could perceive, gave but little satisfaction to any except her husband. He sat with rapture in his eye, and beat time with his hand on the table.

You must observe, my friend, that it is the custom of this country, when a lady or gentleman happens to sing, for the company to sit as mute and as motionless as statues. Every feature, every limb must seem to correspond in fixed attention, and while the song continues, they are to remain in a state of universal petrefaction. In this mortifying situation we had continued for some time, listening to the song, and looking with tranquillity, when the master of the box came to inform us that the water-works were going to begin. At this information, I could instantly perceive the widow bounce from her seat; but correcting herself, she sat down again, repressed by motives of good breeding. Mrs. *Tibbs*, who had seen the water-works an hundred times, resolved not to be interrupted, continued her song without any share of mercy, nor had the smallest pity on our impatience. The widow's face, I own, gave me high entertainment; in it I could plainly read the struggle she felt between good breeding and curiosity; she talked of the water-works the whole evening before, and seemed to have come merely in order to see them; but then she could not bounce out in the very middle of a song, for that would be forfeiting all pretensions to high-life, or high-lived company ever after: Mrs. *Tibbs*, therefore, kept on singing, and we continued to listen, till at last, when the song was just concluded, the waiter came to inform us that the water-works were over!

The water-works over, cried the widow! the water-works over already, that 's impossible, they can't be over so soon! It is not my business, replied the fellow, to contradict your ladyship, I'll run again and see; he went, and soon returned with a confirmation of the dismal tidings. No ceremony could now bind my friend's disappointed mistress, she testified her displeasure in the openest manner; in short, she now began to find fault in turn, and at last, insisted upon going home, just at the time that Mr. and Mrs. *Tibbs* assured the company, that the polite hours were going to begin, and that the ladies would instantaneously be entertained with the horns.

Citizen of the World

287 *The Decoys*

MR. BURCHELL had scarce taken leave, and Sophia consented to dance with the chaplain, when my little ones came running out to tell us that the 'Squire was come with a crowd of company. Upon our return, we found our landlord, with a couple of under gentlemen and two young ladies richly drest, whom he introduced as women of very great distinction and fashion from town. We happened not to have chairs enough for the whole company: but Mr. Thornhill immediately proposed that every gentleman should sit in a lady's lap. This I positively objected to, notwithstanding a look of disapprobation from my wife. Moses was therefore dispatched to borrow a couple of chairs; and as we were in want of ladies also to make up a set at country dances, the two gentlemen went with him in quest of a couple of partners. Chairs and partners were soon provided. The gentlemen returned with my neighbour Flamborough's rosy daughters, flaunting with red top-knots. But there was an unlucky circumstance which was not adverted to; though the Miss Flamborough's were reckoned the very best dancers in the parish, and understood the jig and the round-about to perfection, yet they were totally unacquainted with country dances. This at first discomposed us: however, after a little shoving and dragging, they at last went merrily on. Our music consisted of two fiddles, with a pipe and tabor. The moon shone bright, Mr. Thornhill and my eldest daughter led up the ball, to the great delight of the spectators; for the neighbours, hearing what was going forward, came flocking about us. My girl moved with so much grace and vivacity, that my wife could not avoid discovering the pride of her heart, by assuring me, that though the little chit did it so cleverly, all the steps were stolen from herself. The ladies of the town strove hard to be equally easy, but without success. They swam, sprawled, languished, and frisked; but all would not do: the gazers indeed owned that it was fine; but neighbour Flamborough observed, that Miss Livy's feet seemed as pat to the music as its echo. After the dance had continued about an hour, the two ladies, who were apprehensive of catching cold, moved to break up the ball. One of them, I thought, expressed her sentiments upon this occasion in a very coarse manner, when she observed, that by the *living jingo*, she was all of a muck of sweat. Upon our return to the house, we found a very elegant cold supper, which Mr. Thornhill had ordered to be brought with him. The conversation at this time was more reserved than before. The two ladies threw my girls quite into the shade; for they would talk of nothing but high life, and high-lived company; with other fashionable topics, such as pictures, taste, Shakespear, and the musical glasses. 'Tis true they once or twice mortified us sensibly by slipping out an oath; but that appeared to me as the surest symptom of their distinction, (tho' I am since informed that swearing is perfectly unfashionable). Their finery, however, threw a veil over any grossness in their conversation. My daughters seemed to regard their superior accomplishments with envy; and what appeared amiss was ascribed to tip-top quality breeding. . .

Michaelmas eve happening on the next day, we were invited to burn nuts and play tricks at neighbour Flamborough's. Our late mortifications had humbled us a little, or it is probable we might have rejected such an invitation with contempt: however, we suffered ourselves to be happy. Our honest neighbour's goose and dumplings were fine, and the lamb's-wool, even in the opinion of my wife, who was a connoisseur, was excellent. It is true, his manner of telling stories was not quite so well. They were very long, and very dull, and all about himself, and we had laughed at them ten times before: however, we were kind enough to laugh at them once more.

Mr. Burchell, who was of the party, was always fond of seeing some innocent amusement going forward, and set the boys and girls to blind man's buff. My wife too was perswaded to join in the diversion, and it gave me pleasure to think she was not yet too old. In the mean time, my neighbour and I looked on, laughed at every feat, and praised our own dexterity when we were young. Hot cockles succeeded next, questions and commands followed that, and last of all, they sat down to hunt the slipper. As every person may not be acquainted with this primaeval pastime, it may be necessary to observe, that the company at this play plant themselves in a ring upon the ground all except one who stands in the middle, whose business it is to catch a shoe, which the company shove about their hams from one to another, something like a weaver's shuttle. As it is impossible, in this case, for the lady who is up to face all the company at once, the great beauty of the play lies in hitting her a thump with the heel of the shoe on that side least capable of making a defence. It was in this manner that my eldest daughter was hemmed in, and thumped about, all blowzed, in spirits, and bawling for fair play, fair play, with a voice that might deafen a ballad singer, when, confusion on confusion, who should enter the room but our two great acquaintances from town, Lady Blarney and Miss Carolina Wilhelmina Amelia Skeggs! Description would but beggar, therefore it is unnecessary to describe this new mortification. Death! To be seen by ladies of such high breeding in such vulgar attitudes! Nothing better could ensue from such a vulgar play of Mr. Flamborough's proposing. We seemed stuck to the ground for some time, as if actually petrified with amazement.

The two ladies had been at our house to see us, and finding us from home, came after us hither, as they were uneasy to know what accident could have kept us from church the day before. Olivia undertook to be our prolocutor, and delivered the whole in a summary way, only saying, 'We were thrown from our horses.' At which account the ladies were greatly concerned; but being told the family received no hurt, they were extremely glad; but being informed that we were almost killed by the fright, they were vastly sorry; but hearing that we had a very good night, they were extremely glad again. Nothing could exceed their complaisance to my daughters; their professions the last evening were warm, but now they were ardent. They protested a desire of having a more lasting acquaintance. Lady Blarney was particularly attached to Olivia; Miss Carolina Wilhelmina Amelia Skeggs (I love to give the whole name) took a greater fancy to her sister. They supported the conversation between themselves, while my daughters sate silent, admiring their exalted breeding. But as every reader, however beggarly himself, is fond of high-lived dialogues, with anecdotes of Lords, Ladies, and Knights of the Garter, I must beg leave to give him the concluding part of the present conversation.

'All that I know of the matter,' cried Miss Skeggs, 'is this, that it may be true, or it may not be true: but this I can assure your Ladyship, that the whole rout was in amaze; his Lordship turned all manner of colours, my Lady fell into a sound, but Sir Tomkyn, drawing his sword, swore he was her's to the last drop of his blood.'

'Well,' replied our Peeress, 'this I can say, that the Duchess never told me a syllable of the matter, and I believe her Grace would keep nothing a secret from me. This you may depend on as fact, that the next morning my Lord Duke cried out three times to his valet de chambre, "Jernigan, Jernigan, Jernigan, bring me my garters." '

But previously I should have mentioned the very impolite behaviour of Mr. Burchell, who during this discourse, sate with his face turned to the fire, and at the conclusion of every sentence would cry out *fudge*, an expression which displeased us all, and in some measure damped the rising spirit of the conversation.

'Besides, my dear Skeggs,' continued our Peeress, 'there is nothing of this in the copy of verses that Dr. Burdock made upon the occasion.' *Fudge!*

'I am surprised at that,' cried Miss Skeggs; 'for he seldom leaves any thing out, as he writes only for his own amusement. But can your Ladyship favour me with a sight of them?' *Fudge!*

'My dear creature,' replied our Peeress, 'do you think I carry such things about me? Though they are very fine to be sure, and I think myself something of a judge; at least I know what pleases myself. Indeed I was ever an admirer of all Doctor Burdock's little pieces; for except what he does, and our dear Countess at Hanover Square, there 's nothing comes out but the most lowest stuff in nature ; not a bit of high life among them.' *Fudge !*

'Your Ladyship should except,' says t'other, 'your own things in the Lady's Magazine. I hope you'll say there 's nothing low lived there ? But I suppose we are to have no more from that quarter ? ' *Fudge !*

'Why, my dear,' says the Lady, 'you know my reader and companion has left me, to be married to Captain Roach, and as my poor eyes won't suffer me to write myself, I have been for some time looking out for another. A proper person is no easy matter to find, and to be sure thirty pounds a year is a small stipend for a well-bred girl of character, that can read, write, and behave in company ; as for the chits about town, there is no bearing them about one.' *Fudge !*

'That I know,' cried Miss Skeggs, 'by experience. For of the three companions I had this last half year, one of them refused to do plain-work an hour in the day, another thought twenty-five guineas a year too small a salary, and I was obliged to send away the third, because I suspected an intrigue with the chaplain. Virtue, my dear Lady Blarney, virtue is worth any price ; but where is that to be found ? ' *Fudge !*

My wife had been for a long time all attention to this discourse ; but was particularly struck with the latter part of it. Thirty pounds and twenty-five guineas a year made fifty-six pounds five shillings English money, all which was in a manner going a-begging, and might easily be secured in the family. She for a moment studied my looks for approbation ; and, to own a truth, I was of opinion, that two such places would fit our two daughters exactly.

Vicar of Wakefield

288 *Dedication of the Deserted Village*

To Sir Joshua Reynolds

DEAR SIR,

I CAN have no expectations in an address of this kind, either to add to your reputation, or to establish my own. You can gain nothing from my admiration, as I am ignorant of that art in which you are said to excel; and I may lose much by the severity of your judgment, as few have a juster taste in poetry than you. Setting interest therefore aside, to which I never paid much attention, I must be indulged at present in following my affections. The only dedication I ever made was to my brother, because I loved him better than most other men. He is since dead. Permit me to inscribe this Poem to you.

How far you may be pleased with the versification and meer mechanical parts of this attempt, I don't pretend to enquire; but I know you will object (and indeed several of our best and wisest friends concur in the opinion) that the depopulation it deplores is no where to be seen, and the disorders it laments are only to be found in the poet's own imagination. To this I can scarce make any other answer than that I sincerely believe what I have written; that I have taken all possible pains, in my country excursions, for these four or five years past, to be certain of what I alledge, and that all my views and enquiries have led me to believe those miseries real, which I here attempt to display. But this is not the place to enter into an enquiry, whether the country be depopulating, or not; the discussion would take up much room, and I should prove myself, at best, an indifferent politician, to tire the reader with a long preface, when I want his unfatigued attention to a long poem.

In regretting the depopulation of the country, I inveigh against the increase of our luxuries; and here also I expect the shout of modern politicians against me. For twenty or thirty years past, it has been the fashion to consider luxury as one of the greatest national advantages; and all the wisdom of antiquity in that particular, as erroneous. Still however, I must remain a professed ancient on that head, and continue to think those luxuries prejudicial to states, by which so many vices are introduced, and so many kingdoms have been undone. Indeed so much has been poured out of late on the other side of the question, that, meerly for the sake of novelty and variety, one would sometimes wish to be in the right.

I am,
DEAR SIR,
Your sincere friend,
and ardent admirer,
OLIVER GOLDSMITH.

EDMUND BURKE

1729–1797

289 *The Arena*, 1770

I REMEMBER an old scholastic aphorism, which says 'that the man who lives wholly detached from others, must be either an angel or a devil'. When I see in any of these detached gentlemen of our times the angelic purity, power, and beneficence, I shall admit them to be angels. In the mean time we are born only to be men. We shall do enough if we form ourselves to be good ones. It is therefore our business carefully to cultivate in our minds, to rear to the most perfect vigour and maturity, every sort of generous and honest feeling that belongs to our nature. To bring the dispositions that are lovely in private life into the service and conduct of the commonwealth; so to be patriots, as not to forget we are gentlemen. To cultivate friendships, and to incur enmities. To have both strong, but both selected: in the one, to be placable; in the other, immoveable. To model our principles to our duties and our situation. To be fully persuaded, that all virtue which is impracticable is spurious; and rather to run the risque of falling into faults in a course which leads us to act with effect and energy, than to loiter out our days without blame, and without use. Public life is a situation of power and energy; he trespasses against his duty who sleeps upon his watch, as well as he that goes over to the enemy.

Thoughts on the Present Discontents

290 *Conciliation with America, 1775*

THE last cause of this disobedient spirit in the Colonies is hardly less powerful than the rest, as it is not merely moral, but laid deep in the natural constitution of things. Three thousand miles of ocean lie between you and them. No contrivance can prevent the effect of this distance in weakening Government. Seas roll, and months pass, between the order and the execution; and the want of a speedy explanation of a single point is enough to defeat a whole system. You have, indeed, winged ministers of vengeance, who carry your bolts in their pounces to the remotest verge of the sea. But there a power steps in, that limits the arrogance of raging passions and furious elements, and says, 'So far shalt thou go,

28 *pounces*) *claws*

and no farther.' Who are you, that should fret and rage, and bite the chains of Nature? Nothing worse happens to you than does to all Nations who have extensive Empire; and it happens in all the forms into which Empire can be thrown. In large bodies, the circulation of power must be less vigorous at the extremities. Nature has said it. The Turk cannot govern Ægypt, and Arabia, and Curdistan, as he governs Thrace; nor has he the same dominion in Crimea and Algiers, which he has at Brusa and Smyrna. Despotism itself is obliged to truck and huckster. The Sultan gets such obedience as he can. He governs with a loose rein, that he may govern at all; and the whole of the force and vigour of his authority in his centre is derived from a prudent relaxation in all his borders. Spain, in her provinces, is, perhaps, not so well obeyed as you are in yours. She complies too; she submits; she watches times. This is the immutable condition, the eternal Law, of extensive and detached Empire.

Speech in the House of Commons

291 *Speech at Bristol on declining the Poll, 1780*

Bristol, Saturday, *Sept.* 9, 1780.

THIS morning the Sheriff and Candidates assembled as usual at the Council House, and from thence proceeded to Guildhall. Proclamation being made for the electors to appear and give their votes, Mr. BURKE stood forward on the Hustings, surrounded by a great number of the Corporation and other principal citizens, and addressed himself to the whole assembly as follows:—

GENTLEMEN,

I decline the election.——It has ever been my rule through life, to observe a proportion between my efforts and my objects. I have never been remarkable for a bold, active, and sanguine pursuit of advantages that are personal to myself.

I have not canvassed the whole of this city in form. But I have taken such a view of it as satisfies my own mind, that your choice will not ultimately fall upon me. Your city, Gentlemen, is in a state of miserable distraction ; and I am resolved to withdraw whatever share my pretensions may have had in its unhappy divisions. I have not been in haste ; I have tried all prudent means ; I have waited for the effect of all contingencies. If I were fond of a contest, by the partiality of my numerous friends (whom you know to be among the most weighty and respectable people of the city), I have the means of a sharp one in my hands. But I thought it far better with my strength unspent, and my reputation unimpaired, to do, early and from foresight, that which I might be obliged to do from necessity at last.

I am not in the least surprised, nor in the least angry at this view of things. I have read the book of life for a long time, and I have read other books a little. Nothing has happened to me, but what has happened to men much better than me, and in times and in nations full as good as the age and country that we live in. To say that I am no way concerned, would be neither decent nor true. The representation of *Bristol* was an object on many accounts dear to me ; and I certainly should very far prefer it to any other in the kingdom. My habits are made to it ; and it is in general more unpleasant to be rejected after long trial, than not to be chosen at all.

But, Gentlemen, I will see nothing except your former kindness, and I will give way to no other sentiments than those of gratitude. From the bottom of my heart I thank you for what you have done for me. You have given me a long term, which is now expired. I have performed the conditions, and enjoyed all the profits to the full; and I now surrender your estate into your hands, without being in a single tile or a single stone impaired or wasted by my use. I have served the public for fifteen years. I have served you in particular for six. What is passed is well stored. It is safe, and out of the power of fortune. What is to come, is in wiser hands than ours: and he, in whose hands it is, best knows whether it is best for you and me that I should be in Parliament, or even in the world.

Gentlemen, the melancholy event of yesterday reads to us an awful lesson against being too much troubled about any of the objects of ordinary ambition. The worthy Gentleman, who has been snatched from us at the moment of the election, and in the middle of the contest, whilst his desires were as warm, and his hopes as eager as ours, has feelingly told us, what shadows we are, and what shadows we pursue.

It has been usual for a candidate who declines, to take his leave by a letter to the Sheriffs; but I received your trust in the face of day: and in the face of day I accept your dismission. I am not,—I am not at all ashamed to look upon you; nor can my presence discompose the order of business here. I humbly and respectfully take my leave of the sheriffs, the candidates, and the electors, wishing heartily that the choice may be for the best, at a time which calls, if ever time did call, for service that is not nominal. It is no plaything you are about. I tremble when I consider the trust I have presumed to ask. I confided perhaps too much in my intentions. They were really fair and upright;

and I am bold to say that I ask no ill thing for you, when on parting from this place I pray that whomever you chuse to succeed me, he may resemble me exactly in all things, except in my abilities to serve, and my fortune to please you.

Speech at Bristol

292 *Marie Antoinette*

IT is now sixteen or seventeen years since I saw the queen of France, then the dauphiness, at Versailles; and surely never lighted on this orb, which she hardly seemed to touch, a more delightful vision. I saw her just above the horizon, decorating and cheering the elevated sphere she just began to move in; glittering like the morning star, full of life, and splendor, and joy. Oh! what a revolution! and what an heart must I have, to contemplate without emotion that elevation and that fall! Little did I dream when she added titles of veneration to those of enthusiastic, distant, respectful love, that she should ever be obliged to carry the sharp antidote against disgrace concealed in that bosom; little did I dream that I should have lived to see such disasters fallen upon her in a nation of gallant men, in a nation of men of honour and of cavaliers. I thought ten thousand swords must have leaped from their scabbards to avenge even a look that threatened her with insult.—But the age of chivalry is gone. That of sophisters, œconomists, and calculators, has succeeded; and the glory of Europe is extinguished for ever. Never, never more, shall we behold that generous loyalty to rank and sex, that proud submission, that dignified obedience, that subordination of the heart, which kept alive, even in servitude itself, the spirit of an exalted freedom. The unbought grace of life, the cheap defence of nations, the nurse of manly sentiment and heroic enterprize, is gone! It is gone, that sensibility of principle, that chastity of honour, which felt a stain like a wound, which inspired courage whilst it mitigated ferocity, which ennobled whatever it touched, and under which vice itself lost half its evil, by losing all its grossness.

Reflections on the Revolution in France

293 'The Labouring Poor'

AN untimely shower, or an unseasonable drought; a frost too long continued, or too suddenly broken up, with rain and tempest; the blight of the spring, or the smut of the harvest; will do more to cause the distress of the belly, than all the contrivances of all Statesmen can do to relieve it. Let Government protect and encourage industry, secure property, repress violence, and discountenance fraud, it is all that they have to do. In other respects, the less they meddle in these affairs the better; the rest is in the hands of our Master and theirs. We are in a constitution of things wherein '*Modo sol nimius, nimius modo corripit imber.*' But I will push this matter no further. As I have said a good deal upon it at various times during my publick service, and have lately written something on it, which may yet see the light, I shall content myself now with observing, that the vigorous and laborious class of life has lately got from the *bon ton* of the humanity of this day, the name of the '*labouring poor.*' We have heard many plans for the relief of the '*Labouring Poor.*' This puling jargon is not as innocent as it is foolish. In meddling with great affairs, weakness is never innoxious. Hitherto the name of Poor (in the sense in which it is used to excite compassion) has not been used for those who can, but for those who cannot labour—for the sick and infirm; for orphan infancy; for languishing and decrepid age: but when we affect to pity as poor, those who must labour or the world cannot exist, we are trifling with the condition of mankind. It is the common doom of man that he must eat his bread by the sweat of his brow, that is, by the sweat of his body, or the sweat of his mind. If this toil was inflicted as a curse, it is as might be expected from the curses of the Father of all Blessings—it is tempered with many alleviations, many comforts. Every attempt to fly from it, and to refuse the very terms of our existence, becomes much more truly a curse, and heavier pains and penalties fall upon those who would elude the tasks which are put upon them by the great Master Workman of the World, who in his dealings with his creatures sympathizes with their weakness, and speaking of a creation wrought by mere will out of nothing, speaks of six days of *labour* and one of *rest.* I do not call a healthy young man, chearful in his mind, and vigorous in his arms—I cannot call such a man, *poor;* I cannot pity my kind as a kind, merely because they are men. This affected pity only tends to dissatisfy them with their condition, and to teach them to seek resources where no resources are to be found—in something else than their own industry, and frugality, and sobriety. Whatever may be the intention (which, because I do not know, I cannot dispute) of those who would discontent mankind by this strange pity, they act towards us, in the consequences, as if they were our worst enemies.

Letters on a Regicide Peace

294 *Thomas Paine*

I HAVE a great opinion of Thomas Paine, and of all his productions. I remember his having been one of the Committee for forming one of their annual Constitutions, I mean the admirable Constitution of 1793—after having been a Chamber Counsel to the no less admirable Constitution of 1791. This pious patriot has his eyes still directed to his dear native country, notwithstanding her ingratitude to so kind a benefactor. This outlaw of England, and lawgiver to France, is now, in secret probably, trying his hand again; and inviting us to him by making his Constitution such, as may give his disciples in England some plausible pretext for going into the house that he has opened. We have discovered, it seems, that all, which the boasted wisdom of our ancestors has laboured to bring to perfection for six or seven centuries, is nearly or altogether matched in six or seven days, at the leisure hours and sober intervals of Citizen Thomas Paine.

> But though the treacherous tapster Thomas
> Hangs a new Angel two doors from us,
> As fine as daubers' hands can make it,
> In hopes that strangers may mistake it;
> We think it both a shame and sin
> To quit the good old Angel Inn.

Indeed in this good old House, where every thing, at least, is well aired, I shall be content to put up my fatigued horses, and here take a bed for the long night that begins to darken upon me. Had I, however, the honour (I must now call it so) of being a Member of any of the Constitutional Clubs, I should think I had carried my point most completely. It is clear, by the applauses bestowed on what the Author calls this new Constitution, a mixed Oligarchy, that the difference between the Clubbists and the old adherents to the Monarchy of this country is hardly worth a scuffle. Let it depart in peace, and light lie the earth on the British Constitution!

Letters on a Regicide Peace

295 *Windsor Castle and the Bedford Level*

SUCH are *their* ideas: such *their* religion, and such *their* law. But as to *our* country and *our* race, as long as the well-compacted structure of our church and state, the sanctuary, the holy of holies of that ancient law, defended by reverence, defended by power, a fortress at once and a temple, shall stand inviolate on the brow of the British Sion—as long as the British monarchy, not more limited than fenced by the orders of the state, shall, like the proud Keep of Windsor, rising in the majesty of proportion, and girt with the double belt of its kindred and coeval towers, as long as this awful structure shall oversee and guard the subjected land—so long the mounds and dykes of the low, fat, Bedford level will have nothing to fear from all the pickaxes of all the levellers of France. As long as our Sovereign Lord the King, and his faithful subjects, the Lords and Commons of this realm,—the triple cord, which no man can break; the solemn, sworn, constitutional frank-pledge of this nation; the firm guarantees of each others' being, and each others' rights; the joint and several securities, each in its place and order, for every kind and every quality, of property and of dignity:—as long as these endure, so long the Duke of Bedford is safe: and we are all safe together—the high from the blights of envy and the spoliations of rapacity; the low from the iron hand of oppression and the insolent spurn of contempt. Amen! and so be it: and so it will be.

> Dum domus Aeneae Capitoli immobile saxum
> Accolet; imperiumque pater Romanus habebit.

Letter to a Noble Lord

WILLIAM COWPER

1731–1800

296 *Recollections of Margate*

WHEN I was at Margate, it was an excursion of pleasure to go to see Ramsgate. The pier, I remember, was accounted a most excellent piece of stone-work, and such I found it. By this time, I suppose, it is finished; and surely it is no small advantage, that you have an opportunity of observing how nicely those great stones are put together, as often as you please, without either trouble or expense. But you think Margate more lively. So is a Cheshire cheese full of mites more lively than a sound one: but that very liveliness only proves its rottenness. I remember, too, that Margate, though full of company, was generally filled with such company, as people who were nice in the choice of their company, were rather fearful of keeping company with. The hoy went to London every week, loaded with mackerel and herrings, and returned loaded with company. The cheapness of the conveyance made it equally commodious for Dead fish and Lively company. So, perhaps, your solitude at Ramsgate may turn out another advantage; at least I should think it one.

There was not, at that time, much to be seen in the Isle of Thanet, besides the beauty of the country, and the fine prospects of the sea, which are nowhere surpassed except in the Isle of Wight, or upon some parts of the coast of Hampshire. One sight, however, I remember, engaged my curiosity, and I went to see it: —a fine piece of ruins, built by the late Lord Holland, at a great expense, which, the day after I saw it, tumbled down for nothing. Perhaps, therefore, it is still a ruin; and if it is, I would advise you by all means to visit it, as it must have been much improved by this fortunate incident. It is hardly possible to put stones together with that air of wild and magnificent disorder which they are sure to acquire by falling of their own accord.

We heartily wish that Mrs. Unwin may receive the utmost benefit of bathing. At the same time we caution *you* against the use of it, however the heat of the weather may seem to recommend it. It is not safe for thin habits, hectically inclined.

I remember,—(the fourth and last thing I mean to remember upon this occasion,) that Sam Cox the counsel, walking by the seaside as if absorbed in deep contemplation, was questioned about what he was musing on. He replied, 'I was wondering that such an almost infinite and unwieldy element should produce a *sprat*.' Our love attends your whole party.—Yours affectionately, W. C.

Letter to the Reverend William Unwin, July 1779

297 *The Colubriad*

IT is a sort of paradox, but it is true: we are never more in danger than when we think ourselves most secure, nor in reality more secure than when we seem to be most in danger. Both sides of this apparent contradiction were lately verified in my experience.—Passing from the greenhouse to the barn, I saw three kittens (for we have so many in our retinue) looking with fixed attention at something, which lay on the threshold of a door, coiled up. I took but little notice of them at first; but a loud hiss engaged me to attend more closely, when behold—a viper! the largest I remember to have seen, rearing itself, darting its forked tongue, and ejaculating the afore-mentioned hiss at the nose of a kitten almost in contact with his lips. I ran into the hall for a hoe with a long handle, with which I intended to assail him, and returning in a few seconds missed him: he was gone, and I feared had escaped me. Still however the kitten sat watching immoveably upon the same spot. I concluded, therefore, that, sliding between the door and the threshold, he had found his way out of the garden into the yard. I went round immediately, and there found him in close conversation with the old cat, whose curiosity being excited by so novel an appearance, inclined her to pat his head repeatedly with her fore foot; with her claws however sheathed, and not in anger; but in the way of philosophical inquiry and examination. To prevent her falling a victim to so laudable an exercise of her talents, I interposed in a moment with the hoe, and performed upon him an act of decapitation, which though not immediately mortal, proved so in the end. Had he slid into the passages, where it is dark, or had he, when in the yard, met with no interruption from the cat, and secreted himself in any of the outhouses, it is hardly possible but that some of the family must have been bitten; he might have been trodden upon without being perceived, and have slipped away before the sufferer could have well distinguished what foe had wounded him. Three years ago we discovered one in the same place, which the barber slew with a trowel.

Letter to the Reverend William Unwin, 3 Aug. 1782

298 *A Candidate for Parliament*

AS when the sea is uncommonly agitated, the water finds its way into creeks and holes of rocks, which in its calmer state it never reaches, in like manner the effect of these turbulent times is felt even at Orchard side, where in general we live as undisturbed by the political element, as shrimps or cockles that have been accidentally deposited in some hollow beyond the water mark, by the usual dashing of the waves. We were sitting yesterday after dinner, the two ladies and myself, very composedly, and without the least apprehension of any such intrusion in our snug parlour, one lady knitting, the other netting, and the gentleman winding worsted, when to our unspeakable surprise a mob appeared before the window; a smart rap was heard at the door, the boys halloo'd, and the maid announced Mr. Grenville.

Puss was unfortunately let out of her box, so that the candidate, with all his good friends at his heels, was refused admittance at the grand entry, and referred to the back door, as the only possible way of approach.

Candidates are creatures not very susceptible of affronts, and would rather, I suppose, climb in at a window, than be absolutely excluded. In a minute, the yard, the kitchen, and the parlour, were filled. Mr. Grenville, advancing toward me, shook me by the hand with a degree of cordiality that was extremely seducing. As soon as he and as many more as could find chairs were seated, he began to open the intent of his visit. I told him I had no vote, for which he readily gave me credit. I assured him I had no influence, which he was not equally inclined to believe, and the less, no doubt, because Mr. Ashburner, the draper, addressing himself to me at this moment, informed me that I had a great deal. Supposing that I could not be possessed of such a treasure without knowing it, I ventured to confirm my first assertion, by saying, that if I had any I was utterly at a loss to imagine where it could be, or wherein it consisted. Thus ended the conference. Mr. Grenville squeezed me by the hand again, kissed the ladies, and withdrew. He kissed likewise the maid in the kitchen, and seemed upon the whole a most loving, kissing, kind-hearted gentleman. He is very young, genteel, and handsome. He has a pair of very good eyes in his head, which not being sufficient as it should seem for the many nice and difficult purposes of a senator, he has a third also, which he wore suspended by a riband from his button-hole. The boys halloo'd, the dogs barked, Puss scampered, the hero, with his long train of obsequious followers, withdrew. We made ourselves very merry with the adventure, and in a short time settled into our former tranquillity, never probably to be thus interrupted more.

Letter to the Reverend John Newton, 29 March 1784

299 *Countryside Music*

MY greenhouse is never so pleasant as when we are just upon the point of being turned out of it. The gentleness of the autumnal suns, and the calmness of this latter season, make it a much more agreeable retreat than we ever find it in summer; when, the winds being generally brisk, we cannot cool it by admitting a sufficient quantity of air, without being at the same time incommoded by it. But now I sit with all the windows and the door wide open, and am regaled with the scent of every flower in a garden as full of flowers as I have known how to make it. We keep no bees, but if I lived in a hive I should hardly hear more of their music. All the bees in the neighbourhood resort to a bed of mignonette, opposite to the window, and pay me for the honey they get out of it by a hum, which, though rather monotonous, is as agreeable to my ear as the whistling of my linnets. All the sounds that nature utters are delightful,—at least in this country. I should not perhaps find the roaring of lions in Africa, or of bears in Russia, very pleasing; but I know no beast in England whose voice I do not account musical, save and except always the braying of an ass. The notes of all our birds and fowls please me, without one exception. I should not indeed think of keeping a goose in a cage, that I might hang him up in the parlour for the sake of his melody, but a goose upon a common, or in a farm-yard, is no bad performer; and as to insects, if the black beetle, and beetles indeed of all hues, will keep out of my way, I have no objection to any of the rest; on the contrary, in whatever key they sing, from the gnat's fine treble to the bass of the humble-bee, I admire them all.

Letter to the Reverend John Newton, 18 Sept. 1784

300 *The Promised Visit*

AND now, my dear, let me tell you once more, that your kindness in promising us a visit has charmed us both. I shall see you again. I shall hear your voice. We shall take walks together. I will show you my prospects, the hovel, the alcove, the Ouse, and its banks, everything that I have described. I anticipate the pleasure of those days not very far distant, and feel a part of it at this moment. Talk not of an inn! Mention it not for your life! We have never had so many visitors, but we could easily accommodate them all; though we have received Unwin, and his wife, and his sister, and his son all at once. My dear, I will not let you come till the end of May, or beginning of June, because before that time my greenhouse will not be ready to receive us, and it is the only pleasant room belonging to us. When the plants go out, we go in. I line it with mats, and spread the floor with mats; and there you shall sit with a bed of mignonette at your side, and a hedge of honey-suckles, roses, and jasmine; and I will make you a bouquet of myrtle every day. Sooner than the time I mention the country will not be in complete beauty. And I will tell you what you shall find at your first entrance. *Imprimis*, as soon as you have entered the vestibule, if you cast a look on either side of you, you shall see on the right hand a box of my making. It is the box in which have been lodged all my hares, and in which lodges Puss at present: but he, poor fellow, is worn out with age, and promises to die before you can see him. On the right hand stands a cupboard, the work of the same author; it was once a dove-cage, but I transformed it. Opposite to you stands a table, which I also made: but a merciless servant having scrubbed it until it became paralytic, it serves no purpose now but of ornament; and all my clean shoes stand under it. On the left hand, at the further end of this superb vestibule, you will find the door of the parlour, into which I will conduct you, and where I will introduce you to Mrs. Unwin, unless we should meet her before, and where we will be as happy as the day is long. Order yourself, my Cousin, to the Swan at Newport, and there you shall find me ready to conduct you to Olney.

Letter to Lady Hesketh, 9 Feb. 1786

301 *In at the Death*

ONE day last week, Mrs. Unwin and I, having taken our morning walk and returning homeward through the wilderness, met the Throckmortons. A minute after we had met them, we heard the cry of hounds at no great distance, and mounting the broad stump of an elm which had been felled, and by the aid of which we were enabled to look over the wall, we saw them. They were all at that time in our orchard; presently we heard a terrier, belonging to Mrs. Throckmorton, which you may remember by the name of Fury, yelping with much vehemence, and saw her running through the thickets within a few yards of us at her utmost speed, as if in pursuit of something which we doubted not was the fox. Before we could reach the other end of the wilderness, the hounds entered also; and when we arrived at the gate which opens into the grove, there we found the whole weary cavalcade assembled. The huntsman dismounting, begged leave to follow his hounds on foot, for he was sure, he said, that they had killed him : a conclusion which I suppose he drew from their profound silence. He was accordingly admitted, and with a sagacity that would not have dishonoured the best hound in the world, pursuing precisely the same track which the fox and the dogs had taken, though he had never had a glimpse of either after their first entrance through the rails, arrived where he found the slaughtered prey. He soon produced dead reynard, and rejoined us in the grove with all his dogs about him. Having an opportunity to see a ceremony, which I was pretty sure would never fall in my way again, I determined to stay and to notice all that passed with the most minute attention. The huntsman having by the aid of a pitchfork lodged reynard on the arm of an elm, at the height of about nine feet from the ground, there left him for a considerable time. The gentlemen sat on their horses contemplating the fox, for which they had toiled so hard, and the hounds assembled at the foot of the tree, with faces not less expressive of the most rational delight, contemplated the same object. The huntsman remounted; cut off a foot, and threw it to the hounds ;—one of them swallowed it whole like a bolus. He then once more alighted and drawing down the fox by the hinder legs, desired the people, who were by this time rather numerous, to open a lane for him to the right and left. He was instantly obeyed, when throwing the fox to the distance of some yards, and screaming like a fiend, 'tear him to pieces'—at least six times repeatedly, he consigned him over absolutely to the pack, who in a few minutes devoured him completely. Thus, my dear, as Virgil says, what none of the gods could have ventured to promise me, time itself, pursuing its accustomed course, has of its own accord presented me with. I have been in at the death of a fox, and you now know as much of the matter as I, who am as well informed as any sportsman in England.—Yours, W. C.

Letter to Lady Hesketh, 3 Mar. 1788

EDWARD GIBBON

1737–1794

302 *The Two Antonines*

As soon as Hadrian's passion was either gratified or disappointed, he resolved to deserve the thanks of posterity by placing the most exalted merit on the Roman throne. His discerning eye easily discovered a senator about fifty years of age, blameless in all the offices of life; and a youth of about seventeen, whose riper years opened the fair prospect of every virtue: the elder of these was declared the son and successor of Hadrian, on condition, however, that he himself should immediately adopt the younger. The two Antonines (for it is of them that we are now speaking) governed the Roman world forty-two years with the same invariable spirit of wisdom and virtue. Although Pius had two sons, he preferred the welfare of Rome to the interest of his family, gave his daughter Faustina in marriage to young Marcus, obtained from the senate the tribunitian and proconsular powers, and, with a noble disdain, or rather ignorance, of jealousy, associated him to all the labours of government. Marcus, on the other hand, revered the character of his benefactor, loved him as a parent, obeyed him as his sovereign, and, after he was no more, regulated his own administration by the example and maxims of his predecessor. Their united reigns are possibly the only period of history in which the happiness of a great people was the sole object of government.

Titus Antoninus Pius had been justly denominated a second Numa. The same love of religion, justice, and peace, was the distinguishing characteristic of both princes. But the situation of the latter opened a much larger field for the exercise of those virtues. Numa could only prevent a few neighbouring villages from plundering each other's harvests. Antoninus diffused order and tranquillity over the greatest part of the earth. His reign is marked by the rare advantage of furnishing very few materials for history; which is, indeed, little more than the register of the crimes, follies, and misfortunes of mankind. In private life he was an amiable as well as a good man. The native simplicity of his virtue was a stranger to vanity or affectation. He enjoyed with moderation the conveniences of his fortune, and the innocent pleasures of society; and the benevolence of his soul displayed itself in a cheerful serenity of temper.

The virtue of Marcus Aurelius Antoninus was of a severer and more laborious kind. It was the well-earned harvest of many a learned conference, of many a patient lecture, and many a midnight lucubration. At the age of twelve years he embraced the rigid system of the Stoics, which taught him to submit his body to his mind, his passions to his reason; to consider virtue as the only good, vice as the only evil, all things external as things indifferent. His meditations, composed in the tumult of a camp, are still extant; and he even condescended to give lessons on philosophy, in a more public manner than was perhaps consistent with the modesty of a sage or the dignity of an emperor. But his life was the noblest commentary on the precepts of Zeno. He was severe to himself, indulgent to the imperfection of others, just and beneficent to all mankind. He regretted that Avidius Cassius, who excited a rebellion in Syria, had disappointed him, by a voluntary death, of the pleasure of converting an enemy into a friend; and he justified the sincerity of that sentiment, by moderating the zeal of the senate against the adherents of the traitor. War he detested, as the disgrace and calamity of human nature; but when the necessity of a just defence called upon him to take up arms, he readily exposed his person to eight winter campaigns on the frozen banks of the Danube, the severity of which was at last fatal to the weakness of his constitution. His memory was revered by a grateful posterity, and above a century after his death many persons preserved the image of Marcus Antoninus among those of their household gods.

If a man were called to fix the period in the history of the world during which the condition of the human race was most happy and prosperous, he would, without hesitation, name that which elapsed from the death of Domitian to the accession of Commodus. The vast extent of the Roman empire was governed by absolute power, under the guidance of virtue and wisdom. The armies were restrained by the firm but gentle hand of four successive emperors, whose characters and authority commanded involuntary respect. The forms of the civil administration were carefully preserved by Nerva, Trajan, Hadrian, and the Antonines, who delighted in the image of liberty, and were pleased with considering themselves as the accountable ministers of the laws. Such princes deserved the honour of restoring the republic, had the Romans of their days been capable of enjoying a rational freedom.

Decline and Fall of the Roman Empire

303 *Constantinople*

THE winding channel through which the waters of the Euxine flow with a rapid and incessant course towards the Mediterranean received the appellation of Bosphorus, a name not less celebrated in the history than in the fables of antiquity. A crowd of temples and of votive altars, profusely scattered along its steep and woody banks, attested the unskilfulness, the terrors, and the devotion of the Grecian navigators, who, after the example of the Argonauts, explored the dangers of the inhospitable Euxine. . .

The harbour of Constantinople, which may be considered as an arm of the Bosphorus, obtained, in a very remote period, the denomination of the *Golden Horn*. The curve which it describes might be compared to the horn of a stag, or, as it should seem, with more propriety, to that of an ox. The epithet of *golden* was expressive of the riches which every wind wafted from the most distant countries into the secure and capacious port of Constantinople. The river Lycus, formed by the conflux of two little streams, pours into the harbour a perpetual supply of fresh water, which serves to cleanse the bottom and to invite the periodical shoals of fish to seek their retreat in that convenient recess. As the vicissitudes of tides are scarcely felt in those seas, the constant depth of the harbour allows goods to be landed on the quays without the assistance of boats ; and it has been observed that in many places the largest vessels may rest their prows against the houses, while their sterns are floating in the water. From the mouth of the Lycus to that of the harbour this arm of the Bosphorus is more than seven miles in length. The entrance is about five hundred yards broad, and a strong chain could be occasionally drawn across it, to guard the port and city from the attack of an hostile navy.

Between the Bosphorus and the Hellespont, the shores of Europe and Asia receding on either side inclose the sea of Marmara, which was known to the ancients by the denomination of Propontis. The navigation from the issue of the Bosphorus to the entrance of the Hellespont is about one hundred and twenty miles. Those who steer their westward course through the middle of the Propontis may at once descry the high lands of Thrace and Bithynia, and never lose sight of the lofty summit of Mount Olympus, covered with eternal snows. They leave on the left a deep gulf, at the bottom of which Nicomedia was seated, the imperial residence of Diocletian; and they pass the small islands of Cyzicus and Proconnesus before they cast anchor at Gallipoli; where the sea, which separates Asia from Europe, is again contracted into a narrow channel. . .

We are at present qualified to view the advantageous position of Constantinople; which appears to have been formed by Nature for the centre and capital of a great monarchy. Situated in the forty-first degree of latitude, the Imperial city commanded, from her seven hills, the opposite shores of Europe and Asia; the climate was healthy and temperate, the soil fertile, the harbour secure and capacious; and the approach on the side of the continent was of small extent and easy defence. The Bosphorus and Hellespont may be considered as the two gates of Constantinople ; and the prince who possessed those important passages could always shut them against a naval enemy and open them to the fleets of commerce. The preservation of the eastern provinces may, in some degree, be ascribed to the policy of Constantine, as the Barbarians of the Euxine, who in the preceding age had poured their armaments into the heart of the Mediterranean, soon desisted from the exercise of piracy, and despaired of forcing this insurmountable barrier. When the gates of the Hellespont and Bosphorus were shut, the capital still enjoyed, within their spacious inclosure, every production which could supply the wants, or gratify the luxury, of its numerous inhabitants. The sea-coast of Thrace and Bithynia, which languish under the weight of Turkish oppression, still exhibits a rich prospect of vineyards, of gardens, and of plentiful harvests ; and the Propontis has ever been renowned for an inexhaustible store of the most exquisite fish, that are taken in their stated seasons without skill and almost without labour. But, when the passages of the Straits were thrown open for trade, they alternately admitted the natural and artificial riches of the north and south, of the Euxine, and of the Mediterranean. Whatever rude commodities were collected in the forests of Germany and Scythia, as far as the sources of the Tanais and the Borysthenes ; whatsoever was manufactured by the skill of Europe or Asia ; the corn of Egypt, and the gems and spices of the farthest India, were brought by the varying winds into the port of Constantinople, which, for many ages, attracted the commerce of the ancient world.

Decline and Fall of the Roman Empire

304 *Unworldliness of the Early Christians*

IT is a very honourable circumstance for the morals of the primitive Christians, that even their faults, or rather errors, were derived from an excess of virtue. The bishops and doctors of the church, whose evidence attests, and whose authority might influence, the professions, the principles, and even the practice, of their contemporaries, had studied the scriptures with less skill than devotion, and they often received, in the most literal sense, those rigid precepts of Christ and the apostles to which the prudence of succeeding commentators has applied a looser and more figurative mode of interpretation. Ambitious to exalt the perfection of the gospel above the wisdom of philosophy, the zealous fathers have carried the duties of self-mortification, of purity, and of patience, to a height which it is scarcely possible to attain, and much less to preserve, in our present state of weakness and corruption. A doctrine so extraordinary and so sublime must inevitably command the veneration of the people; but it was ill calculated to obtain the suffrage of those worldly philosophers who, in the conduct of this transitory life, consult only the feelings of nature and the interest of society.

There are two very natural propensities which we may distinguish in the most virtuous and liberal dispositions, the love of pleasure and the love of action. If the former be refined by art and learning, improved by the charms of social intercourse, and corrected by a just regard to economy, to health, and to reputation, it is productive of the greatest part of the happiness of private life. The love of action is a principle of a much stronger and more doubtful nature. It often leads to anger, to ambition, and to revenge ; but, when it is guided by the sense of propriety and benevolence, it becomes the parent of every virtue ; and, if those virtues are accompanied with equal abilities, a family, a state, or an empire may be indebted for their safety and prosperity to the undaunted courage of a single man. To the love of pleasure we may therefore ascribe most of the agreeable, to the love of action we may attribute most of the useful and respectable qualifications. The character in which both the one and the other should be united and harmonised would seem to constitute the most perfect idea of human nature. The insensible and inactive disposition, which should be supposed alike destitute of both, would be rejected, by the common consent of mankind, as utterly incapable of procuring any happiness to the individual, or any public benefit to the world. But it was not in *this* world that the primitive Christians were desirous of making themselves either agreeable or useful.

Decline and Fall of the Roman Empire

305 *On his Life-Work*

i

IT was at Rome, on the 15th of October 1764, as I sat musing amidst the ruins of the Capitol, while the bare-footed fryars were singing vespers in the Temple of Jupiter, that the idea of writing the decline and fall of the city first started to my mind. But my original plan was circumscribed to the decay of the city rather than of the empire : and, though my reading and reflections began to point towards that object, some years elapsed, and several avocations intervened, before I was seriously engaged in the execution of that laborious work.

EDWARD GIBBON

ii

I have presumed to mark the moment of conception: I shall now commemorate the hour of my final deliverance. It was on the day, or rather night, of the 27th of June 1787, between the hours of eleven and twelve, that I wrote the last lines of the last page, in a summer-house in my garden. After laying down my pen, I took several turns in a *berceau*, or covered walk of acacias, which commands a prospect of the country, the lake, and the mountains. The air was temperate, the sky was serene, the silver orb of the moon was reflected from the waters, and all nature was silent. I will not dissemble the first emotions of joy on the recovery of my freedom, and, perhaps, the establishment of my fame. But my pride was soon humbled, and a sober melancholy was spread over my mind, by the idea that I had taken an everlasting leave of an old and agreeable companion, and that whatsoever might be the future date of my History, the life of the historian must be short and precarious.

Memoirs of my Life and Writings

JAMES BOSWELL

1740–1795

306 *Johnson at Oxford*

HE, however, went to Oxford, and was entered a Commoner of Pembroke College on the 31st of October 1728, being then in his nineteenth year.

The Reverend Dr. Adams, who afterwards presided over Pembroke College with universal esteem, told me he was present, and gave me some account of what passed on the night of Johnson's arrival at Oxford. On that evening, his father, who had anxiously accompanied him, found means to have him introduced to Mr. Jorden, who was to be his tutor. His being put under any tutor reminds us of what Wood says of Robert Burton, author of the *Anatomy of Melancholy*, when elected student of Christ Church: 'for form's sake, *though he wanted not a tutor*, he was put under the tuition of Dr. John Bancroft, afterwards Bishop of Oxon.'

His father seemed very full of the merits of his son, and told the company he was a good scholar, and a poet, and wrote Latin verses. His figure and manner appeared strange to them; but he behaved modestly, and sat silent, till upon something which occurred in the course of conversation, he suddenly struck in and quoted Macrobius; and thus he gave the first impression of that more extensive reading in which he had indulged himself.

His tutor, Mr. Jorden, fellow of Pembroke, was not, it seems, a man of such abilities as we should conceive requisite for the instructor of Samuel Johnson, who gave me the following account of him. 'He was a very worthy man, but a heavy man, and I did not profit much by his instructions. Indeed, I did not attend him much. The first day after I came to college I waited upon him, and then stayed away four. On the sixth, Mr. Jorden asked me why I had not attended. I answered I had been sliding in Christ Church meadow. And this I said with as much *nonchalance* as I am now talking to you. I had no notion that I was wrong or irreverent to my tutor.' BOSWELL: 'That, Sir, was great fortitude of mind.' JOHNSON: 'No, Sir; stark insensibility.'

He had a love and respect for Jorden, not for his literature, but for his worth. 'Whenever (said he) a young man becomes Jorden's pupil, he becomes his son.' . . .

No man had a more ardent love of literature, or a higher respect for it than Johnson. His apartment in Pembroke College was that upon the second floor, over the gateway. The enthusiasts of learning will ever contemplate it with veneration. One day, while he was sitting in it quite alone, Dr. Panting, then master of the College, whom he called 'a fine Jacobite fellow', overheard him uttering this soliloquy in his strong, emphatick voice: 'Well, I have a mind to see what is done in other places of learning. I'll go and visit the Universities abroad. I'll go to France and Italy. I'll go to Padua.—And I'll mind my business. For an *Athenian* blockhead is the worst of all blockheads.'

Dr. Adams told me that Johnson, while he was at Pembroke College, 'was caressed and loved by all about him, was a gay and frolicksome fellow, and passed there the happiest part of his life.' But this is a striking proof of the fallacy of appearances, and how little any of us know of the real internal state even of those whom we see most frequently; for the truth is, that he was then depressed by poverty, and irritated by disease. When I mentioned to him this account as given me by Dr. Adams, he said, 'Ah, Sir, I was mad and violent. It was bitterness which they mistook for frolick. I was miserably poor, and I thought to fight my way by my literature and my wit; so I disregarded all power and all authority.' . . .

I do not find that he formed any close intimacies with his fellow collegians. But Dr. Adams told me that he contracted a love and regard for Pembroke College, which he retained to the last. A short time before his death he sent to that College a present of all his works, to be deposited in their library; and he had thoughts of leaving to it his house at Lichfield; but his friends who were about him very properly dissuaded him from it, and he bequeathed it to some poor relations. He took a pleasure in boasting of the many eminent men who had been educated at Pembroke. In this list are found the names of Mr. Hawkins the Poetry Professor, Mr. Shenstone, Sir William Blackstone, and others; not forgetting the celebrated popular preacher, Mr. George Whitefield, of whom, though Dr. Johnson did not think very highly, it must be acknowledged that his eloquence was powerful, his views pious and charitable, his assiduity almost incredible; and, that since his death, the integrity of his character has been fully vindicated. Being himself a poet, Johnson was peculiarly happy in mentioning how many of the sons of Pembroke were poets; adding, with a smile of sportive triumph, 'Sir, we are a nest of singing birds.'

Life of Johnson

307 *The Doctor has a Frolic*

ONE night when Beauclerk and Langton had supped at a tavern in London, and sat till about three in the morning, it came into their heads to go and knock up Johnson, and see if they could prevail on him to join them in a ramble. They rapped violently at the door of his chambers in the Temple, till at last he appeared in his shirt, with his little black wig on the top of his head, instead of a nightcap, and a poker in his hand, imagining, probably, that some ruffians were coming to attack him. When he discovered who they were, and was told their errand, he smiled, and with great good humour agreed to their proposal: 'What, is it you, you dogs! I'll have a frisk with you.' He was soon dressed, and they sallied forth together into Covent-Garden, where the green-grocers and fruiterers were beginning to arrange their hampers, just come in from the country. Johnson made some attempts to help them; but the honest gardeners stared so at his figure and manner, and odd interference, that he soon saw his services were not relished. They then repaired to one of the neighbouring taverns, and made a bowl of that liquor called *Bishop*, which Johnson had always liked; while in joyous contempt of sleep, from which he had been roused, he repeated the festive lines,

Short, O short then be thy reign,
And give us to the world again!

They did not stay long, but walked down to the Thames, took a boat, and rowed to Billingsgate. Beauclerk and Johnson were so well pleased with their amusement, that they resolved to persevere in dissipation for the rest of the day: but Langton deserted them, being engaged to breakfast with some young ladies. Johnson scolded him for 'leaving his social friends, to go and sit with a set of wretched *un-idea'd* girls'. Garrick being told of this ramble, said to him smartly, 'I heard of your frolick t'other night. You'll be in the Chronicle.' Upon which Johnson afterwards observed, '*He* durst not do such a thing. His *wife* would not *let* him!'

Life of Johnson

308 *First Meeting with Johnson*

MR. THOMAS DAVIES the actor, who then kept a bookseller's shop in Russel-Street, Covent-Garden, told me that Johnson was very much his friend, and came frequently to his house, where he more than once invited me to meet him; but by some unlucky accident or other he was prevented from coming to us.

Mr. Thomas Davies was a man of good understanding and talents, with the advantage of a liberal education. Though somewhat pompous, he was an entertaining companion; and his literary performances have no inconsiderable share of merit. He was a friendly and very hospitable man. Both he and his wife (who has been celebrated for her beauty), though upon the stage for many years, maintained an uniform decency of character; and Johnson esteemed them, and lived in as easy an intimacy with them, as with any family which he used to visit. Mr. Davies recollected several of Johnson's remarkable sayings, and was one of the best of the many imitators of his voice and manner, while relating them. He increased my impatience more and more to see the extraordinary man whose works I highly valued, and whose conversation was reported to be so peculiarly excellent.

At last, on Monday the 16th of May, when I was sitting in Mr. Davies's back parlour, after having drunk tea with him and Mrs. Davies, Johnson unexpectedly came into the shop; and Mr. Davies having perceived him through the glass-door in the room in which we were sitting, advancing towards us,—he announced his aweful approach to me, somewhat in the manner of an actor in the part of Horatio, when he addresses Hamlet on the appearance of his father's ghost, 'Look, my Lord, it comes.' I found that I had a very perfect idea of Johnson's figure, from the portrait of him painted by Sir Joshua Reynolds soon after he had published his Dictionary, in the attitude of sitting in his easy chair in deep meditation, which was the first picture his friend did for him, which Sir Joshua has very kindly presented to me, and from which an engraving has been made for this work. Mr. Davies mentioned my name, and respectfully introduced me to him. I was much agitated; and recollecting his prejudice against the Scotch, of which I had heard much, I said to Davies, 'Don't tell where I come from.'—'From Scotland,' cried Davies roguishly. 'Mr. Johnson (said I), I do indeed come from Scotland, but I cannot help it.' I am willing to flatter myself that I meant this as light pleasantry to soothe and conciliate him, and not as an humiliating abasement at the expence of my country. But however that might be, this speech was somewhat unlucky; for with that quickness of wit for which he was so remarkable, he seized the expression 'come from Scotland', which I used in the sense of being of that country; and, as if I had said that I had come away from it, or left it, retorted, 'That, Sir, I find, is what a very great many of your countrymen cannot help.' This stroke stunned me a good deal; and when we had sat down, I felt myself not a little embarrassed, and apprehensive of what might come next. He then addressed himself to Davies: 'What do you think of Garrick? He has refused me an order for the play for Miss Williams, because he knows the house will be full, and that an order would be worth three shillings.' Eager to take any opening to get into conversation with him, I ventured to say, 'O, Sir, I cannot think Mr. Garrick would grudge such a trifle to you.' 'Sir (said he with a stern look), I have known David Garrick longer than you have done: and I know no right you have to talk to me on the subject.' Perhaps I deserved this check; for it was rather presumptuous in me, an entire stranger, to express any doubt of the justice of his animadversion upon his old acquaintance and pupil. I now felt myself much mortified, and began to think that the hope which I had long indulged of obtaining his acquaintance was blasted. And, in truth, had not my ardour been uncommonly strong, and my resolution uncommonly persevering, so rough a reception might have deterred me for ever from making any further attempts. Fortunately, however, I remained upon the field not wholly discomfited; and was soon rewarded by hearing some of his conversation, of which I preserved the following short minute, without marking the questions and observations by which it was produced.

'People (he remarked) may be taken in once, who imagine that an author is greater in private life than other men. Uncommon parts require uncommon opportunities for their exertion.

'In barbarous society, superiority of parts is of real consequence. Great strength or great wisdom is of much value to an individual. But in more polished times there are people to do everything for money; and then there are a number of other superiorities, such as those of birth and fortune, and rank, that dissipate men's attention, and leave no extraordinary share of respect for personal and intellectual superiority. This is wisely ordered by Providence, to preserve some equality among mankind.'

'Sir, this book ('The Elements of Criticism', which he had taken up) is a pretty essay, and deserves to be held in some estimation, though much of it is chimerical.'

Speaking of one who with more than ordinary boldness attacked public measures and the royal family, he said, 'I think he is safe from the law, but he is an abusive scoundrel; and instead of applying to my Lord Chief Justice to punish him, I would send half a dozen footmen and have him well ducked.'

'The notion of liberty amuses the people of England, and helps to keep off the *taedium vitae*. When a butcher tells you that his heart bleeds for his country, he has, in fact, no uneasy feeling.' . . .

I was highly pleased with the extraordinary vigour of his conversation, and regretted that I was drawn away from it by an engagement at another place. I had, for a part of the evening, been left alone with him, and had ventured to make an observation now and then, which he received very civilly; so that I was satisfied that though there was a roughness in his manner, there was no ill-nature in his disposition. Davies followed me to the door, and when I complained to him a little of the hard blows which the great man had given me, he kindly took upon him to console me by saying, 'Don't be uneasy. I can see he likes you very well.'

Life of Johnson

'JUNIUS'

? SIR PHILIP FRANCIS 1740–1818

309 *To the Duke of Grafton*

If I were personally your enemy, I might pity and forgive you. You have every claim to compassion, that can arise from misery and distress. The condition you are reduced to would disarm a private enemy of his resentment, and leave no consolation to the most vindictive spirit, but that such an object, as you are, would disgrace the dignity of revenge. But in the relation you have borne to this country, you have no title to indulgence; and if I had followed the dictates of my own opinion, I never should have allowed you the respite of a moment. In your public character, you have injured every subject of the empire; and though an individual is not authorised to forgive the injuries done to society, he is called upon to assert his separate share in the public resentment. I submitted however to the judgment of men, more moderate, perhaps more candid than myself. For my own part, I do not pretend to understand those prudent forms of decorum, those gentle rules of discretion, which some men endeavour to unite with the conduct of the greatest and most hazardous affairs. Engaged in the defence of an honourable cause, I would take a decisive part.—I should scorn to provide for a future retreat, or to keep terms with a man, who preserves no measures with the public. Neither the abject submission of deserting his post in the hour of danger, nor even the sacred shield of cowardice should protect him. I would pursue him through life, and try the last exertion of my abilities to preserve the perishable infamy of his name, and make it immortal.

The Letters of Junius

WILLIAM PALEY

1743–1805

310 *Ingratitude for Common Benefits*

ONE great cause of our insensibility to the goodness of the Creator is the very *extensiveness* of his bounty. We prize but little, what we share only in common with the rest, or with the generality, of our species. When we hear of blessings, we think forthwith of successes, of prosperous fortunes, of honors, riches, preferments, i. e. of those advantages and superiorities over others, which we happen either to possess, or to be in pursuit of, or to covet. The common benefits of our nature entirely escape us. Yet these are the great things. These constitute, what most properly ought to be accounted blessings of Providence; what alone, if we might so speak, are worthy of its care. Nightly rest and daily bread, the ordinary use of our limbs, and senses, and understandings, are gifts which admit of no comparison with any other. Yet, because almost every man we meet with possesses these, we leave them out of our enumeration. They raise no sentiment: they move no gratitude. Now, herein, is our judgement perverted by our selfishness. A blessing ought in truth to be the *more* satisfactory, the bounty at least of the donor is rendered more conspicuous, by its very diffusion, its commonness, its cheapness; by its falling to the lot, and forming the happiness, of the great bulk and body of our species, as well as of ourselves. Nay even when we do not possess it, it ought to be matter of thankfulness that others do.

Natural Theology

THOMAS HOLCROFT

1745–1809

311 *Life in a Racing-Stable*

ALL the boys in the stable rise at the same hour, from half-past two in spring, to between four and five in the depth of winter. The horses hear them when they awaken each other, and neigh, to denote their eagerness to be fed. Being dressed, the boy begins with carefully clearing out the manger, and giving a feed of oats, which he is obliged no less carefully to sift. He then proceeds to dress the litter; that is, to shake the bed on which the horse has been lying, remove whatever is wet or unclean, and keep the remaining straw in the stable for another time. The whole stables are then thoroughly swept, the few places for fresh air are kept open, the great heat of the stable gradually cooled, and the horse, having ended his first feed, is roughly cleaned and dressed. In about half an hour after they begin, or a little better, the horses have been rubbed down, and reclothed, saddled, each turned in his stall, then bridled, mounted, and the whole string goes out to morning exercise; he that leads being the first: for each boy knows his place.

Except by accident, the race-horse never trots. He must either walk or gallop; and in exercise, even when it is the hardest, the gallop begins slowly and gradually, and increases till the horse is nearly at full speed. When he has galloped half a mile, the boy begins to push him forward, without relaxation, for another half-mile. This is at the period when the horses are in full exercise, to which they come by degrees. The boy that can best regulate these degrees among those of light weight, is generally chosen to lead the gallop; that is, he goes first out of the stable, and first returns. . .

The morning's exercise often extends to four hours, and the evening's to much about the same time. Being once in the stable, each lad begins his labour. He leads the horse into his stall, ties him up, rubs down his legs with straw, takes off his saddle and body clothes; curries him carefully, then with both curry-comb and brush, never leaves him till he has thoroughly cleaned his skin, so that neither spot nor wet, nor any appearance of neglect may be seen about him. The horse is then reclothed, and suffered to repose for some time, which is first employed in gratifying his hunger, and recovering from his weariness. All this is performed, and the stables are once more shut up, about nine o'clock.

Accustomed to this life, the boys are very little overcome by fatigue, except that early in the morning they may be drowsy. I have sometimes fallen slightly asleep at the beginning of the first brushing gallop. But if they are not weary, they are hungry, and they make themselves ample amends for all they have done. Nothing perhaps can exceed the enjoyment of a stable-boy's breakfast: what then may not be said of mine, who had so long been used to suffer hunger, and so seldom found the means of satisfying it? Our breakfast consisted of new milk, or milk porridge, then the cold meat of the preceding day, most exquisite Gloucester cheese, fine white bread, and concluded with plentiful draughts of table beer. All this did not overload the stomach, or in the least deprive me of my youthful activity, except that like others I might sometimes take a nap for an hour, after so small a portion of sleep.

For my own part, so total and striking was the change which had taken place in my situation, that I could not but feel it very sensibly. I was more conscious of it than most boys would have been, and therefore not a little satisfied. The former part of my life had most of it been spent in turmoil, and often in singular wretchedness. I had been exposed to every want, every weariness, and every occasion of despondency, except that such poor sufferers become reconciled to, and almost insensible of suffering, and boyhood and beggary are fortunately not prone to despond. Happy had been the meal where I had enough; rich to me was the rag that kept me warm; and heavenly the pillow, no matter what, or how hard, on which I could lay my head to sleep.

Memoirs, written by Himself

PAUL JONES

(John Paul) 1747–1792

312 *Naval Strategy*

IN my judgment, there has never been an occasion in all the naval wars between France and England when the opportunity was so distinctly and so overwhelmingly on the side of France as in those few October days in 1781, off the Capes of the Chesapeake —when France actually had, for the moment, command of the sea.

Now, my dear Kersaint, you know me too well to accuse me of self-vaunting. You will not consider me vain, in view of your knowledge of what happened in the past off Carrickfergus, off Old Flamboro' Head, and off the Liman in the Black Sea, if I say that, had I stood—fortunately or unfortunately—in the shoes of de Grasse, there would have been disaster to some one off the Capes of the Chesapeake ; disaster of more lasting significance than an orderly retreat of a beaten fleet to a safe port. To put it a little more strongly, there was a moment when the chance to destroy the enemy's fleet would have driven from me all thought of the conjoint strategy of the campaign as a whole.

I could not have helped it.

And I have never since ceased to mourn the failure of the Count de Grasse to be as imprudent as I could not have helped being on that grandest of all occasions.

Howbeit, as I have already said, the object of grand strategy in that operation was accomplished by the manœuvring of the Count de Grasse without general action-in-line. But I confess that under similar conditions the temptation to destroy as well as repulse the fleet of the enemy would have been resistless, had I been the commander. It would have cost more men and perhaps a ship or two ; but, in my opinion, success in naval warfare is measured more perfectly by the extent to which you can capture or sink the ships and kill the seamen of the enemy than by the promptness with which you can force him, by skilful manœuvre or distant cannonade, to sheer off and thereby, with your consent, avoid a conflict that could hardly result otherwise than in conquest for you and destruction to him.

You will by no means infer from these cursory observations that I fail to appreciate, within my limited capacity, the grandeur of the tactical combinations, the skill of the intricate manœuvres, and the far-sighted, long thought-out demonstrations by which the Count de Toulouse drove Rooke out of the Mediterranean in August, 1704, with no more ado than the comparatively bloodless battle off Malaga; or the address with which La Galissonière repulsed Byng from Minorca in 1756 by a long-range battle of which the only notable casualty was the subsequent execution of Byng by his own Government for the alleged crime of failing to destroy the fleet opposed to him! or the brilliant campaign of my noble friend, the Count D'Orvilliers, off Ushant in July, 1778, when he forced Keppel to retreat ignominiously to England; not by stress of defeat, but by the cunningly planned and adroitly executed expedient of avoiding, on any terms but his own, the battle which Keppel vainly tried to force upon him. Let me assure you that none of these great events has been lost upon my sense of admiration.

And yet, my dear Kersaint, one reflection persecutes me, to mar all my memories and baffle all my admiration. This is the undeniable fact that the English ships and English sailors whom La Galissonière manœuvred away from Minorca, under Byng, in 1756, remained intact and lived to ruin Conflans in Quiberon Bay three years later under Sir Edward Hawke; and that the ships and the seamen of Graves, whom de Grasse permitted to escape from his clutches off the Capes of the Chesapeake in October, 1781, were left intact, and lived to discomfit de Grasse himself off Santa Lucia and Dominica in April, 1782, under Rodney.

You know, of course, my dear Kersaint, that my own opportunities in naval warfare have been but few and feeble in comparison with such as I have mentioned. But I do not doubt your ready agreement with me if I say that the hostile ships and commanders that I have thus far enjoyed the opportunity of meeting did not give any one much trouble thereafter. True, this has been on a small scale; but that was no fault of mine. I did my best with the weapons given to me. The rules of conduct, the maxims of action, and the tactical instincts that serve to gain small victories may always be expanded into the winning of great ones with suitable opportunity; because in human affairs the sources of success are ever to be found in the fountains of quick resolve and swift stroke; and it seems to be a law inflexible and inexorable that he who will not risk cannot win.

Letter to Vice-Admiral the Comte de Kersaint, 1791

FANNY BURNEY

1752–1840

313 *The Holborn Beau*

I COULD almost have laughed when I looked at Mr. Smith, who no sooner saw me addressed by Sir Clement, than, retreating aloof from the company, he seemed to lose at once all his happy self-sufficiency and conceit: looking now at the baronet, now at himself; surveying, with sorrowful eyes, his dress, struck with his air, his gestures, his easy gaiety; he gazed at him with envious admiration, and seemed himself, with conscious inferiority, to shrink into nothing.

Observing that Sir Clement seemed disposed to renew his enquiries, I turned towards one of the paintings, and, pretending to be very much occupied in looking at it, asked M. Du Bois some questions concerning the figures.

'O! *Mon Dieu!*' cried Madame Duval, 'don't ask him; your best way is to ask Mr. Smith, for he 's been here the oftenest. Come, Mr. Smith, I dare say you can tell us all about them.'

'Why, yes, Ma'am, yes,' said Mr. Smith: who, brightening up at this application, advanced towards us with an air of assumed importance, which, however, sat very uneasily upon him, and begged to know what he should explain first: 'For I have attended,' said he, 'to all these paintings, and know every thing in them perfectly well; for I am rather fond of pictures, Ma'am; and, really, I must say, I think a pretty picture is a—a very—is really a very—is something very pretty—'

'So do I too,' said Madame Duval; 'but pray now, Sir, tell us who that is meant for,' pointing to a figure of Neptune.

'That!—why, that, Ma'am, is,—Lord bless me, I can't think how I come to be so stupid, but really I have forgot his name;—and yet, I know it as well as my own too:—however, he 's a *General*, Ma'am, they are all Generals.'

I saw Sir Clement bite his lips; and, indeed, so did I mine.

'Well,' said Madame Duval, 'it 's the oddest dress for a General ever I see!'

'He seems so capital a figure,' said Sir Clement, to Mr. Smith, 'that I imagine he must be *Generalissimo* of the whole army.'

'Yes, Sir, yes,' answered Mr. Smith, respectfully bowing, and highly delighted at being thus referred to, 'you are perfectly right;—but I cannot for my life think of his name;—perhaps, Sir, you may remember it?'

'No, really,' replied Sir Clement, 'my acquaintance among the Generals is not so extensive.'

The ironical tone of voice in which Sir Clement spoke entirely disconcerted Mr. Smith; who again retiring to an humble distance, seemed sensibly mortified at the failure of his attempt to recover his consequence.

Evelina

314 *Impeachment of Hastings*

HIS [Burke's] opening had struck me with the highest admiration of his powers, from the eloquence, the imagination, the fire, the diversity of expression, and the ready flow of language, with which he seemed gifted, in a most superior manner, for any and every purpose to which rhetoric could lead. 'And when he came to his two narratives,' I continued, 'when he related the particulars of those dreadful murders, he interested, he engaged, he at last overpowered me; I felt my cause lost. I could hardly keep my seat. My eyes dreaded a single glance towards a man so accused as Mr. Hastings; I wanted to sink on the floor, that they might be saved so painful a sight. I had no hope he could clear himself; not another wish in his favour remained. But when from this narration Mr. Burke proceeded to his own comments and declamation—when the charges of rapacity, cruelty, tyranny were general, and made with all the violence of personal detestation, and continued and aggravated without any further fact or illustration; then there appeared more of study than of truth, more of invective than of justice; and, in short, so little of proof to so much of passion, that in a very short time I began to lift up my head, my seat was no longer uneasy, my eyes were indifferent which way they looked, or what object caught them; and before I was myself aware of the declension of Mr. Burke's powers over my feelings, I found myself a mere spectator in a public place, and looking all around it, with my opera-glass in my hand!' *Diary*

GEORGE CRABBE

1754–1832

315 *A Letter to Burke*

[1781]

SIR,—I am sensible that I need even your talents to apologize for the freedom I now take; but I have a plea which, however simply urged, will, with a mind like yours, Sir, procure me pardon: I am one of those outcasts on the world who are without a friend, without employment, and without bread.

Pardon me a short preface. I had a partial father, who gave me a better education than his broken fortune would have allowed; and a better than was necessary, as he could give me that only. I was designed for the profession of physic; but not having wherewithal to complete the requisite studies, the design but served to convince me of a parent's affection, and the error it had occasioned. In April last, I came to London, with three pounds, and flattered myself this would be sufficient to supply me with the common necessaries of life, till my abilities should procure me more; of these I had the highest opinion, and a poetical vanity contributed to my delusion. I knew little of the world, and had read books only: I wrote, and fancied perfection in my compositions; when I wanted bread they promised me affluence, and soothed me with dreams of reputation, whilst my appearance subjected me to contempt.

Time, reflection, and want, have shown me my mistake. I see my trifles in that which I think the true light; and whilst I deem them such, have yet the opinion that holds them superior to the common run of poetical publications. . . .

Can you, Sir, in any degree, aid me with propriety? Will you ask any demonstrations of my veracity? I have imposed upon myself, but I have been guilty of no other imposition. Let me, if possible, interest your compassion. I know those of rank and fortune are teased with frequent petitions, and are compelled to refuse the requests even of those whom they know to be in distress; it is, therefore, with a distant hope I ventured to solicit such favour; but you will forgive me, Sir, if you do not think proper to relieve. It is impossible that sentiments like yours can proceed from any but a humane and generous heart.

I will call upon you, Sir, to-morrow, and if I have not the happiness to obtain credit with you, I must submit to my fate. My existence is a pain to myself, and every one near and dear to me are distressed in my distresses. G. CRABBE.

WILLIAM COBBETT

1762–1835

316 *The Sandpit*

IN quitting Tilford we came on to the land belonging to Waverly Abbey, and then, instead of going on to the town of Farnham, veered away to the left towards *Wrecklesham*, in order to cross the Farnham and Alton turnpike-road, and to come on by the side of *Crondall* to *Odiham*. We went a little out of the way to go to a place called the *Bourn*, which lies in the heath at about a mile from Farnham. It is a winding narrow valley, down which, during the wet season of the year, there runs a stream beginning at the *Holt Forest*, and emptying itself into the *Wey* just below Moor-Park, which was the seat of *Sir William Temple* when *Swift* was residing with him. We went to this Bourn in order that I might show my son the spot where I received the rudiments of my education. There is a little hop-garden in which I used to work when from eight to ten years old; from which I have scores of times run to follow the hounds, leaving the hoe to do the best that it could to destroy the weeds; but the most interesting thing was a *sand-hill*, which goes from a part of the heath down to the rivulet. As a due mixture of pleasure with toil, I, with two brothers, used occasionally to *disport* ourselves, as the lawyers call it, at this sand-hill. Our diversion was this: we used to go to the top of the hill, which was steeper than the roof of a house; one used to draw his arms out of the sleeves of his smock-frock, and lay himself down with his arms by his sides; and then the others, one at head, and the other at feet, sent him rolling down the hill like a barrel or a log of wood. By the time he got to the bottom, his hair, eyes, ears, nose, and mouth, were all full of this loose sand; then the others took their turn, and at every roll, there was a monstrous spell of laughter. I had often told my sons of this while they were very little, and I now took one of them to see the spot. But, that was not all. This was the spot where I was receiving my *education*; and this was the sort of education; and I am perfectly satisfied that if I had not received such an education, or something very much like it; that, if I had been brought up a milksop, with a nursery-maid everlastingly at my heels, I should have been at this day as great a fool, as inefficient a mortal, as any of those frivolous idiots that are turned out from Winchester and Westminster School, or from any of those dens of dunces called Colleges and Universities. It is impossible to say how much I owe to that sand-hill; and I went to return it my thanks for the ability which it probably gave me to be one of the greatest terrors, to one of the greatest and most powerful bodies of knaves and fools, that ever were permitted to afflict this or any other country.

Rural Rides

JOHN NYREN

1764–1837

317 *Tom Walker*

AND now for those anointed clod-stumpers, the WALKERS, TOM and HARRY. Never sure came two such unadulterated rustics into a civilized community. How strongly are the figures of the men (of Tom's in particular) brought to my mind when they first presented themselves to the club upon Windmill-down. Tom's hard, ungain, scrag-of-mutton frame; wilted, apple-john face (he always looked twenty years older than he really was), his long spider legs, as thick at the ankles as at the hips, and perfectly straight all the way down—for the embellishment of a calf in Tom's leg Dame Nature had considered would be but a wanton superfluity. Tom was the driest and most rigid-limbed chap I ever knew; his skin was like the rind of an old oak, and as sapless. I have seen his knuckles handsomely knocked about from Harris's bowling; but never saw any blood upon his hands—you might just as well attempt to phlebotomize a mummy. This rigidity of muscle (or rather I should say of tendon, for muscle was another ingredient economized in the process of Tom's configuration)—this rigidity, I say, was carried into every motion. He moved like the rude machinery of a steam-engine in the infancy of construction, and when he ran, every member seemed ready to fly to the four winds. He toiled like a tar on horseback. The uncouth actions of these men furnished us, who prided ourselves upon a certain grace in movement and finished air, with an everlasting fund of amusement, and for some time they took no great fancy to me, because I used to worry, and tell them they could not play. They were, however, good hands when they first came among us, and had evidently received most excellent instruction; but after they had derived the advantage of first-rate practice, they became most admirable batters, and were the trustiest fellows (particularly Tom) in cases of emergency or difficulty. They were devilish troublesome customers to get out. I have very frequently known Tom to go in first, and remain to the very last man. He was the coolest, the most imperturbable fellow in existence: it used to be said of him that he had no nerves at all. Whether he was only practising, or whether he knew that the game was in a critical state, and that much depended upon his play, he was the same phlegmatic, unmoved man—he was the Washington of cricketers. Neither he nor his brother were active, yet both were effective fieldsmen. Upon one occasion, on the Mary-le-bone grounds, I remember Tom going in first, and Lord Frederick Beauclerc giving him the first four balls, all of an excellent length. First four or last four made no difference to Tom—he was always the same cool, collected fellow. Every ball he dropped down just before his bat. Off went his lordship's white hat—dash upon the ground (his constant action when disappointed)—calling him at the same time 'a confounded old beast'.—'I doan't care what ee zays,' said Tom, when one close by asked if he had heard Lord Frederick call him 'an old beast'. No, no; Tom was not the man to be flustered.

Young Cricketer's Tutor

ARTHUR WELLESLEY, DUKE OF WELLINGTON

1769–1852

318 *Chaplains for the Army*

I BELIEVE that you have attended a good deal to the establishment of the chaplains to the army, upon which I am now about to trouble you.

Notwithstanding all that has been done upon the subject, with a view to making their situation such as to induce respectable persons to accept of them, I fear that they are not yet sufficiently advantageous to insure the object. I believe the income, while they are employed abroad, to be sufficiently good, but that of retired chaplains, after service, is not; and the period of service required of them is too long.

You will observe that a man can scarcely be eligible to be an army chaplain till he is six or eight and twenty, after an expensive education; and it can scarcely be said that the pay of a retired chaplain, at thirty-six years of age, is what a respectable person would have acquired if he had followed any other line of the clerical profession besides the army. . .

I am very anxious upon this subject, not only from the desire which every man must have that so many persons as there are in this army should have the advantage of religious instruction, but from a knowledge that it is the greatest support and aid to military discipline and order.

It has, besides, come to my knowledge that Methodism is spreading very fast in the army. There are two, if not three, Methodist meetings in this town, of which one is in the Guards. The men meet in the evening, and sing psalms; and I believe a sergeant (Stephens) now and then gives them a sermon. Mr. Briscall has his eye upon these transactions, and would give me notice were they growing into anything which ought to be put a stop to; and the respectability of his character and conduct has given him an influence over these people which will prevent them from going wrong.

These meetings likewise prevail in other parts of the army. In the 9th Regiment there is one, at which two officers attend, Lieutenant —— and Dr. ——; and the commanding officer of the regiment has not yet been able to prevail upon them to discontinue this practice. Here, and in similar circumstances, we want the assistance of a respectable clergyman. By his personal influence and advice, and by that of true religion, he would moderate the zeal and enthusiasm of these gentlemen, and would prevent their meetings from being mischievous, if he did not prevail upon them to discontinue them entirely.

This is the only mode in which, in my opinion, we can touch these meetings. The meeting of soldiers in their cantonments to sing psalms or hear a sermon read by one of their comrades is, in the abstract, perfectly innocent, and it is a better way of spending their time than many others to which they are addicted; but it may become otherwise, and yet, till the abuse has made some progress, the commanding officer would have no knowledge of it, nor could he interfere. Even at last his interference must be guided by discretion, otherwise he will do more harm than good; and it can in no case be so effectual as that of a respectable clergyman.

I wish, therefore, you would turn your mind a little more to this subject, and arrange some plan by which the number of respectable and efficient clergymen with the army may be increased.

Dispatches

WILLIAM WORDSWORTH

1770–1850

319 *Sinews of Patriotism*

i

'IF my Neighbour fails,' says the true Patriot, 'more devolves upon me.' Discord and even treason are not, in a country situated as Spain is, the pure evils which, upon a superficial view, they appear to be. Never are a people so livelily admonished of the love they bear their country, and of the pride which they have in their common parent, as when they hear of some parricidal attempt of a false brother. For this cause chiefly, in times of national danger, are their fancies so busy in suspicion; which under such shape, though oftentimes producing dire and pitiable effects, is notwithstanding in its general character no other than that habit which has grown out of the instinct of self-preservation—elevated into a wakeful and affectionate apprehension for the whole, and ennobling its private and baser ways by the generous use to which they are converted. Nor ever has a good and loyal man such a swell of mind, such a clear insight into the constitution of virtue, and such a sublime sense of its power, as at the first tidings of some atrocious act of perfidy; when, having taken the alarm for human nature, a second thought recovers him; and his faith returns—gladsome from what has been revealed within himself, and awful from participation of the secrets in the profaner grove of humanity which that momentary blast laid open to his view.

The Convention of Cintra

ii

WOE be to that country whose military power is irresistible! I deprecate such an event for Great Britain scarcely less than for any other land. Scipio foresaw the evils with which Rome would be visited when no Carthage should be in existence for her to contend with. If a nation have nothing to oppose or to fear without, it cannot escape decay and concussion within. Universal triumph and absolute security soon betray a state into abandonment of that discipline, civil and military, by which its victories were secured. If the time should ever come when this island shall have no more formidable enemies by land than it has at this moment by sea, the extinction of all that it previously contained of good and great would soon follow. Indefinite progress, undoubtedly, there ought to be somewhere; but let that be in knowledge, in science, in civilization, in the increase of the numbers of the people, and in the augmentation of their virtue and happiness. But progress in conquest cannot be indefinite; and for that very reason, if for no other, it cannot be a fit object for the exertions of a people, I mean beyond certain limits, which, of course, will vary with circumstances. My prayer, as a patriot, is, that we may always have, somewhere or other, enemies capable of resisting us, and keeping us at arm's length.

Letter to Captain Pasley, 28 March 1811

320 *The Poet*

TO this knowledge which all men carry about with them, and to these sympathies in which, without any other discipline than that of our daily life, we are fitted to take delight, the Poet principally directs his attention. He considers man and nature as essentially adapted to each other, and the mind of man as naturally the mirror of the fairest and most interesting properties of nature. And thus the Poet, prompted by this feeling of pleasure, which accompanies him through the whole course of his studies, converses with general nature, with affections akin to those, which, through labour and length of time, the Man of Science has raised up in himself, by conversing with those particular parts of nature which are the objects of his studies. The knowledge both of the Poet and the Man of Science is pleasure; but the knowledge of the one cleaves to us as a necessary part of our existence, our natural and unalienable inheritance; the other is a personal and individual acquisition, slow to come to us, and by no habitual and direct sympathy connecting us with our fellow-beings. The Man of Science seeks truth as a remote and unknown benefactor; he cherishes and loves it in his solitude: the Poet, singing a song in which all human beings join with him, rejoices in the presence of truth as our visible friend and hourly companion. Poetry is the breath and finer spirit of all knowledge; it is the impassioned expression which is in the countenance of all Science. Emphatically may it be said of the Poet, as Shakespeare hath said of man, 'that he looks before and after.' He is the rock of defence for human nature; an upholder and preserver, carrying everywhere with him relationship and love. In spite of difference of soil and climate, of language and manners, of laws and customs: in spite of things silently gone out of mind, and things violently destroyed; the Poet binds together by passion and knowledge the vast empire of human society, as it is spread over the whole earth, and over all time. *Preface to Lyrical Ballads*

DOROTHY WORDSWORTH

1771–1855

321 *i. The Beggars*

A VERY tall woman, tall much beyond the measure of tall women, called at the door. She had on a very long brown cloak and a very white cap, without bonnet. Her face was excessively brown, but it had plainly once been fair. She led a little bare-footed child about two years old by the hand, and said her husband, who was a tinker, was gone before with the other children. I gave her a piece of bread. Afterwards on my way to Ambleside, beside the bridge at Rydale, I saw her husband sitting by the roadside, his two asses feeding beside him, and the two young children at play upon the grass. The man did not beg. I passed on and about a quarter of a mile further

I saw two boys before me, one about 10, the other about 8 years old, at play chasing a butterfly. They were wild figures, not very ragged, but without shoes and stockings. The hat of the elder was wreathed round with yellow flowers, the younger, whose hat was only a rimless crown, had stuck it round with laurel leaves. They continued at play till I drew very near, and then they addressed me with the begging cant and the whining voice of sorrow. I said 'I served your mother this morning.' (The boys were so like the woman who had called at . . . that I could not be mistaken.) 'O!' says the elder, 'you could not serve my mother for she 's dead, and my father 's on at the next town—he 's a potter.' I persisted in my assertion, and that I would give them nothing. Says the elder, 'Let's away,' and away they flew like lightning. They had however sauntered so long in their road that they did not reach Ambleside before me, and I saw them go up to Matthew Harrison's house with their wallet upon the elder's shoulder, and creeping with a beggar's complaining foot. On my return through Ambleside I met in the street the mother driving her asses, in the two panniers of one of which were the two little children, whom she was chiding and threatening with a wand which she used to drive on her asses, while the little things hung in wantonness over the pannier's edge.

ii. Friday 14th May 1802

A VERY cold morning—hail and snow showers all day. We went to Brothers wood, intending to get plants, and to go along the shore of the lake to the foot. We did go a part of the way, but there was no pleasure in stepping along that difficult sauntering road in this ungenial weather. We turned again, and walked backwards and forwards in Brothers wood. William tired himself with seeking an epithet for the cuckoo. I sate a while upon my last summer seat, the mossy stone. William's, unoccupied, beside me, and the space between, where Coleridge has so often lain. The oak trees are just putting forth yellow knots of leaves. The ashes with their flowers passing away, and leaves coming out; the blue hyacinth is not quite full blown; gowans are coming out; marsh marigolds in full glory; the little star plant, a star without a flower. We took home a great load of gowans, and planted them about the orchard. After dinner I worked bread, then came and mended stockings beside William; he fell asleep. After tea I walked to Rydale for letters. It was a strange night. The hills were covered over with a slight covering of hail or snow, just so as to give them a hoary winter look with the black rocks. The woods looked miserable, the coppices green as grass, which looked quite unnatural, and they seemed half shrivelled up, as if they shrank from the air. O, thought I! what a beautiful thing God has made winter to be, by stripping the trees, and letting us see their shapes and forms. What a freedom does it seem to give to the storms! There were several new flowers out, but I had no pleasure in looking at them. I walked as fast as I could back again with my letter from S. H. . . . Met William at the top of White Moss. . . . Near ten we came in. William and Molly had dug the ground and planted potatoes in my absence. We wrote to Coleridge; sent off bread and frocks to the C.'s. Went to bed at half-past eleven. William very nervous. After he was in bed, haunted with altering *The Rainbow*.

Journal

SIR WALTER SCOTT

1771–1832

322 *The Laird Evicts the Gipsies*

CERTAIN qualms of feeling had deterred Ellangowan from attending in person to see his tenants expelled. He left the executive part of the business to the officers of the law. . .

Mr. Bertram himself chose that day to make a visit to a friend at some distance. But it so happened, notwithstanding his precautions, that he could not avoid meeting his late tenants during their retreat from his property.

It was in a hollow way, near the top of a steep ascent, upon the verge of the Ellangowan estate, that Mr. Bertram met the gipsy procession. Four or five men formed the advanced guard, wrapped in long loose great-coats that hid their tall slender figures, as the large slouched hats, drawn over their brows, concealed their wild features, dark eyes, and swarthy faces. Two of them carried long fowling-pieces, one wore a broadsword without a sheath, and all had the Highland dirk, though they did not wear that weapon openly or ostentatiously. Behind them followed the train of laden asses, and small carts, or *tumblers* as they were called in that country, on which were laid the decrepit and the helpless, the aged and infant part of the exiled community. The women in their red cloaks and straw hats, the elder children with bare heads and bare feet, and almost naked bodies, had the immediate care of the little caravan. The road was narrow, running between two broken banks of sand. . .

When the Laird had pressed on with difficulty among a crowd of familiar faces, which had on all former occasions marked his approach with the reverence due to that of a superior being, but in which he now only read hatred and contempt, and had got clear of the throng, he could not help turning his horse, and looking back to mark the progress of their march. . .

The van had already reached a small and stunted thicket, which was at the bottom of the hill, and which gradually hid the line of march until the last stragglers disappeared.

His sensations were bitter enough. The race, it is true, which he had thus summarily dismissed from their ancient place of refuge, was idle and vicious; but had he endeavoured to render them otherwise? They were not more irregular characters now, than they had been while they were admitted to consider themselves as a sort of subordinate dependants of his family; and ought the mere circumstance of his becoming a magistrate to have made at once such a change in his conduct towards them? Some means of reformation ought at least to have been tried, before sending seven families at once upon the wide world, and depriving them of a degree of countenance which withheld them at least from atrocious guilt. There was also a natural yearning of heart on parting with so many known and familiar faces; and to this feeling Godfrey Bertram was peculiarly accessible, from the limited qualities of his mind, which sought its principal amusements among the petty objects around him. As he was about to turn his horse's head to pursue his journey, Meg Merrilies, who had lagged behind the troop, unexpectedly presented herself.

She was standing upon one of those high precipitous banks, which, as we before noticed, overhung the road;

so that she was placed considerably higher than Ellangowan, even though he was on horseback; and her tall figure, relieved against the clear blue sky, seemed almost of supernatural stature. We have noticed that there was in her general attire, or rather in her mode of adjusting it, somewhat of a foreign costume, artfully adopted perhaps for the purpose of adding to the effect of her spells and predictions, or perhaps from some traditional notions respecting the dress of her ancestors. On this occasion, she had a large piece of red cotton cloth rolled about her head in the form of a turban, from beneath which her dark eyes flashed with uncommon lustre. Her long and tangled black hair fell in elf-locks from the folds of this singular head-gear. Her attitude was that of a sibyl in frenzy, and she stretched out in her right hand a sapling bough, which seemed just pulled.

'I'll be d——d,' said the groom, 'if she has not been cutting the young ashes in the Dukit park!'—The Laird made no answer, but continued to look at the figure which was thus perched above his path.

'Ride your ways,' said the gipsy, 'ride your ways, Laird of Ellangowan—ride your ways, Godfrey Bertram!—This day have ye quenched seven smoking hearths—see if the fire in your ain parlour burn the blither for that. Ye have riven the thack off seven cottar houses—look if your ain roof-tree stand the faster.—Ye may stable your stirks in the shealings at Derncleugh—see that the hare does not couch on the hearthstane at Ellangowan.—Ride your ways, Godfrey Bertram—what do ye glower after our folk for?—There's thirty hearts there, that wad hae wanted bread ere ye had wanted sunkets, and spent their life-blood ere ye had scratched your finger.

Yes—there 's thirty yonder, from the auld wife of an hundred to the babe that was born last week, that ye have turned out o' their bits o' bields, to sleep with the tod and the blackcock in the muirs!—Ride your ways, Ellangowan.—Our bairns are hinging at our weary backs—look that your braw cradle at hame be the fairer spread up: not that I'm wishing ill to little Harry, or to the babe that 's yet to be born—God forbid—and make them kind to the poor, and better folk than their father!—And now, ride e'en your ways; for these are the last words ye'll ever hear Meg Merrilies speak, and this is the last reise that I'll ever cut in the bonny woods of Ellangowan.'

So saying, she broke the sapling she held in her hand, and flung it into the road. Margaret of Anjou, bestowing on her triumphant foes her keen-edged malediction, could not have turned from them with a gesture more proudly contemptuous. The Laird was clearing his voice to speak, and thrusting his hand in his pocket to find a half-crown; the gipsy waited neither for his reply nor his donation, but strode down the hill to overtake the caravan.

Ellangowan rode pensively home; and it was remarkable that he did not mention this interview to any of his family. The groom was not so reserved; he told the story at great length to a full audience in the kitchen, and concluded by swearing, that 'if ever the devil spoke by the mouth of a woman, he had spoken by that of Meg Merrilies that blessed day'.

Guy Mannering

323 *The Phoca*

'BUT what is that yonder?' exclaimed Hector, interrupting himself.

'One of the herd of Proteus,' said the Antiquary—'a *phoca*, or seal, lying asleep on the beach.'

Upon which M'Intyre, with the eagerness of a young sportsman, totally forgot both Ossian, Patrick, his uncle, and his wound, and exclaiming—'I shall have her! I shall have her!' snatched the walking-stick out of the hand of the astonished Antiquary, at some risk of throwing him down, and set off at full speed to get between the animal and the sea, to which element, having caught the alarm, she was rapidly retreating.

Not Sancho, when his master interrupted his account of the combatants of Pentapolin with the naked arm to advance in person to the charge of the flock of sheep, stood more confounded than Oldbuck at this sudden escapade of his nephew.

'Is the devil in him,' was his first exclamation, 'to go to disturb the brute that was never thinking of him!'—Then elevating his voice, 'Hector—nephew—fool—let alone the *phoca*—let alone the *phoca!*—they bite, I tell you, like furies. He minds me no more than a post. There—there they are at it—Gad, the *phoca* has the best of it! I am glad to see it,' said he, in the bitterness of his heart, though really alarmed for his nephew's safety—'I am glad to see it, with all my heart and spirit.'

In truth, the seal, finding her retreat intercepted by the light-footed soldier, confronted him manfully, and having sustained a heavy blow without injury, she knitted her brows as is the fashion of the animal when incensed, and making use at once of her forepaws and her unwieldy strength, wrenched the weapon out of the assailant's hand, overturned him on the sands, and scuttled away into the sea, without doing him any further injury. Captain M'Intyre, a good deal out of countenance at the issue of his exploit, just rose in time to receive the ironical congratulations of his uncle upon a single combat worthy to be commemorated by Ossian himself, 'since,' said the Antiquary, 'your magnanimous opponent hath fled, though not upon eagle's wings, from the foe that was low—— Egad, she walloped away with all the grace of triumph, and has carried my stick off also, by way of *spolia opima*.'

M'Intyre had little to answer for himself, except that a Highlander could never pass a deer, a seal, or a salmon, where there was a possibility of having a trial of skill with them, and that he had forgot one of his arms was in a sling. He also made his fall an apology for returning back to Monkbarns, and thus escaped the further raillery of his uncle, as well as his lamentations for his walking-stick.

'I cut it,' he said, 'in the classic woods of Hawthornden, when I did not expect always to have been a bachelor—I would not have given it for an ocean of seals—O Hector! Hector!—thy namesake was born to be the prop of Troy, and thou to be the plague of Monkbarns!'

The Antiquary

324 *A Lost Cause*

AMID this scene of confusion, a gentleman, plainly dressed in a riding-habit, with a black cockade in his hat, but without any arms except a *couteau-de-*

chasse, walked into the apartment without ceremony. He was a tall, thin, gentlemanly man, with a look and bearing decidedly military. He had passed through their guards, if in the confusion they now maintained any, without stop or question, and now stood, almost unarmed, among armed men, who nevertheless gazed on him as on the angel of destruction.

'You look coldly on me, gentlemen,' he said. 'Sir Richard Glendale—my Lord——, we were not always such strangers. Ha, Pate-in-Peril, how is it with you? and you, too, Ingoldsby—I must not call you by any other name—why do you receive an old friend so coldly? But you guess my errand.'

'And are prepared for it, general,' said Redgauntlet; 'we are not men to be penned up like sheep for the slaughter.'

'Pshaw! you take it too seriously—let me speak but one word with you.'

'No words can shake our purpose,' said Redgauntlet, 'were your whole command, as I suppose is the case, drawn round the house.'

'I am certainly not unsupported,' said the general; 'but if you would hear me'——

'Hear *me*, sir,' said the Wanderer, stepping forward; 'I suppose I am the mark you aim at—I surrender myself willingly, to save these gentlemen's danger—let this at least avail in their favour.'

An exclamation of 'Never, never!' broke from the little body of partisans, who threw themselves round the unfortunate prince, and would have seized or struck down Campbell, had it not been that he remained with his arms folded, and a look, rather indicating impatience because they would not hear him, than the least apprehension of violence at their hand.

At length he obtained a moment's silence. 'I do not,' he said, 'know this gentleman'—(making a profound bow to the unfortunate prince)—'I do not wish to know him; it is a knowledge which would suit neither of us.'

'Our ancestors, nevertheless, have been well acquainted,' said Charles, unable to suppress, even at that hour of dread and danger, the painful recollections of fallen royalty.

'In one word, General Campbell,' said Redgauntlet, 'is it to be peace or war? You are a man of honour, and we can trust you.'

'I thank you, sir,' said the general; 'and I reply, that the answer to your question rests with yourself. Come, do not be fools, gentlemen; there was perhaps no great harm meant or intended by your gathering together in this obscure corner, for a bear-bait or a cock-fight, or whatever other amusement you may have intended, but it was a little imprudent, considering how you stand with government, and it has occasioned some anxiety. Exaggerated accounts of your purpose have been laid before government by the information of a traitor in your own counsels; and I was sent down post to take the command of a sufficient number of troops, in case these calumnies should be found to have any real foundation. I have come here, of course, sufficiently supported both with cavalry and infantry, to do whatever might be necessary; but my commands are—and I am sure they agree with my inclination—to make no arrests, nay, to make no further inquiries of any kind, if this good assembly will consider their own interest so far as to give up their immediate purpose, and return quietly home to their own houses.'

'What!—all?' exclaimed Sir Richard Glendale—'all, without exception?'

'ALL, without one single exception,' said the general; 'such are my orders. If you accept my terms, say so, and make haste; for things may happen to interfere with his Majesty's kind purposes towards you all.'

'His Majesty's kind purposes!' said the Wanderer. 'Do I hear you aright, sir?'

'I speak the king's very words, from his very lips,' replied the general. '"I will," said his Majesty, "deserve the confidence of my subjects by reposing my security in the fidelity of the millions who acknowledge my title—in the good sense and prudence of the few who continue, from the errors of education, to disown it." His Majesty will not even believe that the most zealous Jacobites who yet remain can nourish a thought of exciting a civil war, which must be fatal to their families and themselves, besides spreading bloodshed and ruin through a peaceful land. He cannot even believe of his kinsman, that he would engage brave and generous though mistaken men, in an attempt which must ruin all who have escaped former calamities; and he is convinced, that, did curiosity or any other motive lead that person to visit this country, he would soon see it was his wisest course to return to the continent; and his Majesty compassionates his situation too much to offer any obstacle to his doing so.'

'Is this real?' said Redgauntlet. 'Can you mean this? Am I—are all, are any of these gentlemen at liberty, without interruption, to embark in yonder brig, which, I see, is now again approaching the shore?'

'You, sir—all—any of the gentlemen present,' said

the general,—'all whom the vessel can contain, are at liberty to embark uninterrupted by me; but I advise none to go off who have not powerful reasons unconnected with the present meeting, for this will be remembered against no one.'

'Then, gentlemen,' said Redgauntlet, clasping his hands together as the words burst from him, 'the cause is lost for ever!'

Redgauntlet

325 *The Trial of Evan Dhu*

'FERGUS MAC-IVOR of Glennaquoich, otherwise called Vich Ian Vohr, and Evan Mac-Ivor, in the Dhu of Tarrascleugh, otherwise called Evan Dhu, otherwise called Evan Maccombich, or Evan Dhu Maccombich—you, and each of you, stand attainted of high treason. What have you to say for yourselves why the Court should not pronounce judgement against you, that you die according to law?'

Fergus, as the presiding Judge was putting on the fatal cap of judgement, placed his own bonnet upon his head, regarded him with a steadfast and stern look, and replied in a firm voice, 'I cannot let this numerous audience suppose that to such an appeal I have no answer to make. But what I have to say, you would not bear to hear, for my defence would be your condemnation. Proceed, then, in the name of God, to do what is permitted to you. Yesterday, and the day before, you have condemned loyal and honourable blood to be poured forth like water. Spare not mine. Were that of all my ancestors in my veins, I would have perilled it in this quarrel.' He resumed his seat, and refused again to rise.

Evan Maccombich looked at him with great earnestness, and, rising up, seemed anxious to speak; but the confusion of the court, and the perplexity arising from thinking in a language different from that in which he was to express himself, kept him silent. There was a murmur of compassion among the spectators, from an idea that the poor fellow intended to plead the influence of his superior as an excuse for his crime. The Judge commanded silence, and encouraged Evan to proceed.

'I was only ganging to say, my lord,' said Evan, in what he meant to be in an insinuating manner, 'that if your excellent honour, and the honourable Court, would let Vich Ian Vohr go free just this once, and let him gae back to France, and no to trouble King George's government again, that ony six o' the very best of his clan will be willing to be justified in his stead; and if you'll just let me gae down to Glennaquoich, I'll fetch them up to ye mysell, to head or hang, and you may begin wi' me the very first man.'

Notwithstanding the solemnity of the occasion, a sort of laugh was heard in the court at the extraordinary nature of the proposal. The Judge checked this indecency, and Evan, looking sternly around, when the murmur abated, 'If the Saxon gentlemen are laughing,' he said, 'because a poor man, such as me, thinks my life, or the life of six of my degree, is worth that of Vich Ian Vohr, it 's like enough they may be very right; but if they laugh because they think I would not keep my word, and come back to redeem him, I can tell them they ken neither the heart of a Hielandman, nor the honour of a gentleman.'

There was no further inclination to laugh among the audience, and a dead silence ensued.

Waverley

326 *The Banner of England*

THE king was soon at the foot of St. George's Mount, the sides as well as platform of which were now surrounded and crowded, partly by those belonging to the Duke of Austria's retinue, who were celebrating, with shouts of jubilee, the act which they considered as an assertion of national honour; partly by bystanders of different nations, whom dislike to the English, or mere curiosity, had assembled together, to witness the end of these extraordinary proceedings. Through this disorderly troop Richard burst his way, like a goodly ship under full sail, which cleaves her forcible passage through the rolling billows, and heeds not that they unite after her passage and roar upon her stern. . .

'Who has dared,' he said, laying his hands upon the Austrian standard, and speaking in a voice like the sound which precedes an earthquake; 'who has dared to place this paltry rag beside the banner of England?'

The archduke wanted not personal courage, and it was impossible he could hear this question without reply. Yet, so much was he troubled and surprised by the unexpected arrival of Richard, and affected by the general awe inspired by his ardent and unyielding character, that the demand was twice repeated, in a tone which seemed to challenge heaven and earth, ere the archduke replied with such firmness as he could command, 'It was I, Leopold of Austria.'

'Then shall Leopold of Austria,' replied Richard, 'presently see the rate at which his banner and his pretensions are held by Richard of England.'

So saying, he pulled up the standard-spear, splintered it to pieces, threw the banner itself on the ground, and placed his foot upon it.

'Thus,' said he, 'I trample on the banner of Austria —Is there a knight among your Teutonic chivalry, dare impeach my deed?'

There was a momentary silence; but there are no braver men than the Germans.

'I,' and 'I,' and 'I,' was heard from several knights of the duke's followers; and he himself added his voice to those which accepted the King of England's defiance.

'Why do we dally thus?' said the Earl Wallenrode, a gigantic warrior from the frontiers of Hungary: 'Brethren, and noble gentlemen, this man's foot is on the honour of your country—Let us rescue it from violation, and down with the pride of England!'

So saying, he drew his sword, and struck at the king a blow which might have proved fatal, had not the Scot intercepted and caught it upon his shield.

'I have sworn,' said King Richard—and his voice was heard above all the tumult, which now waxed wild and loud—'never to strike one whose shoulder bears the cross; therefore live, Wallenrode—but live to remember Richard of England.'

As he spoke, he grasped the tall Hungarian round the waist, and, unmatched in wrestling as in other military exercises, hurled him backwards with such violence that the mass flew as if discharged from a military engine, not only through the ring of spectators who witnessed the extraordinary scene, but over the edge of the mount itself, down the steep side of which Wallenrode rolled headlong, until, pitching at length upon his shoulder, he dislocated the bone, and lay like one dead.

The Talisman

SYDNEY SMITH

1771–1845

327 *Noodle's Oration*

'WHAT would our ancestors say to this, Sir? How does this measure tally with their institutions? How does it agree with their experience? Are we to put the wisdom of yesterday in competition with the wisdom of centuries? (*Hear, hear!*) Is beardless youth to show no respect for the decisions of mature age? (*Loud cries of hear! hear!*) If this measure be right, would it have escaped the wisdom of those Saxon progenitors to whom we are indebted for so many of our best political institutions? Would the Dane have passed it over? Would the Norman have rejected it? Would such a notable discovery have been reserved for these modern and degenerate times? Besides, Sir, if the measure itself is good, I ask the honourable gentleman if this is the time for carrying it into execution—whether, in fact, a more unfortunate period could have been selected than that which he has chosen? If this were an ordinary measure, I should not oppose it with so much vehemence; but, Sir, it calls in question the wisdom of an irrevocable law—of a law passed at the memorable period of the Revolution. What right have we, Sir, to break down this firm column, on which the great men of that day stamped a character of eternity? Are not all authorities against this measure—Pitt, Fox, Cicero, and the Attorney and Solicitor General? The proposition is new, Sir; it is the first time it was ever heard in this House. I am not prepared, Sir—this House is not prepared, to receive it. The measure implies a distrust of his Majesty's government; their disapproval is sufficient to warrant opposition. Precaution only is requisite where danger is apprehended. Here the high character of the individuals in question is a sufficient guarantee against any ground of alarm. Give not, then, your sanction to this measure; for, whatever be its character, if you do give your sanction to it, the same man by whom this is proposed, will propose to you others to which it will be impossible to give your consent. I care very little, Sir, for the ostensible measure; but what is there behind? What are the honourable gentleman's future schemes? If we pass this bill, what fresh concessions may he not require? What further degradation is he planning for his country? Talk of evil and inconvenience, Sir! look to other countries—study other aggregations and societies of men, and then see whether the laws of this country demand a remedy or deserve a panegyric. Was the honourable gentleman (let me ask him) always of this way of thinking? Do I not remember when he was the advocate in this House of very opposite opinions? I not only quarrel with his present sentiments, Sir, but I declare very frankly, I do not like the party with which he acts. If his own motives were as pure as possible, they cannot but suffer contamination from those with whom he is politically associated. This measure may be a boon to the constitution; but I will accept no favour to the constitution from such hands. (*Loud cries of hear! hear!*) I profess myself, Sir, an honest and upright member of the British Parliament, and I am not afraid to profess myself an enemy to all change and all innovation. I am satisfied with things as they are; and it will be my pride and pleasure to hand down this country to my children as I received it from those who preceded me. The honourable gentleman pretends to justify the severity with which he has attacked the noble Lord who presides in the Court of Chancery; but I say such attacks are pregnant with mischief to Government itself. Oppose Ministers, you oppose Government: disgrace Ministers, you disgrace Government: bring Ministers into contempt, you bring Government into contempt; and anarchy and civil war are the consequences. Besides, Sir, the measure is unnecessary. Nobody complains of disorder in that shape in which it is the aim of your measure to propose a remedy to it. The business is one of the greatest importance; there is need of the greatest caution and circumspection. Do not let us be precipitate, Sir. It is impossible to foresee all consequences. Everything should be gradual: the example of a neighbouring nation should fill us with alarm! The honourable gentleman has taxed me with illiberality, Sir. I deny the charge. I hate innovation; but I love improvement. I am an enemy to the corruption of Government; but I defend its influence. I dread Reform; but I dread it only when it is intemperate. I consider the liberty of the Press as the great Palladium of the Constitution; but, at the same time, I hold the licentiousness of the Press in the greatest abhorrence. Nobody is more conscious than I am of the splendid abilities of the honourable mover; but I tell him at once his scheme is too good to be practicable. It savours of Utopia. It looks well in theory; but it won't do in practice. It will not do, I repeat, Sir, in practice; and so the advocates of the measure will find, if unfortunately it should find its way through Parliament. (*Cheers.*) The source of that corruption to which the honourable member alludes, is in the minds of the people: so rank and extensive is that corruption, that no political reform can have any effect in removing it. Instead of reforming others—instead of reforming the State, the Constitution, and everything that is most excellent, let each man reform himself! let him look at home; he will find there enough to do, without looking abroad, and aiming at what is out of his power. (*Loud Cheers.*) And now, Sir, as it is frequently the custom in this House to end with a quotation, and as the gentleman who preceded me in the debate has anticipated me in my favourite quotation of "The strong pull and the long pull",—I shall end with the memorable words of the assembled Barons—"*Nolumus leges Angliæ mutari.*"'

Bentham on Fallacies

328 *Justice the Root of Patriotism*

THIS is what is called country. Equal rights to unequal possessions, equal justice to the rich and poor: this is what men come out to fight for, and to defend. Such a country has no legal injuries to remember, no legal murders to revenge, no legal robbery to redress; it is strong in its justice; it is then that the use and object of all this assemblage of gentlemen and arrangement of juries, and the deserved veneration in which we hold the character of English judges, is understood in all its bearings, and in its fullest effects; men die for such things—they cannot be subdued by foreign force where such just practices prevail. The sword of ambition is shivered to pieces against such a bulwark. Nations fall where judges are unjust, because there is nothing which the multitude think worth defending;

but nations do not fall which are treated as we are treated, but they rise as we have risen, and they shine as we have shone, and die as we have died, too much used to justice, and too much used to freedom, to care for that life which is not just and free. I call you all to witness if there be any exaggerated picture in this; the sword is just sheathed, the flag is just furled, the last sound of the trumpet has just died away. You all remember what a spectacle this country exhibited; one heart, one voice—one weapon, one purpose. And why? Because this country is a country of the law; because the judge is a judge for the peasant as well as for the palace; because every man's happiness is guarded by fixed rules from tyranny and caprice. This town this week, the business of the next few days, would explain to any enlightened European why other nations *did* fall in the storms of the world, and why we did *not* fall. The Christian patience you may witness, the impartiality of the judgment-seat, the disrespect of persons, the disregard of consequences. These attributes of justice do not end with arranging your conflicting rights, and mine; they give strength to the English people, duration to the English name; they turn the animal courage of this people into moral and religious courage, and present to the lowest of mankind plain reasons and strong motives why they should resist aggression from without, and bind themselves a living rampart round the land of their birth.

The Judge that Smites Contrary to the Law

SAMUEL TAYLOR COLERIDGE

1772–1834

329 *The Vale of Human Life*

THE first range of hills, that encircles the scanty vale of human life, is the horizon for the majority of its inhabitants. On *its* ridges the common sun is born and departs. From *them* the stars rise, and touching *them* they vanish. By the many, even this range, the natural limit and bulwark of the vale, is but imperfectly known. Its higher ascents are too often hidden by mists and clouds from uncultivated swamps, which few have courage or curiosity to penetrate. To the multitude below these vapors appear, now as the dark haunts of terrific agents, on which none may intrude with impunity; and now all *a-glow*, with colors not their own, they are gazed at as the splendid palaces of happiness and power. But in all ages there have been a few who, measuring and sounding the rivers of the vale at the feet of their furthest inaccessible falls, have learned that the sources must be far higher and far inward; a few, who even in the level streams have detected elements, which neither the vale itself or the surrounding mountains contained or could supply. How and whence to these thoughts, these strong probabilities, the ascertaining vision, the intuitive knowledge may finally supervene, can be learnt only by the fact. I might oppose to the question the words with which Plotinus supposes NATURE to answer a similar difficulty. 'Should any one interrogate her, how she works, if graciously she vouchsafe to listen and speak, she will reply, it behoves thee not to disquiet me with interrogatories, but to understand in silence even as I am silent, and work without words.'

Biographia Literaria

330 *Klopstock*

BELIEVE me, I walked with an impression of awe on my spirits, as W—— and myself accompanied Mr. Klopstock to the house of his brother, the poet, which stands about a quarter of a mile from the city gate. It is one of a row of little common-place summer-houses (for so they looked) with four or five rows of young meagre elm trees before the windows, beyond which is a green, and then a dead flat intersected with several roads. Whatever beauty (thought I) may be before the poet's eyes at present, it must certainly be purely of his own creation. We waited a few minutes in a neat little parlour, ornamented with the figures of two of the Muses and with prints, the subjects of which were from Klopstock's odes. The poet entered. I was much disappointed in his countenance, and recognised in it no likeness to the bust. There was no comprehension in the forehead, no weight over the eye-brows, no expression of peculiarity, moral or intellectual, in the eyes, no massiveness in the general countenance. He is, if anything, rather below the middle size. He wore very large half-boots, which his legs filled, so fearfully were they swoln. However, though neither W—— nor myself could discover any indications of sublimity or enthusiasm in his physiognomy, we were both equally impressed with his liveliness, and his kind and ready courtesy. He talked in French with my friend, and with difficulty spoke a few sentences to me in English. His enunciation was not in the least affected by the entire want of his upper teeth. . .

The subject changed to literature, and I inquired

in Latin concerning the History of German poetry and the elder German poets. To my great astonishment he confessed that he knew very little on the subject. He had indeed occasionally read one or two of their elder writers, but not so as to enable him to speak of their merits. Professor Ebeling, he said, would probably give me every information of this kind: the subject had not particularly excited his curiosity. He then talked of Milton and Glover, and thought Glover's blank verse superior to Milton's. . .

He told us that he had read Milton, in a prose translation, when he was fourteen. I understood him thus myself, and W—— interpreted Klopstock's French as I had already construed it. He appeared to know very little of Milton—or indeed of our poets in general. He spoke with great indignation of the English prose translation of his Messiah. All the translations had been bad, very bad—but the English was *no* translation—there were pages on pages not in the original:—and half the original was not to be found in the translation. W—— told him that I intended to translate a few of his odes as specimens of German lyrics—he then said to me in English, 'I wish you would render into English some select passages of the Messiah, and *revenge* me of your countryman!' It was the liveliest thing which he produced in the whole conversation. He told us, that his first ode was fifty years older than his last. I looked at him with much emotion—I considered him as the venerable father of German poetry; as a good man; as a Christian; seventy-four years old; with legs enormously swoln; yet active, lively, chearful, and kind, and communicative. My eyes felt as if a tear were swelling into them. . .

I must remind you, my friend, first, that these notes are not intended as specimens of Klopstock's intellectual power, or even '*colloquial prowess*,' to judge of which by an accidental conversation, and this with strangers, and those too foreigners, would be not only unreasonable, but calumnious. Secondly, I attribute little other interest to the remarks than what is derived from the celebrity of the person who made them. Lastly, if you ask me, whether I have read the Messiah, and what I think of it? I answer—as yet the first four books only: and as to my opinion (the reasons of which hereafter) you may guess it from what I could not help muttering to myself, when the good pastor this morning told me, that Klopstock was the German Milton——'a very *German* Milton indeed!!!'

Biographia Literaria

331 *The Verse and the Gloss*

THE moving Moon went up the sky,
And no where did abide:
Softly she was going up,
And a star or two beside—

In his loneliness and fixedness he yearneth towards the journeying Moon, and the stars that still sojourn, yet still move onward; and every where the blue sky belongs to them, and is their appointed rest, and their native country and their own natural homes, which they enter unannounced, as lords that are certainly expected and yet there is a silent joy at their arrival.

Rime of the Ancient Mariner

332 *Love of Nature*

THE love of Nature is ever returned double to us, not only the delighter in our delight, but by linking our sweetest, but of themselves perishable feelings to distinct and vivid images, which we ourselves, at times, and which a thousand casual recollections, recall to our memory. She is the preserver, the treasurer of our joys. Even in sickness and nervous diseases, she has peopled our imagination with lovely forms which have sometimes overpowered the inward pain and brought with them their old sensations. And even when all men have seemed to desert us and the friend of our heart has passed on, with one glance from his ‘ cold disliking eye ’—yet even then the blue heaven is spread out and bends over us, and the little tree still shelters us under its plumage as a second cope, a domestic firmament, and the low creeping gale will sigh in the heath-plant and soothe us by sound of sympathy till the lulled grief loses itself in fixed gaze on the purple heath-blossom, till the present beauty becomes a vision of memory.

Anima Poetae

ROBERT SOUTHEY

1774–1843

333 *Nelson's Departure from Portsmouth*

EARLY on the following morning he reached Portsmouth; and having dispatched his business on shore, endeavoured to elude the populace by taking a by-way to the beach; but a crowd collected in his train, pressing forward, to obtain a sight of his face: many were in tears, and many knelt down before him, and blessed him as he passed. England has had many heroes; but never one who so entirely possessed the love of his fellow-countrymen as Nelson. All men knew that his heart was as humane as it was fearless; that there was not in his nature the slightest alloy of selfishness or cupidity; but that, with perfect and entire devotion, he served his country with all his heart, and with all his soul, and with all his strength; and, therefore, they loved him as truly as and fervently as he loved England. They pressed upon the parapet, to gaze after him when his barge pushed off, and he was returning their cheers by waving his hat. The sentinels, who endeavoured to prevent them from trespassing upon this ground, were wedged among the crowd; and an officer, who, not very prudently upon such an occasion, ordered them to drive the people down with their bayonets, was compelled speedily to retreat; for the people would not be debarred from gazing, till the last moment, upon the hero—the darling hero of England!

Life of Nelson

334 *The Mourning for Nelson*

THE death of Nelson was felt in England as something more than a public calamity; men started at the intelligence, and turned pale, as if they had heard of the loss of a dear friend. An object of our admiration and affection, of our pride and of our hopes, was suddenly taken from us; and it seemed as if we had never, till then, known how deeply we loved and reverenced him. What the country had lost in its great naval hero—the greatest of our own, and of all former times, was scarcely taken into the account of grief. So perfectly, indeed, had he performed his part, that the maritime war, after the battle of Trafalgar, was considered at an end: the fleets of the enemy were not merely defeated, but destroyed: new navies must be built, and a new race of seamen reared for them, before the possibility of their invading our shores could again be contemplated. It was not, therefore, from any selfish reflection upon the magnitude of our loss that we mourned for him: the general sorrow was of a higher character. The people of England grieved that funeral ceremonies, and public monuments, and posthumous rewards, were all which they could now bestow upon him, whom the king, the legislature, and the nation, would have alike delighted to honour; whom every tongue would have blessed; whose presence in every village through which he might have passed would have wakened the church bells, have given school-boys a holiday, have drawn children from their sports to gaze upon him, and 'old men from the chimney corner', to look upon Nelson ere they died. The victory of Trafalgar was celebrated, indeed, with the usual forms of rejoicing, but they were without joy; for such already was the glory of the British navy, through Nelson's surpassing genius, that it scarcely seemed to receive any addition from the most signal victory that ever was achieved upon the seas: and the destruction of this mighty fleet, by which all the maritime schemes of France were totally frustrated, hardly appeared to add to our security or strength; for, while Nelson was living, to watch the combined squadrons of the enemy, we felt ourselves as secure as now, when they were no longer in existence.

There was reason to suppose, from the appearances

upon opening the body, that, in the course of nature, he might have attained, like his father, to a good old age. Yet he cannot be said to have fallen prematurely whose work was done; nor ought he to be lamented, who died so full of honours, and at the height of human fame. The most triumphant death is that of the martyr; the most awful that of the martyred patriot; the most splendid that of the hero in the hour of victory; and if the chariot and the horses of fire had been vouchsafed for Nelson's translation, he could scarcely have departed in a brighter blaze of glory. He has left us, not indeed his mantle of inspiration, but a name and an example, which are at this hour inspiring thousands of the youth of England: a name which is our pride, and an example which will continue to be our shield and our strength. Thus it is that the spirits of the great and the wise continue to live and to act after them; verifying, in this sense, the language of the old mythologist:

Τοὶ μὲν δαίμονές εἰσι Διὸς μεγάλου διὰ βουλὰς
Ἐσθλοί, ἐπιχθόνιοι, φύλακες θνητῶν ἀνθρώπων.

For gods they are, through high Jove's Counsels good,
Haunting the earth, the guardians of mankind.

Life of Nelson

JANE AUSTEN

1775–1817

335 *The John Dashwoods*

'IT was my father's last request to me,' replied her husband, 'that I should assist his widow and daughters.'

'He did not know what he was talking of, I dare say; ten to one but he was light-headed at the time.

Had he been in his right senses, he could not have thought of such a thing as begging you to give away half your fortune from your own child.'

'He did not stipulate for any particular sum, my dear Fanny; he only requested me, in general terms, to assist them, and make their situation more comfortable than it was in his power to do. Perhaps it would have been as well if he had left it wholly to myself. He could hardly suppose I should neglect them. But as he required the promise, I could not do less than give it: at least I thought so at the time. The promise, therefore, was given, and must be performed. Something must be done for them whenever they leave Norland and settle in a new home.'

'Well, then, *let* something be done for them; but *that* something need not be three thousand pounds. Consider,' she added, 'that when the money is once parted with, it never can return. Your sisters will marry, and it will be gone for ever. If, indeed, it could ever be restored to our poor little boy— '

'Why, to be sure,' said her husband, very gravely, 'that would make a great difference. The time may come when Harry will regret that so large a sum was parted with. If he should have a numerous family, for instance, it would be a very convenient addition.'

'To be sure it would.'

'Perhaps, then, it would be better for all parties if the sum were diminished one-half.—Five hundred pounds would be a prodigious increase to their fortunes!'

'Oh! beyond any thing great! What brother on earth would do half so much for his sisters, even if *really* his sisters! And as it is—only half blood!—But you have such a generous spirit!'

'I would not wish to do anything mean,' he replied.

'One had rather, on such occasions, do too much than too little. No one, at least, can think I have not done enough for them: even themselves, they can hardly expect more.'

'There is no knowing what *they* may expect,' said the lady, 'but we are not to think of their expectations: the question is, what you can afford to do.'

'Certainly—and I think I may afford to give them five hundred pounds a-piece. As it is, without any addition of mine, they will each have above three thousand pounds on their mother's death—a very comfortable fortune for any young woman.'

'To be sure it is: and, indeed, it strikes me that they can want no addition at all. They will have ten thousand pounds divided amongst them. If they marry, they will be sure of doing well, and if they do not, they may all live very comfortably together on the interest of ten thousand pounds.'

'That is very true, and, therefore, I do not know whether, upon the whole, it would not be more advisable to do something for their mother while she lives rather than for them—something of the annuity kind I mean.—My sisters would feel the good effects of it as well as herself. A hundred a year would make them all perfectly comfortable.'

His wife hesitated a little, however, in giving her consent to this plan.

'To be sure,' said she, 'it is better than parting with fifteen hundred pounds at once. But then if Mrs. Dashwood should live fifteen years, we shall be completely taken in.'

'Fifteen years! my dear Fanny; her life cannot be worth half that purchase.'

'Certainly not; but if you observe, people always

live for ever when there is any annuity to be paid them; and she is very stout and healthy, and hardly forty. An annuity is a very serious business; it comes over and over every year, and there is no getting rid of it. You are not aware of what you are doing. I have known a great deal of the trouble of annuities; for my mother was clogged with the payment of three to old superannuated servants by my father's will, and it is amazing how disagreeable she found it. Twice every year these annuities were to be paid; and then there was the trouble of getting it to them; and then one of them was said to have died, and afterwards it turned out to be no such thing. My mother was quite sick of it. Her income was not her own, she said, with such perpetual claims on it; and it was the more unkind in my father, because, otherwise, the money would have been entirely at my mother's disposal, without any restriction whatever. It has given me such an abhorrence of annuities, that I am sure I would not pin myself down to the payment of one for all the world.'

'It is certainly an unpleasant thing,' replied Mr. Dashwood, 'to have those kind of yearly drains on one's income. One's fortune, as your mother justly says, is *not* one's own. To be tied down to the regular payment of such a sum, on every rent day, is by no means desirable: it takes away one's independence.'

'Undoubtedly; and after all you have no thanks for it. They think themselves secure, you do no more than what is expected, and it raises no gratitude at all. If I were you, whatever I did should be done at my own discretion entirely. I would not bind myself to allow them any thing yearly. It may be very inconvenient some years to spare a hundred, or even fifty pounds from our own expences.'

'I believe you are right, my love; it will be better that there should be no annuity in the case; whatever I may give them occasionally will be of far greater assistance than a yearly allowance, because they would only enlarge their style of living if they felt sure of a larger income, and would not be sixpence the richer for it at the end of the year. It will certainly be much the best way. A present of fifty pounds, now and then, will prevent their ever being distressed for money, and will, I think, be amply discharging my promise to my father.'

'To be sure it will. Indeed, to say the truth, I am convinced within myself that your father had no idea of your giving them any money at all. The assistance he thought of, I dare say, was only such as might be reasonably expected of you; for instance, such as looking out for a comfortable small house for them, helping them to move their things, and sending them presents of fish and game, and so forth, whenever they are in season. I'll lay my life that he meant nothing farther; indeed, it would be very strange and unreasonable if he did. Do but consider, my dear Mr. Dashwood, how excessively comfortable your mother-in-law and her daughters may live on the interest of seven thousand pounds, besides the thousand pounds belonging to each of the girls, which brings them in fifty pounds a-year a-piece, and, of course, they will pay their mother for their board out of it. Altogether, they will have five hundred a-year amongst them, and what on earth can four women want for more than that?—They will live so cheap! Their housekeeping will be nothing at all. They will have no carriage, no horses, and hardly any servants; they will keep no company, and can have no expences of any kind! Only conceive how comfortable they will be! Five hundred a-year! I am sure I cannot imagine how they will spend half of it; and as to your giving them more, it is quite absurd to think of it. They will be much more able to give *you* something.'

'Upon my word,' said Mr. Dashwood, 'I believe you are perfectly right. My father certainly could mean nothing more by his request to me than what you say. I clearly understand it now, and I will strictly fulfil my engagement by such acts of assistance and kindness to them as you have described. When my mother removes into another house my services shall be readily given to accommodate her as far as I can. Some little present of furniture too may be acceptable then.'

'Certainly,' returned Mrs. John Dashwood. 'But however, *one* thing must be considered. When your father and mother moved to Norland, though the furniture of Stanhill was sold, all the china, plate, and linen was saved, and is now left to your mother. Her house will therefore be almost completely fitted up as soon as she takes it.'

'That is a material consideration undoubtedly. A valuable legacy indeed! And yet some of the plate would have been a very pleasant addition to our own stock here.'

'Yes; and the set of breakfast china is twice as handsome as what belongs to this house. A great deal too handsome, in my opinion, for any place *they* can ever afford to live in. But, however, so it is. Your father thought only of *them*. And I must say this: that you owe no particular gratitude to him, nor attention to his wishes, for we very well know that if he could, he would have left almost every thing in the world to *them*.'

This argument was irresistible. It gave to his intentions whatever of decision was wanting before; and he finally resolved, that it would be absolutely unnecessary, if not highly indecorous, to do more for the widow and children of his father, than such kind of neighbourly acts as his own wife pointed out.

Sense and Sensibility

336 *Mansfield Park*

ABOUT thirty years ago, Miss Maria Ward of Huntingdon, with only seven thousand pounds, had the good luck to captivate Sir Thomas Bertram, of Mansfield Park, in the county of Northampton, and to be thereby raised to the rank of a baronet's lady, with all the comforts and consequences of an handsome house and large income. All Huntingdon exclaimed on the greatness of the match, and her uncle, the lawyer, himself, allowed her to be at least three thousand pounds short of any equitable claim to it. She had two sisters to be benefited by her elevation; and such of their acquaintance as thought Miss Ward and Miss Frances quite as handsome as Miss Maria, did not scruple to predict their marrying with almost equal advantage. But there certainly are not so many men of large fortune in the world, as there are pretty women to deserve them. Miss Ward, at the end of half a dozen years, found herself obliged to be attached to the Rev. Mr. Norris, a friend of her brother-in-law, with scarcely any private fortune, and Miss Frances fared yet worse. Miss Ward's match, indeed, when it came to the point, was not contemptible, Sir Thomas being happily able to give his friend an income in the living of Mansfield, and Mr. and Mrs. Norris began their career of conjugal felicity with very little less than a thousand a year. But Miss Frances married, in the common phrase, to disoblige her family, and by fixing on a Lieutenant of Marines, without education, fortune, or connections, did it very thoroughly. She could hardly have made a more untoward choice. Sir Thomas Bertram had interest, which, from principle as well as pride, from a general wish of doing right, and a desire of seeing all that were connected with him in situations of respectability, he would have been glad to exert for the advantage of Lady Bertram's sister; but her husband's profession was such as no interest could reach; and before he had time to devise any other method of assisting them, an absolute breach between the sisters had taken place. It was the natural result of the conduct of each party, and such as a very imprudent marriage almost always produces. To save herself from useless remonstrance, Mrs. Price never wrote to her family on the subject till actually married. Lady Bertram, who was a woman of very tranquil feelings, and a temper remarkably easy and indolent, would have contented herself with merely giving up her sister, and thinking no more of the matter: but Mrs. Norris had a spirit of activity, which could not be satisfied till she had written a long and angry letter to Fanny, to point out the folly of her conduct, and threaten her with all its possible ill consequences. Mrs. Price in her turn was injured and angry; and an answer which comprehended each sister in its bitterness, and bestowed such very disrespectful reflections on the pride of Sir Thomas, as

Mrs. Norris could not possibly keep to herself, put an end to all intercourse between them for a considerable period.

Mansfield Park

337 *Miss Bates at the Ball*

MISS BATES and Miss Fairfax, escorted by the two gentlemen, walked into the room; and Mrs. Elton seemed to think it as much her duty as Mrs. Weston's to receive them. Her gestures and movements might be understood by any one who looked on like Emma, but her words, every body's words, were soon lost under the incessant flow of Miss Bates, who came in talking, and had not finished her speech under many minutes after her being admitted into the circle at the fire. As the door opened she was heard,

'So very obliging of you!—No rain at all. Nothing to signify. I do not care for myself. Quite thick shoes. And Jane declares—Well!—(as soon as she was within the door) Well! This is brilliant indeed!—This is admirable!—Excellently contrived, upon my word. Nothing wanting. Could not have imagined it.—So well lighted up.—Jane, Jane, look—did you ever see any thing? Oh! Mr. Weston, you must really have had Aladdin's lamp. Good Mrs. Stokes would not know her own room again. I saw her as I came in; she was standing in the entrance. "Oh! Mrs. Stokes," said I—but I had not time for more.'—She was now met by Mrs. Weston.—'Very well, I thank you, ma'am. I hope you are quite well. Very happy to hear it. So afraid you might have a head-ach!—seeing you pass by so often, and knowing how much trouble you must have. Delighted to hear it indeed. Ah! dear Mrs. Elton, so obliged to you for the carriage!—excellent time.—Jane and I quite ready. Did not keep the horses a moment. Most comfortable carriage.—Oh! and I am sure our thanks are due to you, Mrs. Weston, on that score. Mrs. Elton had most kindly sent Jane a note, or we should have been.—But two such offers in one day!—Never were such neighbours. I said to my mother, "Upon my word, ma'am——." Thank you, my mother is remarkably well. Gone to Mr. Woodhouse's. I made her take her shawl—for the evenings are not warm—her large new shawl—Mrs. Dixon's wedding present.—So kind of her to think of my mother! Bought at Weymouth, you know—Mr. Dixon's choice. There were three others, Jane says, which they hesitated about some time. Colonel Campbell rather preferred an olive. My dear Jane, are you sure you did not wet your feet?—It was but a drop or two, but I am so afraid:—but Mr. Frank Churchill was so extremely—and there was a mat to step upon—I shall never forget his extreme politeness.—Oh! Mr. Frank Churchill, I must tell you my mother's spectacles have never been in fault since; the rivet never came out again. My mother often talks of your goodnature. Does not she, Jane?—Do not we often talk of Mr. Frank Churchill?—Ah! here's Miss Woodhouse.—Dear Miss Woodhouse, how do you do?—Very well I thank you, quite well. This is meeting quite in fairy-land!—Such a transformation!—Must not compliment, I know—(eyeing Emma most complacently)—that would be rude—but upon my word, Miss Woodhouse, you do look—how do you like Jane's hair?—You are a judge.—She did it all herself. Quite wonderful how she does her hair!—No hairdresser from London I think could.—Ah! Dr. Hughes I declare—and Mrs. Hughes. Must go and speak to Dr. and Mrs. Hughes for a moment.—How do you do? How do you do?—Very well, I thank you. This is delightful, is not it?—Where 's dear Mr. Richard?—Oh! there he is. Don't disturb him. Much better employed talking to the young ladies. How do you do, Mr. Richard?—I saw you the other day as you rode through the town——Mrs. Otway, I protest!—and good Mr. Otway, and Miss Otway and Miss Caroline.—Such a host of friends!—and Mr. George and Mr. Arthur!—How do you do? How do you all do?—Quite well, I am much obliged to you. Never better.—Don't I hear another carriage?—Who can this be?—very likely the worthy Coles.—Upon my word, this is charming to be standing about among such friends! And such a noble fire!—I am quite roasted. No coffee, I thank you, for me—never take coffee.—A little tea if you please, sir, by and bye,—no hurry—Oh! here it comes. Everything so good!'

Emma

CHARLES LAMB

1775–1834

338 *The Old Margate Hoy*

ALL this time sat upon the edge of the deck quite a different character. It was a lad, apparently very poor, very infirm, and very patient. His eye was ever on the sea, with a smile: and, if he caught now and then some snatches of these wild legends, it was by accident, and they seemed not to concern him. The waves to him whispered more pleasant stories.

He was as one, being with us, but not of us. He heard the bell of dinner ring without stirring; and when some of us pulled out our private stores—our cold meat and our salads—he produced none, and seemed to want none. Only a solitary biscuit he had laid in; provision for the one or two days and nights, to which these vessels then were oftentimes obliged to prolong their voyage. Upon a nearer acquaintance with him, which he seemed neither to court nor decline, we learned that he was going to Margate, with the hope of being admitted into the Infirmary there for sea-bathing. His disease was a scrofula, which appeared to have eaten all over him. He expressed great hopes of a cure; and when we asked him, whether he had any friends where he was going, he replied, 'he *had* no friends.'

Last Essays of Elia

339 *Amicus redivivus*

Where were ye, Nymphs, when the remorseless deep
Clos'd o'er the head of your loved Lycidas?

I DO not know when I have experienced a stranger sensation, than on seeing my old friend G. D., who had been paying me a morning visit a few Sundays back, at my cottage at Islington, upon taking leave, instead of turning down the right hand path by which he had entered—with staff in hand, and at noon day, deliberately march right forwards into the midst of the stream that runs by us, and totally disappear.

A spectacle like this at dusk would have been appalling enough; but, in the broad open daylight, to witness such an unreserved motion towards self-destruction in a valued friend, took from me all power of speculation.

How I found my feet, I know not. Consciousness was quite gone. Some spirit, not my own, whirled me to the spot. I remember nothing but the silvery apparition of a good white head emerging; nigh which a staff (the hand unseen that wielded it) pointed upwards, as feeling for the skies. In a moment (if time was in that time) he was on my shoulders, and I—freighted with a load more precious than his who bore Anchises.

And here I cannot but do justice to the officious zeal of sundry passers by, who, albeit arriving a little too late to participate in the honours of the rescue, in philanthropic shoals came thronging to communicate their advice as to the recovery; prescribing variously the application, or non-application, of salt, &c., to the person of the patient. Life meantime was ebbing fast away, amidst the stifle of conflicting judgements, when one, more sagacious than the rest, by a bright thought, proposed sending for the Doctor. Trite as the counsel was, and impossible, as one should think, to be missed on,—shall I confess?—in this emergency, it was to me as if an Angel had spoken. Great previous exertions—and mine had not been inconsiderable—are commonly followed by a debility of purpose. This was a moment of irresolution.

Monoculus—for so, in default of catching his true name, I choose to designate the medical gentleman who now appeared—is a grave, middle-aged person, who, without having studied at the college, or truckled to the pedantry of a diploma, hath employed a great portion of his valuable time in experimental processes upon the bodies of unfortunate fellow-creatures, in whom the vital spark, to mere vulgar thinking, would seem extinct, and lost for ever. He omitteth no occasion of obtruding his services, from a case of common surfeit-suffocation to the ignobler obstructions, sometimes induced by a too wilful application of the plant *Cannabis* outwardly. But though he declineth not altogether these drier extinctions, his occupation tendeth for the most part to water-practice; for the convenience of which, he hath judiciously fixed his quarters near the grand repository of the stream mentioned, where, day and night, from his little watch-tower, at the Middleton's-Head, he listeneth to detect the wrecks of drowned mortality—partly, as he saith, to be upon the spot—and partly, because the liquids which he useth to prescribe to himself and his patients, on these distressing occasions, are ordinarily more conveniently to be found at these common hostelries, than in the shops and phials of the apothecaries. His ear hath arrived to such finesse by practice, that it is reported, he can distinguish a plunge at a half furlong distance; and can tell, if it be casual or deliberate. He weareth a medal, suspended over a suit, originally of a sad brown, but which, by time, and frequency of nightly divings, has been dinged into a true professional sable. He passeth by the name of Doctor, and is remarkable for wanting his left eye. His remedy—after a sufficient application of warm blankets, friction, &c., is a simple tumbler, or more, of the purest Cognac, with water, made as hot as the convalescent can bear it. Where he findeth, as in the case of my friend, a squeamish subject, he condescendeth to be the taster; and showeth, by his own example, the innocuous nature of the prescription. Nothing can be more kind or encouraging than this procedure. It addeth confidence to the patient, to see his medical adviser go hand in hand with himself in the remedy. When the doctor swalloweth his own draught, what peevish invalid can refuse to pledge him in the potion? In fine, MONOCULUS is a humane, sensible man, who, for a slender pittance, scarce enough to sustain life, is content to wear it out in the endeavour to save the lives of others—his pretensions so moderate, that with difficulty I could press a crown upon him, for the price of restoring the existence of such an invaluable creature to society as G. D.

It was pleasant to observe the effect of the subsiding alarm upon the nerves of the dear absentee. It seemed to have given a shake to memory, calling up notice after notice, of all the providential deliverances he had experienced in the course of his long and innocent life. Sitting up in my couch—my couch which, naked and void of furniture hitherto, for the salutary repose which it administered, shall be honoured with costly valance, at some price, and henceforth be a state-bed at Colebrooke,—he discoursed of marvellous escapes—by carelessness of nurses—by pails of gelid, and kettles of the boiling element, in infancy—by orchard pranks, and snapping twigs, in schoolboy frolics—by descent of tiles at Trumpington, and of heavier tomes at Pembroke—by studious watchings, inducing frightful vigilance—by want, and the fear of want, and all the sore throbbings of the learned head.—Anon, he would burst out into little fragments of chaunting—of songs long ago—ends of deliverance-hymns, not remembered before since childhood, but coming up now, when his heart was made tender as a child's—for the *tremor cordis*, in the retrospect of a recent deliverance, as in a case of impending danger, acting upon an innocent heart, will produce a self-tenderness, which we should do ill to christen cowardice; and Shakspeare, in the latter crisis, has made his good Sir Hugh to remember the sitting by Babylon, and to mutter of shallow rivers.

Waters of Sir Hugh Middleton—what a spark you were like to have extinguished for ever! Your salubrious streams to this City, for now near two centuries, would hardly have atoned for what you were in a moment washing away. Mockery of a river—liquid artifice—wretched conduit! henceforth rank with canals, and sluggish aqueducts. Was it for this, that, smit in boyhood with the explorations of that Abyssinian traveller, I paced the vales of Amwell to explore your tributary springs, to trace your salutary waters sparkling through green Hertfordshire and cultured Enfield parks?—Ye have no swans—no Naiads—no river God—or did the benevolent hoary aspect of my friend tempt ye to suck him in, that ye also might have the tutelary genius of your waters?

Had he been drowned in Cam there would have been some consonancy in it; but what willows had ye to wave and rustle over his moist sepulture?—or, having no *name*, besides that unmeaning assumption of *eternal novity*, did ye think to get one by the noble prize, and henceforth to be termed the STREAM DYERIAN?

> And could such spacious virtue find a grave
> Beneath the imposthumed bubble of a wave?

I protest, George, you shall not venture out again—no, not by daylight—without a sufficient pair of spectacles—in your musing moods especially. Your absence of mind we have borne, till your presence of body came to be called in question by it. You shall not go wandering into Euripus with Aristotle, if we can help it. Fie, man, to turn dipper at your years, after your many tracts in favour of sprinkling only!

I have nothing but water in my head o' nights since this frightful accident. Sometimes I am with Clarence in his dream. At others, I behold Christian beginning to sink, and crying out to his good brother Hopeful (that is to me), 'I sink in deep waters; the billows go over my head, all the waves go over me. Selah.' Then I have before me Palinurus, just letting go the steerage. I cry out too late to save. Next follow—a mournful procession—*suicidal faces*, saved against their wills from drowning; dolefully trailing a length of reluctant gratefulness, with ropy weeds pendant from locks of watchet hue—constrained Lazari—Pluto's half-subjects—stolen fees from the grave—bilking Charon of his fare. At their head Arion—or is it G. D.?—in his singing garments marcheth singly, with harp in hand, and votive garland, which Machaon (or Dr. Hawes) snatcheth straight, intending to suspend it to the stern God of Sea. Then follow dismal streams of Lethe, in which the half-drenched on earth are constrained to drown downright, by wharfs where Ophelia twice acts her muddy death.

And, doubtless, there is some notice in that invisible world, when one of us approacheth (as my friend did so lately) to their inexorable precincts. When a soul knocks once, twice, at death's door, the sensation aroused within the palace must be considerable; and the grim Feature, by modern science so often dispossessed of his prey, must have learned by this time to pity Tantalus.

A pulse assuredly was felt along the line of the Elysian shades, when the near arrival of G. D. was announced by no equivocal indications. From their seats of Asphodel arose the gentler and the graver ghosts—poet, or historian—of Grecian or of Roman lore—to crown with unfading chaplets the half-finished love-labours of their unwearied scholiast. Him Markland expected—him Tyrwhitt hoped to encounter—him the sweet lyrist of Peter House, whom he had barely seen upon earth, with newest airs prepared to greet ——; and, patron of the gentle Christ's boy,—who should have been his patron through life—the mild Askew, with longing aspirations, leaned foremost from his venerable Æsculapian chair, to welcome into that happy company the matured virtues of the man, whose tender scions in the boy he himself upon earth had so prophetically fed and watered.

Last Essays of Elia

340 *Old China*

I WAS pointing out to my cousin last evening, over our Hyson (which we are old fashioned enough to drink unmixed still of an afternoon) some of these *speciosa miracula* upon a set of extraordinary old blue china (a recent purchase) which we were now for the first time using; and could not help remarking, how favourable circumstances had been to us of late years, that we could afford to please the eye sometimes with trifles of this sort—when a passing sentiment seemed to over-shade the brows of my companion. I am quick at detecting these summer clouds in Bridget.

'I wish the good old times would come again', she said, 'when we were not quite so rich. I do not mean, that I want to be poor; but there was a middle state;' —so she was pleased to ramble on,—'in which I am sure we were a great deal happier. A purchase is but a purchase, now that you have money enough and to spare. Formerly it used to be a triumph. When we coveted a cheap luxury (and, O! how much ado I had to get you to consent in those times!) we were used to have a debate two or three days before, and to weigh the *for* and *against*, and think what we might spare it out of, and what saving we could hit upon, that should be an equivalent. A thing was worth buying then, when we felt the money that we paid for it.

'Do you remember the brown suit, which you made to hang upon you, till all your friends cried shame upon you, it grew so thread-bare—and all because of that folio Beaumont and Fletcher, which you dragged home late at night from Barker's in Covent-garden? Do you remember how we eyed it for weeks before we could make up our minds to the purchase, and had not come to a determination till it was near ten o'clock of the Saturday night, when you set off from Islington, fearing you should be too late—and when the old bookseller with some grumbling opened his shop, and by the twinkling taper (for he was setting bedwards) lighted out the relic from his dusty treasures—and when you lugged it home, wishing it were twice as cumbersome—and when you presented it to me—and when we were exploring the perfectness of it (*collating* you called it)—and while I was repairing some of the loose leaves with paste, which your impatience would not suffer to be left till day-break—was there no pleasure in being a poor man? or can those neat black clothes which you wear now, and are so careful to keep brushed, since we have become rich and finical, give you half the honest vanity, with which you flaunted it about in that over-worn suit—your old corbeau—for four or five weeks longer than you should have done, to pacify your conscience for the mighty sum of fifteen—or sixteen shillings was it?—a great affair we thought it then—which you had lavished on the old folio. Now you can afford to buy any book that pleases you, but I do not see that you ever bring me home any nice old purchases now.

'When you came home with twenty apologies for laying out a less number of shillings upon that print after Lionardo, which we christened the 'Lady Blanch'; when you looked at the purchase, and thought of the money—and thought of the money, and looked again at the picture—was there no pleasure in being a poor man? Now, you have nothing to do but to walk into Colnaghi's, and buy a wilderness of Lionardos. Yet do you?

'Then, do you remember our pleasant walks to Enfield, and Potter's Bar, and Waltham, when we had a holyday—holydays, and all other fun, are gone, now we are rich—and the little hand-basket in which I used to deposit our day's fare of savory cold lamb and salad—and how you would pry about at noon-tide for some decent house, where we might go in, and produce our store—only paying for the ale that you must call for—and speculate upon the looks of the landlady, and whether she was likely to allow us a table-cloth—and wish for such another honest hostess, as Izaak Walton has described many a one on the pleasant banks of the Lea, when he went a fishing—and sometimes they would prove obliging enough, and sometimes they would look grudgingly upon us—but we had cheerful looks still for one another, and would eat our plain food savorily, scarcely grudging Piscator his Trout Hall? Now, when we go out a day's pleasuring, which is seldom moreover, we *ride* part of the way—and go into a fine inn, and order the best of dinners, never debating the expense—which, after all, never has half the relish of those chance country snaps, when we were at the mercy of uncertain usage, and a precarious welcome.

'You are too proud to see a play anywhere now but in the pit. Do you remember where it was we used to sit, when we saw the Battle of Hexham, and the Surrender of Calais, and Bannister and Mrs. Bland in the Children in the Wood—when we squeezed out our shillings a-piece to sit three or four times in a season in the one-shilling gallery—where you felt all the time that you ought not to have brought me—and more strongly I felt obligation to you for having brought me—and the pleasure was the better for a little shame—and when the curtain drew up, what cared we for our place in the house, or what mattered it where we were sitting, when our thoughts were with Rosalind in Arden, or with Viola at the Court of Illyria? You used to say, that the gallery was the best place of all for enjoying a play socially—that the relish of such exhibitions must be in proportion to the infrequency of going—that the company we met there, not being in general readers of plays, were obliged to attend the more, and did attend, to what was going on, on the stage—because a word lost would have been a chasm, which it was impossible for them to fill up. With such reflections we consoled our pride then—and I appeal to you, whether, as a woman, I met generally with less attention and accommodation, than I have done since in more expensive situations in the house? The getting in indeed, and the crowding up those inconvenient staircases, was bad enough,—but there was still a law of civility to women recognised to quite as great an extent as we ever found in the other passages—and how a little difficulty overcome heightened the snug seat, and the play, afterwards! Now we can only pay our money, and walk in. You cannot see, you say, in the galleries now. I am sure we saw, and heard too, well enough then—but sight, and all, I think, is gone with our poverty.'

Last Essays of Elia

341 *Dream Children*

HERE the children fell a crying, and asked if their little mourning which they had on was not for uncle John, and they looked up, and prayed me not to go on about their uncle, but to tell them some stories about their pretty dead mother. Then I told how for seven long years, in hope sometimes, sometimes in despair, yet persisting ever, I courted the fair Alice W—n; and, as much as children could understand, I explained to them what coyness, and difficulty, and denial meant in maidens—when suddenly, turning to Alice, the soul of the first Alice looked out at her eyes with such a reality of re-presentment, that I became in doubt which of them stood there before me, or whose that bright hair was; and while I stood gazing, both the children gradually grew fainter to my view, receding, and still receding till nothing at last but two mournful features were seen in the uttermost distance, which, without speech, strangely impressed upon me the effects of speech: 'We are not of Alice, nor of thee, nor are we children at all. The children of Alice called Bartrum father.

We are nothing; less than nothing, and dreams. We are only what might have been, and must wait upon the tedious shores of Lethe millions of ages before we have existence, and a name'——and immediately awaking, I found myself quietly seated in my bachelor arm-chair, where I had fallen asleep.

Elia

342 *A Londoner in Grain*

I OUGHT before this to have reply'd to your very kind invitation into Cumberland. With you and your Sister I could gang anywhere. But I am afraid whether I shall ever be able to afford so desperate a Journey. Separate from the pleasure of your company, I don't much care if I never see a mountain in my life. I have passed all my days in London, until I have formed as many and intense local attachments, as any of you mountaineers can have done with dead nature. The Lighted shops of the Strand and Fleet Street, the innumerable trades, tradesmen and customers, coaches, waggons, playhouses, all the bustle and wickedness round about Covent Garden, the very women of the Town, the Watchmen, drunken scenes, rattles,—life awake, if you awake, at all hours of the night, the impossibility of being dull in Fleet Street, the crowds, the very dirt & mud, the Sun shining upon houses and pavements, the print shops, the old book stalls, parsons cheap'ning books, coffee houses, steams of soups from kitchens, the pantomimes, London itself a pantomime and a masquerade,—all these things work themselves into my mind and feed me, without a power of satiating me. The wonder of these sights impells me into night-walks about her crowded streets, and

I often shed tears in the Strand from fulness of joy at so much Life.—All these emotions must be strange to you. So are your rural emotions to me. But consider, what must I have been doing all my life, not to have lent great portions of my heart with usury to such scenes?—

My attachments are all local, purely local. I have no passion (or have had none since I was in love, and then it was the spurious engendering of poetry & books) to groves and vallies. The rooms where I was born, the furniture which has been before my eyes all my life, a book case which has followed me about (like a faithful dog, only exceeding him in knowledge) wherever I have moved—old chairs, old tables, streets, squares, where I have sunned myself, my old school,—these are my mistresses. Have I not enough, without your mountains? . . .

Letter to William Wordsworth, 30 Jan. 1801

343 *Writing for Antiquity*

RUMOUR tells us that Miss Holcroft is married. . . Who is Badman, or Bed'em? Have I seen him at Montacute's? I hear he is a great chymist. I am sometimes chymical myself. A thought strikes me with horror. Pray heaven he may not have done it for the sake of trying chymical experiments upon her—young female subjects are so scarce! . . . An't you glad about Burke's case! We may set off the Scotch murders against the Scotch novels—Hare, the Great Unhanged.

M. B. is richly worth your knowing. He is on the top scale of my friendship ladder, on which an angel or two is still climbing, and some, alas! descending. . . Did you see a sonnet of mine in *Blackwood's* last!

Curious construction! *Elaborata facilitas!* And now I'll tell. 'Twas written for 'The Gem,' but the editors declined it, on the plea that it would *shock all mothers*; so they published 'The Widow' instead. I am born out of time. I have no conjecture about what the present world calls delicacy. I thought 'Rosamund Gray' was a pretty modest thing. Hessey assures me that the world would not bear it. I have lived to grow into an indecent character. When my sonnet was rejected, I exclaimed, 'Hang the age, I will write for Antiquity!'..

Blackwood sent me £20 for the drama. Somebody cheated me out of it next day; and my new pair of breeches, just sent home, cracking at first putting on, I exclaimed, in my wrath, 'All tailors are cheats and all men are tailors.' Then I was better.

Letter to Bryan Waller Procter, 22 Jan. 1829

WALTER SAVAGE LANDOR

1775–1864

344 *Mentem mortalia tangunt*

RHODOPE. . . . Let me pause and consider a little, if you please. I begin to suspect that, as gods formerly did, you have been turning men into beasts, and beasts into men. But, Aesop, you should never say the thing that is untrue.

Aesop. We say and do and look no other all our lives.

Rhodope. Do we never know better?

Aesop. Yes; when we cease to please, and to wish it; when death is settling the features, and the cerements are ready to render them unchangeable.

Rhodope. Alas! alas!

Aesop. Breathe, Rhodope! breathe again those painless sighs: they belong to thy vernal season. May thy summer of life be calm, thy autumn calmer, and thy winter never come!

Rhodope. I must die then earlier.

Aesop. Laodameia died; Helen died; Leda, the beloved of Jupiter, went before. It is better to repose in the earth betimes than to sit up late; better, than to cling pertinaciously to what we feel crumbling under us, and to protract an inevitable fall. We may enjoy the present, while we are insensible of infirmity and decay; but the present, like a note in music, is nothing but as it appertains to what is past and what is to come. There are no fields of amaranth on this side of the grave; there are no voices, O Rhodope, that are not soon mute, however tuneful; there is no name, with whatever emphasis of passionate love repeated, of which the echo is not faint at last.

Rhodope. O Aesop! let me rest my head on yours: it throbs and pains me.

Aesop. What are these ideas to thee?

Rhodope. Sad, sorrowful.

Aesop. Harrows that break the soil, preparing it for wisdom. Many flowers must perish ere a grain of corn be ripened. And now remove thy head: the cheek is cool enough after its little shower of tears.

Aesop and Rhodope

345 *Rhodope's Father*

RHODOPE. Never shall I forget the morning when my father, sitting in the coolest part of the house, exchanged his last measure of grain for a chlamys of scarlet cloth fringed with silver. He watched the merchant out of the door, and then looked wistfully into the corn-chest. I, who thought there was something worth seeing, looked in also, and, finding it empty, expressed my disappointment, not thinking however about the corn. A faint and transient smile came over his countenance at the sight of mine. He unfolded the chlamys, stretching it out with both hands before me, and then cast it over my shoulders. I looked down on the glittering fringe and screamed with joy. He then went out; and I know not what flowers he gathered, but he gathered many; and some he placed in my bosom, and some in my hair. But I told him with captious pride, first that I could arrange them better, and again that I would have only the white. However, when he had selected all the white, and I had placed a few of them according to my fancy, I told him (rising in my slipper) he might crown me with the remainder. The splendour of my apparel gave me a sensation of authority. Soon as the flowers had taken their station on my head, I expressed a dignified satisfaction at the taste displayed by my father, just as if I could have seen how they appeared! But he knew that there was at least as much pleasure as pride in it, and perhaps we divided the latter (alas! not both) pretty equally. He now took me into the market-place, where a concourse of people was waiting for the purchase of slaves. Merchants came and looked at me; some commending, others disparaging; but all agreeing that I was slender and delicate, that I could not live long, and that I should give much trouble. Many would have bought the chlamys, but there was something less saleable in the child and flowers.

Aesop. Had thy features been coarse and thy

voice rustic, they would all have patted thy cheeks and found no fault in thee.

Rhodope. As it was, every one had bought exactly such another in time past, and been a loser by it. At these speeches I perceived the flowers tremble slightly on my bosom, from my father's agitation. Although he scoffed at them, knowing my healthiness, he was troubled internally, and said many short prayers, not very unlike imprecations, turning his head aside. Proud was I, prouder than ever, when at last several talents were offered for me, and by the very man who in the beginning had undervalued me the most, and prophesied the worst of me. My father scowled at him, and refused the money. I thought he was playing a game, and began to wonder what it could be, since I never had seen it played before. Then I fancied it might be some celebration because plenty had returned to the city, insomuch that my father had bartered the last of the corn he hoarded. I grew more and more delighted at the sport. But soon there advanced an elderly man, who said gravely, 'Thou hast stolen this child: her vesture alone is worth above a hundred drachmas. Carry her home again to her parents, and do it directly, or Nemesis and the Eumenides will overtake thee.' Knowing the estimation in which my father had always been holden by his fellow citizens, I laughed again, and pinched his ear. He, although naturally choleric, burst forth into no resentment at these reproaches, but said calmly, 'I think I know thee by name, O guest! Surely thou art Xanthus the Samian. Deliver this child from famine.'

Again I laughed aloud and heartily; and, thinking it was now my part of the game, I held out both my arms and protruded my whole body toward the stranger. He would not receive me from my father's neck, but he asked me with benignity and solicitude if I was hungry: at which I laughed again, and more than ever: for it was early in the morning, soon after the first meal, and my father had nourished me most carefully and plentifully in all the days of the famine. But Xanthus, waiting for no answer, took out of a sack, which one of his slaves carried at his side, a cake of wheaten bread and a piece of honey-comb, and gave them to me. I held the honey-comb to my father's mouth, thinking it the most of a dainty. He dashed it to the ground; but, seizing the bread, he began to devour it ferociously. This also I thought was in play; and I clapped my hands at his distortions. But Xanthus looked on him like one afraid, and smote the cake from him, crying aloud, 'Name the price.' My father now placed me in his arms, naming a price much below what the other had offered, saying, 'The Gods are ever with thee, O Xanthus! therefore to thee do I consign my child.' But while Xanthus was counting out the silver, my father seized the cake again, which the slave had taken up and was about to replace in the wallet. His hunger was exasperated by the taste and the delay. Suddenly there arose much tumult. Turning round in the old woman's bosom who had received me from Xanthus, I saw my beloved father struggling on the ground, livid and speechless. The more violent my cries, the more rapidly they hurried me away; and many were soon between us. Little was I suspicious that he had suffered the pangs of famine long before: alas! and he had suffered them for me. Do I weep while I am telling you they ended? I could not have closed his eyes; I was too young; but I might have received his last breath; the only comfort of an orphan's bosom. Do you now think him blameable, O Aesop?

Aesop and Rhodope

346 *The Dream of Boccaccio*

HERE in this chamber she appeared to me more visibly in a dream.

'Thy prayers have been heard, O Giovanni,' said she. I sprang to embrace her.

'Do not spill the water! Ah! you have spilt a part of it.'

I then observed in her hand a crystal vase. A few drops were sparkling on the sides and running down the rim; a few were trickling from the base and from the hand that held it.

'I must go down to the brook,' said she, 'and fill it again as it was filled before.'

What a moment of agony was this to me! Could I be certain how long might be her absence? She went: I was following: she made a sign for me to turn back: I disobeyed her only an instant: yet my sense of disobedience, increasing my feebleness and confusion, made me lose sight of her. In the next moment she was again at my side, with the cup quite full. I stood motionless: I feared my breath might shake the water over. I looked her in the face for her commands—and to see it—to see it so calm, so beneficent, so beautiful. I was forgetting what I had prayed for, when she lowered her head, tasted of the cup, and gave it me. I drank; and suddenly sprang forth before me, many groves and palaces and gardens, and their statues and their avenues, and their labyrinths of alaternus and bay, and alcoves of citron, and watchful loopholes in the retirements of impenetrable pomegranate. Farther off, just below where the fountain slipt away from its marble hall and guardian gods, arose, from their beds of moss and drosera and darkest grass, the sisterhood of oleanders, fond of tantalising with their bosomed flowers and their moist and pouting blossoms the little shy rivulet, and of covering its face with all the colours of the dawn. My dream expanded and moved forward. I trod again the dust of Posilipo, soft as the feathers in the wings of Sleep. I emerged on Baia ; I crossed her innumerable arches ; I loitered in the breezy sunshine of her mole ; I trusted the faithful seclusion of her caverns, the keepers of so many secrets ; and I reposed on the buoyancy of her tepid sea. Then Naples and her theatres and her churches, and grottos and dells and forts and promontories, rushed forward in confusion, now among soft whispers, now among sweetest sounds, and subsided, and sank, and disappeared. Yet a memory seemed to come fresh from every one : each had time enough for its tale, for its pleasure, for its reflection, for its pang. As I mounted with silent steps the narrow staircase of the old palace, how distinctly did I feel against the palm of my hand the coldness of that smooth stone-work, and the greater of the cramps of iron in it !

'Ah me ! is this forgetting ?' cried I anxiously to Fiammetta.

'We must recall these scenes before us,' she replied : 'such is the punishment of them. Let us hope and believe that the apparition, and the compunction which must follow it, will be accepted as the full penalty, and that both will pass away almost together.'

I feared to lose anything attendant on her presence: I feared to approach her forehead with my lips: I feared to touch the lily on its long wavy leaf in her hair, which filled my whole heart with fragrance. Venerating, adoring, I bowed my head at last to kiss her snow-white robe, and trembled at my presumption. And yet the effulgence of her countenance vivified while it chastened me. I loved her—I must not say more than ever—*better* than ever; it was Fiammetta who had inhabited the skies. As my hand opened toward her,

'Beware!' said she, faintly smiling; 'beware, Giovanni. Take only the crystal; take it, and drink again.'

'Must all be then forgotten?' said I sorrowfully.

'Remember your prayer and mine, Giovanni! Shall both have been granted—O how much worse than in vain!'

I drank instantly; I drank largely. How cool my bosom grew; how could it grow so cold before her? But it was not to remain in its quiescency; its trials were not yet over. I will not, Francesco! no, I may not commemorate the incidents she related me, nor which of us said, 'I blush for having loved *first*;' nor which of us replied, 'Say *least*, say *least*, and blush again.'

The charm of the words (for I felt not the encumbrance of the body nor the acuteness of the spirit) seemed to possess me wholly. Although the water gave me strength and comfort, and somewhat of celestial pleasure, many tears fell around the border of the vase as she held it up before me, exhorting me to take courage, and inviting me with more than exhortation to accomplish my deliverance. She came nearer, more tenderly, more earnestly; she held the dewy globe with both hands, leaning forward, and sighed and shook her head, drooping at my pusillanimity. It was only when a ringlet had touched the rim, and perhaps the water (for a sunbeam on the surface could never have given it such a golden hue), that I took courage, clasped it, and exhausted it. Sweet as was the water, sweet as was the serenity it gave me—alas! that also which it moved away from me was sweet!

'This time you can trust me alone,' said she, and parted my hair, and kissed my brow. Again she went toward the brook: again my agitation, my weakness, my doubt, came over me: nor could I see her while she raised the water, nor knew I whence she drew it. When she returned, she was close to me at once: she smiled: her smile pierced me to the bones: it seemed an angel's. She sprinkled the pure water on me; she looked most fondly; she took my hand; she suffered me to press hers to my bosom; but, whether by design I cannot tell, she let fall a few drops of the chilly element between.

'And now, O my beloved!' said she, 'we have consigned to the bosom of God our earthly joys and sorrows. The joys cannot return, let not the sorrows. These alone would trouble my repose among the blessed.'

'Trouble thy repose! Fiammetta! Give me the chalice!' cried I—'not a drop will I leave in it, not a drop.'

'Take it!' said that soft voice. 'O now most dear Giovanni! I know thou hast strength enough; and there is but little—at the bottom lies our first kiss.'

'Mine! didst thou say, beloved one? and is that left thee still?'

'*Mine*,' said she pensively; and as she abased her head, the broad leaf of the lily hid her brow and her eyes; the light of heaven shone through the flower.

'O Fiammetta! Fiammetta!' cried I in agony, 'God is the God of mercy, God is the God of love—can I, can I ever?' I struck the chalice against my head, unmindful that I held it; the water covered my face and my feet. I started up, not yet awake, and I heard the name of Fiammetta in the curtains.

The Pentameron

JAMES WHITE

1775–1820

347 *Davy to Justice Shallow*

MASTER ABRAM is dead, gone, your Worship—dead! Master Abram! Oh! good your Worship, a's gone.—A' never throve, since a' came from Windsor—'twas his death. . . A' took delight in nothing but his book of songs and sonnets—a' would go to the Stroud side under the large beech tree, and sing, till 'twas quite pity of our lives to mark him; for his chin grew as long as a muscle. . . A' died, your Worship, just about one, at the crow of the cock. —I thought how it was with him; for a' talk'd as quick, aye, marry, as glib as your Worship; and a' smiled, and look'd at his own nose, and call'd 'Sweet Ann Page'. I ask'd him if a' would eat—so a' bad us commend him to his Cousin Robert (a' never call'd your Worship so before) and bade us get hot meat, for a' would not say nay to Ann again.—But a' never liv'd to touch it—a' began all in a moment to sing 'Lovers all, a Madrigal'. 'Twas the only song Master Abram ever learnt out of book, and clean by heart, your Worship—and so a' sung, and smiled, and look'd askew at his own nose, and sung, and sung on, till his breath waxed shorter, and shorter, and shorter, and a' fell into a struggle and died. I beseech your Worship to think he was well tended—I look'd to him, your Worship, late and soon, and crept at his heel all day long, an it had been any fallow dog—but I thought a' could never live, for a' did so sing, and then a' never drank with it—I knew 'twas a bad sign—yea, a' sung, your Worship, marry, without drinking a drop.

Alice Shortcake craves, she may make his shroud.—Ah! had your Worship but never ha' taken him to Windsor!

Falstaff Letters

HENRY, LORD BROUGHAM

1778–1868

348 *Political Second-Sight*

IT was in truth a crisis to try men's souls. For a while all was uncertainty and consternation; all were seen fluttering about like birds in an eclipse or a thunderstorm; no man could tell whom he might trust; nay, worse still, no man could tell of whom he might ask anything. It was hard to say, not who were in office, but who were likely to remain in office. All true Scots were in dismay and distraction. It might truly be said they knew not which way to look, or whither to turn. Perhaps it might be yet more truly said, that they knew not *when* to turn. But such a crisis was too sharp to last; it passed away; and then was to be seen a proof of Mr. Dundas's power amongst his countrymen, which transcended all expectation, and almost surpassed belief, if indeed it is not rather to be viewed as an evidence of the acute foresight—the political second-sight—of the Scottish nation. The trusty band in both Houses actually were found adhering to him against the existing Government; nay, he held the proxies of many Scottish Peers in open opposition! Well might his colleague exclaim to the hapless Addington in such unheard-of troubles, 'Doctor, the Thanes fly from us.' When the very Scotch Peers wavered—and when the Grampian hills might next be expected to move about—it was time to think that the end of all things was at hand; and the return of Pitt and security, and patronage and Dundas, speedily ensued to bless old Scotland, and reward her providence, or her fidelity—her attachment at once to her patron—and to herself.

Historical Sketches: Mr. Dundas

WILLIAM HAZLITT

1778–1830

349 *On Going a Journey*

ONE of the pleasantest things in the world is going a journey; but I like to go by myself. I can enjoy society in a room; but out of doors, nature is company enough for me. I am then never less alone than when alone.

The fields his study, nature was his book.

I cannot see the wit of walking and talking at the same time. When I am in the country I wish to vegetate like the country. I am not for criticising hedge-rows and black cattle. I go out of town in order to forget the town and all that is in it. There are those who for this purpose go to watering-places, and carry the metropolis with them. I like more elbow-room and fewer encumbrances. I like solitude, when I give myself up to it, for the sake of solitude; nor do I ask for

> a friend in my retreat,
> Whom I may whisper solitude is sweet.

The soul of a journey is liberty, perfect liberty, to think, feel, do, just as one pleases. We go a journey chiefly to be free of all impediments and of all inconveniences; to leave ourselves behind, much more to get rid of others. It is because I want a little breathing-space to muse on indifferent matters, where Contemplation

> May plume her feathers and let grow her wings,
> That in the various bustle of resort
> Were all too ruffled, and sometimes impair'd,

that I absent myself from the town for a while, without feeling at a loss the moment I am left by myself. Instead of a friend in a postchaise or in a Tilbury, to exchange good things with, and vary the same stale topics over again, for once let me have a truce with impertinence. Give me the clear blue sky over my head, and the green turf beneath my feet, a winding road before me, and a three hours' march to dinner—and then to thinking! It is hard if I cannot start some game on these lone heaths. I laugh, I run, I leap, I sing for joy. From the point of yonder rolling cloud I plunge into my past being, and revel there, as the sun-burnt Indian plunges headlong into the wave that wafts him to his native shore. Then long-forgotten things, like 'sunken wrack and sumless treasuries,' burst upon my eager sight, and I begin to feel, think, and be myself again. Instead of an awkward silence, broken by attempts at wit or dull common-places, mine is that undisturbed silence of the heart which alone is perfect eloquence. No one likes puns, alliterations, antitheses, argument, and analysis better than I do; but I sometimes had rather be without them. 'Leave, oh, leave me to my repose!' I have just now other business in hand, which would seem idle to you, but is with me 'very stuff o' the conscience.' Is not this wild rose sweet without a comment? Does not this daisy leap to my heart set in its coat of emerald?

Table-Talk

350 *The Spirit of Humanity in Shakespeare*

AS good an example as any of this informing and redeeming power in our author's genius might be taken from the comic scenes in both parts of *Henry IV*. Nothing can go much lower in intellect or morals than many of the characters. Here are knaves and fools in abundance, of the meanest order, and stripped stark-naked. But genius, like charity, 'covers a multitude of sins'; we pity as much as we despise them; in spite of our disgust we like them, because they like themselves, and because we are made to sympathize with them; and the ligament, fine as it is, which links them to humanity, is never broken. Who would quarrel with Wart, or Feeble, or Mouldy, or Bull-calf, or even with Pistol, Nym, or Bardolph? None but a hypocrite. The severe censurers of the morals of imaginary characters can generally find a hole for their own vices to creep out at, and yet do not perceive how it is that the imperfect and even deformed characters in Shakespeare's plays, as done to the life, by forming a part of our personal consciousness, claim our personal forgiveness, and suspend or evade our moral judgement, by bribing our self-love to side with them. Not to do so, is not morality, but affectation, stupidity, or ill-nature. I have more sympathy with one of Shakespeare's pick-purses, Gadshill or Peto, than I can possibly have with any member of the Society for the Suppression of Vice, and would by no means assist to deliver the one into the hands of the other. Those who cannot be persuaded to draw a veil over the foibles of ideal characters, may be suspected of wearing a mask over their own! Again, in point of understanding and attainments, Shallow sinks low enough; and yet his cousin Silence is a foil to him; he is the shadow of a shade, glimmers on the very verge of downright imbecility, and totters on the brink of nothing. 'He has been merry twice and once ere now,' and is hardly persuaded to break his silence in a song. Shallow has 'heard the chimes at midnight,' and roared out glees and catches at taverns and inns of court, when he was young. So, at least, he tells his cousin Silence, and Falstaff encourages the loftiness of his pretensions. Shallow would be thought a great man among his dependants and followers; Silence is nobody—not even in his own opinion; yet he sits in the orchard, and eats his caraways and pippins among the rest. Shakespeare takes up the meanest subjects with the same tenderness that we do an insect's wing, and would not kill a fly.

Comic Writers

351 *The Pleasures of Reading*

THE last time I tasted this luxury in its full perfection was one day after a sultry day's walk in summer between Farnham and Alton. I was fairly tired out; I walked into an inn-yard (I think at the latter place); I was shown by the waiter to what looked at first like common outhouses at the other end of it, but they turned out to be a suite of rooms, probably a hundred years old—the one I entered opened into an old-fashioned garden, embellished with beds of larkspur and a leaden Mercury; it was wainscoted, and there was a grave-looking, dark-coloured portrait of Charles II hanging up over the tiled chimneypiece. I had *Love for Love* in my pocket, and began to read; coffee was brought in in a silver coffee-pot; the cream, the bread and butter, every thing was excellent, and the flavour of Congreve's style prevailed over all. I prolonged the entertainment till a late hour, and relished this divine comedy better even than when I used to see it played by Miss Mellon, as Miss Prue; Bob Palmer, as Tattle; and Bannister, as honest Ben. This circumstance happened just five years ago, and it seems like yesterday. If I count my life so by lustres, it will soon glide away; yet I shall not have to repine, if, while it lasts, it is enriched with a few such recollections!

The Plain Speaker

352 *John Cavanagh*

DIED at his house in Burbage Street, St. Giles's, John Cavanagh, the famous hand fives-player. When a person dies who does any one thing better than any one else in the world, which so many others are trying to do well, it leaves a gap in society. It is not likely that any one will now see the game of fives played in its perfection for many years to come—for Cavanagh is dead, and has not left his peer behind him.

It may be said that there are things of more importance than striking a ball against a wall—there are things, indeed, that make more noise and do as little good, such as making war and peace, making speeches and answering them, making verses and blotting them, making money and throwing it away. But the game of fives is what no one despises who has ever played at it. It is the finest exercise for the body, and the best relaxation for the mind. The Roman poet said that 'Care mounted behind the horseman and stuck to his skirts'. But this remark would not have applied to the fives-player. He who takes to playing at fives is twice young. He feels neither the past nor future 'in the instant'. Debts, taxes, 'domestic treason, foreign levy, nothing can touch him further.' He has no other wish, no other thought, from the moment the game begins, but that of striking the ball, of placing it, of *making* it! This Cavanagh was sure to do. Whenever he touched the ball there was an end of the chase. His eye was certain, his hand fatal, his presence of mind complete. He could do what he pleased, and he always knew exactly what to do. He saw the whole game, and played it; took instant advantage of his adversary's weakness, and recovered balls, as if by a miracle and from sudden thought, that every one gave for lost. He had equal power and skill, quickness, and judgement. He could either outwit his antagonist by finesse, or beat him by main strength. Sometimes, when he seemed preparing to send the ball with the full swing of his arm, he would by a slight turn of his wrist drop it within an inch of the line. In general, the ball came from his hand, as if from a racket, in a straight, horizontal line; so that it was in vain to attempt to overtake or stop it. As it was said of a great orator that he never was at a loss for a word, and for the properest word, so Cavanagh always could tell the degree of force necessary to be given to a ball, and the precise direction in which it should be sent. He did his work with the greatest ease; never took more pains than was necessary; and, while others were fagging themselves to death, was as cool and collected as if he had just entered the court. His style of play was as remarkable as his power of execution. He had no affectation, no trifling. He did not throw away the game to show off an attitude or try an experiment. He was a fine, sensible, manly player, who did what he could, but that was more than any one else could even affect to do. His blows were not undecided and ineffectual—lumbering like Mr. Wordsworth's epic poetry, nor wavering like Mr. Coleridge's lyric prose, nor short of the mark like Mr. Brougham's speeches, nor wide of it like Mr. Canning's wit, nor foul like the *Quarterly*, nor *let* balls like the *Edinburgh Review*. Cobbett and Junius together would have made a Cavanagh. He was the best *up-hill* player in the world; even when his adversary was fourteen he would play on the same or better, and as he never flung away the game through carelessness and conceit, he never gave it up through laziness or want of heart. The only peculiarity of his play was that he never *volleyed*, but let the balls hop; but if they rose an inch from the ground he never missed having them. There was not only nobody equal, but nobody second to him. It is supposed that he could give any other player half the game, or beat them with his left hand. . .

Cavanagh was an Irishman by birth, and a house-painter by profession. He had once laid aside his working-dress, and walked up, in his smartest clothes, to the Rosemary Branch to have an afternoon's pleasure. A person accosted him, and asked him if he would have a game. So they agreed to play for half a crown a game and a bottle of cider. The first game began—it was seven, eight, ten, thirteen, fourteen, all. Cavanagh won it. The next was the same. They played on, and each game was hardly contested. 'There,' said the unconscious fives-player, 'there was a stroke that Cavanagh could not take: I never played better in my life, and yet I can't win a game. I don't know how it is!' However, they played on, Cavanagh winning every game, and the bystanders drinking the cider and laughing all the time. In the twelfth game, when Cavanagh was only four, and the stranger thirteen, a person came in and said, 'What! are you here, Cavanagh?' The words were no sooner pronounced than the astonished player let the ball drop from his hand, and saying, 'What! have I been breaking my heart all this time to beat Cavanagh?' refused to make another effort. 'And yet, I give you my word,' said Cavanagh, telling the story with some triumph, 'I played all the while with my clenched fist.' . .

He could not have shown himself in any ground in England but he would have been immediately surrounded with inquisitive gazers, trying to find out in what part of his frame his unrivalled skill lay, as politicians wonder to see the balance of Europe suspended in

Lord Castlereagh's face, and admire the trophies of the British Navy lurking under Mr. Croker's hanging brow. Now Cavanagh was as good-looking a man as the noble Lord, and much better looking than the Right Hon. Secretary. He had a clear, open countenance, and did not look sideways or down, like Mr. Murray the bookseller. He was a young fellow of sense, humour, and courage. He once had a quarrel with a waterman at Hungerford Stairs, and, they say, served him out in great style. In a word, there are hundreds at this day who cannot mention his name without admiration, as the best fives-player that perhaps ever lived (the greatest excellence of which they have any notion); and the noisy shout of the ring happily stood him in stead of the unheard voice of posterity! . . We have paid this willing tribute to his memory.

Let no rude hand deface it
And his forlorn '*Hic Jacet*'.

Table-Talk

JANE TAYLOR

1783–1824

353 *A Young Lady's Education*

WELL! . . my education is at last finished: indeed it would be strange, if, after five years' hard application, anything were left incomplete. Happily that is all over now; and I have nothing to do, but to exercise my various accomplishments.

Let me see!—as to French, I am mistress of that, and speak it, if possible, with more fluency than English. Italian I can read with ease, and pronounce very well: as well, at least, and better, than any of my friends; and that is all one need wish for in

Italian. Music I have learned till I am perfectly sick of it. But, now that we have a grand piano, it will be delightful to play when we have company. I must still continue to practise a little;—the only thing, I think, that I need now to improve myself in. And then there are my Italian songs! which everybody allows I sing with taste, and as it is what so few people can pretend to, I am particularly glad that I can.

My drawings are universally admired; especially the shells and flowers; which are beautiful, certainly; besides this, I have a decided taste in all kinds of fancy ornaments.

And then my dancing and waltzing! in which our master himself owned that he could take me no farther!—just the figure for it certainly; it would be unpardonable if I did not excel.

As to common things, geography, and history, and poetry, and philosophy, thank my stars, I have got through them all! so that I may consider myself not only perfectly accomplished, but also thoroughly well-informed.

Well, to be sure, how much have I fagged through—; the only wonder is that one head can contain it all.

Contributions of Q.Q.

WASHINGTON IRVING

1783–1859

354 *The Stage Coach*

IN the course of a December tour in Yorkshire, I rode for a long distance in one of the public coaches, on the day preceding Christmas. The coach was crowded, both inside and out, with passengers, who, by their talk, seemed principally bound to the mansions of relations or friends, to eat the Christmas dinner. It was loaded also with hampers of game, and baskets and boxes of delicacies; and hares hung dangling their long ears about the coachman's box, presents from distant friends for the impending feast. I had three fine rosy-cheeked school-boys for my fellow-passengers inside, full of the buxom health and manly spirit which I have observed in the children of this country. They were returning home for the holidays in high glee, and promising themselves a world of enjoyment. It was delightful to hear the gigantic plans of the little rogues, and the impracticable feats they were to perform during their six weeks' emancipation from the abhorred thraldom of book, birch, and pedagogue. They were full of anticipations of the meeting with the family and household, down to the very cat and dog; and of the joy they were to give their little sisters by the presents with which their pockets were crammed; but the meeting to which they seemed to look forward with the greatest impatience was with Bantam, which I found to be a pony, and according to their talk, possessed of more virtues than any steed since the days of Bucephalus. How he could trot! how he could run! and then such leaps as he would take—there was not a hedge in the whole country that he could not clear.

They were under the particular guardianship of the coachman, to whom, whenever an opportunity presented, they addressed a host of questions, and pronounced him one of the best fellows in the world. Indeed, I could not but notice the more than ordinary air of bustle and importance of the coachman, who wore his hat a little on one side, and had a large bunch of Christmas greens stuck in the buttonhole of his coat. He is always a personage full of mighty care and business, but he is particularly so during this season, having so many commissions to execute in consequence of the great interchange of presents. . .

Perhaps it might be owing to the pleasing serenity that reigned in my own mind, that I fancied I saw cheerfulness in every countenance throughout the journey. A stage coach, however, carries animation always with it, and puts the world in motion as it whirls along. The horn, sounded at the entrance of a village, produces a general bustle. Some hasten forth to meet friends; some with bundles and bandboxes to secure places, and in the hurry of the moment can hardly take leave of the group that accompanies them. In the meantime the coachman has a world of small commissions to execute. Sometimes he delivers a hare or pheasant; sometimes jerks a small parcel or newspaper to the door of a public-house; and sometimes, with knowing leer and words of sly import, hands to some half-blushing, half-laughing housemaid an odd-shaped *billet doux* from some rustic admirer. As the coach rattles through the village, every one runs to the window, and you have glances on every side of fresh country faces and blooming giggling girls. At the corners are assembled juntos of village idlers and wise men, who take their stations there for the important purpose of seeing company pass; but the sagest knot is generally at the blacksmith's, to whom the passing of the coach is an event fruitful of much speculation.

The Sketch Book

355 *Dulce Domum*

WE had passed for some time along the wall of a park, and at length the chaise stopped at the gate. It was in a heavy magnificent old style, of iron bars, fancifully wrought at top into flourishes and flowers. The huge square columns that supported the gate were surmounted by the family crest. Close adjoining was the porter's lodge, sheltered under dark fir-trees, and almost buried in shrubbery.

The postboy rang a large porter's bell, which resounded through the still, frosty air, and was answered by the distant barking of dogs, with which the mansion-house seemed garrisoned. An old woman immediately appeared at the gate. As the moonlight fell strongly upon her, I had a full view of a little primitive dame, dressed very much in the antique taste, with a neat kerchief and stomacher, and her silver hair peeping from under a cap of snowy whiteness. She came curtseying forth, with many expressions of simple joy at seeing her young master. Her husband, it seemed, was up at the house keeping Christmas eve in the servants' hall; they could not do without him, as he was the best hand at a song and story in the household.

My friend proposed that we should alight and walk through the park to the hall, which was at no great distance, while the chaise should follow on. Our road wound through a noble avenue of trees, among the naked branches of which the moon glittered as she rolled through the deep vault of a cloudless sky. The lawn beyond was sheeted with a slight covering of snow, which here and there sparkled as the moonbeams caught a frosty crystal; and at a distance might be seen a thin transparent vapour, stealing up from the low grounds and threatening gradually to shroud the landscape.

My companion looked around him with transport :—'How often,' said he, 'have I scampered up this avenue, on returning home on school vacations! How often have I played under these trees when a boy! I feel a degree of filial reverence for them, as we look up to those who have cherished us in childhood. My father was always scrupulous in exacting our holidays, and having us around him on family festivals. He used to direct and superintend our games with the strictness that some parents do the studies of their children. He was very particular that we should play the old English games according to their original form; and consulted old books for precedent and authority for every "merrie disport"; yet I assure you there never was pedantry so delightful. It was the policy of the good old gentleman to make his children feel that home was the happiest place in the world; and I value this delicious home-feeling as one of the choicest gifts a parent could bestow.'

We were interrupted by the clamour of a troop of dogs of all sorts and sizes, 'mongrel, puppy, whelp and hound, and curs of low degree,' that, disturbed by the ring of the porter's bell, and the rattling of the chaise, came bounding, open-mouthed, across the lawn.

'——The little dogs and all,
Tray, Blanch, and Sweetheart—see, they bark at me!'

cried Bracebridge, laughing. At the sound of his voice, the bark was changed into a yelp of delight, and in a moment he was surrounded and almost overpowered by the caresses of the faithful animals.

The Sketch Book

356 *Little Britain*

BUT though thus fallen into decline, Little Britain still bears traces of its former splendour. There are several houses ready to tumble down, the fronts of which are magnificently enriched with old oaken carvings of hideous faces, unknown birds, beasts, and fishes; and fruits and flowers which it would perplex a naturalist to classify. There are also, in Aldersgate Street, certain remains of what were once spacious and lordly family mansions, but which have in latter days been subdivided into several tenements. Here may often be found the family of a petty tradesman, with its trumpery furniture, burrowing among the relics of antiquated finery, in great rambling time-stained apartments, with fretted ceilings, gilded cornices, and enormous marble fireplaces. The lanes and courts also contain many smaller houses, not on so grand a scale, but, like your small ancient gentry, sturdily maintaining their claims to equal antiquity. These have their gable-ends to the street; great bow windows, with diamond panes set in lead, grotesque carvings, and low arched doorways. . .

Little Britain may truly be called the heart's core of the City; the stronghold of true John Bullism. It is a fragment of London as it was in its better days, with its antiquated folks and fashions. Here flourish in great preservation many of the holiday games and customs of yore. The inhabitants most religiously eat pancakes on Shrove Tuesday, hot-cross buns on Good Friday, and roast goose at Michaelmas; they send love-letters on Valentine's Day, burn the Pope on the fifth of November, and kiss all the girls under the mistletoe at Christmas. Roast beef and plum pudding are also held in superstitious veneration, and port and sherry maintain their grounds as the only true English wines; all others being considered vile outlandish beverages.

The Sketch Book

357 *Poets' Corner*

I PASSED some time in Poets' Corner, which occupies an end of one of the transepts or cross aisles of the abbey. The monuments are generally simple; for the lives of literary men afford no striking themes for the sculptor. Shakespeare and Addison have statues erected to their memories; but the greater part have busts, medallions, and sometimes mere inscriptions. Notwithstanding the simplicity of these memorials, I have always observed that the visitors to the abbey remained longest about them. A kinder and fonder feeling takes place of that cold curiosity or vague admiration with which they gaze on the splendid monuments of the great and the heroic. They linger about these as about the tombs of friends and companions; for indeed there is something of companionship between the author and the reader. Other men are known to posterity only through the medium of history, which is continually growing faint and obscure; but the intercourse between the author and his fellow men is ever new, active, and immediate. He has lived for them more than for himself; he has sacrificed surrounding enjoyments, and shut himself up from the delights of social life, that he might the more intimately commune with distant minds and distant ages. Well may the world cherish his renown; for it has been purchased, not by deeds of violence and blood, but by the diligent dispensation of pleasure.

Well may posterity be grateful to his memory; for he has left it an inheritance, not of empty names and sounding actions, but whole treasures of wisdom, bright gems of thought, and golden veins of language.

The Sketch Book

LEIGH HUNT

1784–1859

358 *His Prison*

THE doctor then proposed that I should be removed into the prison infirmary; and this proposal was granted. Infirmary had, I confess, an awkward sound, even to my ears. I fancied a room shared with other sick persons, not the best fitted for companions; but the good-natured doctor (his name was Dixon) undeceived me. The infirmary was divided into four wards, with as many small rooms attached to them. The two upper wards were occupied, but the two on the floor had never been used: and one of these, not very providently (for I had not yet learned to think of money) I turned into a noble room. I papered the walls with a trellis of roses; I had the ceiling coloured with clouds and sky; the barred windows I screened with Venetian blinds; and when my bookcases were set up with their busts, and flowers and a pianoforte made their appearance, perhaps there was not a handsomer room on that side the water. I took a pleasure, when a stranger knocked at the door, to see him come in and stare about him. The surprise on issuing from the Borough, and passing through avenues of a gaol, was dramatic. Charles Lamb declared there was no other such room, except in a fairy tale.

But I possessed another surprise; which was a garden. There was a little yard outside the room, railed off from another belonging to the neighbouring ward. This yard I shut in with green palings, adorned it with a trellis, bordered it with a thick bed of earth from a nursery, and even contrived to have a grass-plot. The earth I filled with flowers and young trees. There was an apple-tree, from which we managed to get a pudding the second year. As to my flowers, they were allowed to be perfect. Thomas Moore, who came to see me with Lord Byron, told me he had seen no such heart's-ease. I bought the *Parnaso Italiano* while in prison, and used often to think of a passage in it, while looking at this miniature piece of horticulture:—

Mio picciol orto,
A me sei vigna, e campo, e selva, e prato.—BALDI.

My little garden,
To me thou'rt vineyard, field, and meadow, and wood.

Here I wrote and read in fine weather, sometimes under an awning. In autumn, my trellises were hung with scarlet-runners, which added to the flowery investment. I used to shut my eyes in my arm-chair, and affect to think myself hundreds of miles off.

But my triumph was in issuing forth of a morning. A wicket out of the garden led into the large one belonging to the prison. The latter was only for vegetables; but it contained a cherry tree, which I saw twice in blossom. I parcelled out the ground in my imagination into favourite districts. I made a point of dressing myself as if for a long walk; and then, putting on my gloves, and taking my book under my arm, stepped forth, requesting my wife not to wait dinner if I was too late. My eldest little boy, to whom Lamb addressed some charming verses on the occasion, was my constant companion, and we used to play all sorts of juvenile games together. It was, probably, in dreaming of one of these games (but the words had a more touching effect on my ear) that he exclaimed one night in his sleep, 'No: I'm not lost; I'm found.' Neither he nor I were very strong at that time; but I have lived to see him a man of eight and forty; and wherever he is found, a generous hand and a great understanding will be found together.

Autobiography

359 *Furze on Wimbledon Common*

THERE is an advertisement in the papers announcing a building project at Wimbledon and Westhill. The houses are to occupy a portion of Wimbledon Park; and boards are put among the trees by the roadside, boasting of the 'fine frontage'. Well may they boast of it, especially at this season of the year. It is a golden undulation; a foreground, and from some points of view, a middle distance, fit to make the richest painter despair; a veritable Field of Cloth of Gold. Morning (Aurora, the golden goddess), when the dawn is of a fineness to match, must look beauty for beauty on it. Sunset is divine. The gold goes stretching away in the distance towards the dark trees, like the rich evening of a poetic life. No wonder Linnaeus, when he came to England and first beheld this glorious shrub in bloom, fell down on his knees and thanked God that he had lived to see it. . . As to figures in the landscape, they are not many, nor discordant; such as a horse or two, a few cattle, now and then a horseman, or a sturdy peasant on foot, or a beauty in a barouche. Sometimes the peasant is aged, but hale; or sturdy, though but a child; signs both of good air, and prosperity, and a true country spot. I hardly know which is the more picturesque sight—a fine ruddy-cheeked little peasant boy, not beyond childhood, coming along with a wheelbarrow full of this golden furze, his face looking like a bud a-top of it; or a bent, hearty, old man (bent with age, not with his perquisite) carrying off a bunch of it on his back, as if he triumphed over time and youth.

Table-Talk

JOHN WILSON (' CHRISTOPHER NORTH ')

1785–1854

360 *Our Country*

NORTH. Yes, James, that is our country—not where we have breathed alone; not that land which we have loved, because it has shown to our opening eyes the brightness of heaven, and the gladness of earth; but the land for which we have hoped and feared,—that is to say, for which our bosom has beat with the consenting hopes and fears of many million hearts; that land, of which we have loved the mighty living and the mighty dead; that land, the Roman and the Greek would have said, where the boy had sung in the pomp that led the sacrifice to the altars of the ancient deities of the soil.

SHEPHERD. And therefore, when a man, he would guard them frae profanation, and had he a thousan' lives, would pour them a' out for sake o' what some micht ca' superstition, but which you and me, and Southside, sittin there wi' his great grey een, would fearna, in the face o' heaven, to ca' religion.

Noctes Ambrosianae 1835

THOMAS DE QUINCEY

1785–1859

361 *A London Waif*

TOWARDS nightfall I went down to Greek Street, and found, on taking possession of my new quarters, that the house already contained one single inmate,—a poor, friendless child, apparently ten years old; but she seemed hunger-bitten; and sufferings of that sort often make children look older than they are. From this forlorn child I learned that she had slept and lived there alone for some time before I came; and great joy the poor creature expressed when she found that I was in future to be her companion through the hours of darkness. The house could hardly be called large—that is, it was not large on each separate storey; but, having four storeys in all, it was large enough to impress vividly the sense of its echoing loneliness; and, from the want of furniture, the noise of the rats made a prodigious uproar on the staircase and hall; so that, amidst the real fleshly ills of cold and hunger, the forsaken child had found leisure to suffer still more from the self-created one of ghosts. Against these enemies I could promise her protection; human companionship was in itself protection; but of other and more needful aid I had, alas! little to offer. We lay upon the floor, with a bundle of law-papers for a pillow, but with no other covering than a large horseman's cloak; afterwards, however, we discovered in a garret an old sofa-cover, a small piece of rug, and some fragments of other articles, which added a little to our comfort. The poor child crept close to me for warmth, and for security against her ghostly enemies. When I was not more than usually ill, I took her into my arms, so that, in general, she was tolerably warm, and often slept when I could not. . .

Whether this child were an illegitimate daughter of Mr. Brunell, or only a servant, I could not ascertain; she did not herself know; but certainly she was treated altogether as a menial servant. No sooner did Mr. Brunell make his appearance than she went below-stairs, brushed his shoes, coat, &c.; and, except when she was summoned to run upon some errand, she never emerged from the dismal Tartarus of the kitchens to the upper air until my welcome knock towards nightfall called up her little trembling footsteps to the front-door. Of her life during the daytime, however, I knew little but what I gathered from her own account at night; for, as soon as the hours of business commenced, I saw that my absence would be acceptable; and, in general, therefore, I went off and sat in the parks or elsewhere until the approach of twilight.

Confessions of an Opium-Eater

362 *News of Talavera*

AS we stayed for three or four minutes, I alighted, and immediately from a dismantled stall in the street, where no doubt she had been presiding through the earlier part of the night, advanced eagerly a middle-aged woman. The sight of my newspaper it was that had drawn her attention upon myself. The victory which we were carrying down to the provinces on *this* occasion, was the imperfect one of Talavera—imperfect for its results, such was the virtual treachery of the Spanish general, Cuesta, but not imperfect in its ever-memorable heroism. I told her the main outline of the battle. The agitation of her enthusiasm had been so conspicuous when listening, and when first applying for information, that I could not but ask her if she had not some relative in the Peninsular army. Oh, yes ; her only son was there. In what regiment? He was a trooper in the 23rd Dragoons. My heart sank within me as she made that answer.

This sublime regiment, which an Englishman should never mention without raising his hat to their memory, had made the most memorable and effective charge recorded in military annals. They leaped their horses —*over* a trench where they could, *into* it, and with the result of death or mutilation where they could *not.* What proportion cleared the trench is nowhere stated. Those who *did,* closed up and went down upon the enemy with such divinity of fervour (I use the word *divinity* by design : the inspiration of God must have prompted this movement to those whom even then He was calling to His presence), that two results followed. As regarded the enemy, this 23rd Dragoons, not, I believe, originally three hundred and fifty strong, paralysed a French column, six thousand strong, then ascended the hill, and fixed the gaze of the whole French army. As regarded themselves, the 23rd were supposed at first to have been barely not annihilated ; but eventually, I believe, about one in four survived. And this, then, was the regiment—a regiment already for some hours glorified and hallowed to the ear of all London . . . in which the young trooper served whose mother was now talking in a spirit of such joyous enthusiasm. Did I tell her the truth? Had I the heart to break up her dreams? No. To-morrow, said I to myself—to-morrow, or the next day, will publish the worst. For one night more, wherefore should she not sleep in peace? After to-morrow, the chances are too many that peace will forsake her pillow. This brief respite, then, let her owe to *my* gift and *my* forbearance. But, if I told her not of the bloody price that had been paid, not, therefore, was I silent on the contributions from her son's regiment to that day's service and glory. I showed her not the funeral banners under which the noble regiment was sleeping. I lifted not the over-shadowing laurels from the bloody trench in which horse and rider lay mangled together. But I told her how these dear children of England, officers and privates, had leaped their horses over all obstacles as gaily as hunters to the morning's chase. I told her how they rode their horses into the mists of death (saying to myself, but not saying to *her*), and laid down their young lives for thee, O mother England! as willingly—poured out their noble blood as cheerfully—as ever, after a long day's sport, when infants, they had rested their wearied heads upon their mother's knees, or had sunk to sleep in her arms.

Strange it is, yet true, that she seemed to have no fears for her son's safety, even after this knowledge that the 23rd Dragoons had been memorably engaged; but so much was she enraptured by the knowledge that *his* regiment, and therefore that *he*, had rendered conspicuous service in the dreadful conflict—a service which had actually made them, within the last twelve hours, the foremost topic of conversation in London—so absolutely was fear swallowed up in joy—that, in the mere simplicity of her fervent nature, the poor woman threw her arms round my neck, as she thought of her son, and gave to *me* the kiss which secretly was meant for *him*.

The English Mail-Coach

THOMAS DE QUINCEY

363 *Our Ladies of Sorrow*

'THESE are the Sorrows; and they are three in number, as the *Graces* are three, who dress man's life with beauty; the *Parcae* are three, who weave the dark arras of man's life in their mysterious loom always with colours sad in part, sometimes angry with tragic crimson and black; the *Furies* are three, who visit with retributions called from the other side of the grave offences that walk upon this; and once even the *Muses* were but three, who fit the harp, the trumpet, or the lute, to the great burdens of man's impassioned creations. These are the Sorrows, all three of whom I know.' The last words I say *now*; but in Oxford I said—' one of whom I know, and the others too surely I *shall* know'. For already, in my fervent youth, I saw (dimly relieved upon the dark background of my dreams) the imperfect lineaments of the awful sisters. . .

The eldest of the three is named *Mater Lachrymarum*, Our Lady of Tears. She it is that night and day raves and moans, calling for vanished faces. She stood in Rama, when a voice was heard of lamentation —Rachel weeping for her children, and refusing to be comforted. She it was that stood in Bethlehem on the night when Herod's sword swept its nurseries of Innocents and the little feet were stiffened for ever, which heard at times as they tottered along floors overhead, woke pulses of love in household hearts that were not unmarked in heaven.

Her eyes are sweet and subtle, wild and sleepy by turns; oftentimes rising to the clouds; oftentimes challenging the heavens. She wears a diadem round her head. And I knew by childish memories that she could go abroad upon the winds, when she heard the sobbing of litanies or the thundering of organs, and when she beheld the mustering of summer clouds. This sister, the elder, it is that carries keys more than papal at her girdle, which open every cottage and every palace. . .

By the power of her keys it is that Our Lady of Tears glides a ghostly intruder into the chambers of sleepless men, sleepless women, sleepless children. . .

Every captive in every dungeon;—all that are betrayed, and all that are rejected; outcasts by traditionary law, and children of *hereditary* disgrace—all these walk with Our Lady of Sighs. She also carries a key; but she needs it little. For her kingdom is chiefly amongst the tents of Shem, and the houseless vagrant of every clime. Yet in the very highest ranks of man she finds chapels of her own; and even in glorious England there are some that, to the world, carry their heads as proudly as the reindeer, who yet secretly have received her mark upon their foreheads.

But the third sister, who is also the youngest—— Hush! whisper, whilst we talk of *her*! Her kingdom is not large, or else no flesh should live; but within that kingdom all power is hers. Her head, turreted like that of Cybele, rises almost beyond the reach of sight. She droops not; and her eyes rising so high, *might* be hidden by distance. But, being what they are, they cannot be hidden; through the treble veil of crape which she wears, the fierce light of a blazing misery, that rests not for matins or for vespers—for noon of day or noon of night—for ebbing or for flowing tide—may be read from the very ground. She is the defier of God. She also is the mother of lunacies, and the suggestress of suicides. Deep lie the roots of her power; but narrow is the nation that she rules. For she can approach only those in whom a profound nature has been upheaved by central convulsions; in whom the heart trembles and the brain rocks under conspiracies of tempest from without and tempest from within. Madonna moves with uncertain steps, fast or slow, but still with tragic grace. Our Lady of Sighs creeps timidly and stealthily. But this youngest sister moves with incalculable motions, bounding, and with a tiger's leaps. She carries no key; for, though coming rarely amongst men, she storms all doors at which she is permitted to enter at all. And *her* name is *Mater Tenebrarum*—Our Lady of Darkness.

These were the *Semnai Theai*, or Sublime Goddesses—these were the *Eumenides*, or Gracious Ladies (so called by antiquity in shuddering propitiation)—of my Oxford dreams.

Suspiria de Profundis

SIR WILLIAM NAPIER

1785–1860

364 *Albuera*

THE Fourth Division was composed of two brigades: one of Portuguese under General Harvey; the other, under Sir William Myers, consisting of the seventh and twenty-third regiments was called the fusilier brigade: Harvey's Portuguese were immediately pushed in between Lumley's dragoons and the hill, where they were charged by some French cavalry, whom they beat off, and meantime Cole led his fusiliers up the contested height. At this time six guns were in the enemy's possession, the whole of Werlé's reserves were coming forward to reinforce the front column of the French, the remnant of Houghton's brigade could no longer maintain its ground, the field was heaped with carcasses, the lancers were riding furiously about the captured artillery on the upper parts of the hill, and behind all, Hamilton's Portuguese and Alten's Germans, now withdrawing from the bridge, seemed to be in full retreat. Soon however Cole's fusiliers, flanked by a battalion of the Lusitanian legion under Colonel Hawkshawe, mounted the hill, drove off the lancers, recovered five of the captured guns and one colour, and appeared on the right of Houghton's brigade, precisely as Abercrombie passed it on the left.

Such a gallant line, issuing from the midst of the smoke and rapidly separating itself from the confused and broken multitude, startled the enemy's masses, which were increasing and pressing onwards as to an assured victory; they wavered, hesitated, and then vomiting forth a storm of fire, hastily endeavoured to enlarge their front, while a fearful discharge of grape from all their artillery whistled through the British ranks. Myers was killed, Cole and the three colonels, Ellis, Blakeney and Hawkshawe, fell wounded, and the fusilier battalions, struck by the iron tempest, reeled and staggered like sinking ships; but suddenly and sternly recovering they closed on their terrible enemies, and then was seen with what a strength and majesty the British soldier fights. In vain did Soult with voice and gesture animate his Frenchmen, in vain did the hardiest veterans break from the crowded columns and sacrifice their lives to gain time for the mass to open out on such a fair field; in vain did the mass itself bear up, and, fiercely striving, fire indiscriminately upon friends and foes, while the horsemen hovering on the flank threatened to charge the advancing line. Nothing could stop that astonishing infantry. No sudden burst of undisciplined valour, no nervous enthusiasm weakened the stability of their order, their flashing eyes were bent on the dark columns in their front, their measured tread shook the ground, their dreadful volleys swept away the head of every formation, their deafening shouts overpowered the dissonant cries that broke from all parts of the tumultuous crowd, as slowly and with a horrid carnage it was pushed by the incessant vigour of the attack to the farthest edge of the hill. In vain did the French reserves mix with the struggling multitude to sustain the fight, their efforts only increased the irremediable confusion, and the mighty mass, breaking off like a loosened cliff, went headlong down the steep: the rain flowed after in streams discoloured with blood, and eighteen hundred unwounded men, the remnant of six thousand unconquerable British soldiers, stood triumphant on the fatal hill!

History of the War in the Peninsula

365 *Salamanca*

THE cannonade now became heavy, and the spectacle surprisingly beautiful, for the lighter smoke and mist, curling up in fantastic pillars, formed a huge and glittering dome tinged of many colours by the rising sun; and through the grosser vapour below, the restless horsemen were seen or lost as the fume thickened from the rapid play of the guns, while the bluff head of land, beyond the Trabancos, covered with French troops, appeared, by an optical deception, close at hand, dilated to the size of a mountain, and crowned with gigantic soldiers, who were continually breaking off and sliding down into the fight. Suddenly a dismounted cavalry officer stalked from the midst of the smoke towards the line of infantry; his gait was peculiarly rigid, and he appeared to hold a bloody handkerchief to his heart, but that which seemed a cloth, was a broad and dreadful wound; a bullet had entirely effaced the flesh from his left shoulder and from his breast, and had carried away part of his ribs, his heart was bared, and its movement plainly discerned. It was a piteous and yet a noble sight, for his countenance though ghastly was firm, his step scarcely indicated weakness, and his voice never faltered. This unyielding man's name was Williams; he died a short distance from the field of battle, and it was said, in the arms of his son, a youth of fourteen, who had followed his father to the Peninsula in hopes of obtaining a commission, for they were not affluent.

History of the War in the Peninsula

THOMAS LOVE PEACOCK

1785–1866

366 *The Learned Friend*

'GOD bless my soul, sir!' exclaimed the Reverend Doctor Folliott, bursting, one fine May morning, into the breakfast-room at Crotchet Castle, 'I am out of all patience with this march of mind. Here has my house been nearly burned down, by my cook taking it into her head to study hydrostatics, in a sixpenny-tract, published by the Steam Intellect Society, and written by a learned friend[1] who is for doing all the world's business as well as his own, and

[1] Lord Brougham.

is equally well qualified to handle every branch of human knowledge. I have a great abomination of this learned friend; as author, lawyer, and politician, he is *triformis*, like Hecate: and in every one of his three forms he is *bifrons*, like Janus; the true Mr. Facing-both-ways of Vanity Fair. My cook must read his rubbish in bed; and as might naturally be expected, she dropped suddenly fast asleep, overturned the candle, and set the curtains in a blaze. Luckily, the footman went into the room at the moment, in time to tear down the curtains and throw them into the chimney, and a pitcher of water on her nightcap extinguished her wick: she is a greasy subject, and would have burned like a short mould.'

Crotchet Castle

367 *Picturesque Gardening*

'MY dear Sir,' said Mr. Milestone, 'accord me your permission to wave the wand of enchantment over your grounds. The rocks shall be blown up, the trees shall be cut down, the wilderness and all its goats shall vanish like mist. Pagodas and Chinese bridges, gravel walks and shrubberies, bowling-greens, canals, and clumps of larch, shall rise upon its ruins. One age, Sir, has brought to light the treasures of ancient learning: a second has penetrated into the depths of metaphysics: a third has brought to perfection the science of astronomy: but it was reserved for the exclusive genius of the present times, to invent the noble art of picturesque gardening, which has given, as it were, a new tint to the complexion of nature, and a new outline to the physiognomy of the universe!'

'Give me leave,' said Sir Patrick O'Prism, 'to take an exception to that same. Your system of levelling, and trimming, and clipping, and docking, and clumping, and polishing, and cropping, and shaving, destroys all the beautiful intricacies of natural luxuriance, and all the graduated harmonies of light and shade, melting into one another, as you see them on that rock over yonder. I never saw one of your improved places, as you call them, and which are nothing but big bowling-greens, like sheets of green paper, with a parcel of round clumps scattered over them like so many spots of ink, flicked at random out of a pen, and a solitary animal here and there looking as if it were lost, that I did not think it was for all the world like Hounslow Heath, thinly sprinkled over with bushes and highwaymen.'

'Sir,' said Mr. Milestone, 'you will have the goodness to make a distinction between the picturesque and the beautiful.'

'Will I?' said Sir Patrick: 'och! but I won't. For what is beautiful? That which pleases the eye. And what pleases the eye? Tints variously broken and blended. Now, tints variously broken and blended constitute the picturesque.'

'Allow me,' said Mr. Gall. 'I distinguish the picturesque and the beautiful, and I add to them, in the laying out of grounds, a third and distinct character, which I call *unexpectedness*.'

'Pray, Sir,' said Mr. Milestone, 'by what name do you distinguish this character, when a person walks round the grounds for the second time?'

Headlong Hall

MARY RUSSELL MITFORD

1787–1855

368

Hannah

SINCE the new marriage act, we, who belong to country magistrates, have gained a priority over the rest of the parish in matrimonial news. We (the privileged) see on a work-day the names which the Sabbath announces to the generality. Many a blushing awkward pair hath our little lame clerk (a sorry Cupid !) ushered in between dark and light to stammer and hacker, to bow and curtsey, to sign or make a mark, as it pleases Heaven. One Saturday, at the usual hour, the limping clerk made his appearance ; and, walking through our little hall, I saw a fine athletic young man, the very image of health and vigour, mental and bodily, holding the hand of a young woman, who, with her head half buried in a geranium in the window, was turning bashfully away, listening, and yet not seeming to listen, to his tender whispers. The shrinking grace of that bending figure, was not to be mistaken. 'Hannah !' and she went aside with me, and a rapid series of questions and answers conveyed the story of the courtship. 'William was', said Hannah, 'a journeyman hatter in B. He had walked over one Sunday evening to see the cricketing, and then he came again. Her mother liked him. Everybody liked her William—and she had promised—she was going—was it wrong ? '—' Oh no !—and where are you to live ? '—' William has got a room in B. He works for Mr. Smith, the rich hatter in the market-place, and Mr. Smith speaks of him—oh so well ! But William will not tell me where our room is. I suppose in some narrow street or lane, which he is afraid I shall not like, as our common is so pleasant.

He little thinks—anywhere.'—She stopped suddenly; but her blush and her clasped hands finished the sentence, 'anywhere with him!'—'And when is the happy day?'—'On Monday fortnight, Madam,' said the bridegroom elect, advancing with the little clerk to summon Hannah to the parlour, 'the earliest day possible.' He drew her arm through his, and we parted.

The Monday fortnight was a glorious morning; one of those rare November days when the sky and air are soft and bright as in April. 'What a beautiful day for Hannah!' was the first exclamation of the breakfast-table. 'Did she tell you where they should dine?'—'No, ma'am; I forgot to ask.'—'I can tell you,' said the master of the house, with somewhat of good-humoured importance in his air, somewhat of the look of a man who, having kept a secret as long as it was necessary, is not sorry to get rid of the burthen. 'I can tell you: in London.'—'In London!'—'Yes. Your little favourite has been in high luck. She has married the only son of one of the best and richest men in B., Mr. Smith, the great hatter. It is quite a romance,' continued he; 'William Smith walked over one Sunday evening to see a match at cricket. He saw our pretty Hannah, and forgot to look at the cricketers. After having gazed his fill, he approached to address her, and the little damsel was off like a bird. William did not like her the less for that, and thought of her the more. He came again, and again; and at last contrived to tame this wild dove, and even to get the *entrée* of the cottage. Hearing Hannah talk is not the way to fall out of love with her. So William, at last finding his case serious, laid the matter before his father, and requested his consent to the marriage. Mr. Smith was at first a little startled; but William is an only son, and an excellent son; and, after talking with me, and looking at Hannah (I believe her sweet face was the more eloquent advocate of the two), he relented; and having a spice of his son's romance, finding that he had not mentioned his situation in life, he made a point of its being kept secret till the wedding-day. We have managed the business of settlements; and William, having discovered that his fair bride has some curiosity to see London, intends taking her thither for a fortnight. He will then bring her home to one of the best houses in B., a fine garden, fine furniture, fine clothes, fine servants, and more money than she will know what to do with. Really the surprise of Lord E.'s farmer's daughter, when, thinking she had married his steward, he brought her to Burleigh, and installed her as its mistress, could hardly have been greater. I hope the shock will not kill Hannah though, as is said to have been the case with that poor lady.'—'Oh no! Hannah loves her husband too well. Anywhere with him!'

And I was right. Hannah has survived the shock. She is returned to B., and I have been to call upon her. I never saw anything so delicate and bride-like as she looked in her white gown and her lace mob, in a room light and simple, and tasteful and elegant, with nothing fine except some beautiful greenhouse plants. Her reception was a charming mixture of sweetness and modesty, a little more respectful than usual, and far more shamefaced! Poor thing! her cheeks must have pained her! But this was the only difference. In everything else she is still the same Hannah, and has lost none of her old habits of kindness and gratitude. She was making a handsome matronly cap, evidently for her mother, and spoke, even with tears, of her new father's goodness to her and to Susan. She would fetch the cake and wine herself, and would gather, in spite of all remonstrance, some of her choice flowers as a parting nosegay. She did, indeed, just hint at her troubles with visitors and servants,—how strange and sad it was! seemed distressed at ringing the bell, and visibly shrank from the sound of a double knock. But, in spite of these calamities, Hannah is a happy woman. The double rap was her husband's; and the glow on her cheek, and the smile of her lips and eyes when he appeared, spoke more plainly than ever, 'Anywhere with him!'

Our Village

SIR HARRY SMITH

1787–1860

369 *The Child of Badajoz*

AFTER the attacks upon the breaches, some time before daylight Lord Fitzroy Somerset came to our Division. I think I was almost the first officer who spoke to him. He said, 'Where is Barnard?' I didn't know, but I assured his Lordship he was neither killed nor wounded. A few minutes after his Lordship said that the Duke desired the Light and 4th Divisions to storm again. 'The devil!' says I. 'Why, we have had enough; we are all knocked to pieces.' Lord Fitzroy says, 'I dare say, but you must try again.' I smiled and said, 'If we could not succeed with two whole fresh and unscathed Divisions, we are likely to make a poor show of it now. But we will try again with all our might.' Scarcely had this conversation occurred when a bugle sounded within the breach, indicating what had occurred at the citadel and Puerto de Olivença ; and here ended all the fighting. Our fellows would have gone at it again when collected and put into shape, but we were just as well pleased that our attempt had so attracted the attention of the enemy as greatly to facilitate that success which assured the prize contended for.

There is no battle, day or night, I would not willingly react except this. . .

The atrocities committed by our soldiers on the poor innocent and defenceless inhabitants of the city, no words suffice to depict. Civilized man, when let loose and the bonds of morality relaxed, is a far greater beast than the savage, more refined in his cruelty, more fiend-like in every act ; and oh, too truly did our heretofore noble soldiers disgrace themselves, though the officers exerted themselves to the utmost to repress it, many who had escaped the enemy being wounded in their merciful attempts ! Yet this scene of debauchery, however cruel to many, to me has been the solace and the whole happiness of my life for thirty-three years. A poor defenceless maiden of thirteen years was thrown upon my generous nature through her sister, as described so ably in Johnny Kincaid's book, of which this is an extract—

'I was conversing with a friend the day after, at the door of his tent, when we observed two ladies coming from the city, who made directly towards us ; they seemed both young, and when they came near, the elder of the two threw back her *mantilla* to address us, showing a remarkably handsome figure, with fine features ; but her sallow, sun-burnt, and careworn, though still youthful, countenance showed that in her " the time for tender thoughts and soft endearments had fled away and gone."

'She at once addressed us in that confident, heroic manner so characteristic of the high-bred Spanish maiden, told us who they were—the last of an ancient and honourable house—and referred to an officer high in rank in our army, who had been quartered there in the days of her prosperity, for the truth of her tale.

'Her husband, she said, was a Spanish officer in a distant part of the kingdom; he might, or he might not, still be living. But yesterday she and this her young sister were able to live in affluence and in a handsome house; to-day they knew not where to lay their heads, where to get a change of raiment or a morsel of bread. Her house, she said, was a wreck; and, to show the indignities to which they had been subjected, she pointed to where the blood was still trickling down their necks, caused by the wrenching of their ear-rings through the flesh by the hands of worse than savages, who would not take the trouble to unclasp them!

'For herself, she said, she cared not; but for the agitated and almost unconscious maiden by her side, whom she had but lately received over from the hands of her conventual instructresses, she was in despair, and knew not what to do; and that, in the rapine and ruin which was at that moment desolating the city, she saw no security for her but the seemingly indelicate one she had adopted—of coming to the camp and throwing themselves upon the protection of any British officer who would afford it; and so great, she said, was her faith in our national character, that she knew the appeal would not be made in vain, nor the confidence abused. Nor was it made in vain! Nor could it be abused, for she stood by the side of an angel! A being more transcendingly lovely I had never before seen—one more amiable I have never yet known!

'Fourteen summers had not yet passed over her youthful countenance, which was of a delicate freshness—more English than Spanish; her face, though not perhaps rigidly beautiful, was nevertheless so remarkably handsome, and so irresistibly attractive, surmounting a figure cast in nature's fairest mould, that to look at her was to love her; and I did love her, but I never told my love, and in the mean time another and more impudent fellow stepped in and won her! But yet I was happy, for in him she found such a one as her loveliness and her misfortunes claimed—a man of honour, and a husband in every way worthy of her!

'That a being so young, so lovely, and so interesting, just emancipated from the gloom of a convent, unknowing of the world and to the world unknown, should thus have been wrecked on a sea of troubles, and thrown on the mercy of strangers under circumstances so dreadful, so uncontrollable, and not have sunk to rise no more, must be the wonder of every one. Yet from the moment she was thrown on her own resources, her star was in the ascendant.

'Guided by a just sense of rectitude, an innate purity of mind, a singleness of purpose which defied malice, and a soul that soared above circumstances, she became alike the adored of the camp and of the drawing-room, and eventually the admired associate of princes. She yet lives, in the affections of her gallant husband, in an elevated situation in life, a pattern to her sex, and everybody's *beau ideal* of what a wife should be.

'Thrown upon each other's acquaintance in a manner so interesting, it is not to be wondered at that she and I conceived a friendship for each other, which has proved as lasting as our lives—a friendship which was cemented by after-circumstances so singularly romantic that imagination may scarcely picture them! The friendship of man is one thing—the friendship of woman another; and those only who have been on the theatre of fierce warfare, and knowing that such a being was on the spot, watching with earnest and increasing solicitude over his safety, alike with those most dear to her, can fully appreciate the additional value which it gives to one's existence.' [1]

[1] From *Random Shots by a Rifleman*, by Sir John Kincaid.

I confess myself to be the 'more impudent fellow', and if any reward is due to a soldier, never was one so honoured and distinguished as I have been by the possession of this dear child (for she was little more than a child at this moment), one with a sense of honour no knight ever exceeded in the most romantic days of chivalry, an understanding superior to her years, a masculine mind with a force of character no consideration could turn from her own just sense of rectitude, and all encased in a frame of Nature's fairest and most delicate moulding, the figure of an angel, with an eye of light and expression which then inspired me with a maddening love which, from that period to this (now thirty-three years), has never abated under many and the most trying circumstances. Thus, as good may come out of evil, this scene of devastation and spoil yielded to me a treasure invaluable; to me who, among so many dear friends, had escaped all dangers; to me, a wild youth not meriting such reward, and, however desirous, never able to express half his gratitude to God Almighty for such signal marks of His blessing shown to so young and so thoughtless a being. From that day to this she has been my guardian angel. She has shared with me the dangers and privations, the hardships and fatigues, of a restless life of war in every quarter of the globe. No murmur has ever escaped her. Bereft of every relative, of every tie to her country but the recollection of it, united to a man of different though Christian religion, yet that man has been and is her all, on whom have hinged the closed portals of hope, happiness, and bliss; if opened, misery, destitution, and bereavement, and every loss language can depict summed up in *one* word, '*He* is lost to me.' But, O my God,

Thou hast kindly spared us for each other ; we have, through thy grace, been but little separated, and we have, in unison of soul, received at Thy holy altar the Blessed Sacrament of the Body and Blood of Christ. May we, through His mediation, be still spared to each other in this life, and in the life to come be eternally united in Heaven ! *Autobiography*

The lady here celebrated lived to give her name to Ladysmith, to be linked with a second great feat of the British arms.

MICHAEL SCOTT

1789–1835

370 *A King's Ship*

THERE was the corvette in very truth—she had just tacked, and was close aboard of us on our lee quarter, within musket-shot at the farthest, bowling along upon a wind, with the green, hissing, multitudinous sea surging along her sides, and washing up in foam, like snow flakes, through the mid-ship ports, far aft on the quarterdeck, to the glorification of Jack, who never minds a wet jacket, so long as he witnesses the discomfiture of his ally, Peter Pipeclay. The press of canvas she was carrying laid her over, until her copper sheathing, clear as glass, and glancing like gold, was seen high above the water, throughout her whole length, above which rose her glossy jet-black bends, surmounted by a milk-white streak, broken at regular intervals into eleven goodly ports, from which the British cannon, ugly customers at the best, were grinning, tompion out, open-mouthed at us ; and above all, the clean, well-stowed white hammocks filled the nettings, from tafferel to cat-head—oh ! that I had been in one of them, snug on the berth deck! Aloft, a cloud of white sail swelled to the breeze, till the cloth seemed inclined to say good-bye to the bolt-ropes, bending the masts like willow-wands (as if the devil, determined to beat Paganini himself, was preparing fiddle-sticks to play a spring with, on the cracking and straining weather shrouds and backstays), and tearing her sharp wedge-like bows out of the bowels of the long swell, until the cutwater, and ten yards of the keel next to it, were hove clean out of the sea, into which she would descend again with a roaring plunge, burying everything up to the hause-holes, and driving the brine into mist, over the fore-top, like vapour from a waterfall, through which, as she rose again, the bright red copper on her bows flashed back the sunbeams in momentary rainbows. We were so near, that I could with the naked eye distinctly see the faces of the men. There were at least 150 determined fellows at quarters, and clustered with muskets in their hands, wherever they could be posted to most advantage.

There they were in groups about the ports (I could even see the captains of the guns, examining the locks), in their clean white frocks and trousers, the officers of the ship, and the marines, clearly distinguishable by their blue or red jackets. *I could discern the very sparkle of the epaulets.*

High overhead, the red cross, that for a thousand years 'has braved the battle and the breeze', blew out strong from the peak, like a sheet of flickering white flame, or a thing instinct with life, struggling to tear away the ensign haulyards, and to escape high into the clouds; while, from the main-royal-masthead, the long white pennant streamed upwards into the azure heavens, like a ray of silver light.

Tom Cringle's Log

PERCY BYSSHE SHELLEY

1792–1822

371 *Poetry*

POETRY is indeed something divine. It is at once the centre and circumference of knowledge; it is that which comprehends all science, and that to which all science must be referred. It is at the same time the root and blossom of all other systems of thought; it is that from which all spring, and that which adorns all; and that which, if blighted, denies the fruit and the seed, and withholds from the barren world the nourishment and the succession of the scions of the tree of life. It is the perfect and consummate surface and bloom of all things; it is as the odour and the colour of the rose to the texture of the elements which compose it, as the form and splendour of unfaded beauty to the secrets of anatomy and corruption. What were virtue, love, patriotism, friendship—what were the scenery of this beautiful universe which we inhabit; what were our consolations on this side of the grave—and what were our aspirations beyond it, if poetry did not ascend to bring light and fire from those eternal regions where the owl-winged faculty of calculation dare not ever soar? Poetry is not like reasoning, a power to be exerted according to the determination of the will. A man cannot say, 'I will compose poetry.' The greatest poet even cannot say it; for the mind in creation is as a fading coal, which some invisible influence, like an inconstant wind, awakens to transitory brightness; this power arises from within, like the colour of a flower which fades and changes as it is developed, and the conscious portions of our natures are unprophetic either of its approach or its departure. Could this influence be durable in its original purity and force, it is impossible to predict the greatness of the results; but when composition begins, inspiration is already on the decline, and the most glorious poetry that has ever been communicated to the world is probably a feeble shadow of the original conceptions of the poet.

Poetry is the record of the best and happiest moments of the happiest and best minds. We are aware of evanescent visitations of thought and feeling sometimes associated with place or person, sometimes regarding our own mind alone, and always arising unforeseen and departing unbidden, but elevating and delightful beyond all expression: so that even in the desire and regret they leave, there cannot but be pleasure, participating as it does in the nature of its object. It is as it were the interpenetration of a diviner nature through our own; but its footsteps are like those of a wind over the sea, which the coming calm erases, and whose traces remain only, as on the wrinkled sand which paves it. These and corresponding conditions of being are experienced principally by those of the most delicate sensibility and the most enlarged imagination; and the state of mind produced by them is at war with every base desire. The enthusiasm of virtue, love, patriotism, and friendship, is essentially linked with such emotions; and whilst they last, self appears as what it is, an atom to a universe. Poets are not only subject to these experiences as spirits of the most refined organization, but they can colour all that they combine with the evanescent hues of this ethereal world; a word, a trait in the representation of a scene or a passion, will touch the enchanted chord, and reanimate, in those who have ever experienced these emotions, the sleeping, the cold, the buried image of the past. Poetry thus makes immortal all that is best and most beautiful in the world; it arrests the vanishing apparitions which haunt the interlunations of life, and veiling them, or in language or in form, sends them forth among mankind, bearing sweet news of kindred joy to those with whom their sisters abide—abide, because there is no portal of expression from the caverns of the spirit which they inhabit into the universe of things. Poetry redeems from decay the visitations of the divinity in man.

A Defence of Poetry

FREDERICK MARRYAT

1792–1848

372 *Naval Politeness*

WHEN Jack Easy had gained the deck he found the sun shining gaily, a soft air blowing from the shore, and the whole of the rigging and every part of the ship loaded with the shirts, trousers, and jackets of the seamen, which had been wetted during the heavy gale, and were now hanging up to dry; all the wet sails were also spread on the booms or triced up in the rigging, and the ship was slowly forging through the blue water. The captain and first lieutenant were standing on the gangway in converse, and the majority of the officers were with their quadrants and sextants ascertaining the latitude at noon. The decks were white and clean, the sweepers had just laid by their brooms, and the men were busy coiling down the ropes. It was a scene of cheerfulness, activity, and order, which lightened his heart after the four days of suffering, close air, and confinement, from which he had just emerged.

The captain, who perceived him, beckoned to him, asked him kindly how he felt; the first lieutenant also smiled upon him, and many of the officers, as well as his messmates, congratulated him upon his recovery. The captain's steward came up to him, touched his hat, and requested the pleasure of his company to dinner in the cabin. Jack was the essence of politeness, took off his hat, and accepted the invitation. Jack was standing on a rope which a seaman was coiling down; the man touched his hat and requested he would be so kind as to take his foot off. Jack took his hat off his head in return, and his foot off the rope. The master touched his hat and reported twelve o'clock to the first lieutenant—the first lieutenant touched his hat and reported twelve o'clock to the captain—the captain touched his hat and told the first lieutenant to make it so. The officer of the watch touched his hat, and asked the captain whether they should pipe to dinner—the captain touched his hat, and said, 'If you please.'

The midshipman received his orders—and touched his hat—which he gave to the head boatswain's mate, who touched his hat, and then the calls whistled cheerily.

'Well,' thought Jack, 'politeness seems to be the order of the day, and every one has an equal respect for the other.' Jack stayed on deck; he peeped through the ports, which were open, and looked down into the deep blue wave; he cast his eyes aloft, and watched the tall spars sweeping and tracing with their points, as it were, a small portion of the clear sky, as they acted in obedience to the motion of the vessel; he looked forward at the range of carronades which lined the sides of the deck, and then he proceeded to climb one of the carronades, and lean over the hammocks to gaze on the distant land.

'Young gentleman, get off those hammocks,' cried the master, who was officer of the watch, in a surly tone.

Jack looked round.

'Do you hear me, sir? I'm speaking to you,' said the master again.

Jack felt very indignant, and he thought that politeness was not quite so general as he supposed.

Mr. Midshipman Easy

373 *Weathering the Point*

ON deck the superior officers were in conversation with the captain, who had expressed the same fear that O'Brien had in our berth. The men, who knew what they had to expect—for this sort of intelligence is soon communicated through a ship—were assembled in knots, looking very grave, but at the same time not wanting in confidence. They knew that they could trust to the captain, as far as skill or courage could avail them; and sailors are too sanguine to despair, even at the last moment. . .

Before twelve o'clock the rocky point which we so much dreaded was in sight, broad on the lee bow; and if the low sandy coast appeared terrible, how much more did this, even at a distance: the black masses of rock covered with foam, which each minute dashed up in the air higher than our lower mast-heads. The captain eyed it for some minutes in silence, as if in calculation.

'Mr. Falcon,' said he at last, 'we must put the mainsail on her.'

'She never can bear it, sir.'

'She *must* bear it,' was the reply. 'Send the men aft to the mainsheet. See that careful men attend the buntlines.'

The mainsail was set, and the effect of it upon the ship was tremendous. She careened over so that her lee channels were under the water; and when pressed by a sea, the lee side of the quarter-deck and gangway were afloat. She now reminded me of a goaded and fiery horse, mad with the stimulus applied; not rising as before, but forcing herself through whole seas, and dividing the waves, which poured in one continual torrent from the forecastle down upon the decks below. Four men were secured to the wheel—the sailors were obliged to cling, to prevent being washed away—the ropes were thrown in confusion to leeward—the shot rolled out of the lockers, and every eye was fixed aloft, watching the masts, which were expected every moment to go over the side. A heavy sea struck us on the broadside, and it was some moments before the ship appeared to recover herself; she reeled, trembled, and stopped her way, as if it had stupefied her. The first lieutenant looked at the captain as if to say, 'This will not do.' 'It is our only chance,' answered the captain to the appeal. That the ship went faster through the water, and held a better wind, was certain; but just before we arrived at the point, the gale increased in force. 'If any thing starts, we are lost, sir,' observed the first lieutenant again.

'I am perfectly aware of it,' replied the captain, in a calm tone. . . ''Twill be touch and go indeed, Falcon.' . . 'Come aft, you and I must take the helm. We shall want *nerve* there, and only there, now.'

The captain and first lieutenant went aft, and took the forespokes of the wheel, and O'Brien, at a sign made by the captain, laid hold of the spokes behind him. An old quarter-master kept his station at the fourth. The roaring of the seas on the rocks, with the howling of the wind, was dreadful; but the sight was more dreadful than the noise. For a few moments I shut my eyes, but anxiety forced me to open them again. As near as I could judge, we were not twenty yards from the rocks, at the time that the ship passed abreast of them. We were in the midst of the foam, which boiled around us; and as the ship was driven nearer to them, and careened with the wave, I thought that our main yard-arm would have touched the rock; and at this moment a gust of wind came on which laid the ship on her beam-ends, and checked her progress through the water, while the accumulated noise was deafening. A few moments more the ship dragged on, another wave dashed over her and spent itself upon the rocks, while the spray was dashed back from them, and returned upon the decks. The main rock was within ten yards of her counter, when another gust of wind laid us on our beam-ends; the foresail and mainsail split, and were blown clean out of the bolt-ropes—the ship righted, trembling fore and aft. I looked astern:—the rocks were to windward on our quarter, and we were safe.

Peter Simple

JOHN GIBSON LOCKHART

1794–1854

374 *The Death of Sir Walter*

As I was dressing on the morning of Monday, the 17th of September, Nicolson came into my room, and told me that his master had awoke in a state of composure and consciousness, and wished to see me immediately. I found him entirely himself, though in the last extreme of feebleness. His eye was clear and calm—every trace of the wild fire of delirium extinguished. 'Lockhart,' he said, 'I may have but a minute to speak to you. My dear, be a good man—be virtuous—be religious—be a good man. Nothing else will give you any comfort when you come to lie here.' He paused, and I said, 'Shall I send for Sophia and Anne?' 'No,' said he, 'don't disturb them. Poor souls! I know they were up all night—God bless you all.' With this he sunk into a very tranquil sleep, and, indeed, he scarcely afterwards gave any sign of consciousness, except for an instant on the arrival of his sons. They, on learning that the scene was about to close, obtained anew leave of absence from their posts, and both reached Abbotsford on the 19th. About half-past one p.m., on the 21st of September, Sir Walter breathed his last, in the presence of all his children. It was a beautiful day—so warm that every window was wide open, and so perfectly still that the sound of all others most delicious to his ear, the gentle ripple of the Tweed over its pebbles, was distinctly audible as we knelt around the bed, and his eldest son kissed and closed his eyes.

Life of Sir Walter Scott

THOMAS CARLYLE

1795–1881

375 *Jocelin of Brakelond*

JOCELIN, we said, was somewhat of a Boswell; but unfortunately, by Nature, he is none of the largest, and distance has now dwarfed him to an extreme degree. His light is most feeble, intermittent, and requires the intensest kindest inspection; otherwise it will disclose mere vacant haze. It must be owned, the good Jocelin, spite of his beautiful childlike character, is but an altogether imperfect 'mirror' of these old-world things! The good man, he looks on us so clear and cheery, and in his neighbourly soft-smiling eyes we see so well our *own* shadow,—we have a longing always to cross-question him, to force from him an explanation of much. But no; Jocelin, though he talks with such clear familiarity, like a next-door neighbour, will not answer any question: that is the peculiarity of him, dead these six hundred and fifty years, and quite deaf to us, though still so audible! The good man, he cannot help it, nor can we.

But truly it is a strange consideration this simple one, as we go on with him, or indeed with any lucid simple-hearted soul like him: Behold therefore, this England of the Year 1200 was no chimerical vacuity or dreamland, peopled with mere vaporous Phantasms, Rymer's Fœdera, and Doctrines of the Constitution; but a green solid place, that grew corn and several other things. The Sun shone on it; the vicissitude of seasons and human fortunes. Cloth was woven and worn; ditches were dug, furrow-fields ploughed, and houses built. Day by day all men and cattle rose to labour, and night by night returned home weary to their several lairs. In wondrous Dualism, then as now, lived nations of breathing men; alternating, in all ways, between Light and Dark; between joy and sorrow, between rest and toil,—between hope, hope reaching high as Heaven, and fear deep as very Hell. Not vapour Phantasms, Rymer's Fœdera at all! Cœur-de-Lion was not a theatrical popinjay with greaves and steel-cap on it, but a man living upon victuals,—*not* imported by Peel's Tariff. Cœur-de-Lion came palpably athwart this Jocelin at St. Edmundsbury; and had almost peeled the sacred gold '*Feretrum*', or St. Edmund Shrine itself, to ransom him out of the Danube Jail.

These clear eyes of neighbour Jocelin looked on the bodily presence of King John; the very John *Sansterre*, or Lackland, who signed *Magna Charta* afterwards in Runnymead. Lackland, with a great retinue, boarded once, for the matter of a fortnight, in St. Edmundsbury Convent; daily in the very eyesight, palpable to the very fingers of our Jocelin: O Jocelin, what did he say, what did he do; how looked he, lived he,—at the very lowest, what coat or breeches had he on? Jocelin is obstinately silent. Jocelin marks down what interests *him*; entirely deaf to *us*. With Jocelin's eyes we discern almost nothing of John Lackland. As through a glass darkly, we with our own eyes and appliances, intensely looking, discern at most: A blustering, dissipated human figure, with a kind of blackguard quality air, in cramoisy velvet, or other uncertain texture, uncertain cut, with much plumage and fringing; amid numerous other human figures of the like; riding abroad with hawks; talking noisy nonsense;—tearing out the bowels of St. Edmundsbury Convent (its larders namely and cellars) in the most ruinous way, by living at rack and manger there. Jocelin notes only, with a slight subacidity of manner, that the King's Majesty, *Dominus Rex*, did leave, as gift for our St. Edmund Shrine, a handsome enough silk cloak,—or rather pretended to leave, for one of his retinue borrowed it of us, and *we* never got sight of it again; and, on the whole, that the *Dominus Rex*, at departing, gave us 'thirteen *sterlingii*', one shilling and one penny, to say a mass for him ; and so departed, —like a shabby Lackland as he was ! 'Thirteen pence sterling,' this was what the Convent got from Lackland, for all the victuals he and his had made away with. We of course said our mass for him, having covenanted to do it,—but let impartial posterity judge with what degree of fervour !

And in this manner vanishes King Lackland; traverses swiftly our strange intermittent magic-mirror, jingling the shabby thirteen pence merely; and rides with his hawks into Egyptian night again. It is Jocelyn's manner with all things ; and it is men's manner and men's necessity. How intermittent is our good Jocelin ; marking down, without eye to *us*, what *he* finds interesting ! How much in Jocelin, as in all History, and indeed in all Nature, is at once inscrutable and certain ; so dim, yet so indubitable; exciting us to endless considerations. For King Lackland *was* there, verily he ; and did leave these *tredecim sterlingii*, if nothing more, and did live and look in one way or the other, and a whole world was living and looking along with him !

Past and Present

376 *Teufelsdröckh's Watch-Tower*

AS for Teufelsdröckh, except by his nightly appearances at the *Grüne Gans*, Weissnichtwo saw little of him, felt little of him. Here, over his tumbler of Gukguk, he sat reading Journals ; sometimes contemplatively looking into the clouds of his tobacco-pipe, without other visible employment : always, from his mild ways, an agreeable phenomenon there ; more especially when he opened his lips for speech ; on which occasions the whole Coffee-house would hush itself into silence, as if sure to hear something noteworthy. Nay, perhaps to hear a whole series and river of the most memorable utterances; such as, when once thawed, he would for hours indulge in, with fit audience: and the more memorable, as issuing from a head apparently not more interested in them, not more conscious of them, than is the sculptured stone head of some public fountain, which through its brass mouth-tube emits water to the worthy and the unworthy; careless whether it be for cooking victuals or quenching conflagrations; indeed, maintains the same earnest assiduous look, whether any water be flowing or not.

To the Editor of these sheets, as to a young enthusiastic Englishman, however unworthy, Teufelsdröckh opened himself perhaps more than to the most. Pity only that we could not then half guess his importance, and scrutinise him with due power of vision! We enjoyed, what not three men in Weissnichtwo could boast of, a certain degree of access to the Professor's private domicile. It was the attic floor of the highest house in the Wahngasse; and might truly be called the pinnacle of Weissnichtwo, for it rose sheer up above the contiguous roofs, themselves rising from elevated ground. Moreover, with its windows it looked towards all the four *Orte*, or as the Scotch say, and we ought to say, *Airts*: the sitting-room itself commanded three; another came to view in the *Schlafgemach* (bed-room) at the opposite end; to say nothing of the kitchen, which offered two, as it were, *duplicates*, and showing nothing new. So that it was in fact the speculum or watch-tower of Teufelsdröckh; wherefrom, sitting at ease, he might see the whole life-circulation of that considerable City; the streets and lanes of which, with all their doing and driving (*Thun und Treiben*), were for the most part visible there.

'I look down into all that wasp-nest or bee-hive,' have we heard him say, 'and witness their wax-laying and honey-making, and poison-brewing, and choking by sulphur. From the Palace esplanade, where music plays while Serene Highness is pleased to eat his victuals, down to the low lane, where in her door-sill the aged widow, knitting for a thin livelihood, sits to feel the afternoon sun, I see it all; for, except the Schlosskirche weather-cock, no biped stands so high. Couriers arrive bestrapped and bebooted, bearing Joy and Sorrow bagged-up in pouches of leather: there, topladen, and with four swift horses, rolls-in the country Baron and his household; here, on timber-leg, the lamed Soldier hops painfully along, begging alms: a thousand carriages, and wains, and cars, come tumbling-in with Food, with young Rusticity, and other Raw Produce, inanimate or animate, and go tumbling out again with Produce manufactured. That living flood, pouring through these streets, of all qualities and ages, knowest thou whence it is coming, whither it is going? *Aus der Ewigkeit, zu der Ewigkeit hin:* From Eternity, onwards to Eternity! These are Apparitions: what else? Are they not Souls rendered visible: in Bodies, that took shape and will lose it, melting into air? Their solid Pavement is a Picture of the Sense; they walk on the bosom of Nothing, blank Time is behind them and before them. Or fanciest thou, the red and yellow Clothes-screen yonder, with spurs on its heels and feather in its crown, is but of To-day, without a Yesterday or a To-morrow; and had not rather its Ancestor alive when Hengst and Horsa overran thy Island? Friend, thou seest here a living link in that Tissue of History, which inweaves all Being: watch well, or it will be past thee, and seen no more.'

Sartor Resartus

377 *Friedrich Wilhelm's Tobacco-Parliament*

A HIGH large Room, as the Engravings (mostly worthless) give it us: contented saturnine human figures, a dozen or so of them, sitting round a large long Table, furnished for the occasion; long Dutch pipe in the mouth of each man; supplies of knaster easily accessible; small pan of burning peat, in the Dutch fashion (sandy native charcoal, which burns slowly without smoke), is at your left hand; at your right a jug, which I find to consist of excellent thin bitter beer. Other costlier materials for drinking, if you want such, are not beyond reach. On side-tables stand wholesome cold-meats, royal rounds of beef not wanting, with bread thinly sliced and buttered: in a rustic but neat and abundant way, such innocent accommodations, narcotic or nutritious, gaseous, fluid and solid, as human nature, bent on contemplation and an evening lounge, can require. Perfect equality is to be the rule; no rising, or notice taken, when anybody enters or leaves. Let the entering man take his place and pipe, without obligatory remarks: if he cannot smoke, which is Seckendorf's case for instance, let him at least affect to do so, and not ruffle the established stream of things. And so, Puff, slowly

Pff!—and any comfortable speech that is in you; or none, if you authentically have not any.

Old official gentlemen, military for most part; Grumkow, Derschau, Old Dessauer (when at hand), Seckendorf, old General Flans (rugged Platt-Deutsch specimen, capable of *tocadille* or backgammon, capable of rough slashes of sarcasm when he opens his old beard for speech): these, and the like of these, intimate confidants of the King, men who could speak a little, or who could be socially silent otherwise,—seem to have been the staple of the Institution. Strangers of mark, who happened to be passing, were occasional guests; Ginckel the Dutch Ambassador, though foreign like Seckendorf, was well seen there; garrulous Pöllnitz, who has wandered over all the world, had a standing invitation. Kings, high Princes on visit, were sure to have the honour. The Crown-Prince, now and afterwards, was often present; oftener than he liked,—in such an atmosphere, in such an element. 'The little Princes were all wont to come in,' doffing their bits of triangular hats, 'and bid Papa goodnight. One of the old Generals would sometimes put them through their exercise; and the little creatures were unwilling to go away to bed.'

In such Assemblage, when business of importance, foreign or domestic, was not occupying the royal thoughts,—the Talk, we can believe, was rambling and multifarious: the day's hunting, if at Wusterhausen; the day's news, if at Berlin or Potsdam; old reminiscences, too, I can fancy, turning up, and talk, even in Seckendorf's own time, about Siege of Menin (where your Majesty first did me the honour of some notice), Siege of Stralsund, and—duly on September 11th at least—Malplaquet, with Marlborough and

Eugene: what Marlborough said, looked: and especially Lottum, late Feldmarschall Lottum; and how the Prussian Infantry held firm, like a wall of rocks, when the horse were swept away,—rocks highly volcanic, and capable of rolling forward too; and 'how a certain Adjutant' (Derschau smokes harder, and blushes brown) 'snatched poor Tettau on his back, bleeding to death, amid the iron whirlwinds, and brought him out of shot-range.'—'Hm, na, such a Day, that, Herr Feldzeugmeister, as we shall not see again till the Last of the Days!'

Frederick the Great

JOHN KEATS

1795–1821

378 *The Harp Æolian*

MY dear Reynolds—I had an idea that a Man might pass a very pleasant life in this manner—Let him on a certain day read a certain page of full Poesy or distilled Prose, and let him wander with it, and muse upon it, and reflect from it, and bring home to it, and prophesy upon it, and dream upon it: until it becomes stale—But when will it do so? Never—When Man has arrived at a certain ripeness in intellect any one grand and spiritual passage serves him as a starting-post towards all 'the two-and-thirty Palaces.' How happy is such a voyage of conception, what delicious diligent indolence! A doze upon a sofa does not hinder it, and a nap upon Clover engenders ethereal finger-pointings—the prattle of a child gives it wings, and the converse of middle-age a strength to beat them—a strain of music conducts to 'an odd angle of the Isle,' and when the leaves whisper it puts a girdle round the earth.—Nor will this sparing touch of noble Books be any irreverence to their Writers—for perhaps the honors paid by Man to Man are trifles in comparison to the benefit done by great works to the 'spirit and pulse of good' by their mere passive existence. Memory should not be called Knowledge—Many have original minds who do not think it—they are led away by Custom. Now it appears to me that almost any Man may like the spider spin from his own inwards his own airy Citadel—the points of leaves and twigs on which the spider begins her work are few, and she fills the air with a beautiful circuiting. Man should be content with as few points to tip with the fine Web of his Soul, and weave a tapestry empyrean—full of symbols for his spiritual eye, of softness for his spiritual touch, of space for his wandering, of distinctness for his luxury. But the minds of mortals are so different and bent on such diverse journeys that it may at first appear impossible for any common taste and fellowship to exist between two or three under these suppositions. It is however quite the contrary. Minds would leave each other in contrary directions, traverse each other in numberless points, and at last greet each other at the journey's end. An old man and a child would talk together and the old man be led on his path and the child left thinking. Man should not dispute or assert, but whisper results to his Neighbour, and thus by every germ of spirit sucking the sap from mould ethereal every human might become great, and humanity instead of being a wide heath of furze and briars, with here and there a remote Oak or Pine, would become a grand democracy of forest trees. . . Now it is more noble to sit like Jove than to fly like Mercury :

—let us not therefore go hurrying about and collecting honey, bee-like, buzzing here and there impatiently from a knowledge of what is to be arrived at. But let us open our leaves like a flower, and be passive and receptive; budding patiently under the eye of Apollo and taking hints from every noble insect that favours us with a visit—Sap will be given us for meat, and dew for drink. I was led into these thoughts, my dear Reynolds, by the beauty of the morning operating on a sense of Idleness. I have not read any Books—the Morning said I was right—I had no idea but of the Morning, and the Thrush said I was right.

Letters

379 *Axioms of Poetry*

IN Endymion, I have most likely but moved into the go-cart from the leading-strings—In poetry I have a few axioms, and you will see how far I am from their centre.

1st. I think poetry should surprise by a fine excess, and not by singularity; It should strike the reader as a wording of his own highest thoughts, and appear almost a remembrance.

2d. Its touches of beauty should never be half-way, thereby making the reader breathless, instead of content. The rise, the progress, the setting of Imagery should, like the sun, come natural to him, shine over him, and set soberly, although in magnificence, leaving him in the luxury of twilight. But it is easier to think what poetry should be, than to write it—And this leads me to

Another axiom—That if poetry comes not as naturally as the leaves to a tree, it had better not come at all.—However it may be with me, I cannot help looking into new countries with 'O for a Muse of Fire to ascend!' If Endymion serves me as a pioneer, perhaps I ought to be content—I have great reason to be content, for thank God I can read, and perhaps understand Shakspeare to his depths; and I have, I am sure, many friends, who, if I fail, will attribute any change in my life and temper to humbleness rather than pride—to a cowering under the wings of great poets, rather than to a bitterness that I am not appreciated.

Letter to John Taylor, 27 February 1818

WILLIAM H. PRESCOTT

1796–1859

380 *The First Sight of Mexico*

THEY had not advanced far, when, turning an angle of the sierra, they suddenly came on a view which more than compensated the toils of the preceding day. It was that of the valley of Mexico, or Tenochtitlan, as more commonly called by the natives; which, with its picturesque assemblage of water, woodland, and cultivated plains, its shining cities and shadowy hills, was spread out like some gay and gorgeous panorama before them. In the highly rarefied atmosphere of these upper regions, even remote objects have a brilliancy of colouring and a distinctness of outline which seem to annihilate distance. Stretching far away at their feet were seen noble forests of oak, sycamore, and cedar, and beyond, yellow fields of maize and the towering maguey, intermingled with orchards and blooming gardens; for flowers, in such demand for their religious festivals, were even more abundant in this populous valley than in other parts of Anahuac. In the centre of the great basin were beheld the lakes, occupying then a much larger portion of its surface than at present; their borders thickly studded with towns and hamlets, and, in the midst—like some Indian empress with her coronal of pearls—the fair city of Mexico, with her white towers and pyramidal temples, reposing, as it were, on the bosom of the waters—the far-famed 'Venice of the Aztecs'. High over all rose the royal hill of Chapoltepec, the residence of the Mexican monarchs, crowned with the same grove of gigantic cypresses which at this day fling their broad shadows over the land. In the distance beyond the blue waters of the lake, and nearly screened by intervening foliage, was seen a shining speck, the rival capital of Tezcuco, and, still further on, the dark belt of porphyry, girdling the valley around like a rich setting which Nature had devised for the fairest of her jewels.

Such was the beautiful vision which broke on the eyes of the Conquerors. And even now, when so sad a change has come over the scene; when the stately forests have been laid low, and the soil, unsheltered from the fierce radiance of a tropical sun, is in many places abandoned to sterility; when the waters have retired, leaving a broad and ghastly margin white with the incrustation of salts, while the cities and hamlets on their borders have mouldered into ruins;—even now that desolation broods over the landscape, so indestructible are the lines of beauty which Nature has traced on its features, that no traveller, however cold, can gaze on them with any other emotions than those of astonishment and rapture.

What, then, must have been the emotions of the

Spaniards, when, after working their toilsome way into the upper air, the cloudy tabernacle parted before their eyes, and they beheld these fair scenes in all their pristine magnificence and beauty! It was like the spectacle which greeted the eyes of Moses from the summit of Pisgah; and, in the warm glow of their feelings, they cried out, 'It is the promised land!'

History of the Conquest of Mexico

GEORGE ROBERT GLEIG

1796–1888

381 *Waterloo*

IT was now eight o'clock in the evening, or perhaps a little later. The physical strength of the combatants on both sides had become well nigh exhausted, and on the part of the English there was a feverish desire to close with the enemy, and bring matters to an issue. Up to the present moment, however, the Duke had firmly restrained them. For all purposes of defensive warfare they were excellent troops; the same blood was in their veins which had stirred their more veteran comrades of the Peninsula, but, as has elsewhere been explained, four-fifths of the English regiments were raw levies—second battalions, to manœuvre with which in the presence of a skilful enemy might have been dangerous. Steadily therefore, and with a wise caution, the Duke held them in hand, giving positive orders to each of his generals that they should not follow up any temporary success, so as to endanger the consistency of their lines, but return after every charge to the crest of the hill, and be content with holding that. Now, however, the moment was come for acting on a different principle. Not by Adam and Maitland alone, but by the brigades of Ompteda, Pack, Kempt, and Lambert, the enemy had been overthrown with prodigious slaughter, and all equally panted to be let loose. Moreover, from minute to minute the sound of firing in the direction of Planchenoit became more audible. It was clear, therefore, that even young troops might be slipped in pursuit without much hazard to their own safety, and the Duke let his people go. The lines of infantry were simultaneously formed, the cavalry mounted and rode on, and then a cheer began on the right, which flew like electricity throughout the entire extent of the position. Well was it understood, especially by those who, on a different soil and under a warmer sun, had often listened to similar music.

Story of the Battle of Waterloo

THOMAS BABINGTON, LORD MACAULAY

1800–1859

382 *Clive at Plassey*

CLIVE was in a painfully anxious situation. He could place no confidence in the sincerity or in the courage of his confederate: and, whatever confidence he might place in his own military talents, and in the valour and discipline of his troops, it was no light thing to engage an army twenty times as numerous as his own. Before him lay a river over which it was easy to advance, but over which, if things went ill, not one of his little band would ever return. On this occasion, for the first and for the last time, his dauntless spirit, during a few hours, shrank from the fearful responsibility of making a decision. He called a council of war. The majority pronounced against fighting; and Clive declared his concurrence with the majority. Long afterwards, he said that he had never called but one council of war, and that, if he had taken the advice of that council, the British would never have been masters of Bengal. But scarcely had the meeting broken up when he was himself again. He retired alone under the shade of some trees, and passed near an hour there in thought. He came back determined to put everything to the hazard, and gave orders that all should be in readiness for passing the river on the morrow.

The river was passed; and, at the close of a toilsome day's march, the army, long after sunset, took up its quarters in a grove of mango-trees near Plassey, within a mile of the enemy. Clive was unable to sleep; he heard, through the whole night, the sound of drums and cymbals from the vast camp of the Nabob. It is not strange that even his stout heart should now and then have sunk, when he reflected against what odds, and for what a prize, he was in a few hours to contend.

Nor was the rest of Surajah Dowlah more peaceful. His mind, at once weak and stormy, was distracted by wild and horrible apprehensions. Appalled by the greatness and nearness of the crisis, distrusting his captains, dreading every one who approached him, dreading to be left alone, he sat gloomily in his tent, haunted, a Greek poet would have said, by the furies of those who had cursed him with their last breath in the Black Hole.

The day broke, the day which was to decide the fate of India. At sunrise the army of the Nabob, pouring through many openings from the camp, began to move towards the grove where the English lay. Forty thousand infantry, armed with firelocks, pikes, swords, bows and arrows, covered the plain. They were accompanied by fifty pieces of ordnance of the largest size, each tugged by a long team of white oxen, and each pushed on from behind by an elephant. Some smaller guns, under the direction of a few French auxiliaries, were perhaps more formidable. The cavalry were fifteen thousand, drawn, not from the effeminate population of Bengal, but from the bolder race which inhabits the northern provinces ; and the practised eye of Clive could perceive that both the men and the horses were more powerful than those of the Carnatic. The force which he had to oppose to this great multitude consisted of only three thousand men. But of these nearly a thousand were English ; and all were led by English officers, and trained in the English discipline. Conspicuous in the ranks of the little army were the men of the Thirty-Ninth Regiment, which still bears on its colours, amidst many honourable additions won under Wellington in Spain and Gascony, the name of Plassey, and the proud motto, *Primus in Indis*.

The battle commenced with a cannonade in which the artillery of the Nabob did scarcely any execution, while the few field-pieces of the English produced great effect. Several of the most distinguished officers in Surajah Dowlah's service fell. Disorder began to spread through his ranks. His own terror increased every moment. One of the conspirators urged on him the expediency of retreating. The insidious advice, agreeing as it did with what his own terrors suggested, was readily received. He ordered his army to fall back, and this order decided his fate. Clive snatched the moment, and ordered his troops to advance. The confused and dispirited multitude gave way before the onset of disciplined valour. No mob attacked by regular soldiers was ever more completely routed. The little band of Frenchmen, who alone ventured to confront the English, were swept down the stream of fugitives. In an hour the forces of Surajah Dowlah were dispersed, never to reassemble. Only five hundred of the vanquished were slain. But their camp, their guns, their baggage, innumerable wagons, innumerable cattle, remained in the power of the conquerors. With the loss of twenty-two soldiers killed and fifty wounded, Clive had scattered an army of near sixty thousand men, and subdued an empire larger and more populous than Great Britain.

Essays

383 *Warren Hastings*

THE culprit was indeed not unworthy of that great presence. He had ruled an extensive and populous country, had made laws and treaties, had sent forth armies, had set up and pulled down princes. And in his high place he had so borne himself, that all had feared him, that most had loved him, and that hatred itself could deny him no title to glory, except virtue. He looked like a great man, and not like a bad man. A person small and emaciated, yet deriving dignity from a carriage which, while it indicated deference to the court, indicated also habitual self-possession and self-respect, a high and intellectual forehead, a brow pensive, but not gloomy, a mouth of inflexible decision, a face pale and worn, but serene, on which was written, as legibly as under the picture in the council-chamber at Calcutta, *Mens aequa in arduis*; such was the aspect with which the great Proconsul presented himself to his judges.

Essays

384 *Londonderry*

IT was the twenty-eighth of July. The sun had just set: the evening sermon in the cathedral was over; and the heartbroken congregation had separated; when the sentinels on the tower saw the sails of three vessels coming up the Foyle. Soon there was a stir in the Irish camp. The besiegers were on the alert for miles along both shores. The ships were in extreme peril: for the river was low; and the only navigable channel ran very near to the left bank, where the headquarters of the enemy had been fixed, and where the batteries were most numerous. Leake performed his duty with a skill and spirit worthy of his noble profession, exposed his frigate to cover the merchantmen, and used his guns with great effect. At length the little squadron came to the place of peril. Then the Mountjoy took the lead, and went right at the boom. The huge barricade cracked and gave way: but the shock was such that the Mountjoy rebounded, and stuck in the mud. A yell of triumph rose from the banks: the Irish rushed to their boats, and were preparing to board; but the Dartmouth poured on them a well-directed broadside, which threw them into disorder. Just then the Phœnix dashed at the breach which the Mountjoy had made, and was in a moment within the fence. Meantime the tide was rising fast. The Mountjoy began to move, and soon passed safe through the broken stakes and floating spars. But her brave master was no more. A shot from one of the batteries had struck him; and he died by the most enviable of all deaths, in sight of the city which was his birthplace, which was his home, and which had just been saved by his courage and self-devotion from the most frightful form of destruction. The night had closed in before the conflict at the boom began: but the flash of the guns was seen, and the noise heard, by the lean and ghastly multitude which covered the walls of the city. When the Mountjoy grounded, and when the shout of triumph rose from the Irish on both sides of the river, the hearts of the besieged died within them. One who endured the unutterable anguish of that moment has told us that they looked fearfully livid in each other's eyes. Even after the barricade had been passed, there was a terrible half hour of suspense. It was ten o'clock before the ships arrived at the quay. The whole population was there to welcome them. A screen made of casks filled with earth was hastily thrown up to protect the landing place from the batteries on the other side of the river; and then the work of unloading began. First were rolled on shore barrels containing six thousand bushels of meal. Then came great cheeses, casks of beef, flitches of bacon, kegs of butter, sacks of pease and biscuit, ankers of brandy. Not many hours before, half a pound of tallow and three quarters of a pound of salted hide had been weighed out with niggardly care to every fighting man. The ration which each now received was three pounds of flour, two pounds of beef, and a pint of pease. It is easy to imagine with what tears grace was said over the suppers of that evening. There was little sleep on either side of the wall. The bonfires shone bright along the whole circuit of the ramparts. The Irish guns continued to roar all night; and all night the bells of the rescued city made answer to the Irish guns with a peal of joyous defiance. Through the three following days the batteries of the enemy continued to play. But, on the third night, flames were seen arising from the camp; and, when the first of August dawned, a line of smoking ruins marked the site lately occupied by the huts of the besiegers; and the citizens saw far off the long column of pikes and standards retreating up the left bank of the Foyle towards Strabane.

So ended this great siege, the most memorable in the annals of the British Isles. It had lasted a hundred and five days. The garrison had been reduced from about seven thousand effective men to about three thousand. The loss of the besiegers cannot be precisely ascertained. Walker estimated it at eight thousand men. It is certain from the despatches of Avaux that the regiments which returned from the blockade had been so much thinned that many of them were not more than two hundred strong. Of thirty-six French gunners who had superintended the cannonading, thirty-one had been killed or disabled. The means both of attack and of defence had undoubtedly been such as would have moved the great warriors of the Continent to laughter; and this is the very circumstance which gives so peculiar an interest to the history of the contest. It was a contest, not between engineers, but between nations; and the victory remained with the nation which, though inferior in number, was superior in civilization, in capacity for self-government, and in stubbornness of resolution.

History of England

385 'And Calm of Mind, all Passion spent'

IT chanced in the warm and beautiful spring of the year 1665, a little before the saddest summer that ever London saw, that I went to the Bowling Green at Piccadilly, whither at that time the best gentry made continual resorts. There I met Mr. Cowley, who had lately left Barnelms. . . . I entreated him to dine with me at my lodging in the Temple, which he most courteously promised. And that so eminent a guest might not lack better entertainment than cooks or vintners can provide, I sent to the house of Mr. John Milton, in the Artillery Walk, to beg that he would also be my guest, . . . for I hoped that they would think themselves rather united by their common art than divided by their different factions. And so, indeed, it proved. For while we sat at table they talked freely of men and things, as well ancient as modern, with much civility. Nay, Mr. Milton, who seldom tasted wine, both because of his singular temperance and because of his gout, did more than once pledge Mr. Cowley, who was indeed no hermit in diet. At last, being heated, Mr. Milton begged that I would open the windows. 'Nay,' said I, 'if you desire fresh air and coolness, what would hinder us, as the evening is fair, from sailing for an hour upon the river?' To this they both cheerfully consented; and forth we walked, Mr. Cowley and I leading Mr. Milton between us to the Temple Stairs. There we took a boat, and thence we were rowed up the river.

The wind was pleasant, the evening fine; the sky,

the earth, and the water beautiful to look upon. But Mr. Cowley and I held our peace, and said nothing of the gay sights around us, lest we should too feelingly remind Mr. Milton of his calamity, whereof, however, he needed no monitor; for soon he said sadly: 'Ah, Mr. Cowley, you are a happy man. What would I now give but for one more look at the sun, and the waters, and the gardens of this fair city!'

A Conversation between Mr. Abraham Cowley and Mr. John Milton

JOHN HENRY, CARDINAL NEWMAN

1801–1890

386 *Athens, the Eye of Greece*

MANY a more fruitful coast or isle is washed by the blue Aegean, many a spot is there more beautiful or sublime to see, many a territory more ample; but there was one charm in Attica, which in the same perfection was nowhere else. The deep pastures of Arcadia, the plain of Argos, the Thessalian vale, these had not the gift; Bœotia, which lay to its immediate north, was notorious for its very want of it. The heavy atmosphere of that Bœotia might be good for vegetation, but it was associated in popular belief with the dulness of the Bœotian intellect: on the contrary, the special purity, elasticity, clearness, and salubrity of the air of Attica, fit concomitant and emblem of its genius, did that for it which earth did not;—it brought out every bright hue and tender shade of the landscape over which it was spread, and would have illuminated the face even of a more bare and rugged country.

JOHN HENRY NEWMAN

A confined triangle, perhaps fifty miles its greatest length, and thirty its greatest breadth; two elevated rocky barriers, meeting at an angle; three prominent mountains, commanding the plain,—Parnes, Pentelicus, and Hymettus; an unsatisfactory soil; some streams, not always full;—such is about the report which the agent of a London company would have made of Attica. He would report that the climate was mild; the hills were limestone; there was plenty of good marble; more pasture land than at first survey might have been expected, sufficient certainly for sheep and goats; fisheries productive; silver mines once, but long since worked out; figs fair; oil first-rate; olives in profusion. But what he would not think of noting down, was, that that olive tree was so choice in nature and so noble in shape, that it excited a religious veneration; and that it took so kindly to the light soil, as to expand into woods upon the open plain, and to climb up and fringe the hills. He would not think of writing word to his employers, how that clear air, of which I have spoken, brought out, yet blended and subdued, the colours on the marble, till they had a softness and harmony, for all their richness, which in a picture looks exaggerated, yet is after all within the truth. He would not tell, how that same delicate and brilliant atmosphere freshened up the pale olive, till the olive forgot its monotony, and its cheek glowed like the arbutus or beech of the Umbrian hills. He would say nothing of the thyme and thousand fragrant herbs which carpeted Hymettus; he would hear nothing of the hum of its bees; nor take much account of the rare flavour of its honey, since Gozo and Minorca were sufficient for the English demand. He would look over the Aegean from the height he had ascended; he would follow with his eye the chain of islands, which, starting from the Sunian headland, seemed to offer the fabled divinities of Attica, when they would visit their Ionian cousins, a sort of viaduct thereto across the sea: but that fancy would not occur to him, nor any admiration of the dark violet billows with their white edges down below; nor of those graceful, fan-like jets of silver upon the rocks, which slowly rise aloft like water spirits from the deep, then shiver, and break, and spread, and shroud themselves, and disappear, in a soft mist of foam; nor of the gentle, incessant heaving and panting of the whole liquid plain; nor of the long waves, keeping steady time, like a line of soldiery, as they resound upon the hollow shore,—he would not deign to notice that restless living element at all, except to bless his stars that he was not upon it. Nor the distinct detail, nor the refined colouring, nor the graceful outline and roseate golden hue of the jutting crags, nor the bold shadows cast from Otus or Laurium by the declining sun;—our agent of a mercantile firm would not value these matters even at a low figure. Rather we must turn for the sympathy we seek to yon pilgrim student, come from a semi-barbarous land to that small corner of the earth, as to a shrine, where he might take his fill of gazing on those emblems and coruscations of invisible unoriginate perfection. It was the stranger from a remote province, from Britain or from Mauritania, who in a scene so different from that of his chilly, woody swamps, or of his fiery choking sands, learned at once what a real University must be, by coming to understand the sort of country, which was its suitable home.

Historical Sketches

387 *The Classics*

LET us consider, too, how differently young and old are affected by the words of some classic author, such as Homer or Horace. Passages, which to a boy are but rhetorical common-places, neither better nor worse than a hundred others which any clever writer might supply, which he gets by heart and thinks very fine, and imitates, as he thinks, successfully, in his own flowing versification, at length come home to him, when long years have passed, and he has had experience of life, and pierce him, as if he had never known them, with their sad earnestness and vivid exactness. Then he comes to understand how it is that lines, the birth of some chance morning or evening at an Ionian festival, or among the Sabine hills, have lasted generation after generation, for thousands of years, with a power over the mind, and a charm, which the current literature of his own day, with all its obvious advantages, is utterly unable to rival. Perhaps this is the reason of the mediaeval opinion about Virgil, as of a prophet or magician; his single words and phrases, his pathetic half lines, giving utterance, as the voice of Nature herself, to that pain and weariness, yet hope of better things, which is the experience of her children in every time.

Grammar of Assent

388 *Definition of a Gentleman*

HENCE it is, that it is almost a definition of a gentleman, to say he is one who never inflicts pain. This description is both refined and, as far as it goes, accurate. He is mainly occupied in merely removing the obstacles which hinder the free and unembarrassed action of those about him; and he concurs with their movements rather than takes the initiative himself. His benefits may be considered as parallel to what are called comforts or conveniences in arrangements of a personal nature: like an easy chair or a good fire, which do their part in dispelling cold and fatigue, though nature provides both means of rest and animal heat without them. The true gentleman in like manner carefully avoids whatever may cause a jar or a jolt in the minds of those with whom he is cast;—all clashing of opinion, or collision of feeling, all restraint, or suspicion, or gloom, or resentment; his great concern being to make every one at their ease and at home. He has his eyes on all his company; he is tender towards the bashful, gentle towards the distant, and merciful towards the absurd; he can recollect to whom he is speaking; he guards against unseasonable allusions, or topics which may irritate; he is seldom prominent in conversation, and never wearisome. He makes light of favours while he does them, and seems to be receiving when he is conferring. He never speaks of himself except when compelled, never defends himself by a mere retort, he has no ears for slander or gossip, is scrupulous in imputing motives to those who interfere with him, and interprets everything for the best. He is never mean or little in his disputes, never takes unfair advantage, never mistakes personalities or sharp sayings for arguments, or insinuates evil which he dare not say out. From a long-sighted prudence, he observes the maxim of the ancient sage, that we should ever conduct ourselves towards our enemy as if he were one day to be our friend. He has too much good sense to be affronted at insults, he is too well employed to remember injuries, and too indolent to bear malice. He is patient, forbearing, and resigned, on philosophical principles; he submits to pain, because it is inevitable, to bereavement, because it is irreparable, and to death, because it is his destiny. If he engages in controversy of any kind, his disciplined intellect preserves him from the blundering discourtesy of better, though less educated minds; who, like blunt weapons, tear and hack instead of cutting clean, who mistake the point in argument, waste their strength on trifles, misconceive their adversary, and leave the question more involved than they find it. He may be right or wrong in his opinion, but he is too clear-headed to be unjust; he is as simple as he is forcible, and as brief as he is decisive.

Idea of a University

389 *Leaving Oxford*

I LEFT Oxford for good on Monday, February 23, 1846. On the Saturday and Sunday before, I was in my House at Littlemore simply by myself, as I had been for the first day or two when I had originally taken possession of it. I slept on Sunday night at my dear friend's, Mr. Johnson's, at the Observatory. Various friends came to see the last of me; Mr. Copeland, Mr. Church, Mr. Buckle, Mr. Pattison, and Mr. Lewis. Dr. Pusey too came up to take leave of me; and I called on Dr. Ogle, one of my very oldest friends, for he was my private Tutor, when I was an Undergraduate. In him I took leave of my first College, Trinity, which was so dear to me, and which held on its foundation so many who have been kind to me both when I was a boy, and all through my Oxford life. Trinity had never been unkind to me. There used to be much snap-dragon growing on the walls opposite my freshman's rooms there, and I had for years taken it as the emblem of my own perpetual residence even unto death in my University.

On the morning of the 23rd I left the Observatory. I have never seen Oxford since, excepting its spires, as they are seen from the railway.

Apologia pro Vita Sua

HUGH MILLER

1802–1856

390 *His First Day as Quarry-Boy*

IT was twenty years last February since I set out, a little before sunrise, to make my first acquaintance with a life of labour and restraint; and I have rarely had a heavier heart than on that morning. I was but a slim, loose-jointed boy at the time, fond of the pretty intangibilities of romance, and of dreaming when broad awake; and, woful change! I was now going to work at what Burns has instanced, in his 'Twa Dogs', as one of the most disagreeable of all employments,—to work in a quarry. Bating the passing uneasinesses occasioned by a few gloomy anticipations, the portion of my life which had already gone by had been happy beyond the common lot. I had been a wanderer among rocks and woods, a reader of curious books when I could get them, a gleaner of old traditionary stories; and now I was going to exchange all my day-dreams, and all my amusements, for the kind of life in which men toil every day that they may be enabled to eat, and eat every day that they may be enabled to toil!

The quarry in which I wrought lay on the southern shore of a noble inland bay, or frith rather, with a little clear stream on the one side, and a thick fir wood on the other. It had been opened in the Old Red Sandstone of the district, and was overtopped by a huge bank of diluvial clay, which rose over it in some places to the height of nearly thirty feet, and which at this time was rent and shivered, wherever it presented an open front to the weather, by a recent frost. A heap of loose fragments, which had fallen from above, blocked up the face of the quarry and my first employment was to clear them away. The friction of the shovel soon blistered my hands, but the pain was by no means very severe, and I wrought hard and willingly, that I might see how the huge strata below, which presented so firm and unbroken a frontage, were to be torn up and removed. Picks, and wedges, and levers, were applied by my brother-workmen; and, simple and rude as I had been accustomed to regard these implements, I found I had much to learn in the way of using them. They all proved inefficient, however, and the workmen had to bore into one of the inferior strata, and employ gunpowder. The process was new to me, and I deemed it a highly amusing one: it had the merit, too, of being attended with some such degree of danger as a boating or rock excursion, and had thus an interest independent of its novelty. We had a few capital shots: the fragments flew in every direction; and an immense mass of the diluvium came toppling down, bearing with it two dead birds, that in a recent storm had crept into one of the deeper fissures, to die in the shelter. I felt a new interest in examining them. The one was a pretty cock goldfinch, with its hood of vermilion and its wings inlaid with the gold to which it owes its name, as unsoiled and smooth as if it had been preserved for a museum. The other, a somewhat rarer bird, of the woodpecker tribe, was variegated with light blue and a grayish yellow. I was engaged in admiring the poor little things, more disposed to be sentimental, perhaps, than if I had been ten years older, and thinking of the contrast between the warmth and jollity of their green summer haunts, and the cold and darkness of their last retreat, when I heard our employer bidding the workmen lay by their tools. I looked up and saw the sun sinking behind the thick fir wood beside us, and the long dark shadows of the trees stretching downward towards the shore.

Old Red Sandstone

ROBERT SMITH SURTEES

1803–1864

391 *Mr. Jorrocks, M.F.H., arrives at Handley Cross*

THE clear bright beauty of the day, combined with the attraction of a stranger coming to fill so important a situation as master of fox-hounds, drew many to the Datton railway station who were previously unacquainted even with the name of 'Jorrocks'. . .

All the flys, hack horses, donkeys, and ponies, were bespoke as usual; and many set out at noon to secure good berths at the station. . . Precisely at three-quarters of a minute before three, a wild shrill whistle, that seemed to issue from the bowels of the earth and to run right up into mid-air, was heard at the back of

Shavington Hill, and, in an instant, the engine and long train rounded the base, the engine smoking and snorting like an exasperated crocodile. Nearer and nearer it comes with a thundering sort of hum that sounds throughout the country. The wondering ploughman stops his team. The cows and sheep stand staring with astonishment, while the horses take a look, and then gallop about the fields, kicking up their heels and snorting with delight. The guard's red coat on the engine is visible—next his gold hatband appears—now we read the 'Hercules' on the engine, and anon it pulls up with a whiff, a puff, and a whistle, under the slate-covered shed, to give the Hercules his water, and set down and take up passengers and goods. Seven first-class passenger carriages follow the engine, all smart, clean, and yellow, with appropriate names on each door panel—The Prince Albert, Queen Victoria, and the Prince of Wales, The Venus, The Mercury, The Comet, and The Star; next come ten second-class ones, green, with covered tops and half-covered sides, but in neither set is there anything at all like the Jorrocks party. Cattle-pens follow, holding sheep, swine, donkeys, and poultry; then come an open platform with a broken britzka, followed by a curious looking nondescript one horse vehicle, containing a fat man in a low-crowned hat, and a versatio or reversible coat, with the preferable side outwards. Along with him were two ladies muffled up in cloaks, and at the back was a good looking servant-maid. From the bottom of the carriage swung a couple of hams, and a large warming pan. 'Pray is Mr. Jorrocks here?' inquired the elegant M.C., who had persuaded the station-master to let him in upon the line, riding his white charger near the door of the first-class carriage, and raising his hat as he spoke ; but getting no answer, he continued his interrogatory down the whole set until he came to the end, when casting a despairing glance at the cattle pens, he was about to wheel round, when the gentlemen in the versatio coat, in a very stentorian voice, roared out, ‘ I say, Sir ! Bain't this the 'Andley Cross station ? ’ ‘ It is, Sir,’ replied Captain Doleful, in his most dignified manner, ‘ The Datton station for Handley Cross at least.’

‘ Then I want to land,’ responded the same sweet voice.

‘ Here 's a gentleman wants to be down,’ observed Captain Doleful to the scarlet-coated guard, who came bustling past with a pen of Cochin-Chinas to put upon the train.

‘ Yes, a gentleman and two ladies,’ roared our friend ; ‘ Mister and Missis Jorrocks in fact, and Miss Jorrocks ! ’ . .

Thereupon the Captain beckoned the guard, and Mr. Jorrocks, standing up in the vehicle, looking very like a hay-stack with a hat on the top, bounded to the ground. Mrs. Jorrocks, in a black velvet bonnet lined with pink satin, and her body all shrouded in a sea green silk cloak, then accepted the offer of the Captain's arm, and descended with caution and due state while Belinda, with the spring of youth and elasticity in her limbs, bounded on to the foot-way beyond the rail. Benjamin, who was asleep in the horse-box, being considerately kicked awake by Mr. Jorrocks, the porters cut off the last joints of the train, when away it went, hissing and snorting through the quiet country, leaving our party to the undisturbed observation of the Handley Cross company.

Handley Cross

ROBERT SMITH SURTEES

392 *A Morning Find*

'DASH it, wot a mornin' it is!' exclaimed Mr. Jorrocks, turning up his jolly face, beaming with exultation; 'wot a many delicious moments one loses by smooterin i' bed!—dash my vig! if I won't get up at five every mornin' as long as I live! Glad I've got on my cords 'stead o' my shags, for it 's goin' to be werry 'ot,' continued he, looking down on a pair of second or third-hand whites. 'Yooi over, in there!' to the hounds, with a wave of his hand, as Pigg's horn announced he had taken his station.

In the hounds flew, with a chirp and a whimper; and the crack of Pigg's whip on the far side sounded like a gun in the silence around. 'Yooi, spread and try for him, my beauties!' holloaed Mr. Jorrocks, riding into cover among the stunted underwood. The pack spread, and try in all directions—now here, now there, now whiffing with curious nose round the hollies, and now trying up the rides.

'There 's a touch of a fox,' said Mr. Jorrocks to himself, as Priestess put her nose to the ground, and ran mute across the road, lashing her sides with her stern. A gentle whimper followed, and Mr. Jorrocks cheered her to the echo. 'The warmint's a-stir,' said he; 'that's jest where we hit on him last time.' Now Priestess speaks again in fuller and deeper notes, and Ravager and Lavender, and the rest of the pack rush to the spot. How beautifully they flourish—eager, and yet none will go an inch without the scent. 'Vell done, old 'ooman! speak to him again!' exclaimed Mr. Jorrocks, delighted to hear the old bitch's tongue; 'a fox for a pund; ten if you like!'

Handley Cross

GEORGE BORROW

1803–1881

393 *The Wind on the Heath*

I NOW wandered along the heath, till I came to a place where, beside a thick furze, sat a man, his eyes fixed intently on the red ball of the setting sun.

'That's not you, Jasper?'

'Indeed, brother!'

'I've not seen you for years.'

'How should you, brother?'

'What brings you here?'

'The fight, brother.'

'Where are the tents?'

'On the old spot, brother.'

'Any news since we parted?'

'Two deaths, brother.'

'Who are dead, Jasper?'

'Father and mother, brother.' . .

'Where did they die?'

'Where they were sent, brother.'

'What is your opinion of death, Mr. Petulengro?' said I, as I sat down beside him.

'My opinion of death, brother, is much the same as that in the old song of Pharaoh, which I have heard my grandam sing:—

> Cana marel o manus chivios andé puv,
> Ta rovel pa leste o chavo ta romi.

When a man dies, he is cast into the earth, and his wife and child sorrow over him. If he has neither wife nor child, then his father and mother, I suppose; and if he is quite alone in the world, why, then, he is cast into the earth, and there is an end of the matter.'

'And do you think that is the end of man?'

'There's an end of him, brother, more's the pity.'

'Why do you say so?'

'Life is sweet, brother.'

'Do you think so?'

'Think so! There's night and day, brother, both sweet things; sun, moon, and stars, brother, all sweet things; there's likewise a wind on the heath. Life is very sweet, brother; who would wish to die?'

'I would wish to die——'

'You talk like a Gorgio—which is the same as talking like a fool. Were you a Romany Chal, you would talk wiser. Wish to die, indeed! A Romany Chal would wish to live for ever!'

'In sickness, Jasper?'

'There's the sun and stars, brother.'

'In blindness, Jasper?'

'There's the wind on the heath, brother; if I could only feel that, I would gladly live for ever. Dosta, we'll now go to the tents and put on the gloves; and I'll try to make you feel what a sweet thing it is to be alive, brother.'

Lavengro

394 *The Prize Fight*

LET no one sneer at the bruisers of England. What were the gladiators of Rome, or the bull-fighters of Spain, in its palmiest days, compared to England's bruisers? Pity that ever corruption should have crept in amongst them—but of that I wish not to talk; let us still hope that a spark of the old religion, of which they were the priests, still lingers in the breasts of Englishmen. There they come, the bruisers, far from London, or from wherever else they might chance to be at that time, to the great rendezvous in the old city. Some came one way, some another: some of tip-top reputation came with peers in their chariots, for glory and fame are such fair things, that even peers are proud to have those invested therewith by their sides: others came in their own gigs, driving their own bits of blood, and I heard one say: 'I have driven through at a heat the whole hundred and eleven miles, and only stopped to bait twice.' Oh, the blood-horses of old England! But they too have had their day—for everything beneath the sun there is a season and a time. But the greater number come just as they can contrive—on the tops of coaches, for example—and amongst these there are fellows with dark sallow faces, and sharp shining eyes; and it is these that have planted rottenness in the core of pugilism, for they are Jews, and, true to their kind, have only base lucre in view. . .

So the bruisers of England are come to be present at the grand fight speedily coming off; there they are met in the precincts of the old town, near the field of the chapel, planted with tender saplings at the restoration of sporting Charles, which are now become venerable elms as high as many a steeple. There they are met at a fitting rendezvous, where a retired coachman, with one leg, keeps an hotel and a bowling-green. I think I now see them upon the bowling-green, the men of renown, amidst hundreds of people with no renown at all, who gaze upon them with timid wonder. Fame, after all, is a glorious thing, though it lasts only for a day. There 's Cribb, the champion of England, and perhaps the best man in England; there he is, with his huge, massive figure, and face wonderfully like that of a lion. There is Belcher, the younger, not the mighty one, who is gone to his place, but the Teucer Belcher, the most scientific pugilist that ever entered a ring, only wanting strength to be, I won't say what. He appears to walk before me now, as he did that evening, with his white hat, white great-coat, thin genteel figure, springy step, and keen, determined eye. Crosses him, what a contrast! grim, savage Shelton, who has a civil word for nobody, and a hard blow for anybody—hard! one blow, given with the proper play of his athletic arm, will unsense a giant. Yonder individual, who strolls about with his hands behind him, supporting his brown coat lappets, under-sized, and who looks anything but what he is, is the king of the light weights, so called — Randall! the terrible Randall, who has Irish blood in his veins—not the better for that, nor the worse; and not far from him is his last antagonist, Ned Turner, who, though beaten by him, still thinks himself as good a man, in which he is, perhaps, right, for it was a near thing; and 'a better shentleman,' in which he is quite right, for he is a Welshman. But how shall I name them all? They were there by dozens, and all tremendous in their way. There was Bulldog Hudson, and fearless Scroggins, who beat the conqueror of Sam the Jew. There was Black Richmond—no, he was not there, but I knew him well; he was the most dangerous of blacks, even with a broken thigh. There was Purcell, who could never conquer till all seemed over with him. There was—what! shall I name thee last? ay, why not? I believe that thou art the last of all that strong family still above the sod, where mayest thou long continue—true piece of English stuff, Tom of Bedford—sharp as winter, kind as spring.

Hail to thee, Tom of Bedford, or by whatever name

it may please thee to be called, Spring or Winter. Hail to thee, six-foot Englishman of the brown eye, worthy to have carried a six-foot bow at Flodden, where England's yeomen triumphed over Scotland's king, his clans and chivalry. Hail to thee, last of England's bruisers, after all the many victories which thou hast achieved—true English victories, unbought by yellow gold; need I recount them? Nay, nay! they are already well known to fame—sufficient to say that Bristol's Bull and Ireland's Champion were vanquished by thee, and one mightier still, gold itself, thou didst overcome; for gold itself strove in vain to deaden the power of thy arm; and thus thou didst proceed till men left off challenging thee, the unvanquishable, the incorruptible. 'Tis a treat to see thee, Tom of Bedford, in thy 'public' in Holborn way, whither thou hast retired with thy well-earned bays. 'Tis Friday night, and nine by Holborn clock. There sits the yeoman at the end of his long room, surrounded by his friends. Glasses are filled, and a song is the cry, and a song is sung well suited to the place; it finds an echo in every heart—fists are clenched, arms are waved, and the portraits of the mighty fighting men of yore, Broughton, and Slack, and Ben, which adorn the walls, appear to smile grim approbation, whilst many a manly voice joins in the bold chorus:

'Here 's a health to old honest John Bull,
When he's gone we sha'n't find such another,
And with hearts and with glasses brim full,
We will drink to old England, his mother.'

But the fight! with respect to the fight, what shall I say? Little can be said about it—it was soon over. Some said that the brave from town, who was reputed the best man of the two, and whose form was a perfect model of athletic beauty, allowed himself, for lucre vile, to be vanquished by the massive champion with the flattened nose. One thing is certain, that the former was suddenly seen to sink to the earth before a blow of by no means extraordinary power. Time, time! was called, but there he lay upon the ground apparently senseless, and from thence he did not lift his head till several seconds after the umpires had declared his adversary victor.

Lavengro

RALPH WALDO EMERSON

1803–1882

395 *The Universal in Man*

THERE is one mind common to all individual men. Every man is an inlet to the same and to all of the same. He that is once admitted to the right of reason is made a freeman of the whole estate. What Plato has thought he may think; what a saint has felt he may feel; what at any time has befallen any man he can understand. Who hath access to this universal mind is a party to all that is or can be done, for this is the only and sovereign agent. . .

Of the universal mind each individual man is one more incarnation. All its properties consist in him. Each new fact in his private experience flashes a light on what great bodies of men have done, and the crises of his life refer to national crises. Every revolution was first a thought in one man's mind, and when the same thought occurs to another man it is the key to that era. Every reform was once a private opinion, and when it shall be a private opinion again it will solve the problem of the age. . .

It is remarkable that involuntarily we always read as superior beings. Universal history, the poets, the romancers, do not in their stateliest pictures—in the sacerdotal, the imperial palaces, in the triumphs of will or of genius—anywhere lose our ear, anywhere make us feel that we intrude, that this is for better men; but rather is it true, that in their grandest strokes we feel most at home. All that Shakespeare says of the king, yonder slip of a boy that reads in the corner feels to be true of himself. We sympathize in the great moments of history, in the great discoveries, the great resistances, the great prosperities of men;—because there law was enacted, the sea was searched, the land was found, or the blow was struck *for us*, as we ourselves in that place would have done or applauded. . .

A true aspirant, therefore, never needs look for allusions personal and laudatory in discourse. He hears the commendation, not of himself, but more sweet, of that character he seeks, in every word that is said concerning character, yea, further, in every fact and circumstance—in the running river and the rustling corn. Praise is looked, homage tendered, love flows from mute nature, from the mountains and the lights of the firmament.

Essays: History

396 *A Defence of Frankness*

SOME of my friends have complained that we discussed Fate, Power, and Wealth on too low a platform; gave too much line to the evil spirit of the times; too many cakes to Cerberus; that we ran Cudworth's risk of making, by excess of candour, the argument of atheism so strong, that he could not answer it. I have no fears of being forced in my own despite to play, as we say, the devil's attorney. I have no infirmity of faith; no belief that it is of much importance what I or any man may say: I am sure that a certain truth will be said through me, though I should be dumb, or though I should try to say the reverse. Nor do I fear scepticism for any good soul. A just thinker will allow full swing to his scepticism. I dip my pen in the blackest ink, because I am not afraid of falling into my inkpot. I have no sympathy with a poor man I knew, who, when suicides abounded, told me he dared not look at his razor. We are of different opinions at different hours, but we always may be said to be at heart on the side of truth.

I see not why we should give ourselves such sanctified airs. If the Divine Providence has hid from men neither disease, nor deformity, nor corrupt society, but has stated itself out in passions, in war, in trade, in the love of power and pleasure, in hunger and need, in tyrannies, literatures, and arts,—let us not be so nice that we cannot write these facts down coarsely as they stand, or doubt but there is a counter-statement as ponderous, which we can arrive at, and which, being put, will make all square. The solar system has no anxiety about its reputation, and the credit of truth and honesty is as safe; nor have I any fear that a sceptical bias can be given by leaning hard on the sides of fate, of practical power, or of trade, which the doctrine of Faith cannot down-weigh. The strength of that principle is not measured in ounces and pounds: it tyrannizes at the centre of Nature.

Conduct of Life: Worship

BENJAMIN DISRAELI, EARL OF BEACONSFIELD

1804–1881

397 *A Fisher of Men*

IT is proverbial to what drowning men will cling. Lothair, in his utter hopelessness, made a distinction between the Cardinal and the conspirators. The Cardinal had been absent from Rome during the greater portion of the residence of Lothair in that city. The Cardinal was his father's friend, an English gentleman, with an English education, once an Anglican, a man of the world, a man of honour, a good, kind-hearted man. Lothair explained the apparent and occasional co-operation of his Eminence with the others, by their making use of him without a due consciousness of their purpose on his part. Lothair remembered how delicately his former guardian had always treated the subject of religion in their conversations. The announcement of his visit instead of aggravating the distresses of Lothair, seemed, as all these considerations rapidly occurred to him, almost to impart a ray of hope.

'I see,' said the Cardinal, as he entered serene and graceful as usual, and glancing at the table, 'that you have been reading the account of our great act of yesterday.'

'Yes; and I have been reading it,' said Lothair reddening, 'with indignation; with alarm; I should add, with disgust.'

'How is this?' said the Cardinal, feeling or affecting surprise.

'It is a tissue of falsehood and imposture,' continued Lothair; 'and I will take care that my opinion is known of it.'

'Do nothing rashly,' said the Cardinal. 'This is an official journal, and I have reason to believe that nothing appears in it which is not drawn up, or well considered, by truly pious men.'

'You yourself, sir, must know,' continued Lothair, 'that the whole of this statement is founded on falsehood.'

'Indeed I should be sorry to believe,' said the Cardinal, 'that there was a particle of misstatement, or even exaggeration, either in the base or the superstructure of the narrative.'

'Good God!' exclaimed Lothair. 'Why! take the very first allegation, that I fell at Mentana fighting in the ranks of the Holy Father. Every one knows that I fell fighting against him, and that I was almost slain by one of his chassepots. It is notorious; and though, as a matter of taste, I have not obtruded the fact in the society in which I have been recently living, I have never attempted to conceal it, and have not the slightest doubt that it must be as familiar to every member of that society as to your Eminence.'

'I know there are two narratives of your relations with the battle of Mentana,' observed the Cardinal quietly. 'The one accepted as authentic is that which appears in this journal; the other account, which can only be traced to yourself, bears no doubt a somewhat different character; but considering that it is in the highest degree improbable, and that there is not a tittle of confirmatory or collateral evidence to extenuate its absolute unlikelihood, I hardly think you are justified in using, with reference to the statement in this article, the harsh expression which I am persuaded, on reflection, you will feel you have hastily used.'

'I think,' said Lothair with a kindling eye and a burning cheek, 'that I am the best judge of what I did at Mentana.'

'Well, well,' said the Cardinal with dulcet calmness, 'you naturally think so; but you must remember you have been very ill, my dear young friend, and labouring under much excitement. If I were you, and I speak as your friend, I hope your best one, I would not dwell too much on this fancy of yours about the battle of Mentana. I would myself always deal tenderly with a fixed idea: harsh attempts to terminate hallucination are seldom successful. Nevertheless, in the case of a public event, a matter of fact, if a man finds that he is of one opinion and all orders of society of another, he should not be encouraged to dwell on a perverted view; he should be gradually weaned from it.'

'You amaze me!' said Lothair.

'Not at all,' said the Cardinal. 'I am sure you will benefit by my advice. And you must already perceive that, assuming the interpretation which the world without exception places on your conduct in the field to be the just one, there really is not a single circumstance in the whole of this interesting and important statement, the accuracy of which you yourself would for a moment dispute.'

'What is there said about me at Mentana makes me doubt of all the rest,' said Lothair.

'Well, we will not dwell on Mentana,' said the Cardinal with a sweet smile; 'I have treated of that point. Your case is by no means an uncommon one. It will wear off with returning health. King George IV believed that he was at the battle of Waterloo, and indeed commanded there; and his friends were at one time a little alarmed; but Knighton, who was a sensible man, said, "His Majesty has only to leave off Curaçoa, and rest assured he will gain no more victories."'

Lothair

NATHANIEL HAWTHORNE

1804–1864

398 *Phœbe's Bedchamber*

PHŒBE PYNCHEON slept, on the night of her arrival, in a chamber that looked down on the garden of the old house. It fronted towards the east, so that at a very seasonable hour a glow of crimson light came flooding through the window, and bathed the dingy ceiling and paper-hangings in its own hue. There were curtains to Phœbe's bed; a dark, antique canopy and ponderous festoons, of a stuff which had been rich, and even magnificent, in its time; but which now brooded over the girl like a cloud, making a night in that one corner, while elsewhere it was beginning to be day. The morning light, however, soon stole into the aperture at the foot of the bed, betwixt those faded curtains. Finding the new guest there,—with a bloom on her cheeks like the morning's own, and a gentle stir of departing slumber in her limbs, as when an early breeze moves the foliage,—the dawn kissed her brow. It was the caress which a dewy maiden—such as the Dawn is, immortally—gives to her sleeping sister, partly from the impulse of irresistible fondness, and partly as a pretty hint that it is time now to unclose her eyes.

At the touch of those lips of light, Phœbe quietly awoke, and, for a moment, did not recognize where she was, nor how those heavy curtains chanced to be festooned around her. Nothing, indeed, was absolutely plain to her, except that it was now early morning, and that, whatever might happen next, it was proper, first of all, to get up and say her prayers. She was the more inclined to devotion, from the grim aspect of the chamber and its furniture, especially the tall stiff chairs; one of which stood close by her bedside, and looked as if some old-fashioned personage had been sitting there all night, and had vanished only just in season to escape discovery.

When Phœbe was quite dressed, she peeped out of the window, and saw a rose-bush in the garden. Being a very tall one, and of luxurious growth, it had been propped up against the side of the house, and was literally covered with a rare and very beautiful species of white rose. . . Hastening down the creaking and carpetless staircase, she found her way into the garden, gathered some of the most perfect of the roses, and brought them to her chamber.

Little Phœbe was one of those persons who possess, as their exclusive patrimony, the gift of practical arrangement. It is a kind of natural magic that enables these favoured ones to bring out the hidden capabilities of things around them; and particularly to give a look of comfort and habitableness to any place which, for however brief a period, may happen to be their home. A wild hut of underbrush, tossed together by wayfarers through the primitive forest, would acquire the home aspect by one night's lodging of such a woman, and would retain it long after her quiet figure had disappeared into the surrounding shade. No less a portion of such homely witchcraft was requisite, to reclaim, as it were, Phœbe's waste, cheerless, and dusky chamber, which had been untenanted so long—except by spiders, and mice, and rats, and ghosts—that it was all overgrown with the desolation which watches to obliterate every trace of man's happier hours. What was precisely Phœbe's process, we find it impossible to say. She appeared to have no preliminary design, but gave a touch here and another there; brought some articles of furniture to light, and dragged others into the shadow; looped up or let down a window-curtain; and, in the course of half an hour, had fully succeeded in throwing a kindly and hospitable smile over the apartment.

House of the Seven Gables

CHARLES LEVER

1806–1872

399 *With the Galway Hunt*

BY the time that we reached the foot of the hill, the fox, followed closely by the hounds, had passed through a breach in the wall, while Matthew Blake, with the huntsmen and whipper-in, were riding along in search of a gap to lead the horses through. Before I put spurs to Badger, to face the hill, I turned one look towards Hammersley. There was a slight curl, half-smile, half-sneer upon his lip, that actually maddened me, and had a precipice yawned beneath my feet, I should have dashed at it after that. The ascent was so steep that I was obliged to take the hill in a slanting direction, and even thus, the loose footing rendered it dangerous in the extreme. At length I reached the crest, where the wall, more than five feet in height, stood frowning above and seeming to defy me. I turned my horse full round, so that his very chest almost touched the stones, and, with a bold cut of the whip and a loud halloo, the gallant animal rose, as if rearing, pawed for an instant to regain his balance, and then with a frightful struggle fell backwards, and rolled from top to bottom of the hill, carrying me along with him; the last object that crossed my sight, as I lay bruised and motionless, being the captain as he took the wall in a flying leap, and disappeared at the other side. After a few scrambling efforts to rise, Badger regained his legs, and stood beside me; but such was the shock and concussion of my fall, that all the objects around seemed wavering and floating before me, while showers of bright sparks fell in myriads before my eyes. I tried to rise, but fell back helpless. Cold perspiration broke over my forehead, and I fainted. From that moment I can remember nothing, till I felt myself galloping along at full speed upon a level table land, with the hounds about three fields in advance, Hammersley riding foremost, and taking all his leaps coolly as ever. As I swayed to either side upon my saddle, from weakness, I was lost to all thought or recollection, save a flickering memory of some plan of vengeance, which still urged me forward. The chase had now lasted above an hour, and both hounds and horses began to feel the pace at which they were going. As for me, I rode mechanically; I neither knew nor cared for the dangers before me. My eye rested on but one object; my whole being was concentrated upon one vague and undetermined sense of revenge. At this instant the huntsman came alongside of me.

'Are you hurted, Misther Charles? did you fall?—your cheek is all blood, and your coat is torn in two;

and, Mother o' God, his boot is ground to powder; he does not hear me. Oh, pull up—pull, for the love of the Virgin; there 's the clover field, and the sunk fence before you, and you'll be killed on the spot.' . .

I dashed the rowels into my horse's flanks, and in an instant was beyond the reach of the poor fellow's remonstrances. Another moment, I was beside the captain. He turned round as I came up; the same smile was upon his mouth—I could have struck him. About three hundred yards before us lay the sunk fence; its breadth was about twenty feet, and a wall of close brickwork formed its face. Over this the hounds were now clambering; some succeeded in crossing, but by far the greater number fell back howling into the ditch.

I turned towards Hammersley. He was standing high in his stirrups, and, as he looked towards the yawning fence, down which the dogs were tumbling in masses, I thought (perhaps it was but a thought) that his cheek was paler. I looked again, he was pulling at his horse; ha! it was true then, he would not face it. I turned round in my saddle—looked him full in the face, and, as I pointed with my whip to the leap, called out in a voice hoarse with passion, 'come on.' I saw no more. All objects were lost to me from that moment. When next my senses cleared I was standing amid the dogs, where they had just killed. . . I turned a vague look upon him, and my eyes fell upon the figure of a man that lay stretched and bleeding upon a door before me. His pale face was crossed with a purple stream of blood, that trickled from a wound beside his eye-brow; his arms lay motionless and heavily at either side. I knew him not. A loud report of a pistol aroused me from my stupor; I looked back. I saw a crowd that broke suddenly asunder and fled right and left. I heard a heavy crash upon the ground; I pointed with my finger, for I could not utter a word.

'It is the English mare, yer honour; she was a beauty this morning, but she 's broke her collar bone, and both her legs, and it was best to put her out of pain.'

Charles O'Malley

JOHN STUART MILL

1806–1873

400 *Liberty of the Individual*

THERE is a sphere of action in which society, as distinguished from the individual, has, if any, only an indirect interest; comprehending all that portion of a person's life and conduct which affects only himself, or if it also affects others, only with their free, voluntary, and undeceived consent and participation. When I say only himself, I mean directly, and in the first instance: for whatever affects himself, may affect others through himself; and the objection which may be grounded on this contingency, will receive consideration in the sequel. This, then, is the appropriate region of human liberty. It comprises, first, the inward domain of consciousness; demanding liberty of conscience, in the most comprehensive sense; liberty of thought and feeling; absolute freedom of opinion and sentiment on all subjects, practical or speculative, scientific, moral, or theological. The liberty of expressing and publishing opinions may seem to fall under a different principle, since it belongs to that part of the conduct of an individual which concerns other people; but, being almost of as much importance as the liberty of thought itself, and resting in great part on the same reasons, is practically inseparable from it. Secondly, the principle requires liberty of tastes and pursuits; of framing the plan of our life to suit our own character; of doing as we like, subject to such consequences as may follow: without impediment from our fellow creatures, so long as what we do does not harm them, even though they should think our conduct foolish, perverse, or wrong. Thirdly, from this liberty of each individual, follows the liberty, within the same limits, of combination among individuals; freedom to unite, for any purpose not involving harm to others: the persons combining being supposed to be of full age, and not forced or deceived.

No society in which these liberties are not, on the whole, respected, is free, whatever may be its form of government; and never is completely free in which they do not exist absolute and unqualified.

On Liberty

JAMES FREDERICK FERRIER

1808–1864

401 *The True End of Man*

THE philosophy of the Cyrenaic school, founded by Aristippus, proceeds on the assumption that happiness is, in point of fact, the good, the supreme good, or chief end of man; and this assumption, so far from being discountenanced by the philosophy of Socrates, is involved in that philosophy as one of its most vital principles. Viewed as a matter of fact, we must admit that his own happiness, whatever it may consist in, or whatever may be the means to be employed in the attainment, is the end which each individual has most at heart, and at which he ultimately aims. This is the end after which all men most eagerly strive. Happiness is the goal which, consciously or unconsciously, we are all struggling to reach. Milton has written two epic poems in which he commemorates our fallen and our restored condition. He has written 'Paradise Lost' and 'Paradise Regained.' But the true epic of humanity—the epic which is in a constant course of evolution from the beginning until the end of time, the epic which is daily poured forth from the heart of the whole human race, sometimes in rejoicing paeans, but oftener amid woeful lamentation, tears, and disappointed hopes—what is it but Paradise sought for?

Lectures on Greek Philosophy

JAMES SPEDDING

1808–1881

402 *Bacon and Bribery*

I KNOW nothing more inexplicable than Bacon's unconsciousness of the state of his own case, unless it be the case itself. That he, of all men, whose fault had always been too much carelessness about money—who though always too ready to borrow, to give, to lend, and to spend, had never been either a bargainer or a grasper or a hoarder—and whose professional experience must have continually reminded him of the peril of meddling with any thing that could be construed into corruption,—that he should have allowed himself on any account to accept money from suitors while their cases were before him, is wonderful. That he should have done it without feeling at the time that he was laying himself open to a charge of what in law would be called bribery, is more wonderful still. That he should have done it often, and not lived under an abiding sense of insecurity—from the consciousness that he had secrets to conceal, of which the disclosure would be fatal to his reputation, yet the safe keeping did not rest solely with himself,—is most wonderful of all. Give him credit for nothing more than ordinary intelligence and ordinary prudence—wisdom for a man's self—and it seems almost incredible. And yet I believe it was the fact. The whole course of his behaviour, from the first rumour to the final sentence, convinces me that not the discovery of the thing only, but the thing itself, came upon him as a surprise; and that if anybody had told him the day before that he stood in danger of a charge of taking bribes, he would have received the suggestion with unaffected incredulity. How far I am justified in thinking so the reader shall judge for himself; for the impression is derived solely from the tenor of the correspondence which will be laid before him in due order.

The Life and Letters of Francis Bacon

EDWARD FITZGERALD

1809–1883

403 *The Boat Race*

SHORTLY after this, the rest of us agreed it was time to be gone. We walked along the fields past the church, crossed the boat-house ferry, and mingled with the crowd upon the opposite bank. Townsmen and Gownsmen, with the laced Fellow-commoner sprinkled among them here and there—reading men and sporting men—Fellows, and even Masters of Colleges, not indifferent to the prowess of their respective crews—all these, conversing on all topics, from the slang in Bell's Life to the last new German Revelation, and moving in ever-changing groups down the banks, where, at the farthest visible bend of the river, was a little knot of ladies gathered upon a green knoll, faced and illuminated by the beams of the setting sun. Beyond which point was heard at length some indistinct shouting, which gradually increased, until 'They are off—they are coming!' suspended other conversation among ourselves: and suddenly the head of the first boat turned the corner, and then another close upon it, and then a third; the crews pulling with all their might, but in perfect rhythm and order; and the crowd upon the bank turning round to follow along with them, cheering, 'Bravo, St. John's,' 'Go it, Trinity,' and waving hats and caps—the high crest and blowing forelock of Phidippus's mare, and he himself shouting encouragement to his crew, conspicuous over all—until, the boats reaching us, we also were caught up in the returning tide of spectators, and hurried back toward the boat-house; where we arrived just in time to see the ensign of Trinity lowered from its pride of place, and the eagle of St. John's soaring there instead. Then, waiting a while to hear how it was the winner had won, and the loser had lost, and watching Phidippus engaged in eager conversation with his defeated brethren, I took Euphranor and Lexilogus, one under each arm (Lycion having strayed into better company elsewhere), and walked home with them across the meadow that lies between the river and the town, whither the dusky troops of gownsmen were evaporating, while twilight gathered over all, and the nightingale began to be heard among the flowering chestnuts of Jesus.

Euphranor

404 *Spedding's Forehead*

DEAR FREDERIC,—I have just concluded, with all the throes of imprudent pleasure, the purchase of a large picture by Constable, of which, if I can continue in the mood, I will enclose you a sketch. It is very good: but how you and Morton would abuse it! Yet this, being a sketch, escapes some of Constable's faults, and might escape some of your censures. The trees are not splashed with that white sky-mud, which (according to Constable's theory) the Earth scatters up with her wheels in travelling so briskly round the sun; and there is a dash and felicity in the execution that gives one a thrill of good digestion in one's room, and the thought of which makes one inclined to jump over the children's heads in the streets. But if you could see my great enormous Venetian picture you would be extonished. Does the thought ever strike you, when looking at pictures in a house, that you are to run and jump at one, and go right through it into some behind-scene world on the other side, as Harlequins do? A steady portrait especially invites one to do so: the quietude of it ironically tempts one to outrage it: one feels it would close again over the panel, like water, as if nothing had happened. That portrait of Spedding, for instance, which Laurence has given me: not swords, nor cannon, nor all the bulls of Bashan butting at it, could, I feel sure, discompose that venerable forehead. No wonder that no hair can grow at such an altitude: no wonder his view of Bacon's virtue is so rarefied that the common consciences of men cannot endure it. Thackeray and I occasionally amuse ourselves with the idea of Spedding's forehead: we find it somehow or other in all things, just peering out of all things: you see it in a milestone, Thackeray says. He also draws the forehead rising with a sober light over Mont Blanc, and reflected in the lake of Geneva. We have great laughing over this. The forehead is at present in Pembrokeshire I believe: or Glamorganshire: or Monmouthshire: it is hard to say which. It has gone to spend its Christmas there.

Letter to Frederick Tennyson, 16 January 1841

OLIVER WENDELL HOLMES

1809–1894

405 *The Lost Sloop*

THE firing of the great guns at the Navy-yard is easily heard at the place where I was born and lived. 'There is a ship of war come in,' they used to say, when they heard them. Of course, I supposed that such vessels came in unexpectedly, after indefinite years of absence,—suddenly as falling stones; and that the great guns roared in their astonishment and delight at the sight of the old war-ship splitting the bay with her cutwater. Now the sloop-of-war the *Wasp*, Captain Blakely, after gloriously capturing the *Reindeer* and the *Avon*, had disappeared from the face of the ocean, and was supposed to be lost. But there was no proof of it, and, of course, for a time, hopes were entertained that she might be heard from. Long after the last real chance had utterly vanished, I pleased myself with the fond illusion that somewhere on the waste of waters she was still floating, and there were *years* during which I never heard the sound of the great gun booming inland from the Navy-yard without saying to myself, 'The *Wasp* has come!' and almost thinking I could see her, as she rolled in, crumpling the water before her, weather-beaten, barnacled, with shattered spars and threadbare canvas, welcomed by the shouts and tears of thousands. This was one of those dreams that I nursed and never told.—Let me make a clean breast of it now and say, that, so late as to have outgrown childhood, perhaps to have got far on toward manhood, when the roar of the cannon has struck suddenly on my ear, I have started with a thrill of vague expectation and tremulous delight, and the long-unspoken words have articulated themselves in the mind's dumb whisper, *The Wasp has come!*

The Autocrat of the Breakfast-Table

ALEXANDER WILLIAM KINGLAKE

1809–1891

406 *Scarlett's Three Hundred*
(Balaclava)

THE difference that there was in the temperaments of the two comrade regiments showed itself in the last moments of the onset. The Scots Greys gave no utterance except to a low, eager, fierce moan of rapture—the moan of outbursting desire. The Inniskillings went in with a cheer.

With a rolling prolongation of clangour which resulted from the bends of a line now deformed by its speed, the 'three hundred' crashed in upon the front of the column. They crashed in with a momentum so strong that no cavalry, extended in line and halted, could well have withstood the shock if it had been physically able to turn and fall back; but whatever might be their inclination, the front-rank men of the Russian column were debarred, as we saw, from all means of breaking away to the rear by the weight of their own serried squadrons sloping up the hillside close behind them; and it being too late for them to evade the concussion by a lateral flight, they had no choice—it was a cruel trial for cavalry to have to endure at the halt—they had no choice but to await and suffer the onslaught. On the other hand, it was certain that if the Russian hussar being halted should so plant and keep himself counter to his assailant as to be brought into diametric collision with the heavier man and the heavier horse of the Inniskillings or the Greys whilst charging direct at his front, he must and would be overborne. It might, therefore, be imagined that many of the troopers in the front rank of the Russian column would now be perforce overthrown, that numbers of our dragoons would in their turn be brought to the ground by that very obstacle—the obstacle of over-turned horses and horsemen—which their onset seemed about to build up, and that far along the front of the column the field would be encumbered with a heap or bank of prostrated riders and chargers, where Russians would be struggling for extrication intermingled with Inniskillings or Greys. Such a result would apparently have been an evil one for the 'three hundred,' because it would have enabled the unshattered masses of the enemy to bring their numbers to bear against such of the red-coats as might still remain in their saddles.

It was not thus, however, that the charge wrought its effect. What had first been done by Scarlett and the three horsemen with him, what had next been done by the leaders of the Greys and the 2d squadron of the Inniskillings, and next again by the squadron-leaders and other regimental officers whose place was in front of their men, that now, after more or less struggle, the whole of these charging 'three hundred' were enabled to achieve.

The result of their contact with the enemy was a phenomenon so much spoken of in the days of the old war against the French Empire, that it used to be then described by a peculiar but recognised phrase. Whether our people spoke with knowledge of fact, or whether they spoke in their pride, I do not here stay to question; but in describing the supposed issue of conflicts in which a mass of Continental soldiery was assailed by English troops extended in line, it used to be said of the foreigners that they 'accepted the files.' This meant, it seems, that instead of opposing his body to that of the islander with such rigid determination as to necessitate a front-to-front clash, and a front-to-front trial of weight and power, the foreigner who might be steadfast enough to keep his place in the foremost rank of the assailed mass would still be so far yielding as to let the intruder thrust past him and drive a way into the column.

Whatever was the foundation for this superb faith, the phrase, as above interpreted, represents with a singular exactness what the front rank of the Russian column now did. Being physically barred towards their rear by their own dense and close-pressing squadrons, these horsemen could not fall back under the impact of the charge; and, on the other hand, they did not so plant themselves as to be each of them a directly opposing hindrance to an assailant. They found and took a third course. They 'accepted the files.' Here, there, and almost everywhere along the assailed part of the column, the troopers who stood in front rank so sidled and shrank that they suffered the Grey or the Inniskillinger to tear in between them with the licence accorded to a cannon-ball which is seen to be coming, and must not be obstructed, but shunned. So, although, by their charge, these few horsemen could deliver no blow of such weight as to shake the depths of a column extending far up the hillside, they more or less shivered or sundered the front rank of the mass, and then, by dint of sheer wedge-work and fighting, they opened and cut their way in. It was in the nature of things that at some parts of the line the hindrance should be greater than at others; but, speaking in general terms, it can be said that, as Scarlett had led, so his first line righteously followed; and that, within a brief space from the moment of the first crash, the 'three hundred', after more or less strife, were received into the enemy's column.

Invasion of the Crimea

407 *Damascus*

BUT its gardens are the delight—the delight and the pride of Damascus; they are not the formal parterres which you might expect from the Oriental taste; rather, they bring back to your mind the memory of some dark old shrubbery in our northern isle that has been charmingly *un*-' kept up ' for many and many a day. . .

Wild as that, the nighest woodland of a deserted home in England, but without its sweet sadness, is the sumptuous garden of Damascus. Forest trees, tall and stately enough, if you could see their lofty crests, yet lead a tussling life of it below, with their branches struggling against strong numbers of bushes and wilful shrubs. The shade upon the earth is black as night. High, high above your head, and on every side all down to the ground, the thicket is hemmed in, and choked up by the interlacing boughs that droop with the weight of roses, and load the slow air with their damask breath. There are no other flowers. Here and there, there are patches of ground made clear from the cover, and these are either carelessly planted with some common and useful vegetable, or else are left free to the wayward ways of Nature, and bear rank weeds, moist-looking, and cool to your eyes, and freshening the sense with their earthly and bitter fragrance. There is a lane opened through the thicket, so broad in some places, that you can pass along side by side—in some, so narrow (the shrubs are for ever encroaching) that you ought, if you can, to go on the first, and hold back the bough of the rose tree. And through the sweet wilderness a loud rushing stream flows tumbling along, till it is halted at last in the lowest corner of the garden, and there tossed up in a fountain by the side of the simple alcove. This is all.

Eothen

408 *Homer and the Child*

I, TOO, loved Homer, but not with a scholar's love. The most humble and pious among women, was yet so proud a mother that she could teach her first-born son, no Watts's hymns—no collects for the day; she could teach him in earliest childhood, no less than this—to find a home in his saddle, and love old Homer, and all that Homer sung. True it is, that the Greek was ingeniously rendered into English—the English of Pope, but not even a mesh like that can screen an earnest child from the fire of Homer's battles.

I pored over the Odyssey as over a story-book, hoping and fearing for the hero whom yet I partly scorned. But the Iliad—line by line, I clasped it to my brain with reverence as well as with love. As an old woman deeply trustful sits reading her Bible because of the world to come, so, as though it would fit me for the coming strife of this temporal world, I read, and read the Iliad. Even outwardly it was not like other books; it was throned in towering folios. There was a preface or dissertation printed in type still more majestic than the rest of the book; this I read, but not till my enthusiasm for the Iliad had already run high. The writer compiling the opinions of many men, and chiefly of the ancients, set forth, I know not how quaintly, that the Iliad was all in all to the human race—that it was history—poetry—revelation—that the works of men's hands were folly and vanity, and would pass away like the dreams of a child, but that the kingdom of Homer would endure for ever and ever.

I assented with all my soul. I read, and still read; I came to know Homer. A learned commentator knows something of the Greeks, in the same sense as an oil and colour man may be said to know something of painting; but take an untamed child, and leave him alone for twelve months with any translation of Homer, and he will be nearer by twenty centuries to the spirit of old Greece: *he* does not stop in the ninth year of the siege to admire this or that group of words—*he* has no books in his tent, but he shares in vital counsels with the 'King of men,' and knows the inmost souls of the impending gods; how profanely he exults over the powers divine when they are taught to dread the prowess of mortals! and most of all how he rejoices when the God of War flies howling from the spear of Diomed, and mounts into heaven for safety! Then the beautiful episode of the 6th book: the way to feel this is not to go casting about, and learning from pastors and masters how best to admire it: the impatient child is not grubbing for beauties, but pushing the siege; the women vex him with their delays and their talking—the mention of the nurse is personal, and little sympathy has he for the child that is young enough to be frightened at the nodding plume of a helmet; but all the while that he thus chafes at the pausing of the action, the strong vertical light of Homer's poetry is blazing so full upon the people and things of the Iliad, that soon to the eyes of the child they grow familiar as his mother's shawl; yet of this great gain he is unconscious, and on he goes, vengefully thirsting for the best blood of Troy, and never remitting his fierceness, till almost suddenly it is changed for sorrow—the new and generous sorrow that he learns to feel, when the noblest of all his foes lies sadly dying at the Scaean gate.

Eothen

ABRAHAM LINCOLN

1809–1865

409 *Gettysburg*

FOURSCORE and seven years ago our fathers brought forth upon this continent a new nation, conceived in liberty, and dedicated to the proposition that all men are created equal. Now we are engaged in a great civil war, testing whether that nation, or any nation so conceived and so dedicated, can long endure. We are met on a great battle-field of that war. We have come to dedicate a portion of that field as a final resting-place of those who here gave their lives that that nation might live. It is altogether fitting and proper that we should do this. But in a larger sense we cannot dedicate, we cannot consecrate, we cannot hallow this ground. The brave men, living and dead, who struggled here, have consecrated it far above our power to add or detract. The world will little note, nor long remember, what we say here, but it can never forget what they did here. It is for us, the living, rather to be dedicated here to the unfinished work they have thus far so nobly advanced. It is rather for us to be here dedicated to the great task remaining before us, that from these honored dead we take increased devotion to that cause for which they here gave the last full measure of devotion; that we here highly resolve that the dead shall not have died in vain, that the nation shall, under God, have a new birth of freedom, and that the government of the people, by the people, and for the people, shall not perish from the earth.

Dedicatory Address at Gettysburg Cemetery, 19 Nov. 1863

JOHN BROWN

1810–1882

410 *A Dog Fight*

FOUR-AND-THIRTY years ago, Bob Ainslie and I were coming up Infirmary Street from the High School, our heads together, and our arms intertwisted, as only lovers and boys know how, or why.

When we got to the top of the street, and turned north, we espied a crowd at the Tron Church. 'A dog-fight!' shouted Bob, and was off; and so was I, both of us all but praying that it might not be over before we got up! And is not this boy-nature? and human nature too? and don't we all wish a house on fire not to be out before we see it? . .

Does any curious and finely-ignorant woman wish to know how Bob's eye at a glance announced a dog-fight to his brain? He did not, he could not see the dogs fighting; it was a flash of an inference, a rapid induction. The crowd round a couple of dogs fighting, is a crowd masculine mainly, with an occasional active, compassionate woman, fluttering wildly round the outside, and using her tongue and her hands freely upon the men, as so many 'brutes'; it is a crowd annular, compact, and mobile; a crowd centripetal, having its eyes and its heads all bent downwards and inwards, to one common focus.

Well, Bob and I are up, and find it is not over: a small thoroughbred, white bull-terrier, is busy throttling a large shepherd's dog, unaccustomed to war, but not to be trifled with. They are hard at it; the scientific little fellow doing his work in great style, his pastoral enemy fighting wildly, but with the sharpest of teeth and a great courage. Science and breeding, however, soon had their own; the Game Chicken, as the premature Bob called him, working his way up, took his final grip of poor Yarrow's throat,—and he lay gasping and done for. His master, a brown, handsome, big young shepherd from Tweedsmuir, would have liked to have knocked down any man, would 'drink up Esil, or eat a crocodile,' for that part, if he had a chance: it was no use kicking the little dog; that would only make him hold the closer. Many were the means shouted out in mouthfuls, of the best possible ways of ending it. 'Water!' but there was none near, and many cried for it who might have got it from the well at Blackfriar's Wynd. 'Bite the tail!' and a large, vague, benevolent, middle-aged man, more desirous than wise, with some struggle got the bushy end of *Yarrow's* tail into his ample mouth, and bit it with all his might. This was more than enough for the much-enduring, much-perspiring shepherd, who, with a gleam of joy over his broad visage, delivered a terrific facer upon our large, vague, benevolent, middle-aged friend,—who went down like a shot.

Still the Chicken holds: death not far off. 'Snuff! a pinch of snuff!' observed a calm, highly-dressed young buck, with an eye-glass in his eye. 'Snuff, indeed!' growled the angry crowd, affronted and glaring. 'Snuff! a pinch of snuff!' again observes the buck, but with more urgency; whereon were produced several open boxes, and from a mull which may have been at Culloden, he took a pinch, knelt down, and presented it to the nose of the Chicken. The laws of physiology and of snuff take their course; the Chicken sneezes, and Yarrow is free!

The young pastoral giant stalks off with Yarrow in his arms,—comforting him.

But the Bull Terrier's blood is up, and his soul

unsatisfied; he grips the first dog he meets, and discovering she is not a dog, in Homeric phrase, he makes a brief sort of *amende*, and is off. The boys, with Bob and me at their head, are after him: down Niddry Street he goes, bent on mischief; up the Cowgate like an arrow—Bob and I, and our small men, panting behind.

Rab and his Friends

411 *Presence of Mind*

DR. CHALMERS used to say that in the dynamics of human affairs, two qualities were essential to greatness—Power and Promptitude. One man might have both, another power without promptitude, another promptitude without power. We must all feel the common sense of this, and can readily see how it applies to a general in the field, to a pilot in a storm, to a sportsman, to a fencer, to a debater. It is the same with an operating surgeon at all times, and may be at any time with the practitioner of the art of healing. He must be ready for what are called emergencies—cases which rise up at your feet, and must be dealt with on the instant,—he must have power and promptitude.

It is a curious condition of mind that this requires: it is like sleeping with your pistol under your pillow, and it on full cock; a moment lost and all may be lost. There is the very nick of time. This is what we mean by presence of mind; by a man having such a subject at his finger-ends; that part of the mind lying nearest the outer world, and having to act on it through the bodily organs, through the will—the outposts must be always awake. It is of course, so to speak, only a portion of the mind that is thus needed and thus available; if the whole mind were for ever at the advanced post, it would soon lose itself in this endeavour to keep it... We must have just enough of the right knowledge and no more; we must have the habit of using this; we must have self-reliance, and the consentaneousness of the entire mind; and whatsoever our hand finds to do, we must do it with our might. Therefore it is that this master act of the man, under some sudden and great unexpected crisis, is in a great measure performed unconsciously as to its mental means. The man is so *totus in illo*, that there is no bit of the mind left to watch and record the acts of the rest; therefore men, when they have done some signal feat of presence of mind, if asked how they did it, generally don't very well know—they just did it: it was, in fact, done and then thought of, not thought of and then done, in which case it would likely never have been done. Not that the act was uncaused by mind; it is one of the highest powers of mind thus to act; but it is done, if I may use the phrase, by an acquired instinct. You will find all this in that wonderful old Greek who was Alexander the Great's and the old world's schoolmaster, and ours if we were wise,—whose truthfulness and clear insight one wonders at the longer he lives. He seems to have seen the human mind as a bird or an engineer does the earth—he knew the plan of it. We now-a-days see it as one sees a country, athwart and in perspective, and from the side; he saw it from above and from below. There are therefore no shadows, no foreshortenings, no clear-obscure, indeed no disturbing medium; it is as if he examined everything *in vacuo*. I refer my readers to what he says on Ἀγχίνοια and Εὐστοχία.

Horae Subsecivae

ELIZABETH GASKELL

1810–1865

412 *Miss Matty goes Visiting*

A FEW days after, a note came from Mr. Holbrook, asking us—impartially asking both of us—in a formal, old-fashioned style, to spend a day at his house—a long June day—for it was June now. He named that he had also invited his cousin, Miss Pole; so that we might join in a fly, which could be put up at his house.

I expected Miss Matty to jump at this invitation; but, no! Miss Pole and I had the greatest difficulty in persuading her to go. She thought it was improper; and was even half annoyed when we utterly ignored the idea of any impropriety in her going with two other ladies to see her old lover. Then came a more serious difficulty. She did not think Deborah would have liked her to go. This took us half a day's good hard talking to get over; but, at the first sentence of relenting, I seized the opportunity, and wrote and dispatched an acceptance in her name—fixing day and hour, that all might be decided and done with. . .

She was in a state of silent agitation all the way to Woodley. She had evidently never been there before; and, although she little dreamt I knew anything of her early story, I could perceive she was in a tremor at the thought of seeing the place which might have been her home, and round which it is probable that many of her innocent girlish imaginations had clustered. It was a long drive there, through paved jolting lanes. Miss Matilda sat bolt upright, and looked wistfully out of the windows, as we drew near the end of our journey. The aspect of the country was quiet and pastoral. Woodley stood among fields; and there was an old-fashioned garden, where roses and currant-bushes touched each other, and where the feathery asparagus formed a pretty background to the pinks and gilly-flowers; there was no drive up to the door: we got out at a little gate, and walked up a straight box-edged path.

'My cousin might make a drive, I think,' said Miss Pole, who was afraid of earache, and had only her cap on.

'I think it is very pretty,' said Miss Matty, with a soft plaintiveness in her voice, and almost in a whisper; for just then Mr. Holbrook appeared at the door, rubbing his hands in very effervescence of hospitality. He looked more like my idea of Don Quixote than ever, and yet the likeness was only external. His respectable housekeeper stood modestly at the door to bid us welcome; and while she led the elder ladies upstairs to a bedroom, I begged to look about the garden. My request evidently pleased the old gentleman; who took me all round the place, and showed me his six-and-twenty cows, named after the different letters of the alphabet. . .

When he and I went in, we found that dinner was nearly ready in the kitchen,—for so I suppose the room ought to be called, as there were oak dressers and cupboards all round, an oven by the side of the fireplace, and only a small Turkey carpet in the middle of the flag-floor. . .

When the ducks and green peas came, we looked at each other in dismay; we had only two-pronged, black-handled forks. It is true, the steel was as bright as silver; but what were we to do? Miss Matty picked up her peas, one by one, on the point

25 *an oven) Text gives 'all over', an obvious misprint repeated in all editions*

of the prongs, much as Aminé ate her grains of rice after her previous feast with the Ghoul. Miss Pole sighed over her delicate young peas as she left them on one side of her plate untasted; for they *would* drop between the prongs. I looked at my host: the peas were going wholesale into his capacious mouth, shovelled up by his large round-ended knife. I saw, I imitated, I survived! My friends, in spite of my precedent, could not muster up courage enough to do an ungenteel thing; and, if Mr. Holbrook had not been so heartily hungry, he would probably have seen that the good peas went away almost untouched.

After dinner, a clay pipe was brought in, and a spittoon; and, asking us to retire to another room, where he would soon join us, if we disliked tobacco-smoke, he presented his pipe to Miss Matty, and requested her to fill the bowl. This was a compliment to a lady in his youth; but it was rather inappropriate to propose it as an honour to Miss Matty, who had been trained by her sister to hold smoking of every kind in utter abhorrence. But if it was a shock to her refinement, it was also a gratification to her feelings to be thus selected; so she daintily stuffed the strong tobacco into the pipe; and then we withdrew.

'It is very pleasant dining with a bachelor,' said Miss Matty, softly, as we settled ourselves in the counting-house. 'I only hope it is not improper; so many pleasant things are!'

Cranford

413 *Phillis in Love*

THEN we talked about the different broods of chickens, and she showed me the hens that were good mothers, and told me the characters of all the poultry with the utmost good faith; and in all good faith I listened, for I believe there was a great deal of truth in all she said. And then we strolled on into the wood beyond the ash-meadow, and both of us sought for early primroses, amid the fresh green crinkled leaves. She was not afraid of being alone with me after the first day. I never saw her so lovely, or so happy. I think she hardly knew why she was so happy all the time. I can see her now, standing under the budding branches of the grey trees, over which a tinge of green seemed to be deepening day after day, her sun-bonnet fallen back on her neck, her hands full of delicate wood-flowers, quite unconscious of my gaze, but intent on sweet mockery of some bird in neighbouring bush or tree. She had the art of warbling, and replying to the notes of different birds, and knew their song, their habits and ways, more accurately than any one else I ever knew. She had often done it at my request the spring before; but this year she really gurgled, and whistled, and warbled just as they did, out of the very fullness and joy of her heart. She was more than ever the very apple of her father's eye; her mother gave her both her own share of love and that of the dead child who had died in infancy. I have heard cousin Holman murmur, after a long dreamy look at Phillis, and tell herself how like she was growing to Johnnie, and soothe herself with plaintive inarticulate sounds, and many gentle shakes of the head, for the aching sense of loss she would never get over in this world. The old servants about the place had the dumb loyal attachment to the child of the land, common to most agricultural labourers; not often stirred into activity or expression. My cousin Phillis was like a rose that

5 *amid) texts repeat the misprint* '*and*'

had come to full bloom on the sunny side of a lonely house, sheltered from storms. I have read in some book of poetry—

> A maid whom there were none to praise,
> And very few to love.

And somehow those lines always reminded me of Phillis; yet they were not true of her either. I never heard her praised; and out of her own household there were very few to love her; but though no one spoke out their approbation, she always did right in her parents' eyes, out of her natural simple goodness and wisdom. Holdsworth's name was never mentioned between us when we were alone; but I had sent on his letters to the minister, as I have said; and more than once he began to talk about our absent friend, when he was smoking his pipe after the day's work was done. Then Phillis hung her head a little over her work, and listened in silence.

Cousin Phillis

JOHN BRIGHT

1811–1889

414 *The Angel of Death*

I APPEAL to the noble lord at the head of the Government and to this House; I am not now complaining of the war—I am not now complaining of the terms of peace, nor, indeed, of anything that has been done—but I wish to suggest to this House what, I believe, thousands, and tens of thousands, of the most educated and of the most Christian portion of the people of this country are feeling upon this subject, although, indeed, in the midst of a certain clamour in the country, they do not give public expression to their feelings. Your country is not in an advantageous state at this moment; from one end of the kingdom to the other there is a general collapse of industry. Those members of this House not intimately acquainted with the trade and commerce of the country do not fully comprehend our position as to the diminution of employment and the lessening of wages. An increase in the cost of living is finding its way to the homes and hearts of a vast number of the labouring population. At the same time there is growing up—and, notwithstanding what some hon. members of this House may think of me, no man regrets it more than I do—a bitter and angry feeling against that class which has for a long period conducted the public affairs of this country. I like political changes when such changes are made as the result, not of passion, but of deliberation and reason. Changes so made are safe, but changes made under the influence of violent exaggeration, or of the violent passions of public meetings, are not changes usually approved by this House or advantageous to the country. I cannot but notice, in speaking to gentlemen who sit on either side of this House, or in speaking to any one I meet between this House and any of those localities we frequent when this House is up—I cannot, I say, but notice that an uneasy feeling exists as to the news that may arrive by the very next mail from the East. I do not suppose that your troops are to be beaten in actual conflict with the foe, or that they will be driven into the sea; but I am certain that many homes in England in which there now exists a fond hope that the distant one may return—many such homes may be rendered desolate when the next mail shall arrive. The angel of death has been abroad throughout the land; you may almost hear the beating of his wings. There is no one, as when the first-born were slain of old, to sprinkle with blood the lintel and the two sideposts of our doors, that he may spare and pass on; he takes his victims from the castle of the noble, the mansion of the wealthy, and the cottage of the poor and the lowly, and it is on behalf of all these classes that I make this solemn appeal.

Speech in the House of Commons on the Crimean War
23 Feb. 1855

WILLIAM MAKEPEACE THACKERAY

1811–1863

415 *Sir Pitt Crawley in Town*

JOHN, the groom, who had driven the carriage alone, did not care to descend to ring the bell; and so prayed a passing milk-boy to perform that office for him. When the bell was rung, a head appeared between the interstices of the dining-room shutters, and the door was opened by a man in drab breeches and gaiters, with a dirty old coat, a foul old neckcloth lashed round his bristly neck, a shining bald head, a leering red face, a pair of twinkling grey eyes, and a mouth perpetually on the grin.

'This Sir Pitt Crawley's?' says John, from the box.

'Ees,' says the man at the door with a nod.

'Hand down these 'ere trunks then,' said John.

'Hand 'n down yourself,' said the porter.

'Don't you see I can't leave my hosses? Come, bear a hand, my fine feller, and miss will give you some beer,' said John, with a horse-laugh, for he was no longer respectful to Miss Sharp, as her connexion with the family was broken off, and as she had given nothing to the servants on coming away.

The bald-headed man, taking his hands out of his breeches-pockets, advanced on this summons, and throwing Miss Sharp's trunk over his shoulder, carried it into the house.

'Take this basket and shawl, if you please, and open the door,' said Miss Sharp, and descended from the carriage in much indignation. 'I shall write to Mr. Sedley, and inform him of your conduct,' said she to the groom.

'Don't,' replied that functionary. 'I hope you've forgot nothink? Miss 'Melia's gownds—have you got them—as the lady's maid was to have 'ad? I hope they'll fit you. Shut the door, Jim, you'll get no good out of '*er*,' continued John, pointing with his thumb towards Miss Sharp: 'a bad lot, I tell you, a bad lot,' and so saying, Mr. Sedley's groom drove away. The truth is, he was attached to the lady's maid in question, and indignant that she should have been robbed of her perquisites.

On entering the dining-room, by the orders of the individual in gaiters, Rebecca found that apartment not more cheerful than such rooms usually are, when genteel families are out of town. The faithful chambers seem, as it were, to mourn the absence of their masters. The Turkey carpet has rolled itself up, and retired sulkily under the sideboard: the pictures have hidden their faces behind old sheets of brown paper: the ceiling-lamp is muffled up in a dismal sack of brown holland: the window-curtains have disappeared under all sorts of shabby envelopes: the marble bust of Sir Walpole Crawley is looking from its black corner at the bare boards and the oiled fire-irons, and the empty card-racks over the mantelpiece: the cellaret has lurked away behind the carpet: the chairs are turned up heads and tails along the walls; and in the dark corner opposite the statue, is an old-fashioned crabbed knife-box, locked and sitting on a dumb-waiter.

Two kitchen-chairs, and a round table, and an attentuated old poker and tongs were, however, gathered round the fireplace, as was a saucepan over a feeble sputtering fire. There was a bit of cheese and bread, and a tin candlestick on the table, and a little black porter in a pint-pot.

'Had your dinner, I suppose? It is not too warm for you? Like a drop of beer?'

'Where is Sir Pitt Crawley?' said Miss Sharp, majestically.

'He, he! *I*'m Sir Pitt Crawley. Reklect you owe me a pint for bringing down your luggage. He, he! Ask Tinker if I aynt. Mrs. Tinker, Miss Sharp! Miss Governess, Mrs. Charwoman. Ho, ho!'

The lady addressed as Mrs. Tinker at this moment made her appearance with a pipe and a paper of tobacco for which she had been dispatched a minute before Miss Sharp's arrival; and she handed the articles over to Sir Pitt, who had taken his seat by the fire.

'Where 's the farden?' said he. 'I gave you three half-pence. Where 's the change, old Tinker?'

'There!' replied Mrs. Tinker, flinging down the coin; 'it 's only baronets as cares about farthings.'

'A farthing a day is seven shillings a year,' answered the M.P.; 'seven shillings a year is the interest of seven guineas. Take care of your farthings.'

Vanity Fair

416 *Waterloo*

ALL our friends took their share and fought like men in the great field. All day long, whilst women were praying ten miles away, the lines of the dauntless English infantry were receiving and repelling the furious charges of the French horsemen. Guns which were heard at Brussels were ploughing up their ranks, and comrades falling, and the resolute survivors closing in. Towards evening, the attack of the French, repeated and resisted so bravely, slackened in its fury. They had other foes besides the British to engage, or were preparing for a final onset. It came at last: the columns of the Imperial Guard marched up the hill of St. Jean, at length and at once to sweep the English from the height which they had maintained all day, and spite of all: unscared by the thunder of the artillery, which hurled death from the English line—the dark rolling column pressed on and up the hill. It seemed almost to crest the eminence, when it began to wave and falter. Then it stopped, still facing the shot. Then at last the English troops rushed from the post from which no enemy had been able to dislodge them, and the Guard turned and fled.

No more firing was heard at Brussels—the pursuit rolled miles away. Darkness came down on the field and city: and Amelia was praying for George, who was lying on his face, dead, with a bullet through his heart.

Vanity Fair

417 *Mother and Daughter*

i. O matre pulchra

SHE gave him her hand, her little fair hand: there was only her marriage ring on it. The quarrel was all over. The year of grief and estrangement was passed. They never had been separated. His mistress had never been out of his mind all that time. No, not once. No, not in the prison; nor in the camp; nor on shore before the enemy; nor at sea under the stars of solemn midnight, nor as he watched the glorious rising of the dawn: not even at the table, where he sat carousing with friends, or at the theatre yonder, where he tried to fancy that other eyes were brighter than hers. Brighter eyes there might be, and faces more beautiful, but none so dear—no voice so sweet as that of his beloved mistress, who had been sister, mother, goddess to him during his youth—goddess now no more, for he knew of her weaknesses; and by thought, by suffering, and that experience it brings, was older now than she; but more fondly cherished as woman perhaps than ever she had been adored as divinity. What is it? Where lies it? the secret which makes one little hand the dearest of all? Whoever can unriddle that mystery? Here she was, her son by his side, his dear boy. Here she was, weeping and happy. She took his hand in both hers; he felt her tears...

They walked as though they had never been parted, slowly, with the grey twilight closing round them.

'And now we are drawing near to home,' she continued, 'I knew you would come, Harry, if—if it was but to forgive me for having spoken unjustly to you after that horrid—horrid misfortune. I was half frantic with grief then when I saw you. And I know now—they have told me. That wretch, whose name I can never mention, even has said it: how you tried to avert the quarrel, and would have taken it on yourself, my poor child: but it was God's will that I should be punished, and that my dear lord should fall.'

'He gave me his blessing on his death-bed,' Esmond said. 'Thank God for that legacy!'

'Amen, amen! dear Henry,' says the lady, pressing his arm. 'I knew it. Mr. Atterbury, of St. Bride's, who was called to him, told me so. And I thanked God, too, and in my prayers ever since remembered it.'

'You had spared me many a bitter night, had you told me sooner,' Mr. Esmond said.

'I know it, I know it,' she answered, in a tone of such sweet humility, as made Esmond repent that he should ever have dared to reproach her. 'I know how wicked my heart has been; and I have suffered too, my dear. I confessed to Mr. Atterbury—I must not tell any more. He—I said I would not write to you or go to you—and it was better even that, having parted, we should part. But I knew you would come back—I own that. That is no one's fault. And to-day, Henry, in the anthem, when they sang it, 'When the Lord turned the captivity of Zion, we were like them that dream,' I thought, yes, like them that dream—them that dream. And then it went, 'They that sow in tears shall reap in joy; and he that goeth forth and weepeth, shall doubtless come home again with rejoicing, bringing his sheaves with him'; I looked up from the book, and saw you. I was not surprised when I saw you. I knew you would come, my dear, and saw the gold sunshine round your head.'

She smiled an almost wild smile as she looked up at him. The moon was up by this time, glittering keen in the frosty sky. He could see, for the first time now clearly, her sweet careworn face.

'Do you know what day it is?' she continued. 'It is the 29th of December—it is your birthday! But last year we did not drink it—no, no. My Lord was cold, and my Harry was likely to die: and my brain was in a fever; and we had no wine. But now—now you are come again, bringing your sheaves with you—your sheaves with you!

ii. *filia pulchrior*

As they came up to the house at Walcote, the windows from within were lighted up with friendly welcome; the supper-table was spread in the oak-parlour; it seemed as if forgiveness and love were awaiting the returning prodigal. Two or three familiar faces of domestics were on the look-out at the porch—the old housekeeper was there, and young Lockwood from Castlewood in my Lord's livery of tawny and blue. His dear mistress pressed his arm as they passed into the hall. Her eyes beamed out on him with affection indescribable. 'Welcome,' was all she said, as she looked up, putting back her fair curls and black hood. A sweet rosy smile blushed on her face: Harry thought he had never seen her look so charming. Her face was lighted with a joy that was brighter than beauty—she took a hand of her son who was in the hall waiting his mother—she did not quit Esmond's arm.

'Welcome, Harry!' my young Lord echoed after her. 'Here we are all come to say so. Here's old Pincot, hasn't she grown handsome?' and Pincot, who was older, and no handsomer than usual, made a curtsy to the captain, as she called Esmond, and told my Lord to 'Have done, now.'

'And here's Jack Lockwood. He'll make a famous grenadier, Jack; and so shall I; we'll both 'list under you, Cousin. As soon as I am seventeen, I go to the army—every gentleman goes to the army. Look! who comes here—ho, ho!' he burst into a laugh. ''Tis Mistress Trix, with a new ribbon; I knew she would put one on as soon as she heard a captain was coming to supper.'

This laughing colloquy took place in the hall of Walcote House: in the midst of which is a staircase that leads from an open gallery, where are the doors of the sleeping-chambers: and from one of these, a wax candle in her hand, and illuminating her, came Mistress Beatrix—the light falling indeed upon the scarlet ribbon which she wore, and upon the most brilliant white neck in the world.

Esmond had left a child and found a woman, grown beyond the common height; and arrived at such a dazzling completeness of beauty, that his eyes might well show surprise and delight at beholding her. In hers there was a brightness so lustrous and melting, that I have seen a whole assembly follow her as if by an attraction irresistible: and that night the great Duke was at the playhouse after Ramillies, every soul turned and looked (she chanced to enter at the opposite side of the theatre at the same moment) at her, and not at him. She was a brown beauty: that is, her eyes, hair, and eyebrows and eyelashes, were dark: her hair curling with rich undulations, and waving over her shoulders; but her complexion was as dazzling white as snow in sunshine; except her cheeks, which were a bright red, and her lips, which were of a still deeper crimson. Her mouth and chin, they said, were too large and full, and so they might be for a goddess in marble, but not for a woman whose eyes were fire, whose look was love, whose voice was the sweetest low song, whose shape was perfect symmetry, health, decision, activity, whose foot as it planted itself on the ground, was firm but flexible, and whose motion, whether rapid or slow, was always perfect grace—agile as a nymph, lofty as a queen—now melting, now imperious, now sarcastic, there was no single movement of hers but was beautiful. As he thinks of her, he who writes feels young again, and remembers a paragon.

So she came holding her dress with one fair rounded arm, and her taper before her, tripping down the stair to greet Esmond.

'She hath put on her scarlet stockings and white shoes,' says my Lord, still laughing. 'Oh my fine mistress! is this the way you set your cap at the captain!' She approached, shining smiles upon Esmond, who could look at nothing but her eyes. She advanced holding forward her head, as if she would have him kiss her as he used to do when she was a child.

'Stop,' she said, 'I am grown too big! Welcome, Cousin Harry,' and she made him an arch curtsey, sweeping down to the ground almost, with the most gracious bend, looking up the while with the brightest eyes and sweetest smile. Love seemed to radiate from her. Harry eyed her with such a rapture as the first lover is described as having by Milton.

'*N'est-ce pas?*' says my Lady, in a low, sweet voice, still hanging on his arm.

The History of Henry Esmond

418 *Pulvis et Umbra*

AS Esmond and the dean walked away from Kensington discoursing of this tragedy, and how fatal it was to the cause which they both had at heart; the street-criers were already out with their broadsides, shouting through the town the full, true, and horrible account of the death of Lord Mohun and Duke Hamilton in a duel. A fellow had got to Kensington, and was crying it in the square there at very early morning, when Mr. Esmond happened to pass by. He drove the man from under Beatrix's very window, whereof the casement had been set open. The sun was shining though 'twas November: he had seen the market-carts rolling into London, the guard relieved at the Palace, the labourers trudging to their work in the gardens between Kensington and the City—the wandering merchants and hawkers filling the air with their cries. The world was going to its business again, although dukes lay dead and ladies mourned for them; and kings, very likely, lost their chances. So night and day pass away, and to-morrow comes, and our place knows us not. Esmond thought of the courier, now galloping on the north road to inform him, who was Earl of Arran yesterday, that he was Duke of Hamilton to-day, and of a thousand great schemes, hopes, ambitions, that were alive in the gallant heart, beating a few hours since, and now in a little dust quiescent.

The History of Henry Esmond

419 *'The Steps of a Good Man'*

THE custom of the school is, that on the 12th of December, the Founder's Day, the head gown-boy shall recite a Latin oration, in praise *Fundatoris*

Nostri, and upon other subjects; and a goodly company of old Cistercians is generally brought together to attend this oration: after which we go to chapel and hear a sermon; after which we adjourn to a great dinner, where old condisciples meet, old toasts are given, and speeches are made. Before marching from the oration-hall to chapel, the stewards of the day's dinner, according to old-fashioned rite, have wands put into their hands, walk to church at the head of the procession, and sit there in places of honour. The boys are already in their seats, with smug fresh faces, and shining white collars; the old black-gowned pensioners are on their benches; the chapel is lighted, and Founder's Tomb, with its grotesque carvings, monsters, heraldries, darkles and shines with the most wonderful shadows and lights. There he lies, Fundator Noster, in his ruff and gown, awaiting the great Examination Day. We oldsters, be we ever so old, become boys again as we look at that familiar old tomb, and think how the seats are altered since we were here, and how the doctor—not the present doctor, the doctor of *our* time—used to sit yonder, and his awful eye used to frighten us shuddering boys, on whom it lighted; and how the boy next us *would* kick our shins during service time, and how the monitor would cane us afterwards because our shins were kicked. Yonder sit forty cherry-cheeked boys, thinking about home and holidays to-morrow. Yonder sit some threescore old gentlemen pensioners of the hospital, listening to the prayers and the psalms. You hear them coughing feebly in the twilight—the old reverend blackgowns. Is Codd Ajax alive, you wonder?—the Cistercian lads called these old gentlemen Codds, I know not wherefore—I know not wherefore—but is old Codd Ajax alive, I wonder? or Codd Soldier? or kind old Codd Gentleman, or has the grave closed over them? A plenty of candles lights up this chapel, and this scene of age and youth, and early memories, and pompous death. How solemn the well-remembered prayers are, here uttered again in the place where in childhood we used to hear them! How beautiful and decorous the rite; how noble the ancient words of the supplications which the priest utters, and to which generations of fresh children, and troops of bygone seniors have cried Amen under those arches! The service for Founder's Day is a special one; one of the psalms selected being the thirty-seventh, and we hear——

23. The steps of a good man are ordered by the Lord, and he delighteth in his way.

24. Though he fall, he shall not be utterly cast down, for the Lord upholdeth him with His hand.

25. I have been young, and now am old, yet have I not seen the righteous forsaken, nor his seed begging their bread.

As we came to this verse, I chanced to look up from my book towards the swarm of black-coated pensioners: and amongst them—amongst them—sat Thomas Newcome.

His dear old head was bent down over his Prayer-book; there was no mistaking him. He wore the black gown of the pensioners of the Hospital of Grey Friars. His Order of the Bath was on his breast. He stood there amongst the poor brethren, uttering the responses to the psalm. The steps of this good man had been ordered hither by Heaven's decree: to this Alms-house! Here it was ordained that a life all love, and kindness and honour, should end! I heard no more of prayers, and psalms, and sermon, after that.

The Newcomes

WILLIAM MAKEPEACE THACKERAY

420 *Chur in the Grisons*

I HAVE seldom seen a place more quaint, pretty, calm, and pastoral, than this remote little Chur. What need have the inhabitants for walls and ramparts, except to build summer-houses, to trail vines, and hang clothes to dry? No enemies approach the great mouldering gates: only at morn and even, the cows come lowing past them, the village maidens chatter merrily round the fountains, and babble like the ever-voluble stream that flows under the old walls. The schoolboys, with book and satchel, in smart uniforms, march up to the gymnasium, and return thence at their stated time. There is one coffee-house in the town, and I see one old gentleman goes to it. There are shops with no customers seemingly, and the lazy tradesmen look out of their little windows at the single stranger sauntering by. There is a stall with baskets of queer little black grapes and apples, and a pretty brisk trade with half a dozen urchins standing round. But, beyond this, there is scarce any talk or movement in the street. There 's nobody at the book-shop. 'If you will have the goodness to come again in an hour,' says the banker, with his mouth full of dinner at one o'clock, 'you can have the money.' There is nobody at the hotel, save the good landlady, the kind waiters, the brisk young cook who ministers to you. Nobody is in the Protestant church—(oh! strange sight, the two confessions are here at peace!)—nobody in the Catholic church: until the sacristan, from his snug abode in the cathedral close, espies the traveller eyeing the monsters and pillars before the old shark-toothed arch of his cathedral, and comes out (with a view to remuneration possibly) and opens the gate, and shows you the venerable church, and the queer old relics in the sacristy, and the ancient vestments (a black velvet cope, amongst other robes, as fresh as yesterday, and presented by that notorious 'pervert,' Henry of Navarre and France), and the statue of Saint Lucius, who built St. Peter's Church, opposite No. 65, Cornhill.

Roundabout Papers

CHARLES DICKENS

1812–1870

421 *David's Library*

MY father had left a small collection of books in a little room up-stairs, to which I had access (for it adjoined my own) and which nobody else in our house ever troubled. From that blessed little room, Roderick Random, Peregrine Pickle, Humphrey Clinker, Tom Jones, the Vicar of Wakefield, Don Quixote, Gil Blas, and Robinson Crusoe, came out, a glorious host, to keep me company. They kept alive my fancy, and my hope of something beyond that place and time,—they, and the Arabian Nights, and the Tales of the Genii,—and did me no harm; for whatever harm was in some of them was not there for me; *I* knew nothing of it. It is astonishing to me now, how I found time, in the midst of my porings and blunderings over heavier themes, to read those books as I did. It is curious to me how I could ever have consoled myself under my small troubles (which were great troubles to me), by impersonating my favourite characters in them—as I did—and by putting Mr. and Miss Murdstone into all the bad ones—which

I did too. I have been Tom Jones (a child's Tom Jones, a harmless creature) for a week together. I have sustained my own idea of Roderick Random for a month at a stretch, I verily believe. I had a greedy relish for a few volumes of Voyages and Travels—I forget what, now—that were on those shelves ; and for days and days I can remember to have gone about my region of our house, armed with the centre-piece out of an old set of boot-trees—the perfect realisation of Captain Somebody, of the Royal British Navy, in danger of being beset by savages, and resolved to sell his life at a great price. The Captain never lost dignity, from having his ears boxed with the Latin Grammar. I did ; but the Captain was a Captain and a hero, in despite of all the grammars of all the languages in the world, dead or alive.

This was my only and my constant comfort. When I think of it, the picture always rises in my mind, of a summer evening, the boys at play in the churchyard, and I sitting on my bed, reading as if for life. Every barn in the neighbourhood, every stone in the church, and every foot of the churchyard, had some association of its own, in my mind, connected with these books, and stood for some locality made famous in them. I have seen Tom Pipes go climbing up the church-steeple ; I have watched Strap, with the knapsack on his back, stopping to rest himself upon the wicket-gate ; and I *know* that Commodore Trunnion held that club with Mr. Pickle, in the parlour of our little village alehouse.

David Copperfield

422 *The Widow at the Grave*

SHE was looking at a humble stone which told of a young man who had died at twenty-three years old, fifty-five years ago, when she heard a faltering step approaching, and looking round saw a feeble woman bent with the weight of years, who tottered to the foot of that same grave and asked her to read the writing on the stone. The old woman thanked her when she had done, saying that she had had the words by heart for many a long, long year, but could not see them now.

'Were you his mother?' said the child.

'I was his wife, my dear.'

She the wife of a young man of three-and-twenty! Ah, true! It was fifty-five years ago.

'You wonder to hear me say that,' remarked the old woman, shaking her head. 'You're not the first. Older folk than you have wondered at the same thing before now. Yes, I was his wife. Death doesn't change us more than life, my dear.'

'Do you come here often?' asked the child.

'I sit here very often in the summer-time,' she answered. 'I used to come here once to cry and mourn, but that was a weary while ago, bless God!'

'I pluck the daisies as they grow, and take them home,' said the old woman after a short silence. 'I like no flowers so well as these, and haven't for five-and-fifty years. It's a long time, and I'm getting very old!'

Then growing garrulous upon a theme which was new to one listener though it were but a child, she told her how she had wept and moaned and prayed to die herself, when this happened; and how when she first came to that place, a young creature strong in love and grief, she had hoped that her heart was breaking as it seemed to be. But that time passed by, and although she continued to be sad when she came there, still she could bear to come, and so went on until it was pain no longer, but a solemn pleasure, and a duty she had learned to like. And now that five-and-fifty years were gone, she spoke of the dead man as if he had been her son or grandson, with a kind of pity for his youth, growing out of her own old age, and an exalting of his strength and manly beauty as compared with her own weakness and decay; and yet she spoke about him as her husband too, and thinking of herself in connexion with him, as she used to be and not as she was now, talked of their meeting in another world, as if he were dead but yesterday, and she, separated from her former self, were thinking of the happiness of that comely girl who seemed to have died with him.

The Old Curiosity Shop

423 *Mrs. Gamp on Steam-Engines*

IT was so amusing, that Tom, with Ruth upon his arm, stood looking down from the wharf, as nearly regardless as it was in the nature of flesh and blood to be, of an elderly lady behind him, who had brought a large umbrella with her, and didn't know what to do with it. This tremendous instrument had a hooked handle; and its vicinity was first made known to him by a painful pressure on the windpipe, consequent upon its having caught him round the throat. Soon after disengaging himself with perfect good humour, he had a sensation of the ferule in his back; immediately afterwards, of the hook entangling his ankles; then of the umbrella generally, wandering about his hat, and flapping at it like a great bird ; and, lastly, of a poke or thrust below the ribs, which gave him such exceeding anguish, that he could not refrain from turning round to offer a mild remonstrance.

Upon his turning round, he found the owner of the umbrella struggling on tip-toe, with a countenance expressive of violent animosity, to look down upon the steam-boats ; from which he inferred that she had attacked him, standing in the front row, by design, and as her natural enemy.

'What a very ill-natured person you must be!' said Tom.

The lady cried out fiercely, 'Where 's the pelisse!' meaning the constabulary—and went on to say, shaking the handle of the umbrella at Tom, that but for them fellers never being in the way when they was wanted, she'd have given him in charge, she would.

'If they greased their whiskers less, and minded the duties which they're paid so heavy for, a little more,' she observed, 'no one needn't be drove mad by scrouding so!'

She had been grievously knocked about, no doubt, for her bonnet was bent into the shape of a cocked hat. Being a fat little woman, too, she was in a state of great exhaustion and intense heat. Instead of pursuing the altercation, therefore, Tom civilly inquired what boat she wanted to go on board of?

'I suppose,' returned the lady, 'as nobody but yourself can want to look at a steam package, without wanting to go a-boarding of it, can they! Booby!'

'Which one do you want to look at then?' said Tom. 'We'll make room for you if we can. Don't be so ill-tempered.'

'No blessed creetur as ever I was with in trying times,' returned the lady, somewhat softened, 'and they're a many in their numbers, ever brought it as a charge again myself that I was anythin' but mild and equal in my spirits. Never mind a-contradicting of me, if you seems to feel it does you good, ma'am, I often says, for well you know that Sairey may be trusted not to give it back again. But I will not denige that I am worrited and wexed this day, and with good reagion, Lord forbid!'

By this time, Mrs. Gamp (for it was no other than that experienced practitioner) had, with Tom's assistance, squeezed and worked herself into a small corner between Ruth and the rail; where, after breathing very hard for some little time, and performing a short series of dangerous evolutions with her umbrella, she managed to establish herself pretty comfortably.

'And which of all them smoking monsters is the Ankworks boat, I wonder. Goodness me!' cried Mrs. Gamp.

'What boat did you want?' asked Ruth.

'The Ankworks package,' Mrs. Gamp replied. 'I will not deceive you, my sweet. Why should I?'

'That is the Antwerp packet in the middle,' said Ruth.

'And I wish it was in Jonadge's belly, I do,' cried Mrs. Gamp; appearing to confound the prophet with the whale in this miraculous aspiration.

Ruth said nothing in reply; but, as Mrs. Gamp, laying her chin against the cool iron of the rail, continued to look intently at the Antwerp boat, and every now and then to give a little groan, she inquired whether any child of hers was going abroad that morning? Or perhaps her husband, she said kindly.

'Which shows,' said Mrs. Gamp, casting up her eyes, 'what a little way you've travelled into this wale of life, my dear young creetur! As a good friend of mine has frequent made remark to me, which her name, my love, is Harris, Mrs. Harris through the square and up the steps a-turnin' round by the tobacker shop, "Oh Sairey, Sairey, little do we know wot lays afore us!" "Mrs. Harris, ma'am," I says, "not much, it 's true, but more than you suppoge. Our calcilations, ma'am," I says, "respectin' wot the number of a family will be, comes most times within one, and oftener than you would suppoge, exact." "Sairey," says Mrs. Harris, in a awful way, "Tell me wot is my indiwidgle number." "No, Mrs. Harris," I says to her, "ex-cuge me, if you please. My own," I says, "has fallen out of three-pair backs, and had damp doorsteps settled on their lungs, and one was turned up smilin' in a bedstead, unbeknown. Therefore, ma'am," I says, "seek not to proticipate, but take 'em as they come and as they go." Mine,' said Mrs. Gamp, 'mine is all gone, my dear young chick. And as to husbands, there's a wooden leg gone likeways home to its account, which in its constancy of walkin' into wine vaults, and never comin' out again 'till fetched by force, was quite as weak as flesh, if not weaker.'

When she had delivered this oration, Mrs. Gamp leaned her chin upon the cool iron again; and looking intently at the Antwerp packet, shook her head and groaned.

'I wouldn't,' said Mrs. Gamp, 'I wouldn't be a man and have such a think upon my mind!—but nobody as owned the name of man, could do it!'

Tom and his sister glanced at each other; and Ruth,

after a moment's hesitation, asked Mrs. Gamp what troubled her so much.

'My dear,' returned that lady, dropping her voice, 'you are single, ain't you?'

Ruth laughed, blushed, and said 'Yes.'

'Worse luck,' proceeded Mrs. Gamp, 'for all parties! But others is married, and in the marriage state; and there is a dear young creetur a-comin' down this mornin' to that very package, which is no more fit to trust herself to sea, than nothin' is!'

She paused here to look over the deck of the packet in question, and on the steps leading down to it, and on the gangways. Seeming to have thus assured herself that the object of her commiseration had not yet arrived, she raised her eyes gradually up to the top of the escape-pipe, and indignantly apostrophised the vessel:

'Oh, drat you!' said Mrs. Gamp, shaking her umbrella at it, 'you're a nice spluttering nisy monster for a delicate young creetur to go and be a passinger by; ain't you! *You* never do no harm in that way, do you? With your hammering, and roaring, and hissing, and lamp-iling, you brute! Them confugion steamers,' said Mrs. Gamp, shaking her umbrella again, 'has done more to throw us out of our reg'lar work and bring ewents on at times when nobody counted on 'em (especially them screeching railroad ones), than all the other frights that ever was took. I have heerd of one young man, a guard upon a railway, only three years opened—well does Mrs. Harris know him, which indeed he is her own relation by her sister's marriage with a master sawyer—as is godfather at this present time to six-and-twenty blessed little strangers, equally unexpected, and all on 'em named after the

Ingeins as was the cause. Ugh!' said Mrs. Gamp, resuming her apostrophe, 'one might easy know you was a man's inwention, from your disregardlessness of the weakness of our naturs, so one might, you brute!'

Martin Chuzzlewit

424 *The Pale Young Gentleman*

WHEN I had exhausted the garden and a greenhouse with nothing in it but a fallen-down grape-vine and some bottles, I found myself in the dismal corner upon which I had looked out of window. Never questioning for a moment that the house was now empty, I looked in at another window, and found myself, to my great surprise, exchanging a broad stare with a pale young gentleman with red eyelids and light hair.

This pale young gentleman quickly disappeared, and reappeared beside me. He had been at his books when I had found myself staring at him, and I now saw that he was inky.

'Halloa!' said he, 'young fellow!'

Halloa being a general observation which I had usually observed to be best answered by itself, *I* said 'Halloa!' politely omitting young fellow.

'Who let *you* in?' said he.

'Miss Estella.'

'Who gave you leave to prowl about?'

'Miss Estella.'

'Come and fight,' said the pale young gentleman.

What could I do but follow him? I have often asked myself the question since: but what else could I do? His manner was so final and I was so astonished, that I followed where he led, as if I had been under a spell.

'Stop a minute, though,' he said, wheeling round before we had gone many paces. 'I ought to give you a reason for fighting, too. There it is!' In a most irritating manner he instantly slapped his hands against one another, daintily flung one of his legs up behind him, pulled my hair, slapped his hands again, dipped his head, and butted it into my stomach.

The bull-like proceeding last mentioned, besides that it was unquestionably to be regarded in the light of a liberty, was particularly disagreeable just after bread and meat. I therefore hit out at him, and was going to hit out again, when he said, 'Aha! Would you?' and began dancing backwards and forwards in a manner quite unparalleled within my limited experience.

'Laws of the game!' said he. Here, he skipped from his left leg on to his right. 'Regular rules!' Here, he skipped from his right leg on to his left. 'Come to the ground, and go through the preliminaries!' Here, he dodged backwards and forwards, and did all sorts of things while I looked helplessly at him.

I was secretly afraid of him when I saw him so dexterous; but I felt morally and physically convinced that his light head of hair could have had no business in the pit of my stomach, and that I had a right to consider it irrelevant when so obtruded on my attention. Therefore, I followed him without a word, to a retired nook of the garden, formed by the junction of two walls and screened by some rubbish. On his asking me if I was satisfied with the ground, and on my replying Yes, he begged my leave to absent himself for a moment, and quickly returned with a bottle of water and a sponge dipped in vinegar. 'Available for both,' he said, placing these against the wall. And then fell to pulling off, not only his jacket and waistcoat, but his shirt too, in a manner at once light-hearted, business-like, and blood-thirsty.

Although he did not look very healthy—having pimples on his face, and a breaking out on his mouth—these dreadful preparations quite appalled me. I judged him to be about my own age, but he was much taller, and he had a way of spinning himself about that was full of appearance. For the rest, he was a young gentleman in a grey suit (when not denuded for battle), with his elbows, knees, wrists, and heels considerably in advance of the rest of him as to development.

My heart failed me when I saw him squaring at me with every demonstration of mechanical nicety, and eyeing my anatomy as if he were minutely choosing his bone. I never have been so surprised in my life, as I was when I let out the first blow, and saw him lying on his back, looking up at me with a bloody nose and his face exceedingly fore-shortened.

But he was on his feet directly, and after sponging himself with a great show of dexterity began squaring again. The second greatest surprise I have ever had in my life was seeing him on his back again, looking up at me out of a black eye.

His spirit inspired me with great respect. He seemed to have no strength, and he never once hit me hard, and he was always knocked down ; but he would be up again in a moment, sponging himself or drinking out of the water-bottle, with the greatest satisfaction in seconding himself according to form, and then came at me with an air and a show that made me believe he really was going to do for me at last. He got heavily bruised, for I am sorry to record that the more I hit him, the harder I hit him; but he came up again and again and again, until at last he got a bad fall with the back of his head against the wall. Even after that crisis in our affairs, he got up and turned round and round confusedly a few times, not knowing where I was; but finally went on his knees to his sponge and threw it up: at the same time panting out, 'That means you have won.'

He seemed so brave and innocent, that although I had not proposed the contest, I felt but a gloomy satisfaction in my victory. Indeed, I go so far as to hope that I regarded myself while dressing, as a species of savage young wolf, or other wild beast. However, I got dressed, darkly wiping my sanguinary face at intervals, and I said, 'Can I help you?' and he said, 'No thankee,' and I said, 'Good afternoon,' and *he* said, 'Same to you.'

Great Expectations

425 *The Haymakers*

SUCH was the surrounding of one City churchyard that I saw last summer, on a Volunteering Saturday evening towards eight of the clock, when with astonishment I beheld an old old man and an old old woman in it, making hay. Yes, of all occupations in this world, making hay! It was a very confined patch of churchyard lying between Gracechurch-street and the Tower, capable of yielding, say an apronful of hay. By what means the old old man and woman had got into it, with an almost toothless hay-making rake, I could not fathom. No open window was within view; no window at all was within view, sufficiently near the ground to have enabled their old legs to descend from it; the rusty churchyard-gate was locked, the mouldy church was locked. Gravely among the graves, they made hay, all alone by themselves. They looked like Time and his wife. There was but the one rake between them, and they both had hold of it in a pastorally-loving manner, and there was hay on the old woman's black bonnet, as if the old man had recently been playful. The old man was quite an obsolete old man, in knee-breeches and coarse grey stockings, and the old woman wore mittens like unto his stockings in texture and in colour. They took no heed of me as I looked on, unable to account for them. The old woman was much too bright for a pew-opener, the old man much too meek for a beadle. On an old tombstone in the foreground between me and them, were two cherubim; but for those celestial embellishments being represented as having no possible use for knee-breeches, stockings, or mittens, I should have compared them with the hay-makers, and sought a likeness. I coughed and awoke the echoes, but the hay-makers never looked at me. They used the rake with a measured action, drawing the scanty crop towards them; and so I was fain to leave them under three yards and a half of darkening sky, gravely making hay among the graves, all alone by themselves.

The Uncommercial Traveller

MARK PATTISON

1813–1884

426 *The Instinct of Pilgrimage*

THE truth is, that that magnetic influence which irresistibly draws our feet to spots on which our imagination has long fed, is an instinct of our nature, and that in this, as in other respects, the Church did but take into her service, and propose a fitting object to, an impulse which will vent itself in some form or other. There have been pilgrims both before and since the ages of faith, the ages when the Church bore sway over every action of life. Only she sent them to the tombs of saints, and martyrs, and filled their paths with sacred associations, instead of leaving them to roam at will in search of the relics of pagans or infidels, with Byron or Rousseau in their pockets as the companions of their way. The Church cannot be said to have created pilgrimages, or even to have encouraged them—she suffered them, and gave them a direction which might, at least, edify. But *qui multum peregrinantur, raro sanctificantur* is her doctrine. . .

This is a taste quite distinct from a love of grand scenery—a love of nature. For this we must go to particular spots of the earth, where there are mountains, rocks, lakes. North America or South Africa, lands the least interesting to the historical traveller, will supply the richest objects to the lover of scenery. It is the old historical lands of Europe that the lover of history longs to explore. None of these are more attractive to him than France. Its natural scenery, pre-eminently in Western Europe at least, is tame, and uniform; but rich beyond all others in the traces of the men of old, and the associations of the past. For ourselves, at least were we younger, we could gaze for hours, with Froissart on our knee, over that boundless plain of Languedoc, convicted of all guide-books of being arid, brown, and wholly uninteresting. This old Languedoc, Roman and Gothic still. 'Descend from Cahors,' says Michelet, 'its slopes clothed with vines, and you will find yourself in the country of the mulberries. Spread before you a landscape of some thirty or forty leagues, a vast ocean of tillage, a confused mass, losing itself in the vapour of the distant horizon, above which rises the fantastic outline of the Pyrenees with their silvery peaks. Oxen, yoked together by the horns, slowly, beneath the eye of an ardent sun, labour this fertile valley. At mid-day, a storm; the ground becomes a lake; in an hour the sun has restored it to its state of dust. At night you enter some big dull town; Toulouse, if you will. . .

Nor, we hope, are we singular. Among the shoals of the frivolous and dissipated which this country annually discharges upon the Continent, there are, we would hope, to be found some few thoughtful travellers who are attracted to foreign lands by a love of the localities associated with the memory of the great and the saintly of ancient times. Such is perhaps the nearest approach we may make to the motives of the Christian pilgrim. Such a voyager, if it has ever been his hap to turn his feet to Orleans, and descending to the water-side to embark in one of the tiny iron steamers belonging to M. Larochejacquelin, glide with sinuous course down the Loire, its banks still clad with the broom which gives their title to the Plantagenets, the sunny and laughing landscape once only gloomily broken as we sweep beneath the frowning

Blois ; such a voyager will seldom feel this spell upon his spirit more powerfully than when, before sunset of a long summer's day, the little vessel is moored to the quay of Tours.

Essays : Gregory of Tours

JOHN LOTHROP MOTLEY

1814–1877

427 *William of Orange*

HE possessed, too, that which to the heathen philosopher seemed the greatest good—the sound mind in the sound body. His physical frame was after death found so perfect that a long life might have been in store for him, notwithstanding all which he had endured. The desperate illness of 1574, the frightful gunshot wound inflicted by Jaureguy in 1582, had left no traces. The physicians pronounced that his body presented an aspect of perfect health. His temperament was cheerful. At table, the pleasures of which, in moderation, were his only relaxation, he was always animated and merry, and this jocoseness was partly natural, partly intentional. In the darkest hours of his country's trial, he affected a serenity which he was far from feeling, so that his apparent gaiety at momentous epochs was even censured by dullards, who could not comprehend its philosophy, nor applaud the flippancy of William the Silent.

He went through life bearing the load of a people's sorrows upon his shoulders with a smiling face. Their name was the last word upon his lips, save the simple affirmative, with which the soldier who had been battling for the right all his lifetime, commended his soul in dying 'to his great Captain, Christ.' The people were grateful and affectionate, for they trusted the character of their 'Father William,' and not all the clouds which calumny could collect ever dimmed to their eyes the radiance of that lofty mind to which they were accustomed, in their darkest calamities, to look for light. As long as he lived, he was the guiding-star of a brave nation, and when he died the little children cried in the streets.

Rise of the Dutch Republic

CHARLES READE

1814–1884

428 *The Gallows*

AT the edge of the wood they came upon something so mysterious that they stopped to gaze at it, before going up to it. Two white pillars rose in the air, distant a few paces from each other; and between them stood many figures, that looked like human forms.

'I go no farther till I know what this is,' said Gerard, in an agitated whisper. 'Are they effigies of the saints, for men to pray to on the road? or live robbers waiting to shoot down honest travellers? Nay, living men they cannot be, for they stand on nothing that I see. Oh! Denys, let us turn back till daybreak: this is no mortal sight.'

Denys halted, and peered long and keenly. 'They are men,' said he, at last. Gerard was for turning back all the more.

'But men that will never hurt us, nor we them. Look not to their feet for that they stand on!'

'Where, then, i' the name of all the saints?'

'Look over their heads,' said Denys, gravely.

Following this direction, Gerard presently discerned the outline of a dark wooden beam passing from pillar to pillar; and, as the pair got nearer, walking now on tiptoe, one by one dark snake-like cords came out in the moonlight, each pendent from the beam to a dead man, and tight as wire.

Now as they came under this awful monument of crime and wholesale vengeance, a light air swept by, and several of the corpses swung, or gently gyrated, and every rope creaked. Gerard shuddered at this ghastly salute. So thoroughly had the gibbet, with its sickening load, seized and held their eyes, that it was but now they perceived a fire right underneath, and a living figure sitting huddled over it. His axe lay beside him, the bright blade shining red in the glow. He was asleep.

Gerard started, but Denys only whispered, 'Courage, comrade, here is a fire.'

'Ay! but there is a man at it.'

'There will soon be three:' and he began to heap some wood on it that the watcher had prepared; during which the prudent Gerard seized the man's axe, and sat down tight on it, grasping his own, and examining the sleeper. There was nothing outwardly distinctive in the man. He wore the dress of the country folk, and the hat of the district, a three-cornered hat called a Brunswicker, stiff enough to turn a sword-cut, and with a thick brass hat-band. The weight of the whole thing had turned his ears entirely down, like a fancy rabbit's in our century; but even this, though it spoiled him as a man, was nothing remarkable. They had of late met scores of these dog's-eared rustics. The peculiarity was—this clown watching under a laden gallows. What for?

Denys, if he felt curious, would not show it; he took out two bears' ears from his bundle, and running sticks through them began to toast them. ''Twill be eating coined money,' said he; 'for the burgomaster of Dusseldorf had given us a rix-dollar for these ears, as proving the death of their owners; but better a lean purse than a lere stomach.'

'Unhappy man!' cried Gerard, 'could you eat food *here*?'

'Where the fire is lighted there must the meat roast, and where it roasts there must it be eaten; for nought travels worse than your roasted meat.'

'Well, eat thou, Denys, an thou canst! but I am cold and sick; there is no room for hunger in my heart after what mine eyes have seen,' and he shuddered over the fire; 'oh! how they creak! and who is this man I wonder? what an ill-favoured churl!'

Denys examined him like a connoisseur looking at a picture; and in due course delivered judgment. 'I take him to be of the refuse of that company, whereof these (pointing carelessly upward) were the cream, and so ran their heads into danger.'

'At that rate, why not stun him before he wakes?' and Gerard fidgeted where he sat.

Denys opened his eyes with humorous surprise. 'For one who sets up for a milksop you have the readiest hand. Why should two stun one? tush! he wakes; note now what he says at waking, and tell me.'

These last words were hardly whispered when the watcher opened his eyes. At sight of the fire made up, and two strangers eyeing him keenly, he stared, and there was a severe and pretty successful effort to be calm; still a perceptible tremor ran all over him. Soon he manned himself, and said gruffly,

'Good morrow.' But, at the very moment of saying it, he missed his axe, and saw how Gerard was sitting upon it with his own laid ready to his hand. He lost countenance again directly. Denys smiled grimly at this bit of by-play.

'Good morrow!' said Gerard quietly, keeping his eye on him.

The watcher was now too ill at ease to be silent. 'You make free with my fire,' said he; but he added in a somewhat faltering voice, 'you are welcome.'

Denys whispered Gerard. The watcher eyed them askant.

'My comrade says, sith we share your fire, you shall share his meat.'

'So be it,' said the man, warmly. 'I have half a kid hanging on a bush hard by, I'll go fetch it;' and he arose with a cheerful and obliging countenance, and was retiring.

Denys caught up his cross-bow, and levelled it at his head. The man fell on his knees.

Denys lowered his weapon, and pointed him back to his place. He rose and went back slowly and unsteadily, like one disjointed; and sick at heart as the mouse, that the cat lets go a little way, and then darts and replaces.

'Sit down, friend,' said Denys grimly, in French.

The man obeyed finger and tone, though he knew not a word of French.

'Tell him the fire is not big enough for more than three. He will take my meaning.'

This being communicated by Gerard, the man grinned; ever since Denys spoke he had seemed greatly relieved. 'I wist not ye were strangers,' said he to Gerard.

Denys cut a piece of bear's ear, and offered it with grace to him he had just levelled cross-bow at.

He took it calmly, and drew a piece of bread from his wallet, and divided it with the pair. Nay, more, he winked and thrust his hand into the heap of leaves he sat on (Gerard grasped his axe ready to brain him) and produced a leathern bottle holding full two gallons. He put it to his mouth, and drank their healths, then handed it to Gerard; he passed it untouched to Denys.

'Mort de ma vie!' cried the soldier, 'it is Rhenish wine, and fit for the gullet of an archbishop. Here 's to thee, thou prince of good fellows, wishing thee a short life and a merry one! Come, Gerard, sup! sup! Pshaw, never heed them, man! they heed not thee. Natheless, did I hang over such a skin of Rhenish as this, and three churls sat beneath a drinking it and offered me not a drop, I'd soon be down among them.'

'Denys! Denys!'

'My spirit would cut the cord, and womp would come my body amongst ye, with a hand on the bottle, and one eye winking, t'other——'

Gerard started up with a cry of horror and his fingers to his ears, and was running from the place, when his eye fell on the watcher's axe. The tangible danger brought him back. He sat down again on the axe with his fingers in his ears.

'Courage, l'ami, le diable est mort!' shouted Denys gaily, and offered him a piece of bear's ear, put it right under his nose as he stopped his ears. Gerard turned his head away with loathing. 'Wine!' he gasped. 'Heaven knows I have much need of it, with such companions as thee and——'

He took a long draught of the Rhenish wine: it

ran glowing through his veins, and warmed and strengthened his heart; but could not check his tremors whenever a gust of wind came. As for Denys and the other, they feasted recklessly, and plied the bottle unceasingly, and drank healths and caroused beneath that creaking sepulchre and its ghastly tenants.

The Cloister and the Hearth

429 *The English Skylark in Australia*

THE house was thatched and whitewashed, and English was written on it and on every foot of ground round it. A furze bush had been planted by the door. Vertical oak palings were the fence, with a five-barred gate in the middle of them. From the little plantation all the magnificent trees and shrubs of Australia had been excluded with amazing resolution and consistency, and oak and ash reigned safe from overtowering rivals. They passed to the back of the house, and there George's countenance fell a little, for on the oval grass-plot and gravel-walk he found from thirty to forty rough fellows, most of them diggers.

'Ah! well,' said he, on reflection, 'we could not expect to have it all to ourselves, and indeed it would be a sin to wish it, you know. Now, Tom, come this way; here it is—here it is—there.' Tom looked up, and in a gigantic cage was a light-brown bird. . . Like most singers, he kept them waiting a bit. But at last, just at noon, when the mistress of the house had warranted him to sing, the little feathered exile began as it were to tune his pipes. The savage men gathered round the cage that moment, and amidst a dead stillness the bird uttered some very uncertain chirps, but after a while he seemed to revive his memories, and call his ancient cadences back to him one by one, and string them *sotto voce*.

And then the same sun that had warmed his little heart at home came glowing down on him here, and he gave music back for it more and more, till at last, amidst breathless silence and glistening eyes of the rough diggers hanging on his voice, out burst in that distant land his English song.

It swelled his little throat and gushed from him with thrilling force and plenty, and every time he checked his song to think of its theme, the green meadows, the quiet stealing streams, the clover he first soared from and the Spring he sang so well, a loud sigh from many a rough bosom, many a wild and wicked heart, told how tight the listeners had held their breath to hear him; and when he swelled with song again, and poured with all his soul the green meadows, the quiet brooks, the honey clover, and the English Spring, the rugged mouths opened and so stayed, and the shaggy lips trembled, and more than one drop trickled from fierce unbridled hearts down bronzed and rugged cheeks. *Dulce domum!*

And these shaggy men, full of oaths and strife and cupidity, had once been white-headed boys, and had strolled about the English fields with little sisters and little brothers, and seen the lark rise, and heard him sing this very song. The little playmates lay in the churchyard, and they were full of oaths and drink and lusts and remorses, but no note was changed in this immortal song. And so for a moment or two years of vice rolled away like a dark cloud from the memory, and the past shone out in the song-shine; they came back, bright as the immortal notes that lighted them, those faded pictures and those fleeted days; the cottage, the old mother's tears when he left her without one grain of sorrow; the village church and its simple chimes; the clover field hard by in which he lay and gambolled, while the lark praised God over-head, the chubby playmates that never grew to be wicked, the sweet hours of youth, and innocence, and home!

It is Never too Late to Mend

RICHARD WILLIAM CHURCH, DEAN OF ST. PAUL'S

1815–1890

430 *Spenser's Ideal Gentleman*

THE unity of a story, or an allegory—that chain and backbone of continuous interest, implying a progress and leading up to a climax, which holds together the great poems of the world, the *Iliad* and *Odyssey*, the *Æneid*, the *Commedia*, the *Paradise Lost*, the *Jerusalem Delivered*—this is wanting in the *Faery Queen*. The unity is one of character and its ideal. That character of the completed man, raised above what is poor and low, and governed by noble tempers and pure principles, has in Spenser two conspicuous elements. In the first place, it is based on manliness. In the personages which illustrate the different virtues, Holiness, Justice, Courtesy, and the rest, the distinction is not in nicely discriminated features or shades of expression, but in the trials and the occasions which call forth a particular action or effort: yet the manliness which is at the foundation of all that is good in them is a universal quality common to them all, rooted and imbedded in the governing idea or standard of moral character in the poem. It is not merely courage, it is not merely energy, it is not merely strength. It is the quality of soul which frankly accepts the conditions in human life, of labour, of obedience, of effort, of unequal success; which does not quarrel with them or evade them, but takes for granted with unquestioning alacrity that man is called—by his call to high aims and destiny—to a continual struggle with difficulty, with pain, with evil, and makes it the point of honour not to be dismayed or wearied out by them. It is a cheerful and serious willingness for hard work and endurance, as being inevitable and very bearable necessities, together with even a pleasure in encountering trials which put a man on his mettle, an enjoyment of the contest and the risk, even in play. It is the quality which seizes on the paramount idea of duty, as something which leaves a man no choice; which despises and breaks through the inferior considerations and motives—trouble, uncertainty, doubt, curiosity—which hang about and impede duty; which is impatient with the idleness and childishness of a life of mere amusement, or mere looking on, of continued and self-satisfied levity, of vacillation, of clever and ingenious trifling.

Spenser

ANTHONY TROLLOPE

1815–1882

431 *The Plumstead Foxes*

THERE was a string of narrow woods called Plumstead Coppices which ran from a point near the church right across the parish, dividing the archdeacon's land from the Ullathorne estate, and these coppices, or belts of woodland, belonged to the archdeacon. On the morning of which we are speaking, the archdeacon, mounted on his cob, still thinking of his son's iniquity and of his own fixed resolve to punish him as he had said that he would punish him, opened with his whip a woodland gate, from which a green muddy lane led through the trees up to the house of his gamekeeper. The man's wife was ill, and in his ordinary way of business the archdeacon was about to call and ask after her health. At the door of the cottage he found the man, who was woodman as well as gamekeeper, and was responsible for fences and faggots, as well as for foxes and pheasants' eggs.

'How 's Martha, Flurry? ' said the archdeacon.

'Thanking your reverence, she be a deal improved since the mistress was here—last Tuesday it was, I think.'

'I'm glad of that. It was only rheumatism, I suppose? '

'Just a tich of fever with it, your reverence, the doctor said.'

'Tell her I was asking after it. I won't mind getting down to-day, as I am rather busy. She has had what she wanted from the house? '

'The mistress has been very good in that way. She always is, God bless her ! '

'Good-day to you, Flurry. I'll ask Mr. Sims to come and read to her a bit this afternoon, or to-morrow morning.'

The archdeacon kept two curates, and Mr. Sims was one of them.

'She'll take it very kindly, your reverence. But while you are here, sir, there 's just a word I'd like to say. I didn't happen to catch Mr. Henry when he was here the other day.'

'Never mind Mr. Henry; what is it you have to say?'

'I do think, I do indeed, sir, that Mr. Thorne's man ain't dealing fairly along of the foxes. I wouldn't say a word about it, only that Mr. Henry is so particular.'

'What about the foxes? What is he doing with the foxes?'

'Well, sir, he 's a trapping on 'em. He is, indeed, your reverence. I wouldn't speak if I warn't well nigh mortial sure.'

Now the archdeacon had never been a hunting man, though in his early days many a clergyman had been in the habit of hunting without losing his clerical character by doing so; but he had lived all his life among gentlemen in a hunting county, and had his own very strong ideas about the trapping of foxes. Foxes first, and pheasants afterwards, had always been the rule with him as to any land of which he himself had had the management. . . But now his heart was not with the foxes—and especially not with the foxes on behalf of his son Henry. 'I can't have any meddling with Mr. Thorne,' he said; 'I can't, and I won't.'

'But I don't suppose it can be Mr. Thorne's order, your reverence; and Mr. Henry is so particular.'

'Of course it isn't Mr. Thorne's order. Mr. Thorne has been a hunting man all his life.'

'But he have guv' up now, your reverence. He ain't a hunted these two years.'

'I'm sure he wouldn't have the foxes trapped.'

'Not if he knowed it, he wouldn't, your reverence. A gentleman of the likes of him, who 's been a hunting over fifty year, wouldn't do the likes of that ; but the foxes *is* trapped, and Mr. Henry 'll be a putting it on me if I don't speak out. They is Plumstead foxes too ; and a vixen was trapped just across the field yonder, in Goshall Springs, no later than yesterday morning.' Flurry was now thoroughly in earnest ; and, indeed, the trapping of a vixen in February is a serious thing.

'Goshall Springs don't belong to me,' said the archdeacon.

'No, your reverence ; they're on the Ullathorne property. But a word from your reverence would do it. Mr. Henry thinks more of the foxes than anything. The last word he told me was that it would break his heart if he saw the coppices drawn blank.' . .

'I will have no meddling in the matter, Flurry. Whether there are foxes or whether there are not, is matter of no great moment. I will not have a word said to annoy Mr. Thorne.'

Then he rode away, back through the wood and out on to the road, and the horse walked with him leisurely on, whither the archdeacon hardly knew—for he was thinking, thinking, thinking. . .

He could have heard nothing of his son to stir him more in his favour than this strong evidence of his partiality for foxes. I do not mean it to be understood that the archdeacon regarded foxes as better than active charity, or a contented mind, or a meek spirit, or than self-denying temperance. No doubt all these virtues did hold in his mind their proper place, altogether beyond contamination of foxes. But he had prided himself on thinking that his son should be a country gentleman, and, probably nothing doubting as to the major's active charity and other virtues, was delighted to receive evidence of those tastes which he had ever wished to encourage in his son's character. Or rather, such evidence would have delighted him at any other time than the present. Now it only added more gall to his cup.

'Why should he teach himself to care for such things, when he has not the spirit to enjoy them,' said the archdeacon to himself. 'He is a fool—a fool. A man that has been married once, to go crazy after a little girl, that has hardly a dress to her back, and who never was in a drawing-room in her life!' . . On the [next] morning the archdeacon wrote the following note: 'DEAR THORNE,—My man tells me that foxes have been trapped on Darvell's farm, just outside the coppices. I know nothing of it myself, but I am sure you'll look to it.—

Yours always,

T. GRANTLY.'

The Last Chronicle of Barset

432 *Mr. Harding's Funeral*

THEY buried him in the cathedral which he had loved so well, and in which nearly all the work of his life had been done; and all Barchester was there to see him laid in his grave within the cloisters. There was no procession of coaches, no hearse, nor was there any attempt at funereal pomp. From the dean's side-door, across the vaulted passage, and into the transept —over the little step upon which he had so nearly fallen when last he made his way out of the building— the coffin was carried on men's shoulders. It was but a short journey from his bedroom to his grave. But the bell had been tolling sadly all the morning, and the nave and the aisles and the transepts, close up to the door leading from the transept into the cloister, were crowded with those who had known the name and the figure and the voice of Mr. Harding as long as they had known anything. Up to this day no one would have said specially that Mr. Harding was a favourite in the town. He had never been forward enough in anything to become the acknowledged possessor of popularity. But, now that he was gone, men and women told each other how good he had been. They remembered the sweetness of his smile, and talked of loving little words which he had spoken to them—either years ago or the other day, for his words had always been loving.

The dean and the archdeacon came first, shoulder to shoulder, and after them came their wives. I do not know that it was the proper order for mourning, but it was a touching sight to be seen, and was long remembered in Barchester. Painful as it was for them, the two women would be there, and the two sisters would walk together;—nor would they go before their husbands. Then there were the archdeacon's two sons—for the Rev. Charles Grantly had come to Plumstead on the occasion. And in the vaulted passage which runs between the deanery and the end of the transept, all the chapter, with the choir, the prebendaries, with the fat old chancellor, the precentor and the minor canons down to the little choristers—they all were there, and followed in at the transept door, two by two. And in the transept they were joined by another clergyman, whom no one had expected to see that day. The bishop was there, looking old and worn—almost as though he was unconscious of what he was doing. Since his wife's death no one had seen him out of the palace or of the palace grounds till that day. But there he was—and they made way for him into the procession, behind the two ladies—and the archdeacon, when he saw it, resolved that there should be peace in his heart, if peace might be possible.

They made their way into the cloisters where the grave had been dug—as many as might be allowed to follow. The place indeed was open to all who chose to come; but they who had only slightly known the man, refrained from pressing upon those who had a right to stand around his coffin. But there was one other there whom the faithful chronicler of Barchester should mention. Before any other one had reached the spot, the sexton and the verger had led in between them, among the graves beneath the cloisters, a blind man, very old, with a wondrous stoop, but who must have owned a grand stature before extreme old age had bent him; and they placed him sitting on a stone in the corner of the archway. But as soon as the shuffling of steps reached his ears, he raised himself with the aid of his stick, and stood during the service leaning against the pillar. The blind man was so old that he might almost have been Mr. Harding's father. This was John Bunce, a bedesman from Hiram's Hospital—and none perhaps there had known Mr. Harding better than he had known him. When the earth had been thrown on to the coffin, and the service was over, and they were about to disperse, Mrs. Arabin went up to the old man, and taking his hand between hers whispered a word into his ear. 'Oh, Miss Eleanor,' he said. 'Oh, Miss Eleanor!' Within a fortnight he also was lying within the cathedral precincts.

ANTHONY TROLLOPE

And so they buried Mr. Septimus Harding, formerly Warden of Hiram's Hospital in the city of Barchester, of whom the chronicler may say that that city never knew a sweeter gentleman or a better Christian.

The Last Chronicle of Barset

CHARLOTTE BRONTË

1816–1855

433 *On 'Wuthering Heights'*

WHETHER it is right or advisable to create beings like Heathcliff, I do not know: I scarcely think it is. But this I know; the writer who possesses the creative gift owns something of which he is not always master—something that, at times, strangely wills and works for itself. He may lay down rules and devise principles, and to rules and principles it will perhaps for years lie in subjection; and then, haply without any warning of revolt, there comes a time when it will no longer consent to 'harrow the valleys, or be bound with a band in the furrow'—when it 'laughs at the multitude of the city, and regards not the crying of the driver'—when, refusing absolutely to make ropes out of sea-sand any longer, it sets to work on statue-hewing, and you have a Pluto or a Jove, a Tisiphone or a Psyche, a Mermaid or a Madonna, as Fate or Inspiration direct. Be the work grim or glorious, dread or divine, you have little choice left but quiescent adoption. As for you—the nominal artist—your share in it has been to work passively under dictates you neither delivered nor could question—that would not be uttered at your prayer, nor suppressed nor changed at your caprice. If the result be attractive, the World will praise you, who little deserve praise; if it be repulsive, the same World will blame you, who almost as little deserve blame.

Wuthering Heights was hewn in a wild workshop, with simple tools, out of homely materials. The statuary found a granite block on a solitary moor; gazing thereon, he saw how from the crag might be elicited a head, savage, swart, sinister; a form moulded with at least one element of grandeur—power. He wrought with a rude chisel, and from no model but the vision of his meditations. With time and labour, the crag took human shape; and there it stands colossal, dark, and frowning, half statue, half rock: in the former sense, terrible and goblin-like; in the latter, almost beautiful, for its colouring is of mellow grey, and moorland moss clothes it; and heath, with its blooming bells and balmy fragrance, grows faithfully close to the giant's foot.

Introduction to Wuthering Heights

434 *Rachel*

THE theatre was full—crammed to its roof: royal and noble were there: palace and hotel had emptied their inmates into those tiers so thronged and so hushed. Deeply did I feel myself privileged in having a place before that stage; I longed to see a being of whose powers I had heard reports which made me conceive peculiar anticipations. I wondered if she would justify her renown: with strange curiosity, with feelings severe and austere, yet of riveted interest, I waited. She was a study of such nature as had not encountered my eyes yet: a great and new planet she was: but in what shape? I waited her rising.

She rose at nine that December night; above the horizon I saw her come. She could shine yet with pale grandeur and steady might; but that star verged already on its judgment day. Seen near—it was a chaos—hollow, half consumed: an orb perished or perishing—half lava, half glow.

I had heard this woman termed 'plain,' and I expected bony harshness and grimness—something large, angular, sallow. What I saw was the shadow of a royal Vashti: a queen, fair as the day once, turned pale now like twilight, and wasted like wax in flame.

For a while—a long while—I thought it was only a woman, though an unique woman, who moved in might and grace before this multitude. By-and-by I recognised my mistake. Behold! I found upon her something neither of woman nor of man: in each of her eyes sat a devil. These evil forces bore her through the tragedy, kept up her feeble strength—for she was but a frail creature; and as the action rose and the stir deepened, how wildly they shook her with their passions of the pit! They wrote HELL on her straight, haughty brow. They tuned her voice to the note of torment. They writhed her regal face to a demoniac mask. Hate, and Murder, and Madness incarnate she stood.

It was a marvellous sight: a mighty revelation.

It was a spectacle low, horrible, immoral.

Swordsmen thrust through, and dying in their blood on the arena sand; bulls goring horses disembowelled, made a meeker vision for the public—a milder condiment for a people's palate—than Vashti torn by seven devils: devils which cried sore and rent the tenement they haunted, but still refused to be exorcised.

Suffering had struck that stage empress; and she stood before her audience neither yielding to, nor enduring, nor in finite measure, resenting it: she stood locked in struggle, rigid in resistance. She stood, not dressed, but draped in pale antique folds, long and regular like sculpture. A background and entourage and flooring of deepest crimson threw her out, white like alabaster—like silver: rather, be it said, like Death. . .

I have said that she does not *resent* her grief. No; the weakness of that word would make it a lie. To her, what hurts becomes immediately embodied: she looks on it as a thing that can be attacked, worried down, torn in shreds. Scarcely a substance herself, she grapples to conflict with abstractions. Before calamity she is a tigress; she rends her woes, shivers them in compulsed abhorrence. Pain, for her, has no result in good; tears water no harvest of wisdom: on sickness, on death itself, she looks with the eye of a rebel. Wicked, perhaps, she is, but also she is strong; and her strength has conquered Beauty, has overcome Grace, and bound both at her side, captives peerlessly fair, and docile as fair. Even in the uttermost frenzy of energy is each mænad movement royally, imperially, incedingly upborne. Her hair, flying loose in revel or war, is still an angel's hair, and glorious under a halo. Fallen, insurgent, banished, she remembers the heaven where she rebelled. Heaven's light, following her exile, pierces its confines, and discloses their forlorn remoteness.

Villette

FREDERICK WILLIAM ROBERTSON

1816–1853

435 *The Crystal Palace and Sabbatarianism*

LATELY projects have been devised, one of which in importance surpasses all the rest, for providing places of public recreation for the people: and it has been announced, with the sanction of government, that such a place will be held open during a part at least of the day of rest. By a large section of sincerely religious persons this announcement has been received with considerable alarm, and strenuous opposition. It has seemed to them that such a desecration would be a national crime: for, holding the sabbath to be God's sign between Himself and His people, they cannot but view the desecration of the sign as a forfeiture of His covenant, and an act which will assuredly call down national judgments: . . Now when men are rigorous in the enforcement and reverence paid to laws positive, the tendency is to a corresponding indifference to the laws of eternal Right. The written supersedes in their hearts the moral. The mental history of the ancient Pharisees who observed the sabbath, and tithed mint, anise, and cummin, neglecting justice, mercy, and truth, is the history of a most dangerous, but universal tendency of the human heart. And so, many a man whose heart swells with what he thinks pious horror when he sees the letter delivered or the train run upon the sabbath-day, can pass through the streets at night, undepressed and unshocked by the evidences of the wide-spreading profligacy which has eaten deep into his country's heart. And many a man who would gaze upon the domes of a Crystal Palace, rising above the trees, with somewhat of the same feeling with which he would look on a temple dedicated to Juggernaut and who would fancy that something of the spirit of an ancient prophet was burning in his bosom, when his lips pronounced the Woe! Woe! of a coming doom, would sit calmly in a social circle of English life, and scarcely feel uneasy in listening to its uncharitableness and its slanders . . . would survey the relations of the rich and poor in this country, and remain calmly satisfied that there is nothing false in them, unbrotherly and wrong. No, my brethren! let us think clearly and strongly on this matter. It may be that God has a controversy with this people. It may be, as they say, that our Father will chasten us by the sword of the foreigner. But if He does, and if judgments are in store for our country, they will fall,—not because the correspondence of the land is carried on upon the sabbath-day: nor because Sunday trains are not arrested by the legislature: nor because a public permission is given to the working-classes for a few hours' recreation on the day of rest:—but because we are selfish men; and because we prefer Pleasure to Duty, and Traffic to Honour; and because we love our party more than our Church, and our Church more than our Christianity; and our Christianity more than Truth, and ourselves more than all. These are the things that defile a nation; but the labour and the recreation of its Poor, these are not the things that defile a nation.

Sermons: Second Series

BENJAMIN JOWETT

1817–1893

436 *Belief in Immortality*

CONSIDERING the 'feebleness of the human faculties and the uncertainty of the subject', we are inclined to believe that the fewer our words the better. At the approach of death there is not much said; good men are too honest to go out of the world professing more than they know. There is perhaps no important subject about which, at any time, even religious people speak so little to one another. In the fulness of life the thought of death is mostly awakened by the sight or recollection of the death of others rather than by the prospect of our own. We must also acknowledge that there are degrees of the belief in immortality, and many forms in which it presents itself to the mind. Some persons will say no more than that they trust in God, and that they leave all to Him. It is a great part of true religion not to pretend to know more than we do. Others when they quit this world are comforted with the hope 'That they will see and know their friends in heaven'. But it is better to leave them in the hands of God and to be assured that 'no evil shall touch them'. There are others again to whom the belief in a divine personality has ceased to have any longer a meaning; yet they are satisfied that the end of all is not here, but that something still remains to us, 'and some better thing for the good than for the evil'. They are persuaded, in spite of their theological nihilism, that the ideas of justice and truth and holiness and love are realities. They cherish an enthusiastic devotion to the first principles of morality. Through these they see, or seem to see, darkly, and in a figure, that the soul is immortal.

Introduction to the Phaedo

437 *Socrates under Sentence of Death hears the Voice of the Laws of Athens*

HAS a philosopher like you failed to discover that our country is more to be valued and higher and holier far than mother or father or any ancestor, and more to be regarded in the eyes of the gods and of men of understanding? also to be soothed, and gently and reverently entreated when angry, even more than a father, and either to be persuaded, or if not persuaded, to be obeyed? And when we are punished by her, whether with imprisonment or stripes, the punishment is to be endured in silence; and if she lead us to wounds or death in battle, thither we follow as is right; neither may any one yield or retreat or leave his rank, but whether in battle or in a court of law, or in any other place, he must do what his city and his country order him; or he must change their view of what is just: and if he may do no violence to his father or mother, much less may he do violence to his country.

Translation of the Crito

438 *The Death of Socrates*

NOW the hour of sunset was near, for a good deal of time had passed while he was within. When he came out, he sat down with us again after his bath, but not much was said. Soon the jailer, who was the servant of the Eleven, entered and stood by him, saying:—To you, Socrates, whom I know to be the noblest and gentlest and best of all who ever came to this place, I will not impute the angry feelings of other men, who rage and swear at me, when, in obedience to the authorities, I bid them drink the poison—indeed, I am sure that you will not be angry with me; for others, as you are aware, and not I, are to blame. And so fare you well, and try to bear lightly what must needs be—you know my errand. Then bursting into tears he turned away and went out.

Socrates looked at him and said: I return your good wishes, and will do as you bid. Then turning to us, he said, How charming the man is: since I have been in prison he has always been coming to see me, and at times he would talk to me, and was as good to me as could be, and now see how generously he sorrows on my account. We must do as he says, Crito; and therefore let the cup be brought, if the poison is prepared: if not, let the attendant prepare some.

Yet, said Crito, the sun is still upon the hill tops, and I know that many a one has taken the draught late, and after the announcement has been made to him, he has eaten and drunk, and enjoyed the society of his beloved; do not hurry—there is time enough.

Socrates said: Yes, Crito, and they of whom you speak are right in so acting, for they think that they will be gainers by the delay; but I am right in not following their example, for I do not think that I should gain anything by drinking the poison a little later; I should only be ridiculous in my own eyes for sparing and saving a life which is already forfeit. Please then to do as I say, and not to refuse me.

Crito made a sign to the servant, who was standing

by; and he went out, and having been absent for some time, returned with the jailer carrying the cup of poison. Socrates said: You, my good friend, who are experienced in these matters, shall give me directions how I am to proceed. The man answered: You have only to walk about until your legs are heavy, and then to lie down, and the poison will act. At the same time he handed the cup to Socrates, who in the easiest and gentlest manner, without the least fear or change of colour or feature, looking at the man with all his eyes, Echecrates, as his manner was, took the cup and said: What do you say about making a libation out of this cup to any god? May I, or not? The man answered: We only prepare, Socrates, just so much as we deem enough. I understand, he said: but I may and must ask the gods to prosper my journey from this to the other world—even so—and so be it according to my prayer. Then raising the cup to his lips, quite readily and cheerfully he drank off the poison. And hitherto most of us had been able to control our sorrow; but now when we saw him drinking, and saw too that he had finished the draught, we could no longer forbear, and in spite of myself my own tears were flowing fast; so that I covered my face and wept, not for him, but at the thought of my own calamity in having to part from such a friend. Nor was I the first; for Crito, when he found himself unable to restrain his tears, had got up, and I followed; and at that moment, Apollodorus, who had been weeping all the time, broke out in a loud and passionate cry which made cowards of us all. Socrates alone retained his calmness: What is this strange outcry? he said. I sent away the women mainly in order that they might not misbehave in this way, for I have been told that a man should die in peace. Be quiet then, and have patience. When we heard his words we were ashamed, and refrained our tears; and he walked about until, as he said, his legs began to fail, and then he lay on his back, according to the directions, and the man who gave him the poison now and then looked at his feet and legs; and after a while he pressed his foot hard, and asked him if he could feel; and he said, No; and then his leg, and so upwards and upwards, and showed us that he was cold and stiff. And he felt them himself, and said: When the poison reaches the heart, that will be the end. He was beginning to grow cold about the groin, when he uncovered his face, for he had covered himself up, and said—they were his last words—he said: Crito, I owe a cock to Asclepius; will you remember to pay the debt? The debt shall be paid, said Crito; is there anything else? There was no answer to this question; but in a minute or two a movement was heard, and the attendants uncovered him; his eyes were set, and Crito closed his eyes and mouth.

Such was the end, Echecrates, of our friend; concerning whom I may truly say, that of all the men of his time whom I have known, he was the wisest and justest and best.

Translation of the Phaedo

439 *Last Words on Plato*

AND so having brought into the world 'noble children', he rests from the labours of authorship. More than two thousand two hundred years have passed away since he returned to the place of Apollo and the Muses. Yet the echo of his words continues to be heard among men, because of all philosophers he has the most melodious voice. He is the inspired prophet or teacher who can never die, the only one in whom the outward form adequately represents the fair soul within; in whom the thoughts of all who went before him are reflected and of all who come after him are partly anticipated. Other teachers of philosophy are dried up and withered, —after a few centuries they have become dust; but he is fresh and blooming, and is always begetting new ideas in the minds of men. They are one-sided and abstract; but he has many sides of wisdom. Nor is he always consistent with himself, because he is always moving onward, and knows that there are many more things in philosophy than can be expressed in words, and that truth is greater than consistency. He who approaches him in the most reverent spirit shall reap most of the fruit of his wisdom; he who reads him by the light of ancient commentators will have the least understanding of him.

We may see him with the eye of the mind in the groves of the Academy, or on the banks of the Ilissus, or in the streets of Athens, alone or walking with Socrates, full of those thoughts which have since become the common possession of mankind. Or we may compare him to a statue hid away in some temple of Zeus or Apollo, no longer existing on earth, a statue which has a look as of the God himself. Or we may once more imagine him following in another state of being the great company of heaven which he beheld of old in a vision. So, 'partly trifling, but with a certain degree of seriousness', we linger around the memory of a world which has passed away.

Introduction to the Laws of Plato

HENRY DAVID THOREAU

1817–1862

440 *The Lure of the River*

THE Mississippi, the Ganges, and the Nile, those journeying atoms from the Rocky Mountains, the Himmaleh, and Mountains of the Moon, have a kind of personal importance in the annals of the world. The heavens are not yet drained over their sources, but the Mountains of the Moon still send their annual tribute to the Pasha without fail, as they did to the Pharaohs, though he must collect the rest of his revenue at the point of the sword. Rivers must have been the guides which conducted the footsteps of the first travellers. They are the constant lure, when they flow by our doors, to distant enterprise and adventure; and, by a natural impulse, the dwellers on the banks will at length accompany their currents to the lowlands of the globe, or explore at their invitation the interior of continents. They are the natural highways of all nations, not only levelling the ground and removing obstacles from the path of the traveller, quenching his thirst and bearing him on their bosoms, but conducting him through the most interesting scenery, the most populous portions of the globe, and where the animal and vegetable kingdoms attain their greatest perfection.

I had often stood on the banks of the Concord, watching the lapse of the current, an emblem of all progress, following the same law with the system, with time, and all that is made; the weeds at the bottom gently bending down the stream, shaken by the watery wind, still planted where their seeds had sunk, but erelong to die and go down likewise; the shining pebbles, not yet anxious to better their condition, the chips and weeds, and occasional logs and stems of trees that floated past, fulfilling their fate, were objects of singular interest to me, and at last I resolved to launch myself on its bosom and float whither it would bear me.

Week on the Concord

441 *The Shipwreck*

ABOUT a mile south we could see, rising above the rocks, the masts of the British brig which the St. John had endeavoured to follow, which had slipped her cables, and, by good luck, run into the mouth of Cohasset Harbour. A little further along the shore we saw a man's clothes on a rock; further, a woman's scarf, a gown, a straw bonnet, the brig's caboose, and one of her masts high and dry, broken into several pieces. In another rocky cove, several rods from the water, and behind rocks twenty feet high, lay a part of one side of the vessel, still hanging together. It was, perhaps, forty feet long, by fourteen wide. I was even more surprised at the power of the waves, exhibited on this shattered fragment, than I had been at the sight of the smaller fragments before. The largest timbers and iron braces were broken superfluously, and I saw that no material could withstand the power of the waves; that iron must go to pieces in such a case, and an iron vessel would be cracked up like an egg-shell on the rocks. Some of these timbers, however, were so rotten that I could almost thrust my umbrella through them. They told us that some were saved on this piece, and also showed where the sea had heaved it into this cove, which was now dry. When I saw where it had come in, and in what condition, I wondered that any had been saved on it. A little further on a crowd of men was collected around the mate of the St. John, who was telling his story. He was a slim-looking youth, who spoke of the captain as the master, and seemed a little excited. He was saying that when they jumped into the boat, she filled, and, the vessel lurching, the weight of the water in the boat caused the painter to break, and so they were separated. Whereat one man came away, saying,—

'Well, I don't see but he tells a straight story enough. You see, the weight of the water in the boat broke the painter. A boat full of water is very heavy,' —and so on, in a loud and impertinently earnest tone, as if he had a bet depending on it, but had no humane interest in the matter.

Another, a large man, stood near by upon a rock, gazing into the sea, and chewing large quids of tobacco, as if that habit were forever confirmed with him.

'Come,' says another to his companion, 'let 's be off. We've seen the whole of it. It 's no use to stay to the funeral.'

Further, we saw one standing upon a rock, who, we were told, was one that was saved. He was a sober-looking man, dressed in a jacket and gray pantaloons, with his hands in the pockets. I asked him a few questions, which he answered; but he seemed unwilling to talk about it, and soon walked away. By his side stood one of the lifeboat men, in an oil-cloth jacket, who told us how they went to the relief of the British brig, thinking that the boat of the St. John, which they passed on the way, held all her crew,— for the waves prevented their seeing those who were on the vessel, though they might have saved some had they known there were any there. A little further was the flag of the St. John spread on a rock to dry, and held down by stones at the corners. This frail, but essential and significant portion of the vessel, which had so long been the sport of the winds, was sure to reach the shore. There were one or two houses visible from these rocks, in which were some of the survivors recovering from the shock which their bodies and minds had sustained. One was not expected to live.

Cape Cod

442 *Chanticleer*

ABOVE all, we cannot afford not to live in the present. He is blessed over all mortals who loses no moment of the passing life in remembering the past. Unless our philosophy hears the cock crow in every barn-yard within our horizon, it is belated. That sound commonly reminds us that we are growing rusty and antique in our employments and habits of thought. His philosophy comes down to a more recent time than ours. There is something suggested by it that is a newer testament—the gospel according to this moment. He has not fallen astern; he has got up early and kept up early, and to be where he is is to be in season, in the foremost rank of time. It is an expression of the health and soundness of nature, a brag for all the world,—healthiness as of a spring burst forth, a new fountain of the Muses, to celebrate this last instant of time. Where he lives no fugitive slave laws are passed. Who has not betrayed his master many times since last he heard that note?

The merit of this bird's strain is in its freedom from all plaintiveness. The singer can easily move us to tears or to laughter, but where is he who can excite in us a pure morning joy? When, in doleful dumps, breaking the awful stillness of our wooden sidewalk on a Sunday, or, perchance, a watcher in the house of mourning, I hear a cockerel crow far or near, I think to myself, 'There is one of us well, at any rate,'—and with a sudden gush return to my senses.

Essays: Walking

443 *Autumn Sunset*

THE sun sets on some retired meadow, where no house is visible, with all the glory and splendour that it lavishes on cities, and, perchance, as it has never set before,—where there is but a solitary marsh-hawk to have his wings gilded by it, or only a musquash looks out from his cabin, and there is some little black-veined brook in the midst of the marsh, just beginning to meander, winding slowly round a decaying stump. We walked in so pure and bright a light, gilding the withered grass and leaves, so softly and serenely bright, I thought I had never bathed in such a golden flood, without a ripple or a murmur to it. The west side of every wood and rising ground gleamed like a boundary of Elysium, and the sun on our backs seemed like a gentle herdsman driving us home at evening.

So we saunter toward the Holy Land, till one day the sun shall shine more brightly than ever he has done, shall perchance shine into our minds and hearts, and light up our whole lives with a great awakening light, as warm and serene and golden as on a bank-side in autumn.

Essays: Walking

EMILY BRONTË

1818–1848

444 *The Dream*

THIS time, I remembered I was lying in the oak closet, and I heard distinctly the gusty wind, and the driving of the snow; I heard, also, the fir-bough repeat its teasing sound, and ascribed it to the right cause: but it annoyed me so much, that I resolved to silence it, if possible; and, I thought, I rose and endeavoured to unhasp the casement. The hook was soldered into the staple: a circumstance observed by me when awake, but forgotten. 'I must stop it, nevertheless!' I muttered, knocking my knuckles through the glass, and stretching an arm out to seize the importunate branch; instead of which, my fingers closed on the fingers of a little, ice-cold hand! The intense horror of nightmare came over me: I tried to draw back my arm, but the hand clung to it, and a most melancholy voice sobbed, 'Let me in—let me in!' 'Who are you?' I asked, struggling, meanwhile, to disengage myself. 'Catherine Linton,' it replied shiveringly (why did I think of *Linton*? I had read *Earnshaw* twenty times for Linton). 'I'm come home: I'd lost my way on the moor!' As it spoke, I discerned, obscurely, a child's face looking through the window. Terror made me cruel; and, finding it useless to attempt shaking the creature off, I pulled its wrist on to the broken pane, and rubbed it to and fro till the blood ran down and soaked the bedclothes: still it wailed, 'Let me in!' and maintained its tenacious gripe, almost maddening me with fear. 'How can I!' I said at length. 'Let *me* go, if you want me to let you in!' The fingers relaxed, I snatched mine through the hole, hurriedly piled the books up in a pyramid against it, and stopped my ears to exclude the lamentable prayer. I seemed to keep them closed above a quarter of an hour; yet, the instant I listened again, there was the doleful cry moaning on! 'Begone!' I shouted, 'I'll never let you in, not if you beg for twenty years.' 'It is twenty years,' mourned the voice: 'twenty years. I've been a waif for twenty years!' Thereat began a feeble scratching outside, and the pile of books moved as if thrust forward. I tried to jump up; but could not stir a limb; and so yelled aloud, in a frenzy of fright. To my confusion, I discovered the yell was not ideal: hasty footsteps approached my chamber door; somebody pushed it open, with a vigorous hand, and a light glimmered through the squares at the top of the bed. I sat shuddering yet, and wiping the perspiration from my forehead: the intruder appeared to hesitate, and muttered to himself. At last, he said in a half-whisper, plainly not expecting an answer, 'Is any one here?' I considered it best to confess my presence; for I knew Heathcliff's accents, and feared he might search further, if I kept quiet. With this intention, I turned and opened the panels.

Wuthering Heights

JAMES ANTHONY FROUDE

1818–1894

445 *The End of the Middle Age*

FOR, indeed, a change was coming upon the world, the meaning and direction of which even still is hidden from us, a change from era to era. The paths trodden by the footsteps of ages were broken up;

old things were passing away, and the faith and the life of ten centuries were dissolving like a dream. Chivalry was dying; the abbey and the castle were soon together to crumble into ruins; and all the forms, desires, beliefs, convictions of the old world were passing away, never to return. A new continent had risen up beyond the western sea. The floor of heaven, inlaid with stars, had sunk back into an infinite abyss of immeasurable space; and the firm earth itself, unfixed from its foundations, was seen to be but a small atom in the awful vastness of the universe. In the fabric of habit in which they had so laboriously built for themselves, mankind were to remain no longer.

And now it is all gone—like an unsubstantial pageant faded; and between us and the old English there lies a gulf of mystery which the prose of the historian will never adequately bridge. They cannot come to us, and our imagination can but feebly penetrate to them. Only among the aisles of our cathedrals, only as we gaze upon their silent figures sleeping on their tombs, some faint conceptions float before us of what these men were when they were alive; and perhaps in the sound of church bells, that peculiar creation of mediæval age, which falls upon the ear like the echo of a vanished world.

History of England

446 *The Taking of the 'Cacafuego'*

DRAKE began to realise that he was now entirely alone, and had only himself and his own crew to depend on. There was nothing to do but to go through with it, danger adding to the interest. Arica was the next point visited. Half a hundred blocks of silver were picked up at Arica. After Arica came Lima, the chief depôt of all, where the grandest haul was looked for. At Lima, alas! they were just too late. Twelve great hulks lay anchored there. The sails were unbent, the men were ashore. They contained nothing but some chests of reals and a few bales of silk and linen. But a thirteenth, called by the gods *Our Lady of the Conception*, called by men *Cacafuego*, a name incapable of translation, had sailed a few days before for the isthmus, with the whole produce of the Lima mines for the season. Her ballast was silver, her cargo gold and emeralds and rubies. Drake deliberately cut the cables of the ships in the roads, that they might drive ashore and be unable to follow him. The *Pelican* spread her wings, every feather of them, and sped away in pursuit. He would know the *Cacafuego*, so he learnt at Lima, by the peculiar cut of her sails. The first man who caught sight of her was promised a gold chain for his reward. A sail was seen on the second day. It was not the chase, but it was worth stopping for. Eighty pounds' worth of gold was found, and a great gold crucifix, set with emeralds said to be as large as pigeons' eggs. They took the kernel. They left the shell. Still on and on. We learn from the Spanish accounts that the Viceroy of Lima, as soon as he recovered from his astonishment, despatched ships in pursuit. They came up with the last plundered vessel, heard terrible tales of the rovers' strength, and went back for a larger force. The *Pelican* meanwhile went along upon her course for 800 miles. At length, when in the latitude of Quito and close under the shore, the *Cacafuego's* peculiar sails were sighted, and the gold chain was claimed. There she was, freighted with the fruit of Aladdin's garden, going lazily along a few miles ahead. Care was needed in approaching her. If she guessed the *Pelican's* character, she would run in upon the land and they would lose her. It was afternoon. The sun was still above the horizon, and Drake meant to wait till night, when the breeze would be off the shore, as in the tropics it always is.

The *Pelican* sailed two feet to the *Cacafuego's* one. Drake filled his empty wine-skins with water and trailed them astern to stop his way. The chase supposed that she was followed by some heavy-loaded trader, and, wishing for company on a lonely voyage, she slackened sail and waited for him to come up. At length the sun went down into the ocean, the rosy light faded from off the snows of the Andes; and when both ships had become invisible from the shore, the skins were hauled in, the night wind rose, and the water began to ripple under the *Pelican's* bows. The *Cacafuego* was swiftly overtaken, and when within a cable's length a voice hailed her to put her head into the wind. The Spanish commander, not understanding so strange an order, held on his course. A broadside brought down his mainyard, and a flight of arrows rattled on his deck. He was himself wounded. In a few minutes he was a prisoner, and *Our Lady of the Conception* and her precious freight were in the corsair's power. The wreck was cut away; the ship was cleared; a prize crew was put on board. Both vessels turned their heads to the sea. At daybreak no land was to be seen, and the examination of the prize began. The full value was never acknowledged. The invoice, if there was one, was destroyed. The accurate figures were known only to Drake and Queen Elizabeth. A published schedule acknowledged to twenty tons of silver bullion, thirteen chests of silver coins, and a hundredweight of gold, but there were gold nuggets besides in indefinite quantity, and 'a great store' of pearls, emeralds, and diamonds. The Spanish Government proved a loss of a million and a half of ducats, excluding what belonged to private persons. The total capture was immeasurably greater.

Drake, we are told, was greatly satisfied. He thought it prudent to stay in the neighbourhood no longer than necessary. He went north with all sail set, taking his prize along with him. The master, San Juan de Anton, was removed on board the *Pelican* to have his wound attended to. He remained as Drake's guest for a week, and sent in a report of what he observed to the Spanish Government. One at least of Drake's party spoke excellent Spanish. This person took San Juan over the ship. She showed signs, San Juan said, of rough service, but was still in fine condition, with ample arms, spare rope, mattocks, carpenter's tools of all descriptions. There were eighty-five men on board all told, fifty of them men-of-war, the rest young fellows, ship-boys and the like. Drake himself was treated with great reverence; a sentinel stood always at his cabin door. He dined alone with music.

English Seamen in the Sixteenth Century

447 *Oxford Revisited*

MANY long years had passed since I visited Oxford,—some twenty-eight or more. I had friends among the resident members of that venerable domicile of learning. Pleasant had been the time that I had spent there, of which intervening years had not diminished the remembrance—perhaps heightened the tone of its colouring. On many accounts I regarded that beautiful city with affectionate veneration. There were more than local attractions to render it interesting. There were the recollections of those who ceased in the interval to be denizens of this world. These could not but breathe sadness over the noble edifices that recalled men, conversations, and convivialities which, however long departed, shadowed upon the mind its own inevitable destiny. Again were those venerable buildings before me in their architectural richness. There were tower, and roof, and gateway, in all their variety of outline, defined with the sharp light and shade peculiar to ecclesiastical architecture. There were tufted groves overshadowing the haunts of learning; and there, too, was old Magdalen, which used to greet our sight so pleasantly upon our approach to the city. I began to fancy I had leaped no gulf of time since, for the Cherwell ran on as of old. I felt that the happy allusion of Quevedo to the Tiber was not out of place here, 'The fugitive is alone permanent.' The same river ran on as it had run on before, but the cheerful faces that had been once reflected in its stream had passed away. I saw things once familiar as I saw them before; but 'the fathers, where were they?' I was in this respect like one awaked from the slumber of an age, who found himself a stranger in his own land. . .

At length I adjourned to the Star, somewhat moody, more than half wishing I had not entered the city. I ordered my solitary meal, and began ruminating, as we all do, over the thousandth-time told tale of human destiny by generation after generation. I am not sure I did not greet with sullen pleasure a heavy, dark, dense mass of cloud that at that moment canopied the city. The mind finds all kinds of congenialities grateful at such moments. Some drops of rain fell; then a shower, tolerably heavy. I could not go out again as I intended doing. I sat and sipped my wine, thinking of the fate of cities,—of Nineveh the renowned, of the marbles lately recovered from thence with the mysterious arrow-headed characters. I thought that some future Layard might exhume the cornices of the Oxford temples. The deaths of cities were as inevitable as those of men. I felt that my missing friends had only a priority in mortality, and that the law of the Supreme existed to be obeyed without man's questionings.

But a sun-burst took place, the shower ceased, all became fresh and clear. I saw several gownsmen pass down the street, and I sallied forth again. Several who were in front of me, so full was I of old imaginings, I thought might be old friends whom I should recognize. How idle! I strolled to the Isis. It was all glitter and gaiety. The sun shone out warmly and covered the surface of the river with gold. Numerous skiffs of the university-men were alive on the water, realizing the lines,—

'Some lightly o'er the current swim,
Some show their gaily gilded trim
Quick glancing to the sun.'

Here was the repetition of an old performance, but the actors were new. I too had once floated over that glittering water, or lain up by the bank in conversation, or reciting verses, or, perhaps, in that silent, dreamy vacancy, in which the mind ruminates or rests folded up within itself in the consciousness of its own immortality.

There seems of late years much less of that feeling for poetry than once existed; the same may be observed in respect to classical learning. Few now regard how perished nations lived and passed away,—how men thought, acted, and were moved, for example, in the time of Pericles or the Roman Augustus. What are they to us? What is blind Maeonides to us, or that Roman who wrote odes so beautifully—who understood so well the philosophy of life and the poetry of life at the spring of Bandusia? In the past generation, a part of the adolescent being and of manhood extended a kindly feeling towards them. We hear no admiration of those immortal strains now. We must turn for them to our universities. People are getting shy of them, as rich men shirk poor friends. Are we in the declining state, that of 'mechanical arts and merchandize,' to use Lord Bacon's phrase, and is our middle age of learning past? Even then, thank Heaven, we have our universities still, where we may, for a time at least, enter and converse with the spirits of the good, that 'sit in the clouds and mock' the rest of the greedy world. They will last our time—glorious mementos of the anxiety of our forefathers for the preservation of learning; hallowed by grateful recollections, by time, renown, virtue, conquests over ignorance, imperishable gratitude, a proud roll of mighty names in their sons, and the prospect of continuing to be monuments of glory to unborn generations. Long may Oxford and Cambridge stand and brighten with years, though to some they may not, as they do to me, exhibit a title to the gratitude and admiration of Old England, to which it would be difficult to point out worthy rivals.

Words about Oxford

GEORGE ELIOT
(MARY ANN EVANS)

1819–1880

448 *Maggie and the Doll*

'MAGGIE, Maggie,' exclaimed Mrs. Tulliver, sitting stout and helpless with the brushes on her lap, 'what is to become of you, if you're so naughty? I'll tell your aunt Glegg and your aunt Pullet when they come next week, and they'll never love you any more. O dear, O dear! look at your clean pinafore, wet from top to bottom. Folks 'ull think it 's a judgment on me as I've got such a child—they'll think I've done summat wicked.'

Before this remonstrance was finished, Maggie was already out of hearing, making her way towards the great attic that ran under the old high-pitched roof, shaking the water from her black locks as she ran, like a Skye terrier escaped from his bath. This attic was Maggie's favourite retreat on a wet day, when the weather was not too cold; here she fretted out all her ill-humours, and talked aloud to the worm-eaten floors and the worm-eaten shelves, and the dark rafters festooned with cobwebs; and here she kept a Fetish which she punished for all her misfortunes. This was the trunk of a large wooden doll, which once stared with the roundest of eyes above the reddest of cheeks; but was now entirely defaced by a long career of vicarious suffering. Three nails driven into the head commemorated as many crises in Maggie's nine years of earthly struggle; that luxury of vengeance having been suggested to her by the picture of Jael destroying Sisera in the old Bible. The last nail had been driven in with a fiercer stroke than usual, for the Fetish on that occasion represented aunt Glegg. But immediately afterwards Maggie had reflected that if she drove many nails in, she would not be so well able to fancy that the head was hurt when she knocked it against the wall, nor to comfort it, and make believe to poultice it, when her fury was abated; for even aunt Glegg would be pitiable when she had been hurt very much, and thoroughly humiliated, so as to beg her niece's pardon. Since then she had driven no more nails in, but had soothed herself by alternately grinding and beating the wooden head against the rough brick of the great chimneys that made two square pillars supporting the roof. That was what she did this morning on reaching the attic, sobbing all the while with a passion that expelled every other form of consciousness—even the memory of the grievance that had caused it. As at last the sobs were getting quieter, and the grinding less fierce, a sudden beam of sunshine, falling through the wire lattice across the worm-eaten shelves, made her throw away the Fetish and run to the window. The sun was really breaking out; the sound of the mill seemed cheerful again; the granary doors were open; and there was Yap, the queer white-and-brown terrier with one ear turned back trotting about and sniffing vaguely, as if he were in search of a companion. It was irresistible. Maggie tossed her hair back and ran down-stairs, seized her bonnet without putting it on, peeped, and then dashed along the passage lest she should encounter her mother, and was quickly out in the yard, whirling round like a Pythoness, and singing as she whirled, 'Yap, Yap, Tom's coming home!' while Yap danced and barked round her, as much as to say, if there was any noise wanted he was the dog for it.

The Mill on the Floss

449 *Mrs. Linnet's Reading*

MRS. LINNET had become a reader of religious books since Mr. Tryan's advent, and as she was in the habit of confining her perusal to the purely secular portions, which bore a very small proportion to the whole, she could make rapid progress through a large number of volumes. On taking up the biography of a celebrated preacher, she immediately turned to the end to see what disease he died of; and if his legs swelled, as her own occasionally did, she felt a stronger interest in ascertaining any earlier facts in the history of the dropsical divine—whether he had ever fallen off a stage coach, whether he had married more than one wife, and, in general, any adventures or repartees recorded of him previous to the epoch of his conversion. She then glanced over the letters and diary, and wherever there was a predominance of Zion, the River of Life, and notes of exclamation, she turned over to the next page; but any passage in which she saw such promising nouns as 'smallpox,' 'pony,' or 'boots and shoes,' at once arrested her.

Scenes of Clerical Life

450 *The Archery Meeting*

BRACKENSHAW PARK, where the Archery Meeting was held, looked out from its gentle heights far over the neighbouring valley to the outlying eastern downs and the broad slow rise of cultivated country hanging like a vast curtain towards the west. The castle, which stood on the highest platform of the clustered hills, was built of rough-hewn limestone, full of lights and shadows made by the dark dust of lichens and the washings of the rain. Masses of beech and fir sheltered it on the north, and spread down here and there along the green slopes like flocks seeking the water which gleamed below. The archery-ground was a carefully-kept enclosure on a bit of table-land at the farthest end of the park, protected towards the south-west by tall elms and a thick screen of hollies, which kept the gravel walk and the bit of newly-mown turf where the targets were placed in agreeable afternoon shade. The Archery Hall with an arcade in front showed like a white temple against the greenery on the northern side.

What could make a better background for the flower-groups of ladies, moving and bowing and turning their necks as it would become the leisurely lilies to do if they took to locomotion? The sounds too were very pleasant to hear, even when the military band from Wancester ceased to play: musical laughs in all the registers and a harmony of happy friendly speeches, now rising towards mild excitement, now sinking to an agreeable murmur. . .

Who can deny that bows and arrows are among the prettiest weapons in the world for feminine forms to play with? They prompt attitudes full of grace and power, where that fine concentration of energy seen in all markmanship, is freed from associations of bloodshed. . . Archery has no ugly smell of brimstone; breaks nobody's shins, breeds no athletic monsters; its only danger is that of failing, which for generous blood is enough to mould skilful action. And among the Brackenshaw archers the prizes were all of the nobler symbolic kind: not property to be carried off in a parcel, degrading honour into gain; but the gold arrow and the silver, the gold star and the silver, to be worn for a time in sign of achievement and then transferred to the next who did excellently. These signs of pre-eminence had the virtue of wreaths without their inconveniences, which might have produced a melancholy effect in the heat of the ball-room. Altogether the Brackenshaw Archery Club was an institution framed with good taste, so as not to have by necessity any ridiculous incidents.

And to-day all incalculable elements were in its favour. There was mild warmth, and no wind to disturb either hair or drapery or the course of the arrow; all skilful preparation had fair play, and when there was a general march to extract the arrows, the promenade of joyous young creatures in light speech and laughter, the graceful movement in common towards a common object, was a show worth looking at. Here Gwendolen seemed a Calypso among her nymphs. It was in her attitudes and movements that every one was obliged to admit her surpassing charm.

Daniel Deronda

CHARLES KINGSLEY

1819–1875

451 *Amyas on the Cliff*

SO on they went to the point, where the cyclopean wall of granite cliff which forms the western side of Lundy, ends sheer in a precipice of some three hundred feet, topped by a pile of snow-white rock, bespangled with golden lichens. As they approached, a raven, who sat upon the topmost stone, black against the bright blue sky, flapped lazily away, and sank down the abysses of the cliff, as if he scented the corpses underneath the surge. Below them from the Gull-rock rose a thousand birds, and filled the air with sound; the choughs cackled, the hacklets wailed, the great blackbacks laughed querulous defiance at the intruders, and a single falcon, with an angry bark, dashed out from beneath their feet, and hung poised high aloft, watching the sea-fowl which swung slowly round and round below.

It was a glorious sight, upon a glorious day. To the northward the glens rushed down toward the cliff, crowned with grey crags, and carpeted with purple heather and green fern; and from their feet stretched away to the westward the sapphire rollers of the vast Atlantic, crowned with a thousand crests of flying foam. On their left hand, some ten miles to the south, stood out against the sky the purple wall of Hartland cliffs, sinking lower and lower as they trended away to the southward along the lonely iron-bound shores of Cornwall, until they faded, dim and blue, into the blue horizon forty miles away.

The sky was flecked with clouds, which rushed toward them fast upon the roaring south-west wind; and the warm ocean breeze swept up the cliffs, and whistled through the heather-bells, and howled in cranny and in crag,

> Till the pillars and clefts of the granite
> Rang like a God-swept lyre;

while Amyas, a proud smile upon his lips, stood breasting that genial stream of airy wine with swelling nostrils and fast-heaving chest, and seemed to drink in life from every gust. All three were silent for awhile; and Jack and Cary, gazing downward with delight upon the glory and the grandeur of the sight, forgot for awhile that their companion saw it not. Yet when they started sadly, and looked into his face, did he not see it? So wide and eager were his eyes, so bright and calm his face, that they fancied for an instant that he was once more even as they.

A deep sigh undeceived them. 'I know it is all here—the dear old sea, where I would live and die. And my eyes feel for it; feel for it—and cannot find it; never, never will find it again for ever! God's will be done!'

'Do you say that?' asked Brimblecombe, eagerly.

'Why should I not? Why have I been raving in hell-fire for I know not how many days, but to find out that, John Brimblecombe, thou better man than I?'

'Not that last: but Amen! Amen! and the Lord has indeed had mercy upon thee!' said Jack, through his honest tears.'

'Amen!' said Amyas. 'Now set me where I can rest among the rocks without fear of falling—for life is sweet still, even without eyes, friends—and leave me to myself awhile.'

It was no easy matter to find a safe place; for from the foot of the crag the heathery turf slopes down all but upright, on one side to a cliff which overhangs a shoreless cove of deep dark sea, and on the other to an abyss even more hideous, where the solid rock has sunk away, and opened inland in the hillside a smooth-walled pit, some sixty feet square and some hundred and fifty in depth, aptly known then as now, as the Devil's-limekiln; the mouth of which, as old wives say, was once closed by the Shutter-rock itself, till the fiend in malice hurled it into the sea, to be a pest to mariners. A narrow and untrodden cavern at the bottom connects it with the outer sea; they could even then hear the mysterious thunder and gurgle of the surge in the subterranean adit, as it rolled huge boulders to and fro in darkness, and forced before it gusts of pent-up air. It was a spot to curdle weak blood, and to make weak heads reel: but all the fitter on that account for Amyas and his fancy.

'You can sit here as in an arm-chair,' said Cary, helping him down to one of those square natural seats so common in the granite tors.

'Good; now turn my face to the Shutter. Be sure and exact. So. Do I face it full?'

'Full,' said Cary.

'Then I need no eyes wherewith to see what is before me,' said he with a sad smile. 'I know every stone and every headland, and every wave too, I may say, far beyond aught that eye can reach. Now go, and leave me alone with God and with the dead!'

They retired a little space and watched him. He never stirred for many minutes; then leaned his elbows on his knees, and his head upon his hands, and so was still again. He remained so long thus, that the pair became anxious, and went towards him. He was asleep, and breathing quick and heavily.

'He will take a fever,' said Brimblecombe, 'if he sleeps much longer with his head down in the sunshine.'

'We must wake him gently, if we wake him at all.' And Cary moved forward to him.

As he did so, Amyas lifted his head, and turning it to right and left, felt round him with his sightless eyes.

'You have been asleep, Amyas.'

'Have I? I have not slept back my eyes, then. Take up this great useless carcase of mine, and lead me home. I shall buy me a dog when I get to Burrough, I think, and make him tow me in a string, eh? So! Give me your hand. Now, march!'

His guides heard with surprise this new cheerfulness.

'Thank God, Sir, that your heart is so light already,' said good Jack; 'it makes me feel quite upraised myself, like.'

'I have reason to be cheerful, Sir John; I have left a heavy load behind me. I have been wilful, and proud, and a blasphemer, and swollen with cruelty and pride; and God has brought me low for it, and cut me off from my evil delight. No more Spaniard-hunting for me now, my masters. God will send no such fools as I upon His errands.'

'You do not repent of fighting the Spaniards?'

'Not I: but of hating even the worst of them. Listen to me, Will and Jack. If that man wronged me, I wronged him likewise. I have been a fiend when I thought myself the grandest of men, yea, a very avenging angel out of heaven. But God has shown me my sin, and we have made up our quarrel for ever.'

'Made it up?'

'Made it up, thank God. But I am weary. Set me down awhile, and I will tell you how it befel.'

Wondering, they set him down upon the heather, while the bees hummed round them in the sun; and Amyas felt for a hand of each, and clasped it in his own hand, and began—

'When you left me there upon the rock, lads, I looked away and out to sea, to get one last snuff of the merry sea-breeze, which will never sail me again. And as I looked, I tell you truth, I could see the water and the sky; as plain as ever I saw them, till I thought my sight was come again. But soon I knew it was not so; for I saw more than man could see; right over the ocean, as I live, and away to the Spanish Main.

26 *The prose is from this point deliberately metrical.*

And I saw Barbados, and Grenada, and all the isles that we ever sailed by; and La Guayra in Caraccas, and the Silla, and the house beneath it where she lived. And I saw him walking with her, on the barbecue, and he loved her then. I saw what I saw; and he loved her; and I say he loves her still.

'Then I saw the cliffs beneath me, and the Gull-rock, and the Shutter, and the Ledge; I saw them, William Cary, and the weeds beneath the merry blue sea. And I saw the grand old galleon, Will; she has righted with the sweeping of the tide. She lies in fifteen fathoms, at the edge of the rocks, upon the sand; and her men are all lying around her, asleep until the Judgement Day.'

Cary and Jack looked at him, and then at each other. His eyes were clear, and bright, and full of meaning; and yet they knew that he was blind. His voice was shaping itself into a song. Was he inspired? Insane? What was it? And they listened with awe-struck faces, as the giant pointed down into the blue depths far below, and went on.

'And I saw him sitting in his cabin, like a valiant gentleman of Spain; and his officers were sitting round him, with their swords upon the table, at the wine. And the prawns and the crayfish and the rockling, they swam in and out above their heads: but Don Guzman he never heeded, but sat still, and drank his wine. Then he took a locket from his bosom; and I heard him speak, Will, and he said: "Here's the picture of my fair and true lady; drink to her, Señors all." Then he spoke to me, Will, and called me, right up through the oar-weed and the sea: "We have had a fair quarrel, Señor; it is time to be friends once more. My wife and your brother have forgiven me; so your honour takes no stain." And I answered, "We are friends, Don Guzman; God has judged our quarrel, and not we." Then he said, "I sinned, and I am punished." And I said, "And, Señor, so am I." Then he held out his hand to me, Cary; and I stooped to take it, and awoke.'

Westward Ho!

452 *Salmon Rivers*

AND when the daylight came, Tom found himself out in the salmon river.

And what sort of a river was it? Was it like an Irish stream, winding through the brown bogs, where the wild ducks squatter up from among the white water-lilies, and the curlews flit to and fro, crying 'Tullie-wheep, mind your sheep'; and Dennis tells you strange stories of the Peishtamore, the great bogy-snake which lies in the black peat pools, among the old pine-stems, and puts his head out at night to snap at the cattle as they come down to drink? . .

Or was it like a Welsh salmon river, which is remarkable chiefly (at least, till this last year) for containing no salmon, as they have been all poached out by the enlightened peasantry, to prevent the *Cythrawl Sassenach* (which means you, my little dear, your kith and kin, and signifies much the same as the Chinese *Fan Quei*) from coming bothering into Wales, with good tackle, and ready money, and civilisation, and common honesty, and other like things of which the Cymry stand in no need whatsoever?

Or was it such a salmon stream as I trust you will see among the Hampshire water-meadows before your hairs are grey, under the wise new fishing-laws?—

when Winchester apprentices shall covenant, as they did three hundred years ago, not to be made to eat salmon more than three days a week; and fresh-run fish shall be as plentiful under Salisbury spire as they are in Holly-hole at Christchurch; in the good time coming, when folks shall see that, of all Heaven's gifts of food, the one to be protected most carefully is that worthy gentleman salmon, who is generous enough to go down to the sea weighing five ounces, and to come back next year weighing five pounds, without having cost the soil or the state one farthing?

Or was it like a Scotch stream, such as Arthur Clough drew in his 'Bothie':—

Where over a ledge of granite
Into a granite bason the amber torrent descended. . .
Beautiful there for the colour derived from green rocks under;
Beautiful most of all, where beads of foam uprising
Mingle their clouds of white with the delicate hue of the stillness. . .
Cliff over cliff for its sides, with rowan and pendent birch boughs. . .

Ah, my little man, when you are a big man, and fish such a stream as that, you will hardly care, I think, whether she be roaring down in full spate, like coffee covered with scald cream, while the fish are swirling at your fly as an oar-blade swirls in a boat-race, or flashing up the cataract like silver arrows, out of the fiercest of the foam; or whether the fall be dwindled to a single thread, and the shingle below be as white and dusty as a turnpike road, while the salmon huddle together in one dark cloud in the clear amber pool, sleeping away their time till the rain creeps back again off the sea. You will not care much, if you have eyes and brains; for you will lay down your rod contentedly, and drink in at your eyes the beauty of that glorious place; and listen to the water-ouzel piping on the stones, and watch the yellow roes come down to drink and look up at you with their great soft trustful eyes, as much as to say, 'You could not have the heart to shoot at us?'. .

No. It was none of these, the salmon stream at Harthover. It was such a stream as you see in dear old Bewick.

The Water Babies

453 *Finding a Fox*

A SILENT, dim, distanceless, steaming, rotting day in March. The last brown oak-leaf which had stood out the winter's frost spun and quivered plump down, and then lay; as if ashamed to have broken for a moment the ghastly stillness, like an awkward guest at a great dumb dinner-party. A cold suck of wind just proved its existence, by toothaches on the north side of all faces. The spiders, having been weather-bewitched the night before, had unanimously agreed to cover every brake and brier with gossamer-cradles, and never a fly to be caught in them; like Manchester cotton-spinners madly glutting the markets in the teeth of 'no demand.' The steam crawled out of the dank turf, and reeked off the flanks and nostrils of the shivering horses, and clung with clammy paws to frosted hats and dripping boughs. A soulless, skyless, catarrhal day, as if that bustling dowager, old mother Earth—what with match-making in spring, and *fêtes champêtres* in summer, and dinner-giving in autumn—was fairly worn out, and put to bed with the influenza, under wet blankets and the cold-water cure.

There sat Lancelot by the cover-side, his knees

aching with cold and wet, thanking his stars that he was not one of the whippers-in who were lashing about in the dripping cover. . .

But 'all things do end,' and so did this; and the silence of the hounds also; . . and Lancelot began to stalk slowly with a dozen horsemen up the wood-ride, to a fitful accompaniment of wandering hound-music, where the choristers were as invisible as nightingales among the thick cover. And hark! . . the sweet hubbub suddenly crashed out into one jubilant shriek, and then swept away fainter and fainter among the trees. The walk became a trot—the trot a canter. Then a faint melancholy shout at a distance, answered by a 'Stole away!' from the fields; a doleful 'toot!' of the horn; the dull thunder of many horse-hoofs rolling along the further wood-side. Then red coats, flashing like sparks of fire across the grey gap of mist at the ride's-mouth, then a whipper-in, bringing up a belated hound, burst into the pathway, smashing and plunging, with shut eyes, through ash-saplings and hassock-grass; then a fat farmer, sedulously pounding through the mud, was overtaken and bespattered in spite of all his struggles;—until the line streamed out into the wide rushy pasture, starting up pewits and curlews, as horsemen poured in from every side, and cunning old farmers rode off at inexplicable angles to some well-known haunts of pug: and right ahead, chiming and jangling sweet madness, the dappled pack glanced and wavered through the veil of soft grey mist.

Yeast

JAMES RUSSELL LOWELL

1819–1891

454 *Evening Thoughts after War-Time*

WALKING one day toward the Village, as we used to call it in the good old days when almost every dweller in the town had been born in it, I was enjoying that delicious sense of disenthralment from the actual which the deepening twilight brings with it, giving, as it does, a sort of obscure novelty to things familiar. . .

I love old ways, and the path I was walking felt kindly to the feet it had known for almost fifty years. How many fleeting impressions it had shared with me! How many times I had lingered to study the shadows of the leaves mezzotinted upon the turf that edged it by the moon, of the bare boughs etched with a touch beyond Rembrandt by the same unconscious artist on the smooth page of snow! If I turned round, through dusky tree-gaps came the first twinkle of evening lamps in the dear old homestead. On Corey's hill I could see these tiny pharoses of love and home and sweet domestic thoughts flash out one by one across the blackening salt-meadow between. How much has not kerosene added to the cheerfulness of our evening landscape! A pair of night-herons flapped heavily over me toward the hidden river. The war was ended. I might walk townward without that aching dread of bulletins that had darkened the July sunshine, and twice made the scarlet leaves of October seem stained with blood. I remembered with a pang, half proud, half painful, how so many years ago I had walked over the same path and felt round my finger the soft pressure of a little hand that was one day to harden with faithful grip of sabre. On how many paths, leading to how many homes where proud Memory does all she can to fill up the fireside gaps with shining shapes, must not men be walking in just such pensive mood as I? Ah, young heroes, safe in immortal youth as those of Homer, you at least carried your ideal hence untarnished! It is locked for you beyond moth or rust in the treasure-chamber of Death.

On a Certain Condescension in Foreigners

HERMAN MELVILLE

1819–1891

455 *Fayaway*

WE had a very pleasant day; my trusty valet plied the paddle and swept us gently along the margin of the water, beneath the shades of the overhanging thickets. Fayaway and I reclined in the stern of the canoe, on the very best terms possible with one another; the gentle nymph occasionally placing her pipe to her lip, and exhaling the mild fumes of the tobacco, to which her rosy breath added a fresh perfume. . .

We floated about thus for several hours, when I looked up to the warm, glowing, tropical sky, and then down into the transparent depths below; and when my eye, wandering from the bewitching scenery around, fell upon the grotesquely-tattooed form of Kory-Kory, and finally encountered the pensive gaze of Fayaway, I thought I had been transported to some fairy region, so unreal did everything appear.

This lovely piece of water was the coolest spot in all the valley, and I now made it a place of continual resort during the hottest period of the day. One side of it lay near the termination of a long gradually expanding gorge, which mounted to the heights that environed the vale. The strong trade wind, met in its course by these elevations, circled and eddied about their summits, and was sometimes driven down the steep ravine and swept across the valley, ruffling in its passage the otherwise tranquil surface of the lake.

One day, after we had been paddling about for some time, I disembarked Kory-Kory, and paddled the canoe to the windward side of the lake. As I turned the canoe, Fayaway, who was with me, seemed all at once to be struck with some happy idea. With a wild exclamation of delight, she disengaged from her person the ample robe of tappa which was knotted over her shoulder (for the purpose of shielding her from the sun), and spreading it out like a sail, stood erect with upraised arms in the head of the canoe. We American sailors pride ourselves upon our straight clean spars, but a prettier little mast than Fayaway made was never shipped a-board of any craft.

In a moment the tappa was distended by the breeze—the long brown tresses of Fayaway streamed in the air—and the canoe glided rapidly through the water, and shot towards the shore. Seated in the stern, I directed its course with my paddle until it dashed up the soft sloping bank, and Fayaway, with a light spring, alighted on the ground; whilst Kory-Kory, who had watched our manœuvres with admiration, now clapped his hands in transport, and shouted like a madman. Many a time afterwards was this feat repeated.

Typee

456 *Sighting the Whale*

IT was a cloudy, sultry afternoon; the seamen were lazily lounging about the decks, or vacantly gazing over into the lead-colored waters. Queequeg and I were mildly employed weaving what is called a sword-mat, for an additional lashing to our boat. So still and subdued and yet somehow preluding was all the scene, and such an incantation of revelry lurked in the air, that each silent sailor seemed resolved into his own invisible self.

I was the attendant or page of Queequeg, while busy at the mat. As I kept passing and repassing the filling or woof of marline between the long yarns of the warp, using my own hand for the shuttle, and as Queequeg, standing sideways, ever and anon slid his heavy oaken sword between the threads, and idly looking off upon the water, carelessly and unthinkingly drove home every yarn: I say so strange a dreaminess did there then reign all over the ship and all over the sea, only broken by the intermitting dull sound of the sword, that it seemed as if this were the Loom of Time, and I myself were a shuttle mechanically weaving and weaving away at the Fates. There lay the fixed threads of the warp subject to but one single, ever returning, unchanging vibration, and that vibration merely enough to admit of the crosswise interblending of other threads with its own. This warp seemed necessity; and here, thought I, with my own hand I ply my own shuttle and weave my own destiny into these unalterable threads. Meantime, Queequeg's impulsive, indifferent sword, sometimes hitting the woof slantingly, or crookedly, or strongly, or weakly, as the case might be; and by this difference in the concluding blow producing a corresponding contrast in the final aspect of the completed fabric; this savage's sword, thought I, which thus finally shapes and fashions both warp and woof; this easy, indifferent sword must be chance—aye, chance, free will, and necessity—no wise incompatible—all interweavingly working together. The straight warp of necessity, not to be swerved from its ultimate course—its every alternating vibration, indeed, only tending to that; free will still free to ply her shuttle between given threads; and chance, though restrained in its play within the right lines of necessity, and sideways in its motions directed by free will, though thus prescribed to by both, chance by turns rules either, and has the last featuring blow at events.

* * * * * * *

Thus we were weaving and weaving away when I started at a sound so strange, long drawn, and musically wild and unearthly, that the ball of free will dropped from my hand, and I stood gazing up at the clouds whence that voice dropped like a wing. High aloft in the cross-trees was that mad Gay-Header, Tashtego. His body was reaching eagerly forward, his hand stretched out like a wand, and at brief sudden intervals he continued his cries. To be sure the same sound was that very moment perhaps being heard all over the seas, from hundreds of whalemen's look-outs perched as high in the air; but from few of those lungs could that accustomed old cry have derived such a marvellous cadence as from Tashtego the Indian's.

As he stood hovering over you half suspended in air, so wildly and eagerly peering towards the horizon, you would have thought him some prophet or seer beholding the shadows of Fate, and by those wild cries announcing their coming.

'There she blows! there! there! there! she blows! she blows!'

'Where-away?'

'On the lee-beam, about two miles off! a school of them!'

Moby Dick

JOHN RUSKIN

1819–1900

457 *A Cathedral Close*

AND now I wish that the reader, before I bring him into St. Mark's Place, would imagine himself for a little time in a quiet English cathedral town, and walk with me to the west front of its cathedral. Let us go together up the more retired street, at the end of which we can see the pinnacles of one of the towers, and then through the low grey gateway, with its battlemented top and small latticed window in the centre, into the inner private-looking road or close, where nothing goes in but the carts of the tradesmen who supply the bishop and the chapter, and where there are little shaven grass-plots, fenced in by neat rails, before old-fashioned groups of somewhat diminutive and excessively trim houses, with little oriel and bay windows jutting out here and there, and deep wooden cornices and eaves painted cream colour and white, and small porches to their doors in the shape of cockle-shells, or little, crooked, thick, indescribable wooden gables warped a little on one side; and so forward till we come to larger houses, also old-fashioned, but of red brick, and with gardens behind them, and fruit walls, which show here and there, among the nectarines, the vestiges of an old cloister arch or shaft, and looking in front on the cathedral square itself, laid out in rigid divisions of smooth grass and gravel walk, yet not uncheerful, especially on the sunny side, where the canons' children are walking with their nurserymaids. And so, taking care not to tread on the grass, we will go along the straight walk to the west front, and there stand for a time, looking up at its deep-pointed porches, and the dark places between their pillars where there were statues once, and where the fragments, here and there, of a stately figure are still left, which has in it the likeness of a king, perhaps indeed a king on earth, perhaps a saintly king long ago in heaven ; and so higher and higher up to the great mouldering wall of rugged sculpture and confused arcades, shattered, and grey, and grisly with heads of dragons and mocking fiends, worn by the rain and swirling winds into yet unseemlier shape, and coloured on their stony scales by the deep russet-orange lichen, melancholy gold ; and so, higher still, to the bleak towers, so far above that the eye loses itself among the bosses of their traceries, though they are rude and strong, and only sees like a drift of eddying black points, now closing, now scattering, and now settling suddenly into invisible places among the bosses and flowers, the crowd of restless birds that fill the whole square with that strange clangour of theirs, so harsh and yet so soothing, like the cries of birds on a solitary coast between the cliffs and sea.

Think for a little while of that scene, and the meaning of all its small formalisms, mixed with its serene sublimity. Estimate its secluded, continuous, drowsy felicities, and its evidence of the sense and steady performance of such kind of duties as can be regulated by the cathedral clock; and weigh the influence of those dark towers on all who have passed through the lonely square at their feet for centuries, and on all who have seen them rising far away over the wooded plain, or catching on their square masses the last rays of the sunset, when the city at their feet was indicated only by the mist at the bend of the river.

The Stones of Venice

458 *The Two Boyhoods*

i. Giorgione

HAVE you ever thought what a world his eyes opened on—fair, searching eyes of youth? What a world of mighty life, from those mountain roots to the shore;—of loveliest life, when he went down, yet so young, to the marble city—and became himself as a fiery heart to it?

A city of marble, did I say? nay, rather a golden city, paved with emerald. For truly, every pinnacle and turret glanced or glowed, overlaid with gold, or bossed with jasper. Beneath, the unsullied sea drew in deep breathing, to and fro, its eddies of green wave. Deep-hearted, majestic, terrible as the sea,—the men of Venice moved in sway of power and war; pure as her pillars of alabaster, stood her mothers and maidens; from foot to brow, all noble, walked her knights; the low bronzed gleaming of sea-rusted armour shot angrily under their blood-red mantle-folds. Fearless, faithful, patient, impenetrable, implacable,—every word a fate—sate her senate. In hope and honour, lulled by flowing of wave around their isles of sacred sand, each with his name written and the cross graved at his side, lay her dead. A wonderful piece of world. Rather, itself a world. It lay along the face of the waters, no larger, as its captains saw it from their masts at evening, than a bar of sunset that could not pass away; but for its power, it must have seemed to them as if they were sailing in the expanse of heaven, and this a great planet, whose orient edge widened through ether. A world from which all ignoble care and petty thoughts were banished, with all the common and poor elements of life. No foulness, nor tumult, in those tremulous streets, that filled, or fell, beneath the moon; but rippled music of majestic change, or thrilling silence. No weak walls could rise above them; no low-roofed cottage, nor straw-built shed. Only the strength as of rock, and the finished setting of stones most precious. And around them, far as the eye could reach, still the soft moving of stainless waters, proudly pure; as not the flower, so neither the thorn nor the thistle, could grow in the glancing fields. Ethereal strength of Alps, dreamlike, vanishing in high procession beyond the Torcellan shore; blue islands of Paduan hills, poised in the golden west. Above, free winds and fiery clouds ranging at their will;—brightness out of the north, and balm from the south, and the stars of the evening and morning clear in the limitless light of arched heaven and circling sea.

ii. Turner

NEAR the south-west corner of Covent Garden, a square brick pit or well is formed by a close-set block of houses, to the back windows of which it admits a few rays of light. Access to the bottom of it is obtained out of Maiden Lane, through a low archway and an iron gate; and if you stand long enough under the archway to accustom your eyes to the darkness you may see on the left hand a narrow door, which formerly gave quiet access to a respectable barber's shop, of which the front window, looking into Maiden Lane, is still extant, filled, in this year (1860), with a row of bottles, connected, in some defunct manner, with a brewer's business. A more fashionable neighbourhood, it is said, eighty years ago than now—never certainly a cheerful one—wherein a boy being born on St. George's day, 1775, began soon after to take interest in the world of Covent Garden, and put to service such spectacles of life as it afforded.

No knights to be seen there, nor, I imagine, many beautiful ladies; their costume at least disadvantageous, depending much on incumbency of hat and feather, and short waists; the majesty of men founded similarly on shoebuckles and wigs;—impressive enough when Reynolds will do his best for it; but not suggestive of much ideal delight to a boy.

'Bello ovile dov' io dormii agnello:' of things beautiful, besides men and women, dusty sunbeams up or down the street on summer mornings; deep furrowed cabbage-leaves at the greengrocer's; magnificence of oranges in wheelbarrows round the corner; and Thames' shore within three minutes' race.

None of these things very glorious; the best, however, that England, it seems, was then able to provide for a boy of gift: who, such as they are, loves them—never, indeed, forgets them. The short waists modify to the last his visions of Greek ideal. His foregrounds had always a succulent cluster or two of greengrocery at the corners. Enchanted oranges gleam in Covent Gardens of the Hesperides; and great ships go to pieces in order to scatter chests of them on the waves. That mist of early sunbeams in the London dawn crosses, many and many a time, the clearness of Italian air; and by Thames' shore, with its stranded barges and glidings of red sail, dearer to us than Lucerne lake or Venetian lagoon,—by Thames' shore we will die.

Modern Painters

WALT WHITMAN

1819–1892

459 *Starlight, and Carlyle Dying*

FOR the last three years we in America have had transmitted glimpses of a thin-bodied, lonesome, wifeless, childless, very old man, lying on a sofa, kept out of bed by indomitable will, but, of late, never well enough to take the open air. I have noted this news from time to time in brief descriptions in the papers. A week ago I read such an item just before I started out for my customary evening stroll between eight and nine. In the fine cold night, unusually clear (Feb. 5, '81), as I walk'd some open grounds adjacent, the condition of Carlyle, and his approaching—perhaps even then actual—death, filled me with thoughts eluding statement, and curiously blending with the scene. The planet Venus, an hour high in the west, with all her volume and lustre recover'd (she has been shorn and languid for nearly a year), including an additional sentiment I never noticed before—not merely voluptuous, Paphian, steeping, fascinating—now with calm commanding seriousness and hauteur—the Milo Venus now. Upward to the zenith, Jupiter, Saturn, and the moon past her quarter, trailing in procession, with the Pleiades following, and the constellation Taurus, and red Aldebaran. Not a cloud in heaven. Orion strode through the south-east, with his glittering belt—and a trifle below hung the sun of the night, Sirius. Every star dilated, more vitreous, nearer than usual. Not as in some clear nights when the larger stars entirely outshine the rest. Every little star or cluster just as distinctly visible, and just as nigh. Berenice's hair showing every gem, and new ones. To the north-east and north the Sickle, the Goat and kids, Cassiopeia, Castor and Pollux, and the two Dippers. While through the whole of this silent indescribable show, inclosing and bathing my whole receptivity, ran the thought of Carlyle dying. (To soothe and spiritualize, and, as far as may be, solve the mysteries of death and genius, consider them under the stars at midnight.)

And now that he has gone hence, can it be that Thomas Carlyle, soon to chemically dissolve in ashes and by winds, remains an identity still? In ways perhaps eluding all the statements, lore, and speculations of ten thousand years—eluding all possible statements to mortal sense—does he yet exist, a definite, vital being, a spirit, an individual—perhaps now wafted in space among those stellar systems, which, suggestive and limitless as they are, merely edge more limitless, far more suggestive systems? I have no doubt of it. In silence, of a fine night, such questions are answer'd to the soul.

Specimen Days in America

HENRY LONGUEVILLE MANSEL

1820–1871

460 *Against Rational Theology*

IF there is one dream of a godless philosophy to which, beyond all others, every moment of our consciousness gives the lie, it is that which subordinates the individual to the universal, the person to the species; which deifies kinds and realizes classifications; which sees Being in generalization, and Appearance in limitation; which regards the living and conscious man as a wave on the ocean of the unconscious infinite; his life, a momentary tossing to and fro on the shifting tide; his destiny, to be swallowed up in the formless and boundless universe. The final conclusion of this philosophy, in direct antagonism to the voice of consciousness, is 'I think; therefore I am not.' When men look around them in bewilderment for that which lies within them; when they talk of the enduring species and the perishing individual, and would find, in the abstractions which their own minds have made, a higher and truer existence than in the mind which made them; they seek for that which they know, and know not that for which they seek. They would fain lift up the curtain of their own being, to view the picture which it conceals. Like the painter of old, they know not that the curtain *is* the picture.

It is our duty, then, to think of God as personal; and it is our duty to believe that He is infinite. It is true that we cannot reconcile these two representations with each other; as our conception of personality involves attributes apparently contradictory to the notion of infinity. But it does not follow that this contradiction exists anywhere but in our own minds:

it does not follow that it implies any impossibility in the absolute nature of God. The apparent contradiction, in this case, as in those previously noticed, is the necessary consequence of an attempt on the part of the human thinker to transcend the boundaries of his own consciousness. It proves that there are limits to man's power of thought; and it proves no more.

The preceding considerations are equally conclusive against both the methods of metaphysical theology described in my last Lecture; that which commences with the divine to reason down to the human, and that which commences with the human to reason up to the divine. For though the mere abstract expression of *the infinite*, when regarded as indicating nothing more than the negation of limitation, and therefore of conceivability, is not contradictory in itself, it becomes so the instant we attempt to apply it in reasoning to any object of thought. A thing, an object, an attribute, a person, or any other term signifying one out of many possible objects of consciousness, is by that very relation necessarily declared to be finite. An infinite thing, or object, or attribute, or person, is therefore in the same moment declared to be both finite and infinite. We cannot, therefore, start from any abstract assumption of the divine infinity, to reason downwards to any object of human thought. And on the other hand, if all human attributes are conceived under the conditions of difference, and relation, and time, and personality, we cannot represent in thought any such attribute magnified to infinity; for this again is to conceive it as finite and infinite at the same time. We can conceive such attributes, at the utmost, only *indefinitely*: that is to say, we may withdraw our thought, for the moment, from the fact of their being limited; but we cannot conceive them as *infinite*: that is to say, we cannot positively think of the absence of the limit; for, the instant we attempt to do so, the antagonist elements of the conception exclude one another, and annihilate the whole.

The Limits of Religious Thought Examined

MATTHEW ARNOLD

1822–1888

461 *Ideas in England*

IN our greatest literary epoch, that of the Elizabethan age, English society at large was accessible to ideas, was permeated by them, was vivified by them, to a degree which has never been reached in England since. Hence the unique greatness in English literature of Shakspeare and his contemporaries; they were powerfully upheld by the intellectual life of their nation; they applied freely in literature the then modern ideas,—the ideas of the Renaissance and the Reformation. A few years afterwards the great English middle class, the kernel of the nation, the class whose intelligent sympathy had upheld a Shakspeare, entered the prison of Puritanism, and had the key turned on its spirit there for two hundred years. *He enlargeth a nation*, says Job, *and straiteneth it again.* In the literary movement of the beginning of the nineteenth century the signal attempt to apply freely the modern spirit was made in England by two members of the aristocratic class, Byron and Shelley. Aristocracies are, as such, naturally impenetrable by ideas; but their individual members have a high courage and a turn for breaking bounds; and a man of genius, who is the born child of the idea, happening to be born in the aristocratic ranks, chafes against the obstacles which prevent him from freely developing it. But Byron and Shelley did not succeed in their attempt freely to apply the modern spirit in English literature; they could not succeed in it; the resistance to baffle them, the want of intelligent sympathy to guide and uphold them, were too great. Their literary creation, compared with the literary creation of Shakspeare and Spenser, compared with the literary creation of Goethe and Heine, is a failure. The best literary creation of that time in England proceeded from men who did not make the same bold attempt as Byron and Shelley. What, in fact, was the career of the chief English men of letters, their contemporaries? The greatest of them, Wordsworth, retired (in Middle-Age phrase) into a monastery. I mean, he plunged himself in the inward life, he voluntarily cut himself off from the modern spirit. Coleridge took to opium. Scott became the historiographer-royal of feudalism. Keats passionately gave himself up to a sensuous genius, to his faculty for interpreting nature; and he died of consumption at twenty-five. Wordsworth, Scott, and Keats have left admirable works; far more solid and complete works than those which Byron and Shelley have left. But their works have this defect;—they do not belong to that which is the main current of the literature of modern epochs, they do not apply modern ideas to life; they constitute, therefore, *minor currents*, and all other literary work of our day, however popular, which has the same defect, also constitutes but a minor current. Byron and Shelley will long be remembered, long after the inadequacy of their actual work is clearly recognised, for their passionate, their

Titanic effort to flow in the main stream of modern literature; their names will be greater than their writings; *stat magni nominis umbra.*

Essays in Criticism

462 *Oxford*

NO, we are all seekers still! seekers often make mistakes, and I wish mine to redound to my own discredit only, and not to touch Oxford. Beautiful city! so venerable, so lovely, so unravaged by the fierce intellectual life of our century, so serene!

'There are our young barbarians all at play!'

And yet, steeped in sentiment as she lies, spreading her gardens to the moonlight, and whispering from her towers the last enchantments of the Middle Age, who will deny that Oxford, by her ineffable charm, keeps ever calling us nearer to the true goal of all of us, to the ideal, to perfection,—to beauty, in a word, which is only truth seen from another side?—nearer, perhaps, than all the science of Tübingen. Adorable dreamer, whose heart has been so romantic! who hast given thyself so prodigally, given thyself to sides and to heroes not mine, only never to the Philistines! home of lost causes, and forsaken beliefs, and unpopular names, and impossible loyalties! what example could ever so inspire us to keep down the Philistine in ourselves, what teacher could ever so save us from that bondage to which we are all prone, that bondage which Goethe, in those incomparable lines on the death of Schiller, makes it his friend's highest praise (and nobly did Schiller deserve the praise) to have left miles out of sight behind him;—the bondage of '*was uns alle bändigt,* DAS GEMEINE!' She will forgive me, even if I have unwittingly drawn upon her a shot or two aimed at her unworthy son; for she is generous, and the cause in which I fight is, after all, hers. Apparitions of a day, what is our puny warfare against the Philistines, compared with the warfare which this queen of romance has been waging against them for centuries, and will wage after we are gone?

Essays in Criticism

463 *Milton*

THE verse of the poets of Greece and Rome no translation can adequately reproduce. Prose cannot have the power of verse; verse-translation may give whatever of charm is in the soul and talent of the translator himself, but never the specific charm of the verse and poet translated. In our race are thousands of readers, presently there will be millions, who know not a word of Greek and Latin, and will never learn those languages. If this host of readers are ever to gain any sense of the power and charm of the great poets of antiquity, their way to gain it is not through translations of the ancients, but through the original poetry of Milton, who has the like power and charm, because he has the like great style.

Through Milton they may gain it, for, in conclusion, Milton is English; this master in the great style of the ancients is English. Virgil, whom Milton loved and honoured, has at the end of the *Æneid* a noble passage, where Juno, seeing the defeat of Turnus and the Italians imminent, the victory of the Trojan invaders assured, entreats Jupiter that Italy may nevertheless survive and be herself still, may retain her own mind, manners, and language, and not adopt those of the conqueror.

'Sit Latium, sint Albani per secula reges!'

Jupiter grants the prayer; he promises perpetuity and the future to Italy—Italy reinforced by whatever virtue the Trojan race has, but Italy, not Troy. This we may take as a sort of parable suiting ourselves. All the Anglo-Saxon contagion, all the flood of Anglo-Saxon commonness, beats vainly against the great style but cannot shake it, and has to accept its triumph. But it triumphs in Milton, in one of our own race, tongue, faith, and morals. Milton has made the great style no longer an exotic here; he has made it an inmate amongst us, a leaven, and a power. Nevertheless he, and his hearers on both sides of the Atlantic, are English, and will remain English

'Sermonem Ausonii patrium moresque tenebunt.'

The English race overspreads the world, and at the same time the ideal of an excellence the most high and the most rare abides a possession with it for ever.

Essays in Criticism: Second Series

HENRY JAMES SUMNER MAINE

1822–1888

464 *Political Parties*

PARTY has many strong affinities with religion. Its devotees, like those of a religious creed, are apt to substitute the fiction that they have adopted it upon mature deliberation for the fact that they were born into it or stumbled into it. But they are in the highest degree reluctant to come to an open breach with it; they count it shame to speak of its weak points, except to co-religionists; and, whenever it is in serious difficulty, they return to its assistance or rescue. Their relation to those outside the pale—the relation of Whig to Tory, of Conservative to Liberal—is on the whole exceedingly like that of Jew to Samaritan. But the closest resemblances are between party discipline and military discipline; and indeed, historically speaking, Party is probably nothing more than a survival and a consequence of the primitive combativeness of mankind. It is war without the city transmuted into war within the city, but mitigated in the process. The best historical justification which can be offered for it is that it has often enabled portions of the nation, who would otherwise be armed enemies, to be only factions. Party strife, like strife in arms, develops many high but imperfect and one-sided virtues; it is fruitful of self-denial and self-sacrifice. But wherever it prevails, a great part of ordinary morality is unquestionably suspended; a number of maxims are received, which are not those of religion or ethics; and men do acts which, except as between enemies, and except as between political opponents, would be very generally classed as either immoralities or sins.

Popular Government

THOMAS HUGHES

1822–1896

465 *Coaching to School*

TOM stands up on the coach and looks back at his father's figure as long as he can see it, and then the guard, having disposed of his luggage, comes to an anchor, and finishes his buttonings and other preparations for facing the three hours before dawn ; no joke for those who minded cold, on a fast coach in November, in the reign of his late Majesty.

I sometimes think that you boys of this generation are a deal tenderer fellows than we used to be. At any rate you're much more comfortable travellers, for I see every one of you with his rug or plaid, and other dodges for preserving the caloric, and most of you going in those fuzzy, dusty, padded first-class carriages. It was another affair altogether, a dark ride on the top of the Tally-ho, I can tell you, in a tight Petersham coat, and your feet dangling six inches from the floor. Then you knew what cold was, and what it was to be without legs, for not a bit of feeling had you in them after the first half-hour. But it had its pleasures, the old dark ride. First there was the consciousness of silent endurance, so dear to every Englishman,—of standing out against something, and not giving in. Then there was the music of the rattling harness, and the ring of the horses' feet on the hard road, and the glare of the two bright lamps through the steaming hoar frost, over the leaders' ears, into the darkness ; and the cheery toot of the guard's horn, to warn some drowsy pikeman or the ostler at the next change ; and the looking forward to daylight—and last but not least, the delight of returning sensation in your toes.

Then the break of dawn and the sunrise, where can they be ever seen in perfection but from a coach roof? You want motion and change and music to see them in their glory ; not the music of singing-men and singing-women, but good silent music, which sets itself in your own head, the accompaniment of work and getting over the ground.

The Tally-ho is past St. Alban's, and Tom is enjoying the ride, though half-frozen. The guard, who is alone with him on the back of the coach, is silent, but has muffled Tom's feet up in straw, and put the end of an oat-sack over his knees. The darkness has driven him inwards, and he has gone over his little past life, and thought of all his doings and promises, and of his mother and sister, and his father's last words ; and has made fifty good resolutions, and means to bear himself like a brave Brown as he is, though a young one. Then he has been forward into the mysterious boy-future, speculating as to what sort of a place Rugby is, and what they do there, and calling up all the stories of public schools which he has heard from big boys in the holidays. He is chock full of hope and life, notwithstanding the cold, and kicks his heels against the back board, and would like to sing, only he doesn't know how his friend the silent guard might take it. . .

And now they begin to see, and the early life of the country-side comes out ; a market-cart or two, men in smock-frocks going to their work pipe in mouth, a whiff of which is no bad smell this bright morning. The sun gets up, and the mist shines like silver gauze. They pass the hounds jogging along to a distant meet, at the heels of the huntsman's hack, whose face is about the colour of the tails of his old pink, as he exchanges greetings with coachman and guard. Now they pull up at a lodge, and take on board a well-muffled-up sportsman, with his gun-case and carpet-bag. An early up-coach meets them, and the coachmen gather up their horses, and pass one another with the accustomed lift of the elbow, each team doing eleven miles an hour, with a mile to spare behind if necessary. And here comes breakfast.

'Twenty minutes here, gentlemen,' says the coachman, as they pull up at half-past seven at the inn-door.

Tom Brown's Schooldays

466 *The First Bump*

THERE it comes, at last—the flash of the starting gun. Long before the sound of the report can roll up the river, the whole pent-up life and energy which has been held in leash, as it were, for the last six minutes, is let loose, and breaks away with a bound and a dash which he who has felt it will remember for his life, but the like of which, will he ever feel again? The starting ropes drop from the coxswains' hands, the oars flash into the water, and gleam on the feather, the spray flies from them, and the boats leap forward.

The crowds on the bank scatter, and rush along, each keeping as near as it may be to its own boat. Some of the men on the towing path, some on the very edge of, often in, the water—some slightly in advance, as if they could help to drag their boat forward—some behind, where they can see the pulling better—but all at full speed, in wild excitement, and shouting at the top of their voices to those on whom the honour of the college is laid.

'Well pulled, all!' 'Pick her up there, five!' 'You're gaining, every stroke!' 'Time in the bows!' 'Bravo, St. Ambrose!'

On they rushed by the side of the boats, jostling one another, stumbling, struggling, and panting along.

For a quarter of a mile along the bank the glorious maddening hurly-burly extends, and rolls up the side of the stream.

For the first ten strokes Tom was in too great fear

of making a mistake to feel or hear or see. His whole soul was glued to the back of the man before him, his one thought to keep time, and get his strength into the stroke. But as the crew settled down into the well-known long sweep, what we may call consciousness returned; and while every muscle in his body was straining, and his chest heaved, and his heart leapt, every nerve seemed to be gathering new life, and his senses to wake into unwonted acuteness. He caught the scent of the wild thyme in the air, and found room in his brain to wonder how it could have got there, as he had never seen the plant near the river, or smelt it before. Though his eye never wandered from the back of Diogenes, he seemed to see all things at once. The boat behind, which seemed to be gaining—it was all he could do to prevent himself from quickening on the stroke as he fancied that—the eager face of Miller, with his compressed lips, and eyes fixed so earnestly ahead that Tom could almost feel the glance passing over his right shoulder; the flying banks and the shouting crowd; see them with his bodily eyes he could not, but he knew nevertheless that Grey had been upset and nearly rolled down the bank into the water in the first hundred yards, that Jack was bounding and scrambling and barking along by the very edge of the stream; above all, he was just as well aware as if he had been looking at it, of a stalwart form in cap and gown, bounding along, brandishing the long boat-hook, and always keeping just opposite the boat; and amid all the Babel of voices, and the dash and pulse of the stroke, and the labouring of his own breathing, he heard Hardy's voice coming to him again and again, and clear as if there had been no other sound in the air, 'Steady, two! steady! well pulled! steady, steady!' The voice seemed to give him strength and keep him to his work. And what work it was! he had had many a hard pull in the last six weeks, but 'never aught like this.'

But it can't last for ever; men's muscles are not steel, or their lungs bull's hide, and hearts can't go on pumping a hundred miles an hour long without bursting. The St. Ambrose boat is well away from the boat behind, there is a great gap between the accompanying crowds; and now, as they near the Gut, she hangs for a moment or two in hand, though the roar from the bank grows louder and louder, and Tom is already aware that the St. Ambrose crowd is melting into the one ahead of them.

'We must be close to Exeter!' The thought flashes into him, and it would seem into the rest of the crew at the same moment. For, all at once, the strain seems taken off their arms again; there is no more drag; she springs to the stroke as she did at the start; and Miller's face, which had darkened for a few seconds, lightens up again.

Miller's face and attitude are a study. Coiled up into the smallest possible space, his chin almost resting on his knees, his hands close to his sides, firmly but lightly feeling the rudder, as a good horseman handles the mouth of a free-going hunter,—if a coxswain could make a bump by his own exertions, surely he will do it. No sudden jerks of the St. Ambrose rudder will you see, watch as you will from the bank; the boat never hangs through fault of his, but easily and gracefully rounds every point. 'You're gaining! you're gaining!' he now and then mutters to the Captain, who responds with a wink, keeping his breath for other matters. Isn't he grand, the Captain, as he comes forward like lightning, stroke after stroke, his back flat, his teeth set, his whole frame working from the hips with the regularity of a machine? As the space still narrows, the eyes of the fiery little coxswain flash with excitement, but he is far too good a judge to hurry the final effort before the victory is safe in his grasp.

The two crowds are mingled now, and no mistake; and the shouts come all in a heap over the water. 'Now, St. Ambrose, six strokes more.' 'Now, Exeter, you're gaining; pick her up.' 'Mind the Gut, Exeter.' 'Bravo, St. Ambrose.' The water rushes by, still eddying from the strokes of the boat ahead. Tom fancies now he can hear their oars and the workings of their rudder, and the voice of their coxswain. In another moment both boats are in the Gut, and a perfect storm of shouts reaches them from the crowd, as it rushes madly off to the left to the footbridge, amidst which 'Oh, well steered, well steered, St. Ambrose!' is the prevailing cry. Then Miller, motionless as a statue till now, lifts his right hand and whirls the tassel round his head: 'Give it her now, boys; six strokes and we're into them.' Old Jervis lays down that great broad back, and lashes his oar through the water with the might of a giant, the crew catch him up in another stroke, the tight new boat answers to the spurt, and Tom feels a little shock behind him, and then a grating sound, as Miller shouts, 'Unship oars bow and three,' and the nose of the St. Ambrose boat glides quietly up the side of the Exeter, till it touches their stroke oar.

Tom Brown at Oxford

COVENTRY PATMORE

1823–1896

467 *Noble Manners*

THERE is nothing comparable for moral force to the charm of truly noble manners. The mind is, in comparison, only slightly and transiently impressed by heroic actions, for these are felt to be but uncertain signs of a heroic soul; nothing less than a series of them, more sustained and varied than circumstances are ever found to demand, could assure us, with the infallible certainty required for the highest power of example, that they were the faithful reflex of the ordinary spirit of the actor. The spectacle of patient suffering, though not so striking, is morally more impressive; for we know that

> Action is transitory—a step, a blow,
> The motion of a muscle this way or that—
> Tis done; and, in the after vacancy,
> We wonder at ourselves, like men betrayed;
> Suffering is permanent, obscure, and dark,
> And has the nature of infinity.

The mind, however, has a very natural repugnance to the sustained contemplation of this species of example, and is much more willingly persuaded by a spectacle precisely the reverse—namely, that of goodness actually upon the earth triumphant, and bearing in its ordinary demeanour, under whatever circumstances, the lovely stamp of obedience to that highest and most rarely-fulfilled commandment, 'Rejoice evermore.' Unlike action or suffering, such obedience is not so much the way to heaven, as a picture, say rather a part, of heaven itself; and truly beautiful manners will be found upon inspection to involve a continual and visible compliance with that apostolical injunction. A right obedience of this kind must be the crown and completion of all lower kinds of obedience. It is not compatible with the bitter humiliations of the habit of any actual sin; it excludes selfishness, since the condition of joy, as distinguished from pleasure, is generosity, and a soul in the practice of going forth from itself; it is no sensual partiality for the 'bright side' of things, no unholy repugnance to the consideration of sorrow; but a habit of lifting life to a height at which all sides of it become bright, and all moral difficulties intelligible: in action it is a salubrity about which doctors will not disagree; in the countenance it is a loveliness which connoisseurs will not dispute; in the demeanour it is a lofty gentleness, which, without pride, patronises all the world, and which, without omitting the minutest temporal obligations or amenities, does everything with an air of immortality.

Principle in Art

FRANCIS PARKMAN

1823–1893

468 *The Heights of Abraham*

FOR full two hours the procession of boats, borne on the current, steered silently down the St. Lawrence. The stars were visible, but the night was moonless and sufficiently dark. The General was in one of the foremost boats, and near him was a young midshipman, John Robison, afterwards professor of natural philosophy in the University of Edinburgh. He used to tell in his later life how Wolfe, with a low voice, repeated Gray's *Elegy in a Country Churchyard* to the officers about him. Probably it was to relieve the intense strain of his thoughts. Among the rest was the verse which his own fate was soon to illustrate—

'The paths of glory lead but to the grave.'

'Gentlemen,' he said, as his recital ended, 'I would rather have written those lines than take Quebec.' None were there to tell him that the hero is greater than the poet.

As they neared their destination, the tide bore them in towards the shore, and the mighty wall of rock and forest towered in darkness on their left. The dead stillness was suddenly broken by the sharp *Qui vive!* of a French sentry, invisible in the thick gloom. *France!* answered a Highland officer of Fraser's regiment from one of the boats of the light infantry. He had served in Holland, and spoke French fluently.

À quel régiment?

De la Reine, replied the Highlander. He knew that a part of that corps was with Bougainville. The sentry, expecting the convoy of provisions, was satisfied, and did not ask for the password.

Soon after, the foremost boats were passing the heights of Samos, when another sentry challenged them, and they could see him through the darkness running down to the edge of the water, within range of a pistol-shot. In answer to his questions, the same officer replied, in French: 'Provision-boats. Don't make a noise; the English will hear us.' In fact, the sloop-of-war 'Hunter' was anchored in the stream not far off. This time, again, the sentry let them pass. In a few moments they rounded the headland above the Anse du Foulon. There was no sentry there. The strong current swept the boats of the light infantry a little below the intended landing-place. They disembarked on a narrow strand at the foot of heights as steep as a hill covered with trees can be. The twenty-four volunteers led the way, climbing with what silence they might, closely followed by a much larger body. When they reached the top they saw in the dim light a cluster of tents at a short distance, and immediately made a dash at them. Vergor leaped from bed and tried to run off, but was shot in the heel and captured. His men, taken by surprise, made little resistance. One or two were caught, and the rest fled.

The main body of troops waited in their boats by the edge of the strand. The heights near by were cleft by a great ravine choked with forest trees; and in its depths ran a little brook called Ruisseau St.-Denis, which, swollen by the late rains, fell plashing in the stillness over a rock. Other than this no sound could reach the strained ear of Wolfe but the gurgle of the tide and the cautious climbing of his advance-parties as they mounted the steeps at some little distance from where he sat listening. At length from the top came a sound of musket-shots, followed by loud huzzas, and he knew that his men were masters of the position. The word was given; the troops leaped from the boats and scaled the heights, some here, some there, clutching at trees and bushes, their muskets slung at their backs. Tradition still points out the place, near the mouth of the ravine, where the foremost reached the top. Wolfe said to an officer near him: 'You can try it, but I don't think you'll get up.' He himself, however, found strength to drag himself up with the rest. The narrow slanting path on the face of the heights had been made impassable by trenches and abattis; but all obstructions were soon cleared away, and then the descent was easy. In the gray of the morning the long file of red-coated soldiers moved quickly upward, and formed in order on the plateau above.

Montcalm and Wolfe

HENRY WALTER BATES

1825–1892

469 *A Naturalist's Day in the Tropics*

WE used to rise soon after dawn, when Isidoro would go down to the city, after supplying us with a cup of coffee, to purchase the fresh provisions for the day. The two hours before breakfast were devoted to ornithology. At that early period of the day the sky was invariably cloudless (the thermometer marking 72° or 73° Fahr.); the heavy dew or the previous night's rain, which lay on the moist foliage, becoming quickly dissipated by the glowing sun, which, rising straight out of the east, mounted rapidly towards the zenith. All nature was fresh, new leaf and flower-buds expanding rapidly. Some mornings a single tree would appear in flower amidst what was the preceding evening a uniform green mass of forest—a dome of blossom suddenly created as if by magic. The birds were all active; from the wild-fruit trees, not far off, we often heard the shrill yelping of the Toucans (*Rhamphastos vitellinus*). Small flocks of parrots flew over on most mornings, at a great height, appearing in distinct relief against the blue sky, always two by two, chattering to each other, the pairs being separated by regular intervals; their bright colours, however, were not apparent at that height. After breakfast we devoted the hours from 10 a.m. to 2 or 3 p.m. to entomology; the best time for insects in the forest being a little before the greatest heat of the day. We did not find them at all numerous, although of great variety as to species. . . After several years' observation, I came to the conclusion that the increase of these creatures was checked by the close persecution of insectivorous animals, which are excessively numerous in this country. The check operates at all periods of life—on the eggs, the larvae, and the perfect insects.

The heat increased rapidly towards two o'clock (92° and 93° Fahr.), by which time every voice of bird or mammal was hushed; only in the trees was heard at intervals the harsh whirr of a cicada. The leaves, which were so moist and fresh in early morning, now became lax and drooping; the flowers shed their petals. Our neighbours, the Indian and Mulatto inhabitants of the open palm-thatched huts, as we returned home fatigued with our ramble, were either asleep in their hammocks or seated on mats in the shade, too languid even to talk. On most days in June and July a heavy shower would fall some time in the afternoon, producing a most welcome coolness. The approach of the rain-clouds was after a uniform fashion, very interesting to observe. First, the cool sea-breeze, which commenced to blow about 10 o'clock, and which had increased in force with the increasing power of the sun, would flag and finally die away. The heat and electric tension of the atmosphere would then become almost insupportable. Languor and uneasiness would seize on every one; even the denizens of the forest betraying it by their motions.

White clouds would appear in the east and gather into cumuli, with an increasing blackness along their lower portions. The whole eastern horizon would become almost suddenly black, and this would spread upwards, the sun at length becoming obscured. Then the rush of a mighty wind is heard through the forest, swaying the tree-tops ; a vivid flash of lightning bursts forth, then a crash of thunder, and down streams the deluging rain. Such storms soon cease, leaving bluish-black motionless clouds in the sky until night. Meantime all nature is refreshed ; but heaps of flower-petals and fallen leaves are seen under the trees. Towards evening life revives again, and the ringing uproar is resumed from bush and tree. The following morning the sun again rises in a cloudless sky, and so the cycle is completed ; spring, summer, and autumn, as it were, in one tropical day. . .

In Europe, a woodland scene has its spring, its summer, its autumnal, and its winter aspects. In the equatorial forests the aspect is the same or nearly so every day in the year : budding, flowering, fruiting, and leaf-shedding are always going on in one species or other. The activity of birds and insects proceeds without interruption, each species having its own separate times ; the colonies of wasps, for instance, do not die off annually, leaving only the queens, as in cold climates ; but the succession of generations and colonies goes on incessantly. It is never either spring, summer, or autumn, but each day is a combination of all three. With the day and night always of equal length, the atmospheric disturbances of each day neutralising themselves before each succeeding morn ; with the sun in its course proceeding mid-way across the sky, and the daily temperature the same within two or three degrees throughout the year—how grand in its perfect equilibrium and simplicity is the march of Nature under the equator!

A Naturalist on the Amazons

THOMAS HENRY HUXLEY

1825–1895

470 *A Game of Chess*

SUPPOSE it were perfectly certain that the life and fortune of every one of us would, one day or other, depend upon his winning or losing a game at chess.

Don't you think that we should all consider it to be a primary duty to learn at least the names and the moves of the pieces; to have a notion of a gambit, and a keen eye for all the means of giving and getting out of check? Do you not think that we should look with a disapprobation amounting to scorn, upon the father who allowed his son, or the state which allowed its members, to grow up without knowing a pawn from a knight?

Yet it is a very plain and elementary truth, that the life, the fortune, and the happiness of every one of us, and, more or less, of those who are connected with us, do depend upon our knowing something of the rules of a game infinitely more difficult and complicated than chess. It is a game which has been played for untold ages, every man and woman of us being one of the two players in a game of his or her own. The chess-board is the world, the pieces are the phenomena of the universe, the rules of the game are what we call the laws of Nature.

The player on the other side is hidden from us.

We know that his play is always fair, just, and patient. But also we know, to our cost, that he never overlooks a mistake, or makes the smallest allowance for ignorance. To the man who plays well, the highest stakes are paid, with that sort of overflowing generosity with which the strong shows delight in strength. And one who plays ill is checkmated—without haste, but without remorse.

My metaphor will remind some of you of the famous picture in which Retzsch has depicted Satan playing at chess with man for his soul. Substitute for the mocking fiend in that picture, a calm, strong angel who is playing for love, as we say, and would rather lose than win—and I should accept it as an image of human life.

Lay Sermons

'LORD' GEORGE SANGER

1825–1911

471 *A Fair and a Fire*

I HAVE reason to remember that particular Stepney Fair. . . There was an enormous rope factory on one side of the green, an establishment that extended over a piece of ground running quite into the country, and on the last day of the fair this was suddenly discovered to be on fire. It was just towards dusk when the flames were first seen, and in a very little time they had made tremendous headway. The excitement was intense, the people flocking from the fair to witness the fire and to render what assistance they could. With the pleasure seekers went the showmen, one and all, to give what aid was possible, and an extraordinary scene was the result. There was no time to take off dresses, and amid the flying sparks, and in and about the burning buildings, could be seen clowns, knights in armour, Indian chiefs, jugglers in tights and spangles, rope walkers in fleshings—in fact, all the characters of the fair in full dress, striving with might and main to combat the flames. Here would be seen clown, pantaloon, harlequin, and demon passing buckets from hand to hand, while at another point was the feeble parish engine, manned by sweating Saracens, Crusaders, Roman gladiators, and such-like, pumping as though their very lives depended on their exertions. Up on the building, running along beams with crowbars and hatchets, were the tight-rope walkers, vaulters, and acrobats, whose training enabled them to go where no other persons could possibly have clambered, breaking away roofs and walls to prevent the spread of the fire. Over all was the glow of the flames lighting up the faces of the dense multitude that surged and swung and shouted its approval of the efforts of the motley-garbed show-folk to check the advance of the enemy.

It was a picture that would have delighted a painter of weird scenes, though he might have despaired of ever putting its wavering lights and shadows and the strange characters glancing through them effectively on canvas. I know it impressed itself indelibly on my memory, as in my Hamlet dress I took my share of work with the others in checking the roaring flames. At last our efforts told, and we did check them, but not until enormous damage had been done. A big part of the works was, however, saved, and so pleased were the authorities at the spirit the showmen had exhibited that they gave orders for the fair to continue another day to help make up any losses we had sustained through leaving our booths to become fire fighters.

We did rare business on the extra day, for the story of the fire had spread, and the public came in crowds to view the scene and to patronize the showmen who had worked so well.

Seventy Years of a Showman's Life

WALTER BAGEHOT

1826–1877

472 *The Old Private Banker*

I CAN imagine nothing better in theory or more successful in practice than private banks as they were in the beginning. A man of known wealth, known integrity, and known ability is largely entrusted with the money of his neighbours. The confidence is strictly personal. His neighbours know him, and trust him because they know him. They see daily his manner of life, and judge from it that their confidence is deserved. In rural districts, and in former times, it was difficult for a man to ruin himself except at the place in which he lived; for the most part he spent his money there, and speculated there if he speculated at all. Those who lived there also would soon see if he was acting in a manner to shake their confidence. Even in large cities, as cities then were, it was possible for most persons to ascertain with fair certainty the real position of conspicuous persons, and to learn all which was material in fixing their credit. Accordingly the bankers who for a long series of years passed successfully this strict and continual investigation, became very wealthy and very powerful.

The name 'London Banker' had especially a charmed value. He was supposed to represent, and often did represent, a certain union of pecuniary sagacity and educated refinement which was scarcely to be found in any other part of society. In a time when the trading classes were much ruder than they now are, many private bankers possessed a variety of knowledge and a delicacy of attainment which would even now be very rare. Such a position is indeed singularly favourable. The calling is hereditary; the credit of the bank descends from father to son: this inherited wealth soon brings inherited refinement. Banking is a watchful, but not a laborious trade. A banker, even in large business, can feel pretty sure that all his transactions are sound, and yet have much spare mind. A certain part of his time, and a considerable part of his thoughts, he can readily devote to other pursuits. And a London banker can also have the most intellectual society in the world if he chooses it. There has probably very rarely ever been so happy a position as that of a London private banker; and never perhaps a happier.

Lombard Street

GEORGE MEREDITH

1828–1909

473 *Diversion on a Penny Whistle*

AWAY with Systems! Away with a corrupt World! Let us breathe the air of the Enchanted Island.

Golden lie the meadows: golden run the streams; red gold is on the pine-stems. The sun is coming down to earth, and walks the fields and the waters.

The sun is coming down to earth, and the fields and the waters shout to him golden shouts. He comes, and his heralds run before him, and touch the leaves of oaks and planes and beeches lucid green, and the pine-stems redder gold; leaving brightest footprints upon thickly-weeded banks, where the foxglove's last upper-bells incline, and bramble-shoots wander amid moist rich herbage. The plumes of the woodland are alight; and beyond them, over the open, 'tis a race with the long-thrown shadows; a race across the heaths and up the hills, till, at the farthest bourne of mounted eastern cloud, the heralds of the sun lay rosy fingers and rest.

Sweet are the shy recesses of the woodland. The ray treads softly there. A film athwart the pathway quivers many-hued against purple shade fragrant with warm pines, deep moss-beds, feathery ferns. The little brown squirrel drops tail, and leaps; the inmost bird is startled to a chance tuneless note. From silence into silence things move.

Peeps of the revelling splendour above and around enliven the conscious full heart within. The flaming West, the crimson heights, shower their glories through voluminous leafage. But these are bowers where deep bliss dwells, imperial joy, that owes no fealty to yonder glories, in which the young lamb gambols and the spirits of men are glad. Descend, great Radiance! embrace creation with beneficent fire, and pass from us! You and the vice-regal light that succeeds to you, and all heavenly pageants, are the ministers and the slaves of the throbbing content within.

For this is the home of the enchantment. Here, secluded from vexed shores, the prince and princess of the island meet: here like darkling nightingales they sit, and into eyes and ears and hands pour endless ever-fresh treasures of their souls.

Roll on, grinding wheels of the world: cries of ships going down in a calm, groans of a System which will not know its rightful hour of exultation, complain to the universe. You are not heard here.

He calls her by her name, Lucy: and she, blushing at her great boldness, has called him by his, Richard. Those two names are the key-notes of the wonderful harmonies the angels sing aloft.

'Lucy! my beloved!'

'O Richard!'

Out in the world there, on the skirts of the woodland, a sheep-boy pipes to meditative eve on a penny whistle.

Love's musical instrument is as old, and as poor: it has but two stops; and yet, you see, the cunning musician does thus much with it!

The Ordeal of Richard Feverel

474 *Clara Middleton*

SHE had the mouth that smiles in repose. The lips met full on the centre of the bow and thinned along to a lifting dimple; the eyelids also lifted slightly at the outer corners and seemed, like the lip into the limpid cheek, quickening up the temples, as with a run of light, or the ascension indicated off a shoot of colour. Her features were playfellows of one another, none of them pretending to rigid correctness, nor the nose to the ordinary dignity of governess among merry girls, despite which the nose was of a fair design, not acutely interrogative or inviting to gambols. Aspens imaged in water, waiting for the breeze, would offer a susceptible lover some suggestion of her face: a pure smooth-white face, tenderly flushed in the cheeks, where the gentle dints were faintly intermelting even during quietness. Her eyes were brown, set well between mild lids, often shadowed, not unwakeful. Her hair of lighter brown, swelling above her temples on the sweep to the knot, imposed the triangle of the fabulous wild woodland visage from brow to mouth and chin, evidently in agreement with her taste; and the triangle suited her; but her face was not significant of a tameless wildness or of weakness; her equable shut mouth threw its long curve to guard the small round chin from that effect; her eyes wavered only in humour, they were steady when thoughtfulness was awakened; and at such seasons the build of her winter-beechwood hair lost the touch of nymph-like and whimsical, and strangely, by mere outline, added to her appearance of studious concentration. Observe the hawk on stretched wings over the prey he spies, for an idea of this change in the look of a young lady whom Vernon Whitford could liken to the Mountain Echo, and Mrs. Mountstuart Jenkinson pronounced to be 'a dainty rogue in porcelain.'

The Egoist

475 *Dawn in the Mountains*

BEYOND the firwood light was visibly the dawn's. Half-way down the ravines it resembled the light cast off a torrent water. It lay on the grass like a sheet of unreflecting steel, and was a face without a smile above. Their childhood ran along the tracks to the forest by the light, which was neither dim nor cold, but grave; presenting tree and shrub and dwarf growth and grass austerely, not deepening or confusing them. They wound their way by borders of crag, seeing in a dell below the mouth of the idle mine begirt with weedy and shrub-hung rock, a dripping semicircle. Farther up they came on the flat juniper and crossed a wet ground-thicket of whortleberry: their feet were in the moist moss among sprigs of heath; and a great fir tree stretched his length, a peeled multitude of his dead fellows leaned and stood upright in the midst of scattered fire-stained members, and through their skeleton limbs the sheer precipice of slate-rock of the bulk across the chasm, nursery of hawk and eagle, wore a thin blue tinge, the sign of warmer light abroad.

'This way, my brother!' cried Carinthia, shuddering at a path he was about to follow.

Dawn in the mountain-land is a meeting of many friends. The pinnacle, the forest-head, the latschen-tufted mound, rock-bastion and defiant cliff and giant of the triple peak, were in view, clearly lined for a common recognition, but all were figures of solid gloom, unfeatured and bloomless. Another minute and they had flung off their mail and changed to various indented, intricate, succinct in ridge, scar and channel; and they had all a look of watchfulness that made them one company. The smell of rock-waters and roots of herb and moss grew keen; air became a wine that raised the breast high to breathe it; an uplifting coolness pervaded the heights. What wonder that the mountain-bred girl should let fly her voice. The natural carol woke an echo. She did not repeat it.

'And we will not forget our home, Chillon,' she said, touching him gently to comfort some saddened feeling.

The plumes of cloud now slowly entered into the lofty arch of dawn and melted from brown to purple-black. The upper sky swam with violet; and in a moment each stray cloud-feather was edged with rose, and then suffused. It seemed that the heights fronted East to eye the interflooding of colours, and it was imaginable that all turned to the giant whose forehead first kindled to the sun: a greeting of god and king.

On the morning of a farewell we fluctuate sharply between the very distant and the close and homely: and even in memory the fluctuation occurs, the grander scene casting us back on the modestly nestling, and that, when it has refreshed us, conjuring imagination to embrace the splendour and wonder. But the wrench of an immediate division from what we love makes the things within reach the dearest, we put out our hands for them, as violently-parted lovers do, though the soul in days to come would know a craving, and imagination flap a leaden wing, if we had not looked beyond them.

'Shall we go down?' said Carinthia, for she knew a little cascade near the house, showering on rock and fern, and longed to have it round her.

They descended, Chillon saying that they would soon have the mists rising, and must not delay to start on their journey.

The armies of the young sunrise in mountain-lands neighbouring the plains, vast shadows, were marching over woods and meads, black against the edge of golden; and great heights were cut with them, and bounding waters took the leap in a silvery radiance to gloom; the bright and dark-banded valleys were like night and morning taking hands down the sweep of their rivers. Immense was the range of vision scudding the peaks and over the illimitable Eastward plains flat to the very East and sources of the sun.

The Amazing Marriage

DANTE GABRIEL ROSSETTI

1828–1882

476 *Dante's Dream*

AT the first, it seemed to me that I saw certain faces of women with their hair loosened, which called out to me, 'Thou shalt surely die'; after the which, other terrible and unknown appearances said unto me, 'Thou art dead.' At length, as my phantasy held on in its wanderings, I came to be I knew not where, and to behold a throng of dishevelled ladies wonderfully sad, who kept going hither and thither weeping. Then the sun went out, so that the stars showed themselves, and they were of such a colour that I knew they must be weeping: and it seemed to me that the birds fell dead out of the sky, and that there were great earthquakes. With that, while I wondered in my trance, and was filled with a grievous fear, I conceived that a certain friend came unto me and said: 'Hast thou not heard? She that was thine excellent lady hath been taken out of life.' Then I began to weep very piteously; and not only in mine imagination, but with mine eyes, which were wet with tears. And I seemed to look towards Heaven, and to behold a multitude of angels who were returning upwards, having before them an exceedingly white cloud: and these angels were singing together gloriously, and the words of their song were these: '*Osanna in excelsis*'; and there was no more that I heard. Then my heart that was so full of love said unto me: 'It is true that our lady lieth dead'; and it seemed to me that I went to look upon the body wherein that blessed and most noble spirit had had its abiding-place. And so strong was this idle imagining, that it made me to behold my lady in death, whose head certain ladies seemed to be covering with a white veil; and who was so humble of her aspect that it was as though she had said, 'I have attained to look on the beginning of peace'.

Early Italian Poets

ALEXANDER SMITH

1830–1867

477 *Dreamthorp*

THE village stands far inland; and the streams that trot through the soft green valleys all about have as little knowledge of the sea, as the three-years' child of the storms and passions of manhood. The surrounding country is smooth and green, full of undulations; and pleasant country roads strike through it in every direction, bound for distant towns and villages, yet in no hurry to reach them. On these roads the lark in summer is continually heard; nests are plentiful in the hedges and dry ditches; and on the grassy banks, and at the feet of the bowed dikes, the blue-eyed speedwell smiles its benison on the passing wayfarer. On these roads you may walk for a year and encounter nothing more remarkable than the country cart, troops of tawny children from the woods, laden with primroses, and at long intervals—for people in this district live to a ripe age—a black funeral creeping in from some remote hamlet ; and to this last the people reverently doff their hats and stand aside. Death does not walk about here often, but when he does, he receives as much respect as the squire himself. Everything round one is unhurried, quiet, moss-grown, and orderly. Season follows in the track of season, and one year can hardly be distinguished from another. Time should be measured here by the silent dial, rather than by the ticking clock, or by the chimes of the church. Dreamthorp can boast of a respectable antiquity, and in it the trade of the builder is unknown. Ever since I remember, not a single stone has been laid on the top of another. . .

The houses are old, and remote dates may yet be deciphered on the stones above the doors ; the apple-trees are mossed and ancient ; countless generations of sparrows have bred in the thatched roofs, and thereon have chirped out their lives. In every room of the place men have been born, men have died. On Dreamthorp centuries have fallen, and have left no more trace than have last winter's snowflakes. This commonplace sequence and flowing on of life is immeasurably affecting. That winter morning when Charles lost his head in front of the banqueting-hall of his own palace, the icicles hung from the eaves of the houses here, and the clown kicked the snowballs from his clouted shoon, and thought but of his supper when, at three o'clock, the red sun set in the purple mist. On that Sunday in June while Waterloo was going on, the gossips, after morning service, stood on the country roads discussing agricultural prospects, without the slightest suspicion that the day passing over their heads would be a famous one in the calendar. Battles have been fought, kings have died, history has transacted itself; but, all unheeding and untouched, Dreamthorp has watched apple-trees redden, and wheat ripen, and smoked its pipe, and quaffed its mug of beer, and rejoiced over its newborn children, and with proper solemnity carried its dead to the churchyard.

Dreamthorp

HENRY KINGSLEY

1830–1876

478 *The Children at a Wedding*

I WAITED till the procession had gone in, and then I found that the tail of it was composed of Gus, Flora, and Archy, with their nurse. If a bachelor is worth his salt, he will make himself useful. I saw that nurse was in distress and anxious, so I stayed with her.

Archy was really as good as gold till he met with his accident. He walked up the steps with nurse as quiet as possible. But even at first I began to get anxious about Gus and Flora. They were excited. Gus wouldn't walk up the steps; but he put his two heels together, and jumped up them one at a time, and Flora walked backwards, looking at him sarcastically. At the top step but one Gus stumbled; whereupon Flora said, 'Goozlemy, goozlemy, goozlemy.'

And Gus said, 'You wait a minute, my lady, till we get into church,' after which awful speech I felt as if I was smoking in a powder magazine.

I was put into a pew with Gus, and Flora, and Archy. Nurse, in her modesty, went into the pew behind us.

I am sorry to say that these dear children, with whom I had no previous acquaintance, were very naughty.

The ceremony began by Archy getting too near the edge of his hassock, falling off, pitching against the pew door, bursting it open, and flying out among the free seats, head foremost. Nurse, a nimble and dexterous woman, dashed out, and caught him up, and actually got him out of the church door before he had time to fetch his breath for a scream. Gus and Flora were left alone with me.

Flora had a great scarlet and gold church service. As soon as she opened it, she disconcerted me by saying aloud, to an imaginary female friend, 'My dear, there is going to be a collection; and I have left my purse on the piano.'

At this time, also, Gus, seeing that the business was well begun, removed to the further end of the pew, sat down on the hassock, and took from his trousers' pocket a large tin trumpet.

I broke out all over in a cold perspiration as I looked at him. He saw my distress, and putting it to his lips, puffed out his cheeks. Flora administered comfort to me. She said, 'You are looking at that foolish boy. Perhaps he won't blow it, after all. He mayn't if you don't look at him. At all events, he probably won't blow it till the organ begins; and then it won't matter so much.' . .

I wish those dear children (not meaning them any harm) had been, to put it mildly, at play on the village green, that blessed day.

When I looked at Gus again, he was still on the hassock, threatening propriety with his trumpet. I hoped for the best. Flora had her prayer-book open, and was playing the piano on each side of it, with her fingers. After a time she looked up at me, and said out loud——

'I suppose you have heard that Archy's cat has kittened?'

I said, 'No.'

'Oh, yes, it has,' she said. 'Archy harnessed it to his meal cart, which turns a mill, and plays music when the wheels go round; and it ran downstairs with the cart; and we heard the music playing as it went; and it kittened in the wood-basket immediately afterwards; and Alwright says she don't wonder at it; and no more do I; and the steward's-room boy is going to drown some. But you mustn't tell Archy, because, if you do, he won't say his prayers; and if he don't say his prayers, he will—etc., etc.' Very emphatically, and in a loud tone of voice.

This was very charming. If I could only answer for Gus, and keep Flora busy, it was wildly possible that we might pull through. If I had not been a madman, I should have noticed that Gus had disappeared.

He had. And the pew door had never opened, and I was utterly unconscious. Gus had crawled up, on all fours, under the seat of the pew, until he was opposite the calves of his sister's legs, against which calves, *horresco referens*, he put his trumpet and blew a long shrill blast. Flora behaved very well and courageously. She only gave one long, wild shriek, as from a lunatic in a padded cell at Bedlam, and then, hurling her prayer-book at him, she turned round and tried to kick him in the face.

This was the culminating point of my misfortunes. After this, they behaved better. . . Gus only made an impertinent remark about Flora's garters, and Flora only drew a short, but trenchant, historical parallel between Gus and Judas Iscariot.

Ravenshoe

EDWARD LORD MACNAGHTEN

1830–1913

479 *Gluckstein v. Barnes: Pleading*

THESE gentlemen set about forming a company to pay them a handsome sum for taking off their hands a property which they had contracted to buy with that end in view. They bring the company into existence by means of the usual machinery. They appoint themselves sole guardians and protectors of this creature of theirs, half-fledged and just struggling into life, bound hand and foot while yet unborn by contracts tending to their private advantage, and so fashioned by its makers that it could only act by their hands and only see through their eyes. They issue a prospectus representing that they had agreed to purchase the property for a sum largely in excess of the amount which they had, in fact, to pay. On the faith of this prospectus they collect subscriptions from a confiding and credulous public. And then comes the last act. Secretly, and therefore dishonestly, they put into their own pockets the difference between the real and the pretended price. After a brief career the company is ordered to be wound up. In the course of the liquidation the trick is discovered. Mr. Gluckstein is called upon to make good a portion of the sum which he and his associates had misappropriated. Why Mr. Gluckstein alone was selected for attack I do not know any more than I know why he was only asked to pay back a fraction of the money improperly withdrawn from the coffers of the company. . . In these two matters Mr. Gluckstein has been in my opinion extremely fortunate. But he complains that he may have a difficulty in recovering from his co-directors their share of the spoil, and he asks that the official liquidator may proceed against his associates before calling upon him to make good the whole amount with which he has been charged. My Lords, there may be occasions in which that would be a proper course to take. But I cannot think that this is a case in which any indulgence ought to be shown to Mr. Gluckstein. He may or may not be able to recover a contribution from those who joined with him in defrauding the company. He can bring an action at law if he likes. If he hesitates to take that course or takes it and fails, then his only remedy lies in an appeal to that sense of honour which is popularly supposed to exist among robbers of a humbler type.

Law Reports

MARK RUTHERFORD (WILLIAM HALE WHITE)

1831–1913

480 *Injustice*

A NOTION, self-begotten in me, of the limitations of my friend is answerable for the barrenness of my intercourse with him. I set him down as hard; I speak to him as if he were hard and from that which is hard in myself. Naturally I evoke only that which is hard, although there may be fountains of tenderness in him of which I am altogether unaware. It is far better in conversation not to regulate it according to supposed capacities or tempers, which are generally those of some fictitious being, but to be simply ourselves. We shall often find unexpected and welcome response.

Our estimates of persons, unless they are frequently revived by personal intercourse, are apt to alter insensibly and to become untrue. They acquire increased definiteness but they lose in comprehensiveness.

Especially is this true of those who are dead. If I do not read a great author for some time my mental abstract of him becomes summary and false. I turn to him again, all summary judgments upon him become impossible, and he partakes of infinitude. Writers, and people who are in society and talk much are apt to be satisfied with an algebraic symbol for a man of note, and their work is done not with him but with *x*.

Pages from a Journal

481 *A Londoner's Holiday*

ONE Sunday we determined upon a holiday. It was a bold adventure for us, but we had made up our minds. There was an excursion train to Hastings, and accordingly Ellen, Marie, and myself were at London Bridge Station early in the morning. It was a lovely summer's day in mid-July. The journey down was uncomfortable enough in consequence of the heat and dust, but we heeded neither one nor the other in the hope of seeing the sea. We reached Hastings at about eleven o'clock, and strolled westwards towards Bexhill. Our pleasure was exquisite. Who can tell, save the imprisoned Londoner, the joy of walking on the clean sea-sand! What a delight that was, to say nothing of the beauty of the scenery! To be free of the litter and filth of a London suburb, of its broken hedges, its brickbats, its torn advertisements, its worn and trampled grass in fields half given over to the speculative builder: in place of this, to tread the immaculate shore over which breathed a wind not charged with soot; to replace the dull, shrouding obscurity of the smoke by a distance so distinct that the masts of the ships whose hulls were buried below the horizon were visible—all this was perfect bliss. It was not very poetic bliss, perhaps; but nevertheless it is a fact that the cleanness of the sea and the sea air was as attractive to us as any of the sea attributes. We had a wonderful time. Only in the country is it possible to note the change of morning into mid-day, of mid-day into afternoon, and of afternoon into evening; and it is only in the country, therefore, that a day seems stretched out into its proper length. We had brought all our food with us, and sat upon the shore in the shadow of a piece of the cliff. A row of heavy white clouds lay along the horizon almost unchangeable and immovable, with their summit-lines and the part of the mass just below them steeped in sunlight. The level opaline water differed only from a floor by a scarcely perceptible heaving motion, which broke into the faintest of ripples at our feet. So still was the great ocean, so quietly did everything lie in it, that the wavelets which licked the beach were as pure and bright as if they were a part of the mid-ocean depths. About a mile from us, at one o'clock, a long row of porpoises appeared, showing themselves in graceful curves for half-an-hour or so, till they went out farther to sea off Fairlight. Some fishing-boats were becalmed just in front of us. Their shadows slept, or almost slept, upon the water, a gentle quivering alone showing that it was not complete sleep, or if sleep, that it was sleep with dreams. The intensity of the sunlight sharpened the outlines of every little piece of rock, and of the pebbles, in a manner which seemed supernatural to us Londoners. In London we get the heat of the sun, but not his light, and the separation of individual parts into such vivid isolation was so surprising that even Marie noticed it, and said it 'all seemed as if she were looking through a glass'. It was perfect—perfect in its beauty—and perfect because, from the sun in the heavens down to the fly with burnished wings on the hot rock, there was nothing out of harmony. Everything breathed one spirit. Marie played near us; Ellen and I sat still, doing nothing. We wanted nothing, we had nothing to achieve; there were no curiosities to be seen, there was no particular place to be reached, no 'plan of operations', and London was forgotten for the time. It lay behind us in the north-west, and the cliff was at the back of us shutting out all thought of it. No reminiscences and no anticipations disturbed us; the present was sufficient, and occupied us totally.

Mark Rutherford's Deliverance

LEONARD LORD COURTNEY OF PENWITH

1832–1918

482 *Justice*

IF we could get rid of injustice! How shall we labour to bring about that great result? How shall we get the rulers of nations to cease to aspire to obtain power over others; how shall we get the members of nations to be just to one another, so that they shall not even tolerate the thought of wrong-doing? How shall we get amongst the nations what we have succeeded in obtaining within nations—a reference to law instead of to force, an appeal to the privileges and powers of society for enforcing justice, instead of a resort on one's own account to the force which one may command to compel justice? How, I say, can we hope to bring about this great result?

After all, the machinery of justice involves this fundamental notion, that when two persons are in disagreement there is a tribunal to which they can appeal. In a perfect form that tribunal is always in action, and each of the litigants can compel the other to come before it. Then you have established a law which does away with private violence, and if you got that among the nations you would have a law that did away with national violence.

The first thing to which I would direct your attention is to use all your powers, all your opportunities to develop the strength, the scope, the purity of international law. Do as much as you can as individuals, influence your rulers as much as you can as citizens of free communities, to develop, strengthen, and purify international law—international law which rises above the separate nations, just as the municipal law of a community rises above its separate citizens.

The temptation to lust and rapine of unchecked human nature is under coercion in every society; and lovers of the larger civilization of the world must rejoice in the restraint of temptation which is found in compacts of international peace.

Without justice we can have no guarantee of permanent peace. With justice the peace of the world is unassailable.

Addresses 1908–1909

JOSEPH HENRY SHORTHOUSE

1834–1903

483 *The Pavilion in the Wood*

PRESENTLY, in the brilliant moonlight, they saw the pointed roofs of the pavilion on a little rising-ground, with the forest trees coming up closely to the walls. The moon was now high in the heavens, and it was as light as day. The upper windows of the pavilion were open, and within it lights were burning. The door was opened to them before they knocked, and the keeper of the pavilion came to meet them, accompanied by a boy who took the horses. The man showed no surprise at their coming, only saying some servants of the Duchess had been there a few hours previously, and had prepared a repast in the dining-room, forewarning him that he should expect visitors. He accompanied them upstairs, for they saw nothing of the other inmates of the place. The rooms were arranged with a sort of rustic luxury, and were evidently intended for repose during the heat of the day. A plentiful and delicate collation was spread on one of the tables, with abundance of fruit and wine. The place looked like the magic creation of an enchanter's wand, raised for purposes of evil from the unhealthy marsh, and ready to sink again, when that malefic purpose was fulfilled, into the weird depths from which it rose.

The old man showed them the other rooms of the apartment, and left them. At the door he turned back and said,—

'I should not advise the lady to sleep here; the miasma from the forest is very fatal to such as are not used to it.'

Inglesant looked at him, but could not perceive that he intended his word to have any deeper meaning than the obvious one. He said,—

'We shall stay only an hour or two; let the horses be ready to go on.'

The man left them, and they sat down at the table. . . The night air was heavy and close, not a breath of wind stirred the lights, though every window was thrown open, and the shutters that closed the loggia outside were drawn back. In the brilliant moonlight every leaf of the great forest shone with an unnatural distinctness, which, set in a perfect silence, became terrible to see. The sylvan arcades seemed like a painted scene-piece upon a Satanic stage, supernaturally alight to further deeds of sin, and silent and unpeopled, lest the wrong should be interrupted or checked. . . The two found their eyes drawn with a kind of fascination to this strange sight, and Inglesant arose and closed the shutters before the nearest casement.

They felt more at ease when the mysterious forest was shut out. But Lauretta was silent and troubled, and Inglesant's efforts to cheer and enliven her were not successful. . . At last she refused to drink, and rising up suddenly, she exclaimed,—

'Oh, it is terribly hot. I cannot bear it. I wish we had not come.'

She wandered from the room in which they sat, through the curtained doorway into the next, which was furnished with couches, and sank down on one of them. Inglesant followed her, and, as if the heat felt stifling also to him, went out upon the open verandah...

He gazed another moment over the illumined forest, which seemed transfigured in the moonlight and the stillness into an unreal landscape of the dead. The poisonous mists crept over the tops of the cork trees, and flitted across the long vistas in spectral forms, cowled and shrouded for the grave. Beneath the gloom indistinct figures seemed to glide,—the personation of the miasma that made the place so fatal to human life.

He turned to enter the room, but even as he turned a sudden change came over the scene. The deadly glamour of the moonlight faded suddenly, a calm pale solemn light settled over the forest, the distant line of hills shone out distinct and clear, the evil mystery of the place departed whence it came, a fresh and cooling breeze sprang up and passed through the rustling wood, breathing pureness and life. The dayspring was at hand in the eastern sky.

The rustling breeze was like a whisper from heaven that reminded him of his better self. It would seem that hell overdid it; the very stillness for miles around, the almost concerted plan, sent flashing through his brain the remembrance of another house, equally guarded for a like purpose—a house at Newnham near Oxford, into which years ago he had himself forced his way to render help in such a case as this. Here was the same thing happening over again with the actors changed; was it possible that such a change had been wrought in him? The long past life of those days rushed into his mind; the sacramental Sundays, the repeated vows, the light of heaven in the soul, the kneeling forms in Little Gidding Chapel, the face of Mary Collet, the loveliness that blessed the earth where she walked, her deathbed, and her dying words. What so rarely happens happened here. The revulsion of feeling, the rush of recollection and association, was too powerful for the flesh. . . But the struggle was fierce; he was torn like the demon-haunted child in the gospel story; but, as in that story, the demon was expelled.

He came back into the room. Lauretta lay upon a couch with rich drapery and cushions. . . As he entered she raised her head from her hands, and looked at him with a strange, apprehensive, expectant gaze. He remained for a moment silent, his face very pale; then he said, slowly and uncertainly, like a man speaking in a dream,—

'The fatal miasma is rising from the plain. Lauretta, this place is safe for neither of us, we had better go on.'

John Inglesant

WILLIAM MORRIS

1834–1896

484 *Kelmscott*

IN a few minutes we had passed through a deep eddying pool into the sharp stream that ran from the ford, and beached our craft on a tiny strand of limestone-gravel, and stepped ashore into the arms of our up-river friends, our journey done.

I disentangled myself from the merry throng, and mounting on the cart-road that ran along the river some feet above the water, I looked round about me. The river came down through a wide meadow on my left, which was grey now with the ripened seeding grasses; the gleaming water was lost presently by a turn of the bank, but over the meadow I could see the mingled gables of a building where I knew the lock must be, and which now seemed to combine a mill with it. A low wooded ridge bounded the river-plain to the south and south-east, whence we had come, and a few low houses lay about its feet and up its slope. I turned a little to my right, and through the hawthorn sprays and long shoots of the wild roses could see the flat country spreading out far away under the sun of the calm evening, till something that might be called hills with a look of sheep-pastures about them bounded it with a soft blue line. Before me, the elm-boughs still hid most of what houses there might be in this river-side dwelling of men, but to the right of the cart-road a few grey buildings of the simplest kind showed here and there.

There I stood in a dreamy mood, and rubbed my eyes as if I were not wholly awake, and half expected to see the gay-clad company of beautiful men and women change to two or three spindle-legged back-bowed men, and haggard, hollow-eyed, ill-favoured women, who once wore down the soil of this land with their heavy hopeless feet, from day to day, and season to season, and year to year. But no change came as yet, and my heart swelled with joy as I thought of all the beautiful grey villages from the river to the plain and the plain to the uplands, which I could picture to myself so well, all peopled now with this happy and lovely folk, who had cast away riches and attained to wealth. As I stood there Ellen detached herself from our happy friends who still stood on the little strand and came up to me. She took me by the hand, and said softly, 'Take me on to the house at once; we need not wait for the others: I had rather not.'

I had a mind to say that I did not know the way thither, and that the river-side dwellers should lead; but almost without my will my feet moved on along the road they knew. The raised way led us into a little field bounded by a backwater of the river on one side; on the right hand we could see a cluster of small houses and barns, new and old, and before us a grey stone barn and a wall partly overgrown with ivy, over which a few grey gables showed. The village road ended in the shallow of the aforesaid backwater. We crossed the road, and again almost without my will my hand raised the latch of a door in the wall, and we stood presently on a stone path which led up to the old house to which fate in the shape of Dick had so strangely brought me in this new world of men. My companion gave a sigh of pleased surprise and enjoyment; nor did I wonder, for the garden between the wall and the house was redolent of the June flowers, and the roses were rolling over one another with that delicious superabundance of small well-tended gardens which at first sight takes away all thought from the beholder save that of beauty. The blackbirds were singing their loudest, the doves were cooing on the roof-ridge, the rooks in the high elm-trees beyond were garrulous among the young leaves, and the swifts wheeled whining about the gables. And the house itself was a fit guardian for all the beauty of this heart of summer.

News from Nowhere

JAMES ABBOTT McNEILL WHISTLER

1834–1903

485 *Nature and Art*

NATURE contains the elements, in colour and form, of all pictures, as the keyboard contains the notes of all music.

But the artist is born to pick, and choose, and group

with science, these elements, that the result may be beautiful—as the musician gathers his notes, and forms his chords, until he bring forth from chaos glorious harmony.

To say to the painter, that Nature is to be taken as she is, is to say to the player, that he may sit on the piano. . .

The dignity of the snow-capped mountain is lost in distinctness, but the joy of the tourist is to recognize the traveller on the top. The desire to see, for the sake of seeing, is, with the mass, alone the one to be gratified, hence the delight in detail.

And when the evening mist clothes the riverside with poetry, as with a veil, and the poor buildings lose themselves in the dim sky, and the tall chimneys become campanili, and the warehouses are palaces in the night, and the whole city hangs in the heavens, and fairy-land is before us—then the wayfarer hastens home; the working man and the cultured one, the wise man and the one of pleasure, cease to understand, as they have ceased to see, and Nature, who, for once, has sung in tune, sings her exquisite song to the artist alone, her son and her master—her son in that he loves her, her master in that he knows her.

To him her secrets are unfolded, to him her lessons have become gradually clear. He looks at her flower, not with the enlarging lens, that he may gather facts for the botanist, but with the light of the one who sees in her choice selection of brilliant tones and delicate tints, suggestions of future harmonies.

He does not confine himself to purposeless copying, without thought, each blade of grass, as commended by the inconsequent, but, in the long curve of the narrow leaf, corrected by the straight tall stem, he learns how grace is wedded to dignity, how strength enhances sweetness, that elegance shall be the result.

In the citron wing of the pale butterfly, with its dainty spots of orange, he sees before him the stately halls of fair gold, with their slender saffron pillars, and is taught how the delicate drawing high upon the walls shall be traced in tender tones of orpiment, and repeated by the base in notes of graver hue.

In all that is dainty and lovable he finds hints for his own combinations, and *thus* is Nature ever his resource and always at his service, and to him is naught refused.

Through his brain, as through the last alembic, is distilled the refined essence of that thought which began with the Gods, and which they left him to carry out.

Set apart by them to complete their works, he produces that wondrous thing called the masterpiece, which surpasses in perfection all that they have contrived in what is called Nature; and the Gods stand by and marvel, and perceive how far away more beautiful is the Venus of Melos than was their own Eve.

The Gentle Art of Making Enemies

WILLIAM STANLEY JEVONS

1835–1882

486 *True Science*

FROM science, modestly pursued, with a due consciousness of the extreme finitude of our intellectual powers, there can arise only nobler and wider notions of the purpose of Creation. Our philosophy will be an affirmative one, not the false and negative dogmas of Auguste Comte, which have usurped the name, and misrepresented the tendencies of a true *positive philosophy*. True science will not deny the existence of things because they cannot be weighed and measured. It will rather lead us to believe that the wonders and subtleties of possible existence surpass all that our mental powers allow us clearly to perceive. The study of logical and mathematical forms has convinced me that even space itself is no requisite condition of conceivable existence. Everything, we are told by materialists, must be here or there, nearer or further, before or after. I deny this—and point to logical relations as my proof.

. . So far am I from accepting Kant's doctrine that space is a necessary form of thought, that I regard it as an accident, and an impediment to pure logical reasoning. Material existences must exist in space, no doubt, but intellectual existences may be neither in space nor out of space; they may have no relation to space at all, just as space itself has no relation to time. For all that I can see, then, there may be intellectual existences to which both time and space are nullities.

Now among the most unquestionable rules of scientific method is that first law that *whatever phenomenon is, is*. We must ignore no existence whatever; we may variously interpret or explain its meaning and origin, but, if a phenomenon does exist, it demands some kind of explanation. If then there is to be competition for scientific recognition, the world without us must yield to the undoubted existence of the spirit within. Our own hopes and wishes and determinations are the most undoubted phenomena within the sphere of consciousness. If men do act, feel, and live as if they were not merely the brief products of a casual conjunction of atoms, but the instruments of a far-reaching purpose, are we to record all other phenomena and pass over these? We investigate the instincts of the ant and the bee and the beaver, and discover that they are led by an inscrutable agency to work towards a distant purpose. Let us be faithful to our scientific method, and investigate also those instincts of the human mind by which man is led to work as if the approval of a Higher Being were the aim of life.

The Principles of Science

CHARLES SYNGE CHRISTOPHER LORD JUSTICE BOWEN

1835–1894

487 *Mogul Steamship Company v. McGregor Gow & Co.: Judgement*

WE were told that competition ceases to be the lawful exercise of trade, and so to be a lawful excuse for what will harm another, if carried to a length which is not fair or reasonable. The offering of reduced rates by the defendants in the present case is said to have been ' unfair '. This seems to assume that, apart from fraud, intimidation, molestation, or obstruction, of some other personal right *in rem* or *in personam*, there is some natural standard of ' fairness ' or ' reasonableness ' (to be determined by the internal consciousness of judges and juries) beyond which competition ought not in law to go. There seems to be no authority, and I think, with submission, that there is no sufficient reason for such a proposition. It would impose a novel fetter upon trade. The defendants, we are told by the plaintiffs' counsel, might lawfully lower rates provided they did not lower them beyond a 'fair freight', whatever that may mean. But where is it established that there is any such restriction upon commerce? And what is to be the definition of a 'fair freight'? It is said that it ought to be a normal rate of freight, such as is reasonably remunerative to the shipowner. But over what period of time is the average of this reasonable remunerativeness to be calculated? All commercial men with capital are acquainted with the ordinary expedient of sowing one year a crop of apparently unfruitful prices, in order by driving competition away to reap a fuller harvest of profit in the future; and until the present argument at the bar it may be doubted whether shipowners or merchants were ever deemed to be bound by law to conform to some imaginary 'normal' standard of freights or prices, or that Law Courts had a right to say to them in respect of their competitive tariffs, 'Thus far shalt thou go and no further'. To attempt to limit English competition in this way would probably be as hopeless an endeavour as the experiment of King Canute.

Law Reports

WILLIAM EDWARD HALL

1835–1894

488 *A Prophecy*

LOOKING back over the last couple of centuries we see International Law at the close of each fifty years in a more solid position than that which it occupied at the beginning of the period. Progressively it has taken firmer hold, it has extended its sphere of operation, it has ceased to trouble itself about trivial formalities, it has more and more dared to grapple in detail with the fundamental facts in the relations of states. The area within which it reigns beyond dispute has in that time been infinitely enlarged, and it has been greatly enlarged within the memory of living men. But it would be idle to pretend that this progress has gone on without check. In times when wars have been both long and bitter, in moments of revolutionary passion, on occasions when temptation and opportunity of selfishness on the part of neutrals have been great, men have fallen back into disregard of law and even into true lawlessness. And it would be idle also to pretend that Europe is not now in great likelihood moving towards a time at which the strength of International Law will be too hardly tried. Probably in the next great war the questions which have accumulated during the last half-century and more, will all be given their answers at once. Some hates moreover will crave for satisfaction; much envy and greed will be at work; but above all, and at the bottom of all, there will be the hard sense of necessity. Whole nations will be in the field; the commerce of the world may be on the sea to win or lose; national existences will be at stake; men will be tempted to do anything which will shorten hostilities and tend to a decisive issue. Conduct in the next great war will certainly be hard; it is very doubtful if it will be scrupulous, whether on the part of belligerents or neutrals; and most likely the next war will be great. But there can be very little doubt that if the next war is unscrupulously waged, it also will be followed by a reaction towards increased stringency of law. In a community, as in an individual, passionate excess is followed by a reaction of lassitude and to some extent of conscience. On the whole the collective seems to exert itself in this way more surely than the individual conscience; and in things within the scope of International Law, conscience, if it works less impulsively, can at least work more freely than in home affairs. Continuing temptation ceases with the war. At any rate it is a matter of experience that times, in which International Law has been seriously disregarded, have been followed by periods in which the European conscience has done penance by putting itself under straiter obligations than those which it before acknowledged. There is no reason to suppose that things will be otherwise in the future. I therefore look forward with much misgiving to the manner in which the next great war will be waged, but with no misgiving at all as to the character of the rules which will be acknowledged ten years after its termination, by comparison with the rules now considered to exist.

Preface to the Third Edition of International Law

SAMUEL BUTLER

1835–1902

489 *The Turtle*

WALKING the other day in Cheapside I saw some turtles in Mr. Sweeting's window, and was tempted to stay and look at them. As I did so I was struck not more by the defences with which they were hedged about, than by the fatuousness of trying to hedge that in at all which, if hedged thoroughly, must die of its own defencefulness. The holes for the head and feet through which the turtle leaks out, as it were, on to the exterior world, and through which it again absorbs the exterior world into itself—'catching on' through them to things that are thus both turtle and not turtle at one and the same time—these holes stultify the armour, and show it to have been designed by a creature with more of faithfulness to a fixed idea, and hence onesidedness, than of that quick sense of relative importances and their changes, which is the main factor of good living.

The turtle obviously had no sense of proportion; it differed so widely from myself that I could not comprehend it; and as this word occurred to me, it occurred also that until my body comprehended its body in a physical material sense, neither would my mind be able to comprehend its mind with any thoroughness. For unity of mind can only be consummated by unity of body; everything, therefore, must be in some respects both knave and fool to all that which has not eaten it, or by which it has not been eaten. As long as the turtle was in the window and I in the street outside, there was no chance of our comprehending one another.

Nevertheless, I knew that I could get it to agree with me if I could so effectually buttonhole and fasten on to it as to eat it. Most men have an easy method with turtle soup, and I had no misgiving but that if I could bring my first premise to bear I should prove the better reasoner. My difficulty lay in this initial process, for I had not with me the argument that would alone compel Mr. Sweeting to think that I ought to be allowed to convert the turtles—I mean I had no money in my pocket. No missionary enterprise can be carried on without any money at all, but even so small a sum as half a crown would, I suppose, have enabled me to bring the turtle partly round, and with many half-crowns I could in time no doubt convert the lot, for the turtle needs must go where the money drives. If, as is alleged, the world stands on a turtle, the turtle stands on money. No money no turtle.

Ramblings in Cheapside

490 *The Statues*

I PASSED along the western side of the lake, where the ground was easier, and when I had got about half way I expected that I should see the plains which I had already seen from the opposite mountains; but it was not to be so, for the clouds rolled up to the very summit of the pass, though they did not overlip it on to the side from which I had come. I therefore soon found myself enshrouded by a cold thin vapour, which prevented me seeing more than a very few yards in front of me. Then I came upon a large patch of old snow, in which I could distinctly trace the half-melted tracks of goats—and in one place, as it seemed to me, there had been a dog following them. Had I lighted upon a land of shepherds? The ground, where not covered with snow, was so poor and stony, and there was so little herbage, that I could see no sign of a path or regular sheep-track. But I could not help feeling rather uneasy as I wondered what sort of a reception I might meet with if I were to come suddenly upon inhabitants. I was thinking of this, and proceeding cautiously through the mist, when I began to fancy that I saw some objects darker than the cloud looming in front of me. A few steps brought me nearer, and a shudder of unutterable horror ran through me when I saw a circle of gigantic forms, many times higher than myself, upstanding grim and grey through the veil of cloud before me.

I suppose I must have fainted, for I found myself some time afterwards sitting upon the ground, sick and deadly cold. There were the figures, quite still and silent, seen vaguely through the thick gloom, but in human shape indisputably.

A sudden thought occurred to me, which would have doubtless struck me at once had I not been prepossessed with forebodings at the time that I first saw the figures, and had not the cloud concealed them from me—I mean that they were not living beings, but statues. I determined that I would count fifty slowly, and was sure that the objects were not alive if during that time I could detect no sign of motion.

How thankful was I when I came to the end of my fifty and there had been no movement!

I counted a second time—but again all was still.

I then advanced timidly forward, and in another moment I saw that my surmise was correct. I had come upon a sort of Stonehenge of rude and barbaric figures, seated as Chowbok had sat when I questioned him in the wool-shed, and with the same superhumanly malevolent expression upon their faces. They had been all seated, but two had fallen. They were barbarous—neither Egyptian, nor Assyrian, nor Japanese—different from any of these, and yet akin to all. They were six or seven times larger than life, of great antiquity, worn and lichen grown. They were ten in number. There was snow upon their heads and wherever snow could lodge. Each statue had been built of four or five enormous blocks, but how these had been raised and put together is known to those alone who raised them. Each was terrible after a different kind. One was raging furiously, as in pain and great despair; another was lean and cadaverous with famine; another cruel and idiotic, but with the silliest simper that can be conceived—this one had fallen, and looked exquisitely ludicrous in his fall—the mouths of all were more or less open, and as I looked at them from behind, I saw that their heads had been hollowed. . .

Then came a gust of howling wind, accompanied with a moan from one of the statues above me. I clasped my hands in fear. I felt like a rat caught in a trap, as though I would have turned and bitten at whatever thing was nearest me. The wildness of the wind increased, the moans grew shriller, coming from several statues, and swelling into a chorus. I almost immediately knew what it was, but the sound was so unearthly that this was but little consolation. The inhuman beings into whose hearts the Evil One had put it to conceive these statues, had made their heads into a sort of organ-pipe, so that their mouths should catch the wind and sound with its blowing. It was horrible. However brave a man might be, he could never stand such a concert, from such lips, and in such a place. I heaped every invective upon them that my tongue could utter as I rushed away from them into the mist, and even after I had lost sight of them, and turning my head round could see nothing but the storm-wraiths driving behind me, I heard their ghostly chanting, and felt as though one of them would rush after me and grip me in his hand and throttle me.

Erewhon

JOHN RICHARD GREEN

1837–1883

491 *The Universities and Feudalism*

THE feudal and ecclesiastical order of the old mediæval world were both alike threatened by the power that had so strangely sprung up in the midst of them. Feudalism rested on local isolation, on the severance of kingdom from kingdom and barony from barony, on the distinction of blood and race, on the supremacy of material or brute force, on an allegiance determined by accidents of place and social position. The University, on the other hand, was a protest against this isolation of man from man. The smallest school was European and not local. Not merely every province of France, but every people of Christendom, had its place among the 'nations' of Paris or Padua. A common language, the Latin tongue, superseded within academical bounds the warring tongues of Europe. A common intellectual kinship and rivalry took the place of the petty strifes which parted province from province or realm from realm. What the Church and Empire had both aimed at and both failed in, the knitting of Christian nations together into a vast commonwealth, the Universities for a time actually did. Dante felt himself as little a stranger in the 'Latin' quarter around Mont Ste Geneviève as under the arches of Bologna. Wandering Oxford scholars carried the writings of Wyclif to the libraries of Prague. In England the work of provincial fusion was less difficult or important than elsewhere, but even in England work had to be done. The feuds of Northerner and Southerner which so long disturbed the discipline of Oxford witnessed at any rate to the fact that Northerner and Southerner had at last been brought face to face in its streets. And here as elsewhere the spirit of national isolation was held in check by the larger comprehensiveness of the University. After the dissensions that threatened the prosperity of Paris in the thirteenth century, Norman and Gascon mingled with Englishmen in Oxford lecture-halls. At a later time the rebellion of Owen Glyndwr found hundreds of Welshmen gathered round its teachers. And within this strangely mingled mass, society and government rested on a purely democratic basis. Among Oxford scholars the son of the noble stood on precisely the same footing with the poorest mendicant. Wealth, physical strength, skill in arms, pride of ancestry and blood, the very grounds on which feudal society rested, went for nothing in the lecture-room. The University was a state absolutely self-governed, and whose citizens were admitted by a purely intellectual franchise. Knowledge made the 'master'. To know more than one's fellows was a man's sole claim to be a 'ruler' in the schools: and within this intellectual aristocracy all were equal. When the free commonwealth of the masters gathered in the aisles of S. Mary's all had an equal right to counsel, all had an equal vote in the final decision. Treasury and library were at their complete disposal. It was their voice that named every officer, that proposed and sanctioned every statute. Even the Chancellor, their head, who had at first been an officer of the Bishop, became an elected officer of their own.

Short History of the English People

ALGERNON CHARLES SWINBURNE

1837–1909

492 *Philip the Bastard*

FAR beyond the reach of any but his maker's hand is the pattern of a perfect English warrior, set once for all before the eyes of all ages in the figure of the noble Bastard. The national side of Shakespeare's genius, the heroic vein of patriotism that runs like a thread of living fire through the world-wide range of his omnipresent spirit, has never, to my thinking, found vent or expression to such glorious purpose as here. Not even in Hotspur or Prince Hal has he mixed with more godlike sleight of hand all the lighter and graver good qualities of the national character, or compounded of them all so lovable a nature as this. In those others we admire and enjoy the same bright fiery temper of soul, the same buoyant and fearless mastery of fate or fortune, the same gladness and glory of life made lovely with all the labour and laughter of its full fresh days; but no quality of theirs binds our hearts to them as they are bound to Philip—not by his loyal valour, his keen young wit, his kindliness, constancy, readiness of service as swift and sure in the day of his master's bitterest shame and shamefullest trouble as in the blithest hour of battle and that first good fight which won back his father's spoils from his father's slayer; but more than all these, for that lightning of divine rage and pity, of tenderness that speaks in thunder and indignation that makes fire of its tears, in the horror of great compassion which falls on him, the tempest and storm of a beautiful and godlike anger which shakes his strength of spirit and bows his high heart down at sight of Arthur dead.

A Study of Shakespeare

ALGERNON CHARLES SWINBURNE

493 *Byron*

HIS work was done at Missolonghi; all of his work for which the fates could spare him time. A little space was allowed him to show at least a heroic purpose, and attest a high design; then, with all things unfinished before him and behind, he fell asleep after many troubles and triumphs. Few can ever have gone wearier to the grave; none with less fear. He had done enough to earn his rest. Forgetful now and set free for ever from all faults and foes, he passed through the doorway of no ignoble death out of reach of time, out of sight of love, out of hearing of hatred, beyond the blame of England and the praise of Greece. In the full strength of spirit and of body his destiny overtook him, and made an end of all his labours. He had seen and borne and achieved more than most men on record. 'He was a great man, good at many things, and now he has attained this also, to be at rest.'

Introduction to a Selection from the Works of Lord Byron

WILLIAM EDWARD HARTPOLE LECKY

1838–1903

494 *Party Votes*

A MEMBER of Parliament must often feel himself in the position of a private in an army, or a player in a game, or an advocate in a law case. On many questions each party represents and defends the special interests of some particular classes in the country. When there are two plausible alternative courses to be pursued which divide public opinion, the

Opposition is almost bound by its position to enforce the merits of the course opposed to that adopted by the Government. In theory nothing could seem more absurd than a system of government in which, as it has been said, the ablest men in Parliament are divided into two classes, one side being charged with the duty of carrying on the government and the other with that of obstructing and opposing them in their task, and in which, on a vast multitude of unconnected questions, these two great bodies of very competent men, with the same facts and arguments before them, habitually go into opposite lobbies. In practice, however, parliamentary government by great parties, in countries where it is fully understood and practised, is found to be admirably efficacious in representing every variety of political opinion; in securing a constant supervision and criticism of men and measures; and in forming a safety valve through which the dangerous humours of society can expand without evil to the community.

This, however, is only accomplished by constant compromises which are seldom successfully carried out without a long national experience. Party must exist. It must be maintained as an essential condition of good government, but it must be subordinated to the public interests, and in the public interests it must be in many cases suspended. There are subjects which cannot be introduced without the gravest danger into the arena of party controversy. Indian politics are a conspicuous example, and, although foreign policy cannot be kept wholly outside it, the dangers connected with its party treatment are extremely great. Many measures of a different kind are conducted with the concurrence of the two front benches. A cordial union on large classes of questions between the heads of the rival parties is one of the first conditions of successful parliamentary government. The Opposition leader must have a voice in the conduct of business, on the questions that should be brought forward, and on the questions that it is for the public interest to keep back. He is the official leader of systematic, organised opposition to the Government, yet he is on a large number of questions their most powerful ally. He must frequently have confidential relations with them, and one of his most useful functions is to prevent sections of his party from endeavouring to snatch party advantages by courses which might endanger public interests. If the country is to be well governed there must be a large amount of continuity in its policy; certain conditions and principles of administration must be inflexibly maintained, and in great national emergencies all parties must unite.

The Map of Life

JOHN VISCOUNT MORLEY OF BLACKBURN

1838–1923

495 *Eighteenth-Century Verse*

TO find beautiful and pathetic language, set to harmonious numbers, for the common impressions of meditative minds, is no small part of the poet's task. That part has never been achieved by any poet in any tongue, with more complete perfection and success than in the immortal *Elegy*, of which we may truly say that it has for nearly a century and a half given to greater multitudes of men more of the exquisite pleasure of poetry than any other single piece in all the glorious treasury of English verse. It abounds, as Johnson says, 'with images which find a mirror in every mind, and with sentiments to which every bosom returns an echo.' These moving commonplaces of the human lot, Gray approached through books and studious contemplation; not, as Wordsworth approached them, by daily contact with the lives and habit of men and the forces and magical apparitions of external nature. But it is a narrow view to suppose that the men of the eighteenth century did not look through the literary conventions of the day to the truths of life and nature behind them. The conventions have gone, or are changed, and we are all glad of it. Wordsworth effected a wholesome deliverance when he attacked the artificial diction, the personifications, the allegories, the antitheses, the barren rhymes and monotonous metres, which the reigning taste had approved. But while welcoming the new freshness, sincerity, and direct and fertile return on nature, that is a very bad reason why we should disparage poetry so genial, so simple, so humane, and so perpetually pleasing as the best verse of the rationalistic century.

Introduction to Wordsworth's Poetical Works

ANNE THACKERAY (LADY RITCHIE)

1838–1919

496 *The Children's Hour*

AS I write the snow lies thick upon the ground outside, upon the branches of the trees, upon the lawns. Here, within, the fire leaps brightly in its iron cage; the children cluster round the chair by the chimney corner, where the mother sits reading their beloved fairy tales. The hearth was empty once—the home was desolate; but time after time, day by day, we see the phoenix of home and of love springing from the dead ashes; love kindles and warms chilled hearts to life.

Take courage, say the happy to those in sorrow and trouble; are there not many mansions even here? seasons in their course; harvests in their season, thanks be to the merciful ordinance that metes out sorrow and peace, and longing and fulfilment, and rest after the storm. Take courage, say the happy—the message of the sorrowful is harder to understand. The echoes come from afar, and reach beyond our ken. And the cry passes beyond us into the awful unknown, we feel that this is, perhaps, the voice in life that reaches beyond life itself. Not of harvests to come, not of peaceful home hearths do they speak in their sorrow. Their fires are out, their hearths are in ashes, but see, it was the sunlight that extinguished the flame.

Old Kensington

WALTER PATER

1839–1894

497 *Monna Lisa*

THE presence that thus rose so strangely beside the waters, is expressive of what in the ways of a thousand years men had come to desire. Hers is the head upon which all 'the ends of the world are come,' and the eyelids are a little weary. It is a beauty wrought out from within upon the flesh, the deposit, little cell by cell, of strange thoughts and fantastic reveries and exquisite passions. Set it for a moment beside one of those white Greek goddesses or beautiful women of antiquity, and how would they be troubled by this beauty, into which the soul with all its maladies has passed? All the thoughts and experience of the world have etched and moulded there, in that which they have of power to refine and make expressive the outward form, the animalism of Greece, the lust of Rome, the reverie of the middle age with its spiritual ambition and imaginative loves, the return of the Pagan world, the sins of the Borgias. She is older than the rocks among which she sits; like the vampire, she has been dead many times, and learned the secrets of the grave; and has been a diver in deep seas, and keeps their fallen day about her; and trafficked for strange webs with Eastern merchants: and, as Leda, was the mother of Helen of Troy, and, as Saint Anne, the mother of Mary; and all this has been to her but as the sound of lyres and flutes, and lives only in the delicacy with which it has moulded the changing lineaments, and tinged the eyelids and the hands. The fancy of a perpetual life, sweeping together ten thousand experiences, is an old one; and modern thought has conceived the idea of humanity as wrought upon by, and summing up in itself, all modes of thought and life. Certainly Lady Lisa might stand as the embodiment of the old fancy, the symbol of the modern idea. *The Renaissance*

498 The Religion of Numa

THE day of the 'little' or private *Ambarvalia* was come, to be celebrated by a single family for the welfare of all belonging to it, as the great college of the Arval Brothers officiated at Rome in the interest of the whole state. At the appointed time all work ceases;

the instruments of labour lie untouched, hung with wreaths of flowers, while masters and servants together go in solemn procession along the dry paths of vineyard and cornfield, conducting the victims whose blood is presently to be shed for the purification from all natural or supernatural taint of the lands they have 'gone about.' The old Latin words of the liturgy, to be said as the procession moved on its way, though their precise meaning was long since become unintelligible, were recited from an ancient illuminated roll, kept in the painted chest in the hall, together with the family records. Early on that day the girls of the farm had been busy in the great portico, filling large baskets with flowers plucked short from branches of apple and cherry, then in spacious bloom, to strew before the quaint images of the gods—Ceres and Bacchus and the yet more mysterious Dea Dia—as they passed through the fields, carried in their little houses on the shoulders of white-clad youths, who were understood to proceed to this office in perfect temperance, as pure in soul and body as the air they breathed in the firm weather of that early summer-time. The clean lustral water and the full incense-box were carried after them. The altars were gay with garlands of wool and the more sumptuous sort of blossom and green herbs to be thrown into the sacrificial fire, fresh-gathered this morning from a particular plot in the old garden, set apart for the purpose. Just then the young leaves were almost as fragrant as flowers, and the scent of the bean-fields mingled pleasantly with the cloud of incense. But for the monotonous intonation of the liturgy by the priests, clad in their strange, stiff, antique vestments, and bearing ears of green corn upon their heads, secured by flowing bands of white, the procession moved in absolute stillness, all persons, even the children, abstaining from speech after the utterance of the pontifical formula, *Favete linguis!*—Silence! Propitious Silence!—lest any words save those proper to the occasion should hinder the religious efficacy of the rite.

With the lad Marius, who as the head of his house took a leading part in the ceremonies of the day, there was a devout effort to complete this impressive outward silence by that inward tacitness of mind, esteemed so important by religious Romans in the performance of these sacred functions. To him the sustained stillness without seemed really but to be waiting upon that interior, mental condition of preparation or expectancy, for which he was just then intently striving.

Marius the Epicurean

499 *The Poetry of Ronsard*

IN such condition of mind, how deeply, delightfully, must the poetry of Ronsard and his fellows have moved him, when he became aware, as from age to age inquisitive youth by good luck does become aware, of the literature of his own day, confirming—more than confirming—anticipation! Here was a poetry which boldly assumed the dress, the words, the habits, the very trick, of contemporary life, and turned them into gold. It took possession of the lily in one's hand, and projecting it into a visionary distance, shed upon the body of the flower the soul of its beauty. Things were become at once more deeply sensuous and more deeply ideal. As at the touch of a wizard, something more came into the rose than its own natural blush. Occupied so closely with the visible, this new poetry had so profound an intuition of what can only be felt, and maintained that mood in speaking of such objects as wine, fruit, the plume in the cap, the ring on the finger. And still that was no dubious or generalised form it gave to flower or bird, but the exact pressure of the jay at the window ; you could count the petals,—of the exact natural number ; no expression could be too faithful to the precise texture of things ; words, too, must embroider, be twisted and spun, like silk or golden hair. Here were real people, in their real, delightful attire, and you understood how they moved ; the visible was more visible than ever before, just because soul had come to its surface. The juice in the flowers, when Ronsard named them, was like wine or blood. It was such a coloured thing ; though the grey things also, the cool things, all the fresher for the contrast—with a freshness, again, that seemed to touch and cool the soul—found their account there ; the clangorous passage of the birds at night foretokening rain, the moan of the wind at the door, the wind's self made visible over the yielding corn.

Gaston de Latour

500 *Montaigne*

SOCIABLE, of sociable intellect, and still inclining instinctively, as became his fresh and agreeable person, from the midway of life, towards its youthful side, he was ever on the alert for a likely interlocutor to take part in the conversation, which (pleasantest, truly ! of all modes of human commerce) was also of ulterior service as stimulating that endless *inward* converse from which the essays were a kind of abstract. For him, as for Plato, for Socrates whom he cites so often, the essential dialogue was that of the mind with itself; but this dialogue throve best with, often actually needed, outward stimulus—physical motion, some text shot from a book, the queries and objections of a living voice.—'My thoughts sleep, if I sit still.' Neither 'thoughts,' nor 'dialogues,' exclusively, but thoughts still partly implicate in the dialogues which had evoked them, and therefore not without many seemingly arbitrary transitions, many links of connexion to be supposed by the reader, constituting their characteristic difficulty, the Essays owed their actual publication at last to none of the usual literary motives—desire for fame, to instruct, to amuse, to sell—but to the sociable desire for a still wider range of conversation with others. He wrote for companionship, 'if but one sincere man would make his acquaintance'; speaking on paper, as he 'did to the first person he met.'—'If there be any person, any knot of good company, in France or elsewhere, who can like my humour, and whose humours I can like, let them but whistle, and I will run!' *Gaston de Latour*

ANONYMOUS

501 *The Poetry of Gardening*

1839

OF all the vain assumptions of these coxcomical times, that which arrogates the pre-eminence in the true science of gardening is the vainest. True, our conservatories are full of the choicest plants from every clime; we ripen the grape and the pine-apple with an art unknown before, and even the mango, the mangosteen, and the guava are made to yield their matured fruits; but the real beauty and poetry of a garden are lost in our efforts after rarity, and strangeness, and variety. To be the possessor of a unique pansy, the introducer of a new specimen of the Orchidaceae, or the cultivator of five hundred choice varieties of the dahlia, is now the only claim to gardening celebrity and Horticultural medals.

And then our lot has fallen in the evil days of System. We are proud of our natural or English style; and scores of unmeaning flower-beds, disfiguring the lawn in the shapes of kidneys, and tadpoles and sausages, and leeches, and commas, are the result. Landscape-gardening has encroached too much upon gardening-proper; and this has had the same effect upon our gardens that horticultural societies have had on our fruits—to make us entertain the vulgar notion, that size is virtue. . .

If we review the various styles that have prevailed in England, from the knotted gardens of Elizabeth, the pleach-work and intricate flower-borders of James I, the painted Dutch statues and canals of William and Mary, the winding gravel walks and lace-making of Brown, to poor Shenstone's sentimental farm and the landscape-fashion of the present day—we shall have little reason to pride ourselves on the advance which national taste has made upon the earliest efforts in this department. . .

My garden should lie to the south of the house; the ground gradually sloping for some short way till it falls abruptly into the dark and tangled shrubberies that all but hide the winding brook below. A broad terrace, half as wide, at least, as the house is high, should run along the whole southern length of the building, extending to the western side also, whence, over the distant country, I may catch the last red light of the setting sun. I must have some musk and noisette roses, and jasmine, to run up the mullions of my oriel window, and honeysuckles and clematis, the white, the purple, and the blue, to cluster round the top. The upper terrace should be strictly architectural, and no plants are to be harboured there, save such as twine among the balustrades, or fix themselves in the mouldering crevices of the stone. I can endure no plants in pots—a plant in a pot is like a bird in a cage. The gourd alone throws out its vigorous tendrils, and displays its green and golden fruit from the vases that surmount the broad flight of stone steps that lead to the lower terrace; while a vase of larger dimensions and bolder sculpture at the western corner is backed by the heads of a mass of crimson, rose, and straw-coloured hollyhocks that spring up from the bank below. The lower terrace is twice the width of the one above, of the most velvety turf, laid out in an elaborate pattern of the Italian style. Here are collected the choicest flowers of the garden, the Dalmatic purple of the gentianella, the dazzling scarlet of the verbena, the fulgent lobelia, the bright yellows and rich browns of the calceolaria here luxuriate in their trimly cut parterres, and with colours as brilliant as the mosaic of an old cathedral painted window

> Broider the ground
> With rich inlay.

> Tot fuerant illic, quot habet natura, colores :
> Pictaque dissimili flore nitebat humus. *Ovid.*

But you must leave this mass of gorgeous colouring and the two pretty fountains that play in their basins of native rock, while you descend the flight of steps, simpler than those of the upper terrace, and turn to the left hand, where a broad gravel walk will lead you to the kitchen-garden, through an avenue splendid in autumn with hollyhocks, dahlias, China asters, nasturtians, and African marigolds.

We will stop short of the walled garden to turn among the clipt hedges of box, and yew, and hornbeam which surround the bowling-green, and lead to a curiously formed labyrinth, in the centre of which, perched up on a triangular mound, is a fanciful old summer-house, with a gilded roof, that commands the view of the whole surrounding country.

The Carthusian

AUSTIN DOBSON

1840–1921

502 *Mrs. Hogarth*

TOWARD the close of the last century, the regular attendants upon the ministrations of the Rev. James Trebeck in the picturesque old church at the end of Chiswick Mall, must often have witnessed the arrival of a well-known member of the congregation. Year after year had been wheeled, in a Bath chair, from a little villa under the wing of the Duke of Devonshire's mansion hard by, a stately old lady between seventy and eighty years of age, whose habitual costume was a silk sacque, a raised head-dress, and a black calash. Leaning heavily upon her crutched cane, and aided by the arm of a portly female relative in similar attire, she would make her way slowly and with much dignity up the nave, being generally preceded by a bent and white-haired man-servant, who, after carrying the prayer-books into the pew, and carefully closing the door upon his mistress and her companion, would himself retire to a remoter part of the building. From the frequenters of the place, the little procession attracted no more notice than any other recognized ceremonial, of which the intermission would alone have been remarkable; but it seldom failed to excite the curiosity of those wayfarers who, under the third George, already sought reverently, along the pleasant riverside, for that house in Mawson's Buildings where the great Mr. Pope wrote part of his 'Iliad,' or for the garden of Richard, Earl of Burlington, where idle John Gay gorged himself with apricots and peaches. They would be told that the elder lady was the widow of the famous painter, William Hogarth, who lay buried under the teacaddy-like tomb in the neighbouring churchyard; that her companion was her cousin, Mary Lewis, in whose arms he died; and that the old servant's name was Samuel. For five and twenty years Mrs. Hogarth survived her husband, during all of which time she faithfully cherished his memory. Those who visited her at her Chiswick home (for she had another in Leicester Fields) would recall with what tenacity she was wont to combat the view that he was a mere maker of caricatura, or, at best, 'a writer of comedy with the pencil,' as Mr. Horace Walpole (whose over-critical book she had not even condescended to acknowledge) had thought fit to designate him. It was as a painter pure and simple, as a rival of the Guidos and Correggios, that she mainly valued her William. 'They said he could not colour!' she would cry, pointing, it may be, as a protest against the words, to the brilliant sketch of the 'Shrimp Girl,' now in the National Gallery, but then upon her walls.

Eighteenth Century Vignettes, First Series

THOMAS HARDY

1840–

503 *Midnight on St. Thomas's Eve*

THE sky was clear—remarkably clear—and the twinkling of all the stars seemed to be but throbs of one body, timed by a common pulse. The North Star was directly in the wind's eye, and since evening the Bear had swung round it outwardly to the east, till he was now at a right angle with the meridian. A difference of colour in the stars—oftener read of than seen in England—was really perceptible here. The sovereign brilliancy of Sirius pierced the eye with a steely glitter, the star called Capella was yellow, Aldebaran and Betelgueux shone with a fiery red.

To persons standing alone on a hill during a clear midnight such as this, the roll of the world eastward is almost a palpable movement. The sensation may be caused by the panoramic glide of the stars past earthly objects, which is perceptible in a few minutes of stillness, or by the better outlook upon space that a hill affords, or by the wind, or by the solitude; but whatever be its origin the impression of riding along is vivid and abiding. The poetry of motion is a phrase much in use, and to enjoy the epic form of that gratification it is necessary to stand on a hill at a small hour of the night, and, having first expanded with a sense of difference from the mass of civilized mankind, who are dreamwrapt and disregardful of all such proceedings at this time, long and quietly watch your stately progress through the stars. After such a nocturnal reconnoitre it is hard to get back to earth, and to believe that the consciousness of such majestic speeding is derived from a tiny human frame.

Far from the Madding Crowd

504 *The 'Victory' Passes*

THE wild, herbless, weather-worn promontory was quite a solitude, and, saving the one old lighthouse about fifty yards up the slope, scarce a mark was visible to show that humanity had ever been near the spot. Anne found herself a seat on a stone, and swept with her eyes the tremulous expanse of water around her that seemed to utter a ceaseless unintelligible incantation. Out of the three hundred and sixty degrees of her complete horizon two hundred and fifty were covered by waves, the *coup d'œil* including the area of troubled waters known as the Race, where two seas met to effect the destruction of such vessels as could not be mastered by one. She counted the craft within her view: there were five; no, there were only four; no, there were seven, some of the specks having resolved themselves into two. They were all small coasters, and kept well within sight of land.

Anne sank into a reverie. Then she heard a slight noise on her left hand, and turning beheld an old sailor, who had approached with a glass. He was levelling it over the sea in a direction to the south-east, and somewhat removed from that in which her own eyes had been wandering. Anne moved a few steps thitherward, so as to unclose to her view a deeper sweep on that side, and by this discovered a ship of far larger size than any which had yet dotted the main before her. Its sails were for the most part new and clean, and in comparison with its rapid progress before the wind the small brigs and ketches seemed standing still. Upon this striking object the old man's glass was bent.

'What do you see, sailor?' she asked.

'Almost nothing,' he answered. 'My sight is so gone off lately that things, one and all, be but a November mist to me. And yet I fain would see to-day. I am looking for the *Victory*.'

'Why?' she said quickly.

'I have a son aboard her. He 's one of three from these parts. There 's the captain, there 's my son Jim, and there 's young Loveday of Overcombe—he that lately joined.'

'Shall I look for you?' said Anne, after a pause.

'Certainly, mis'ess, if so be you please.'

Anne took the glass, and he supported it by his arm. 'It is a large ship,' she said, 'with three masts, three rows of guns along the side, and all her sails set.'

'I guessed as much.'

'There is a little flag in front—over her bow-sprit.'

'The jack.'

'And there 's a large one flying at her stern.'

'The ensign.'

'And a white one on her fore-topmast.'

'That 's the admiral's flag, the flag of my Lord Nelson. What is her figure-head, my dear?'

'A coat-of-arms, supported on this side by a sailor.'

Her companion nodded with satisfaction. 'On the other side of that figure-head is a marine.'

'She is twisting round in a curious way, and her sails sink in like old cheeks, and she shivers like a leaf upon a tree.'

'She is in stays, for the larboard tack. I can see what she 's been doing. She 's been re'ching close in to avoid the flood tide, as the wind is to the sou'-west, and she 's bound down; but as soon as the ebb made, d'ye see, they made sail to the west'ard. Captain

Hardy may be depended upon for that; he knows every current about here, being a native.'

'And now I can see the other side; it is a soldier where a sailor was before. You are *sure* it is the *Victory*?'

'I am sure.' . .

The great silent ship, with her population of blue-jackets, marines, officers, captain, and the admiral who was not to return alive, passed like a phantom the meridian of the Bill. Sometimes her aspect was that of a large white bat, sometimes that of a grey one. In the course of time the watching girl saw that the ship had passed her nearest point; the breadth of her sails diminished by foreshortening, till she assumed the form of an egg on end. After this something seemed to twinkle, and Anne, who had previously withdrawn from the old sailor, went back to him, and looked again through the glass. The twinkling was the light falling upon the cabin windows of the ship's stern. She explained it to the old man.

'Then we see now what the enemy have seen but once. That was in seventy-nine, when she sighted the French and Spanish fleet off Scilly, and she retreated because she feared a landing. Well, 'tis a brave ship, and she carries brave men!' . .

The courses of the *Victory* were absorbed into the main, then her topsails went, and then her top-gallants. She was now no more than a dead fly's wing on a sheet of spider's web; and even this fragment diminished. Anne could hardly bear to see the end, and yet she resolved not to flinch. The admiral's flag sank behind the watery line, and in a minute the very truck of the last topmast stole away. The *Victory* was gone.

The Trumpet Major

505 *A Tree-Planting*

HE descended the path, and looked out, and beheld Marty South, dressed for out-door work.

'Why didn't you come, Mr. Winterborne?' she said; 'I've been waiting there hours and hours, and at last I thought I must try to find you!'

'Bless my soul, I'd quite forgot!' said Giles.

What he had forgotten was that there were a thousand young fir trees to be planted in a neighbouring spot which had been cleared by the wood-cutters, and that he had arranged to plant them with his own hands. He had a marvellous power of making trees grow. Although he would seem to shovel in the earth quite carelessly there was a sort of sympathy between himself and the fir, oak, or beech that he was operating on; so that the roots took hold of the soil in a few days. When, on the other hand, any of the journeymen planted, although they seemed to go through an identically similar process, one quarter of the trees would die away during the ensuing August.

Hence Winterborne found delight in the work even when, as at present, he contracted to do it on portions of the woodland in which he had no personal interest. Marty, who turned her hand to anything, was usually the one who performed the part of keeping the trees in a perpendicular position whilst he threw in the mould.

He accompanied her towards the spot, being inclined yet further to proceed with the work by the knowledge that the ground was close to the roadside along which Grace must pass on her way from Hintock House.

'You've a cold in the head, Marty,' he said as they walked. 'That comes of cutting off your hair.'

'I suppose it do. Yes; I've three headaches going on in my head at the same time.'

'Three headaches!'

'Yes, Mr. Winterborne: a rheumatic headache in my poll, a sick headache over my eyes, and a misery headache in the middle of my brain. However, I came out, for I thought you might be waiting and grumbling like anything if I was not there.'

The holes were already dug, and they set to work. Winterborne's fingers were endowed with a gentle conjuror's touch in spreading the roots of each little tree, resulting in a sort of caress under which the delicate fibres all laid themselves out in their proper directions for growth. He put most of these roots towards the south-west; for, he said, in forty years' time, when some great gale is blowing from that quarter, the trees will require the strongest holdfast on that side to stand against it and not fall.

'How they sigh directly we put 'em upright, though while they are lying down they don't sigh at all,' said Marty.

'Do they?' said Giles. 'I've never noticed it.'

She erected one of the young pines into its hole, and held up her finger; the soft musical breathing instantly set in which was not to cease night or day till the grown tree should be felled—probably long after the two planters had been felled themselves.

'It seems to me,' the girl continued, 'as if they sigh because they are very sorry to begin life in earnest—just as we be.'

'Just as we be?' He looked critically at her. 'You ought not to feel like that, Marty.'

Her only reply was turning to take up the next tree; and they planted on through a great part of the day, almost without another word.

The Woodlanders

506 *Marty has her Reward*

MELBURY now returned to the room, and the men having declared themselves refreshed they all started on the homeward journey, which was by no means cheerless under the rays of the high moon. Having to walk the whole distance they came by a footpath rather shorter than the highway, though difficult except to those who knew the country well. This brought them by way of the church: and passing the graveyard they observed as they talked a motionless figure standing by the gate.

'I think it was Marty South,' said the hollow-turner parenthetically.

'I think 'twas; 'a was always a lonely maid,' said Upjohn. And they passed on homeward, and thought of the matter no more.

It was Marty, as they had supposed. That evening had been the particular one of the week upon which Grace and herself had been accustomed to privately deposit flowers on Giles's grave, and this was the first occasion since his death eight months earlier on which Grace had failed to keep her appointment. Marty had waited in the road just outside Melbury's, where her fellow-pilgrim had been wont to join her, till she was weary; and at last, thinking that Grace had missed her, and gone on alone, she followed the way to the church, but saw no Grace in front of her. It got later, and Marty continued her walk till she reached the churchyard gate; but still no Grace. Yet her sense of comradeship would not allow her to go on to the grave alone, and still thinking the delay had been unavoidable she stood there with her little basket of flowers in her clasped hands, and her feet chilled by the damp ground, till more than two hours had passed. She then heard the footsteps of Melbury's men, who presently passed on their return from the search. In the silence of the night Marty could not help hearing fragments of their conversation, from which she acquired a general idea of what had occurred, and that Mrs. Fitzpiers was by that time in the arms of another man than Giles.

Immediately they had dropped down the hill she entered the churchyard, going to a secluded corner behind the bushes where rose the unadorned stone that marked the last bed of Giles Winterborne. As this solitary and silent girl stood there in the moonlight, a straight slim figure, clothed in a plaitless gown, the contours of womanhood so undeveloped as to be scarcely perceptible in her, the marks of poverty and toil effaced by the misty hour, she touched sublimity at points, and looked almost like a being who had rejected with indifference the attribute of sex for the loftier quality of abstract humanism. She stooped down and cleared away the withered flowers that Grace and herself had laid there the previous week, and put her fresh ones in their place.

'Now, my own, own love,' she whispered, 'you are mine, and only mine; for she has forgot 'ee at last, although for her you died! But I—whenever I get up I'll think of 'ee, and whenever I lie down I'll think of 'ee again. Whenever I plant the young larches I'll think that none can plant as you planted; and whenever I split a gad, and whenever I turn the cider wring, I'll say none could do it like you. If ever I forget your name let me forget home and heaven! .. But no, no, my love, I never can forget 'ee; for you was a good man, and did good things!'

The Woodlanders

W. H. HUDSON

1841–1922

507 *The Return of the Chiff-Chaff*

ON a warm, brilliant morning in late April I paid a visit to a shallow lakelet or pond five or six acres in extent which I had discovered some weeks before hidden in a depression in the land, among luxuriant furze, bramble, and blackthorn bushes. Between the thickets the boggy ground was everywhere covered with great tussocks of last year's dead and faded marsh grass—a wet, rough, lonely place where a lover of solitude need have no fear of being intruded on by a being of his own species, or even a wandering moorland donkey. On arriving at the pond I was surprised and delighted to find half the surface covered with a thick growth of bog-bean just coming into flower. The quaint three-lobed leaves, shaped like a grebe's foot, were still small, and the flower-stocks, thick as corn in a field, were crowned with pyramids of buds, cream and rosy-red like the opening dropwort clusters, and at the lower end of the spikes were the full-blown singular, snow-white, cottony flowers—our strange and beautiful water edelweiss.

A group of ancient, gnarled and twisted alder bushes, with trunks like trees, grew just on the margin of the pond, and by-and-by I found a comfortable arm-chair on the lower stout horizontal branches overhanging the water, and on that seat I rested for a long time, enjoying the sight of that rare unexpected loveliness.

The chiff-chaff, the common warbler of this moorland district, was now abundant, more so than anywhere else in England; two or three were flitting about among the alder leaves within a few feet of my head, and a dozen at least were singing within hearing, chiff-chaffing near and far, their notes sounding strangely loud at that still, sequestered spot. Listening to that insistent sound I was reminded of Warde Fowler's words about the sweet season which brings new life and hope to men, and how a seal and sanction is put on it by that same small bird's clear resonant voice. I endeavoured to recall the passage, saying to myself that in order to enter fully into the feeling expressed it is sometimes essential to know an author's exact words. Failing in this, I listened again to the bird, then let my eyes rest on the expanse of red and cream-coloured spikes before me, then on the masses of flame-yellow furze beyond, then on something else. I was endeavouring to keep my attention on these extraneous things, to shut my mind resolutely against a thought, intolerably sad, which had surprised me in that quiet solitary place. Surely, I said, this spring-time verdure and bloom, this fragrance of the furze, the infinite blue of heaven, the bell-like double note of this my little feathered neighbour in the alder tree, flitting hither and thither, light and airy himself as a wind-fluttered alder leaf—surely this is enough to fill and to satisfy any heart, leaving no room for a grief so vain and barren, which nothing in nature suggested! That it should find me out here in this wilderness of all places—the place to which a man might come to divest himself of himself—that second self which he has unconsciously acquired—to be like the trees and animals, outside of the sad atmosphere of human life and its eternal tragedy! A vain effort and a vain thought, since that from which I sought to escape came from nature itself, from every visible thing;

every leaf and flower and blade was eloquent of it, and the very sunshine, that gave life and brilliance to all things, was turned to darkness by it.

A Traveller in Little Things

508 *Birds and Death*

THE bird, however hard the frost may be, flies briskly to his customary roosting-place, and, with beak tucked into his wing, falls asleep. He has no apprehensions; only the hot blood grows colder and colder, the pulse feebler as he sleeps, and at midnight, or in the early morning, he drops from his perch—dead.

Yesterday he lived and moved, responsive to a thousand external influences, reflecting earth and sky in his small brilliant brain as in a looking-glass; also he had a various language, the inherited knowledge of his race, and the faculty of flight, by means of which he could shoot, meteor-like, across the sky, and pass swiftly from place to place; and with it such perfect control over all his organs, such marvellous certitude in all his motions, as to be able to drop himself plumb down from the tallest tree-top, or out of the void air, on to a slender spray, and scarcely cause its leaves to tremble. Now, on this morning, he lies stiff and motionless; if you were to take him up and drop him from your hand, he would fall to the ground like a stone or a lump of clay—so easy and swift is the passage from life to death in wild nature! But he was never miserable.

Birds in Town and Village

W. H. HUDSON

509 *Pilgrims at the Land's End*

THERE were days at the headland when I observed a goodish number of elderly men among the pilgrims, some very old, and this at first surprised me, but by-and-by it began to seem only natural. I was particularly impressed one day at noon in early spring in clear but cold weather with a biting north-east wind, when I found six or seven aged men sitting about on the rocks that lie scattered over the green slope behind the famous promontory. They were too old or too feeble to venture down on the rough headland: their companions had strayed away, some to the fishing cove, others along the higher cliffs, and left them there to rest. They were in great-coats with scarves and comforters round their necks, and hats or caps drawn well down; and they sat mostly in dejected attitudes, bending forward, their hands resting on the handles of their sticks, some with their chins on their hands, but all gazed in one direction over the cold grey sea. Strangers to each other, unlike in life and character, coming from widely separated places, some probably from countries beyond the ocean, yet all here, silently gazing in one direction beyond that rocky foreland, with the same look of infinite weariness on their grey faces and in their dim sad eyes, as if one thought and feeling and motive had drawn them to this spot. Can it be that the sentiment or fancy which is sown in our minds in childhood and lies asleep and forgotten in us through most of our years, revives and acquires towards the end a new and strange significance when we have entered upon our second childhood? The period, I mean, when we recover our ancient mental possessions—the heirlooms which cannot be alienated or lost, which have descended to us from our remotest progenitors through centuries and thousands of years. These old men cannot see the objects which appear to younger eyes—the distant passing ships, and the land—that dim, broken line, as of a low cloud on the horizon, of the islands : their sight is altered from what it was, yet is, perhaps, now able to discern things invisible to us—other islands, uncharted, not the Cassiterides. What are they, these other islands, and what do we know of them? Nothing at all; indeed, nothing can be known to the generality; only these life-weary ancients, sitting on rocks and gazing at vacancy, might enlighten us if they would. Undoubtedly there are differences of sight among them which would make their descriptions vary, but they would probably all agree in affirming that the scene before them has no resemblance to the earlier vision. This grey-faced very old man with his chin on his hands, who looks as if he had not smiled these many years, would perhaps smile now if he were to recall that former vision, which came by teaching and served well enough during his hot youth and strenuous middle age. He does not see before him a beautiful blessed land bright with fadeless flowers, nor a great multitude of people in shining garments and garlands who will come down to the shore to welcome him with sounds of shouting and singing and playing on instruments of divers forms, and who will lead him in triumph to the gardens of everlasting delight and to mansions of crystal with emerald and amethyst colonnades and opal domes and turrets and pinnacles. Those glories and populous realms of joy have quite vanished: he sees now only what his heart desires—a silent land of rest. No person will greet him there; he will land and go up alone into that empty and solitary place, a still grey wilderness extending inland and upward hundreds of leagues, an immeasurable distance, into infinity, and rising to mountain ridges compared with which the Himalayas are but molehills. The sky in that still land is always pale grey-blue in colour, and the earth, too, is grey like the rocks, and the trees have a grey-green foliage—trees more ancient in appearance than the worn granite hills, with gnarled and buttressed trunks like vast towers and immense horizontal branches, casting a slight shade over many acres of ground. Onwards and upwards, with eyes downcast, he will slowly take his devious way to the interior, feeling the earth with his staff, in search of a suitable last resting-place. And when he has travelled many, many leagues and has found it—a spot not too sunny nor too deeply shaded, where the old fallen dead leaves and dry moss have formed a thick soft couch to recline on and a grey exposed root winding over the earth offers a rest to his back—there at length he will settle himself. There he will remain motionless and contented for ever in that remote desert land where is no sound of singing bird nor of running water nor of rain or wind in the grey ancient trees: waking and sleeping he will rest there, dreaming little and thinking less, while year by year and age by age the memory of the world of passion and striving of which he was so unutterably tired grows fainter and fainter in his mind. And he will have neither joy nor sorrow, nor love nor hate, nor wish to know them any more; and when he remembers his fellow-men it will comfort him to think that his peace will never be broken by the sight of human face or the sound of human speech, since never by any chance will any wanderer from the world discover him in that illimitable wilderness.

The Land's End

HENRY DUFF TRAILL

1842–1900

510 *Plato and Landor in Elysium*

PLATO. I am persuaded, my friend, that you think too ill of your country and its manners. . . Do they not send us more poets? Do they not send us more painters?

Landor. Ay, truly; they send us any number—and all of them immortal. It is true they are a little difficult to distinguish from each other. The poets seem to have written all their poems with a paint-brush, and the painters were apparently unable to complete their pictures without the pen. But what has this to do with the things of the mind?

Plato. Much, surely; unless poetry and art among you have ceased to be an exercise of the faculties according to a law of right reason. Have they?

Landor. I would rather let the painters answer for themselves. But as for the poets, I do not feel justified in associating the name of reason with many of their performances; nor, exceptions excepted, can I even think of them in connexion with the idea of 'law'.

Plato. Do you mean that they reject the supreme authority of reason as a guide and moderator in their compositions?

Landor. I mean that they not only reject but insult it. A poem by one of these poets is either a riot of the imagination or a mutiny of the passions, and Reason would present herself there with as much rashness as an unpopular magistrate at a tumult among the cobblers. They would pelt her from the scene with rotten adjectives.

Plato. You are, indeed, describing a lawless and

licentious class of men. . . Yet even these express reverence for Greek art, and for the Greek spirit, and, I doubt not, feel it.

Landor. It is impossible, O Plato, that you can have met any of them, or you would never think so.

Plato. Nay, I have been in their company more than once.

Landor. And failed to convict them of imposture? —Perhaps, then, it *was* all Socrates. There may be something in the Boswell theory of the Platonic Dialogues after all.

Plato. I cannot hear what you are saying.

Landor. I was merely repeating to myself a passage from one of the Homeric hymns. . .

The New Lucian

WILLIAM JAMES

1842–1910

511 *The Will to Believe*

I CONFESS that I do not see why the very existence of an invisible world may not in part depend on the personal response which any one of us may make to the religious appeal. God himself, in short, may draw vital strength and increase of very being from our fidelity. For my own part, I do not know what the sweat and blood and tragedy of this life mean, if they mean anything short of this. If this life be not a real fight, in which something is eternally gained for the universe by success, it is no better than a game of private theatricals from which one may withdraw at will. But it *feels* like a real fight,—as if there were something really wild in the universe which we, with all our idealities and faithfulnesses, are needed to redeem ; and first of all to redeem our own hearts from atheisms and fears. For such a half-wild, half-saved universe our nature is adapted. The deepest thing in our nature is . . . this dumb region of the heart in which we dwell alone with our willingnesses and unwillingnesses, our faiths and fears. As through the cracks and crannies of caverns those waters exude from the earth's bosom which then form the fountain-heads of springs, so in these crepuscular depths of personality the sources of all our outer deeds and decisions take their rise. Here is our deepest organ of communication with the nature of things ; and compared with these concrete movements of our soul all abstract statements and scientific arguments—the veto, for example, which the strict positivist pronounces upon our faith—sound to us like mere chatterings of the teeth. . .

These then are my last words to you : Be not afraid of life. Believe that life *is* worth living, and your belief will help create the fact. The 'scientific proof' that you are right may not be clear before the day of judgment (or some stage of being which that expression may serve to symbolize) is reached. But the faithful fighters of this hour, or the beings that then and there will represent them, may then turn to the faint-hearted, who here decline to go on, with words like those with which Henry IV greeted the tardy Crillon after a great victory had been gained : 'Hang yourself, brave Crillon ! we fought at Arques, and you were not there.'

The Will to Believe

CHARLES DOUGHTY

1843–

512 *The Deaf and Dumb*

As we sat, one came in who but then returned from an absence; as the custom is he would first declare his tidings in the mejlis, and afterward go home to his own household. He sat down on his knee, but was so poor a man, there was none in the sheykhly company that rose to kiss him: with a solemn look he stayed him a moment on his camel-stick, and then pointing gravely with it to every man, one after other, he saluted him with an hollow voice, by his name, saying, 'The Lord strengthen thee!' A poor old Beduin wife, when she heard that her son was come again, had followed him over the hot sand hither; now she stood to await him, faintly leaning upon a stake of the beyt a little without, since it is not for any woman to enter where the men's mejlis is sitting. His tidings told, he stepped abroad to greet his mother, who ran and cast her weak arms about his manly neck, trembling for age and tenderness, to see him alive again and sound; and kissing him she could not speak, but uttered little cries. Some of the coffee-drinkers laughed roughly, and mocked her drivelling, but Motlog said, 'Wherefore laugh? is not this the love of a mother?'

Travels in Arabia Deserta

513 *The Desert Day*

The summer's night at end, the sun stands up as a crown of hostile flames from that huge covert of inhospitable sandstone bergs; the desert day dawns not little and little, but it is noontide in an hour.

3 *mejlis) assembly* 14 *beyt) booth*

The sun, entering as a tyrant upon the waste landscape, darts upon us a torment of fiery beams, not to be remitted till the far-off evening.—No matins here of birds; not a rock partridge-cock, calling with blithesome chuckle over the extreme waterless desolation. Grave is that giddy heat upon the crown of the head; the ears tingle with a flickering shrillness, a subtle crepitation it seems, in the glassiness of this sun-stricken nature: the hot sand-blink is in the eyes, and there is little refreshment to find in the tents' shelter; the worsted booths leak to this fiery rain of sunny light. Mountains looming like dry bones through the thin air, stand far around about us: the savage flank of Ybba Moghrair, the high spire and ruinous stacks of el-Jebâl, Chebàd, the coast of Helwàn! Herds of weak nomad camels waver dispersedly, seeking pasture in the midst of this hollow fainting country, where but lately the swarming locusts have fretted every green thing. This silent air burning about us, we endure breathless till the assr: when the dazing Arabs in the tents revive after their heavy hours. The lingering day draws down to the sun-setting; the herdsmen, weary of the sun, come again with the cattle, to taste in their menzils the first sweetness of mirth and repose.—The day is done, and there rises the nightly freshness of this purest mountain air: and then to the cheerful song and the cup at the common fire. The moon rises ruddy from that solemn obscurity of jebel like a mighty beacon:—and the morrow will be as this day, days deadly drowned in the sun of the summer wilderness.

Travels in Arabia Deserta

20 *assr*) *hour of the third prayer* 24 *menzils*) *camping-grounds*
29 *jebel*) *mountain*

HENRY JAMES

1843–1916

514 *An Archangel Slightly Damaged*

SUDDENLY, at the end of twenty minutes, there was projected across this clearness the image of a massive, middle-aged man seated on a bench, under a tree, with sad, far-wandering eyes and plump white hands folded on the head of a stick—a stick I recognised, a stout gold-headed staff that I had given him in devoted days. I stopped short as he turned his face to me, and it happened that for some reason or other I took in as I had perhaps never done before the beauty of his rich blank gaze. It was charged with experience as the sky is charged with light, and I felt on the instant as if we had been overspanned and conjoined by the great arch of a bridge or the great dome of a temple. Doubtless I was rendered peculiarly sensitive to it by something in the way I had been giving him up and sinking him. While I met it I stood there smitten, and I felt myself responding to it with a sort of guilty grimace. This brought back his attention in a smile which expressed for me a cheerful, weary patience, a bruised, noble gentleness. I had told Miss Anvoy that he had no dignity, but what did he seem to me, all unbuttoned and fatigued as he waited for me to come up, if he didn't seem unconcerned with small things, didn't seem in short majestic? There was majesty in his mere unconsciousness of our little conferences and puzzlements over his maintenance and his reward.

After I had sat by him a few minutes I passed my arm over his big soft shoulder (wherever you touched him you found equally little firmness) and said in a tone of which the suppliance fell oddly on my own ear: 'Come back to town with me, old friend—come back and spend the evening.' I wanted to hold him, I wanted to keep him, and at Waterloo, an hour later, I telegraphed possessively to the Mulvilles. When he objected, as regards staying all night, that he had no things, I asked him if he hadn't everything of mine. I had abstained from ordering dinner, and it was too late for preliminaries at a club; so we were reduced to tea and fried fish at my rooms—reduced also to the transcendent. Something had come up which made me want him to feel at peace with me—and which, precisely, was all the dear man himself wanted on any occasion. I had too often had to press upon him considerations irrelevant, but it gives me pleasure now to think that on that particular evening I didn't even mention Mrs. Saltram and the children. Late into the night we smoked and talked; old shames and old rigours fell away from us; I only let him see that I was conscious of what I owed him. He was as mild as contrition and as copious as faith; he was never so fine as on a shy return, and even better at forgiving than at being forgiven. I dare say it was a smaller matter than that famous night at Wimbledon, the night of the problematical sobriety and of Miss Anvoy's initiation; but I was as much in it on this occasion as I had been out of it then. At about 1.30 he was sublime.

The Coxon Fund

515 *Philosophy of a Grand Dame*

OLD Madame de Mauves had nothing severe but her nose, and she seemed to Euphemia—what indeed she had every claim to pass for—the very image and pattern of an 'historical character'. Belonging to a great order of things, she patronized the young stranger who was ready to sit all day at her feet and listen to anecdotes of the *bon temps* and quotations from the family chronicles. Madame de Mauves was a very honest old woman; she uttered her thoughts with ancient plainness. One day after pushing back Euphemia's shining locks and blinking with some tenderness from behind an immense *face-à-main* that acted as for the relegation of the girl herself to the glass case of a museum, she declared with an energetic shake of the head that she didn't know what to make of such a little person. And in answer to the little person's evident wonder, 'I should like to advise you,' she said, 'but you seem to me so all of a piece that I'm afraid that if I advise you I shall spoil you. It 's easy to see you're not one of us. I don't know whether you're better, but you seem to me to have been wound up by some key that isn't kept by your governess or your confessor or even your mother, but that you wear by a fine black ribbon round your own neck. Little persons in my day—when they were stupid they were very docile, but when they were clever they were very sly! You're clever enough, I imagine, and yet if I guessed all your secrets at this moment is there one I should have to frown at? I can tell you a wickeder one than any you've discovered for yourself. If you wish to live at ease in the *doux pays de France* don't trouble too much about the key of your conscience or even about your conscience itself—I mean your own particular one. You'll fancy it saying things it won't help your case to hear. They'll make you sad, and when you're sad you'll grow plain, and when you're plain you'll grow bitter, and when you're bitter you'll be *peu aimable*. I was brought up to think that a woman's first duty is to be infinitely so, and the happiest women I've known have been in fact those who performed this duty faithfully. As you're not a Catholic I suppose you can't be a dévote; and if you don't take life as a fifty years' mass the only way to take it 's as a game of skill. Listen to this. Not to lose at the game of life you must—I don't say cheat, but not be too sure your neighbour won't, and not be shocked out of your self-possession if he does. Don't lose, my dear—I beseech you don't lose. Be neither suspicious nor credulous, and if you find your neighbour peeping don't cry out; only very politely wait your own chance. I've had my revenge more than once in my day, but I really think the sweetest I could take, *en somme*, against the past I've known, would be to have your blest innocence profit by my experience.'

Madame de Mauves

516 *The Pont du Gard*

THE ravine is the valley of the Gardon, which the road from Nîmes has followed some time without taking account of it, but which, exactly at the right distance from the aqueduct, deepens and expands and puts on those characteristics which are best suited to give it effect. The gorge becomes romantic, still, and solitary, and, with its white rocks and wild shrubbery, hangs over the clear-coloured river, in whose slow course there is, here and there, a deeper pool. Over the valley, from side to side and ever so high in the air, stretch the three tiers of the tremendous bridge. They are unspeakably imposing, and nothing could well be more Roman. The hugeness, the solidity, the unexpectedness, the monumental rectitude of the whole thing leave you nothing to say—at the time—and make you stand gazing. You simply feel that it is noble and perfect, that it has the quality of greatness. A road, branching from the highway, descends to the level of the river and passes under one of the arches. This road has a wide margin of grass and loose stones, which slopes upward into the bank of the ravine. You may sit here as long as you please, staring up at the light, strong piers ; the spot is sufficiently 'wild', though two or three stone benches have been erected on it. I remained there an hour and got a complete impression ; the place was perfectly soundless and, for the time at least, lonely ; the splendid afternoon had begun to fade, and there was a fascination in the object I had come to see. It came to pass that at the same time I discovered in it a certain stupidity, a vague brutality. That element is rarely absent from great Roman work, which is wanting in the nice adaptation of the means to the end. The means are always exaggerated ; the end is so much more than attained. The Roman rigour was apt to overshoot the mark, and I suppose a race which could do nothing small is as defective as a race that can do nothing great. Of this Roman rigour the Pont du Gard is an admirable example. It would be a great injustice, however, not to insist upon its beauty—a kind of manly beauty, that of an object constructed not to please but to serve, and impressive simply from the scale on which it carries out this intention. The number of arches in each tier is different ; they are smaller and more numerous as they ascend. The preservation of the thing is extraordinary ; nothing has crumbled or collapsed ; every feature remains, and the huge blocks of stone, of a brownish-yellow (as if they had been baked by the Provençal sun for eighteen centuries), pile themselves, without mortar or cement, as evenly as the day they were laid together. All this to carry the water of a couple of springs to a little provincial city! The conduit on the top has retained its shape and traces of the cement with which it was lined. When the vague twilight began to gather, the lonely valley seemed to fill itself with the shadow of the Roman name, as if the mighty empire were still as erect as the supports of the aqueduct; and it was open to a solitary tourist, sitting there sentimental, to believe that no people has ever been, or will ever be, as great as that, measured, as we measure the greatness of an individual, by the push they gave to what they undertook. The Pont du Gard is one of the three or four deepest impressions they have left; it speaks of them in a manner with which they might have been satisfied.

A Little Tour in France

ROBERT BRIDGES

1844–

517 *The Quest*

(*Adapting the version of Edward Bouverie Pusey*, 1800–1882)

AND what is this? I asked the earth and it said, 'I am not He': and whatsoever is in it confessed the same. I asked the sea and the deeps, and all that swimming or creeping live therein, and they answered 'We are not thy God, seek above us'. I asked the wandering winds; and the whole air with his inhabitants spoke 'Anaximenes was deceived, I am not God'. I asked the heavens, sun, moon and stars, 'Nor (say they) are we the God whom thou seekest'.

And I replied unto all those things which encompass the door of my flesh, 'Ye have told me of my God, that ye are not he: tell me something of him'. And they cried all with a great voice, 'He made us'. My questioning them was my mind's desire, and their Beauty was their answer.

From the Confessions of S. Augustine: included in The Spirit of Man

518 *A School Portrait*

I HAD not visited Eton for many years, when one day passing from the Fellows' Library into the Gallery I caught sight of the portrait of my school-friend Digby Dolben hanging just without the door among our most distinguished contemporaries. I was wholly arrested, and as I stood gazing on it, my companion asked me if I knew who it was. I was thinking that, beyond a few whom I could name, I must be almost the only person who would know. Far memories of my boyhood were crowding freshly upon me: he was standing again beside me in the eager promise of his youth; I could hear his voice; nothing of him was changed; while I, wrapt from him in a confused mist of time, was wondering what he would think, could he know that at this actual moment he would have been dead thirty years, and that his memory would be thus preserved and honoured in the beloved school, where his delicate spirit had been so strangely troubled.

This portrait-gallery of old Etonians is very select: preëminent distinction of birth or merit may win you a place there, or again official connection with the school, which rightly loves to keep up an unbroken panorama of its teachers, and to vivify its annals with the faces and figures of the personalities who carried on its traditions. But how came Dolben there? It was because he was a poet,—that I knew;—and yet his poems were not known; they were jealously guarded by his family and a few friends: indeed such of his poems as could have come to the eyes of the authorities who sanctioned this memorial would not justify it. There was another reason; and the portrait bears its own credentials; for though you might not perhaps divine the poet in it, you can see the saint, the soul rapt in contemplation, the habit of stainless life, of devotion, of enthusiasm for high ideals. Such a being must have stood out conspicuously among his fellows; the facts of his life would have been the ground of the faith in his genius; and when his early death endeared and sanctified his memory, loving grief would generously grant him the laurels which he had never worn.

Memoir prefixed to Poems of Digby Mackworth Dolben

ANDREW LANG

1844–1912

519 *Aucassin's Choice*

'FAIR Sir,' said the Captain, 'let these things be. Nicolete is a captive that I did bring from a strange country. Yea, I bought her at my own charges of the Saracens, and I bred her up and baptised her, and made her my daughter in God. And I have cherished her, and one of these days I would have given her a young man, to win her bread honourably. With this hast thou naught to make, but do thou take the daughter of a King or a Count. Nay more, what wouldst thou deem thee to have gained, hadst thou made her thy leman, and taken her to thy bed? Plentiful lack of comfort hadst thou got thereby, for in Hell would thy soul have lain while the world endures, and into Paradise wouldst thou have entered never.'

'In Paradise what have I to win? Therein I seek not to enter, but only to have Nicolete, my sweet lady that I love so well. For into Paradise go none but such folk as I shall tell thee now: Thither go these same old priests, and halt old men and maimed, who all day and night cower continually before the altars, and in the crypts; and such folk as wear old amices and old clouted frocks, and naked folk and shoeless, and covered with sores, perishing of hunger and thirst, and of cold, and of little ease. These be they that go into Paradise, with them have I naught to make. But into Hell would I fain go; for into Hell fare the goodly clerks, and goodly knights that fall in tourneys and great wars, and stout men-at-arms, and all men noble. With these would I liefly go. And thither pass the sweet ladies and courteous that have two lovers, or three, and their lords also thereto. Thither goes the gold, and the silver, and cloth of vair, and cloth of gris, and harpers, and makers, and the prince of this world. With these I would gladly go, let me but have with me, Nicolete, my sweetest lady.'

Aucassin and Nicolete

520 *Saint Augustine Robs an Orchard*

YET the sin which he regrets most bitterly was nothing more dreadful than the robbery of an orchard! Pears he had in plenty, none the less he went, with a band of roisterers, and pillaged another man's pear tree. 'I loved the sin, not that which I obtained by the same, but I loved the sin itself.' There lay the sting of it! They were not even unusually excellent pears. 'A Peare tree ther was, neere our vineyard, heavy loaden with fruite, which tempted not greatly either the sight or tast. To the shaking and robbing thereof, certaine most wicked youthes (whereof I was one) went late one night. We carried away huge burthens of fruit from thence, not for our owne eating, but to be cast before the hoggs.'

Oh, moonlit night of Africa, and orchard by those wild seabanks where once Dido stood; oh, laughter of boys among the shaken leaves, and sound of falling fruit; how do you live alone out of so many nights that no man remembers? For Carthage is destroyed, indeed, and forsaken of the sea, yet that one hour of summer is to be unforgotten while man has memory of the story of his past.

Adventures among Books

521 *Izaak Walton*

CIRCUMSTANCES and inclination combined to make Walton choose the *fallentis semita vitae*. Without ambition, save to be in the society of good men, he passed through turmoil, ever companioned by content. For him existence had its trials: he saw all that he held most sacred overthrown; laws broken up; his king publicly murdered; his friends outcasts; his worship proscribed; he himself suffered in property from the raid of the Kirk into England. He underwent many bereavements: child after child he lost, but content he did not lose, nor sweetness of heart, nor belief. His was one of those happy characters which are never found disassociated from unquestioning faith. Of old he might have been the ancient religious Athenian in the opening of Plato's *Republic*, or Virgil's aged gardener. The happiness of such natures would be incomplete without religion, but only by such tranquil and blessed souls can religion be accepted with no doubt or scruple, no dread, and no misgiving. In his preface to *Thealma and Clearchus* Walton writes, and we may use his own words about his own works: 'The Reader will here find such various events and rewards of innocent Truth and undissembled Honesty, as is like to leave in him (if he be a good-natured reader) more sympathising and virtuous impressions, than ten times so much time spent in impertinent, critical and needless disputes about religion.' Walton relied on authority; on 'plain, unperplexed catechism'. In an age of the strangest and most dissident theological speculations, an age of Quakers, Anabaptists, Antinomians, Fifth Monarchy Men, Covenanters, Independents, Gibbites, Presbyterians, and what not, Walton was true to the authority of the Church of England, with no prejudice against the ancient Catholic faith. As Gesner was his authority for pickerel weed begetting pike, so the Anglican bishops were security for Walton's creed.

To him, if we may say so, it was easy to be saved, while Bunyan, a greater humorist, could be saved only in following a path that skirted madness, and 'as by fire'. To Bunyan, Walton would have seemed a figure like his own Ignorance; a pilgrim who never stuck in the Slough of Despond, nor met Apollyon in the Valley of the Shadow, nor was captive in Doubting Castle, nor stoned in Vanity Fair. And of

Bunyan, Walton would have said that he was among those Nonconformists who 'might be sincere, well-meaning men, whose indiscreet zeal might be so like charity, as thereby to cover a multitude of errors'. To Walton there seemed spiritual solace in remembering 'that we have comforted and been helpful to a dejected or distressed family'. Bunyan would have regarded this belief as a heresy, and (theoretically) charitable deeds 'as filthy rags'. Differently constituted, these excellent men accepted religion in different ways. Christian bows beneath a burden of sin; Piscator beneath a basket of trout. Let us be grateful for the diversities of human nature, and the dissimilar paths which lead Piscator and Christian alike to the City not built with hands. Both were seekers for a City which to have sought through life, in patience, honesty, loyalty, and love, is to have found it. Of Walton's book we may say:

Laudis amore tumes? Sunt certa piacula quae te
Ter pure lecto poterunt recreare libello.

Essay on Izaak Walton

WILLIAM CLARK RUSSELL

1844–1911

522 *The Last of the Grosvenor*

THE boatswain shoved the boat's head off, and we each shipped an oar and pulled the boat about a quarter of a mile away from the ship; and then, from a strange and wild curiosity to behold the ship sink, and still in our hearts clinging to her, not only as the home wherein we had found shelter for many days past, but as the only visible object in all the stupendous reach of waters, we threw in the oars and sat watching her. . .

Few sailors can behold the ship in which they have sailed sinking before their eyes without the same emotion of distress and pity almost which the spectacle of a drowning man excites in them. She has grown a familiar name, a familiar object; thus far she has borne them in safety; she has been rudely beaten, and yet has done her duty; but the tempest has broken her down at last; all the beauty is shorn from her; she is weary with the long and dreadful struggle with the vast forces that Nature arrayed against her; she sinks, a desolate, abandoned thing in mid-ocean, carrying with her a thousand memories, which surge up in the heart with the pain of a strong man's tears. . .

The sun was now quite close to the horizon, branding the ocean with a purple glare, but itself descending into a cloudless sky. I cannot express how majestic and wonderful the great orb looked to us who were almost level with the water. Its disc seemed vaster than I had ever before seen it, and there was something sublimely solemn in the loneliness of its descent. All the sky about it, and far to the south and north, was changed into the colour of gold by its lustre; and over our heads the heavens were an exquisite tender green, which melted in the east into a dark blue.

I was telling Mary that ere the sun sank again we might be on board a ship, and whispering any words of encouragement and hope to her, when I was startled by the boatswain crying, 'Now she 's gone! Look at her!' I turned my eyes towards the ship, and could scarcely credit my senses when I found that her hull had vanished, and that nothing was to be seen of her but her spars, which were all aslant sternwards.

I held my breath as I saw the masts sink lower and lower. First the crossjack-yard was submerged, then the gaff with the ensign hanging dead at the peak, then the mainyard; presently only the maintopmast cross-trees were visible, a dark cross upon the water: they vanished; at the same moment the sun disappeared behind the horizon; and now we were alone on the great breathing deep, with all the eastern sky growing dark as we watched.

'It 's all over!' said the boatswain, breaking the silence, and speaking in a hollow tone. 'No livin' man'll ever see the *Grosvenor* agin!'

The Wreck of the Grosvenor

GEORGE SAINTSBURY

1845–

523 *The Death of Molière*

MOLIÈRE was not old; he was almost exactly the age of Shakespeare when he too died—less 'tragically', as they say, but also with a parcel of work done, such as makes it, though natural, almost absurd to wish for more. As for the 'tragedy', there was, it may seem to a sober and not too obtuse judgment, little for tears here, little to wail, except in so far as 'the end' is always sad. If God has given you brains, and courage, and the upward countenance; if you have loved; if you have had your day and lived your life, what more do you want? Molière had had and done all this. And as for dying in his vocation, Nelson and he and that saintly hero of Rotrou who elected 'mourir debout et dans son rang', may possibly appeal together to a tribunal which does not judge according to the standard of the Puritan and the Pharisee.

Introduction to the Plays of Molière

FRANCIS HERBERT BRADLEY

1846–1924

524 *Reason and Reality*

WHAT is it guarantees this presumed identity of truth and fact? We have an instinct, no doubt, that leads us to believe in it, but our instincts, if they can not be in error, may at least be mistranslated and misunderstood. And here we seem placed between rival promptings, that contend for mastery over our reason. It is an old preconception that reality and truth must contain the same movement of a single content that, by itself not intellectual, then doubles itself in the glass of reflection. On the other hand it is a certain result that our intellect and the movement of our intellect's content is abstract and discursive, a mere essence distilled from our senses' abundance. And this certainty has inspired an opposite conclusion. Since the rational and the real in truth must be one, and since these vital essences are the life of our reason, then, despite of seeming, the reality too must consist and must live in them. If the real becomes truth, then so without doubt the truth must be real.

In the face of these promptings, I must venture to doubt whether *both* have not branched from one stem of deceit, whether truth, if that stands for the work of the intellect, is ever precisely[1] identical with fact, or claims in the end to possess such identity. To the

[1] precisely *is here emphatic*

arguments urged by the reason, and which demonstrate that an element which is not intelligible is nothing, I possibly might not find an intelligible reply. But I comfort my mind with the thought that if myself, when most truly myself, were pure intelligence, I at least am not likely to survive the discovery, or be myself when I wake from a pleasant delusion. And perhaps it may stand with the philosopher's reason, as it stood with the sculptor who moulded the lion. When in the reason's philosophy the rational appears dominant and sole possessor of the world, we can only wonder what place would be left to it, if the element excluded might break through the charm of the magic circle, and, without growing rational, could find expression. Such an idea may be senseless, and such a thought may contradict itself, but it serves to give voice to an obstinate instinct. Unless thought stands for something that falls beyond mere intelligence, if 'thinking' is not used with some strange implication that never was part of the meaning of the word, a lingering scruple still forbids us to believe that reality can ever be purely[1] rational. It may come from a failure in my metaphysics, or from a weakness of the flesh which continues to blind me, but the notion that existence[2] could be the same as understanding strikes as cold and ghost-like as the dreariest materialism. That the glory of this world in the end is appearance leaves the world more glorious, if we feel it is a show of some fuller splendour; but the sensuous curtain is a deception and a cheat, if it hides some colourless movement of atoms, some spectral woof of impalpable abstractions, or unearthly ballet of bloodless categories. Though dragged to such conclusions, we can not

[1] purely *is here emphatic*

[2] existence *here = reality*

embrace them. Our principles may be true, but they are not reality. They no more *make* that Whole which commands our devotion, than some shredded dissection of human tatters *is* that warm and breathing beauty of flesh which our hearts found delightful.

The Principles of Logic

ARCHIBALD PHILIP PRIMROSE EARL OF ROSEBERY

1847–

525 *The Elder and the Younger Pitt*

IT is perhaps unnecessary to say more of the circumstances and surroundings of Pitt. But it is impossible to complete any sketch of his career, or indeed to form an adequate estimate of his character, without setting him, if only for a moment, by the side of Chatham. Not merely are they father and son; not merely are they the most conspicuous English Ministers of the eighteenth century; but their characters illustrate each other. And yet it is impossible for men to be more different. Pitt was endowed with mental powers of the first order; his readiness, his apprehension, his resource were extraordinary; the daily parliamentary demand on his brain and nerve power he met with serene and inexhaustible affluence; his industry, administrative activity, and public spirit were unrivalled, it was perhaps impossible to carry the force of sheer ability further; he was a portent. Chatham in most of these respects was inferior to his son. He was a political mystic; sometimes sublime, sometimes impossible, and sometimes insane. But he had genius. It was that fitful and undefinable inspiration that gave to his eloquence a piercing and terrible note which no other English eloquence has touched; that made him the idol of his countrymen, though they could scarcely be said to have seen his face or heard his voice or read his speeches; that made him a watchword among those distant insurgents whose wish for independence he yet ardently opposed; that made each remotest soldier and bluejacket feel when he was in office that there was a man in Downing Street, and a man whose eye penetrated everywhere; that made his name at once an inspiration and a dread; that cowed the tumultuous Commons at his frown. Each Pitt possessed in an eminent degree the qualities which the other most lacked: one was formed by nature for peace, the other for war. Chatham could not have filled Pitt's place in the ten years which followed 1783: but, from the time that war was declared, the guidance of Chatham would have been worth an army. No country could have too many Pitts: the more she has the greater will she be. But no country could afford the costly and splendid luxury of many Chathams.

Pitt

RICHARD JEFFERIES

1848–1887

526 *The Wheat*

i

IF you will look at a grain of wheat you will see that it seems folded up: it has crossed its arms and rolled itself up in a cloak, a fold of which forms a groove, and so gone to sleep. If you look at it some time, as people in the old enchanted days used to look into a mirror, or the magic ink, until they saw living figures therein, you can almost trace a miniature human being in the oval of the grain. It is narrow at the top, where the head would be, and broad across the shoulders, and narrow again down towards the feet; a tiny man or woman has wrapped itself round about with a garment and settled to slumber. Up in the far north, where the dead ice reigns, our arctic explorers used to roll themselves in a sleeping-bag like this, to keep the warmth in their bodies against the chilliness of the night. Down in the south, where the heated sands of Egypt never cool, there in the rock-hewn tombs lie the mummies wrapped and lapped and wound about with a hundred yards of linen, in the hope, it may be, that spices and balm might retain within the sarcophagus some small fragment of human organism through endless ages, till at last the gift of life revisited it. Like a grain of wheat the mummy is folded in its cloth. And I do not know really whether I might not say that these little grains of English corn do not hold within them the actual flesh and blood of man. Transubstantiation is a fact there.

Sometimes the grains are dry and shrivelled and hard as shot, sometimes they are large and full and have a juiciness about them, sometimes they are a little bit red, others are golden, many white. The sack stands open in the market—you can thrust your arm in it a foot deep, or take up a handful and let it run back like a liquid stream, or hold it in your palm and balance it, feeling the weight. They are not very heavy as they lie in the palm, yet these little grains are a ponderous weight that rules man's world. Wherever they are there is empire. Could imperial Rome have only grown sufficient wheat in Italy to have fed her legions Caesar would still be master of three-fourths of the earth. Rome thought more in her latter days of grapes and oysters and mullets, that change colour as they die, and singing girls and flute-playing, and cynic verse of Horace—anything rather than corn. Rome is no more, and the lords of the world are they who have mastership of wheat. We have the mastership at this hour by dint of our gold and our hundred-ton guns, but they are telling our farmers to cast aside their corn, and to grow tobacco and fruit and anything else that can be thought of in preference. The gold is slipping away. These sacks in the market open to all to thrust their hands in are not sacks of corn but of golden sovereigns, half-sovereigns, new George and the dragon, old George and the dragon, Sydney mint sovereigns, Napoleons, half-Napoleons, Belgian gold, German gold, Italian gold ; gold scraped and scratched and gathered together like old rags from door to door. Sacks full of gold. . .

ii

The great field you see was filled with gold corn four feet deep as a pitcher is filled with water to the brim. Of yore the rich man is said, in the Roman classic, to have measured his money, so here you might have measured it by the rood. The sunbeams sank deeper and deeper into the wheatears, layer upon layer of light, and the colour deepened by these daily strokes. There was no bulletin to tell the folk of its progress, no Nileometer to mark the rising flood of the wheat to its hour of overflow. Yet there went through the village a sense of expectation, and men said to each other, ' We shall be there soon '. No one knew the day—the last day of doom of the golden race ; every one knew it was nigh. One evening there was a small square piece cut at one side, a little notch, and two shocks stood there in the twilight. Next day the village sent forth its army with their crooked weapons to cut and slay. It used to be an era, let me tell you, when a great farmer gave the signal to his reapers; not a man, woman, or child that did not talk of that. Well-to-do people stopped their vehicles and walked out into the new stubble. Ladies came, farmers, men of low degree, everybody—all to exchange a word or two with the workers. These were so terribly in earnest at the start they could scarcely acknowledge the presence even of the squire. They felt themselves so important, and were so full, and so intense and one-minded in their labour, that the great of the earth might come and go as sparrows for aught they cared. More men and more men were put on day by day, and women to bind the sheaves, till the vast field held the village, yet they seemed but a handful buried in the tunnels of the golden mine: they were lost in it like the hares, for as the wheat fell, the shocks rose behind them, low tents of corn. Your skin or mine could not have stood the scratching of the straw, which is stiff and sharp, and the burning of the sun, which blisters like red-hot iron. No one could stand the harvest-field as a reaper except he had been born and cradled in a cottage, and passed his childhood bareheaded in July heats and January snows. *Field and Hedgerow*

EDMUND GOSSE

1849–

527 *Oddicombe Chapel*

BEFORE our coming, a little flock of persons met in the Room, a community of the indefinite sort just then becoming frequent in the West of England, pious rustics connected with no other recognized body of Christians, and depending directly on the independent study of the Bible. . . The origin of the meeting had been odd. A few years before we came a crew of Cornish fishermen, quite unknown to the villagers, were driven by stress of weather into the haven under the cliff. They landed, and, instead of going to a public-house, they looked about for a room where they could hold a prayer-meeting. They were devout Wesleyans ; they had come from the open sea, they were far from home, and they had been starved by lack of their customary religious privileges. As they stood about in the street before their meeting, they challenged the respectable girls who came out to stare at them, with the question, ' Do you love the Lord Jesus, my maid ? ' Receiving dubious answers, they pressed the inhabitants to come in and pray with them, which several did. Ann Burmington, who long afterwards told me about it, was one of those girls, and she repeated that the fishermen said, ' What a dreadful thing it will be, at the Last Day, when the Lord says, " Come, ye blessed," and says it not to you, and then " Depart, ye cursed," and you maidens have to depart.' They were finely-built young men, with black beards and shining eyes, and I do not question that some flash of sex unconsciously mingled with the curious episode, although their behaviour was in all respects discreet. It was, perhaps, not wholly a coincidence that almost all those particular girls remained unmarried to the end of their lives. After two or three days, the fishermen went off to sea again. They prayed and sailed away, and the girls, who had not even asked their names, never heard of them again. But several of the young women were definitely converted, and they formed the nucleus of our little gathering. *Father and Son*

WILLIAM ERNEST HENLEY

1849–1903

528 *Other Sea-Poets and Longfellow*

THE ocean as confidant, a Laertes that can neither avoid his Hamlets nor bid them hold their peace, is a modern invention. Byron and Shelley discovered it; Heine took it into his confidence, and told it the story of his loves; Wordsworth made it a moral influence; Browning loved it in his way, but his way was not often the poet's; to Matthew Arnold it was the voice of destiny, and its message was a message of despair; Hugo conferred with it as with an humble friend, and uttered such lofty things over it as are rarely heard upon the lips of man. And so with living lyrists each after his kind. . .

But to Longfellow alone was it given to see that stately galley which Count Arnaldos saw; his only to hear the steersman singing that wild and wondrous song which none that hears it can resist, and none that has heard it may forget. Then did he learn the old monster's secret—the word of his charm, the core of his mystery, the human note in his music, the quality of his influence upon the heart and the mind of man; and then did he win himself a place apart among sea-poets. With the most of them it is a case of *Ego et rex meus*: It is I and the sea, and my egoism is as valiant and as vocal as the other's. But Longfellow is the spokesman of a confraternity; what thrills him to utterance is the spirit of that strange and beautiful freemasonry established as long ago as when the first sailor steered the first keel out into the unknown, irresistible water-world, and so established the foundations of the eternal brotherhood of man with ocean. To him the sea is a place of mariners and ships. In his verse the rigging creaks, the white sail fills and crackles, there are blown smells of pine and hemp and tar; you catch the home wind on your cheeks; and old shipmen, their eyeballs white in their bronzed faces, with silver rings and gaudy handkerchiefs, come in and tell you moving stories of the immemorial, incommunicable deep. He abides in a port; he goes down to the docks, and loiters among the galiots and brigantines; he hears the melancholy song of the chanty-men; he sees the chips flying under the shipwright's adze; he smells the pitch that smokes and bubbles in the caldron. And straightway he falls to singing his variations on the ballad of Count Arnaldos; and the world listens, for its heart beats in his song.

Views and Reviews: Literature

529 *Raeburn*

THE material Raeburn found in his native place was of the finest quality. The blessing of the Union was everywhere apparent, but Scotland was not yet Anglicized, and Edinburgh was still her capital in fact as well as in name. As the city at once of Walter Scott and of the Great Unknown, it was a metropolis of poetry and fiction; as the city of Jeffrey and *Maga*, it was a centre of so-called criticism; as the city of Raeburn and John Thomson, it was a high place of portraiture and landscape; as the city of Archibald Constable and the Ballantynes, it was a headquarters of bookselling and printing. It was the city of Reid and Dugald Stewart, of Erskine and Henry Dundas, of John Home and Henry Mackenzie, of Braxfield and Newton and Clerk of Eldin, of Francis Horner and Neil Gow; and as Raeburn painted the most of these—and indeed there was scarce an eminent Scotsman but sat to him—his achievement may be said to mirror some thirty years of the Scots nation's life. Scarce anywhere could he have found better models; which, for their part, were thrice fortunate in their painter. Honourable as were his beginnings, they scarce gave earnest of the results of his later years. His genius, essentially symmetrical and sane, did but mature with time; artistic from the first, his accomplishment was finest at his death; his vision was at its keenest in his latest efforts; his life, in fine, was a piece of work as sound and healthy and manly as his art. Thus: 'he is said to have lost a great deal of money by becoming security for a relative, but he bore his loss with great composure, and painted no more industriously after than before'; he spent much of his leisure in 'mechanics and natural philosophy'; he practised sculpture—it is said that when he was studying under Michelangelo in Rome, he came near to preferring it before painting—with a certain diligence; he 'excelled', says his biographer, 'at archery, golf, and other Scottish exercises'; he laid out and built 'on so judicious and tasteful a plan' that his estate became in no great while 'the most extensive suburb attached to Edinburgh'; he was an excellent talker; he appears to have been singularly fortunate in his domestic relations; he enjoyed the friendship as he commanded the admiration of the most distinguished men of his time; his health was perfect;

he stood upwards of six foot two in his boots; 'it may be added that, while engaged in painting, his step and attitudes were at once stately and graceful'. His character and his career, indeed, have all the balance, the unity, the symmetrical completeness, of his genius and his achievement; and the rhythm to which they moved—large, dignified, consummate: like that of a Handelian chorus—remained unbroken until the end. It came in 1823. He was now a man of sixty-seven; his health was apparently imperturbable; with Scott and Adam and Shepherd, he had been for some years in the habit of 'interposing a parenthesis into the chapter of public business for the purpose of visiting objects of historical interest and curiosity'; and this year he had not only 'visited with enthusiasm the ancient ruins of St. Andrews, of Pittenweem, and other remains of antiquity', but had also 'contributed much to the hilarity of the party'. Returning to Edinburgh, he had been honoured with a sitting from Sir Walter, of whom he was anxious to finish two presentments, one for himself and one for Lord Montagu; and 'within a day or two afterwards' he was 'suddenly affected with a general decay and debility',—a condition 'not accompanied by any visible complaint'. He lingered no more than a week; and so it befell that the portrait of the author of *Waverley* was the last to make any call upon a capacity of brain and hand unequalled in that owner's day. Thus does Scotland work: she has the genius of fitness, so that to the world without her achievement seems ever instinct with the very spirit of romance. There are two great artists in the Edinburgh of 1823, and the one dies painting the other (the fact remains 'a subject of affectionate regret' to the survivor). I think of Hugo—of the *Je crois en Dieu* of his last will and testament, his careful provision of a pauper's hearse. And I revert with pride and gratitude to the supreme experience of this august pair of friends.

Views and Reviews: Art

AUGUSTINE BIRRELL

1850–

530 *John Wesley's Journal*

WHERE the reader of the Journal will be shocked is when his attention is called to the public side of the country—to the state of the gaols, to Newgate, to Bethlehem, to the criminal code, to the brutality of so many of the judges and the harshness of the magistrates, to the supineness of the bishops, to the extinction in high places of the missionary spirit—in short, to the heavy slumber of humanity.

Wesley was full of compassion—of a compassion wholly free from hysterics and credulity. In public affairs his was the composed zeal of a Howard. His efforts to penetrate the dark places were long in vain. He says in his dry way: 'They won't let me go to Bedlam because they say I make the inmates mad, or into Newgate because I make them wicked.' The reader of the Journal will be at no loss to see what these sapient magistrates meant. Wesley was a terribly exciting preacher, quiet though his manner was. He pushed matters home without flinching. He made people cry out and fall down, nor did it surprise him that they should. You will find some strange biographies in the Journal. Consider that of John

Lancaster for a moment. He was a young fellow who fell into bad company, stole some velvet, and was sentenced to death, and lay for awhile in Newgate awaiting his hour. A good Methodist woman, Sarah Peters, obtained permission to visit him, though the fever was raging in the prison at the time. Lancaster had no difficulty in collecting six or seven other prisoners, all like himself waiting to be strangled, and Sarah Peters prayed with them and sang hymns, the clergy of the diocese being otherwise occupied. When the eve of their execution arrived, the poor creatures begged that Sarah Peters might be allowed to remain with them to continue her exhortations; but this could not be. In her absence, however, they contrived to console one another, for that devilish device of a later age, solitary confinement, was then unknown. When the bellman came round at midnight to tell them, 'Remember you are to die to-day,' they cried out: 'Welcome news—welcome news!' How they met their deaths you can read for yourselves in the Journal, which concludes the narrative with a true eighteenth-century touch: 'John Lancaster's body was carried away by a company hired by the surgeons, but a crew of sailors pursued them, took it from them by force, and delivered it to his mother, by which means it was decently interred in the presence of many who praised God on his behalf.'

If you want to get into the last century, to feel its pulses throb beneath your finger, be content sometimes to leave the letters of Horace Walpole unturned, resist the drowsy temptation to waste your time over the learned triflers who sleep in the seventeen volumes of Nichols—nay, even deny yourself your annual reading of Boswell or your biennial retreat with Sterne, and ride up and down the country with the greatest force of the eighteenth century in England

No man lived nearer the centre than John Wesley, neither Clive nor Pitt, neither Mansfield nor Johnson. You cannot cut him out of our national life. No single figure influenced so many minds, no single voice touched so many hearts. No other man did such a life's work for England. As a writer he has not achieved distinction. He was no Athanasius, no Augustine. He was ever a preacher and an organizer, a labourer in the service of humanity; but, happily for us, his Journals remain, and from them we can learn better than from anywhere else what manner of man he was, and the character of the times during which he lived and moved and had his being.

Miscellanies

FREDERIC WILLIAM MAITLAND

1850–1906

531 *The Voice of the Majority*

ONE of the great books that remain to be written is The History of the Majority. Our habit of treating the voice of a majority as equivalent to the voice of an all is so deeply engrained that we hardly think that it has a history. But a history it has, and there is fiction there: not fiction if that term implies falsehood or caprice, but a slow extension of old words and old thoughts beyond the old facts. In the earlier middle ages it is unanimity that is wanted; it is unanimity that is chronicled; it is unanimity that is after a sort obtained. A shout is the test, and in form it is the primary test today in the House of Commons.

But the few should not go on shouting when they know that they are few. If they do, measures can be taken to make them hold their peace. In the end the assembly has but one voice, one audible voice; it is unanimous. The transition to a process which merely counts heads or hands is the slower because in some manner that no arithmetic can express the voices of the older, wiser, more worshipful, more substantial men are the weightiest. The disputed, the double elections that we read of in every quarter, from the papal and imperial downwards, tell a very curious story of constitutional immaturity. But until men will say plainly that a vote carried by a majority of one is for certain purposes every whit as effectual as an unanimous vote, one main contrast between corporate ownership and mere community escapes them.

Township and Borough

LAFCADIO HEARN

1850–1904

532 *A Japanese Garden*

NO effort to create an impossible or purely ideal landscape is made in the Japanese garden. Its artistic purpose is to copy faithfully the attractions of a veritable landscape, and to convey the real impression that a real landscape communicates. It is therefore at once a picture and a poem; perhaps even more a poem than a picture. For as nature's scenery, in its varying aspects, affects us with sensations of joy or of solemnity, of grimness or of sweetness, of force or of peace, so must the true reflection of it in the labor of the landscape gardener create not merely an impression of beauty, but a mood in the soul. The grand old landscape gardeners, those Buddhist monks who first introduced the art into Japan, and subsequently developed it into an almost occult science, carried their theory yet farther than this. They held it possible to express moral lessons in the design of a garden, and abstract ideas, such as Chastity, Faith, Piety, Content, Calm, and Connubial Bliss. Therefore were gardens contrived according to the character of the owner, whether poet, warrior, philosopher, or priest. In those ancient gardens (the art, alas, is passing away under the withering influence of the utterly commonplace Western taste) there were expressed both a mood of nature and some rare Oriental conception of a mood of man.

I do not know what human sentiment the principal division of my garden was intended to reflect; and there is none to tell me. Those by whom it was made passed away long generations ago, in the eternal transmigration of souls. But as a poem of nature it requires no interpreter. It occupies the front portion of the grounds, facing south; and it also extends west to the verge of the northern division of the garden, from which it is partly separated by a curious screen-fence structure. There are large rocks in it, heavily mossed; and divers fantastic basins of stone for holding water; and stone lamps green with years; and a shachihoko, such as one sees at the peaked angles of castle roofs,—a great stone fish, an idealized porpoise, with its nose in the ground and its tail in the air. There are miniature hills, with old trees upon them; and there are long slopes of green, shadowed by flowering shrubs, like river banks; and there are green knolls like islets. All these verdant elevations rise from spaces of pale yellow sand, smooth as a surface of silk and miming the curves and meanderings of a river course. These sanded spaces are not to be trodden upon; they are much too beautiful for that. The least speck of dirt would mar their effect; and it requires the trained skill of an experienced native gardener—a delightful old man he is—to keep them in perfect form. But they are traversed in various directions by lines of flat unhewn rock slabs, placed at slightly irregular distances from one another, exactly like stepping-stones across a brook. The whole effect is that of the shores of a still stream in some lovely, lonesome, drowsy place.

There is nothing to break the illusion, so secluded the garden is. High walls and fences shut out streets and contiguous things; and the shrubs and the trees, heightening and thickening toward the boundaries, conceal from view even the roofs of the neighbouring katchiū-yashiki. Softly beautiful are the tremulous shadows of leaves on the sunned sand; and the scent of flowers comes thinly sweet with every waft of tepid air; and there is a humming of bees.

Glimpses of Unfamiliar Japan

ROBERT LOUIS STEVENSON

1850–1894

533 *The English Admirals*

ALMOST everybody in our land, except humanitarians and a few persons whose youth has been depressed by exceptionally æsthetic surroundings, can understand and sympathise with an Admiral or a prize-fighter. I do not wish to bracket Benbow and Tom Cribb; but, depend upon it, they are practically bracketed for admiration in the minds of many frequenters of ale-houses. If you told them about Germanicus and the eagles, or Regulus going back to Carthage, they would very likely fall asleep; but tell them about Harry Pearce and Jem Belcher, or about Nelson and the Nile, and they put down their pipes to listen. I have by me a copy of *Boxiana*, on the fly-leaves of which a youthful member of the fancy kept a chronicle of remarkable events and an obituary of great men. Here we find piously chronicled the demise of jockeys, watermen, and pugilists—Johnny Moore, of the Liverpool Prize Ring; Tom Spring, aged fifty-six; 'Pierce Egan, senior, writer of *Boxiana* and other sporting works'—and among all these, the Duke of Wellington! If Benbow had lived in the time of this annalist, do you suppose his name would not have been added to the glorious roll? In short, we do not all feel warmly towards Wesley or Laud, we cannot all take pleasure in *Paradise Lost*; but there are certain common sentiments and touches of nature by which the whole nation is made to feel kinship. A little while ago everybody, from Hazlitt and John Wilson down to the imbecile creature who scribbled his register on the fly-leaves of *Boxiana*, felt a more or less shamefaced satisfaction in the exploits of prize-fighters. And the exploits of the Admirals are popular to the same degree, and tell in all ranks of society. Their sayings and doings stir English blood like the sound of a trumpet; and if the Indian Empire, the trade of London, and all the outward and visible ensigns of our greatness should pass away, we should still leave behind us a durable monument of what we were in these sayings and doings of the English Admirals.

Virginibus Puerisque

534 *Children*

THEY are wheeled in perambulators or dragged about by nurses in a pleasing stupor. A vague, faint, abiding wonderment possesses them. Here and there some specially remarkable circumstance, such as a water-cart or a guardsman, fairly penetrates into the seat of thought and calls them, for half a moment, out of themselves; and you may see them, still towed forward sideways by the inexorable nurse as by a sort of destiny, but still staring at the bright object in their wake. It may be some minutes before another such moving spectacle reawakens them to the world in which they dwell. For other children, they almost invariably show some intelligent sympathy. 'There is a fine fellow making mud pies,' they seem to say; 'that I can understand, there is some sense in mud pies.' But the doings of their elders, unless where they are speakingly picturesque or recommend themselves by the quality of being easily imitable, they let them go over their heads (as we say) without the least regard. If it were not for this perpetual imitation, we should be tempted to fancy they despised us outright, or only considered us in the light of creatures brutally strong and brutally silly; among whom they condescended to dwell in obedience like a philosopher at a barbarous court.

Virginibus Puerisque

535 *Night among the Pines*

A FAINT wind, more like a moving coolness than a stream of air, passed down the glade from time to time; so that even in my great chamber the air was being renewed all night long. I thought with horror of the inn at Chasseradès and the congregated nightcaps; with horror of the nocturnal prowesses of clerks and students, of hot theatres and pass-keys and close rooms. I have not often enjoyed a more serene possession of myself, nor felt more independent of material aids. The outer world, from which we cower into our houses, seemed after all a gentle habitable place; and night after night a man's bed, it seemed, was laid and waiting for him in the fields, where God keeps an open house. I thought I had rediscovered one of those truths which are revealed to savages and hid from political economists: at the least, I had discovered a new pleasure for myself. And yet even while I was exulting in my solitude I became aware of a strange lack. I wished a companion to lie near me in the starlight, silent and not moving, but ever within touch. For there is a fellowship more quiet even than solitude, and which, rightly understood, is solitude made perfect. And to live out of doors with the woman a man loves is of all lives the most complete and free.

As I thus lay, between content and longing, a faint noise stole towards me through the pines. I thought, at first, it was the crowing of cocks or the barking of dogs at some very distant farm; but steadily and gradually it took articulate shape in my ears, until I became aware that a passenger was going by upon the high-road in the valley, and singing loudly as he went. There was more of good-will than grace in his performance; but he trolled with ample lungs; and the sound of his voice took hold upon the hillside and set the air shaking in the leafy glens. I have heard people passing by night in sleeping cities; some of them sang; one, I remember, played loudly on the bagpipes. I have heard the rattle of a cart or carriage spring up suddenly after hours of stillness, and pass, for some minutes, within the range of my hearing as I lay abed. There is a romance about all who are abroad in the black hours, and with something of a thrill we try to guess their business. But here the romance was double: first, this glad passenger, lit internally with wine, who sent up his voice in music through the night; and then I, on the other hand, buckled into my sack, and smoking alone in the pine-woods between four and five thousand feet towards the stars.

Travels with a Donkey

536 *A Midnight Flitting*

ONCE in my own room, I made the customary motions of undressing, so that I might time myself; and when the cycle was complete, set my tinder-box ready, and blew out my taper. The matter of an hour afterward I made a light again, put on my shoes of list that I had worn by my lord's sick-bed, and set forth into the house to call the voyagers. All were dressed and waiting—my lord, my lady, Miss Katharine, Mr. Alexander, my lady's woman Christie; and I observed the effect of secrecy even upon quite innocent persons, that one after another showed in the chink of the door a face as white as paper. We slipped out of the side postern into a night of darkness, scarce broken by a star or two; so that at first we groped and stumbled and fell among the bushes. A few hundred yards up the wood-path Macconochie was waiting us with a great lantern; so the rest of the way we went easy enough, but still in a kind of guilty silence. A little beyond the abbey the path debouched on the main road; and some quarter of a mile farther, at the place called Eagles, where the moors begin, we saw the lights of the two carriages stand shining by the wayside. Scarce a word or two was uttered at our parting, and these regarded business: a silent grasping of hands, a turning of faces aside, and the thing was over; the horses broke into a trot, the lamplight sped like Will-o'-the-Wisp upon the broken moorland, it dipped beyond Stony Brae; and there were Macconochie and I alone with our lantern on the road. There was one thing more to wait for, and that was the reappearance of the coach upon Cartmore. It seems they must have pulled up upon the summit, looked back for a last time, and seen our lantern not yet moved away from the place of separation. For a lamp was taken from a carriage, and waved three times up and down by way of a farewell. And then they were gone indeed, having looked their last on the kind roof of Durrisdeer, their faces toward a barbarous country. I never knew before, the greatness of that vault of night in which we two poor serving-men—the one old, and the one elderly—stood for the first time deserted; I had never felt before my own dependency upon the countenance of others. The sense of isolation burned in my bowels like a fire. It seemed that we who remained at home were the true exiles, and that Durrisdeer and Solwayside, and all that made my country native, its air good to me, and its language welcome, had gone forth and was far over the sea with my old masters.

The Master of Ballantrae

ROBERT LOUIS STEVENSON

537 *Kirstie*

SHE lay tossing in bed that night, besieged with feverish thoughts. There were dangerous matters pending, a battle was toward, over the fate of which she hung in jealousy, sympathy, fear, and alternate loyalty and disloyalty to either side. Now she was reincarnated in her niece, and now in Archie. Now she saw, through the girl's eyes, the youth on his knees to her, heard his persuasive instances with a deadly weakness, and received his overmastering caresses. Anon, with a revulsion, her temper raged to see such utmost favours of fortune and love squandered on a brat of a girl, one of her own house, using her own name—a deadly ingredient—and that 'didna ken her ain mind an' was as black 's your hat.' Now she trembled lest her deity should plead in vain, loving the idea of success for him like a triumph of nature ; anon, with returning loyalty to her own family and sex, she trembled for Kirstie and the credit of the Elliotts. And again she had a vision of herself, the day over for her old-world tales and local gossip, bidding farewell to her last link with life and brightness and love ; and behind and beyond, she saw but the blank butt-end where she must crawl to die. Had she then come to the lees? she, so great, so beautiful, with a heart as fresh as a girl's and strong as womanhood? It could not be, and yet it was so ; and for a moment her bed was horrible to her as the sides of the grave. And she looked forward over a waste of hours, and saw herself go on to rage, and tremble, and be softened, and rage again, until the day came and the labours of the day must be renewed.

Suddenly she heard feet on the stairs—his feet, and soon after the sound of a window-sash flung open.

She sat up with her heart beating. He had gone to his room alone, and he had not gone to bed. She might again have one of her night cracks; and at the entrancing prospect, a change came over her mind; with the approach of this hope of pleasure, all the baser metal became immediately obliterated from her thoughts. She rose, all woman, and all the best of woman, tender, pitiful, hating the wrong, loyal to her own sex—and all the weakest of that dear miscellany, nourishing, cherishing next her soft heart, voicelessly flattering, hopes that she would have died sooner than have acknowledged. She tore off her nightcap, and her hair fell about her shoulders in profusion. Undying coquetry awoke. By the faint light of her nocturnal rush, she stood before the looking-glass, carried her shapely arms above her head, and gathered up the treasures of her tresses. She was never backward to admire herself; that kind of modesty was a stranger to her nature; and she paused, struck with a pleased wonder at the sight. 'Ye daft auld wife!' she said, answering a thought that was not; and she blushed with the innocent consciousness of a child. Hastily she did up the massive and shining coils, hastily donned a wrapper, and with the rushlight in her hand, stole into the hall. Below stairs she heard the clock ticking the deliberate seconds, and Frank jingling with the decanters in the dining-room. Aversion rose in her, bitter and momentary. 'Nesty, tippling puggy!' she thought; and the next moment she had knocked guardedly at Archie's door and was bidden enter.

Weir of Hermiston

FREDERICK YORK POWELL

1850–1904

538 *Alfred*

TO the statesman and warrior that saved his own country in her hour of need, preserved her national individuality, and paved the way to her future unity; to the scholar and man of letters that first made of our English tongue an avenue to all the knowledge of the past, a vehicle for the highest expression of human thought that the world was then capable of; that raised his vernacular to the rank of a classic language, is due, at least, the gratitude of those whom he has benefited. Alfred's life was not an easy one: 'Hardship and grief not a king but would desire to be free of if he could, but I know that he cannot.' He bade a man do his duty and look to no reward but God, but the good report of his fellows was dear to him as it was to the greatest of his time. A northern contemporary, one of his foemen, possibly, has put this strong Teutonic feeling in a simple and direct way:

Cattle die, kinsfolk die,
  Land and lea are wasted,
One thing that never dies I know—
  Men's judgement on the dead.

Cattle die, kinsfolk die,
  And man himself dies,
But never dies good report
  Away from him that won it.

And Alfred himself has recorded in well-known words his heart's desire: 'This I can now most truly say, that I have desired to live worthily while I lived, and after my life to leave to the men that should be after me a remembrance in good works.'

Life, Letters, and Writings

539 *Omar Khayyàm*

AND for Omar the Persian there were many gratifications, and among them those that thrill, and rightly, the bodily senses. He was no despiser of the common joys of mankind, he acknowledged their blessedness. For him, as for Blake, Earth was a beautiful place; like brother Martin, he loved wine and song and woman. The perpetual miracle of the spring did not appeal to him in vain. The odour of roses came to him as a very breath from heaven. But his paradise was not as simple as Muhammad's.

Toward his fellows he was largely tolerant. He abhorred hypocrisy, but he was not too stern with the hypocrite; he loathed bigotry, but yet he did not deeply condemn the bigot who yearned to murder him. He revolted openly at the cruelties and tragedies of life, but he did not wholly accuse the Universe that baffled him. A man could never be prevented from doing his duty. He would not allow the Unknowable to confound him, and his humour does not quail before any imaginable thing or being.

There is a frank courage about him; he dealt with life as with his mathematics. He was no *quietist.* We cannot steer our drifting raft, nor stem the resistless current; but we have it in our power to behave decently, to share the meagre stock of victuals fairly as long as they last, to take the good and evil as it comes, and even to hope, if we choose to do so, for a fair haven.

Omar has no heaven to offer, no hell to threaten with. His appeal is not to spiritualities, his deity is more *fainéant* than even the gods of Epicurus. To Omar the fair mirage is but a bright reflection, and he will not mistake it for the city that is very far off. He is a plain, downright man, and his 'message' is only a friendly whisper to them that care to sit near him, bidding them trust to the real and front life squarely.

Life, Letters, and Writings

ROBERT BONTINE CUNNINGHAME GRAHAM

1852–

540 *On the 'Santa Barbara'*

EVEN to Cartagena there came echoes of the war. An old, condemned stern-wheeler, lofty of side, beam-engined, crank as a coracle, and quite unseaworthy, had lain for three years in the mud at Maracaibo. Her seams all gaped, her paint was cracked and blistered by the sun, her engines rusty, and round her garboard strakes festoons of seaweed had gathered into a veritable forest, clinging to the barnacles. What her name had been when she toiled up against the muddy waters of the Mississippi I cannot tell. The company that bought her named her the *Santa Barbara*. They set her to run from Cartagena to Quibdó, the capital of the Chocó, up the Atrato River, and down the coast, touching at Tolú, Cispata, and other little ports, after a summary repair. . .

Her crew were negroes and nondescripts, and her engineer, of course, a Scotsman, known as Scottie, stricken in drink and years ; but capable and brave to rashness, as he had proved a hundred times by venturing his life in such a Babylonia as was the rechristened *Santa Barbara*. That nothing should be wanting, and that the link should be supplied between this antique vessel worthy to have convoyed La Pinta and La Santa Maria in their memorable voyage from Palos, had they not outsailed her, a young German mate, from one of the Boche steamers, interned in the bay, acted as captain. He proved himself a sailor and a man. The *Santa Barbara*, after the usual delay of several hours, cleared out of Cartagena in a calm afternoon. She passed into the Caño, at whose mouth the village of Pasacaballos is situated; then out into the great lagoon beyond it. There, she met the gale that seems to have been blowing since the days of the Conquistadores, and is most likely blowing as I write. She rolled like a galleon, the heavy upper decks catching the wind like sails. Seas came aboard of her and set the packages and bales upon her decks awash. The miserable passengers were soaked, and as the evening advanced the seas grew heavier, and still the Point of Tigua loomed a league or two in front of her as she lay labouring in the sea.

The German captain dived into the engine-room and then emerged without his cap, his hair tossed in the wind, and scanned the horizon anxiously. After a look about the deck, . . he took his resolution. Advancing to an Englishman who was sheltering behind a deck-house, he drew his feet together, clicked his heels, and said, 'My name is Einstein, Second-Lieutenant of the Reserve of German Navy,' and raised his fingers mechanically, forgetting he had lost his cap. 'We are at war,' he said; 'but what of that?—no one cares to die without a fight. You see that headland? It is the Point of Tigua. The sea is breaking heavily upon it, and if we drift there we are lost. Only a month ago a steamer failed to weather it, and not a soul was saved. Those that were not dashed on the rocks, the sharks soon tore to pieces. Upon the other side of it we shall be in shelter ; but the swine firemen are frightened and refuse to work. Come down with me, and . . . ah, that is right, you have a pistol : we will help Scottie to persuade them to work on.'

The Englishman, muttering 'All right,' went down below into the engine-room. The firemen, huddled in a heap, had turned that ashy-grey colour that comes into a negro's face at the approach of death, or strongly moved by fear. A foot or two from the ship's furnaces the water lapped up dangerously. Holding their pistols in their hands, the enemies, made comrades by the deadly peril they were in, distributed a hearty kick or two and forced the negroes to fire up.

When they had passed the Point of Tigua, and the old *Santa Barbara* had got under shelter, shaking the water off her decks, as a Newfoundland dog shakes himself on emerging from a swim, they left the engine-room and came up on deck. The two men looked at one another and said nothing, and then instinctively their hands stole out towards each other. The Englishman, half shyly, muttered, 'You are a damned good Boche. My name is Brown.'

Cartagena and the Banks of the Sinú

ARTHUR SHADWELL

AND *c.* 1821

ROBERT HENRY LYTTELTON

1854–

541 *Oxford* v. *Cambridge*

i

Septem Contra Camum: 1843

THE Rev. Arthur Shadwell, who steered the seven-oared crew, has kindly furnished me with the following particulars concerning the race and the circumstances attending on it:

'When the deciding heat for the Grand Challenge Cup was about to come off, Mr. Fletcher Menzies, captain and stroke oar of the Oxford University crew, fainted while stepping into his boat. A deputation from that crew immediately proceeded across the river to inform the holders of the cup, the Cambridge Subscription Rooms crew, of this accident: they found them taking their places to row down to the course. They asked if an eighth man might be allowed them to fill the captain's place. No one was specially proposed to be his substitute, but the rules of the regatta, which had been drawn up in accordance with a remonstrance made by Oxford in the preceding year, did not allow any one to be substituted for a man who had already rowed in a heat: it must be the same crew in its entirety throughout the races. The Cambridge Rooms, indeed, were not willing to grant the petition, but neither was it in their power to grant it. The Oxford men then asked for a delay to enable them to make arrangements: some of the opposite crew were unwilling at first to grant this, but their objections were overruled, and it was finally arranged that the competitors should meet in an hour's time.

Oxford then shifted their No. 7 to 8, and their bow man to No. 7, and taking up their station close under the lee of the Oxfordshire bank, to be out of the wind, then blowing fresh, were enabled to hold with their opponents from the very first, and then gradually drawing ahead crossed over with a clear lead to the Berkshire bank, and won by two lengths between the two boats. Such is the account of this the most remarkable race on record. The truth was that the winning crew was not only composed of the heaviest and finest material ever brought together in an eight-oar, but they had been gradually forming with incessant care from the October term preceding, and had been handled in their practice as though they were preparing for a race on the London long course. No less pains had been bestowed upon their boat itself, which was truly worthy to carry them. Its subsequent history is remarkable. A few days after the Henley match it defeated the Leander club: in the next summer it beat both Cambridge University and the Leander; and after lasting for years as a kind of sacred model, it was dismembered to form souvenirs of every kind, oars, rudders, and snuff-boxes; till at last the portion containing the coxswain's thwart was converted into a presidential chair of state for the University Boat Club barge twenty-five years after its launch.'

The Oxford and Cambridge Boat Races from 1829 to 1869

ii

Cobden's Over: 1870

HE had not now to receive the ball, for Mr. Hill, who was bustling the field a good deal, stood at his place ready to play, and amidst dead silence the ball was tossed to Mr. Cobden.

We say with confidence that never can one over bowled by any bowler at any future time surpass the over that Cobden was about to deliver then, and it deserves a minute description. Cobden took a long run and bowled very fast, and on the whole was for his pace a straight bowler. But he bowled with little or no break, had not got a puzzling delivery, and though effective against inferior bats, would never have succeeded in bowling out a man like Mr. Ottaway if he had sent a thousand balls to him. However, on the present occasion Ottaway was out, those he had to bowl to were not first-rate batsmen, and Cobden could bowl a good yorker.

You might almost have heard a pin drop as Cobden began his run and the ball whizzed from his hand. Crack! was heard as Mr. Hill's bat met the ball plump and hard, and a yell that beat Donnybrook burst from several thousand Oxford throats. The Oxford eleven still sat at the threshold of the pavilion ready to welcome their comrades after the winning hit was made, and they yelled louder than the rest. The ball was hit hard and low in the direction of long-off, where stood Mr. Bourne, a safe fieldsman; but that he could save this ball from going to the ropes and winning the match by three wickets nobody dreamt. However, the yell of Oxford subdued to a gentler tone, and it was seen that Mr. Bourne had got his left hand in the way and converted a fourer into a single; as the match stood, Oxford wanted 2 to tie and 3 to win and three wickets to go down: Mr. Butler to receive the ball. The second ball that Cobden bowled was very similar to the first, straight and well up on the off stump. Mr. Butler did what anybody else except Louis Hall or Shrewsbury would have done, namely, let drive vigorously. Unfortunately he did not keep the ball down, and it went straight and hard a catch to Mr. Bourne, to whom everlasting credit is due, for he held it, and away went Mr. Butler —amidst Cambridge shouts this time. The position was getting serious, for neither Mr. Stewart nor Mr. Belcher was renowned as a batsman. Rather pale, but with a jaunty air that cricketers are well aware frequently conceals a sickly feeling of nervousness, Mr. Belcher walked to the wicket and took his guard. He felt that if only he could stop one ball and be bowled out the next, still Mr. Hill would get another chance of a knock and the match would probably be won. Cobden had bowled two balls, and two more wickets had to be got; if therefore a wicket was got each ball the match would be won by Cambridge, and Mr. Hill would have no further opportunity of distinguishing himself. In a dead silence Cobden again took the ball. Everybody knows that the sight of a yorker raises hope in a batsman's breast that either a full pitch or a half-volley is coming. To play either of these balls ninety-nine players out of a hundred raise their bat off the ground as a first preliminary. If you are not a quick player the raising of the bat sometimes means nothing less than opening the door of defence, and the ball getting underneath. This is precisely what happened on the present occasion, and Cobden shot in a very fast yorker. A vision of the winning hit flashed across Mr. Belcher's brain, and he raised his bat preparatory to performing great things. He had not seen till too late that neither a full pitch nor a half-volley had been bowled; he could not get his bat down again in time, the ball went under, and his wicket was shattered. There was still one more ball wanted to complete, and Mr. Belcher, a sad man, walked away amid an uproarious storm of cheers.

Matters were becoming distinctly grave, and very irritating must it have been to Mr. Hill, who was like a billiard-player watching his rival in the middle of a big break; he could say a good deal and think a lot, but he could do nothing. Mr. Stewart, *spes ultima* of Oxford, with feelings that are utterly impossible to describe, padded and gloved, nervously took off his coat in the pavilion. If ever a man deserved pity, Mr. Stewart deserved it on that occasion. He did not profess to be a good bat, and his friends did not claim so much for him; he was an excellent wicket-keeper, but he had to go in at a crisis that the best bat in England would not like to face. Mr. Pauncefote, the Oxford captain, was seen addressing a few words of earnest exhortation to him, and with a rather sick feeling Mr. Stewart went to the wicket. Mr. Hill looked at him cheerfully, but very earnestly did Mr. Stewart wish the next ball well over. He took his guard and held his hands low on the bat handle, which was fixed fast as a tree on the block-hole; for Mr. Pauncefote, having seen that Mr. Belcher lost his wicket by raising his bat and letting the ball get under it, had earnestly entreated Mr. Stewart to put the bat straight in the block-hole and keep it there without moving it. This was not by any means bad advice, for the bat covers a great deal of the wicket, and though it is a piece of counsel not likely to be offered to W. G. Grace or Daft, it might not have been inexpedient to offer it to Mr. Stewart. Here, then, was the situation—Mr. Stewart standing manfully up to the wicket, Mr. Cobden beginning his run, and a perfectly dead silence in the crowd. Whiz went the ball, Stewart received the same on his right thigh, fly went the bails, the batsman was bowled off his legs, and Cambridge had won the match by 2 runs! The situation was bewildering. Nobody could quite realize what had happened for a second or so, but then —up went Mr. Absalom's hat, down the pavilion steps with miraculous rapidity flew the Rev. A. R. Ward, and smash went Mr. Charles Marsham's umbrella against the pavilion brickwork.

The Badminton Library: Cricket

ARTHUR BINGHAM WALKLEY

1855–

542 *The National Gallery*

WHO was it who said that, whenever a new book came out, he went and read an old one? It sounds like Lamb or Hazlitt and, I believe, is generally attributed to one or other of the pair, but I have never succeeded in tracing it. Whenever, with each recurrent May, the 'Academy' reopens, I resolve to visit it, so as to be abreast of the times, to have a presentable opinion about 'the picture of the year', and to deplore with actual instances the present condition of British art, but it always ends in my going to the National Gallery instead.

The truth is, brand-new pictures intimidate me. They are aggressive and garish, like the 'new rich'; uncomfortable, like new boots; indigestible, like new vintage port; disconcerting, like the new Regent Street. They challenge a precipitate judgement. It seems absurd to regard things with the paint hardly dry on them *sub specie aeternitatis*. 'Sir, it is driving on the system of life,' and so, I suppose, they must continue to be painted. But I cannot abide them. 'The old masters were very fine,' said Mr. Ramsay MacDonald the other day, 'but we could not live on the old masters alone.' Well, the old masters suffice me. They do not impertinently compete with nature, they have become part of it. Mousehold Heath may be elsewhere on the map, but for me it is situate on the N. side of Trafalgar Square. Endymion Porter may have a history of his own, but for me he is just two portraits, remarkably dissimilar, and an unforgettable name of romance. The Wertheimer family of Mr. Sargent have become as 'legendary', belong as much to the world of imagination as Hogarth's 'Family Group', who it seems were in real life named Strode and had a butler named Jonathan Powell—but have now all changed their names to Hogarth. When the earliest of Mr. Sargent's Wertheimers appeared it created, I believe, what people call a 'sensation'. It was a new picture and the vulgar had their opportunity of gloating over novelty. Now it is an old master, and we can placidly enjoy it, as we placidly enjoy Holbein's Duchess of Milan or Constable's Malvern Hall. I mention these two last, because they are things, unlike the Wertheimer, of pure beauty. 'The Sicilian expedition,' wrote Gray to his friend West, who was reading Thucydides, 'is it or is it not the very finest thing you ever read in your life?' So I would ask of Constable's 'Malvern Hall', is it or is it not the very finest bit of English Landscape you ever saw in your life?

I shall very likely be called a Philistine for my pains—be told that I like English park scenery and enjoy the Constable because it depicts that: in other words, that I appreciate not the art but the subject, which is an aesthetic heresy, &c., &c. I do not plead guilty. The colouring of the picture, the dark blue-greens of the trees against the pale red of the Georgian house; the elegant symmetry of the design, with the reflection of the house in the lake; above all, what I must inadequately call the feeling of the whole composition —all these things affect me. That the subject is a beautiful one in itself 'spoils nothing', as the French say. But what a wonderful corner that is where this gem modestly glows! The 'Flatford Mill' is close by it, and the 'Frosty Morning' on the next wall. These are pictures that make one glad to be an Englishman, with an affectionate heart for the English countryside. It is a perpetual miracle to me that one can mount a few steps out of Trafalgar Square into a quiet room there, and, all of a sudden, enjoy these things, be transported and transformed by them, be changed by them into a different being. We become, for the time, Constables and Turners ourselves, see with their eyes, feel with their emotions.

Still More Prejudice

OSCAR WILDE

1856–1900

543 *The Critic as Artist*

THE world is made by the singer for the dreamer... On the mouldering citadel of Troy lies the lizard like a thing of green bronze. The owl has built her nest in the palace of Priam. Over the empty plain wander shepherd and goatherd with their flocks, and where, on the wine-surfaced, oily sea, *οἶνοψ πόντος*, as Homer calls it, copper-prowed and streaked with vermilion, the great galleys of the Danaoi came in their gleaming crescent, the lonely tunny-fisher sits in his little boat and watches the bobbing corks of his net. Yet, every morning the doors of the city are thrown open, and on foot, or in horse-drawn chariot, the warriors go forth to battle, and mock their enemies from behind their iron masks. All day long the fight rages, and when night comes the torches gleam by the tents, and the cresset burns in the hall. Those who live in marble or on painted panel, know of life but a single exquisite instant, eternal indeed in its beauty, but limited to one note of passion or one mood of calm. Those whom the poet makes live have their myriad emotions of joy and terror, of courage and despair, of pleasure and of suffering. The seasons come and go in glad or saddening pageant, and with winged or leaden feet the years pass by before them. They have their youth and their manhood, they are children, and they grow old. It is always dawn for St. Helena, as Veronese saw her at the window. Through the still morning air the angels bring her the symbol of God's pain. The cool breezes of the morning lift the gilt threads from her brow. On that little hill by the city of Florence, where the lovers of Giorgione are lying, it is always the solstice of noon, of noon made so languorous by summer suns that hardly can the slim naked girl dip into the marble tank the round bubble of clear glass, and the long fingers of the lute-player rest idly upon the chords. It is twilight always for the dancing nymphs whom Corot set free among the silver poplars of France. In eternal twilight they move, those frail diaphanous figures, whose tremulous white feet seem not to touch the dew-drenched grass they tread on. But those who walk in epos, drama, or romance, see through the labouring months the young moons wax and wane, and watch the night from evening unto morning star, and from sunrise unto sunsetting, can note the shifting day with all its gold and shadow. For them, as for us, the flowers bloom and wither, and the Earth, that Green-tressed Goddess as Coleridge calls her, alters her raiment for their pleasure. The statue is concentrated to one moment of perfection. The image stained upon the canvas possesses no spiritual element of growth or change. If they know nothing of death, it is because they know little of life, for the secrets of life and death belong to those, and those only, whom the sequence of time affects, and who possess not merely the present but the future, and can rise or fall from a past of glory or of shame. Movement, that problem of the visible arts, can be truly realized by Literature alone. It is Literature that shows us the body in its swiftness and the soul in its unrest.

Intentions

GEORGE BERNARD SHAW

1856–

544 *The Artist-Philosopher*

THAT the author of Everyman was no mere artist, but an artist-philosopher, and that the artist-philosophers are the only sort of artists I take quite seriously, will be no news to you. Even Plato and Boswell, as the dramatists who invented Socrates and Dr. Johnson, impress me more deeply than the romantic playwrights. Ever since, as a boy, I first breathed the air of the transcendental regions at a performance of Mozart's Zauberflöte, I have been proof against the garish splendors and alcoholic excitements of the ordinary stage combinations of Tappertitian romance with the police intelligence. Bunyan, Blake, Hogarth and Turner (these four apart and above all the English classics), Goethe, Shelley, Schopenhauer, Wagner, Ibsen, Morris, Tolstoy and Nietzsche are among the writers whose peculiar sense of the world I recognize as more or less akin to my own. Mark the word peculiar. I read Dickens and Shakespear without shame or stint; but their pregnant observations and demonstrations of life are not co-ordinated into any philosophy or religion: on the contrary, Dickens's sentimental assumptions are violently contradicted by his observations; and Shakespear's pessimism is only his wounded humanity. Both have the specific genius of the fictionist and the common sympathies of human feeling and thought in pre-eminent degree. They are often saner and shrewder than the philosophers just as Sancho Panza was often saner and shrewder than Don Quixote. They clear away vast masses of oppressive gravity by their sense of the ridiculous, which is at bottom a combination of sound moral judgment with light-hearted good humor. But they are concerned with the diversities of the world instead of with its unities...

Now you cannot say this of the works of the artist-philosophers. You cannot say it, for instance, of The Pilgrim's Progress. Put your Shakespearian hero and coward, Henry V and Pistol or Parolles, beside Mr. Valiant and Mr. Fearing, and you have a sudden revelation of the abyss that lies between the fashionable author who could see nothing in the world but personal aims and the tragedy of their disappointment or the comedy of their incongruity, and the field preacher who achieved virtue and courage by identifying himself with the purpose of the world as he understood it. The contrast is enormous: Bunyan's coward stirs your blood more than Shakespear's hero, who actually leaves you cold and secretly hostile. You suddenly see that Shakespear, with all his flashes and divinations, never understood virtue and courage, never conceived how any man who was not a fool could, like Bunyan's hero, look back from the brink of the river of death over the strife and labour of his pilgrimage, and say 'yet do I not repent me'; or, with the panache of a millionaire, bequeath 'my sword to him that shall succeed me in my pilgrimage, and my courage and skill to him that can get it.' This is the true joy in life, the being used for a purpose recognized by yourself as a mighty one; the being thoroughly worn out before you are thrown on the scrap heap; the being a force of Nature instead of a feverish selfish little clod of ailments and grievances complaining that the world will not devote itself to making you happy. And also the only real tragedy in life is the being used by personally minded men for purposes which you recognize to be base. All the rest is at worst mere misfortune or mortality: this alone is misery, slavery, hell on earth; and the revolt against it is the only force that offers a man's work to the poor artist, whom our personally minded rich people would so willingly employ as pandar, buffoon, beauty monger, sentimentalizer and the like.

Man and Superman. Epistle Dedicatory to Arthur Bingham Walkley

GEORGE GISSING

1857–1903

545 *Shakespeare's Island*

TO-DAY I have read *The Tempest*. . . Among the many reasons which make me glad to have been born in England, one of the first is that I read Shakespeare in my mother tongue. If I try to imagine myself as one who cannot know him face to face, who hears him only speaking from afar, and that in accents which only through the labouring intelligence can touch the living soul, there comes upon me a sense of chill discouragement, of dreary deprivation. I am wont to think that I can read Homer, and, assuredly, if any man enjoys him, it is I; but can I for a moment dream that Homer yields me all his music, that his word is to me as to him who walked by the Hellenic shore when Hellas lived? I know that there reaches me across the vast of time no more than a faint and broken echo; I know that it would be fainter still, but for its blending with those memories of youth which are as a glimmer of the world's primeval glory. Let every land have joy of its poet; for the poet is the land itself, all its greatness and its sweetness, all that incommunicable heritage for which men live and die. As I close the book, love and reverence possess me. Whether does my full heart turn to the great Enchanter, or to the Island upon which he has laid his spell? I know not. I cannot think of them apart. In the love and reverence awakened by that voice of voices, Shakespeare and England are but one.

Private Papers of Henry Ryecroft

JOSEPH CONRAD

1857–1924

546 *A Close Shave*

HOW he first got in touch with his captain's wife Powell relates in this way. It was long before his memorable conversation with the mate and shortly after getting clear of the channel. It was gloomy weather; dead head wind, blowing quite half a gale; the *Ferndale* under reduced sail was stretching close-hauled across the track of the homeward-bound ships, just moving through the water and no more, since there was no object in pressing her and the weather looked threatening. About ten o'clock at night he was alone on the poop, in charge, keeping well aft by the weather rail and staring to windward, when amongst the white, breaking seas, under the black sky, he made out the lights of a ship. He watched them for some time. She was running dead before the wind of course. She will pass jolly close—he said to himself; and then suddenly he felt a great mistrust of that approaching ship. She 's heading straight for us—he thought. It was not his business to get out of the way. On the contrary. And his uneasiness grew by the recollection of the forty tons of dynamite in the body of the *Ferndale*; not the sort of cargo one thinks of with equanimity in connection with a threatened collision. He gazed at the two small lights in the dark immensity filled with the angry noise of the seas. They fascinated him till their plainness to his sight gave him a conviction that there was danger there. He knew in his mind what to do in the emergency, but very properly he felt that he must call the captain at once.

He crossed the deck in one bound. By the immemorial custom and usage of the sea the captain's room is on the starboard side. You would just as soon expect your captain to have his nose at the back of his head as to have his stateroom on the port side of the ship. Powell forgot all about the direction on that point given him by the chief. He flew over as I said, stamped with his foot and then putting his face to the cowl of the big ventilator shouted down there: 'Please come on deck, sir,' in a voice which was not trembling or scared but which we may call fairly expressive. There could not be a mistake as to the urgence of the call. But instead of the expected alert 'All right!' and the sound of a rush down there, he heard only a faint exclamation—then silence.

Think of his astonishment! He remained there, his ear in the cowl of the ventilator, his eyes fastened on those menacing sidelights dancing on the gusts of wind which swept the angry darkness of the sea. It was as though he had waited an hour but it was something much less than a minute before he fairly bellowed into the wide tube 'Captain Anthony!' An agitated 'What is it?' was what he heard down there in Mrs. Anthony's voice, light rapid footsteps. . . Why didn't she try to wake him up! 'I want the captain,' he shouted, then gave it up, making a dash at the companion where a blue light was kept, resolved to act for himself.

On the way he glanced at the helmsman whose face lighted up by the binnacle lamps was calm. He said rapidly to him: 'Stand by to spin that helm up at the first word.' The answer 'Aye, aye, sir,' was delivered in a steady voice. Then Mr. Powell, after a shout for the watch on deck to 'lay aft,' ran to the ship's side and struck the blue light on the rail.

A sort of nasty little spitting of sparks was all that came. The light (perhaps affected by damp) had failed to ignite. The time of all these various acts must be counted in seconds. Powell confessed to me that at this failure he experienced a paralysis of thought, of voice, of limbs. The unexpectedness of this misfire positively overcame his faculties. It was the only thing for which his imagination was not prepared. It was knocked clean over. When it got up it was with the suggestion that he must do something at once or there would be a broadside smash accompanied by the explosion of dynamite, in which both ships would be blown up and every soul on board of them would vanish off the earth in an enormous flame and uproar.

He saw the catastrophe happening and at the same moment, before he could open his mouth or stir a limb to ward off the vision, a voice very near his ear, the measured voice of Captain Anthony, said: 'Wouldn't light—eh? Throw it down! Jump for the flare-up.'

The spring of activity in Mr. Powell was released with great force. He jumped. The flare-up was kept inside the companion with a box of matches ready to hand. Almost before he knew he had moved he was diving under the companion slide. He got hold of the can in the dark and tried to strike a light. But he had to press the flare-holder to his breast with one arm, his fingers were damp and stiff, his hands trembled a little. One match broke. Another went out. In its flame he saw the colourless face of Mrs. Anthony a little below him, standing on the cabin stairs. Her eyes which were very close to his (he was in a crouching posture on the top step) seemed to burn darkly in the vanishing light. On deck the captain's voice was heard sudden and unexpectedly sardonic: 'You had better look sharp, if you want to be in time.'

'Let me have the box,' said Mrs. Anthony in a hurried and familiar whisper which sounded amused as if they had been a couple of children up to some lark behind a wall. He was glad of the offer which seemed to him very natural, and without ceremony—

'Here you are. Catch hold.'

Their hands touched in the dark and she took the box while he held the paraffin-soaked torch in its iron holder. He thought of warning her: 'Look out for yourself.' But before he had the time to finish the sentence the flare blazed up violently between them and he saw her throw herself back with an arm across her face. 'Hallo,' he exclaimed; only he could not stop a moment to ask if she was hurt. He bolted out of the companion straight into his captain who took the flare from him and held it high above his head.

The fierce flame fluttered like a silk flag, throwing an angry swaying glare mingled with moving shadows over the poop, lighting up the concave surfaces of the sails, gleaming on the wet paint of the white rails. And young Powell turned his eyes to windward with a catch in his breath.

The strange ship, a darker shape in the night, did not seem to be moving onwards but only to grow more distinct right abeam, staring at the *Ferndale* with one green and one red eye which swayed and tossed as if they belonged to the restless head of some invisible monster ambushed in the night amongst the waves. A moment, long like eternity, elapsed, and, suddenly, the monster which seemed to take to itself the shape of a mountain shut its green eye without as much as a preparatory wink.

Mr. Powell drew a free breath. 'All right now,' said Captain Anthony in a quiet undertone. He gave the blazing flare to Powell and walked aft to watch the passing of that menace of destruction coming blindly with its parti-coloured stare out of a blind night on the wings of a sweeping wind. Her very form could be distinguished now black and elongated amongst the hissing patches of foam bursting along her path.

As is always the case with a ship running before wind and sea she did not seem to an onlooker to move very fast; but to be progressing indolently in long leisurely bounds and pauses in the midst of the overtaking waves. It was only when actually passing the stern within easy hail of the *Ferndale* that her headlong speed became apparent to the eye. With the red light shut off and soaring like an immense shadow on the crest of a wave she was lost to view in one great, forward swing, melting into the lightless space.

'Close shave,' said Captain Anthony in an indifferent voice just raised enough to be heard in the wind. 'A blind lot on board that ship. Put out the flare now.'

Chance

547 *The Tartane*

JUST about sunset, which is the time of burials at sea, the *Amelia* was hove to and, the rope being manned, the tartane was brought alongside and her two keepers ordered on board their ship. Captain Vincent, leaning over with his elbows on the rail, seemed lost in thought. At last the first lieutenant spoke.

'What are we going to do with that tartane, sir? Our men are on board.'

'We are going to sink her by gunfire,' declared Captain Vincent suddenly. 'His ship makes a very good coffin for a seaman, and those men deserve better than to be thrown overboard to roll on the waves. Let them rest quietly at the bottom of the sea in the craft to which they had stuck so well.'

The lieutenant, making no reply, waited for some more positive order. Every eye in the ship was turned on the captain. But Captain Vincent said nothing and seemed unable or unwilling to give it yet. He was feeling vaguely that in all his good intentions there was something wanting.

'Ah! Mr. Bolt,' he said, catching sight of the master's mate in the waist. 'Did they have a flag on board that craft?'

'I think she had a tiny bit of ensign when the chase began, sir, but it must have blown away. It is not at the end of her mainyard now.' He looked over the side. 'The halliards are rove, though,' he added.

'We must have a French ensign somewhere on board,' said Captain Vincent.

'Certainly, sir,' struck in the master, who was listening.

'Well, Mr. Bolt,' said Captain Vincent, 'you have had most to do with all this. Take a few men with you, bend the French ensign on the halliards and sway his mainyard to the masthead.' He smiled at all the faces turned towards him. 'After all, they never surrendered and, by heavens, gentlemen, we will let them go down with their colours flying.'

The Rover

YOUTH

548 *i. The Leak*

AND we pumped. And there was no break in the weather. The sea was white like a sheet of foam, like a caldron of boiling milk; there was not a break in the clouds, no—not the size of a man's hand—no, not for so much as ten seconds. There was for us no sky, there were for us no stars, no sun, no universe—nothing but angry clouds and an infuriated sea. We pumped watch and watch, for dear life; and it seemed to last for months, for years, for all eternity, as though we had been dead and gone to a hell for sailors. We forgot the day of the week, the name of the month, what year it was, and whether we had ever been ashore. The sails blew away, she lay broadside on under a weather-cloth, the ocean poured over her, and we did not care. We turned those handles, and had the eyes of idiots. As soon as we had crawled on deck I used to take a round turn with a rope about the men, the pumps, and the mainmast, and we turned, we turned incessantly, with the water to our waists, to our necks, over our heads. It was all one. We had forgotten how it felt to be dry.

And there was somewhere in me the thought: By Jove! this is the deuce of an adventure—something you read about; and it is my first voyage as second mate—and I am only twenty—and here I am lasting it out as well as any of these men, and keeping my chaps up to the mark. I was pleased. I would not have given up the experience for worlds. I had moments of exultation. Whenever the old dismantled craft pitched heavily with her counter high in the air, she seemed to me to throw up, like an appeal, like a defiance, like a cry to the clouds without mercy, the words written on her stern: '*Judea*, London. Do or Die.'

O youth! The strength of it, the faith of it, the imagination of it! To me she was not an old rattle-trap carting about the world a lot of coal for a freight—to me she was the endeavour, the test, the trial of life. I think of her with pleasure, with affection, with regret—as you would think of some one dead you have loved. I shall never forget her. . . Pass the bottle.

ii. Ship on Fire

I WALKED up to the skipper and shook him by the shoulder. At last he opened his eyes, but did not move. 'Time to leave her, sir,' I said, quietly.

He got up painfully, looked at the flames, at the sea sparkling round the ship, and black, black as ink farther away; he looked at the stars shining dim through a thin veil of smoke in a sky black, black as Erebus.

'Youngest first,' he said.

And the ordinary seaman, wiping his mouth with the back of his hand, got up, clambered over the taffrail, and vanished. Others followed. One, on the point of going over, stopped short to drain his bottle, and with a great swing of his arm flung it at the fire. 'Take this!' he cried.

The skipper lingered disconsolately, and we left him to commune alone for a while with his first command. Then I went up again and brought him away at last. It was time. The ironwork on the poop was hot to the touch.

Then the painter of the long-boat was cut, and the three boats, tied together, drifted clear of the ship. It was just sixteen hours after the explosion when we abandoned her. Mahon had charge of the second boat, and I had the smallest—the 14-foot thing. The long-boat would have taken the lot of us; but the skipper said we must save as much property as we could —for the underwriters—and so I got my first command. I had two men with me, a bag of biscuits, a few tins of meat, and a breaker of water. I was ordered to keep close to the long-boat, that in case of bad weather we might be taken into her.

And do you know what I thought? I thought I would part company as soon as I could. I wanted to have my first command all to myself. I wasn't going to sail in a squadron if there was a chance for independent cruising. I would make land by myself. I would beat the other boats. Youth! All youth! The silly, charming, beautiful youth.

But we did not make a start at once. We must see the last of the ship. And so the boats drifted about that night, heaving and setting on the swell. The men dozed, waked, sighed, groaned. I looked at the burning ship.

Between the darkness of earth and heaven she was burning fiercely upon a disc of purple sea shot by the blood-red play of gleams; upon a disc of water, glittering and sinister. A high, clear flame, an immense and lonely flame, ascended from the ocean, and from its summit the black smoke poured continuously at the sky. She burned furiously; mournful and imposing like a funeral pile kindled in the night, surrounded by the sea, watched over by the stars. A magnificent death had come like a grace, like a gift, like a reward to that old ship at the end of her laborious days. The surrender of her weary ghost to the keeping of stars and sea was stirring like the sight of a glorious triumph. The masts fell just before daybreak, and for a moment there was a burst and turmoil of sparks that seemed to fill with flying fire the night patient and watchful, the vast night lying silent upon the sea. At daylight she was only a charred shell, floating still under a cloud of smoke and bearing a glowing mass of coal within.

Then the oars were got out, and the boats forming in a line moved round her remains as if in procession—the long-boat leading. As we pulled across her stern a slim dart of fire shot out viciously at us, and suddenly she went down, head first, in a great hiss of steam. The unconsumed stern was the last to sink ; but the paint had gone, had cracked, had peeled off, and there were no letters, there was no word, no stubborn device that was like her soul, to flash at the rising sun her creed and her name.

We made our way north.

iii. The Landfall

I NEED not tell you what it is to be knocking about in an open boat. I remember nights and days of calm, when we pulled, we pulled, and the boat seemed to stand still, as if bewitched within the circle of the sea horizon. I remember the heat, the deluge of rain-squalls that kept us baling for dear life (but filled our water-cask), and I remember sixteen hours on end with a mouth dry as a cinder and a steering-oar over the stern to keep my first command head on to a breaking sea. I did not know how good a man I was till then. I remember the drawn faces, the dejected figures of my two men, and I remember my youth and the feeling that will never come back any more—the feeling that I could last for ever, outlast the sea, the earth, and all men; the deceitful feeling that lures us on to joys, to perils, to love, to vain effort—to death; the triumphant conviction of strength, the heat of life in the handful of dust, the glow in the heart that with every year grows dim, grows cold, grows small, and expires—and expires, too soon, too soon—before life itself.

And this is how I see the East. I have seen its secret places and have looked into its very soul; but now I see it always from a small boat, a high outline of mountains, blue and afar in the morning; like faint mist at noon; a jagged wall of purple at sunset. I have the feel of the oar in my hand, the vision of a scorching blue sea in my eyes. And I see a bay, a wide bay, smooth as glass and polished like ice, shimmering in the dark. A red light burns far off upon the gloom of the land, and the night is soft and warm. We drag at the oars with aching arms, and suddenly a puff of wind, a puff faint and tepid and laden with strange odours of blossoms, of aromatic wood, comes out of the still night—the first sigh of the East on my face. That I can never forget. It was impalpable and enslaving, like a charm, like a whispered promise of mysterious delight.

We had been pulling this finishing spell for eleven hours. Two pulled, and he whose turn it was to rest sat at the tiller. We had made out the red light in that bay and steered for it, guessing it must mark some small coasting port. We passed two vessels, outlandish and high-sterned, sleeping at anchor, and, approaching the light, now very dim, ran the boat's nose against the end of a jutting wharf. We were blind with fatigue. My men dropped the oars and fell off the thwarts as if dead. I made fast to a pile. A current rippled softly. The scented obscurity of the shore was grouped into vast masses, a density of colossal clumps of vegetation, probably—mute and fantastic shapes. And at their foot the semi-circle of a beach gleamed faintly, like an illusion. There was not a light, not a stir, not a sound. The mysterious East faced me, perfumed like a flower, silent like death, dark like a grave.

And I sat weary beyond expression, exulting like a conqueror, sleepless and entranced as if before a profound, a fateful enigma.

A splashing of oars, a measured dip reverberating on the level of water, intensified by the silence of the shore into loud claps, made me jump up. A boat, a European boat, was coming in. I invoked the name of the dead; I hailed: *Judea* ahoy! A thin shout answered.

It was the captain, I had beaten the flagship by three hours, and I was glad to hear the old man's voice again, tremulous and tired. 'Is it you, Marlow?' 'Mind the end of that jetty, sir,' I cried.

iv. The East

I PULLED back, made fast again to the jetty, and then went to sleep at last. I had faced the silence of the East. I had heard some of its language. But when I opened my eyes again the silence was as complete as though it had never been broken. I was lying in a flood of light, and the sky had never looked so far, so high, before. I opened my eyes and lay without moving.

And then I saw the men of the East—they were

looking at me. The whole length of the jetty was full of people. I saw brown, bronze, yellow faces, the black eyes, the glitter, the colour of an Eastern crowd. And all these beings stared without a murmur, without a sigh, without a movement. They stared down at the boats, at the sleeping men who at night had come to them from the sea. Nothing moved. The fronds of palms stood still against the sky. Not a branch stirred along the shore, and the brown roofs of hidden houses peeped through the green foliage, through the big leaves that hung shining and still like leaves forged of heavy metal. This was the East of the ancient navigators, so old, so mysterious, resplendent and sombre, living and unchanged, full of danger and promise. And these were the men. I sat up suddenly. A wave of movement passed through the crowd from end to end, passed along the heads, swayed the bodies, ran along the jetty like a ripple on the water, like a breath of wind on a field—and all was still again. I see it now—the wide sweep of the bay, the glittering sands, the wealth of green infinite and varied, the sea blue like the sea of a dream, the crowd of attentive faces, the blaze of vivid colour—the water reflecting it all, the curve of the shore, the jetty, the high-sterned outlandish craft floating still, and the three boats with the tired men from the West sleeping, unconscious of the land and the people and of the violence of sunshine. They slept thrown across the thwarts, curled on bottom-boards, in the careless attitudes of death. The head of the old skipper, leaning back in the stern of the long-boat, had fallen on his breast, and he looked as though he would never wake. Farther out old Mahon's face was upturned to the sky, with the long white beard spread out on his breast, as though he had been shot where he sat at the tiller ; and a man, all in a heap in the bows of the boat, slept with both arms embracing the stem-head and with his cheek laid on the gunwale. The East looked at them without a sound.

I have known its fascination since ; I have seen the mysterious shores, the still water, the lands of brown nations, where a stealthy Nemesis lies in wait, pursues, overtakes so many of the conquering race, who are proud of their wisdom, of their knowledge, of their strength. But for me all the East is contained in that vision of my youth. It is all in that moment when I opened my young eyes on it. I came upon it from a tussle with the sea—and I was young—and I saw it looking at me. And this is all that is left of it! Only a moment ; a moment of strength, of romance, of glamour—of youth ! . . A flick of sunshine upon a strange shore, the time to remember, the time for a sigh, and—good-bye !—Night—Good-bye ! . .

He drank.

Ah ! The good old time—the good old time. Youth and the sea. Glamour and the sea ! The good, strong sea, the salt, bitter sea, that could whisper to you and roar at you and knock your breath out of you.

He drank again.

By all that 's wonderful it is the sea, I believe, the sea itself—or is it youth alone? Who can tell? But you here—you all had something out of life : money, love—whatever one gets on shore—and, tell me, wasn't that the best time, that time when we were young at sea ; young and had nothing, on the sea that gives nothing, except hard knocks—and sometimes a chance to feel your strength—that only—what you all regret?

Youth

GEORGE MOORE

1857–

549 *Esther's Son*

AT twelve o'clock Esther and Mrs. Barfield walked out on the lawn. A loud wind came up from the sea, and it shook the evergreens as if it were angry with them. A rook carried a stick to the tops of the tall trees, and the women drew their cloaks about them. The train passed across the vista, and the women wondered how long it would take Jack to walk from the station. Then another rook stooped to the edge of the plantation, gathered a twig, and carried it away. The wind was rough; it caught the evergreens underneath and blew them out like umbrellas; the grass had not yet begun to grow, and the grey sea harmonized with the grey-green land. The women waited on the windy lawn, their skirts blown against their legs, keeping their hats on with difficulty. It was too cold for standing still. They turned and walked a few steps towards the house, and then looked round.

A tall soldier came through the gate. He wore a long red cloak, and a small cap jauntily set on the side of his close-clipped head. Esther uttered a little exclamation, and ran to meet him. He took his mother in his arms, kissed her, and they walked towards Mrs. Barfield together. All was forgotten in the happiness of the moment—the long fight for his life, and the possibility that any moment might declare him to be mere food for powder and shot. She was only conscious that she had accomplished her woman's work—she had brought him up to man's estate; and that was her sufficient reward. What a fine fellow he was! She did not know he was so handsome, and blushing with pleasure and pride she glanced shyly at him out of the corners of her eyes as she introduced him to her mistress.

'This is my son, ma'am.'

Mrs. Barfield held out her hand to the young soldier.

'I have heard a great deal about you from your mother.'

'And I of you, ma'am. You've been very kind to my mother. I don't know how to thank you.'

And in silence they walked towards the house.

Esther Waters

550 *Hail and Farewell!*

IT was very sad leaving those ten years of my life, and next morning, a grey misty morning in February, the train took me to Kingstown, a very different departure from the one that I had long been meditating. The ideal departure should have been on an evening in May, and with the golden west behind me I should have watched from the vessel's stern the beautiful outlines of the coast and the lovely shapes of Howth, thinking a last farewell. I should have murmured the words of Catullus when he journeyed over land and sea to burn the body of his brother, and to fit them to my circumstance a change of a single word would have been enough:

ATQUE IN PERPETUUM, MATER, AVE ATQUE VALE.

Our dreams and our circumstances are often in conflict, and never were they in greater opposition than the day the train took me from Westland Row to Kingstown—a long, barren tract of sand: a grey sky hanging low over the grey sea without a ripple in it, like glass. If the evening had been a golden evening my heart might have overflowed with fine sentiments;

it is on golden evenings that fine sentiments overflow the heart; then it is like crystal that the least touch will break; but on a cold, bleak, February morning the prophet is as uninspired as his humblest fellow, and a very humble fellow, forgetful of Ireland, forgetful of Catholicism, forgetful of literature, went below to think of the friends he had left behind him—Æ and the rest.

Hail and Farewell! Vale

CHARLES CANNAN

AND 1858–1919

ROBERT W. CHAPMAN

1881–

551 *Ingram Bywater*

i

AT the Clarendon Press, to which so much devoted service is given by the members of its Board, Bywater's thirty-five years of heavy work will stand unrivalled. He took a personal interest in every piece of sound learning that was offered for publication. 'That book of ——,' he said, 'has given me a horrible interest in mediaeval geography, and there is no subject so remote from my proper studies.' He found—or made—time to assist or direct all kinds of undertakings in very different fields. He studied, for instance, not merely all the proofs of the Oxford Classical Texts (which were planned on the model of his own edition of the Ethics) but huge slices of the English Dictionary. When everyone else had failed to find the word *inferentia*, and when at least one dissertation had proved that it could not have been used in Latin, Bywater produced a quotation from Abelard. 'Murray,' he said, 'asked me for an early instance of *poetria* ('poetry'), and when I tell you that I found it at last in a seventh-century scholium to the Epistles of Horace, you may imagine that it took me some time: but I am sometimes lucky on Sunday.' Another Sunday produced—by telegram on Monday morning—a Gladstonian use of 'science' in the old Oxford sense of metaphysics. Bywater's immense bibliographical knowledge in many fields of learning enabled him to estimate with accuracy the value of a new book, regarded as a contribution to the common stock; and his long experience gave him an uncanny skill in predicting without arithmetical data the cost of production and the willingness—or unwillingness—of the public to buy. He never missed an opportunity of getting a good piece of work before the world; and if he sometimes set limits to an enterprise, or relegated what was conceived to be a book 'to the pages of a learned periodical,' it was not a scholar's hypercriticism but a practical man's estimate of possibilities and values that suggested his caution. To all the problems of practical administration he brought a very shrewd and incisive appreciation of the governing factors; and in his long tenure of office the sum of his work at the Press, or in connection with it, must be quite comparable to that which eminent private publishers find necessary for their business.

The Journal of Philology

ii

THE subject of my portrait was a great scholar, as only those few can be who laboriously cultivate a rare natural gift. The penetralia of the ancient world are not to be reached save through the long and dusty corridors of modern learning; and only by a saving grace of genius will the student reach the farther end with senses unimpaired. Our scholar knew the history of classical learning as it is unlikely it will ever be known again, and read ancient literature with a taste and feeling undimmed by a cobweb. He told me once, he had read the *Choephoroe* in the train that morning: 'You know, it 's monstrously good.' The quotation does feeble justice to my vivid sense of his being as intimate with Aeschylus as he was with Browning, and as intimate with Politian as with either. He was so profoundly versed in the literature and the manners of many ages, that he would speak of Sir Thomas More, or of Burke, very much as he spoke of Swinburne; as if he had known them.

Few even of his friends, I imagine, suspected the prodigious range of his attainments. He did not suspect it himself. He had no vulgar avidity of information or conceit of versatility, and of many branches of modern scientific and mechanical knowledge was content to remain as ignorant as a gentleman need be. He acquired his knowledge with an easy deliberation, and kept it by mere tenacity and a sure instinct for selection. In conversation his native courtesy chose subjects with which he knew his interlocutor to be familiar; and the Renaissance scholar who knew that he lived on terms of close intimacy with Erasmus and the Scaligers might well remain in ignorance of his equal familiarity with Diogenes Laertius, or the Elizabethan dramatists, or the historians of the Peninsular War. Till he warmed to a subject his knowledge was always shy; he was not to be drawn; and it was felt that the attempt would be indecent. The loftiness of his own standard was more surely betrayed by the alarm he evinced at the rare discovery of a gap in his knowledge. At a meeting of a learned society over which he presided, a member, while reading a commentator's note, boggled at a word and applied to the president for its meaning. '*Sicilicus—sicilicus!*' There was a silence as he made his way to the dictionary. '*Sicilicus.* It means the forty-eighth part of an *as*, and, by metonymy, it means a comma.' Then, replacing the book and turning to his audience, in accents of unfeigned dismay—'I didn't *know that!*'

The Portrait of a Scholar

FRANCIS THOMPSON

1859–1907

552 *Shelley*

ENCHANTED child, born into a world unchildlike; spoiled darling of Nature, playmate of her elemental daughters; 'pard-like spirit, beautiful and swift,' laired amidst the burning fastnesses of his own fervid mind; bold foot along the verges of precipitous dream; light leaper from crag to crag of inaccessible fancies; towering Genius, whose soul rose like a ladder between heaven and earth with the angels of song ascending and descending it;—he is shrunken into the little vessel of death, and sealed with the unshatterable seal of doom, and cast down deep below the rolling tides of Time.

Mighty meat for little guests, when the heart of Shelley was laid in the cemetery of Caius Cestius! Beauty, music, sweetness, tears—the mouth of the worm has fed of them all. Into that sacred bridal-gloom of death where he holds his nuptials with eternity let not our rash speculations follow him;

let us hope rather that as, amidst material nature, where our dull eyes see only ruin, the finer eye of science has discovered life in putridity and vigour in decay, seeing dissolution even and disintegration, which in the mouth of man symbolize disorder, to be in the works of God undeviating order, and the manner of our corruption to be no less wonderful than the manner of our health,—so, amidst the supernatural universe, some tender undreamed surprise of life in doom awaited that wild nature, which, worn by warfare with itself, its Maker, and all the world, now

> Sleeps, and never palates more the dug,
> The beggar's nurse, and Cæsar's.

Shelley

KENNETH GRAHAME

1859–

553 *The Roman Road*

ALL the roads of our neighbourhood were cheerful and friendly, having each of them pleasant qualities of their own; but this one seemed different from the others in its masterful suggestion of a serious purpose, speeding you along with a strange uplifting of the heart. The others tempted chiefly with their treasures of hedge and ditch; the rapt surprise of the first lords-and-ladies, the rustle of a field-mouse, the splash of a frog; while cool noses of brother-beasts were pushed at you through gate or gap.

A loiterer you had need to be, did you choose one of them; so many were the tiny hands thrust out to detain you, from this side and that. But this one was of a sterner sort, and even in its shedding off of bank and hedgerow as it marched straight and full for the open downs, it seemed to declare its contempt for adventitious trappings to catch the shallow-pated. . .

'The Knights' Road' we children had named it, from a sort of feeling that, if from any quarter at all, it would be down this track we might some day see Lancelot and his peers come pacing on their great war-horses; supposing that any of the stout band still survived, in nooks and unexplored places. Grown-up people sometimes spoke of it as the 'Pilgrims' Way'; but I didn't know much about pilgrims—except Walter in the Horselberg story. Him I sometimes saw, breaking with haggard eyes out of yonder copse, and calling to the pilgrims as they hurried along on their desperate march to the Holy City, where peace and pardon were awaiting them. 'All roads lead to Rome', I had heard somebody say; and I had taken the remark very seriously, of course, and puzzled over it many days. There must have been some mistake, I concluded at last; but of one road at least I intuitively felt it to be true. . .

Rome! It was fascinating to think that it lay at the other end of this white ribbon that rolled itself off from my feet over the distant downs. I was not quite so uninstructed as to imagine I could reach it that afternoon; but some day, I thought, if things went on being as unpleasant as they were now—some day . . . we would see.

The Golden Age

554 *The Water Rat and the Sea Rat*

BY this time their meal was over, and the Seafarer, refreshed and strengthened, his voice more vibrant, his eye lit with a brightness that seemed caught from some far-away sea-beacon, filled his glass with the red and glowing vintage of the South, and, leaning towards the Water Rat, compelled his gaze and held him, body and soul, while he talked. Those eyes were of the changing foam-streaked grey-green of leaping Northern seas; in the glass shone a hot ruby that seemed the very heart of the South, beating for him who had courage to respond to its pulsation. The twin lights, the shifting grey and the steadfast red, mastered the Water Rat and held him bound, fascinated, powerless. The quiet world outside their rays receded far away and ceased to be. And the talk, the wonderful talk flowed on—or was it speech entirely, or did it pass at times into song—chanty of the sailors weighing the dripping anchor, sonorous hum of the shrouds in a tearing North-Easter, ballad of the fisherman hauling his nets at sundown against an apricot sky, chords of guitar and mandoline from gondola or caique? Did it change into the cry of the wind, plaintive at first, angrily shrill as it freshened, rising to a tearing whistle, sinking to a musical trickle of air from the leech of the bellying sail? All these sounds the spellbound listener seemed to hear, and with them the hungry complaint of the gulls and the sea-mews, the soft thunder of the breaking wave, the cry of the protesting shingle. Back into speech again it passed, and with beating heart he was following the adventures of a dozen seaports, the fights, the escapes, the rallies, the comradeships, the gallant undertakings; or he searched islands for treasure, fished in still lagoons and dozed day-long on warm white sand. Of deep-sea fishings he heard tell, and mighty silver gatherings of the mile-long net; of sudden perils, noise of breakers on a moonless night, or the tall bows of the great liner taking shape overhead through the fog; of the merry home-coming, the headland rounded, the harbour lights opened out; the groups seen dimly on the quay, the cheery hail, the splash of the hawser; the trudge up the steep little street towards the comforting glow of red-curtained windows.

Lastly, in his waking dream it seemed to him that the Adventurer had risen to his feet, but was still speaking, still holding him fast with his sea-grey eyes. 'And now,' he was softly saying, 'I take to the road again, holding on south-westwards for many a long and dusty day; till at last I reach the little grey sea town I know so well, that clings along one steep side of the harbour. There through dark doorways you look down flights of stone steps, overhung by great pink tufts of valerian and ending in a patch of sparkling blue water. The little boats that lie tethered to the rings and stanchions of the old sea-wall are gaily painted as those I clambered in and out of in my own childhood; the salmon leap on the flood tide, schools of mackerel flash and play past quay-sides and foreshores, and by the windows the great vessels glide, night and day, up to their moorings or forth to the open sea. There, sooner or later, the ships of all seafaring nations arrive; and there, at its destined hour, the ship of my choice will let go its anchor. I shall take my time, I shall tarry and bide, till at last the right one lies waiting for me, warped out into mid-stream, loaded low, her bowsprit pointing down harbour. I shall slip on board, by boat or along hawser; and then one morning I shall wake to the song and tramp of the sailors, the clink of the capstan, and the rattle of the anchor-chain coming merrily in. We shall break out the jib and the foresail, the white houses on the harbour side will glide slowly past us as she gathers steering-way, and the voyage will have begun! As she forges towards the headland she will clothe herself with canvas; and then, once outside, the sounding slap of great green seas as she heels to the wind, pointing South!

And you, you will come too, young brother; for the days pass, and never return, and the South still waits for you. Take the Adventure, heed the call, now ere the irrevocable moment passes! 'Tis but a banging of the door behind you, a blithesome step forward, and you are out of the old life and into the new! Then some day, some day long hence, jog home here if you will, when the cup has been drained and the play has been played, and sit down by your quiet river with a store of goodly memories for company. You can easily overtake me on the road, for you are young, and I am ageing and go softly. I will linger, and look back; and at last I will surely see you coming, eager and light-hearted, with all the South in your face!'

The voice died away and ceased, as an insect's tiny trumpet dwindles swiftly into silence; and the Water Rat, paralysed and staring, saw at last but a distant speck on the white surface of the road.

The Wind in the Willows

HENRY FIELDING HALL

1859–

555 *A Burmese on the English*

IT is not only that when you get an order you obey it, though it come from so very far away—that is wonderful enough to us—but you obey it willingly. You act as if it was something you wanted to do yourself, something you thought of in yourself for your own advantage. You understand not only what the order says but what it means, almost as if you yourself had said it. You are not servants who obey orders, you are as the hand or foot that acts as the brain designs. You live here widely separated, many thousand miles from your small island, but yet you are not divided from it. You are all held together by nerves in the invisible air that make you one. Therefore your Government is you, not your master, your teacher, your commander, but yourself. You feel as we do about our family and our village, that it is ourselves. That is what we notice and wonder at in you. When we see two or three Englishmen alone governing a great district, you appear to us not individuals but tiny finger-tips of a great living thing whose heart and brain are far away. Yet if the finger-tip be touched the whole responds. And what one of you does, that is the act of the whole.

The Inward Light

OLIVE SCHREINER

1859–1920

556 *Waldo*

SITTING there with his arms folded on his knees, and his hat slouched down over his face, Waldo looked out into the yellow sunshine that tinted even the very air with the colour of ripe corn, and was happy.

He was an uncouth creature with small learning, and no prospect in the future but that of making endless tables and stone walls, yet it seemed to him as he sat there that life was a rare and very rich thing. He rubbed his hands in the sunshine. Ah, to live on so, year after year, how well! Always in the present; letting each day glide, bringing its own labour, and its own beauty; the gradual lighting up of the hills, night and the stars, firelight and the coals! To live on so, calmly, far from the paths of men; and to look at the lives of clouds and insects; to look deep into the heart of flowers, and see how lovingly the pistil and the stamens nestle there together; and to see in the thorn-pods how the little seeds suck their life through the delicate curled-up string, and how the little embryo sleeps inside! Well, how well, to sit so on one side, taking no part in the world's life; but when great men blossom into books looking into those flowers also, to see how the world of men too opens beautifully, leaf after leaf. Ah! life is delicious; well to live long, and see the darkness breaking, and the day coming. The day when soul shall not thrust back soul that would come to it; when men shall not be driven to seek solitude, because of the crying out of their hearts for love and sympathy. Well to live long and see the new time breaking! Well to live long; life is sweet, sweet, sweet! In his breast pocket, where of old the broken slate used to be, there was now a little dancing shoe of his friend who was sleeping. He could feel it when he folded his arm tight against his breast; and that was well also. He drew his hat lower over his eyes, and sat so motionless that the chickens thought he was asleep, and gathered closer around him. One even ventured to peck at his boot; but he ran away quickly. Tiny, yellow fellow that he was, he knew that men were dangerous; even sleeping they might awake. But Waldo did not sleep, and coming back from his sunshiny dream, stretched out his hand for the tiny thing to mount. But the chicken eyed the hand askance, and then ran off to hide under its mother's wing, and from beneath it it sometimes put out its round head to peep at the great figure sitting there. Presently its brothers ran off after a little white moth, and it ran out to join them; and when the moth fluttered away over their heads they stood looking up disappointed, and then ran back to their mother.

Waldo through his half-closed eyes looked at them. Thinking, fearing, craving, those tiny sparks of brother life, what were they, so real there in that old yard on that sunshiny afternoon? A few years—where would they be? Strange little brother spirits! He stretched his hand towards them, for his heart went out to them; but not one of the little creatures came nearer him, and he watched them gravely for a time; then he smiled, and began muttering to himself after his old fashion. Afterwards he folded his arms upon his knees, and rested his forehead on them. And so he sat there in the yellow sunshine, muttering, muttering, muttering to himself.

It was not very long after when Em came out at the back-door with a towel thrown across her head, and in her hand a cup of milk.

'Ah,' she said, coming close to him, 'he is sleeping now. He will find it when he wakes, and be glad of it.'

She put it down upon the ground beside him. The mother-hen was at work still among the stones, but the chickens had climbed about him, and were perching on him. One stood upon his shoulder, and rubbed its little head softly against his black curls; another tried to balance itself on the very edge of the old felt hat. One tiny fellow stood upon his hand, and tried to crow; another had nestled itself down comfortably on the old coat-sleeve, and gone to sleep there.

Em did not drive them away ; but she covered the glass softly at his side. 'He will wake soon,' she said, 'and be glad of it.'

But the chickens were wiser.

The Story of an African Farm

JOHN ANDREW HAMILTON, LORD SUMNER OF IBSTONE

1859–

557 *Bowman v. Secular Society Ltd.: Judgement*

THE words, as well as the acts, which tend to endanger society differ from time to time in proportion as society is stable or insecure in fact, or is believed by its reasonable members to be open to assault. In the present day meetings or processions are held lawful which a hundred and fifty years ago would have been deemed seditious, and this is not because the law is weaker or has changed, but because the times having changed, society is stronger than before. In the present day reasonable men do not apprehend the dissolution or downfall of society because religion is publicly assailed by methods not scandalous. Whether it is possible that in the future irreligious attacks, designed to undermine fundamental institutions of our society, may come to be criminal in themselves, as constituting a public danger, is a matter that does not arise. The fact that opinion grounded on experience has moved one way does not in law preclude the possibility of its moving on fresh experience in the other ; nor does it bind succeeding generations, when conditions have again changed. After all, the question whether a given opinion is a danger to society is a question of the times and is a question of fact. I desire to say nothing that would limit the right of society to protect itself by process of law from the dangers of the moment, whatever that right may be, but only to say that, experience having proved dangers once thought real to be now negligible, and dangers once very possibly imminent to have now passed away, there is nothing in the general rules as to blasphemy and irreligion, as known to the law, which prevents us from varying their application to the particular circumstances of our time in accordance with that experience.

Law Reports

CHARLES WHIBLEY

1859–

558 *Rabelais*

HIS scheme of education was more wholesome and practical than the vaunted system of our public schools. Read how Gargantua was instructed by Ponocrates, and note that nothing was neglected that might strengthen his body or set a fine edge upon his wit. Good order was always observed, and the young giant was even 'combed, curled, trimmed and perfumed'. Then after three good hours of lecture, he went into the meadows, where they played at the ball, 'most gallantly exercising their bodies, as formerly they had done their mindes'. And sport was as little an infliction as study: 'All their play was but in liberty, for they left off when they pleased, and that was commonly when they did sweat over all their body, or were otherwayes weary. Then were they very well wiped and rubbed, shifted their shirts, and, walking soberly, went to see if dinner was ready. . . In the mean time Master Appetite came, and then very orderly sate they down at table ; at the beginning of the meale, there was read some pleasant history of the warlike actions of former times, until he had taken a glasse of wine '. Thereafter were discussed ' the nature and efficacy of all that was served at table ', and such appropriate authors as Athenæus, Pliny, and Aristotle were quoted. At last, after some ' fine Canticks made in praise of the divine bounty and munificence ', cards were brought, not for play, but to learn a thousand pretty tricks founded on arithmetic, and so the science of numbers was encouraged. Then came music and sports of all kinds, until at ' last they prayed unto God the Creator, in falling down before him, and strengthening their faith towards him, and glorifying him for his boundlesse bounty for the time that was past, they recommended themselves to his divine clemency for the future, which being done, they went to bed, and betook themselves to their repose and rest '. Thus he sketched an education which might have befitted a great king, without a word of ribaldry or scorn, and in such a spirit as proves that he gravely condemned the lazy, lither system of the monasteries.

Being a true man of letters, he loved best of all the ' celestial manna of honest literature ', and he has composed in Gargantua's letter to Pantagruel the simple gospel of humanism. This eloquent plea for the liberal arts, for the dignity of the classics, above all for the supremacy of Greek, is as good an argument against the superstition of the Church as may be found in the books of the century. Moreover, the famous letter is inspired with a lofty intelligence and a wise fervour which the enemies of Rabelais do not suspect. 'But because, as the wise man Solomon saith'—thus he writes—'Wisdome entereth not into a malicious minde; that knowledge without conscience is but the ruine of the soule, it behooveth thee to serve, to love, to feare God, and on him to cast all thy thoughts and all thy hope, and by faith formed in charity to cleave unto him, so that thou mayest never be separated from him by thy sins.' Knowledge, without conscience, is but the ruin of the soul! The man who echoed that profound sentence was no buffoon, and it is only a perverse criticism which has obscured the real character of his book. The world has lived nearly four centuries since Rabelais, and we are not within a league of realizing his noble, humane ideal of education.

Literary Portraits

559 *George Brummel*

BRUMMEL, then, was to himself a work of art, which should be embellished by perfect manners, perfect taste, and a cunning tailor; nor is it surprising that the finished work inspired the whole of English society with an admiring awe. . . He arrived at the moment when the democratic spirit had killed elegance. The Revolution had done its work, and Charles Fox, himself a Dandy of the second class, had preached the doctrine of equality. The old picturesqueness was dead; the cocked hat had been vanquished by the topper; and Brummel had no less a task than to construct a noble costume from this wreckage of republican principles. And what poor material had he whereon to work! A coat, a waistcoat, and a pair of trousers! Yet he was no fanatic to restore the ancient mode; his greatness consisted in the proper adaptation of the poor materials left to his hand. He did not neglect their shape and contour; but that their poverty of design might be less noticed, he drew off the attention to the cravat.

This, indeed, was the masterpiece of his invention. The cravat of Brummel was the envy of crowned heads; yet nothing could have been more simple. It was half-starched, and it went twice round; its glory began and ended in the perfect arrangement of its folds; and Brummel was so delicate an artist that he discarded a cravat which was not flawless at the first attempt. He would insult neither himself nor his cravat by a second trial, and the famous story is a proper index of his greatness. A friend one day encountered his valet carrying with him a tray-full of discarded cravats. 'What are these?' asked the eager friend, with half a hope that he might penetrate a long-kept secret. 'These', replied the valet, 'are some of our failures.' And in that simple phrase did Brummel reveal his true, imperishable temperament.

Introduction to The Pageantry of Life

JAMES MATTHEW BARRIE

1860–

560 *The Chairs*

ON the day I was born we bought six hair-bottomed chairs, and in our little house it was an event, the first great victory in a woman's long campaign; how they had been laboured for, the pound-note and the thirty threepenny-bits they cost, what anxiety there was about the purchase, the show they made in possession of the west room, my father's unnatural coolness when he brought them in (but his face was white)—I so often heard the tale afterwards, and shared as boy and man in so many similar triumphs, that the coming of the chairs seems to be something I remember, as if I had jumped out of bed on that first day, and run ben to see how they looked. I am sure my mother's feet were ettling to be ben long before they could be trusted, and that the moment after she was left alone with me she was discovered barefooted in the west room, doctoring a scar (which she had been the first to detect) on one of the chairs, or sitting on them regally, or withdrawing and re-opening the door suddenly to take the six by surprise. And then, I think, a shawl was flung over her (it is strange to me to think it was not I who ran after her with the shawl), and she was escorted sternly back to bed and reminded that she had promised not to budge, to which her reply was probably that she had been gone but an instant, and the implication that therefore she had not been gone at all. Thus was one little bit of her revealed to me at once: I wonder if I took note of it.

Neighbours came in to see the boy and the chairs. I wonder if she deceived me when she affected to think that there were others like us, or whether I saw through her from the first, she was so easily seen through.

Margaret Ogilvy

MARY ELIZABETH COLERIDGE

1861–1907

The Knight of Malta: a Florentine Portrait in the National Gallery

561

A YOUNG man, dressed in black with the White Cross of the Knights of Malta, leans against a parapet, holding an open letter in his hand. Behind him is a square of blue tranquillity, brightening into pure light towards the horizon; on the left the usual slender little tree, divided into symmetrical branches, and leaves that one could count; round about, rocks and houses and a tiny bridge, gay in the sunshine. The Knight stands dark and lonely. The letter that he holds has blotted out the landscape. Henceforward he will not notice bright colouring.

'The world is painted in black and white.'

He has the dreamy abstraction of a man whose eyes, fixed as they are upon the world within, see little of that without. It is impossible to help gazing at them; who could resist peering into his neighbour's house, if he were sure that he should find the occupant, and that the occupant would never see him? The lamp of this fair house was Memory; it still burns through the windows. Nine times out of ten it is Memory that makes a man gentle, and gentleness is the soul of a Knight's courage. The Knight is young. There is but a slight down on the upper lip, and cheek and brow are smooth, while the mouth is tremulous with emotion; yet there is nothing of the rebellion of youth against the first order it receives to march joylessly. He is a dignified person; he has not borne, but he knows how to bear. The Knight's fidelity is his. . .

Tar : ublia : chi : bien : eima. 'Slowly he forgets who loves well.' That is the inscription upon the parapet.

Non Sequitur

WALTER RALEIGH

1861–1922

562 *The Book of the Courtier*

i

THAT the vogue of the book in England should have coincided exactly with the Elizabethan Age is something other than an accident. The literature of that age was a literature of the Court, as surely as the literature of the age of Anne was a literature of the Town. The way to political influence, to social advancement, to power and consideration and fame, lay through the Court, in England as in Italy. Now that the Court has dwindled into a drawing-room, it is perhaps not wholly easy to realize what once it meant to the nation. It was the centre, not of government alone, but of the fine arts: the exemplar of culture and civilization. Few great Englishmen of the nineteenth century have been intimately connected with the Court; few indeed of the great Elizabethans were not. The names of Charles Darwin, Robert Browning, and Charles George Gordon on the one hand, of Francis Bacon, Edmund Spenser, and Sir Philip Sidney on the other, sufficiently point the contrast. Even Shakespeare, the High Bailiff's son, was something of a Courtier; he paid the most magnificent of courtly tributes to Queen Elizabeth in certain lines:

> And the imperial votaress passed on
> In maiden meditation, fancy free:

and he (or his editors) inserted in the play of *Macbeth* sundry passages which can only be called skilful pieces of flattery designed to gratify King James. In those flourishing days of adventure, the successful adventurer found himself, sooner or later, brought into contact with the Court. Francis Drake, when he had sailed round the world, entertained Queen Elizabeth on board his ship at Deptford; and William Lithgow, the Scottish pedestrian, after escaping with his life from the tortures of the Spanish Inquisition, was carried on a feather-bed to Theobalds, that he might narrate the wonders of his travels to King James. The Courtier was the embodiment and type of the civilization of the Renaissance, as the Orator was the typical product of the civilization of ancient Rome. And the treatises of Cicero and Quintilian, wherein is set forth the character of the perfect orator, have their exact counterpart in the books written by the Italians of the sixteenth century for the instruction of the Perfect Courtier.

ii

In our own time, if the very existence of the Scholar-Gentleman be threatened, it is not so much by revolutionary morals as by the enormous growth of specialized knowledge, which divides human life into many departments, organized under learned barbarism. But the many-sided ideal has always been strong in England. Even in the eighteenth century, Congreve surprised and disgusted Voltaire by refusing the status of a professional author; and it is a criticism of modern France, passed upon English painters, that they aspire to be *grands seigneurs*. There was something profoundly sane, after all, in the ambitions that built New Place and Abbotsford. At the close of a revolutionary century, now that the fogs of a crude moral theory are dissipating, and the dream of a mechanical Utopia, a mere nightmare produced by a surfeit of science, is passing away, it is time to remember our ancestry. Our proudest title is not that we are the contemporaries of Darwin, but that we are the descendants of Shakespeare; we too are men of the Renaissance, inheritors of that large and noble conception of humanity and art to which a monument is erected in this Book of the Courtier.

Sir Thomas Hoby

563 *Quae stulta sunt mundi elegit Deus*

THESE two moods, the mood of Quixote and the mood of Sancho, seem to divide between them most of the splendours and most of the comforts of human life. It is rare to find either mood in its perfection. A man who should consistently indulge in himself the mood of the unregenerate Sancho would be a rogue, though, if he preserved good temper in his doings, he would be a pleasant rogue. The man who should maintain in himself the mood of Quixote would be something very like a saint. The saints of the Church Militant would find no puzzle and no obscurity in the character of the Knight of La Mancha. Some of them, perhaps, would understand, better than Don Quixote understood, that the full record of his doings, compiled by Cervantes, is both a tribute to the saintly character, and a criticism of it. They certainly could not fail to discover the religious kernel of the book, as the world, in the easy confidence of its own superiority, has failed to discover it. They would know that whoso loseth his life shall save it; they would not find it difficult to understand how Don Quixote, and, in his own degree, Sancho, was willing to be a fool, that he, and the world with him, might be made wise. Above all, they would appreciate the more squalid misadventures of Don Quixote, for, unlike the public, which recognizes the saint by his aureole, they would know, none better, that the way they have chosen is the way of contempt, and that Christianity was nursed in a manger.

Don Quixote

MAURICE HEWLETT

1861–1923

564 *Mascalls*

WE cut out of the high road by a sunk lane between dogwood hedges and ragged elms, I and a young squire of my acquaintance who lives and reigns not far from here. Beyond the trees there showed up the gable-end and chimneys of a house, and anon we came to a flint-and-stone wall, a blank space of masonry, wherein one barred window. The place might have been a convent in some Tuscan *vicolo*, so blind a look it had; but in our country, when a little house faces the sun, it has no use for windows to the north. We reached a door in the wall, tumbled down a flight of steps, and stood, as it were, upon the shore of a lake of light, with nothing before us but sunshot air, and across that radiant emptiness the further hills rolling away towards Somerset. Two great ilexes guard the entry, and make so dry a shelter that the angle of the wall with their covering serves as a wood-shed. A terrace-walk runs along the rim of the vale, from which the garden, enclosed in its white wall and red-tile coping, falls sharply down to the river. The wall ends there in a freakish gazebo overhanging the water, which once might have covered a boat-house, but now has a homelier use. Upon the terrace is Mascalls, the old stone house.

Mascalls has a quiet and seemly, plain face, much like that of some old labourer which has been bleached and scorched by the suns of fifty summers. It would be bald-looking, almost too severely to the purpose, but for one ample bow-window, the after-thought of some Mascall of the Regency. That was about the date at which it took its present shape, for while the ashlar might be of any age, and no doubt had served a much older house, its windows were all sashed in the way of 1810 or so, and a line of billets had been set under the eaves when a tile roof took the place of thatch. But antiquity was below us and about us—a mullioned window to the cellar, a huge tithe barn close by, built in Pelasgian blocks. The front door, with a coquettish stuccoed pediment which reminded me somehow of Jane Austen, stood open ; and there, bowing, appealing with her faded eyes, stood the wife of the last Mascall who could be suffered to hold Mascalls, a patient, sad-faced woman, rendered by cares rather than years to look any age. She made us free of the place with a courtesy which never fails her countrywomen, though one of us had decreed that morning that she must leave. We made our rueful survey. We saw the wreck of a sturdy old house. From attic to cellar the tale was the same. Parting walls, sagging ceilings, gaping floor-boards, dry-rotten joists, damp-eaten, rat-gnawed, it was falling about the family's heads. To put the place in order again would cost a small fortune in these days, which could only be recovered by rent. But rent was what the family could not find—so what were you to do? My friend was humane, but he had to pay his way. His land was not a luxury, it was his livelihood. He was in as mortgagee on a foreclosure. The word had been spoken. Mascall could no longer hold Mascalls.

Yet what a pleasant seat for an old house, on a ridge above the eddying chalk-stream, full in the sun, with a view over the valley into the heart of the West! What a shady orchard of cider-apples, what a sheltered, ripe old walled-garden, what a green water-meadow edging the brook! The place is so much 'seated in the mean', as Shakespeare says; it has the homely comfort, the plainness, the gentle every-dayness which makes our country beloved of all who come to know it. A country of half-tones, of silver-greys and amber-yellows, of mild wet winds, misted mornings and temperate noons; a country of Quaker habit. To be driven from it, if you have lived there all your life, and laboured its earth, and gone out and in; brought your bride there, got your children there, seen your old father die and borne him thence to the churchyard, returning then to know that you are Mascall of Mascalls; as it was in the beginning, is now . . . and then—to slip back and back, to feel your hold loosening, to be shiftless to help, in your own holding on sufferance, by squatter's right . . . and then—bidden to go! How can a man bear that?

Wiltshire Essays

ARTHUR CHRISTOPHER BENSON

1862–1925

565 *Henry Bradshaw*

WHEN one speaks of Bradshaw's 'work', it is hard to make the uninitiated quite understand either its extent, its importance, or its perfection. He knew more about printed books than any man living—he could tell at a glance the date and country, generally the town, at which a book was published. And the enormous range of this subject cannot be explained without a technical knowledge of the same. He was one of the foremost of Chaucer scholars, a very efficient linguist in range (though for reading, not speaking purposes), as, for instance, in the case of the old Breton language, which he evolved from notes and glosses, scribbled between the lines and on margins of Mass books—and his joy at the discovery of a word that he had suspected but never encountered was delightful to see. He could acquire a language for practical purposes with great rapidity—as, for instance, Armenian, which he began on a Thursday morning at Venice, and could read, so as to decipher titles for cataloguing, on Saturday night. He had a close and unrivalled knowledge of cathedral statutes and constitutions. He was an advanced student in the origins of liturgies—especially Irish—and, indeed, in the whole of Irish literature and printing he was supreme—and, finally, he was by common consent the best palaeographist, or critic of the date of MSS., in the world.

The story of his adventure in the Parisian Library is worth recording here: a book had been lost for nearly a century; he went over to Paris to see if he could discover it. Search was fruitless, though there was a strong presumption as to the part of the library where it would be found. He stood in one of the classes describing its probable appearance to the librarian, and to illustrate it said, 'About the height, thickness, and of similar binding to this', taking a book out of the shelves as he did so. It was the missing volume. . .

The way in which all this work was done, all this knowledge was accumulated, was, among the other peculiarities of his genius, the most amazing. No man ever seemed to have more leisure; he would talk with perfect readiness not only on any special matter that any friend wished to consult him on, but he enjoyed trivial, leisurely gossip, and never showed impatience to continue his work, or the least desire to return to it. The secret was that he never left off. Except for rare holidays, visits to relations or foreign tours, he never left Cambridge for years. His hours were most perplexing; he would generally work very late at night, sometimes till four or five in the morning, if there was much work on hand, go to the library about eleven, return for lunch, then back to the library again, with perhaps a visit to a Board or Syndicate till tea-time—for he took no exercise except spasmodically. Then he would go into Hall, or not, as the fancy took him, on the majority of days not doing so, and tasting nothing but tea and bread-and-butter in his rooms—and then from eight o'clock he would sit there, working if uninterrupted, but with his doors generally open to welcome all intruders, ceaselessly, patiently acquiring, amassing, disintegrating the enormous mass of delicate and subtle information which not only did he never forget, but all of which he seemed to carry on the surface, and carry so lightly and easily too—for he did not appear to be erudite—he never played the *rôle* of the learned man, though with acquirements as ponderous and detailed, and to the generality of people as uninteresting, as the real or the fictitious Casaubon. . .

And in an instant the whole structure breaks and melts before our eyes: the knowledge gone, God knows whither: the centre of so many quiet activities, of so many dependent lives slipped from its place. However often we say to ourselves that nothing runs to waste, that hoarded experience—gathered painfully in life and seemingly only to be applied in life—thus vanishing in an instant is hidden, not gone, the blank is there. As Bradshaw himself said to a friend after a great trial that he had told him of, which seemed to have in it no wholesome flavour, to be nothing either in prospect or in retrospect but the very root of bitterness itself, 'Everything is the result of something —whether it is our own fault or not, it means something: what we have to do is to try and interpret it.'

Essays

GOLDSWORTHY LOWES DICKINSON

1862–

566 *Literature in Cathay*

IN China letters are respected not merely to a degree but in a sense which must seem, I think, to you unintelligible and overstrained. But there is a reason for it. Our poets and literary men have taught their successors, for long generations, to look for good not in wealth, not in power, not in miscellaneous activity, but in a trained, a choice, an exquisite appreciation of the most simple and universal relations of life. To feel, and in order to feel to express, or at least to understand the expression of all that is lovely in Nature, of all that is poignant and sensitive in man, is to us in itself a sufficient end. A rose in a moonlit garden, the shadow of trees on the turf, almond blossom, scent of pine, the wine-cup and the guitar; these and the pathos of life and death, the long embrace, the hand stretched out in vain, the moment that glides for ever away, with its freight of music and light, into the shadow and hush of the haunted past, all that we have, all that eludes us, a bird on the wing, a perfume escaped on the gale—to all these things we are trained to respond, and the response is what we call literature.

Letters from John Chinaman

HENRY NEWBOLT

1862–

567 *Gardenleigh*

CHANGE has passed lightly over Gardenleigh since the day when William the Norman's fighting bishop, Geoffrey of Coutances, died at enmity with Rufus, and his seventy Somerset manors passed to the Honour of Gloucester, to be parcelled out among the tenants of FitzHamon and De Clare. What it was then, such in all essentials it has been ever since. Five Colthursts, five Marlands, three Romseys, twelve Silvaynes, and three of these new Earnshaws from the North, have all in turn become, by descent, by marriage, or by purchase, the stewards of the commonwealth for Gardenleigh; all in turn have lived here, planted, drained and sown, hunted, and administered the king's most rustic peace, and handed on the place to their successors unimpaired in beauty. It is true that none of them have attained high rank or lasting fame in politics, in war, or in the arts; but they have filled a definite place in English life, and a still more definite place in the history of the land of England.

And what of that land itself? What of the few hundred acres of it which the child-like Saxon in some dim century named Gardenleigh? Is it not a dream? Even as we know it, is it not the dream of seven and twenty generations? Year after year, life after life, century after century, to all who have seen it, whether as squires or serfs, natives or settlers, it has been the fabric upon which the pattern of their days was woven—the perfect setting of high dawns and tender sunsets, of birth, and toil, and passion, and pursuit; of all joys, and many partings and inevitable death. Now they themselves are dust, or less than dust; nothing is left of them but the shrines they built, the woods they planted, the mounds in the churchyard, and a few stones, for the most part long since broken and illegible. But Gardenleigh is still as green as ever. Can it be that the dream has indeed outlasted the dreamers so utterly? Has the slow stream of human life had no effect upon these meadows that it has so long watered? Are they no richer for all this love, no more fertile to the spirit than the raw clearings of yesterday in new-discovered countries? Are there no voices but ours in these old mossy woods and sunlit gardens, no steps but ours by this lake where the stars are mirrored in silence? What, then, is Time, that he should have power to make away with the dearest memories of seven and twenty generations?

The Old Country

E. Œ. SOMERVILLE AND MARTIN ROSS

(MISS VIOLET MARTIN, 1862–1915)

568 *An Outpost of Ireland*

BELOW the Lodge, to the south-east, the restless sand has smothered many a landmark, obliterated many a grave. Lie down in it, it is a soft bed; let it slip through your fingers, dry and fine and delicate, while the sea line is high and blue above you, and the light breaker strikes the slow moments in rhythm. Saint and oratory, cloghaun and cromlech, lie deep in its oblivion, their memory living faintly and more faintly from lip to lip through the years; around the saints their halos still linger, pale in this age's noonday, and the fishermen still strike sail at the corner of the island to the little crumbling tower that is supposed to mark the grave of Saint Gregory.

The ridge of the island runs in tablelands of rock, dropping in cliffs to the sea along its south-western face. These heights are level deserts of stone, streaked with soft grass where the yellow vetch blazes and a myriad wild roses lay their petals against the boulders. Yet even these handmaids of the rock are not the tenderest of its surprises. Look down the slits and fissures as you step across them on a May day, and you will see fronds of maidenhair climbing out of the darkness and warm mud below. A month later they will be strong and tall above the surface; the clots of foam may often strike them when, below their platform, the piled-up Atlantic rolls its vastness to the attack, with the cruel green of the updrawn wave, with the hurl of the pent tons against crag and cliff.

But for us, on that May morning, land and sea lay in rapt accord, and the breast of the brimming tide was laid to the breast of the cliff, with a low and broken voice of joy.

Some Irish Yesterdays

JOHN BURNET

1863–

569 *Ignorance*

THE problem I wish to discuss is the growth of ignorance at the present day, a problem which is generally overlooked just because, instead of beginning with ignorance, we fix our attention on knowledge, which at least appears to be increasing. Moreover, when I speak of the growth of ignorance, I am not referring specially to what are sometimes called 'the masses'. Among them we certainly find a great increase, if not of knowledge, at any rate of the desire for knowledge, and the Labour Party has a sincere belief in education. Unfortunately they are apt to speak as if there existed somewhere a stock of ready-made knowledge which has only to be doled out liberally to satisfy all needs. That was the view of Lord Brougham and other pioneers of popular education in the first half of the nineteenth century, but it is altogether wrong. If we start, as we should, from a consideration of ignorance, we shall be struck first of all, I think, by its passivity and inertness, and this raises a presumption that knowledge is above all, as Plato held it to be, an activity of the soul. But, if so, it follows that it cannot be communicated at all, except in so far as the active soul can induce other souls to share in its activity. What can be supplied from stock is merely the sediment of dead knowledge, though even that is valuable, as I hope to show, since it furnishes us with the necessary tools for the real activity of knowing. But it is not itself the real thing. The only knowledge worth distributing is living, first-hand knowledge, and that, from the nature of the case, can only be realized in its fullness by the few. It is, however, the only reservoir from which the needs of the many can be supplied, and it is therefore important to consider from time to time whether it is being maintained at the proper level. In the long run, everything depends on higher education, and so it remains true that the chief purpose of education is to form an *élite*, not for its own sake, but for that of society. That is Plato's doctrine. The Guardians in the *Republic* are the hardest worked and least remunerated class in the community, and those who have ascended to the light of the true day must descend once more in turn to the Cave to release the prisoners from their bonds.

The Romanes Lecture 1923

GEORGE SANTAYANA

1863–

570 *The Weather in his Soul*

LET me come to the point boldly; what governs the Englishman is his inner atmosphere, the weather in his soul. It is nothing particularly spiritual or mysterious. When he has taken his exercise and is drinking his tea or his beer and lighting his pipe; when, in his garden or by his fire, he sprawls in an aggressively comfortable chair; when, well-washed and well-brushed, he resolutely turns in church to the east and recites the Creed (with genuflexions, if he likes genuflexions) without in the least implying that he believes one word of it; when he hears or sings the most crudely sentimental and thinnest of popular songs, unmoved but not disgusted; when he makes up his mind who is his best friend or his favourite poet; when he adopts a party or a sweetheart; when he is hunting or shooting or boating, or striding through the fields; when he is choosing his clothes or his profession—never is it a precise reason, or purpose, or outer fact that determines him; it is always the atmosphere of his inner man.

To say that this atmosphere was simply a sense of physical well-being, of coursing blood and a prosperous digestion, would be far too gross; for while psychic weather is all that, it is also a witness to some settled disposition, some ripening inclination for this or that, deeply rooted in the soul. It gives a sense of direction in life which is virtually a code of ethics, and a religion behind religion. On the other hand, to say it was the vision of any ideal or allegiance to any principle would be making it far too articulate and abstract. The inner atmosphere, when compelled to condense into words, may precipitate some curt maxim or over-simple theory as a sort of war-cry; but its puerile language does it injustice, because it broods at a much deeper level than language or even thought. It is a mass of dumb instincts and allegiances, the love of a certain quality of life, to be maintained manfully. It is pregnant with many a stubborn assertion and rejection. It fights under its trivial fluttering opinions like a smoking battleship under its flags and signals; you must consider, not what they are, but why they have been hoisted and will not be lowered. One is tempted at times to turn away in despair from the most delightful acquaintance—the picture of manliness, grace, simplicity, and honour, apparently rich in knowledge and humour—because of some enormous platitude he reverts to, some hopelessly stupid little dogma from which one knows that nothing can ever liberate him. The reformer must give him up; but why should one wish to reform a person so much better than oneself? He is like a thoroughbred horse, satisfying to the trained eye, docile to the light touch, and coursing in most wonderful unison with you through the open world. What do you care what words he uses? Are you impatient with the lark because he sings rather than talks? and if he could talk, would you be irritated by his curious opinions? Of course, if any one positively asserts what is contrary to fact, there is an error, though the error may be harmless; and most divergencies between men should interest us rather than offend us, because they are effects of perspective, or of legitimate diversity in experience and interests. Trust the man who hesitates in his speech and is quick and steady in action, but beware of long arguments and long beards. Jupiter decided the most intricate questions with a nod, and a very few words and no gestures suffice for the Englishman to make his inner mind felt most unequivocally when occasion requires.

Instinctively the Englishman is no missionary, no conqueror. He prefers the country to the town, and home to foreign parts. He is rather glad and relieved if only natives will remain natives and strangers strangers, and at a comfortable distance from himself. Yet outwardly he is most hospitable and accepts almost anybody for the time being; he travels and conquers without a settled design, because he has the instinct of exploration. His adventures are all external; they change him so little that he is not afraid of them. He carries his English weather in his heart wherever he goes, and it becomes a cool spot in the desert, and a steady and sane oracle amongst all the deliriums of mankind. Never since the heroic days of Greece has the world had such a sweet, just, boyish master. It will be a black day for the human race when scientific blackguards, conspirators, churls, and fanatics manage to supplant him.

Soliloquies in England

571 *Religio Stoici*

THERE is a philosophic piety which has the universe for its object. This feeling, common to ancient and modern Stoics, has an obvious justification in man's dependence upon the natural world and in its service to many sides of the mind. Such justification of cosmic piety is rather obscured than supported by the euphemisms and ambiguities in which these philosophers usually indulge in their attempt to preserve the customary religious unction. For the more they personify the universe and give it the name of God the more they turn it into a devil. The universe, so far as we can observe it, is a wonderful and immense engine; its extent, its order, its beauty, its cruelty, make it alike impressive. If we dramatize its life and conceive its spirit, we are filled with wonder, terror, and amusement, so magnificent is that spirit, so prolific, inexorable, grammatical, and dull. Like all animals and plants, the cosmos has its own way of doing things, not wholly rational nor ideally best, but patient, fatal, and fruitful. Great is this organism of mud and fire, terrible this vast, painful, glorious experiment. Why should we not look on the universe with piety? Is it not our substance? Are we made of other clay? All our possibilities lie from eternity hidden in its bosom. It is the dispenser of all our joys. We may address it without superstitious terrors; it is not wicked. It follows its own habits abstractedly; it can be trusted to be true to its word. Society is not impossible between it and us, and since it is the source of all our energies, the home of all our happiness, shall we not cling to it and praise it, seeing that it vegetates so grandly and so sadly, and that it is not for us to blame it for what, doubtless, it never knew that it did? Where there is such infinite and laborious potency there is room for every hope.

Little Essays

RUDYARD KIPLING

1865–

572 *With the Main Guard*

'GUARRD, TURN OUT!'

The Relief had come; it was four o'clock. 'I'll catch a kyart for you, Sorr,' said Mulvaney. diving hastily into his accoutrements. 'Come up to the top av the Fort an' we'll pershue our invistigations into M'Grath's shtable.' The relieved guard strolled round the main bastion on its way to the swimming-bath. . .

'Fwhat 's here?' said Mulvaney, checking at a blur of white by the foot of the old sentry-box. He stooped and touched it. 'It 's Norah—Norah M'Taggart! Why, Nonie darlin', fwhat are ye doin' out av your mother's bed at this time?'

The two-year-old child of Sergeant M'Taggart must have wandered for a breath of cool air to the very verge of the parapet of the Fort ditch. Her tiny night-shift was gathered into a wisp round her neck and she moaned in her sleep. 'See there!' said Mulvaney; 'poor lamb! Look at the heat-rash on the innocint skin av her. 'Tis hard—crool hard even for us. Fwhat must it be for these? Wake up, Nonie, your mother will be woild about you. Begad, the child might ha' fallen into the ditch!'

He picked her up in the growing light, and set her on his shoulder, and her fair curls touched the grizzled stubble of his temples. Ortheris and Learoyd followed snapping their fingers, while Norah smiled at them a sleepy smile. Then carolled Mulvaney, clear as a lark, dancing the baby on his arm—

'If any young man should marry you,
  Say nothin' about the joke;
That iver ye slep' in a sinthry-box,
  Wrapped up in a soldier's cloak.'

'Though, on my sowl, Nonie,' he said gravely, 'there was not much cloak about you. Niver mind, you won't dhress like this ten years to come. Kiss your friends an' run along to your mother.'

Nonie, set down close to the Married Quarters, nodded with the quiet obedience of the soldier's child, but, ere she pattered off over the flagged path, held up her lips to be kissed by the Three Musketeers. Ortheris wiped his mouth with the back of his hand and swore sentimentally; Learoyd turned pink; and the two walked away together. The Yorkshireman lifted up his voice and gave in thunder the chorus of *The Sentry-Box*, while Ortheris piped at his side.

'Bin to a bloomin' sing-song, you two?' said the Artilleryman, who was taking his cartridge down to the Morning Gun. 'You're over merry for these dashed days.'

'I bid ye take care o' the brat, said he,
For it comes of a noble race,'

Learoyd bellowed. The voices died out in the swimming-bath.

'Oh, Terence!' I said, dropping into Mulvaney's speech, when we were alone, 'it 's you that have the Tongue!'

He looked at me wearily; his eyes were sunk in his head, and his face was drawn and white. 'Eyah!' said he; 'I've blandandhered thim through the night somehow, but can thim that helps others help thimselves? Answer me that, Sorr!'

And over the bastions of Fort Amara broke the pitiless day.

Soldiers Three

573 *The Spring Running*

IT was a perfect white night, as they call it. All green things seemed to have made a month's growth since the morning. The branch that was yellow-leaved the day before dripped sap when Mowgli broke it. The mosses curled deep and warm over his feet, the young grass had no cutting edges, and all the voices of the Jungle boomed like one deep harpstring touched by the moon—the Moon of New Talk, who splashed her light full on rock and pool, slipped it between trunk and creeper, and sifted it through a million leaves. Forgetting his unhappiness, Mowgli sang aloud with pure delight as he settled into his stride. It was more like flying than anything else, for he had chosen the long downward slope that leads to the Northern Marshes through the heart of the main Jungle, where the springy ground deadened the fall of his feet. A man-taught man would have picked his way with many stumbles through the cheating moonlight, but Mowgli's muscles, trained by years of experience, bore him up as though he were a feather. When a rotten log or a hidden stone turned under his foot he saved himself, never checking his pace, without effort and without thought. When he tired of ground-going he threw up his hands monkey-fashion to the nearest creeper, and seemed to float rather than to climb up into the thin branches, whence he would follow a tree-road till his mood changed, and he shot downward in a long, leafy curve to the levels again. There were still, hot hollows surrounded by wet rocks where he could hardly breathe for the heavy scents of the night flowers and the bloom along the creeper buds; dark avenues where the moonlight lay in belts as regular as checkered marbles in a church aisle; thickets where the wet young growth stood breast-high about him and threw its arms round his waist; and hilltops crowned with broken rock, where he leaped from stone to stone above the lairs of the frightened little foxes. He would hear, very faint and far off, the *chug-drug* of a boar sharpening his tusks on a bole; and would come across the great gray brute all alone, scribing and rending the bark of a tall tree, his mouth dripping with foam, and his eyes blazing like fire. Or he would turn aside to the sound of clashing horns and hissing grunts, and dash past a couple of furious sambhur, staggering to and fro with lowered heads, striped with blood that showed black in the moonlight. Or at some rushing ford he would hear Jacala the Crocodile bellowing like a bull, or disturb a twined knot of the Poison People, but before they could strike he would be away and across the glistening shingle, and deep in the Jungle again.

So he ran, sometimes shouting, sometimes singing to himself, the happiest thing in all the Jungle that night, till the smell of the flowers warned him that he was near the marshes, and those lay far beyond his farthest hunting-grounds.

The Second Jungle Book

574 *The Great Wall*

'"ROME'S Race—Rome's Pace", as the proverb says. Twenty-four miles in eight hours, neither more nor less. Head and spear up, shield on your back, cuirass-collar open one hand's breadth—and that 's how you take the Eagles through Britain.'

'And did you meet any adventures?' said Dan.

'There are no adventures South the Wall,' said Parnesius. 'The worst thing that happened me was having to appear before a magistrate up North, where a wandering philosopher had jeered at the Eagles. I was able to show that the old man had deliberately blocked our road; and the magistrate told him, out of his own Book, I believe, that, whatever his Gods might be, he should pay proper respect to Caesar.'

'What did you do?' said Dan.

'Went on. Why should *I* care for such things, my business being to reach my station? It took me twenty days.

'Of course, the farther North you go the emptier are the roads. At last you fetch clear of the forests and climb bare hills, where wolves howl in the ruins of our cities that have been. No more pretty girls; no more jolly magistrates who knew your Father when he was young, and invite you to stay with them; no news at the temples and way-stations except bad news of wild beasts. There 's where you meet hunters, and trappers for the Circuses, prodding along chained bears and muzzled wolves. Your pony shies at them, and your men laugh.

'The houses change from gardened villas to shut forts with watch-towers of grey stone, and great stone-walled sheepfolds, guarded by armed Britons of the North Shore. In the naked hills beyond the naked houses, where the shadows of the clouds play like cavalry charging, you see puffs of black smoke from the mines. The hard road goes on and on—and the wind sings through your helmet-plume—past altars to Legions and Generals forgotten, and broken statues of Gods and Heroes, and thousands of graves where the mountain foxes and hares peep at you. Red-hot in summer, freezing in winter, is that big, purple heather country of broken stone.

'Just when you think you are at the world's end, you see a smoke from East to West as far as the eye can turn, and then, under it, also as far as the eye can stretch, houses and temples, shops and theatres, barracks and granaries, trickling along like dice behind—always behind—one long, low, rising and falling, and hiding and showing line of towers. And that is the Wall!'

'Ah!' said the children, taking breath.

'You may well,' said Parnesius. 'Old men who have followed the Eagles since boyhood say nothing in the Empire is more wonderful than first sight of the Wall!'

'Is it just *a* Wall? Like the one round the kitchen-garden?' said Dan.

'No, no! It is *the* Wall. Along the top are towers with guard-houses, small towers, between. Even on the narrowest part of it three men with shields can walk abreast, from guard-house to guard-house. A little curtain wall, no higher than a man's neck, runs along the top of the thick wall, so that from a distance you see the helmets of the sentries sliding back and forth like beads. Thirty feet high is the Wall, and on the Picts' side, the North, is a ditch, strewn with blades of old swords and spear-heads set in wood, and tyres of wheels joined by chains. The Little People come there to steal iron for their arrow-heads.

'But the Wall itself is not more wonderful than the town behind it. Long ago there were great ramparts and ditches on the South side, and no one was allowed to build there. Now the ramparts are partly pulled down and built over, from end to end of the Wall; making a thin town eighty miles long. Think of it! One roaring, rioting, cock-fighting, wolf-baiting, horse-racing town, from Ituna on the West to Segedunum on the cold eastern beach! On one side heather, woods and ruins where Picts hide, and on the other, a vast town—long like a snake, and wicked like a snake. Yes, a snake basking beside a warm wall!

'My Cohort, I was told, lay at Hunno, where the Great North Road runs through the Wall into the Province of Valentia.' Parnesius laughed scornfully. 'The Province of Valentia! We followed the road, therefore, into Hunno town, and stood astonished. The place was a fair—a fair of peoples from every corner of the Empire. Some were racing horses: some sat in wine-shops: some watched dogs baiting bears, and many gathered in a ditch to see cocks fight. A boy not much older than myself, but I could see he was an officer, reined up before me and asked what I wanted.

'"My station," I said, and showed him my shield.' Parnesius held up his broad shield with its three X's like letters on a beer-cask.

'"Lucky omen!" said he. "Your Cohort 's the next tower to us, but they're all at the cock-fight. This is a happy place. Come and wet the Eagles." He meant to offer me a drink.

'"When I've handed over my men," I said. I felt angry and ashamed.

'"Oh, you'll soon outgrow that sort of nonsense," he answered. "But don't let me interfere with your hopes. Go on to the Statue of Roma Dea. You can't miss it. The main road into Valentia!" and he laughed and rode off. I could see the statue not a quarter of a mile away, and there I went. At some time or other the Great North Road ran under it into Valentia; but the far end had been blocked up because of the Picts, and on the plaster a man had scratched, "Finish!" It was like marching into a cave. We grounded spears together, my little thirty, and it echoed in the barrel of the arch, but none came. There was a door at one side painted with our number. We prowled in, and I found a cook asleep, and ordered him to give us food. Then I climbed to the top of the Wall, and looked out over the Pict country, and I—thought,' said Parnesius. 'The bricked-up arch with "Finish!" on the plaster was what shook me, for I was not much more than a boy.'

Puck of Pook's Hill

HERBERT GEORGE WELLS

1866–

575 *The Potwell Inn*

IT was about two o'clock in the afternoon, one hot day in May, when Mr. Polly, unhurrying and serene, came upon that broad bend of the river to which the little lawn and garden of the Potwell Inn run down. He stopped at the sight of the place and surveyed its deep tiled roof, nestling under big trees—you never get a decently big, decently shaped tree by the seaside—its sign towards the roadway, its sun-blistered green bench and tables, its shapely white windows and its row of upshooting hollyhock plants in the garden. A hedge separated the premises from a buttercup-yellow meadow, and beyond stood three poplars in a group against the sky, three exceptionally tall, graceful, and harmonious poplars. It is hard to say what there was about them that made them so beautiful to Mr. Polly, but they seemed to him to touch a pleasant scene with a distinction almost divine. He stood admiring them quietly for a long time.

At last the need for coarser aesthetic satisfactions arose in him.

'Provinder,' he whispered, drawing near to the inn. 'Cold sirloin, for choice. And nutbrown brew and wheaten bread.'

The nearer he came to the place the more he liked it. The windows on the ground floor were long and low, and they had pleasing red blinds. The green tables outside were agreeably ringed with memories of former drinks, and an extensive grape vine spread level branches across the whole front of the place. Against the wall was a broken oar, two boat-hooks, and the stained and faded red cushions of a pleasure-boat. One went up three steps to the glass-panelled door and peeped into a broad, low room with a bar and a beer-engine, behind which were many bright and helpful-looking bottles against mirrors, and great and little pewter measures, and bottles fastened in brass wire upside down, with their corks replaced by taps, and a white china cask labelled ' Shrub ', and cigar boxes, and boxes of cigarettes, and a couple of Toby jugs and a beautifully coloured hunting scene framed and glazed, showing the most elegant people taking Piper's Cherry Brandy, and cards such as the law requires about the dilution of spirits and the illegality of bringing children into bars, and satirical verses about swearing and asking for credit, and three very bright, red-cheeked wax apples, and a round-shaped clock.

But these were the mere background to the really pleasant thing in the spectacle, which was quite the plumpest woman Mr. Polly had ever seen, seated in an arm-chair in the midst of all these bottles and glasses and glittering things, peacefully and tranquilly, and without the slightest loss of dignity, asleep. Many people would have called her a fat woman, but Mr. Polly's innate sense of epithet told him from the outset that plump was the word. She had shapely brows and a straight, well-shaped nose, kind lines and contentment about her mouth, and beneath it the jolly chins clustered like chubby little cherubim about the feet of an Assumption-ing Madonna. Her plumpness was firm and pink and wholesome, and her hands, dimpled at every joint, were clasped in front of her; she seemed, as it were, to embrace herself with infinite confidence and kindliness, as one who knew herself good in substance, good in essence, and would show her gratitude to God by that ready acceptance of all that He had given her. Her head was a little on one side, not much, but just enough to speak of trustfulness, and rob her of the stiff effect of self-reliance. And she slept.

'*My* sort,' said Mr. Polly, and opened the door very softly, divided between the desire to enter and come nearer, and an instinctive indisposition to break slumbers so manifestly sweet and satisfying.

She awoke with a start, and it amazed Mr. Polly to see swift terror flash into her eyes. Instantly it had gone again.

'Law!' she said, her face softening with relief. 'I thought you was Jim.'

'I'm never Jim,' said Mr. Polly.

'You've got his sort of hat.'

'Ah!' said Mr. Polly, and leant over the bar.

'It just came into my head you was Jim,' said the plump lady, dismissed the topic and stood up. 'I believe I was having forty winks,' she said, 'if all the truth was told. What can I do for you?'

'Cold meat?' said Mr. Polly.

'There *is* cold meat,' the plump woman admitted.

'And room for it.'

The plump woman came and leant over the bar and regarded him judicially but kindly. 'There's some cold boiled beef,' she said, and added, 'A bit of crisp lettuce?'

'New mustard,' said Mr. Polly.

'And a tankard!'

'A tankard.'

They understood each other perfectly.

'Looking for work?' asked the plump woman.

'In a way,' said Mr. Polly.

They smiled like old friends.

Whatever the truth may be about love, there is certainly such a thing as friendship at first sight. They liked each other's voices, they liked each other's way of smiling and speaking.

'It 's such beautiful weather this spring,' said Mr. Polly, explaining everything.

'What sort of work do you want ?' she asked.

'I've never properly thought that out,' said Mr. Polly. 'I've been looking round—for ideas.'

'Will you have your beef in the tap or outside ? That 's the tap.'

Mr. Polly had a glimpse of an oaken settle. 'In the tap will be handier for you,' he said.

'Hear that ?' said the plump lady.

'Hear what ?'

'Listen.'

Presently the silence was broken by a distant howl—'Oooooover !' 'Eh ?' she said.

He nodded.

'That 's the ferry. And there isn't a ferryman.'

'Could I ?'

'Can you punt ?'

'Never tried.'

'Well—pull the pole out before you reach the end of the punt, that 's all. Try.'

Mr. Polly went out again into the sunshine.

At times one can tell so much so briefly. Here are the facts then—bare. He found a punt and a pole, got across to the steps on the opposite side, picked up an elderly gentleman in an alpaca jacket and a pith helmet, cruised with him vaguely for twenty minutes, conveyed him tortuously into the midst of a thicket of forget-me-not spangled sedges, splashed some water-weed over him, hit him twice with the punt pole, and finally landed him, alarmed but abusive, in treacherous soil at the edge of a hay meadow about forty yards down-stream, where he immediately got into difficulties with a noisy, aggressive little white dog, which was guarding a jacket.

Mr. Polly returned in a complicated manner, but with perfect dignity, to his moorings.

He found the plump woman rather flushed and tearful, and seated at one of the green tables outside.

'I been laughing at you,' she said.

'What for ?' asked Mr. Polly.

'I ain't 'ad such a laugh since Jim come 'ome. When you 'it 'is 'ead, it 'urt my side.'

'It didn't hurt his head—not particularly.'

'Did you charge him anything ?'

'Gratis,' said Mr. Polly. 'I never thought of it.'

The plump woman pressed her hands to her sides and laughed silently for a space. 'You ought to 'ave charged 'im Sumpthing,' she said. 'You better come and have your cold meat before you do any more puntin'. You and me'll get on together.'

The History of Mr. Polly

LIONEL JOHNSON

1867–1902

576 *Mannerism in Art*

THE works of a writer past the prime of life are apt to display a certain excess or extravagance: what was once his strength has now become his weakness, and his virtue has changed into his vice. This is most often seen in the case of very strong and masterful writers; those whose good work is all done in some one *annus mirabilis*, or flowering season, fall into mere decay, as Coleridge or as Wordsworth. It is in writers whose whole life has been full of successful toil and untiring effort, that manner degenerates into mannerism. Such writers, and, indeed, all artists of such a kind, are often men who have discovered some new way in art, and who possess a secret and a power proper to themselves ; the world, used to the old and familiar ways, will not at once take notice of them. In proportion to their faith in themselves and their fidelity to their art, these artists, unshaken and undeterred, continue upon their way, rather increasing than relaxing their unappreciated labours. Slowly and gradually the world comes round to their side, is converted to their faith, welcomes them with applause. But what of the artists, all this long time? Is there no danger that, in a kind of unconscious defiance and challenge, they will have gone too far, and grown enamoured of that in their work which the world did well to blame? If the world cried out upon their obscurity, where there was some obscurity but not much, was it not natural in them to have replied with worse obscurities, out of an impatient contempt and exasperation?

Reviews and Critical Papers

ARNOLD BENNETT

1867–

577 *Swinburne*

ON Good Friday night I was out in the High Street, at the cross-roads, where the warp and the woof of the traffic assault each other under a great glare of lamps. The shops were closed and black, except where a tobacconist kept the tobacconist's bright and everlasting vigil; but above the shops occasional rare windows were illuminated, giving hints —dressing-tables, pictures, gas-globes—of intimate private lives. I don't know why such hints should always seem to me pathetic, saddening; but they do. And beneath them, through the dark defile of shutters, motor-omnibuses roared and swayed and curved, too big for the street, and dwarfing it. And automobiles threaded between them, and bicycles dared the spaces that were left. From afar off there came a flying light, like a shot out of a gun, and it grew into a man perched on a shuddering contrivance that might have been invented by H. G. Wells, and swept perilously into the contending currents, and by miracles emerged untouched, and was gone, driven by the desire of the immortal soul within the man. This strange thing happened again and again. The pavements were crowded with hurrying or loitering souls, and the omnibuses and autos were full of them: hundreds passed before the vision every moment. And they were all preoccupied; they nearly all bore the weary, egotistic melancholy that spreads like an infection at the close of a fête day in London; the lights of a motor-omnibus would show the rapt faces of sixteen souls at once in their glass cage, driving the vehicle on by their desires. The policeman and the loafers in the ring of fire made by the public-houses at the cross-roads—even these were grave with the universal affliction of life, and grim with the relentless universal egotism. Lovers walked as though there were no heaven and no earth, but only themselves in space. Nobody but me seemed to guess that the road to Delhi could be as naught to this road, with its dark, fleeing shapes, its shifting beams, its black brick precipices, and its thousand pale, flitting faces of a gloomy and decadent race. As says the Indian proverb, I met ten thousand men on the Putney High Street, and they were all my brothers. But I alone was aware of it. As I stood watching autobus after autobus swing round in a fearful semicircle to begin a new journey, I gazed myself into a mystic comprehension of the significance of what I saw. A few yards beyond where the autobuses turned was a certain house with lighted upper windows, and in that house the greatest lyric versifier that England ever had, and one of the great poets of the whole world and of all the ages, was dying: a name immortal. But nobody looked; nobody seemed to care; I doubt if any one thought of it. This enormous negligence appeared to me to be fine, to be magnificently human.

The next day all the shops were open, and hundreds of fatigued assistants were pouring out their exhaustless patience on thousands of urgent and bright women; and flags waved on high, and the gutters were banked with yellow and white flowers, and the air was brisk and the roadways were clean. The very vital spirit of energy seemed to have scattered the breath of life generously, so that all were intoxicated by it in the gay sunshine. He was dead then. The waving posters said it. . .

Last year I was walking down Putney Hill, and I saw Swinburne for the first and last time. I could see nothing but his face and head. I did not notice those ridiculously short trousers that Putney people invariably mention when mentioning Swinburne. Never have I seen a man's life more clearly written in his eyes and mouth and forehead. The face of a man who had lived with fine, austere, passionate thoughts of his own! By the heavens, it was a noble sight. I have not seen a nobler. Now, I knew by hearsay every crease in his trousers, but nobody had told me that his face was a vision that would never fade from my memory.

Books and Persons

CHARLES EDWARD MONTAGUE

1867–

578 *The Faculty of Delight*

AMONG the mind's powers is one that comes of itself to many children and artists. It need not be lost, to the end of his days, by any one who has ever had it. This is the power of taking delight in a thing, or rather in anything, everything, not as a means to some other end, but just because it is what it is, as the lover dotes on whatever may be the traits of the beloved object. A child in the full health of his mind will put his hand flat on the summer turf, feel it, and give a little shiver of private glee at the elastic firmness of the globe. He is not thinking how well it will do for some game or to feed sheep upon. That would be the way of the wooer whose mind runs on his mistress's money. The child's is sheer affection, the true ecstatic sense of the thing's inherent characteristics. No matter what the things may be, no matter what they are good or no good for, there they are, each with a thrilling unique look and feel of its own, like a face; the iron astringently cool under its paint, the painted wood familiarly warmer, the clod crumbling enchantingly down in the hands, with its little dry smell of the sun and of hot nettles; each common thing a personality marked by delicious differences.

The joy of an Adam new to the garden and just looking round is brought by the normal child to the things that he does as well as those that he sees. To be suffered to do some plain work with the real spade used by mankind can give him a mystical exaltation: to come home with his legs, as the French say, re-entering his body from the fatigue of helping the gardener to weed beds sends him to sleep in the glow of a beatitude that is an end in itself. . .

The right education, if we could find it, would work up this creative faculty of delight into all its branching possibilities of knowledge, wisdom, and nobility. Of all three it is the beginning, condition, or raw material.

Disenchantment

579 *Belated Victory*

THERE were other days, during the following months of worm-eaten success, when some mirage of the greater joys which we had forfeited hung for a few moments over the sand. It must be always a strange delight to an infantryman to explore at his ease, in security, ground that to him has been almost as unimaginable as events after death. There is no describing the vesture of enigmatic remoteness enfolding a long-watched enemy line. Tolstoy has tried, but even he does not come up to it. Vergil alone has expressed one sensation of the British overflow over Lille and Cambrai, Menin (even the Menin Road had an end) and Bruges and Ostend, Le Cateau and Landrecies, Liège and Namur—

> Iuvat ire et Dorica castra
> Desertosque videre locos, litusque relictum.
> Classibus hic locus, hic acie certare solebant,
> Hic Dolopum manus, hic saevus tendebat Achilles.

And then, wherever you went, till the frontier was reached, every one was your host and your friend; all the relations of strangers to one another had been transfigured into the sum of all kindness and courtesy. In one mining village in Flanders, quitted that day by the Germans, a woman rushed out of a house to give me a lump of bread, thinking that we must all be as hungry as she and her neighbours. Late one night in Brussels, just after the Germans had gone, I was walking with another officer down the chief street of the city, then densely crowded with radiant citizens. My friend had a wooden stump leg and could not walk very well; and this figure of a khaki-clad man, maimed in the discharge of an Allied obligation to Belgium, seemed suddenly and almost simultaneously to be seen by the whole of that great crowd in all its symbolic value, so that the crowd fell silent and opened out spontaneously along the whole length of the street and my friend had to hobble down the middle of a long avenue of bareheaded men and bowing women.

Finally—last happy thrill of the war—the first stroke of eleven o'clock, on the morning of Armistice Day, on the town clock of Mons, only captured that morning; Belgian civilians and British soldiers crowding together into the square, shaking each other's hands and singing each other's national anthems; a little toy-like peal of bells in the church contriving to tinkle out 'Tipperary' for our welcome, while our airmen, released from their labours, tumbled and romped overhead like boys turning cartwheels with ecstasy.

What a victory it might have been—the real, the Winged Victory, chivalric, whole and unstained! The bride that our feckless wooing had sought and not won in the generous youth of the war had come to us now: an old woman, or dead, she no longer refused us. We had arrived, like the prince in the poem—

Too late for love, too late for joy,
  Too late, too late!
You loitered on the road too long,
  You trifled at the gate:
The enchanted dove upon her branch
  Died without a mate;
The enchanted princess in her tower
  Slept, died behind the grate:
Her heart was starving all this while
  You made it wait.

Disenchantment

JOHN GALSWORTHY

1867–

580 *Death of Aunt Ann*

UPON arriving, the coffin was borne into the chapel, and, two by two, the mourners filed in behind it. This guard of men, all attached to the dead by the bond of kinship, was an impressive and singular sight in the great city of London, with its overwhelming diversity of life, its innumerable vocations, pleasures, duties, its terrible hardness, its terrible call to individualism.

The family had gathered to triumph over all this, to give a show of tenacious unity, to illustrate gloriously that law of property underlying the growth of their tree, by which it had thriven and spread, trunk and branches, the sap flowing through all, the full growth reached at the appointed time. The spirit of the old woman lying in her last sleep had called them to this demonstration. It was her final appeal to that unity which had been their strength—it was her final triumph that she had died while the tree was yet whole.

She was spared the watching of the branches jut out beyond the point of balance. She could not look into the hearts of her followers. The same law that had worked in her, bringing her up from a tall, straight-backed slip of a girl to a woman strong and grown, from a woman grown to a woman old, angular, feeble, almost witch-like, with individuality all sharpened and sharpened, as all rounding from the world's contact fell off from her—that same law would work, was working, in the family she had watched like a mother.

She had seen it young, and growing, she had seen it strong and grown, and before her old eyes had time or strength to see any more, she died. She would have tried, and who knows but she might have kept it young and strong, with her old fingers, her trembling kisses—a little longer; alas! not even Aunt Ann could fight with Nature.

'Pride comes before a fall!' In accordance with this, the greatest of Nature's ironies, the Forsyte family had gathered for a last proud pageant before they fell. Their faces to right and left, in single lines, were turned for the most part impassively toward the ground, guardians of their thoughts; but here and there, one looking upward, with a line between his brows, seemed to see some sight on the chapel walls too much for him, to be listening to something that appalled. And the responses, low-muttered, in voices through which rose the same tone, the same unseizable family ring, sounded weird, as though murmured in hurried duplication by a single person.

The service in the chapel over, the mourners filed up again to guard the body to the tomb. The vault stood open, and, round it, men in black were waiting.

From that high and sacred field, where thousands of the upper-middle class lay in their last sleep, the eyes of the Forsytes travelled down across the flocks of graves. There—spreading to the distance, lay London, with no sun over it, mourning the loss of its daughter, mourning with this family, so dear, the loss of her who was mother and guardian. A hundred thousand spires and houses, blurred in the great gray web of property, lay there like prostrate worshippers before the grave of this, the oldest Forsyte of them all.

A few words, a sprinkle of earth, the thrusting of the coffin home, and Aunt Ann had passed to her last rest.

Round the vault, trustees of that passing, the five brothers stood, with white heads bowed; they would see that Ann was comfortable where she was going. Her little property must stay behind, but otherwise, all that could be should be done.

Then severally, each stood aside, and putting on his hat, turned back to inspect the new inscription on the marble of the family vault:

SACRED TO THE MEMORY OF
ANN FORSYTE,
THE DAUGHTER OF THE ABOVE
JOLYON AND ANN FORSYTE,
WHO DEPARTED THIS LIFE THE 27TH DAY OF
SEPTEMBER, 1886,
AGED EIGHTY-SEVEN YEARS AND FOUR DAYS.

The Forsyte Saga

ARTHUR CLUTTON-BROCK

1868–1924

581 *The Cardinal Virtue of Prose*

PROSE of its very nature is longer than verse, and the virtues peculiar to it manifest themselves gradually. If the cardinal virtue of poetry is love, the cardinal virtue of prose is justice; and, whereas love makes you act and speak on the spur of the moment, justice needs inquiry, patience, and a control even of the noblest passions... By justice here I do not mean justice only to particular people or ideas, but a habit of justice in all the processes of thought, a style tranquillized and a form moulded by that habit. The master of prose is not cold, but he will not let any word or image inflame him with a heat irrelevant to his purpose. Unhasting, unresting, he pursues it, subduing all the riches of his mind to it, rejecting all beauties that are not germane to it; making his own beauty out of the very accomplishment of it, out of the whole work and its proportions, so that you must read to the end before you know that it is beautiful. But he has his reward, for he is trusted and convinces, as those who are at the mercy of their own eloquence do not; and he gives a pleasure all the greater for being hardly noticed. In the best prose, whether narrative or argument, we are so led on as we read, that we do not stop to applaud the writer, nor do we stop to question him.

Modern Essays

EDWARD VERRALL LUCAS

1868–

582 *The Windmill*

CHANCE recently made me for a while the tenant of a windmill. Not to live in, and unhappily not to grind corn in, but to visit as the mood arose, and see the ships in the harbour from the topmost window, and look down on the sheep and the green world all around. For this mill stands high and white—so white, indeed, that when there is a thunder-cloud behind it, it seems a thing of polished aluminium.

From its windows you can see four other mills, all, like itself, idle, and one merely a ruin and one with only two sweeps left. But just over the next range of hills, out of sight, to the north-east, is a windmill that still merrily goes, and about five miles away to the north-west is another also active; so that things are not quite so bad hereabouts as in many parts of the country, where the good breezes blow altogether in vain. . .

Thinking over the losses which England has had forced upon her by steam and the ingenuity of the engineer, one is disposed to count the decay of the windmill among the first. Perhaps in the matter of pure picturesqueness the most serious thing that ever happened to England was the discovery of galvanized iron roofing; but, after all, there was never anything but quiet and rich and comfortable beauty about red roofs, whereas the living windmill is not only beautiful but romantic too: a willing, man-serving creature, yoked to the elements, a whirling monster, often a thing of terror. No one can stand very near the crashing sweeps of a windmill in half a gale without a tightening of the heart—a feeling comparable to that which comes from watching the waves break over a wall in a storm. And to be within the mill at such a time is to know something of sound's very sources; it is the cave of noise itself. No doubt there are dens of hammering energy which are more shattering, but the noise of a windmill is largely natural, the product of wood striving with the good sou'-wester; it fills the ears rather than assaults them. The effect, moreover, is by no means lessened by the absence of the wind itself and the silent nonchalance of the miller and his man, who move about in the midst of this appalling racket with the quiet efficiency of vergers.

In my mill, of course, there is no such uproar; nothing but the occasional shaking of the cross-pieces of the idle sails. Everything is still; and the pity of it is that everything is in almost perfect order for the day's work. The mill one day—some score years ago—was full of life; the next, and ever after, mute and lifeless, like a stream frozen in a night or the palace in Tennyson's ballad of the 'Sleeping Beauty'. There is no decay—merely inanition. One or two of the apple-wood cogs have been broken from the great wheel; a few floor planks have been rotted; but that is all. A week's overhauling would put everything right. But it will never come, and the cheerful winds that once were to drive a thousand English mills so happily now bustle over the Channel in vain.

Old Lamps for New

ROBERT FALCON SCOTT
AND 1868–1912
CHARLES TURLEY

583 (i) *The Death of Captain Oates*

ON this same day a blizzard met them after they had marched for half an hour, and Scott seeing that not one of them could face such weather, pitched camp and stayed there until the following morning. Then they struggled on again with the sky so overcast that they could see nothing and consequently lost the tracks. At the most they gained little more than six miles during the day, and this they knew was as much as they could hope to do if they got no help from wind or surfaces. 'We have 7 days' food and should be about 55 miles from One Ton Camp to-night, 6 × 7 = 42, leaving us 13 miles short of our distance, even if things get no worse.'

Oates too was, Scott felt, getting very near the end. 'What we or he will do, God only knows. We discussed the matter after breakfast; he is a brave fine fellow and understands the situation, but he practically asked for advice. Nothing could be said but to urge him to march as long as he could. One satisfactory result to the discussion: I practically ordered Wilson to hand over the means of ending our troubles to us, so that any of us may know how to do so. Wilson had no choice between doing so and our ransacking the medicine case.'

Thus Scott wrote on the 11th, and the next days brought more and more misfortunes with them. A strong northerly wind stopped them altogether on the 13th, and although on the following morning they started with a favourable breeze, it soon shifted and blew through their wind-clothes and their mits. 'Poor Wilson horribly cold, could not get off ski for some time. Bowers and I practically made camp, and when we got into the tent at last we were all deadly cold. . . We *must* go on, but now the making of every camp must be more difficult and dangerous. It must be near the end, but a pretty merciful end. . . I shudder to think what it will be like to-morrow.'

Up to this time, incredible as it seems, Scott had only once spared himself the agony of writing in his journal, so nothing could be more pathetic and significant than the fact that at last he was unable any longer to keep a daily record of this magnificent journey.

'Friday, March 16 or Saturday 17. Lost track of dates, but think the last correct,' his next entry begins, but then under the most unendurable conditions he went on to pay a last and imperishable tribute to his dead companion.

'Tragedy all along the line. At lunch, the day before yesterday, poor Titus Oates said he couldn't go on; he proposed we should leave him in his sleeping-bag. That we could not do, and we induced him to come on, on the afternoon march. In spite of its awful nature for him he struggled on and we made a few miles. At night he was worse and we knew the end had come.

'Should this be found I want these facts recorded. Oates' last thoughts were of his Mother, but immediately before he took pride in thinking that his regiment would be pleased with the bold way in which he met his death. We can testify to his bravery. He has borne intense suffering for weeks without complaint, and to the very last was able and willing to discuss outside subjects. He did not—would not—give up hope till the very end. He was a brave soul. This was the end. He slept through the night before last, hoping not to wake; but he woke in the morning—yesterday.

It was blowing a blizzard. He said, "I am just going outside and may be some time." He went out into the blizzard and we have not seen him since.

'I take this opportunity of saying that we have stuck to our sick companions to the last. In case of Edgar Evans, when absolutely out of food and he lay insensible, the safety of the remainder seemed to demand his abandonment, but Providence mercifully removed him at this critical moment. He died a natural death, and we did not leave him till two hours after his death.

'We knew that poor Oates was walking to his death, but though we tried to dissuade him, we knew it was the act of a brave man and an English gentleman. We all hope to meet the end with a similar spirit, and assuredly the end is not far.'

(*ii*) *The End*

'*March* 29.—Since the 21st we have had a continuous gale from W.S.W. and S.W. We had fuel to make two cups of tea apiece, and bare food for two days on the 20th. Every day we have been ready to start for our depot 11 *miles away*, but outside the door of the tent it remains a scene of whirling drift. I do not think we can hope for any better things now. We shall stick it out to the end, but we are getting weaker, of course, and the end cannot be far.

'It seems a pity, but I do not think I can write more.

'R. Scott'

Last entry.

'For God's sake look after our people.'

After Cherry-Garrard and Demetri had returned to Hut Point on March 16 without having seen any signs of the Polar party, Atkinson and Keohane made one more desperate effort to find them. When, however, this had been unsuccessful there was nothing more to be done until the winter was over.

During this long and anxious time the leadership of the party devolved upon Atkinson, who under the most trying circumstances showed qualities that are beyond all praise. At the earliest possible moment (October 30) a large party started south. 'On the night of the 11th and morning of the 12th,' Atkinson says, 'after we had marched 11 miles due south of One Ton, we found the tent. It was an object partially snowed up and looking like a cairn. Before it were the ski sticks and in front of them a bamboo which probably was the mast of the sledge. . .

'Inside the tent were the bodies of Captain Scott, Doctor Wilson, and Lieutenant Bowers. They had pitched their tent well, and it had withstood all the blizzards of an exceptionally hard winter.'

Wilson and Bowers were found in the attitude of sleep, their sleeping-bags closed over their heads as they would naturally close them.

Scott died later. He had thrown back the flaps of his sleeping-bag, and opened his coat. The little wallet containing the three note-books was under his shoulder and his arm flung across Wilson.

Scott's Last Expedition, retold by Charles Turley

MICHAEL FAIRLESS

(MARGARET FAIRLESS BARBER, 1869–1901)

584 *The Roadmender and the Birds*

THE birds have no fear of me; am I not also of the brown brethren in my sober fustian livery? They share my meals—at least the little dun-coated

Franciscans do ; the blackbirds and thrushes care not a whit for such simple food as crumbs, but with legs well apart and claws tense with purchase they disinter poor brother worm, having first mocked him with sound of rain. The robin that lives by the gate regards my heap of stones as subject to his special inspection. He sits atop and practises the trill of his summer song until it shrills above and through the metallic clang of my strokes ; and when I pause he cocks his tail, with a humorous twinkle of his round eye which means—'What! shirking, big brother ?'—and I fall, ashamed, to my mending of roads.

The Roadmender

HILAIRE BELLOC

1870–

585 *The Normans*

THEY have been written of enough to-day, but who has seen them from close by or understood that brilliant interlude of power?

The little bullet-headed men, vivacious, and splendidly brave, we know that they awoke all Europe, that they first provided settled financial systems and settled governments of land, and that everywhere, from the Grampians to Mesopotamia, they were like steel when all other Christians were like wood or like lead.

We know that they were a flash. They were not formed or definable at all before the year 1000 ; by the year 1200 they were gone. Some odd transitory phenomenon of cross-breeding, a very lucky freak in the history of the European family, produced the only body of men who all were lords and who in their collective action showed continually nothing but genius.

We know that they were the spear-head, as it were, of the Gallic spirit: the vanguard of that one of the Gallic expansions which we associate with the opening of the Middle Ages and with the crusades... We know all this and write about it; nevertheless, we do not make enough of the Normans in England.

Here and there a man who really knows his subject and who disdains the market of the school books, puts as it should be put their conquest of this island and their bringing into our blood whatever is still strongest in it. Many (descended from their leaders) have remarked their magical ride through South Italy, their ordering of Sicily, their hand in Palestine. As for the Normans in Normandy, of their exchequer there, of what Rouen was—all that has never been properly written down at all. Their great adventure here in England has been most written of by far; but I say again no one has made enough of them; no one has brought them back out of their graves. The character of what they did has been lost in these silly little modern quarrels about races, which are but the unscholarly expression of a deeper hypocritical quarrel about religion.

Yet it is in England that the Norman can be studied as he can be studied nowhere else. He did not write here (as in Sicily) upon a palimpsest. He was not merged here (as in the Orient) with the rest of the French. He was segregated here; he can be studied in isolation; for though so many that crossed the sea on that September night with William, the big leader of them, held no Norman tenure, yet the spirit of the whole thing was Norman: the regularity, the suddenness, the achievement, and, when the short fighting was over, the creation of a new society. It was the Norman who began everything over again—the first fresh influence since Rome.

The riot of building has not been seized. The island was conquered in 1070. It was a place of heavy foolish men with random laws, pale eyes, and a slow manner; their houses were of wood: sometimes they built (but how painfully, and how childishly!) with stone. There was no height, there was no dignity, there was no sense of permanence. The Norman Government was established. At once rapidity, energy, the clear object of a united and organised power followed. And see what followed in architecture alone, and in what a little space of the earth, and in what a little stretch of time—less than the time that separates us to-day from the year of Disraeli's death or the occupation of Egypt.

The Conquest was achieved in 1070. In that same year they pulled down the wooden shed at Bury St. Edmunds, 'unworthy,' they said, 'of a great saint,' and began the great shrine of stone. Next year it was the castle at Oxford, in 1075 Monkswearmouth, Jarrow, and the church at Chester; in 1077 Rochester and St Alban's; in 1079 Winchester. Ely, Worcester, Thorney, Hurley, Lincoln, followed with the next years; by 1089 they had tackled Gloucester, by 1092 Carlisle, by 1093 Lindisfarne, Christchurch, tall Durham. . . . And this is but a short and random list of some of their greatest works in the space of one boyhood. Hundreds of castles, houses, village churches are unrecorded.

Were they not indeed a people? . .

One may say of the Norman preceding the Gothic what Dante said of Virgil preceding the Faith: Would that they had been born in a time when they could have known it! But the East was not yet open. The mind of Europe had not yet received the great experience of the Crusades; the Normans had no medium wherein to express their mighty soul, save the round arch and the straight line, the capital barbaric or naked, the sullen round shaft of the pillar—more like a drum than like a column. They could build, as it were, with nothing but the last ruins of Rome. They were given no forms but the forms which the fatigue and lethargy of the Dark Ages had repeated for six hundred years. They were capable, even in the north, of impressing even these forms with a superhuman majesty.

Hills and the Sea

JOHN MILLINGTON SYNGE

1871–1909

586 *Riders to the Sea*

MAURYA has gone over and knelt down at the head of the table. The women are keening softly and swaying themselves with a slow movement. CATHLEEN *and* NORA *kneel at the other end of the table. The men kneel near the door.*

MAURYA (*raising her head and speaking as if she did not see the people around her*). They're all gone now, and there isn't anything more the sea can do to me. . . I'll have no call now to be up crying and praying when the wind breaks from the south, and you can hear the surf is in the east, and the surf is in the west, making a great stir with the two noises, and they hitting one on the other. I'll have no call now to be going down and getting Holy Water in the dark nights after Samhain, and I won't care what way the sea is when the other women will be keening. (*To Nora.*) Give me the Holy Water, Nora; there 's a small sup still on the dresser.

Nora gives it to her.

MAURYA (*drops* MICHAEL'S *clothes across* BARTLEY'S *feet, and sprinkles the Holy Water over him*). It isn't that I haven't prayed for you, Bartley, to the Almighty God. It isn't that I haven't said prayers in the dark night till you wouldn't know what I'd be saying; but it 's a great rest I'll have now, and it 's time, surely. It 's a great rest I'll have now, and great sleeping in the long nights after Samhain, if it 's only a bit of wet flour we do have to eat, and maybe a fish that would be stinking.

Riders to the Sea

MAX BEERBOHM

1872–

587 *The Morris Dancers*

IT was in the wide street of a tiny village near Oxford that I saw them. Fantastic—high-fantastical—figures they did cut in their finery. But in demeanour they were quite simple, quite serious, these eight English peasants. They had trudged hither from the neighbouring village that was their home. And they danced quite simply, quite seriously. One of them, I learned, was a cobbler, another a baker, and the rest were farm-labourers. And their fathers and their fathers' fathers had danced here before them, even so, every May-day morning. They were as deeply rooted in antiquity as the elm outside the inn. They were here always in their season as surely as the elm put forth its buds. And the elm, knowing them, approving them, let its green-flecked branches dance in unison with them.

The first dance was in full swing when I approached. Only six of the men were dancers. Of the others, one was the 'minstrel', the other the 'dysard'. The minstrel was playing a flute; and the dysard I knew by the wand and leathern bladder which he brandished as he walked around, keeping a space for the dancers, and chasing and buffeting merrily any man or child who ventured too near. He, like the others, wore a white smock decked with sundry ribands, and a top-hat that must have belonged to his grandfather. Its antiquity of form and texture contrasted strangely with the freshness of the garland of paper roses that wreathed it. I was told that the wife or sweetheart of every Morris-dancer takes special pains to deck her man out more gaily than his fellows. But this pious endeavour had defeated its own end. So bewildering was the amount of brand-new bunting attached to all these eight men that no matron or maiden could for the life of her have determined which was the most splendid of them all. Besides his adventitious finery, every dancer, of course, had in his hands the scarves which are as necessary to his performance of the Morris as are the bells strapped about the calves of his legs. Waving these scarves and jangling these bells with a stolid rhythm, the six peasants danced facing one another, three on either side, while the minstrel fluted and the dysard strutted around. That minstrel's tune runs in my head even now—a queer little stolid tune that recalls vividly to me the aspect of the dance. It is the sort of tune Bottom the Weaver must often have danced to in his youth. . . After they had drunk some ale, they formed up for the second dance—a circular dance. And anon, above the notes of the flute and the jangling of the bells and the stamping of the boots, I seemed to hear the knell actually toll. *Hoot! Hoot! Hoot!* A motor-car came fussing and fuming in its cloud of dust. *Hoot! Hoot!* The dysard ran to meet it, brandishing his wand of office. He had to stand aside. *Hoot!* The dancers had just time to get out of the way. The scowling motorists vanished. Dancers and dysard, presently visible through the subsiding dust, looked rather foolish and crestfallen. And all the branches of the Tory old elm above them seemed to be quivering with indignation.

Yet Again

588 *The Golden Drugget*

IT is on nights when the wind blows its hardest, but makes no rift anywhere for a star to peep through, that the Golden Drugget, as I approach it, gladdens my heart the most. The distance between Rapallo and my home up yonder is rather more than two miles. The road curves and zigzags sharply, for the most part; but at the end of the first mile it runs straight for three or four hundred yards; and, as the inn stands at a point midway on this straight course, the Golden Drugget is visible to me long before I come to it. Even by starlight, it is good to see. How much better, if I happen to be out on a black rough night when nothing is disclosed but this one calm bright thing. Nothing? Well, there has been descriable, all the way, a certain grey glimmer immediately in front of my feet. This, in point of fact, is the road, and by following it carefully I have managed to escape collision with trees, bushes, stone walls. The continuous shrill wailing of trees' branches writhing unseen but near, and the great hoarse roar of the sea against the rocks far down below, are no cheerful accompaniment for the buffeted pilgrim. He feels that he is engaged in single combat with Nature at her unfriendliest. He isn't sure that she hasn't supernatural allies working with her—witches on broomsticks circling closely round him, demons in pursuit of him or waiting to leap out on him. And how about mere robbers and cut-throats? Suppose—but look! that streak, yonder, look!—the Golden Drugget.

There it is, familiar, serene, festal. That the pilgrim knew he would see it in due time does not diminish for him the queer joy of seeing it; nay, this emotion would be far less without that fore-knowledge. Some things are best at first sight. Others—and here is one of them—do ever improve by recognition. I remember that when first I beheld this steady strip of light, shed forth over a threshold level with the road, it seemed to me conceivably sinister. It brought Stevenson to my mind: the chink of doubloons and the clash of cutlasses; and I think I quickened pace as I passed it. But now!—now it inspires in me a sense of deep trust and gratitude; and such awe as I have for it is altogether a loving awe, as for holy ground that should be trod lightly. A drugget of crimson cloth across a London pavement is rather resented by the casual passer-by, as saying to him 'Step across me, stranger, but not along me, not in!' and for answer he spurns it with his heel. 'Stranger, come in!' is the clear message of the Golden Drugget. 'This is but a humble and earthly hostel, yet you will find here a radiant company of angels and archangels.' And always I cherish the belief that if I obeyed the summons I should receive fulfilment of the promise. Well, the beliefs that one most cherishes one is least willing to test. I do not go in at that open door. But lingering, but reluctant, is my tread as I pass by it ; and I pause to bathe in the light that is as the span of our human life, granted between one great darkness and another.

And Even Now

GILBERT KEITH CHESTERTON

1874–

589 *Mr. Pickwick*

PICKWICK goes through life with that god-like gullibility which is the key to all adventures. The greenhorn is the ultimate victor in everything ; it is he that gets the most out of life. Because Pickwick is led away by Jingle, he will be led to the White Hart Inn, and see the only Weller cleaning boots in the courtyard. Because he is bamboozled by Dodson and Fogg, he will enter the prison house like a paladin, and rescue the man and the woman who have wronged him most. His soul will never starve for exploits or excitements who is wise enough to be made a fool of. He will make himself happy in the traps that have been laid for him ; he will roll in their nets and sleep. All doors will fly open to him who has a mildness more defiant than mere courage. The whole is unerringly expressed in one fortunate phrase—he will be always 'taken in.' To be taken in everywhere is to see the inside of everything. It is the hospitality of circumstance. With torches and trumpets, like a guest, the greenhorn is taken in by Life. And the sceptic is cast out by it.

Charles Dickens

590 *The Battle of the Marne*

THE driven and defeated line stood at last almost under the walls of Paris; and the world waited for the doom of the city. The gates seemed to stand open; and the Prussian was to ride into it for the third and the last time: for the end of its long epic of liberty and equality was come. And still the very able and very French individual on whom rested the last hope of the seemingly hopeless Alliance stood unruffled as a rock, in every angle of his sky-blue jacket and his bulldog figure. He had called his bewildered soldiers back when they had broken the invasion at Guise; he had silently digested the responsibility of dragging on the retreat, as in despair, to the last desperate leagues before the capital; and he stood and watched. And even as he watched the whole huge invasion swerved.

Out through Paris and out and round beyond Paris, other men in dim blue coats swung out in long lines upon the plain, slowly folding upon Von Kluck like blue wings. Von Kluck stood an instant; and then, flinging a few secondary forces to delay the wing that was swinging round on him, dashed across the Allies' line at a desperate angle, to smash it in the centre as with a hammer. It was less desperate than it seemed; for he counted, and might well count, on the moral and physical bankruptcy of the British line and the end of the French line immediately in front of him, which for six days and nights he had chased before him like autumn leaves before a whirlwind. Not unlike autumn leaves, red-stained, dust-hued, and tattered, they lay there as if swept into a corner. But even as their conquerors wheeled eastwards, their bugles blew the charge ; and the English went forward through the wood that is called Creçy, and stamped it with their seal for the second time, in the highest moment of all the secular history of man.

But it was not now the Creçy in which English and French knights had met in a more coloured age, in a battle that was rather a tournament. It was a league of all knights for the remains of all knighthood, of all brotherhood in arms or in arts, against that which is and has been radically unknightly and radically unbrotherly from the beginning. Much was to happen after—murder and flaming folly and madness in earth and sea and sky ; but all men knew in their hearts that the third Prussian thrust had failed, and Christendom was delivered once more. The empire of blood and iron rolled slowly back towards the darkness of the northern forests ; and the great nations of the West went forward ; where side by side as after a long lover's quarrel, went the ensigns of St. Denys and St. George.

The Crimes of England

JOHN MASEFIELD

1875–

591 *The Clipper*

WHEN I saw her first there was a smoke of mist about her as high as her foreyard. Her topsails and flying kites had a faint glow upon them where the dawn caught them. Then the mist rolled away from her, so that we could see her hull and the glimmer of the red sidelight as it was hoisted inboard. She was rolling slightly, tracing an arc against the heaven, and as I watched her the glow upon her deepened, till every sail she wore burned rosily like an opal turned to the sun, like a fiery jewel. She was radiant, she was of an immortal beauty, that swaying, delicate clipper. Coming as she came, out of the mist into the dawn, she was like a spirit, like an intellectual presence. Her hull glowed, her rails glowed; there was colour upon the boats and tackling. She was a lofty ship (with skysails and royal staysails), and it was wonderful to watch her, blushing in the sun, swaying and curveting. She was alive with a more than mortal life. One thought that she would speak in some strange language or break out into a music which would express the sea and that great flower in the sky. She came trembling down to us, rising up high and plunging; showing the red lead below her water-line; then diving down till the smother bubbled over her hawseholes. She bowed and curveted; the light caught the skylights on the poop; she gleamed and sparkled; she shook the sea from her as she rose. There was no man aboard of us but was filled with the beauty of that ship. I think they would have cheered her had she been a little nearer to us; but, as it was, we ran up our flags in answer to her, adding our position and comparing our chronometers, then dipping our ensigns and standing away. For some minutes I watched her, as I made up the flags before putting them back in their cupboard. The old mate limped up to me, and spat, and swore. 'That 's one of the beautiful sights of the world,' he said. 'That, and a cornfield, and a woman with her child. It 's beauty and strength. How would you like to have one of them skysails round your neck?' I gave him some answer, and continued to watch her, till the beautiful, precise hull, with all its lovely detail, had become blurred to leeward, where the sun was now marching in triumph, the helm of a golden warrior plumed in cirrus.

A Tarpaulin Muster : A Memory

592 *Clewing up the Royals*

AFTER a day of it, as we sat below, we felt our mad ship taking yet wilder leaps, bounding over yet more boisterous hollows, and shivering and exulting in every inch of her. She seemed filled with a fiery, unquiet life. She seemed inhuman, glorious, spiritual. One forgot that she was man's work. We forgot that we were men. She was alive, immortal, furious. We were her minions and servants. We were the star-dust whirled in the train of the comet. We banged our plates with the joy we had in her. We sang and shouted and called her the glory of the seas.

There is an end to human glory. 'Greatness a period hath, no sta-ti-on.' The end to our glory came when, as we sat at dinner, the door swung back from its hooks and a mate in oilskins bade us come on deck 'without stopping for our clothes'. It was time. She was carrying no longer; she was dragging. To windward the sea was blotted in a squall. The line of the horizon was masked in a grey film. The glory of the sea had given place to greyness and grimness. Her beauty had become savage. The music of the wind had changed to a howl as of hounds.

And then we began to 'take it off her', to snug her down, to check her in her stride. We went to the clewlines and clewed the royals up. Then it was, 'Up there, you boys, and make the royals fast.' My royal was the mizen-royal, a rag of a sail among the clouds, a great grey rag, which was leaping and slatting a hundred and sixty feet above me. The wind beat me down against the shrouds, it banged me and beat me, and blew the tears from my eyes. It seemed to lift me up the futtocks into the top, and up the topmast rigging to the cross-trees. In the cross-trees I learned what wind was.

It came roaring past with a fervour and a fury which struck me breathless. I could only look aloft to the yard I was bound for and heave my panting body up the rigging. And there was the mizen-royal. There was the sail I had come to furl. And a wonder of a sight it was. It was blowing and bellying in the wind, and leaping around 'like a drunken colt', and flying over the yard, and thrashing and flogging. It was roaring like a bull with its slatting and thrashing. The royal mast was bending to the strain of it. To my eyes it was buckling like a piece of whalebone. I lay out on the yard, and the sail hit me in the face and knocked my cap away. It beat me and banged me, and blew from my hands. The wind pinned me flat against the yard, and seemed to be blowing all my clothes to shreds. I felt like a king, like an emperor. I shouted aloud with the joy of that 'rastle' with the sail. Forward of me was the main mast, with another lad, fighting another royal; and beyond him was yet another, whose sail seemed tied in knots. Below me was the ship, a leaping mad thing, with little silly figures, all heads and shoulders, pulling silly strings along the deck. There was the sea, sheer under me, and it looked grey and grim, and streaked with the white of our smother.

A Tarpaulin Muster : Being Ashore

GEORGE MACAULAY TREVELYAN

1876–

593 ### *Garibaldi*

WHEN in 1848 he returned to fight for Italy, in the full strength of matured manhood—at the time of life when Cromwell first drew sword—he had been sheltered, ever since he went to sea at fifteen, from every influence which might have turned him into an ordinary man or an ordinary soldier.

He had had two schools—the seas of romance, and the plateaus of South America. He had lived on shipboard and in the saddle. The man who loved Italy as even she has seldom been loved, scarcely knew her. The soldier of modern enlightenment was himself but dimly enlightened. Rather, his mind was like a vast sea cave, filled with the murmur of dark waters at flow and the stirring of nature's greatest forces, lit here and there by streaks of glorious sunshine bursting in through crevices hewn at random in its rugged sides. He had all the distinctive qualities of the hero, in their highest possible degree, and in their very simplest form. Courage and endurance without limit; tenderness to man and to all living things, which was never blunted by a life-time of war in two hemispheres among combatants often but half civilized; the power to fill men with ardour by his presence and to stir them by his voice to great deeds, but above all the passion to be striking a blow for the oppressed, a passion which could not be quenched by failure, nor checked by reason, nor sated by success, old age, and the worship of the world.

These qualities, perhaps, could not have existed in a degree so pre-eminent, in the person either of a sage or of a saint. Without, on the one hand, the childlike simplicity that often degenerated into folly, and on the other hand, the full store of common human passions that made him one with the multitude, he could never have been so ignorant of despair and doubt, so potent to overawe his followers and to carry men blindfold into enterprises which would have been madness under any other chief. The crowning work of his life was in 1860, when he landed with a thousand ill-armed volunteers in the Island of Sicily, to overcome a garrison of 24,000 well-armed and well-disciplined men. Moltke could no more have conquered Sicily with such means, than Garibaldi could have planned the battle of Sedan.

Garibaldi's Defence of the Roman Republic

594 *Garibaldi in the Assembly*

ABOUT midday on June 30, while Manara was dying in the hospital, Garibaldi was galloping across the Tiber to the Capitol, whither the Assembly of the Roman Republic had summoned him to attend its fateful session. He rode in haste, for though the fighting had died away, he would not consent to be absent from his post longer than one hour. He had missed death in the battle, and his heart was bitter within him. To add to his misery, news had just been brought that his faithful negro friend, Aguyar, who had so often guarded his life in the perils of war, had been killed by a shell whilst walking across a street in the Trastevere. Garibaldi, who was far above base racial pride, and regarded all men as brothers to be valued each according to his deserts, had given his love freely to the noble Othello, who in body and soul alike far surpassed the common type of white man. Sore at heart, and pre-occupied by bitter thoughts, he galloped up to the Capitol, dismounted, and entered the Assembly as he was, his red shirt covered with dust and blood, his face still moist with the sweat of battle, his sword so bent that it stuck half-way out of the scabbard. The members, deeply moved, rose to their feet and cheered, as he walked slowly to the tribune and mounted the steps.

They had sent to ask his advice on the three plans, between which, as Mazzini had told them in his speech that morning, they were now reduced to choose. They could surrender; they could die fighting in the streets; or, lastly, they could make their exodus into the mountains, taking with them the Government and the army. This third plan was that which Garibaldi had for days past been urging on the Triumvirate, and he now pressed the Assembly to adopt it, in a brief and vigorous speech.

He brushed aside the idea of continuing the defence of Rome. It could no longer, he showed them, be carried on even by street fighting, for the Trastevere must be abandoned, and the enemy's cannon from the height of San Pietro in Montorio could reduce the capital of the world to ashes. As to surrender, he does not seem to have discussed it. There remained the third plan—to carry the Government and army into the wilderness. This he approved. '*Dovunque saremo, colà sarà Roma*' ('Wherever we go, there will be Rome'), he said. This was the part he had chosen for himself and for everyone who would come with him. But he wished to have only volunteers, and to take no one on false pretences. He declared that he could promise nothing, and very honestly drew for the senators a picture of the life of danger and hardship to which he invited them.

Altogether it was a wise and noble speech, for it put an end to all thought of bringing further ruin on the buildings of Rome, and at the same time offered a path of glory and sacrifice to those who, like himself, were determined never to treat with the foreigner on Italian soil. Having spoken, he left the hall and galloped back to the Janiculum.

Garibaldi's Defence of the Roman Republic

JAMES HOPWOOD JEANS

1877–

595 *The Services of Astronomy*

TO the fundamental question of the meaning of human existence, astronomy has little of positive value to offer. It must be so, for the discussion of the question turns in the last resort on the ultimate significance of mind and matter. Astronomy knows nothing of mind and must perforce take matter for granted. But she can perhaps render some service in the humbler capacity of checking and criticizing the various conjectures which human thought has put forward as answers. The answers given by the human race in its infancy, the presumptuous answers which assumed in one form or another that terrestrial life was the sole reason for the existence of the myriads of stars in the firmament, met their death at the hands of Copernicus, an astronomer, and of Galileo, another astronomer. The arrogance of this view gave place to the humility of the succeeding view, which held that each of these millions of stars gave heat and light to families of planets peopled by living beings similar to ourselves, and of course quite as important as ourselves. But astronomy now seems to suggest that perhaps the pendulum has swung too far. We begin to suspect that life is not the normal accompaniment of a sun, since planets capable of sustaining life are not the normal accompaniments of suns. Astronomy does not know whether or not life is important in the scheme of nature, but she begins to whisper that it must necessarily be somewhat rare. Her suggestions, although still vague, seem to indicate that our terrestrial life forms a greater proportion of the sum total of all the life of the universe than we at one time thought.

The Nebular Hypothesis and Modern Cosmogony

GILES LYTTON STRACHEY

1880–

596 *The Loss of the Prince Consort*

THE sudden removal of the Prince was not merely a matter of overwhelming personal concern to Victoria; it was an event of national, of European importance. He was only forty-two, and in the ordinary course of nature he might have been expected to live at least thirty years longer. Had he done so it can hardly be doubted that the whole development of the English polity would have been changed. Already at the time of his death he filled a unique place in English public life; already among the inner circle of politicians he was accepted as a necessary and useful part of the mechanism of the State. Lord Clarendon, for instance, spoke of his death as 'a national calamity of far greater importance than the public dream of ', and lamented the loss of his ' sagacity and foresight ', which, he declared, would have been ' more than ever valuable ' in the event of an American war. And, as time went on, the Prince's influence must have enormously increased. For, in addition to his intellectual and moral qualities, he enjoyed, by virtue of his position, one supreme advantage which every other holder of high office in the country was without: he was permanent. Politicians came and went, but the Prince was perpetually installed at the centre of affairs. Who can doubt that, towards the end of the century, such a man, grown grey in the service of the nation, virtuous, intelligent, and with the unexampled experience of a whole lifetime of government, would have acquired an extraordinary prestige? If, in his youth, he had been able to pit the Crown against the mighty Palmerston and to come off with equal honours from the contest, of what might he not have been capable in his old age? What Minister, however able, however popular, could have withstood the wisdom, the irreproachability, the vast prescriptive authority, of the venerable Prince? It is easy to imagine how, under such a ruler, an attempt might have been made to convert England into a State as exactly organized, as elaborately trained, as efficiently equipped, and as autocratically controlled, as Prussia herself. Then perhaps, eventually, under some powerful leader—a Gladstone or a Bright—the democratic forces in the country might have rallied together, and a struggle might have followed in which the Monarchy would have been shaken to its foundations. Or, on the other hand, Disraeli's hypothetical prophecy might have come true. ' With Prince Albert ', he said, ' we have buried our sovereign. This German Prince has governed England for twenty-one years with a wisdom and energy such as none of our kings have ever shown. . . If he had out-lived some of our "old stagers" he would have given us the blessings of absolute Government.'

The English Constitution—that indescribable entity—is a living thing, growing with the growth of men, and assuming ever-varying forms in accordance with the subtle and complex laws of human character. It is the child of wisdom and chance. The wise men of 1688 moulded it into the shape we know; but the chance that George I could not speak English gave it one of its essential peculiarities—the system of a Cabinet independent of the Crown and subordinate to the Prime Minister. The wisdom of Lord Grey saved it from petrifaction and destruction, and set it upon the path of Democracy. Then chance intervened once more; a female sovereign happened to marry an able and pertinacious man; and it seemed likely that an element which had been quiescent within it for years—the element of irresponsible administrative power—was about to become its predominant characteristic and to change completely the direction of its growth. But what chance gave, chance took away. The Consort perished in his prime; and the English Constitution, dropping the dead limb with hardly a tremor, continued its mysterious life as if he had never been.

One human being, and one alone, felt the full force of what had happened. The Baron, by his fireside at Coburg, suddenly saw the tremendous fabric of his creation crash down into sheer and irremediable ruin. Albert was gone, and he had lived in vain.

Even his blackest hypochondria had never envisioned quite so miserable a catastrophe. Victoria wrote to him, visited him, tried to console him by declaring with passionate conviction that she would carry on her husband's work. He smiled a sad smile and looked into the fire. Then he murmured that he was going where Albert was—that he would not be long. He shrank into himself. His children clustered round him and did their best to comfort him, but it was useless: the Baron's heart was broken. He lingered for eighteen months, and then, with his pupil, explored the shadow and the dust.

Queen Victoria

597 *The Passing of Victoria*

WHEN, two days previously, the news of the approaching end had been made public, astonished grief had swept over the country. It appeared as if some monstrous reversal of the course of nature was about to take place. The vast majority of her subjects had never known a time when Queen Victoria had not been reigning over them. She had become an indissoluble part of their whole scheme of things, and that they were about to lose her appeared a scarcely possible thought. She herself, as she lay blind and silent, seemed to those who watched her to be divested of all thinking—to have glided already, unawares, into oblivion. Yet, perhaps, in the secret chambers of consciousness, she had her thoughts, too. Perhaps her fading mind called up once more the shadows of the past to float before it, and retraced, for the last time, the vanished visions of that long history—passing back and back, through the cloud of years, to older and ever older memories—to the spring woods at Osborne, so full of primroses for Lord Beaconsfield—to Lord Palmerston's queer clothes and high demeanour, and Albert's face under the green lamp, and Albert's first stag at Balmoral, and Albert in his blue and silver uniform, and the Baron coming in through a doorway, and Lord M. dreaming at Windsor with the rooks cawing in the elm-trees, and the Archbishop of Canterbury on his knees in the dawn, and the old King's turkey-cock ejaculations, and Uncle Leopold's soft voice at Claremont, and Lehzen with the globes, and her mother's feathers sweeping down towards her, and a great old repeater-watch of her father's in its tortoise-shell case, and a yellow rug, and some friendly flounces of sprigged muslin, and the trees and the grass at Kensington.

Queen Victoria

COMPTON MACKENZIE

1883–

598 'The Basket of Roses'

SOME four-and-twenty miles from Curtain Wells on the Great West Road is a tangle of briers among whose blossoms an old damask rose is sometimes visible. If the curious traveller should pause and examine this fragrant wilderness, he will plainly perceive the remains of an ancient garden, and if he be of an imaginative character of mind will readily recall the legend of the Sleeping Beauty in her mouldering palace; for some enchantment still enthralls the spot, so that he who bravely dares the thorns is well rewarded with pensive dreams and, as he lingers a while gathering the flowers or watching their petals flutter to the green shadows beneath, will haply see elusive Beauty hurry past.

Here at the date of this tale stood the *Basket of Roses* Inn, a mile or so away from a small village. When coaches ceased to run, the house began to lose its custom, and, as stone is scarce hereabouts, was presently pulled down in order to provide the Parson with a peculiarly bleak Parochial Hall.

However, this melancholy fate was still distant, and old Simon Tabrum had a fine custom from the coaches and private travellers who delighted to spend a night in so sweet a lodging.

The *Basket of Roses* was the fairest, dearest inn down all that billowy London road. The counter, sheathed in a case of pewter, the glasses all in a row, the sleek barrels and the irregular lines of home-brewed cordials, charmed the casual visitor to a more intimate acquaintance. Behind the tap was the Travellers' Room, and what a room it was—with great open fireplaces and spits and bubbling kettles and blackened ingles. Long-buried ancestors of the village had carved their rude initials over each high-backed bench and battered the bottoms of the great tankards into unexpected dents by many rollicking choruses in the merry dead past. The walls of this room knew the pedigree of every bullock and the legend of every ghost for many miles round. Here was the cleanest floor, the clearest fire in England.

Old Tabrum the landlord was the very man for the house—the very man to bring out all that was most worthy in his guests. He always produced good wine and a piping hot supper, never asked for his money till his guests were satisfied, and always wore an apron as white as the foam of his cool deep ale.

He was eighty years old now, with a bloom on his cheeks like an autumn pippin and two limpid blue eyes that looked straight into yours and, if you had any reverence at all, made the tears well involuntarily at the sight of such gentle beauty.

Once he was a famous Basso Profundo, but now his voice was high and thin, and seemed already fraught with faint aerial music. The ancient man was a great gardener as properly became a landlord whose sign was a swinging posy. What a garden there was at the back of this florious inn. The bowling-green surrounded by four grey walls was the finest ever known, and as for the borders, deep borders twelve feet wide, they were full of every sweet flower. There were Columbines and Canterbury Bells and blue Bells of Coventry and Lilies and Candy Goldilocks with Penny flowers or White Sattin and Fair Maids of France and Fair Maids of Kent and London Pride.

There was Herb of Grace and Rosemary and Lavender to pluck and crush between your fingers, while some one rolled the jack across the level green of the ground. In Spring there were Tulips and Jacynths, Dames' Violets and Primroses, Cowslips of Jerusalem, Daffodils and Pansies, Lupins like spires in the dusk, and Ladies' Smocks in the shadowed corners. As for Summer, why the very heart of high June and hot July dwelt in that fragrant enclosure. Sweet Johns and Sweet Williams with Dragon flowers and crimson Peaseblossom and tumbling Peonies, Blue Moonwort and the Melancholy Gentlemen, Larksheels, Marigolds, Hearts, Hollyhocks and Candy Tufts. There was Venus' Looking Glass and Flower of Bristol, and Apple of Love and Blue Helmets and Herb Paris and Campion and Love in a Mist and Ladies' Laces and Sweet

Sultans or Turkey Cornflowers, Gillyflower Carnations (Ruffling Rob of Westminster amongst them) with Dittany and Sops in Wine and Floramer, Widow Wail and Bergamot, True Thyme and Gilded Thyme, Good Night at Noon and Flower de Luce, Golden Mouse-ear, Princes' Feathers, Pinks, and deep-red Damask Roses.

It was a very wonderful garden indeed.

The Passionate Elopement

RUPERT BROOKE

1887–1915

599 *1914*

'Her foundations are upon the holy hills'

SOME say the Declaration of War threw us into a primitive abyss of hatred and the lust for blood. Others declare that we behaved very well. I do not know. I only know the thoughts that flowed through the mind of a friend of mine when he heard the news. My friend—I shall make no endeavour to excuse him —is a normal, even ordinary man, wholly English, twenty-four years old, active and given to music. By a chance he was ignorant of the events of the world during the last days of July. He was camping with some friends in a remote part of Cornwall, and had gone on, with a companion, for a four-days' sail. So it wasn't till they beached her again that they heard. A youth ran down to them with a telegram: 'We're at war with Germany. We've joined France and Russia.'

My friend ate and drank, and then climbed a hill of gorse, and sat alone, looking at the sea. His mind was full of confused images, and the sense of strain. In answer to the word 'Germany', a train of vague thoughts dragged across his brain. The pompous middle-class vulgarity of the building of Berlin; the wide and restful beauty of Munich; the taste of beer; innumerable quiet, glittering *cafés*; the *Ring*; the swish of evening air in the face, as one *skis* down past the pines; a certain angle of the eyes in the face; long nights of drinking, and singing, and laughter; the admirable beauty of German wives and mothers; certain friends; some tunes; the quiet length of evening over the Starnberger-See. Between him and the Cornish sea he saw quite clearly an April morning on a lake south of Berlin, the grey water slipping past his little boat, and a peasant-woman, suddenly revealed against apple-blossom, hanging up blue and scarlet garments to dry in the sun. Children played about her; and she sang as she worked. . .

A cloud over the sun woke him to consciousness of his own thoughts; and he found, with perplexity, that they were continually recurring to two periods of his life, the days after the death of his mother, and the time of his first deep estrangement from one he loved. After a bit he understood this. Now, as then, his mind had been completely divided into two parts: the upper running about aimlessly from one half-relevant thought to another, the lower unconscious half labouring with some profound and unknowable change. This feeling of ignorant helplessness linked him with those past crises. His consciousness was like the light scurry of waves at full tide, when the deeper waters are pausing and gathering and turning home. Something was growing in his heart, and he couldn't tell what. But as he thought 'England and Germany', the word 'England' seemed to flash like a line of foam. With a sudden tightening of his heart, he realized that there might be a raid on the English coast. He didn't imagine any possibility of it *succeeding*, but only of enemies and warfare on English soil. The idea sickened him. He was immensely surprised to perceive that the actual earth of England held for him a quality which he found in A—, and in a friend's honour, and scarcely anywhere else, a quality which, if he'd ever been sentimental enough to use the word, he'd have called 'holiness'. His astonishment grew as the full flood of 'England' swept him on from thought to thought. He felt the triumphant helplessness of a lover. Grey, uneven little fields, and small, ancient hedges rushed before him, wild flowers, elms and beeches, gentleness, sedate houses of red brick, proudly unassuming, a countryside of rambling hills and friendly copses. He seemed to be raised high, looking down on a landscape compounded of the western view from the Cotswolds, and the Weald, and the high land in Wiltshire, and the Midlands seen from the hills above Prince's Risborough. And all this to the accompaniment of tunes heard long ago, an intolerable number of them being hymns. There was, in his mind, a confused multitude of faces, to most of which he could not put a name. At one moment he was on an Atlantic liner, sick for home, making Plymouth at nightfall; and at another, diving into a little rocky pool through which the Teign flows, north of Bovey; and again, waking, stiff with dew, to see the dawn come up over the Royston plain. And continually he seemed to see the set of a mouth which he knew for his mother's, and A—'s face, and, inexplicably, the face of an old man he had once passed in a Warwickshire village. To his great disgust, the most commonplace sentiments found utterance in him. At the same time he was extraordinarily happy...

From his last prose writings

O CELESTIAL gift of divine liberality, descending from the Father of light to raise up the rational soul even to heaven. . . Undoubtedly, indeed, thou hast placed thy desirable tabernacle in books, where the Most High, the Light of light, the Book of Life, hath established thee. Here then all who ask receive, all who seek find thee, to those who knock thou openest quickly. In books cherubim expand their wings, that the soul of the student may ascend and look around from pole to pole, from the rising and the setting sun, from the north and from the sea. In them the most high and incomprehensible God Himself is contained and worshipped.

RICHARD DE BURY, 1281–1345, *Philobiblon: translated by John Bellingham Inglis*, 1832

INDEX OF AUTHORS, TITLES AND SOURCES

INDEX OF AUTHORS

TITLES AND SOURCES

INDEX OF AUTHORS

TITLES AND SOURCES

INDEX OF AUTHORS

TITLES AND SOURCES

INDEX OF AUTHORS

TITLES AND SOURCES

INDEX OF AUTHORS

TITLES AND SOURCES

INDEX OF AUTHORS

TITLES AND SOURCES

INDEX OF AUTHORS

TITLES AND SOURCES

INDEX OF AUTHORS

TITLES AND SOURCES

INDEX OF AUTHORS

TITLES AND SOURCES

INDEX OF AUTHORS

TITLES AND SOURCES

TITLES AND SOURCES

INDEX OF AUTHORS

TITLES AND SOURCES

INDEX OF AUTHORS

TITLES AND SOURCES

INDEX OF AUTHORS

Enid,

Christmas, 1932,

from Edwin